The PC Bible

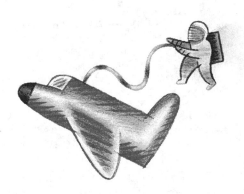

Edited by Eric Knorr

 Peachpit Press

The PC Bible
Edited by Eric Knorr

Peachpit Press
2414 Sixth Street
Berkeley, CA 94710
510/548-4393
510/548-5991 (fax)

Technical editor: TJ Byers
Cover and interior design: YO, San Francisco
Cover and interior illustrations: Bud Peen
Margin icons: Joe Crabtree, Art Parts
Production: The Harbinger Group
Copyediting: Tema Goodwin, John Hammett, Sally Zahner
Index: Steve Rath

Permissions
Portions of Chapter 11: *Health, Safety, and the Environment* are reprinted from material originally published by *PC World*, and are used with its permission.

Trademarks
Throughout this book, trademarked names are used. Rather than put a trademark symbol in every occurrence of a trademarked name, we are using the names only in an editorial fashion and to the benefit of the trademark owner, with no intention of infringement of the trademark.

Notice of Rights

Notice of Liability

Library of Congress Cataloging-in-Publication Data
The PC Bible / edited by Eric Knorr.
        p. cm.
    Includes index.
        1. Microcomputers. 2. IBM compatible computers. I. Knorr, Eric.
QA76.5.P358   1994   94-31629
006—dc20   CIP

ISBN 1-56609-107-1

9 8 7 6 5 4 3 2 1

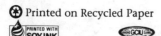

Printed on Recycled Paper

Printed and bound in the United States of America

To Karl Koessel, a technical guru worthy of the name,
whose patient explanations of how computers
work still guide me.

Table of Contents

Chapter 8: Upgrade It Yourself **137**

Chapter 9: Protect Your Data **171**

Chapter 10: When Things Go Wrong **203**

Chapter 11: Health, Safety, and the Environment **221**

Introduction

~~~~~~

You're holding in your hands more useful information about PC hardware and software than has ever been assembled in one book—an extravagant claim, but a truthful one. Want to install an expansion card? You'll find step-by-step instructions in Chapter 10. Forget a DOS command? Chapter 12 will refresh your memory. Itching to get into multimedia? Chapter 23 explains what you need to get rolling. Need to copy formatting fast in *Word for Windows*? Then turn to Chapter 14. Unless you already know everything there is to know about PCs, you'll find something—probably many things—of value in this book.

Yes, this is a monster of a book, but a big, friendly monster. Every effort has been made to strip out jargon, and every necessary technical term has been explained in context and in the glossary. Just as important, all 25 chapters have been organized to provide both quick tutorials for beginners and easy access to hundreds of tips and product evaluations for people who already know what they're doing. In other words, you can browse randomly for tidbits, read sequentially to get a working knowledge of a given area, or use the index to zero in on exactly the information you need.

The secret to this book is in the expertise of its authors. Obviously, there's no way to cover everything about PCs in under 1000 pages. So each of this book's 19 experts had the same mandate: Use the benefit of experience to tell people what they most need to know. With this book, you can get up and running fast with *Excel*, the most popular spreadsheet—but you won't learn about advanced statistical functions or macro programming. You can discover how to get on line and access services like

CompuServe or Internet—but if you want to set up a communications server for a network, look elsewhere. Instead of truly advanced stuff, you'll find concise primers and frank opinions about products, plus some of the hottest tips around.

We hope this book's breadth, usefulness, clarity, and logical organization earns it a place right next to your PC. *The PC Bible* is a work in progress that will hopefully go through many editions. To make it a more effective reference, we invite you to send in your comments when you order your free 30-page update to this edition.

How to Use This Book

The PC Bible is loosely divided into hardware and software testaments. Chapters 1 through 8 are largely devoted to helping you select and install the right hardware. Chapters 9 through 11 explain how to prevent and troubleshoot problems relating to hardware, software, and ergonomics, while Chapters 12 and 13 cover the essential software almost everyone uses: Windows, DOS, and fonts. The remainder of the book covers the 12 major application areas, with special emphasis on word processing and spreadsheets.

Beginners and Raw Beginners

This book is intended for people at various levels of computer expertise. After all, no one knows everything about computers—you may be a spreadsheet wizard, for instance, but be completely at sea when it comes to printers. That's why each chapter has been carefully designed so that you can plunge right in without knowing much about the subject—and usually get the information you need without resorting to the glossary.

However, if you're new to the entire subject of PCs, and terms like "RAM" or "hard disk" leave you scratching your head, go directly to Chapter 1: *For Beginners Only*. There you'll find the basic explanations that will help you understand the rest of this book. If you're a raw beginner and already have a PC, then the next step is Chapter 12: *Windows and DOS*, where a fairly complete tutorial and Cookbook reference will get you acquainted with your PC's most essential software.

Those Little Icons

For those who like to browse, we offer icons to call attention to passages in text and make the browsing more fun. With icons and an abundance of little subheads as signposts, you may not even need to bother with the index when you search for specific information.

HOT TIP

If you're already a PC user, try this experiment: Turn to the chapter that covers the type of software you use most. Then check out the tip icons in the margin (when a whole block of tips run together, you'll see a vertical line next to the icon). Chances are you'll find some tips worth trying.

DANGER

Knowing what you shouldn't do—buy a bad product, press a wrong key, touch a sensitive component—is every bit as important as knowing what you should do. The danger icon is this book's red flag. It's reserved for important warnings that might frighten an ostrich.

REMEMBER

Certain facts should take up residence in the back of your mind as you shop or as you work. This icon highlights these important points. For example, this whole discussion about icons could easily get its own remember icon, but that would look pretty weird.

Note that the icons merely call out some of the most important information—but there's useful stuff on almost every page. If you have a special interest in a subject, checking for tips may not be the best strategy, since information valuable to you may lack an icon entirely.

Product Information

One handy use for *The PC Bible* is as a reference for the top PC products and companies. At the end of nearly every chapter, you'll find a Product Directory listing product names, companies, addresses, and phone numbers for ordering. These directories are not intended to be fully comprehensive, but they do cover major companies in each area, with occasional bias toward those companies deemed the best by the author of each chapter.

Note that information on products, particularly pricing, versions, and models, is subject to swift and sweeping change. We did our best to get the latest data for products in this book, but it will age quickly. Make sure you fill out the coupon in the back of this book to receive your free 30-page update, which will cover many of the key products introduced or revised after this edition went to press.

Typographic Conventions

Throughout this book you'll find keycaps, characters in a special font used to represent keys on the PC keyboard. Keycaps indicate the keys you should press when you enter a command or execute a keyboard "shortcut"—Ctrl B for boldface, for example. However, when you're supposed to enter a whole string of characters, you'll find they appear in Courier, as in copy a:*.*.

Whenever a technical term is introduced, you'll find it italicized and defined in context. Thereafter the term won't be italicized, so if you forget what it means, you can either flip backward in the chapter or check the glossary. Software also gets the italic treatment—but only if you can buy it separately. For example, you can't purchase the Photo-Paint component of *CorelDraw* without buying the whole enchilada, so Photo-Paint doesn't appear in italics.

About the Authors

This book is little more than a distillation of the knowledge and skill of its contributors. Here's the cast of characters:

Rick Altman has authored or co-authored eight books on publishing and graphics software. His International CorelDraw User Conference is attended by over 500 artists and illustrators every year.

Anita Amirrezvani is an editor for the *Contra Costa Times* and a contributing editor for *PC World* magazine. She co-authors *The Green PC*, a nationally syndicated column on environmental computing.

TJ Byers is a freelance writer and contributing editor for *Microcomputer Journal* and *PC World*. He is the author of several books on PC hardware, including *Inside the IBM PC AT*, McGraw-Hill.

George Campbell is a contributing editor for *PC World* and the author of a monthly column, *Word Processing Q&A*. He is also president of OsoSoft, a shareware publishing company.

Steve Cummings is the author or co-author of *DeskJet Unlimited*, *The Little Laptop Book*, and *Jargon*, all from Peachpit Press. He has written hundreds of articles for *PC Magazine*, *MacWeek*, and many other computer publications.

Michael Goodwin is a *PC World* contributing editor. When he's not writing about computers, he is a widely published book and magazine writer in such areas as film, food, and traditional American music and culture.

Judy Heim is a contributing editor and columnist for *PC World*. She has written about PC communications and on-line services for ten years. She also publishes a newsletter about using PCs to track personal investments.

Gregg Keizer is an Oregon-based freelancer who writes about games for a slew of publications, including *Omni, Pulse!, Electronic Entertainment*, and *Family Fun*.

Eric Knorr is a veteran computer journalist and former editor of *PC World* magazine. He is currently recuperating after finishing this book.

Robert Lauriston is a freelance writer and a contributing editor for *Windows* magazine. He has also contributed articles to *Desktop Video World, Keyboard, NewMedia, PowerPC World*, and *Wired* magazines.

Robert Luhn is editor-in-chief of *Computer Currents*, a biweekly national magazine, and co-author of *The Green PC*, a nationally syndicated column. His work has appeared in *Omni*, the *Christian Science Monitor*, and *Mother Jones*.

Celeste Robinson is a consultant, a freelance writer, and a columnist for *PC World*. She writes how-to database books and has a business that specializes in database design and implementation.

Steve Sagman has published six books on presentation graphics, including *Harvard Graphics 2 for Windows* from Peachpit Press. Based in New York, he teaches, writes, and consults.

Richard Scoville is a software training consultant based in Chapel Hill, North Carolina. He is a contributing editor for *PC World* magazine, where he offers monthly how-to advice and frequently reviews spreadsheet software.

Scott Spanbauer is a contributing editor for *PC World* magazine and a frequent contributor to *NewMedia* magazine.

Daniel Tynan is a freelance writer and contributing editor for *Electronic Entertainment, PC World*, and *Publish* magazines.

Daniel Will-Harris is a writer, designer, and noted authority on type. The author of Peachpit's *Dr. Daniel's Windows Diet* and *Typestyle*, he recently hosted a series of software training videos from Learn Key, Inc.

Naomi Wise is a freelance writer whose work has appeared in *PC World*, the *Washington Post Magazine*, the *Village Voice*, and the *San Jose Mercury News*. She also has four cookbooks and a biography to her name.

Kathy Yakal is a freelance writer specializing in personal finance and accounting software. She has contributed many articles to national computer publications, including *PC Magazine*.

Acknowledgments

This book is the brainchild of Neil Salkind, who originally proposed a reference that would provide the same wealth of information to the PC community that *The Macintosh Bible* has provided to the Mac community.. Robert Lauriston contributed not only a huge quantity of excellent copy, but also a wealth of ideas, advice, enthusiasm, and willingness to help move this juggernaut along. Early input from Richard Scoville and George Campbell was also invaluable. Special thanks are due TJ Byers, who doggedly stuck by this project even when the deadlines stretched and the hours got weird. For their endless patience as they waited for pages, Roslyn Bullas, Stephen Long, Mimi Heft, and Greg Hill deserve a lifetime supply of ibuprofen.

A heartfelt thanks also goes to the following people, whose encouragement, tips, insights, comments, corrections, and other contributions helped make this book possible: DJ Anderson, Rex Farrance, Steve Fox, Roberta Furger, Richard Jantz, Caroline Jones, Bob Mahoney, Allison Parker, David Schneider, Jim Schwabe, Don Watkins, and Bob Weibel.

1 For Beginners Only

By Eric Knorr and Naomi Wise

- How to unpack and set up your PC
- A visual glossary of PC components
- Keyboard and mouse basics
- Opening, closing, and saving files

A personal computer is just another appliance, like a blender or a microwave oven. If you want to do something with a PC—write a letter, get the latest stock market quotes, play solitaire—you click the right buttons, and the job is done. True, it's not always obvious *where* the right buttons are. But the most important thing to realize is that you'll find them eventually, without having to learn sleight of hand or mind-bending secret codes.

The main difference between a PC and other appliances is in the variety of jobs it can do. The PC's closest relative is the VCR: Every time you pop in a new videotape, the VCR shows a different movie. Just like a VCR, a PC is merely the required electronic equipment—the *hardware*. Without *software*—the PC's equivalent of the feature film—you wouldn't be able to do anything useful or entertaining with a computer.

When you buy a PC, it comes with a little software to get you started word processing, doing calculations, and playing games. But these simple pieces of software—each one a small *application* because it *applies* to a specific job—are only the beginning.

This book will introduce you to hundreds of the best applications you can buy, help you choose among them, and even lead you step by step through the process of using many of them. You'll also learn how to pick hardware to run that software—Chapter 2, for example, explains how to choose a PC. But if you're really a raw beginner, you need to understand a few things first. Where to start? Well, imagine you just bought a PC and brought it home...

Unpacking and Getting Settled

The best way to unpack new hardware is to get a friend to help. While unpacking, the aim is to place all the components on a desk without destroying the boxes, the styrofoam, or your spine. Remember to keep the packing materials in case you have to return your PC or send it in for repairs—or if you move.

1. **Find a good home.** If you're setting up a PC at work, hopefully your company has prepared a proper work area (see Chapter 11: *Health, Safety, and the Environment*). If you're setting up at home, choose a large desk near an AC outlet with enough space not only for the PC and printer, but also papers, reference materials, and so on (avoid those tiny "computer desks"). The desk should be low enough so your forearms are parallel to the floor when you type—failing that, a keyboard drawer (available at most office supply stores) should do the trick.

2. **Unpack the PC.** Take your PC out of its box first. If you have a helper, the weaker person should hold the box, while the stronger should yank out the PC, which will probably be surrounded by styrofoam. The monitor will probably be heavier and harder to lift.

4. **Prepare to connect.** Carefully set the PC and monitor on your desk. Both the monitor and PC should be angled away from the wall so you can access their backsides and connect up various cables. Look for your floppy disk drives (see "The ABCs of Hardware," below, for their locations), check inside them, and remove any paper, cardboard, or plastic packing material.

5. **Prepare your printer.** Printers often come with a special set of unpacking instructions that tell you how to remove plastic spacers that prevent damage

during shipping. A certain amount of assembly will be required. The user manual will have instructions and a diagram.

6. **Take inventory.** Make a final search of each box (and the indentations in the styrofoam blocks) for additional documentation—not to mention software, cables, or other parts, which are frequently packed in baggies or in small boxes. Check packing lists—especially if you bought the hardware mail order—and make sure all the listed items are there. If not, call whoever sold you the equipment immediately.

Now's an excellent time to put every piece of documentation you've found in a manila folder labeled System Survival Kit and stash it in a place where you'll find it easily. Add the PC manufacturer's tech support number to your Rolodex for good measure.

HOT TIP

In some cases you may need to unpack and connect other *peripherals* (the word for any hardware devices besides the PC itself), such as a *modem*, which enables you to hook your PC to the phone lines and communicate with other computers. The section "Making the Right Connections" will explain what plugs into where.

Don't Try This at Home (or at Work)

Nothing's worse than damaging equipment because you broke some dumb rule about basic system care that you didn't even know about. So here are the rules. Now you don't have an excuse:

- Don't place any piece of hardware in direct sunlight.

- Don't leave anything on the vents atop your monitor. Without circulating air, your monitor's innards won't last as long (confine your rubber alligator to an unvented section.)

- Don't place your PC so its back is less than two inches from a wall, because your PC needs air circulation, too.

- Don't turn on your PC if it's too cold in the room. Warm the room to a comfortable temperature before flipping the switch so any water vapor condensed inside the chassis can evaporate.

- Don't place open containers of liquid (or frozen yogurt bars) on top of or even very near to any of your equipment. Liquid, especially sugary stuff, can severely damage hardware.

- Don't use an extension cord if you can avoid it. Disastrous disconnections may result.

Do use a device with a row of AC outlets called a *power strip*—preferably one with *surge suppression,* which dampens potentially damaging fluctuations in electric power (see Chapter 9: *Protect Your Data*). Plug into one, and you can leave your PC, monitor, and printer turned on and turn everything on and off with the flick of a single switch. Remember to plug the power strip into a three-prong, grounded outlet to guard against problems caused by static electricity and the remote hazard of electric shock.

The ABCs of Hardware

To start computing, all you need is a PC with a monitor, keyboard, and mouse (the mouse may cost extra). The nice little setup shown here also includes a printer for putting your thoughts on paper and a modem for communicating with other computers over the phone lines.

Monitor. Also called the *display* or the *screen,* this device is what your system uses to show you what you're doing and what it's doing. A monitor is much like a TV without the ability to receive broadcasts, but the picture tube is of much higher quality (see Chapter 5: *Monitors, Etc.*).

System unit. Sometimes called "the system" or "the machine," this is the PC itself (although without a keyboard and monitor you couldn't do anything with it). This is where the computer's brains are. Inside, you'll also find the *hard disk,* a small, sealed mechanical device that stores huge quantities of software and data, whether the PC is turned off or on (see Chapter 4: *Disk Drives*).

Printer. The printer makes paper copies of documents, termed *printouts* or *hard copies.* Shown here is a *laser printer,* which produces documents using a technology similar to that of a photocopier (see Chapter 6: *Printers and Printing*).

Floppy disk drives. These devices spin *floppy disks,* inexpensive little magnetic disks that you use to transport small quantities of data—or use to *install* software onto your hard disk (software you buy in stores comes on floppy disks). Almost always, the *A: drive* is above and the *B: drive* is below, although not every system has a B: drive (the hard disk is usually *drive C:*).

Modem. This device hooks your PC to the phone lines so you can communicate with other computers.

Keyboard. With a design similar to a typewriter, the keyboard enables you to type data into your PC and tell your software what to do (see "The Keyboard and the Mouse" later in this chapter).

Mouse. So called because of its small size and tail-like trailing wire, the mouse is used to point at parts of the screen and issue *commands* (the instructions you use to make software do your bidding). Move the mouse, and the pointer moves in the same direction on the screen. An inexpensive *mouse pad,* which is just a piece of plastic over a foam backing, can make mouse operation smoother.

What "IBM Compatible" Really Means

When you get right down to it, there are only two types of personal computers: IBM-compatible PCs—so called because they're fashioned after IBM's original personal computer—and Macintoshes. Although an IBM-compatible setup is shown on the opposite page, your average Mac and its components look very similar. But Macs have one huge difference: They run different software.

Go to the store, and you'll find software packages clearly labeled as being for the Mac or for IBM-compatible PCs (or for Windows or DOS, either of which mean the same thing as IBM compatible). If you try to run Mac software on an IBM-compatible PC, or vice-versa, it simply won't work.

Software incompatibility is the reason people seldom discuss IBM-compatible PCs (call 'em PCs for short) and Macs in the same breath. You may also hear people say that Macs are easier to use than PCs, but this is true only to a slight degree. Anyway, you'll find next to nothing about Macs in this book, mainly because Peachpit Press has another book, *The Macintosh Bible,* that will tell you all you need to know about them.

Making the Right Connections

Let's say everything is out of its box and sitting on the desk, waiting for you to put it all together. Your PC's manual will tell you how to hook things up, but seldom will you find everything explained step by step in one place, as you will here.

Don't be thrown by the fact that there are multiple names for everything—for example, the connectors on the back of your PC are also called *ports*. Note that connectors are either *male* or *female*—that is, they have either small pins or sockets to accommodate those pins.

To help you along, your PC may have small text labels or universal symbols alongside the ports on your PC. Then again, it may not—and the placement of connectors varies from PC to PC, so you should check out the basic diagrams of connectors (below) to see which is which.

1. **Plug in the keyboard.** Usually, the keyboard has a coiled cord that ends in a circular, 5-pin male plug, which fits into a round female port on the back of the PC—although a few PCs have the keyboard connector in the front. (Compaq PCs have a mouse-style connector, while a few other systems use a phone-style

connector.) Line up the pins on the plug with the holes in the keyboard port; a notch usually keeps you from plugging in the wrong way.

2. **Hook up the monitor.** The monitor has two cables: an AC power cord and a video cable. The video cable is as thick (or thicker) than the power cord and ends in a 15-pin male plug known as a *D shell*, so called because its D-like shape keeps you from reversing it. The 15-pin female video port will probably be located on the rear metal bracket of an *expansion card* (a circuit card that fits inside your PC to give it added capabilities). Connect the video cable using gentle pressure and screw in the plug's thumbscrew; then plug the AC cord into the back of the monitor.

3. **Connect the mouse.** If you see a round 5-pin mouse port, plug the mouse into it. If there's no mouse port, plug the mouse into a *serial port* (also known as a *COM* or *communications port*). Serial ports are either 9-pin or 25-pin D shells and are always male. Mice generally have a plug for both a mouse port and a 9-pin serial port; if you have the wrong plug, you can usually buy an adapter (see Chapter 8: *Upgrade It Yourself* for more on mouse installation).

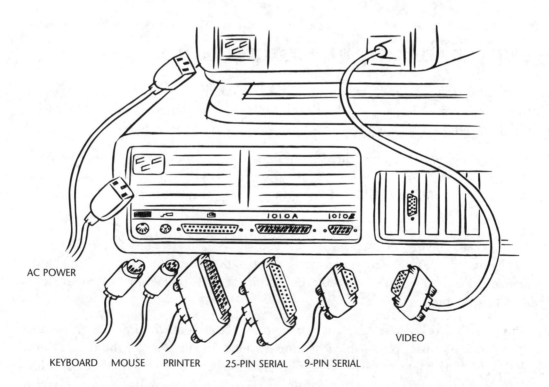

AC POWER

KEYBOARD   MOUSE   PRINTER   25-PIN SERIAL   9-PIN SERIAL

VIDEO

Figure 1: Plugging it all together. Every PC has most of the connectors shown in this rear view, although their locations vary from model to model. The modem plugs into one of the serial ports.

Your PC's Status Lights and What They Mean

On the front of your system unit you'll see several small icons and/or lights—the exact number and type depend on the make and model PC. Here are some common icons and what they indicate:

 Power on. Sometimes you see this icon, sometimes you just see a light on or near the PC's power switch. The power on light is unnecessary because the sound of the cooling fan is the best sign your PC is on.

 Hard disk access. A light next to this icon flashes every time your hard disk does something. If your PC malfunctions, and this light doesn't light up (or stays lit too long), then the disk could be the source of trouble.

 Turbo. The turbo icon, when included, is accompanied by both a light and a small pushbutton. If the turbo light is on, then your PC is running at top speed. The only time when turbo should be off is when you try to run ancient software—which is to say, maybe never.

 Keyboard locked. The *keylock* may be on the face of the system, or on the back. This icon is at the lock's rightmost position, which means your keyboard won't send input to the system no matter how hard you type.

 Keyboard unlocked. This icon is at the keylock's leftmost position, the "normal" position. Few people ever lock their keyboards, in part because everybody seems to lose the key.

4. **Hook up the printer.** The printer has a thick cable that plugs into a *parallel port*, a female D-shell connector with holes for 25-pins (sometimes labeled LPT1 or PRN). Some printers can also connect to a serial port, but the parallel port is always preferable because it's faster. If your printer didn't come with a cable, you'll have to buy it separately (try Radio Shack). Usually, the printer itself has a *Centronics interface*, a special connector that requires a matching plug (check your printer's manual to make sure).

HOT TIP

5. **Plug in the modem.** If the modem is an *external* model, then it simply plugs into a serial port. If it's an *internal* model, then it's an expansion card, and it may be a real pain to install (see Chapter 8: *Upgrade It Yourself*).

Now that everything's connected, you can place your PC in its work position. If you have a standard *desktop* PC, you can either leave it on top of the desk or—if the keyboard, mouse, and monitor cables are long enough—place it underneath to save desk space. If you have a *tower* PC, keep your desktop free and find a home for the tower under your desk (see Chapter 2, Figure 7).

Flicking the Power Switch

Now it's time to *boot up*—computerese for starting your PC. Turn on the monitor first (the On button is usually in front under the screen). The screen won't light up until you turn on the PC, but the monitor's power light should go on right away, unless you forgot to connect the thing to the AC source.

Next look for the PC's power switch. On many models, it's a button or a switch on the front panel. On other PCs, it may be a switch at the rear of the chassis on the right side—or on the back of the machine, out of sight completely. If you have a printer, look for its power switch, too—but be aware that some environmentally correct printers (like the LaserJet 4L) don't have power switches at all. They turn themselves on when you print from an application, and off when you don't print anything for five minutes or so.

If you're using a power strip and nothing happens when you flip all the switches, ask yourself: Is the power strip turned on? If you hear something but see nothing, check your monitor's brightness and contrast controls, usually located below the screen or on the right side, to make sure they're not turned down all the way.

What's It Mumbling to Itself?

The term *booting* or *booting up* derives from "pulling oneself up by the boot-straps." Every time you turn on your PC, the system *BIOS (basic input/output system)*—a smidgen of software permanently stored on a chip inside your computer—checks the computer over. You don't have to do anything while the BIOS does its stuff, but you'll hear all sorts of sounds (whirs, beeps, clicks, grinds) and see a fair quantity of gibberish scrolling

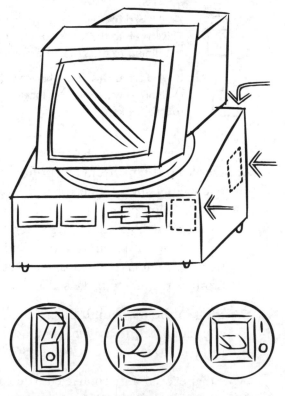

Figure 2: Where's the On button? *Here are some popular PC power switch styles and locations. Note that some power switches are marked by a horizontal line and a circle (the binary digits 1 and 0). The line means "on," the circle means "off."*

quickly on the monitor. Here's what your PC is doing and saying to itself:

1. It checks to see if it has power.

2. It does a self-test of its components. Many PCs display messages on screen that explain what's being tested, so if anything fails, you know immediately. You'll also hear a grinding noise from the floppy drives as the PC checks them out.

3. It looks for an *operating system* in floppy drive A: (at which point the drive grinds again). The operating system

is the software that enables your PC to run. Very likely, your operating system is DOS (an acronym for *disk operating system*) and the manufacturer has already put it on your C: drive (see the beginning of Chapter 12: *Windows and DOS* for more on what an operating system does). If there's no disk in drive A:—and there shouldn't be—the PC continues searching.

4. It looks for an operating system on drive C: (the hard disk) and most probably finds its there. Strictly speaking, booting is the process of *loading* DOS into *memory*—that is, of taking DOS out of *storage* on disk and making it active. Memory (also called *random access memory* or *RAM*) is an array of chips into which the computer puts everything (programs and data) it's actively handling. Storage refers to data and programs on disk that the computer isn't using right away. When the PC boots successfully, it beeps.

The point to remember here is the practical difference between memory and storage: When you turn off your PC, everything in RAM vaporizes, while everything stored on disk stays the same. Whatever you're working on as you compute is held in memory, so if you don't want that work to go to waste, you must copy it from memory to disk before you turn off your PC—a process called *saving* your work.

REMEMBER

Why Your PC Looks in Drive A:

There's a good reason why your PC begins its search for DOS with the A: drive. All the software stored on a PC's hard disk—including the operating system—must be fed to it using floppy disks. If the computer didn't start by looking in the A: drive, you (or rather, the guys at the factory) wouldn't be able to install DOS. Moreover, if your hard disk fails to boot (it happens!), you can start your PC anyhow—and probably revive drive C:, eventually—by slipping a DOS *boot disk* in the A: drive (see Chapter 12 for instructions on how to create a boot disk).

So don't leave your Pokerino game disk in the A: drive overnight. When you turn the PC on again, it'll find a game instead of DOS, and will stop right there ("Non-System disk or disk error," it'll say) until you take the loathsome thing out.

What You See After Your PC Boots Up

Your machine has finished booting. So what will you see on screen? This all depends on how your PC has been set up by the manufacturer. If you see something different than either of the screens shown here, then probably the company that sold you the PC has prepared your system specially in some way, and you should consult your manual (or follow the instructions on screen). If you don't see anything and your PC doesn't beep, either your PC is malfunctioning or no one bothered to put DOS on it. In the latter case, see "How to Install DOS and Windows" in Chapter 12.

Plain Old DOS

Less than half of all PCs go directly to DOS when you turn on your PC for the first time. This is not a fun place to be. If you're in DOS, you'll see a lone *DOS prompt*, which consists of the drive letter, a backslash, and a colon. Next to that will be a little flashing underline called the *cursor*, the point where the first letter of any command you type will appear. Your PC will sit there forever until you type a *DOS command*— that is, until you tell it to do something (see Chapter 12 for a rundown of the basic DOS commands).

In the bad old days of computing, people used DOS applications (some still do) to word process, crunch numbers, and so on. You'd type a command at the DOS prompt to start your DOS application and get to work. DOS applications are usually in *character mode*— that is, everything you see on screen is made up of *ASCII* (pronounced *ASK-ee*) characters, a standard set of 256 letters, numbers, and symbols. Character mode is ugly to look at, DOS applications are often hard to figure out, and DOS itself is notoriously unfriendly. The best thing to do at this point is get out of here and go

Figure 3: Welcome to DOS. *If you see this screen when you turn on your PC, the best thing to do is to head for Windows as quickly as possible.*

into Windows (to learn how to get there, see "The Keyboard and the Mouse," below).

Windows: A Friendlier Place to Be

If you've landed in Windows, you'll find yourself looking at a screen with rows of words along the top and a group of schematic pictures called *icons* in the middle. Windows works in *graphics mode*, which means the images you see on screen are *not* made up entirely of little characters and symbols. Graphics mode means that anything goes—photographic images, text, cartoons, numbers, whatever the programmer who created the software dreamt up.

Figure 4: Welcome to Windows. *There, that's better. If you see this screen when you turn on your PC, you're ready to start playing around with your computer (see Chapter 12: Windows and DOS).*

Because Windows and its applications are in graphics mode, and because they take advantage of that mode by symbolizing commands with fetching little icons, Windows is called a *graphical user interface* (or *GUI*, pronounced *gooey*). *Interface* is computerese for the screen display that enables you to interact with software; an interface is to a computer as a dashboard and steering wheel are to a car. There are several GUIs on the market, but Windows (a program written by Microsoft, the same company that created DOS) is by far the most popular.

Note that Compaq machines boot into something called *TabWorks*, a *Windows shell* that supposedly makes Windows easier to use (see Chapter 21: *Utilities* for more on Windows shells).

The Keyboard and the Mouse

Whether you end up in DOS or Windows, to talk to your PC properly you need two *input devices*: the keyboard and the mouse. Here's a quick look at both these devices and a few hints on how to use them.

A Tour of the Keyboard

A computer keyboard has all the characters of a typewriter keyboard and then some—101 keys in all. A few keyboards have nonstandard layouts, but the basic key placements are pretty much the same. Several keys have the same labels as typewriter keys but have slightly different functions. Some examples:

- Caps Lock works like the typewriter key—except that you only get capital letters when Caps Lock is on. The number keys are not affected by Caps Lock. To get the asterisk (*) on the 8 number key, for instance, you still have to press the Shift key. On most keyboards, a little light stays lit while Caps Lock is on.

- Tab jumps several spaces at a time, according to where you set it, just as with a typewriter. In Windows, Tab moves you to the next selection, while Shift Tab moves to the previous one.

- ←Backspace goes backward one space at a time, all right, but unlike a typewriter's backspace the PC version destroys everything in its path. Held down, it keeps deleting.

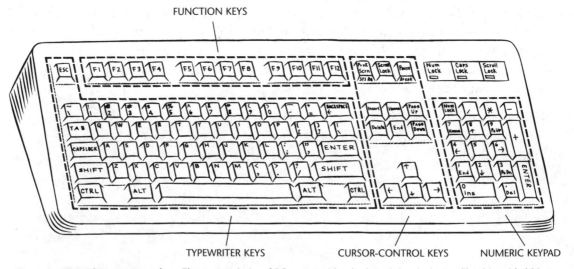

FUNCTION KEYS

TYPEWRITER KEYS   CURSOR-CONTROL KEYS   NUMERIC KEYPAD

Figure 5: More than a typewriter. The vast majority of PCs come with a keyboard that looks just like this, with 101 keys arranged in four basic groups.

The Four Most Important Computer Keys

Here are the four most important keys you'll find on a PC keyboard that you won't find on a typewriter:

- [Enter] starts a new paragraph by moving the cursor one line down. (You don't need to use it to start a new line in the middle of a paragraph; all applications *wrap* the line automatically.) [Enter] also tells the computer that you've completed a command, and that it's time to take action.

- [Esc], "Escape," is used in most applications to tell the computer "cancel that last command" or "stop that right now!" or "let's blow this joint." A very useful key.

- [Ctrl], "Control," is used in many programs as part of a command formed by pressing [Ctrl] and another key at the same time. For example, in Windows word processing programs, pressing [Ctrl][I] italicizes text.

- [Alt], "Alternate," activates the menu bar in Windows and in many DOS applications. Like [Ctrl], [Alt] is often used in combination with other keys to form commands.

If your computer "freezes" or "hangs" when you're trying to make it do something and it just won't unfreeze, simultaneously pressing [Ctrl][Alt][Del] will usually *reboot* your PC without your having to turn it off and back on. Unfortunately, all the work that was in memory will be lost.

REMEMBER

Three Special Key Groups

There are three groups of keys that don't appear on typewriters:

- **Function keys.** Numbered 1 through 10, the function keys line the top edge of the keyboard. With most applications, pressing a function key issues a command specific to that program, such as "print this document" or "go back to the beginning of this line." However, in almost any program, pressing [F1] gets you help with what you're doing in the form of instructions that pop up on the screen.

HOT TIP

- **Cursor keys.** The four "arrow keys," arranged in an upside-down "T," move the cursor up, down, and sideways, as indicated by their arrows. Depending on the application, [Home] takes you to the beginning of a document, the top of the screen, or the beginning of a line, while [End] takes you to the end of a document, screen, or line. [Page Down] advances you by a screen's worth, while [Page Up] goes backward by the same amount. [Insert] toggles between overtyping characters and pushing them to the right as you insert other characters. [Delete] erases the character on which the cursor is resting or any highlighted item (such as a block of text).

Three Keys You May Never Use

Typically, above the cursor pad are three other keys:

- [Print Screen] supposedly causes your printer to print all the text on screen, but this only works in some DOS programs (if the printer is off, [Print Screen] may freeze your computer). In Windows, [Print Screen] copies a picture of whatever is on your screen onto the Clipboard, where the image can be pasted into another document (go to Chapter 12: *Windows and DOS* to see what this is all about). "Sys Rq," on the side of the [Print Screen] key, is short for "System Request." It's a holdover from mainframe terminal days. Ignore it.

- [Scroll Lock] is used in some spreadsheet applications, but most people don't bother. You'll probably never need it.

- [Pause] freezes a scrolling screen in DOS (press [Enter] to start scrolling again). [Break], on the side of the [Pause] key, is accessed by pressing [Shift][Pause]. [Break] is a kind of emergency brake in DOS, enabling you to stop what DOS is doing and return to the DOS prompt. You can accomplish the same thing by pressing [Ctrl][C].

- **Numeric keypad.** With the [Num Lock] key on, this pad is like a 10-key adding machine's keyboard, enabling you to enter numbers and mathematical signs (into a spreadsheet, for instance). The +, -, and = signs are standard, but the asterisk (*) is the multiplier, while the slash (/) indicates division. With [Num Lock] off, the numeric keypad becomes an alternate cursor control pad.

Your First Keyboard Task: Getting to Windows

Most PCs come with Windows already on the hard disk. If you think you have Windows, but the computer left you in DOS, type

```
cd\windows
```

and press [Enter]. If the response is "Invalid directory," try

```
cd\win
```

If *that* doesn't work, see Chapter 12 to learn how to look for Windows and how to install Windows if it's not there. If you're successful—that is, you don't get a message from DOS saying you've done something wrong—type

```
win
```

and press [Enter]. Windows' smiling interface should appear momentarily.

Using a Mouse

You use the mouse to execute commands, jump around in documents, highlight blocks of text, or what have you. As you roll the mouse on your desk, an arrow-shaped *pointer* moves on screen in the same direction your hand moves. The leading end of the mouse is divided into two (or in some cases three) buttons, but the left-hand button is the one you'll use most by far (if you're left-handed, see Chapter 7 to learn how to swap buttons).

If you don't press any buttons, the pointer just floats on top of the application displayed on the screen. Press a button, and things happen. All applications use roughly the same vocabulary to describe mouse actions:

- **Clicking** means pressing the left mouse button once. Depending on where the pointer is, clicking may execute a command, cancel a command, or move you to a different location in a document. Often, to perform a specific action, you click on an item listed on a *menu* (a list of commands).

- **Clicking and dragging** means holding down the left mouse button and moving the pointer at the same time. You can drag a graphic or a chunk of text from one place to another by clicking and dragging, or you can *highlight* text or graphics as if you were using a highlighter pen (usually in preparation for another action, such as deleting).

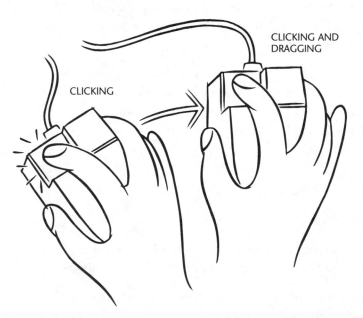

- **Double-clicking** means clicking something twice in very quick succession. Depending on what's beneath the pointer, this may start an application, execute a command, or call up a menu. Many people have difficulty double-clicking at first, because they don't click fast enough. **HOT TIP**

Figure 6: Mouse moves. Click the left mouse button to select an object or perform an action; click and drag to select text or move graphics or text.

- **Right-clicking** means pressing the right mouse button once. In many Windows applications, right-clicking on something brings up a menu of commands relating to whatever you clicked on.

Often, after you click once, the program will ask you to verify, placing a small box in the middle of the screen with a choice of two or more actions. Double-clicking is sort of like saying OK without being asked first.

Floppy Disks and Applications

Although Windows is nice to look at and the little applications that come with it are reasonably fun to use, you will inevitably purchase other software if you want to do serious work or have serious fun. (From the standpoint of the people who sell software, that's the whole point.)

Applications come in a shrink-wrapped cardboard box containing *floppy disks* (along with a manual telling you how to use the program). Floppy disks are like small, portable versions of hard disks. But instead of holding hundreds of megabytes, they generally hold no more than 1.44MB.

Floppies (also called *diskettes*) most often contain software, but they're also a handy way to transport data from one computer to another. If you don't have a modem or if you're not hooked up to a network, floppies are far and away the most convenient way to get data on and off your computer.

Floppies and the floppy drives that run them come in two sizes: $3^{1}/2$ inch and $5^{1}/4$ inch. The $3^{1}/2$-inch size stores more data, is easier to handle, and is less fragile—which is why $5^{1}/4$-inch floppies have all but disappeared. Unfortunately, they haven't *completely* disappeared, so you might want to buy a system with both sizes of drives just in case (see Chapter 4: *Disk Drives* for more on floppy disks).

Floppy Smarts

Here are a few tips to keep the data on your floppies safe:

- **Never touch the disk itself.** The magnetic disk is fully encased in a $3^{1}/2$-inch floppy, but it's easy to put your thumb on the large cutout area on a $5^{1}/4$-inch floppy.

- **Avoid magnets.** This includes not only refrigerator magnets, but also telephone handsets, speakers, or anything with an electric motor.

Bits and Bytes Defined!

Everyone throws *bits, bytes, binary,* and related terms around without knowing their true meanings. With these definitions, you can amaze your friends and maybe get a little better idea of how computers work:

- **Binary logic.** Most of us automatically do our "math thinking" in the decimal system, which is based on the number ten (based, in turn, on the number of fingers our species can count on). Computers use a binary system, which makes complete sense for an electronic brain: The two binary numbers are zero and one, representing "off" and "on." Counting in binary goes: 0, 1, 10, 11, 100, 101, 110, 111, 1000, 1001, and so forth.

- **Bits and bytes.** A *bit* (short for *binary digit*) is the smallest unit of computer information. Eight bits make one *byte*, which is the amount of information that makes up a single character (a letter, number, or symbol). You measure memory and storage in bytes or multiples of bytes.

- **Kilobyte** (abbreviated K) sounds like it ought to be 1000 bytes, but it's actually 1024 bytes. From here on up, all multiples are based on 1024. One K equals approximately one third of a single-spaced page of text.

- **Megabyte** (abbreviated MB) is 1024K or over a million bytes. Your PC's memory and storage capacities are expressed in megabytes. A gigabyte (GB) is 1024MB or over a billion bytes. The biggest hard disks you can buy today store about 2GB of data.

Data, incidentally, is a slippery term. To your computer, data is simply anything that takes up bytes, including *software.* From your perspective, *data* means information you've created or want to change—as opposed to *software,* the tool you use to create or alter information.

- **Keep 'em dry.** Liquids and floppies don't mix. If you spill your drink on one, kiss it goodbye.

- **Do not crush.** Don't place heavy objects on top of disks (even the sturdy 3$1/2$-inch floppies, which aren't floppy at all), because this can grind dust into the surface of the disk.

- **Avoid temperature extremes.** No dashboards or windowsills in summer, no car trunks in the dead of a Minnesota winter.

- **Don't lube it.** Don't spray lubricants (such as WD-40) into your floppy drives, no matter what horrible noises they make. The noises are normal.

Figure 7: Using a 3¹/₂-inch floppy drive. To insert a 3¹/₂-inch floppy, slip in the shiny metal edge first, with the hub side of the disk down. To remove the disk, push the button on the drive. Always wait until the drive light is out before removing!

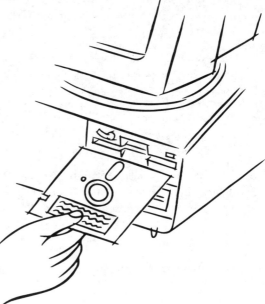

Figure 8: Using a 5¹/₄-inch floppy drive. To insert a 5¹/₄-inch floppy, slide it in label side up, so that the cutout exposing the magnetic surface of the disk goes in first. Flip the lever down to close the drive. Flip the lever up to open the drive and remove the disk—but only after the drive light has gone out!

- **5¹/₄-inch tips.** Put 5¹/₄-inch disks back in their protective sleeves after use. Don't write in ballpoint pen on the disk label, because this may damage the disk itself. Mail 5¹/₄-inch disks inside sturdy cardboard disk mailers.

Avoid working directly on floppies beyond what's necessary. It's faster, easier, and quieter (and causes less wear and tear on the drive and diskette) to copy data to the hard disk and work on it there.

Application Basics

To *install* an application—that is, to copy it from floppies to your hard disk, where every application you own should be stored—you usually slip the floppy disk labeled #1 or Setup into your A: drive. Type `a:install` or `a:setup` and press `Enter`, and nine times out of ten the application's installation "routine" leads you through a step-by-step process that involves shuffling several floppies in and out of the drive. The Cookbook in Chapter 12 provides several handy tips for installing applications.

Once you've installed an application worth using, you're ready to do something meaningful with your new PC. Almost everything you create on a computer will be called a *file*. Files are the basic units that hold data of any sort. A file can be a five-word note to your neighbor or a gigantic collection of information about your business's customers. There are two general types of files:

- **Program files** contain all or part of a program or application (applications are usually big programs made up of many program files).

- **Data files** contain information you've created or want to manipulate, rather than software. A customer file, your latest novel, and a spreadsheet full of meaningless projections are all data files.

Each file should have a unique name. DOS imposes ridiculous restrictions on how you can name files, a sorry state of affairs addressed (along with other file matters) at the beginning of Chapter 12.

Opening, Storing, and Abandoning Files

On a very basic level, every application handles files in the same way. In fact, most applications display a File menu in the upper-left corner of the screen (click on the word File with your mouse to display the menu). Learn your way around this menu, and you can immediately begin work in any application:

- **New** starts a new file, whether a word processing document, a blank spreadsheet, or an empty database. This is your blank slate. Do what you will.

- **Open** loads an existing file. That is, you pick a file by name from a list, and the application copies the file from storage (that is, from the hard or floppy disk) into memory, your computer's work area.

- **Save** copies a new file (or an existing file that you've changed) from memory to the hard disk for safekeeping. If you've created a new file, you give it a name when you save for the first time.

- **Save as** lets you make a second copy of the open file, only you must give it a different name (or store it in a different location).

- **Print** lets you send all or part of your file to the printer.

> ## Data Safety Tip #1
>
> A hard disk stores data like an electronic filing cabinet, keeping it safe and sound even when you turn off your PC. That is, it *usually* keeps your data safe. Hard disks have moving parts that wear out. Computer viruses can do terrible mischief. And sometimes, lightning *does* strike. The only way to keep your data safe is to create a copy of it called a *backup* and store it in a safe place. Before you get very far in your computing career, turn to Chapter 9: *Protect Your Data* and learn how to develop your own daily backup program. Someday—guaranteed—you *will* need that backup copy.

- **Close** abandons a new file or any changes you've made to an existing file. Usually, you use this option when you've messed up an existing file and want to restore the file to its original condition.

- **Exit** gets you out of the application. Remember to save your changes before you Exit.

DANGER

Remember that you must save an open file before you exit your application or turn off your PC, or you lose any changes you've made. Save your work every few minutes—some day, that heater *will* trip the circuit breaker or the computer may freeze up for no reason at all. Experienced PC users get into the habit of saving their work every *10–15 minutes*, or they use automatic options that save the current file in memory at regular intervals.

Bye for Now (Shutting Down)

When you're done working, you can't just switch off the computer. (Life should be simpler than this.) Here's your basic shutdown procedure:

1. **Save your work.** The file you're messing with is in memory while you're working on it, and as you know by now, anything in memory disappears when you turn off your PC. If you don't save the file before you shut down, you'll lose any changes you made, back to the point when you *last* saved the file.

2. **Exit your applications (and Windows).** If Windows or applications are loaded in memory when you turn off your system, damage to the software may result (or at least fragments of program file copies will be scattered around your hard disk and take up space unnecessarily). To get out of Windows, pull down the File menu in the Program Manager, select Exit Windows, and click OK—this will land you at the DOS prompt, which is where you should be at shutdown time.

3. **Turn off your PC.** Now you can flick the power switch. Don't forget to turn off your monitor, too.

Your computing session is now officially over. Easy, right?

If you don't agree with that sentiment, remember that making mistakes is one of the most popular computing activities, and no one has ever damaged the hardware by pressing the wrong key. True, you can completely destroy your data, but if you're a beginner, destroying the small quantity of data you've accumulated probably won't be too tragic. If on the other hand your PC didn't work properly—say, it wouldn't boot, it froze, or it refused to cooperate in some other obtuse way—then you should call your PC manufacturer's technical support line immediately.

If you have all the hardware you think you'll need, and it seems to work all right, then the next logical step after reading this chapter is to turn to Chapter 12: *Windows and DOS* and learn the ins and outs of your most basic and essential software. From there, you can take your pick of the application chapters—Chapter 14: *Word Processing*, Chapter 17: *Graphics*, whatever strikes your fancy. This book is intended to be browsed rather than studied, so kick back, skim a few pages, and see what happens.

2 How to Buy a PC

By Eric Knorr

- The five key points to consider when choosing a system
- The right components to get more speed for your dollar
- Buying enough room for software, data, and options
- Warranty, service, and tech support advice
- Suggested PC configurations for your software and budget

Like many things in life, buying a PC is whole lot easier once you decide what you want. You may already have an idea of how much you want to spend. But do you really know what you're getting?

Don't let a salesperson make up your mind for you. Before you walk into a superstore or order a PC by phone, decide which of the following five things are important to you, and which you can live with less of:

- **Speed.** No one likes to wait for a program to start or a spreadsheet to calculate—the question is how much you're willing to pay to wait less. The *central processing unit* (CPU) has more effect on a PC's speed and price than any other component. There are several dozen CPU types and speeds, and a big part of this chapter is devoted to helping you choose a PC with the right one (see Figure 2). The rule of thumb: Don't buy anything less than a PC with an SX2-66 CPU.

HOT TIP

- **Capacity.** Two factors here: Room on the hard disk, and room for disk drives and expansion cards. You need space on your hard disk to store all the programs and data you think you'll be using, plus at least 50 percent more (a 200MB hard disk is an absolute minimum). As for options, look for at least two empty slots for expansion cards, plus space for a tape backup and a second hard disk.

HOT TIP

- **Reliability.** PCs seldom break beyond repair, but problems often occur, so always get at least a one-year warranty covering parts, labor, and telephone technical support. It's usually worth spending a little more for on-site (that is, to-your-door) service and a two-year warranty.

- **Monitor quality.** Computing is hell on the eyes, but a better monitor can help (see Chapter 5: *Monitors, Etc.*). Monitors that come with PCs aren't always so hot, so you may want to purchase one separately, though doing so usually costs more. Look for sharp focus, low glare, and straight lines, and don't put up with flicker. Monitors that measure 17 inches and larger may cost a bundle, but they're usually high quality and enable you to see a lot more on screen without squinting or scrolling.

- **Multimedia.** Everywhere you turn, you see "multimedia" PCs equipped with sound cards, speakers, and CD ROM drives. What can you do with this extra $300 to $600 worth of hardware? Play flashy games and run educational software, mostly (see Chapter 23: *Multimedia*). If you have little use for either, invest that money in speed, capacity, and so on. You can always add a CD ROM drive or sound card yourself later.

This chapter can help you find a PC with the speed, capacity, and reliability you want at a price you can afford. The idea is to aid you in choosing an appropriate PC *configuration* (that is, combination of components) before you buy, so you won't wish you'd found a better deal later. At the end of this chapter, you'll find several suggested configurations.

Watch Out for Future Software!

As you shop, remember to consider *future* performance and capacity. Today's muscle PC is tomorrow's wimp, because new software keeps getting bigger, better, and hungrier for power. Any "excess" performance and hard disk space you buy now will pay off later in a longer useful life span. Whatever PC you buy, it should be easy to *upgrade* (that is, swap parts in and out of) so you can add more powerful components later, such as a faster CPU (see Chapter 8: *Upgrade It Yourself*).

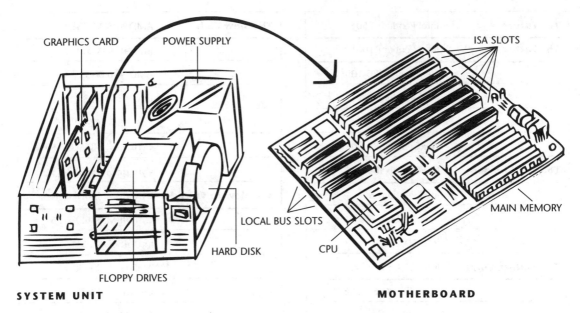

Figure 1: Your PC and its motherboard. *Welcome to the inside of a typical PC. Choose components wisely, and you'll get more performance and capacity for your buck.*

Speed: What to Look For, What to Pay

The CPU isn't the only component that has a big impact on speed. In fact, it's not unusual for two PCs with the same CPU to show a 20 percent difference in performance. That's because memory, the make and model of hard disk, the choice of *graphics controller* (the component that sends data to your screen), and various bits of engineering on the motherboard all have their roles to play in moving data along. Still, it's usually the CPU that makes the difference between a PC that's snappy and one that just shuffles along.

Choosing a PC With the Right CPU

The CPU *is* the computer, the electronic brain where all software commands turn into action. It's the biggest chip on the *motherboard*, the main circuit board that lines the bottom interior of most PCs. Most PC models get their name from the type of CPU inside them (486, DX4, Pentium, and so on). You don't need to know how a CPU works, but you should know how one CPU's performance compares to others' —or you may pay too much for a laggard PC.

The Future	Intel Pentium-150[1]	**The Slow Club**	AMD 486DX-33[1]
The Fastest	Intel Pentium-100[1]		Intel 486DX-33[1]
	NexGen Nx586-100[2]		AMD 486SX-33
	Intel Pentium--90[1]		Intel 486SX-33
	NexGen Nx586-90[2]		Intel 486DX2-40[1]
	NexGen Nx586-80[2]		Cyrix/IBM 486SLC2-50
The Workhorses	NexGen Nx586-75[2]		Cyrix/IBM 486SX3-75
	Intel Pentium-66[1]	**Too Slow to Consider**	Cyrix/IBM 486DLC-40
	Intel Pentium-60[1]		Cyrix/IBM 486SX2-66
	Intel DX4-100[1]		Intel 486DX-25[1]
The Budget Chips	Intel DX4-83[1]		AMD 386DXL-40
	Cyrix/IBM 486DX2-80[1]		Cyrix/IBM 486DLC-33
	Intel DX4-75[1]		Cyrix/IBM 486SLC2-40
	AMD 486DX2-66[1]		Cyrix/IBM 486SX2-50
	Cyrix/IBM 486DX2-66[1]		AMD 486SX-25
	Intel DX2-66[1]		Intel 486SX-25
	AMD 486SX2-66		
	Intel SX2-66		
Bargain Basement	Cyrix/IBM 486SLC2-66		
	AMD 486DX-50[1]		
	Intel 486DX-50[1]		
	Cyrix/IBM 486SX3-100		
	AMD 486DX-40[1]		
	AMD 486SX-40		
	AMD 486DX2-50[1]		
	Cyrix/IBM DX2-50[1]		
	Intel 486DX2-50[1]		
	AMD SX2-50		
	Intel SX2-50		

[1]Includes built-in math coprocessor
[2]Available with or without math coprocessor

Figure 2: How the chips stack up. This chart ranks the most popular CPUs from fastest to slowest—more or less, since different tests show different results, and some of the rankings within each list are based on estimates.
As you might expect, PCs with faster CPUs are generally more expensive, although you may get a break with non-Intel CPUs. In addition, note that AMD, Cyrix/IBM, and Intel processors with the same DX or DX2 designation should perform equally well.

You'll find the relative speeds of the most common CPUs in Figure 2, along with some idea of pricing for PCs that contain them. Note that many of the CPUs have similar names, except for the number following the hyphen. The word or number before the hyphen indicates the CPU's *class*, while the number after the hyphen indicates the CPU's *clock speed* in megahertz (MHz). Clock speed is to processor class as a car's RPMs are to engine size: Run a big engine at the same RPM as a smaller one, and the larger engine can pull a bigger load. That's why, for example, a Pentium-66 is nearly twice as fast as a DX2-66.

Had your fill of CPU jargon? Then let's cut to the chase. The hottest deal you can get is a PC with a NexGen Nx586-90 or Intel Pentium-90 CPU.

HOT TIP

Doing the Numbers: Math Coprocessors

They're called central processing units, but Pentium, DX4, DX2, and DX CPUs are actually two processors in one: a CPU and a *math coprocessor* (also known as a floating-point unit or FPU) together on the same chip. Math coprocessors can speed up spreadsheet financial and statistical functions several times over, and many *computer-aided design (CAD)* programs (used for creating architectural or engineering diagrams) require a math coprocessor in order to function.

What Happened to the Good Old DOS PC?

In case you haven't noticed, the buying recommendations in this chapter assume that you'll be running Windows. Why? Because that's where all the best software is—the best word processors, spreadsheets, graphics programs, you name it. Old DOS programs such as *WordPerfect 5.1* or *1-2-3 2.4* can't hold a candle to the Windows stuff.

The advantage DOS programs have is that you can run them on cheap hardware. For the latest Windows software, you should really have a 486 PC or better, but most DOS programs run just fine on an old-fashioned 386 PC. Few companies sell 386 PCs anymore, but if you order by mail you may be able to buy a 386 PC complete for as little as $500 or $600—considerably less than the cheapest 486. If you're on a very tight budget and you can live with hard-to-use DOS software, a super-cheap 386 might do the trick. You can always give it to the kids when you buy a real computer.

If neither of these software activities sounds like your game, a math coprocessor may not speed things up at all, and you can save money by buying a PC that lacks one. Still, an increasing number of new programs can benefit from a math coprocessor, so I recommend that you opt for one in any case, unless you can save, say, $100 to $200 dollars. True, you can always add a CPU with a math coprocessor later, but it's an expensive upgrade.

HOT TIP

CPU Upgrades

HOT TIP

Make sure the PC you buy can accept an Intel OverDrive. These upgrade CPUs plug either into a special OverDrive socket inside your PC, or into the same socket as the original CPU (which means you have to unplug the original CPU first). Depending on what program you're running, OverDrives typically give your PC a 30 to 70 percent performance boost. They're the easiest, most cost-effective way to upgrade the CPU (and in some cases add a math coprocessor at the same time).

Some PCs also offer *processor card* upgrades. Here, the CPU sits on an expansion card that plugs into a special slot inside the PC. When new software hinders performance, you extract the old card and plug in the new, making your choice of CPU limited only by the imagination of future engineers. Replacing the processor card is an expensive way to upgrade, though, because you pay for both the new CPU and the card itself. Fortunately, most processor cards also accept OverDrive CPUs.

HOT TIP

If the PC you want to buy has an OverDrive socket, in effect that PC is guaranteed to work with an Intel OverDrive chip. If it doesn't have an OverDrive socket, call Intel's "fax-back" line at 800/525-3019 to get a list of systems certified as OverDrive compatible. If your PC is on the list, you get your money back if the upgrade *doesn't* work (for more on CPU upgrades, see Chapter 8: *Upgrade It Yourself*).

The PowerPC and Other New Chips

All the chips in Figure 2 share one salient feature: They run DOS (and Windows, of course). The ability to do this was once the very definition of a PC, but that is changing.

One reason is Windows NT, which comes in several different versions, some of which run on CPUs that are not Intel compatible. NT is designed to replace both DOS and Windows. It looks just like Windows, but more important, it can run most Windows programs, and it's more reliable than Windows itself (see "Windows Alternatives" at the end of Chapter 12: *Windows and DOS*).

The Compatibility Question

Intel, the world's largest chip manufacturer, sets the standard for PC CPUs, so any CPU made by a competing company needs to be compatible with Intel's standard in order to run the huge number of PC programs out there (see "The PowerPC and Other New Chips" for exceptions to this rule). Salespeople and other misinformed individuals sometimes imply that if a CPU isn't made by Intel, its compatibility is questionable. Bunk! I've never heard of any AMD, Cyrix, or IBM chip that was designed to be Intel-compatible having a problem. In fact, you can often get better deals on PCs with CPUs from Intel's competitors, because they tend to sell their chips for less.

What this means, basically, is that you can run your favorite Windows program on any PC with a CPU that runs NT, regardless of whether that chip can run DOS or not. The following Intel-incompatible CPUs can (or will soon be able to) run NT. They can also run DOS and Windows software, but the scheme for doing so makes them slow and inefficient.

- **The PowerPC.** You may have heard of this cheap and very fast CPU because Apple's Power Mac uses it. Not only can this multiple-personality chip run Mac software, but it will also soon be able to run Workplace-OS (IBM's forthcoming NT-like operating system) along with NT itself. Whenever PowerPC versions of the hottest Windows programs arrive, a PC with this CPU could be an attractive choice.

- **DEC Alpha.** Designed to run NT, DEC's Alpha CPU looks faster than Intel's Pentium on paper. But as with the PowerPC, programs need to be modified slightly for the CPU to crank them at top speed, and so far, there aren't that many. Unless you're dying to use a specific program recompiled for the Alpha, a PC with this CPU is not recommended.

- **The MIPS R4000 and R4400.** Just like the Alpha, these chips run NT like blazes, but few NT programs have been recompiled to take advantage of them. You'll get lightning performance out of programs modified for these chips, but other programs will run faster on Intel Pentium PCs.

PCs with PowerPC, Alpha, or MIPS CPUs also tend to cost more than Intel-based systems in roughly the same performance class. If prices come down and enough software you want to use runs quickly on these alternative systems, give them serious consideration. Otherwise, buy a system that uses an Intel chip or one of its compatibles.

HOT TIP

Memory and Performance

Two kinds of memory affect performance: *main memory* and *cache memory*. Main memory is the CPU's work area, into which software and data are copied (or "loaded") from the hard disk. You don't have to worry much about main memory when you're shopping for a PC, but in some cheap PCs a low limit on cache memory can hobble performance.

Main Memory

No PC should have less than 4MB of RAM, or your software will get cramped and you'll feel like you are computing in molasses. Some PCs are sold with less, but that's not a problem. The Single Inline Memory Modules (SIMMs) used by virtually all PCs are so inexpensive and easy to install, many people save money by buying their PCs with minimum memory and purchasing additional SIMMs separately through a discount mail-order firm.

HOT TIP

A comfortable amount of memory for most PCs is 8MB. However, for people who like to run several programs at once, 16MB isn't unusual. Your PC should have room for at least 32MB if you plan on running fancy new Windows NT software, more if you want to set up a network server (see Chapter 22: *About Networks*).

Upgrading memory is easy, physically—you just pop SIMMs in and out—but upgrading can be hard on the wallet if you must discard old SIMMs in order to install new ones. Before you buy, check the system's specifications and see whether it takes 30-pin SIMMs or 72-pin SIMMs. The 72-pin variety is more expensive, but better: You seldom have to chuck old SIMMs when you upgrade memory, as you often must do with the 30-pin variety.

Cache Memory

The trouble with main memory is that it's slow compared to your average CPU. In fact, most CPUs access main memory *directly* as little as possible, because they must slow down to do so. Instead, CPUs prefer to access a superfast (and expensive) memory zone called a memory cache. Special circuitry guesses what the CPU wants from main memory and copies it to the *memory cache*, where the CPU doesn't have to reduce speed to work on it.

All 486 and Pentium CPUs have a memory cache right on the chip. But it's a small one, and oftentimes the CPU can't find what it needs in the cache. To prevent the CPU from having to slow down and resort to main memory, most PCs have a second line of defense called *secondary* (or *external*) cache memory.

HOT TIP

For good performance, a PC with any of the CPUs in Figure 2 should have some kind of secondary memory cache. Figure 4 shows recommended minimums for some of the most popular Intel CPUs; add more and you can often improve performance somewhat. Some secondary memory

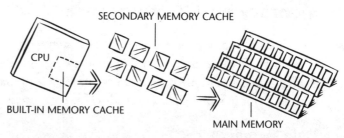

Figure 3: Why you need cache memory. *Main memory is too slow for the CPU to access quickly—so most CPUs have their own fast, on-chip memory cache. If the CPU can't find what it needs there, it turns to the secondary cache before resorting to main memory. A larger secondary cache can yield better performance.*

Recommended Secondary Cache Sizes

PC Type (CPU Class)	Size of Cache on CPU	Recommended Minimum Secondary Cache Size	Typical Main Memory Size
486DX or 486SX	8K	128K	8MB
DX2 or SX2	8K	128K	8MB
DX4	16K	256K	8MB–16MB
Pentium	16K	512K[1]	16MB+

[1]Write-back cache strongly preferred.

Figure 4: If your PC has a secondary cache smaller than that listed here, performance may suffer. Some secondary caches can be upgraded, and some cannot, so check before you buy.

caches can't be upgraded, however, so shop carefully. One final tip: Of the two most common memory-caching methods, "write-back" is generally better than "write-through," and a write-back secondary cache is strongly recommended for Pentium systems.

Fast Graphics and the Local Bus

CPUs are so fast, memory isn't the only thing that has trouble keeping up. Sometimes, the CPU quickly processes a hunk of data but then encounters a bottle-neck or two on the way to the screen. One obstacle could be the graphics controller. The other might be the *bus*—the circuit where the graphics controller and other components reside.

For top performance, look for a PC that has *local bus graphics*. This means the CPU and the graphics controller run at nearly the same speed. Sometimes, the graphics controller is on the motherboard, but more frequently it sits on a local bus graphics card that plugs into one of two or three local bus slots.

HOT TIP

There are two types of local buses: VL and PCI. There's little performance difference between the two, but you'll find more cards for the PCI bus. You probably shouldn't sink more than a couple hundred dollars into a local bus graphics card, because even the cheap ones are pretty quick (see Chapter 5: *Monitors, Etc.*).

Hard Disk Performance

The hard disk is the biggest bottleneck in any system. Unfortunately, unless you run benchmarks on a bunch of PCs before you choose one (not likely), you can't *really* tell which make and model hard disk will be slower, and which will be faster. However, the following specifications can give you a rough idea:

- **Average seek time.** This is the mean time it takes for a hard disk to access any point on a hard disk platter, expressed in milliseconds (ms). Typical average seek times range from 8.5ms to 15ms (the lower number is better). You usually pay more for hard disks with a faster average seek time, but not always.

- **Local bus or not?** Hard disks require an *interface* in order to connect to your PC's motherboard. If the PC you buy has a local bus, and the hard disk interface can plug into it, you may get much better performance (see Chapter 5: *Disk Drives* for more information).

- **Data transfer rate.** This is the amount of data a hard disk can send to memory in one second. Typical data transfer rates range from around 1.5MB per second to 3MB per second, but the variation in real performance is far less dramatic. Drives with SCSI (pronounced "scuzzy") interfaces have the highest potential data transfer rates, but a better reason to buy one is that you can hook up to seven SCSI devices (including CD ROM drives) to a single interface card.

- **Disk rotation speed.** The faster a hard disk's platter spins, the quicker that data can be accessed and transferred. Hard disks are fixed at one speed: from 3600 RPM to 5400 RPM. Few people consider this specification when they buy, but other specs being equal, faster RPM disks consistently perform better.

HOT TIP

HOT TIP

Another big factor in hard disk performance is the *disk cache*. Here, data that the CPU is likely to need is automatically copied into main memory, where it can be accessed quicker than the hard disk can fetch it. You should always use a disk cache—the question is what kind. Don't be snookered into paying extra for an expensive hard disk interface card with a *hardware* disk cache on it. *A software* disk cache called a SmartDrive uses a small portion of your PC's main memory, comes free with DOS, and works nearly as well as a $300 hardware cache card.

Capacity: How Much Room Is Enough?

Software and data grow to fill all available hard disk space. And as the months wear on, you may also find yourself running out of room for such options as tape backup drives, sound cards, CD ROM drives, network cards, and the like. The trade-off is between a sleek little machine with a cramped interior, and a desk hog that can hold anything but makes you wonder where you'll put your mug.

Hard Disks, Limited

It's hard to even *find* a hard disk smaller than 210MB. And a 340MB model costs so little more, you're best advised to start there. In fact, you won't regret buying one in the 540MB range.

HOT TIP

What could you possibly use 540MB for? Well, software takes a lot of room, and future software will take even more. DOS and Windows alone eat up about 14MB, and Windows word processors and spreadsheet programs take from 20MB to 30MB each. Multimedia sound and video *files* may occupy many megabytes. On a personal note, my 340MB hard disk has only 87MB left, I'm not interested in multimdia, and I'm not really sure what happened to the other 253MB. Get the idea?

When my hard disk runs out of space, I probably won't replace it—I'll add a second hard disk instead. Fortunately, there's enough room in my PC to do this, but some PCs are too cramped to oblige. To avoid having to replace *your* hard disk when it fills up, get a PC with room for a second drive.

HOT TIP

Room for Floppy Drives, Etc.

Hard disks can be mounted deep in your PC's innards. But floppy disk drives, CD ROM drives, and tape backup drives need to be mounted where you can slip disks and tapes in and out. Many PCs give you

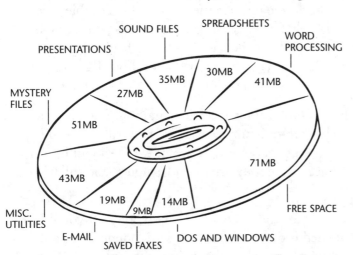

Figure 5: How a 340MB hard disk runs out of space. *Like a garage, a closet, or the bottom drawer of your desk, hard disks collect an amazing amount of stuff. True, this hard disk could probably use a housecleaning— but who has time for that?*

Labels around the disk: PRESENTATIONS · SOUND FILES · SPREADSHEETS · WORD PROCESSING · MYSTERY FILES · MISC. UTILITIES · E-MAIL · SAVED FAXES · DOS AND WINDOWS · FREE SPACE

Values: 35MB · 30MB · 41MB · 27MB · 51MB · 71MB · 43MB · 19MB · 9MB · 14MB external access to two drives at most. That's enough for the bare essentials: one 5 1/4-inch floppy drive and one 3 1/2-inch floppy drive (if you think one type of floppy drive is enough, wait until you run across a vital floppy disk you can't use).

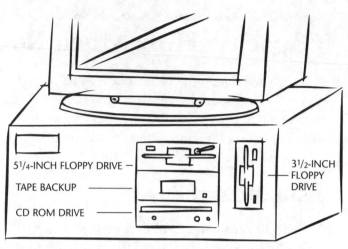

Everyone needs a tape backup drive (a QIC-80 model should add less than $200 to the price; see Chapter 9: *Protect Your Data*). Tape drives that install in your PC cost less than self-contained models—

Figure 6: Why you need room up front. *At the least, a PC should have space for two floppy disk drives so you'll be able to read both kinds of floppy disks. Tape backup and CD ROM drives that install in your PC cost less than self-contained models, so it's nice to have space up front for them, too.*

HOT TIP

so external access to three drives is a very good idea. The same is true of CD ROM drives, so if you plan to add one of those, access to four drives is best.

How Many Slots and What Kind?

The vast majority of PCs have ISA (Industry Standard Architecture) slots. The choice of expansion cards to plug into them is virtually limitless, but the *performance* of the ISA bus is quite limited. That's why they came up with the local bus—to enable cards to run faster and get some processing help from fast CPUs. Up to this point, graphics cards have benefited most from the local bus, but hard disks are beginning to get some of the speed benefits, too. That means you should buy a local bus PC with, in addition to the usual ISA slots, at least two local bus slots.

HOT TIP

So how many slots should a PC have all told? This is a trick question. For example, some PCs have hard disk interfaces built into the motherboard, while others need an interface card to talk to a hard disk. Here's the way to figure it: A PC should have a graphics controller, a hard disk interface, two floppy drives, and a mouse, and still have

REMEMBER

at least two slots free.

I can suggest plenty of expansion cards for those slots, but who knows? If you'll be hooking your PC to a LAN, you'll need room for a network card. Sound cards are a popular item. Modem cards cost less than external modems. Cards that play VCR-like

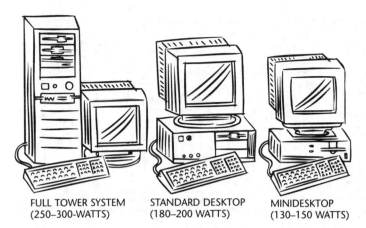

FULL TOWER SYSTEM
(250–300-WATTS)

STANDARD DESKTOP
(180–200 WATTS)

MINIDESKTOP
(130–150 WATTS)

Figure 7: PCs and their power needs. The more drives and cards a PC can hold, the bigger the power supply it needs (hard drives need the most juice). Use these estimates to make sure a PC has what it takes to pull a full load.

video are great if you like that sort of thing. And then there's the other stuff not invented yet. That's why two free slots are the minimum—and three or four are better.

HOT TIP

In place of ordinary ISA slots, some systems come with EISA (Extended Industry Standard Architecture) slots, which accept either ISA or EISA cards. The EISA bus and its cards potentially offer better performance than ISA cards, but the benefits are only significant with network servers. The EISA bus adds to the price of the system and EISA cards are expensive, so if you're buying a desktop PC, don't bother.

Power to Spare

You PC's *power supply*, the box inside your PC that supplies juice to everything except the monitor, must be big enough to handle all the drives and boards you want to install. This is seldom a question—most power supplies can handle a full house with no problem. For example, a 200-watt power supply almost always has sufficient power to support whatever you can load into a standard desktop system.

Unfortunately, some cheap tower PCs have that same 200-watt power supply, even though they can hold nearly twice the cards and drives. Fill one of these babies with drives, and its wimpy power supply could shut itself down (or cause data errors). If you're in the market for a tower, insist on a 250 to 300-watt power supply.

The fans in power supplies sometimes make an obnoxious amount of noise, which can drive you crazy over time. If you're buying by mail, ask about the power supply's noise level; if you're in a store, listen. You can always replace the power supply later if it bothers you—replacements are cheap—but if you buy a quiet one to begin with, you needn't bother.

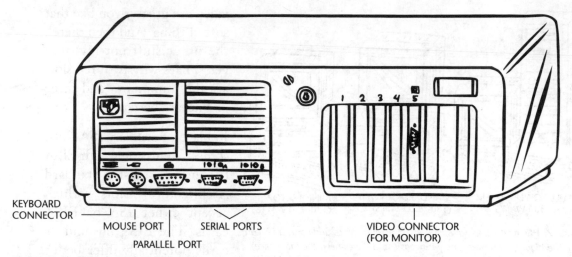

KEYBOARD
CONNECTOR
MOUSE PORT
PARALLEL PORT
SERIAL PORTS
VIDEO CONNECTOR
(FOR MONITOR)

*Figure 8: **Finding the right connections.*** *Here's a typical set of connectors on the back of your average PC. Never buy a system with less than two serial ports (or one serial port and one mouse port).*

All Those Connectors in the Back

The back of every PC has at least four kinds of connectors. You'll find one for the monitor, one for the keyboard, and sometimes one for a mouse. You'll also find at least one serial port and one parallel port (sometimes called a printer port). However, you should insist on two serial ports (or one serial port and one mouse port), since a mouse plus an external modem is a very common combination.

Reliability: Buying Peace of Mind

Sometimes bad things happen to perfectly good PCs. A can of Diet Coke gets spilled on the keyboard, a hard disk freezes, a "we're sorry, but that number..." message comes on when you call tech support. But with a reliable company and a solid warranty, good things can happen to even the worst PC—like, a technician shows up to recover your data or a replacement PC arrives by Fed Ex.

Note that big mail-order companies like Gateway and Dell provide just as much security as companies that sell exclusively through stores (there are few such companies left—even IBM and Compaq sell by mail). Whether you buy from across the street or across the country, your peace of mind depends mostly on the terms of the warranty and how well the company honors it.

What to Look for in a Warranty

Standard two-year warranties are pretty common, so if there are two PCs you like equally, longer-term coverage could be the tiebreaker. Of course, everything hinges on what you get during that period of time.

- **Telephone technical support.** This is your first line of defense, and your most important one—something like 90 percent of all hardware problems can be solved over the phone. If it's not an 800 number, the company is nickle-and-diming you. Long weekday hours and even weekend hours (you never know) can help in a pinch—but not if you get a busy signal. That's why you should always call the company's tech support line to make sure you can get through *before* you buy.

- **On-site service.** Believe it or not, PC companies usually provide this for free. A technician will come to your place and fix your PC if the problem can't be solved over the phone. (Actually, what these techs usually do is replace parts and decide if you need a replacement machine—and they generally take longer to show up than advertised.) Some companies charge a minimal extra fee for on-site service, but it's worth the money.

- **Fax-back.** Here's how this works: You dial into a voice-mail maze, select a technical document about your PC and its problem, and have it faxed to your fax number automatically. I use fax-back services to get fast answers all the time. If you can find the right document, this route is as good as phone support.

- **Bulletin board service (BBS).** You log on, type in your question, and check again in 24 hours to read the response (see Chapter 21: *Communications*). Kind of like phone support in very slow motion.

- **Sending it back.** The last resort! If you don't have on-site service, hopefully you can get the company to pay for shipping when the phone tech says, "OK, I give up, send it to us." (You kept your original packing material, didn't you?) There's also the dreaded carry-in method, where you lug the thing to the nearest service center. Some kind of guaranteed turnaround time is good policy in either case—none of that "You want it when?" stuff.

The most obvious support should be right next to your PC—your manual. Checking the index and flipping to the right page is often the fastest way to answer any question. Buy a PC that doesn't have a manual, and you're asking for trouble. At the very least, the phone lines at the cut-rate company that sold you the PC will be ringing off the wall.

Buying From a No-Name Company

A great service and support agreement won't help if the manufacturer goes belly up. Some people simply avoid risk and buy from a big company like Compaq or IBM, and usually pay more—sometimes much more than the cost of stuff advertised in the back of computer tabloids. If you're not so skittish and have your eye on a faster, cheaper PC from Makeshift Computers, read on.

REMEMBER

• **Pay with a credit card.** Buy by mail and send a check, and the company will cash it right away. If your order gets lost, the company dies, or you're deliberately scammed (this happens more than you might expect), your PC may be a long time coming. Always, always, always pay by credit card. If the worst happens, you'll have a means of recourse and may be able to recover your money.

DANGER

• **Demand a 30-day, unconditional, money-back guarantee.** This is basic stuff, but make sure you get one. Ask what happens if you *do* have to send the system back. Do you pay only for shipping, or also for "restocking"? Some companies charge up to 20 percent of the price of your PC just for putting it back on the shelf.

• **Check references.** Call the Better Business Bureau for the city where the company is located and ask if any complaints have been registered. While you're at it, find out how long the company has been in business; if less than a year, you might want to reconsider. Ask the company to produce a list of customer references—if they hem and haw, it could be a bad sign.

Should You Buy a Used PC?

Not unless you can save a bundle of money. You won't have a warranty or support, and if you check the American Computer Exchange Corporation (ACEC) Index of used computer prices, often published in local computer tabloids, you'll find prices only slightly below those asked by the lowliest mail-order companies. You might have better luck at computer *swap meets,* weekend fairs where you can haggle over used stuff and buy new PCs from companies offering substantial discounts. For swap meet locations and times, check in your local paper or with your local user group.

If you're determined to go the used route, ACEC matches buyers with sellers of used computers, so you might try giving the company a call at 800/786-0717. Whenever you buy any PC not under warranty, make sure you can get skilled, reasonably priced service from a third party nearby. Again, user groups are a great resource for this kind of thing, not to mention good deals on used stuff.

Finally, I hate to indict an entire region, but I must note that more than a few PC scam operations have been operated out of two Southern California towns—Walnut and City of Industry. Generally, these "companies" simply take orders over the phone and don't deliver. There must also be some good computer firms in those towns, so I'm not sure what to tell you. Just pay special attention to the above procedures if you order from this region.

DANGER

Suggested Configurations

One way to choose a PC is to look through recent reviews in the computer press— *PC World* and *PC Magazine* reviews are the most reliable. Not a bad place to start making a list, provided the machines that get good reviews are still around (things change that fast). Unfortunately, your day's research won't save you from having to develop a configuration.

What Every New PC Should Have (At Least)						
Drives	**Memory**	**Slots and Sockets**	**Monitor**	**Connectors**	**Warranty**	**Miscellaneous**
3½-inch floppy	8MB main memory	Two local bus slots	15-inch diagonal or larger	One serial port	One-year coverage	Complete manual
Hard disk (210MB+)	Secondary cache	Two open ISA slots[1]	1024-by-768 resolution[3]	One mouse port or second serial port	30-day, money-back guarantee	Microsoft-compatible mouse
5¼-inch floppy		OverDrive-compatible socket[2]	70-Hz refresh at maximum resolution[3]	One parallel port	Technical phone support	DOS and Windows
Room for a second hard disk			.28mm dot pitch or less	Video	On-site service[4]	
				Keyboard		

[1]With a graphics controller, a hard disk interface, two floppy drives, and a mouse already installed.
[2]Separate socket not required; Intel 486, DX2, DX4, and Pentium CPUs can usually be replaced.
[3]The graphics controller determines the resolution and refresh rate, but the monitor must handle these specs.
[4]Small fee may be required.

Figure 9: *Here's what to look for in a PC, no matter what model you buy. Remember that this is the recommended minimum—two-year warranties are fairly common, and you may well want a larger hard disk, a bigger monitor, or more room for expansion.*

Three Likely Configurations				
	CPU	**Hard Disk**	**Memory**	**Monitor**
Budget Model	SX2-66[1]	340MB	8MB	15-inch
Workhorse	Pentium-66	540MB	8MB to 16MB	15- to 17-inch
PC Maximus	Pentium-90 and up	1GB	16MB or more	17- to 19-inch

[1]Whether you buy an SX or DX CPU depends on whether you need a math coprocessor.

Figure 10: *Faster CPUs should be coupled with more memory and a larger hard disk. And if you can process more data faster, you might as well have a bigger monitor so you can see more of it at one time.*

Figures 9 and 10 pull all the information in this chapter together and suggest some likely combinations of components. I haven't included prices because they fall so quickly—the eternal curse of computing is that whatever system you buy today, you can always find a faster, cheaper one in a few months.

Just to make it more difficult for you to compare models, many companies throw in software extras the way record clubs throw in free CDs. Almost every company includes DOS and Windows, but beyond that, it's all over the map. The key here is simple: Unless you have use for the software offered, don't consider it a buying plus. For example, many PCs come with Microsoft's *Works for Windows*, an integrated group of mini-programs that includes a word processor, spreadsheet, database, and communications program—all much less powerful than the real McCoys.

Who To Buy From

The Product Directory below lists 25 of the biggest and most popular PC manufacturers. The best of the lot is Compaq. Many of this company's low-cost systems are good values, and in 10 years of testing and otherwise fiddling with PCs, I've found that Compaq systems seem to perform well no matter what. AST and Hewlett-Packard also produce very reliable systems, though the price often seems a little high.

IBM's Value Point systems live up to their name, but word on the street is that IBM's subsidiary, Ambra, has trouble delivering hardware as reliable as you might expect. More innuendo: Although you'll find Packard Bell PCs in every superstore from here to Albuquerque, these computers generally perform poorly in tests, and the company's service and support has a bad rep. I've also heard reports that Acer and Insight have had trouble providing good support.

Mail order moguls Dell and Gateway 2000 are hugely popular, and in my opinion they're good companies to buy from. Dell had a few problems with reliability awhile back, but these seem to have been solved, and the company's prompt and courteous support can't be beat. Gateway sells an enormous volume of fast systems priced just far enough below average to be irresistible—so many that the company sometimes has trouble keeping up with tech support calls.

Needless to say, hundreds of manufacturers didn't make it on this list. Some of them may be providing the best deals around as you read this—but no one can keep track of them all. If you're contemplating buying from a company you've never heard of, just make sure you ask a few customers whether they'd buy from that company again, and otherwise observe the advice in the Reliability section of this chapter.

Product Directory

Acer America
2641 Orchard Pkwy.
San Jose, CA 95134
800/733-2237
408/432-6200

ALR, Inc.
9401 Jeronimo
Irvine, CA 92718
714/581-6770

Ambra Computer Corp.
3200 Beachleaf Ct. #1000
Raleigh, NC 27604
800/626-2726
919/713-1550

AST Research Inc.
16215 Alton Pkwy.
Irvine, CA 92718
800/876-4278
714/727-4141

AT&T/NCR
1700 S. Patterson
Dayton, OH 45479
800/637-2600
513/445-5000

Austin Computer Systems
2121 Energy Dr.
Austin, TX 78758
800/752-1577
512/339-3500

Canon USA Computer
Systems
15955 Alton Pkwy.
Irvine, CA 92718
800/848-4123
714/438-3000

Compaq Computer Corp.
20555 SH 249
Houston, TX 77070
800/345-1518
713/250-2930

CompuAdd
12303 Technology Blvd.
Austin, TX 78727
800/925-3000
512/250-1489

DEC
1 Digital Dr.
Merrimack, NH 03054
800/722-9332
508/493-5111

Dell
9505 Arboretum Blvd.
Austin, TX 78759
800/986-3355

DTK Computer
18501 E. Gail Ave. #150
City of Industry, CA 91748
800/289-2385
818/810-8880

Epson America, Inc.
20770 Madrona Ave.
Torrance, CA 90503
800/289-3776
310/782-0770

Everex Systems
5020 Brandon Ct.
Fremont, CA 94538
800/821-0806
510/498-1111

Gateway 2000
610 Gateway Dr.
N. Sioux City, SD 57049
800/846-2000
605/232-2000

Hewlett-Packard
3000 Hanover St.
Palo Alto, CA 94304
800/752-0900
415/857-1501

IBM PC Company
800/426-2968

Insight
1912 W. 4th St.
Tempe, AZ 85281
800/729-0770
602/902-1176

Leading Edge
1107 Flanders Rd.
Westborough, MA 01581
800/874-3340
508/836-4800

Micro Express
1801 Carnegie Ave.
Santa Ana, CA 92705
800/989-9900
714/852-1400

NEC Technologies, Inc.
1255 Michael Dr.
Wood Dale, IL 60191
800/388-8888
708/860-9500

Packard Bell
31717 La Tienda Dr.
Westlake Village, CA 91362
800/733-5858
818/865-1555

Tandy
Contact your local
  Radio Shack dealer

Tri-Star Computer Corp.
2424 W. 14th St.
Tempe, AZ 85281
800/800-7668
602/731-4926

Zeos Int'l. Ltd.
1301 Industrial Blvd. NE
Minneapolis, MN 55413
800/554-7172
612/633-4591

3 Mobile Computing

By Steve Cummings

- Portable speed, battery life, and weight
- Mini screens, hard disks, and keyboards
- Credit card–size communications options
- The top ten tips for mobile computing
- What to look for in a portable printer

It's more fun, and more work, to shop for a mobile PC than for a desktop machine—the little guys come in so many sizes and shapes and seem to have infinite combinations of features. There are four classes of battery-powered mobile PC to choose from, each one defined primarily by its size and weight:

- **Notebooks** are the mobile PCs you won't mind doing some serious Windows computing with—you might even consider one in place of a desktop PC. A typical notebook is about the size of a ream of paper and weighs between 4$1/2$ and 7 pounds. You can get power approaching that of a desktop system—a Pentium model with a 540MB hard disk and a color display may cost a bundle, but you can find one. You generally get a decent keyboard and a sharp, bright screen along with a built-in floppy drive.

- **Subnotebooks** are smaller, lighter versions of notebooks, measuring about an inch less all around and weighing between 2½ and 4½ pounds. Compared with notebooks, they have smaller screens and their keyboards are often cramped. Hard disk capacity is more

limited and the floppy drive is almost always an external option that attaches via cable. The big advantages: You can throw one in a briefcase and have room to spare, and battery charges often last longer than a notebook's.

- **Palmtop computers** weigh a pound or less and come with toylike keyboards that rule out serious computing. They're good for keeping your address list, writing and reading E-mail messages, or running a few spreadsheet calculations—but not for much else. The best, such as Hewlett-Packard's 100LX or the Psion Series 3a, come with their own versions of popular DOS applications.

- **Personal Digital Assistants (PDAs)** are roughly the same size and weight as palmtops, but instead of a little keyboard, you get a "pen"—a plastic stylus—with which to pick commands, fill in forms, or scrawl notes on a small screen. Most PDAs, such as Apple's Newton MessagePad or Tandy's Z-PDA Zoomer, feature handwriting recognition, a technology that produces erratic results. Like palmtops, PDAs are best for electronic communication or collecting a little data; but they can't come close to replacing a desktop PC.

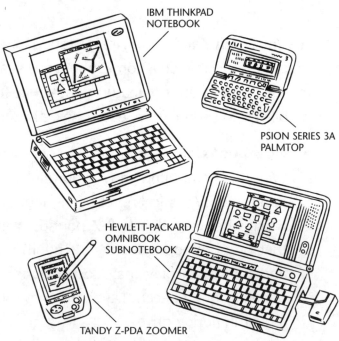

IBM THINKPAD NOTEBOOK

PSION SERIES 3A PALMTOP

HEWLETT-PACKARD OMNIBOOK SUBNOTEBOOK

TANDY Z-PDA ZOOMER

Figure 1: The four types of mobile PCs. Notebooks give you nearly as much computing power as a desktop PC, while subnotebooks trade some of that power for smaller size and lower weight. Palmtops and PDAs are more executive toys than computers.

If you're looking for a computer rather than an elaborate plaything, buy a notebook or a subnotebook. The bulk of this chapter is devoted to helping you find one. Choosing a note or subnote is similar in many ways to shopping for a desktop system, so turn to Chapter 2: *How to Buy a PC* for more detail on speed, data capacity, and reliability. Once you're equipped, turn to the end of this chapter for tips on computing with your mobile PC.

Buyers' Guide to Notes and Subnotes

When it comes to mobile PCs, you often pay more for less. Cramming all that technology into such a small space costs money—notebooks with top-notch color displays are particularly pricey, and the fastest notebook always lags behind the fastest desktop. Expect to pay nearly twice as much for the same speed and capacity in a mobile PC as in a desktop; the same inflation goes for such mobile add-ons as fax modems, memory modules, hard disks, and so on.

Performance on the Road

As with desktops, the central processing unit (CPU) is the component that determines more than any other whether you'll compute in a hurry or at a crawl. Memory size and hard disk speed also affect performance, as does the display's response time:

- **CPU.** While Pentium desktops promise clock speeds of 150 megahertz (MHz), you probably won't be able to buy a Pentium notebook faster than 75 MHz for some time—still plenty of power for most of us. On the low end, remember that if you want to run Windows software without waiting around, you should get a notebook with at least a 486SX, 486DX, or 486SL CPU running at 33 MHz or faster (the latter chip is distinguished by battery conservation features and is being phased out; see Figure 2 in Chapter 2 for specific CPU comparisons). Another approach: Buy a cheap, slow subnotebook you can kick around, and run DOS apps on it.

- **Memory.** Notebooks often come with 4MB of RAM, half the 8MB minimum generally required to keep Windows from bogging down. Although most notebooks can hold up to 20MB of RAM, few accept standard SIMMs, which means you're stuck buying memory modules from the manufacturer (some companies charge four times as much for these modules than for ordinary SIMMs, so make sure you figure that into the price when you shop). And while secondary memory caches are the rule in desktop PCs, few notebooks have them—a major reason why a notebook almost always runs slower than a desktop with the same CPU.

HOT TIP

- **Display response time.** Here's the rule of thumb: An *active-matrix* screen is always much faster (not to mention better looking and more expensive) than a *passive-matrix screen*. And if a notebook has *local-bus video*—that is, graphics processing that runs as fast as the CPU—performance should be better still. For more on mobile PC displays, see "Screen Considerations" later in this chapter.

- **Hard disk speed.** As with ordinary hard disks, a lower average seek time, a faster throughput rate, and faster rotational speed often indicate better hard disk performance. However, the performance of a tiny mobile hard disk seldom fails to lag behind that of a desktop hard disk.

Since mobile PCs run on rechargeable batteries, nearly all offer a *power conservation* mode that may affect performance—to conserve juice the CPU may run at a slower speed, or the hard disk may "spin down" (and take a few seconds to spin up again) if you don't touch the keyboard for a few minutes. If your notebook comes with a power management utility, you can decide which components to throttle down in exchange for a little extra battery life.

Hard and Floppy Disk Drives

Notebooks typically come with a 120MB hard disk, barely enough capacity for day-in, day-out Windows work, but enough for monthly road trips with a few favorite applications. If you plan to use your notebook more often than that, you can usually opt for a 200MB-plus model, and factory-installed 340MB to 540MB hard disks are frequently available—capacity worth the price if your notebook will be your primary computer.

If you run out of disk space, you must usually have an authorized service center or the manufacturer upgrade the hard disk for you. However, a few notebooks make upgrading easy, with removable hard disks that you can swap in and out yourself. This is a good solution if you share a laptop with someone—you have your hard disk, the other person has theirs; but in any case you should buy a big enough hard disk to begin with. Notebook hard disks are expensive, and the limit is usually one per machine, so upgrading is wasteful.

In the cases where you *can* add a second hard disk, you do so by plugging it into a standard slot that goes by the unwieldy acronym *PCMCIA* (for Personal Computer Memory Card International Association, if you care to know). To accommodate a PCMCIA hard disk, your notebook must have a PCMCIA Type III slot, or two Type II slots stacked one above the other (see "PCMCIA: The Standard for Mobile Add-Ons" later in this chapter). However, PCMCIA hard disks have three problems: They're more expensive, they have less capacity, and they're not as fast as ordinary notebook hard disks.

Who Needs a Floppy Drive?

Of course you need a floppy drive when you install software—even the cheapest subnotebook has an external floppy, at least as an option. But when it's time to transfer a couple of files between a notebook and another PC, many people are happier leaving their floppy drive at home. Instead, they link computers with a serial or a parallel cable and run a *file transfer* utility.

DOS comes with a file transfer utility called InterInk. Before you go on the road, set up InterInk by adding the line `device=c:\dos\interlnk.exe` to your notebook's CONFIG.SYS file (see Appendix A). Then, when you want to transfer files, whip out your bidirectional parallel cable (special lightweight versions for travel are available at most superstores) and hook the two computers together by their printer ports.

Now type `interlnk` at your notebook's DOS prompt, and `intersvr` at the other PC's DOS prompt. InterInk treats the drives on the machine you've hooked up with as extra drives on the computer you're using (after the notebook's drive C:, for example, the A: drive on the other computer would be drive D:, B: would be E:, and so on). You can access the other computer's drives in the normal way, and copy as many files as you like.

You can also run out and buy *LapLink,* a low-cost file transfer utility from Traveling Software (800/343-8080) with a nicer interface than DOS's InterInk. *LapLink* even comes with a cable right in the box.

Notebooks have built-in floppy disk drives, but subnotebooks don't. No other method is as convenient for transferring a few files as copying them to a floppy disk, so if you buy a subnotebook, make sure to figure in the cost of an external floppy drive.

REMEMBER

Screen Considerations

All mobile PCs use some type of liquid crystal display (LCD) to produce images. Notebooks with decent color LCD screens are surprisingly affordable—good news if you plan to use Windows on the road, since Windows without color is dull and sometimes confusing, depending on the quality of the screen.

Ultimately, the best way to choose a notebook or subnotebook is to line up several units side by side and have a close look. Choosing the right screen is an important decision, since few models let you upgrade the screen (NEC's Versa line is one of the few exceptions). The following buying tips may help you narrow down your choice:

- **Backlighting.** All color screens need a light source behind them to work, so a screen without backlighting is an option only if you buy a monochrome unit. Even then, few subnotebooks and even fewer notebooks do without backlighting, because no one likes a low-contrast screen that's hard to see in dim light. Consider a nonbacklit screen only if you need long battery life above all else.

REMEMBER

Choosing the Right Screen

	Active-matrix color	Passive-matrix dual-scan color	Passive-matrix single-scan color	Active-matrix mono	Passive-matrix mono	Passive-matrix mono (nonbacklit)
Quality	Excellent	Good to fair	Fair to poor	Excellent	Good to fair	Fair to poor
Speed	Fast	Slow	Slow	Fast	Slow	Slow
Power consumption	High	Moderate	Moderate	Moderate	Low	Very low
Cost	Expensive	Reasonable	Reasonable	Expensive	Cheap	Very cheap
Availability	Common	Common	Uncommon	Very rare	Common	Common

Figure 2: *A dual-scan color screen offers the best trade-off between price and legibility. The size and quality of individual screens varies, so give prospective buys the eyeball test if possible.*

- **Active vs. passive color.** Why are active-matrix screens faster and better looking than passive-matrix screens? With passive matrix, electrodes transmit pulses to liquid crystal molecules, which line up to either block or let through backlight, depending on the polarity. The same process occurs with an active-matrix screen, except that transistors do the work of electrodes—resulting in a faster, sharper, higher-contrast display that rivals the quality of a desktop monitor. Unfortunately, all that silicon is expensive, so you pay hundreds more for active matrix.

- **Single-scan vs. dual-scan color.** *Single-scan* passive matrix delivers as little as a quarter of the contrast of active matrix. A *dual-scan* passive-matrix screen, which is effectively two screens seamlessly butted together, offers twice the contrast of a single-scan screen and costs little more—and the speed is better, too. That's why single-scan is on the way out, and you should accept no less than a dual-scan, passive-matrix screen if you buy a color notebook.

HOT TIP

- **Number of colors or shades.** Shaded or photographic images are appearing in more and more applications. A screen that can produce only 16 colors or gray shades won't do the images justice, and 64 is barely adequate. Demand 256 colors or shades unless graphics are truly unimportant to you.

- **Brightness and contrast controls.** Best case: slide controls or knobs mounted right next to the screen. Worst case: weird key combinations you'll never remember that do the same thing.

As you'll notice if you compare screens live and in person (highly recommended), larger screens are easier to read. Most screens range between 8 and 10 inches diagonally. If you regularly use your notebook to give small on-site presentations, go for the largest active-matrix color screen you can find. A passive-matrix screen becomes unreadable when viewed at an angle, while an active-matrix screen maintains its quality even when viewers have to crane their necks from the wrong side of the conference table.

HOT TIP

Many people like to hook up their notebooks to desktop monitors—either for presentations to a slightly larger group or for a bigger view of their own applications. Notebook and subnotebook screens themselves have a fixed 640-by-480 resolution, but you'll usually also find an external monitor connector that delivers a maximum resolution of 800 by 600 or 1024 by 768. If you plan to connect your notebook to a 17-inch monitor, look for 1024-by-768 capability.

Keyboard Questions

No notebook or subnotebook has as many keys as a desktop keyboard. So some keys must do double duty—for example, you hold down a special key (usually labeled "Fn" or "F" for function), and you can access such keys as Home, End, and so on.

These two-for-one keyboard layouts range from ingenious to very awkward. The main alphabet and number keys are always in the same places, and the first 10 function keys are always on top, but placement of other keys varies from model to model. Personal taste will guide you here, but these rules of thumb may make your evaluation easier:

- **Emulated keys.** Print Screen, Scroll Lock, and Pause can disappear for all I care. But I hate having to press Fn to access Home, End, Page Up, or Page Down. Subnotebooks have smaller keyboards, so you often have to live with such compromises—a significant subnotebook drawback.

REMEMBER

- **Key size and spacing.** Expect notebook keys to be a little smaller or closer together than on a desktop keyboard, which will mean more typing errors, at least while you're getting used to the keyboard. Again, with subnotebooks this is even more of a problem.

- **Cursor keys.** Choose a machine with cursor keys in an "inverted T" configuration, the same arrangement as on a desktop keyboard.

- **Key placement.** You should be able to reach Alt, Ctrl and "Fn" easily with your hands in the standard typing position. Having Alt and Ctrl in their usual locations is also a plus.

As you type, don't expect the same sensation you get on desktop keyboards. Notebook keyboards are thinner, so the key travel—the distance the key moves—is always less than on a desktop keyboard, which may cause you to repeat characters accidentally. As usual, subnotebook size worsens the problem, but some notebooks imitate the feel of a typical desktop keyboard pretty closely.

HOT TIP

Many notebooks and subnotebooks include a port for hooking up a standard, full-size PC keyboard when you're at home or at the office. That's a real plus if you plan to use your mobile machine as your sole computer.

Battery Power Issues

The big power question is: How many hours will the battery last on a full charge? The range is enormous. When a notebook or subnotebook is away from the wall socket, it may run from 2 to 8 hours, depending on the model and on how the unit is being used (subnotebooks tend to run longer because they have fewer features). Magazine reviews can help here—manufacturers generally overstate the charge life, while tests in *PC World* and *PC Magazine* do pretty well at measuring average-use battery depletion times.

Battery Types

Notebooks and subnotebook batteries can be removed easily, so you can replace them yourself when they wear out, or charge a couple in advance and then swap them during a long airline flight. There are three main types of batteries. Sometimes, you get a choice of battery type when you buy a mobile PC:

- **Nickel cadmium (NiCd).** Batteries using this technology are on the way out. They don't last as long as other battery types. And they pollute the environment with highly toxic cadmium.

- **Nickel–metal-hydride (NiMH).** This is the mainstream battery technology. It delivers longer battery life than NiCd, and the materials aren't as toxic.

HOT TIP

- **Lithium ion storage (LIS).** This is the best battery technology of all. LIS batteries last about a third longer than NiMH batteries. They also cost more, but they take longer to die permanently: NiCd and NiMH batteries last for about 500 charges, while LIS batteries can be recharged approximately 1200 times before they go belly up.

LIS batteries also contain the least toxic substances. Remember, though, no matter which type of battery you buy, you should always send it back to the manufacturer for recycling when it has exhausted its usefulness. You wouldn't pour used oil from your car into the gutter, would you?

Power Management

Most notes and subnotes have power conservation features that extend the length of a battery charge by powering down components when you're not actively using the computer. Commonly, if the hard disk isn't being used, the computer turns it off automatically, and if you stop typing for a minute or two, the screen backlight turns off. On the best machines, if the hard disk and keyboard are idle, the CPU itself throttles down, saving even more power. This is the notebook equivalent of a light nap—also known as *standby mode*.

Nearly every mobile PC also has a *sleep* or *suspend* mode. With most models, you press a button, and the system goes catatonic—the screen goes blank, and everything shuts down except for the bare minimum required to keep any unsaved data alive. Press the button again, and the unit comes back to life right where you left off. With some systems, closing the cover immediately kicks the unit into sleep mode—a handy feature, since this keeps you from losing data if you accidentally pack the thing up while it's still on.

Some notes and subnotes keep your unsaved data safe in standby mode for weeks, while others do so for only a couple of hours, so check the specs before you bet your data on this feature. Another consideration: The faster a system wakes up, the better.

DANGER

Convenience Features

Ideally, you should be able to swap batteries while you work so that you don't have to shut the computer off to do the job. To let you know when batteries are low, most notes and subnotes feature a blinking light, which sometimes blinks faster as doom approaches; and sometimes an alarm indicates that you should save immediately while there's still time. Best of all is a gauge (either a software utility or an array of lights) that shows how much juice you have left.

The AC Power Supply

The main thing to consider here is size and weight, since you'll be taking the AC power supply with you. Expect anything from a few ounces and the size of a cigarette pack to over a pound and the dimensions of a small book.

The cord connecting the AC power supply to your laptop should be long enough for you to put the power supply on the floor when the computer is in your lap. And give the power connectors a close look—flimsy connectors are a frequent source of breakdowns for otherwise hardy portables.

DANGER

Going abroad? Then the power supply should be able to adapt automatically to 220-volt operation. If it can't, and you accidentally plug the power supply into the wrong voltage, you may burn it to a crisp. Try replacing one of those in Estonia.

Pointing Devices

Most notes and subnotes come with some type of *pointing device*, a mouse substitute that controls the movement of the mouse cursor. Picking an alternative pointing device is a highly personal matter, and you'll find no shortage of variations. Here are the main types to choose from:

- **Built-in trackball.** A trackball is essentially a mouse flipped on its back. Instead of rolling a critter around your desktop, you save space by rolling a little plastic ball mounted in the computer's casing (buttons flanking the trackball stand in for mouse buttons). The best place for a built-in trackball is in front of the keyboard, where you can reach it easily with either thumb as you type. Some models put the trackball near the screen on the right—a real drag for lefties.

- **External trackball.** This is a trackball that mounts on the side of the keyboard. You hold it like the handle of a gun, with the buttons in trigger position and your thumb on the trackball. It's a very comfortable device, which you can buy separately if your mobile PC lacks a pointing device entirely. Microsoft sells one called the BallPoint; Logitech offers one called TrackMan.

- **TrackPoint II.** Many people love this device. A little red shaft juts out between the G and H keys and acts like a tiny, video-game joystick that you push around with your thumbs. The

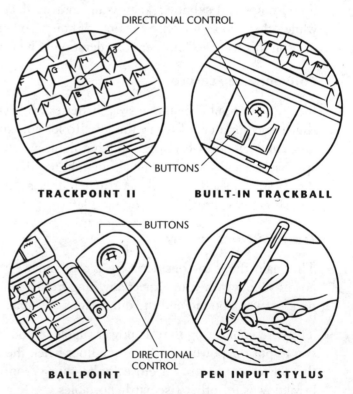

Figure 3: *Where do your hands belong?* Try the four most popular mouse replacements, and decide which feels best.

harder you push, the faster the cursor moves—though never as fast as you can move it with a trackball. You click the buttons, which sit in front of the spacebar, with the heels of your palms.

- **Pen computing.** PDAs aren't the only devices that enable you to make menu choices or write on the screen using a pen. Several notes and subnotes give you a choice of keyboard or pen input—or both, so you can move the mouse cursor with a stylus.

Other pointing devices are worth checking out. Some people with small fingers like Appoint's Thumbelina, a tiny, hand-held trackball. Several notebook models sport a TrackPoint-like device that's really a modified J key, which you rock in the direction you want the pointer to move. Hewlett-Packard OmniBook subnotebooks have a cordless, mouse-like contraption that pops out of the right side of the machine. Try your hand at a few devices before you make up your mind.

Communications

When you're on the road, you'll want to keep in touch. That means you need to hook up to the phone lines using a modem, preferably a fax modem so you can send and receive faxes as well as E-mail messages. You have several choices of modem size and shape, but when it comes to speed, you should probably buy a 14.4kbps fax modem. They're the best deals going. (For more advice on selecting fax modems, see "How to Buy a Fax Modem" near the beginning of Chapter 20: *Communications.*)

For the ultimate in mobile communications, consider a cellular fax modem. This device works in concert with cellular phones, so you don't have to hunt for a phone jack in order to link up. Cellular modems are expensive, they only work with certain cellular phones, and you can expect dropped connections when you drive under a bridge or across cellular communications zones. But the kinks are being worked out, and prices are dropping rapidly.

Want to hook up to a network? Then you need a LAN adapter. The vast majority of PC networks are Ethernet based, so buy a portable Ethernet adapter if you'll be hooking up on the road (see Chapter 22: *About Networks* for more on LAN hardware). If you'll be linking up with your office LAN, check with your network administrator before you buy.

Cellular or otherwise, fax modems and LAN adapters come in three basic varieties:

- **PCMCIA.** On most notes and subnotes, the modem or LAN adapter comes on a card that plugs into a PCMCIA slot. Because PCMCIA is now the standard for notebook options, at least one PCMCIA Type II or Type III slot guarantees you'll

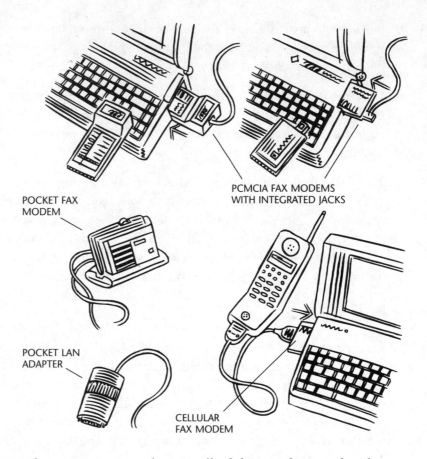

***Figure 4: Mobile com-
munications options.***
*Mobile modems and LAN
adapters come in all
shapes and sizes, but
PCMCIA units are the
most popular. If you buy
a PCMCIA modem, make
sure you get one with an
integrated connector as
shown here.*

POCKET FAX
MODEM

PCMCIA FAX MODEMS
WITH INTEGRATED JACKS

POCKET LAN
ADAPTER

CELLULAR
FAX MODEM

have a wide choice of communications devices, all of them as long and wide as a
credit card. Unfortunately, PCMCIA cards are also thinner than a phone jack—
which in some cases means the phone jack hangs from a wire dangling from the
card, where it can easily break off. PCMCIA modems with integrated jacks (such as
the two shown in Figure 4) are much better.

HOT TIP

- **Portable.** Usually about the size of a cigarette pack, portable modems and LAN
  adapters have one significant advantage: You can use them with your desktop or
  several different laptops, because they screw right onto a serial (or in the case of
  most LAN adapters, parallel) port. They're a pain to lug around, though. For more
  on portable modems, see the conclusion of "How to Buy a Fax Modem" in Chapter 20.

- **Proprietary.** You can buy these devices only from the manufacturer, because they
  fit into a special slot unique to the manufacturer's products. Often these devices are
  more expensive than PCMCIA or portable units. One advantage of proprietary
  modems is that once they're installed, the phone jack is always easy to access and
  securely mounted.

PCMCIA: The Standard for Mobile Add-Ons

As noted earlier in this chapter, PCMCIA stands for Personal Computer Memory Card International Association. This awkward acronym describes an industry standard for all kinds of plug-in devices, including modems, network adapters, hard disks, and yes, memory cards.

Most new notes and subnotes, along with many palmtops and PDAs, have at least one PCMCIA slot. The devices that fit in these slots measure 5.4 centimeters by 8.56cm, or approximately the length and width of a credit card. They come in three thicknesses: Type I (3.3 millimeters), Type II (5mm), and Type III (10.5mm).

Most notes and subnotes have at least one PCMCIA Type II slot, and most PCMCIA cards—including fax modems and LAN adapters—are also Type II. So far so good. All PCMCIA hard disks, however, are Type III devices, so a minority of mobile PCs can accommodate them. In addition, Type III slots can also usually hold two Type II cards—one stacked on top of the other—but not always. Got that?

The PCMCIA standard is supposed to let you safely swap cards without turning off your system, but many users have crashed their systems in the attempt. In fact, there have been a number of compatibility problems between PCMCIA slots and PCMCIA devices, although these seem to be abating as the technology matures. Regardless, always check with the maker of the card to see whether it functions with your particular model, and make sure you get a 30-day, money-back guarantee on any PCMCIA card.

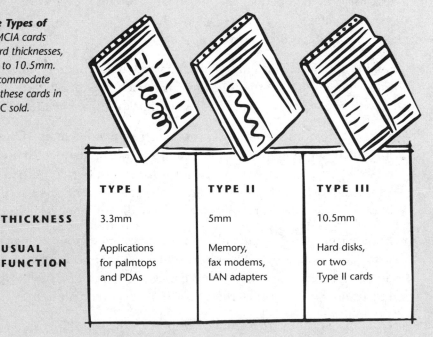

Figure 5: The Three Types of PCMCIA Cards. PCMCIA cards come in three standard thicknesses, ranging from 3.3mm to 10.5mm. You'll find slots to accommodate one or more types of these cards in nearly every mobile PC sold.

	TYPE I	TYPE II	TYPE III
THICKNESS	3.3mm	5mm	10.5mm
USUAL FUNCTION	Applications for palmtops and PDAs	Memory, fax modems, LAN adapters	Hard disks, or two Type II cards

REMEMBER

Make sure you figure the cost of a modem into the price of a note or subnote, since it's a necessity, not an option.

Off-the-Road Connections

Notebooks and subnotebooks usually have one parallel port, a serial port, a video connector for hooking up an external monitor, and either a mouse port or a second serial port. Think twice about buying a machine with less, or you may not be able to hook up a printer or a portable modem along with your pointing device. If

REMEMBER

you plan to use the machine at a desk for extended periods of time, make sure it has a connector for a standard keyboard.

Lost, Found, and Returned

Let people know who owns your mobile machine. If you ever lose the thing, you'll be glad you engraved your name and address in an obvious location on the case. If you never get around to that, at least add your name and number to your AUTOEXEC.BAT file (see Appendix A for instructions on editing this file), so the information will come up every time your computer is turned on. The lines should look something like this:

```
echo This computer is the property of Waldo
Portatif

echo If found, please call collect at 814-555-
1234

pause
```

The PAUSE command temporarily stops your AUTOEXEC.BAT until you press Enter. Who knows? If you're lucky, a curious good Samaritan will find your peripatetic PC, and you'll actually get it back.

Thinking about making a notebook your primary computer? Then you'll also want to consider buying one of the following manufacturer options, which can make using a notebook at your desk as easy and as comfortable as using a desktop PC:

- **Port replicators** are simply two-sided strips of connectors. On the back, you plug in your desktop monitor, mouse, and keyboard, along with a printer if you have one. When you get back from the road, you plug your road machine into the connectors along the front of the replicator—and hook to all the desktop devices in one fell swoop. Port replicators are usually quite inexpensive.

- **Expansion chassis** generally provide the connections of port replicators, along with room for a couple of desktop-style ISA expansion slots—so you can hook right up to the network without the hassle of a mobile LAN adapter, for example. Expansion chassis cost significantly more than port replicators.

- **Docking stations** offer duplicated ports, expansion slots, and sometimes as much room for disk drives as a desktop PC (the notebook still provides all the processing power). With a well-designed docking station, you keep the cover on your note-book closed, slide it into a bay beneath the monitor, and everything comes up just as if you'd turned on a desktop PC. Predictably, most docking stations are expensive.

Not all manufacturers offer these options, so if your notebook will be doing double duty as a desktop, make sure desktop connection and expansion options are available before you buy.

Durability and Security

Kick the tires. More than desktop computers, portables are prone to physical break-downs (as opposed to electronic ones) because they get banged, bumped, dumped, and dropped. Make a judgment about how sturdy the whole unit is, and watch out for trouble spots:

DANGER

- Avoid hinged compartment doors—they break off too easily; look for sliding com-partment covers instead.

- Avoid switches and knobs that project past the main outline of the case—a forceful whack is bound to knock them off eventually.

- Avoid keyboards that flex when you type, or that seem too fragile to take the pun-ishment endured by desktop keyboards.

- Avoid flimsy power connectors or cords on the computer and on the AC adapter.

As for less accidental disasters, some machines have key locks that will at least keep out casual snoopers. Some let you set up a password that you must type in to use the computer—without it, the machine refuses to start. Others come with built-in metal brackets, so you can cable-lock them to a desk.

Service

"Service" is a euphemism for what usually happens when a mobile computer stops working: The manufacturer simply swaps a new machine for the sick one. At whole-sale prices, these computers apparently cost less than a technician's time, and most of the broken computers just get junked.

In any case, be sure you check out the service policy carefully. Find out how many service centers there are, and where they're located. If a traveling computer is critical to your business plan, you want guaranteed on-site service within 24 hours, or a guaranteed overnight exchange policy. Also, ask if you need a credit card to exchange the system via Federal Express or another courier when you're not near a service center. This is

HOT TIP

Pen Notebooks

The pen would seem to be a natural way to interact with computers for certain tasks, such as checking off selections, marking up faxes, and above all, as a way for nontypists to enter information. In truth, pen technology has a way to go before you can write away on your screen and expect handwriting recognition software to keep up—and turn your scrawls into text accurately.

Some companies have had success with custom pen applications for field personnel, where recognition is limited to converting entries on forms to text. Further toward the mainstream, Microsoft's Pen Windows enables you to control a familiar interface with a stylus instead of a mouse. If pen computing sounds attractive, but you don't want to buy an expensive notebook for a pen application alone, consider a hybrid machine like NEC's Versa or Compaq's Concerto. These machines are designed to be used with either a keyboard or a pen; for tasks best suited to pen input, you detach or reverse the keyboard and use the screen as a full-size writing tablet.

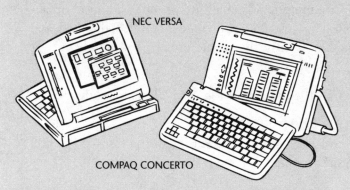

NEC VERSA

COMPAQ CONCERTO

Figure 6: Compaq's Concerto and NEC's Versa notebooks do double duty: You can use them with a keyboard, or for pen-only applications.

common practice among many vendors who want to protect themselves until they can definitively say whether the failure was their fault or yours. Falls kill more portables than anything else. As a result, it's becoming increasingly popular for the vendor to offer extra-cost accident insurance. But check out the rates before you buy.

Ten Tips for Mobile Computing

The following free advice can save frustration when you're traveling with a mobile PC in tow. Note that some of these suggestions may add to the traveling weight—another reason to go with the lightest system you can find that has the features you need.

HOT TIPS

1. **Bring an extension cord.** In some hotel rooms, the phone jack is a mile away from the AC outlet. You want to make both connections simultaneously, since modems suck battery power like crazy.

2. **Carry a spare boot disk.** Any system, mobile or otherwise, should have a nearby floppy disk to boot from should anything go wrong with the hard disk. To learn how to create a boot disk, see "Safety Check" in the last section of Chapter 12: *DOS and Windows.*

3. **Don't sweat airport X-rays.** Some people say you're risking data if you run your mobile PC through a security check's X-ray machine, but they're wrong.

4. **Print by fax.** If you don't have access to a printer, use your computer's fax modem to send the document to the nearest fax machine. The document won't look great, but you'll have a paper copy.

5. **Improve your Windows cursor.** On some passive-matrix screens, the mouse pointer gets lost when you move it, becoming a blurry gray streak. To combat this, double-click on Mouse in Control Panel and check the Mouse Trails box.

6. **Mono madness.** Do you have a monochrome screen? Then graphics and text normally in color may be unreadable. To make software easier to work with, look for a "monochrome" or "laptop" setting in the program's setup routine.

7. **Enlarge Windows text.** Notebook screens are too small for many people to read comfortably. Just about every Windows application enables you to increase the font size of the document you're working on—just choose Font from the Format menu. If you have a Zoom option on your View menu, this works even better, because it won't screw up the line breaks.

8. **Don't forget tech support numbers.** If your hardware is on the fritz, you don't want to wrack your brains trying to remember the city where the manufacturer is so you can call 555-1212. Keep those 800 tech support numbers in your carrying case.

9. **International tip.** You probably know that much of the world uses 220-volt instead of 110-volt AC power. But did you know that Europe alone has over a dozen types of power plugs? If you're going abroad, make sure you have the correct adapter plug; travel specialty stores often sell "universal" ones that fit five or six types of sockets.

10. **Back up before you go.** No matter how durable your mobile PC is, its data is always at greater risk than a deskbound PC's. Before you pack up and move on, at the very least copy the files you've updated to floppy and keep that disk in a safe place separate from your computer.

Printing on the Road

Most of the time, taking a printer on the road makes about as much sense as stuffing your suitcase with a brick—with floppies for backup copies of your work, and electronic mail for communicating, printing can usually wait until you get back home. In some cases, though, you really do need a printed paper copy of that contract, invoice, or estimate.

HOT TIP

If so, you want a plain-paper ink jet printer, because they consume the least battery power, supplies are relatively cheap, and print quality is great (for more on ink jets see Chapter 6: *Printers and Printing*). Canon's BJ-10sx and Kodak's Diconix 701 are two excellent choices. Hewlett-Packard also makes a color portable, the DeskJet 310. The Diconix 701 has the advantage of a built-in sheet feeder.

One other option to consider is the Canon NoteJet 486, a full-fledged notebook PC with a built-in ink jet printer. Though the paper feeding mechanism is a little touchy, and supply costs are above average, the print quality is very good. Only slightly larger and heavier than a regular notebook, the all-in-one package is far easier to haul around than two separate machines.

Product Directory

Mobile PC Manufacturers

AST Research Inc.
16215 Alton Pkwy.
Irvine, CA 92718
800/876-4278
714/727-4141

CAF Technology
1315 Johnson Dr.
City of Industry, CA 91745
818/369-3690

Compaq Computer Corp.
P.O. Box 692000
Houston, TX 77269
800/345-1518
713/378-8820

Dell Computer Corp.
9595 Arboretum Blvd.
Austin, TX 78759
800/289-3355
512/338-4400

Epson America, Inc.
20770 Madrona Ave.
Torrance, CA 90503
800/922-8911

Gateway 2000
610 Gateway Dr.
North Sioux City, SD 57049
800/846-2000
605/232-2000

Hewlett-Packard
19310 Pruneridge Ave.
Cupertino, CA 95014
800/752-0900

IBM Corp.
800/426-7735

NEC Technologies, Inc.
1414 Massachusetts Ave.
Boxborough, MA 01719
800/388-8888
508/264-8000

Sharp Electronics
Sharp Plaza
Mahwah, NJ 07430
800/237-4277
201/529-9593

Tandy
One Tandy Center
Fort Worth, TX 76102
817/390-3011

Texas Instruments
P.O. Box 14949, MS 2240
Austin, TX 78714
800/527-3500
512/795-5970

Toshiba America
  Information Systems
9740 Irvine Blvd.
Irvine, CA 92718
800/334-3445
714/583-3000

Twinhead Corp.
1537 Centre Pointe Dr.
Milpitas, CA 95035
800/545-8946
408/945-0808

Zenith Data Systems
2150 E. Lake Cook Rd.
Buffalo Grove, IL 60089
800/553-0331
708/808-5000

Zeos Int'l, Ltd.
1301 Industrial Blvd.
Minneapolis, MN 55418
800/554-5220
612/362-1234

PCMCIA Card Manufacturers

AST Research Inc.
800/876-4278

Boca Research, Inc.
6413 Congress Blvd.
Boca Raton, FL 33487
407/997-6227

Epson America, Inc.
800/922-8911

Integral Peripherals
5775 Flat Iron Pkwy.
Boulder, CO 80301
800/333-8009
303/449-8009

Megahertz Corp.
605 N. 5600 West
Salt Lake City, UT 84116
800/527-8677
801/272-6006

Input Device Manufacturers

Appoint
6377 Clark Ave. #111
Dublin, CA 94568
800/448-1184
510/803-8850

IMSI
1938 4th St.
San Rafael, CA 94901
800/833-8082
415/454-7101

Logitech
6505 Kaiser Dr.
Freemont, CA 94555
800/732-3127
510/795-8500

Microsoft Corp.
One Microsoft Way
Redmond, WA 98052-6399
800/426-9400
206/882-8080

Portable Printer Manufacturers

Canon Computer
  Systems, Inc.
123 E. Paularino Ave.
Costa Mesa, CA 92628
800/848-4123

Eastman Kodak Co.
  Printer Products
901 Elmgrove Rd.
Rochester, NY 14653
800/344-0006

Hewlett-Packard
16399 W. Bernardo Dr.
San Diego, CA 92127
800/752-0900

Mannesmann Tally
8301 S. 180th St.
Kent, WA 98064
800/843-1347
206/251-5500
614/457-8600

4 Disk Drives

By TJ Byers

- Getting the fastest, biggest hard disk for the price
- Floppy disks, drives, and common data capacities
- A brief buyers' guide to CD ROM drives
- Alternative storage from Bernoulli to floptical

Every day you entrust your data to the slowest, most primitive devices in your PC—the disk drives. These high-speed magnetic record players, each with scores of moving parts that eventually malfunction or wear out, are the most important components in your system. Actually, disk drives are remarkably quick and reliable for all their machinations, but when it comes to your hard disk—your main data repository—you should shop carefully to get the best deal on a roomy drive you can count on.

Most of this chapter deals with choosing the right hard disk. However, you'll also find a little buying advice on floppy disk drives, along with a quick guide to the specifications to look for in that hottest of multimedia accessories, the CD ROM drive. Finally, for those of you who need maximum data capacity and security, a section on alternative storage covers drives with removable disks that hold hundreds of megabytes.

Hard Disks

Most of the time it's much less of a hassle to buy a PC with a hard disk already installed. However, PC companies always give you a choice of hard disk models, and few of us will exhaust the life of our PCs without having to add or replace a hard disk eventually. Use the following guidelines to help you find a hard disk that will meet your current and future requirements.

How Many Megabytes?

HOT TIP

Windows applications go through disk space like kids go through candy—so the classic mistake is purchasing a hard drive you'll outgrow too soon. In fact, you shouldn't buy anything less than a 340MB drive, but that's really a bare minimum. Personally, I wouldn't consider anything less than 540MB, and neither should you. If your budget permits, a 1.2GB (that's 1200MB) drive would be better. At this writing a typical 1.2GB hard disk goes for about $700, while a 540MB drive sells for a little over $300.

Where All Those Megabytes Go	
Application	**Disk space required**
DOS	10MB
Windows	12MB
Excel	12MB
Word for Windows	25MB
PC Tools for Windows	24MB
PowerPoint	17MB
Ventura Publisher	12MB
WordPerfect for Windows	30MB
Adobe Type Manager	6MB

Figure 1: *Why do you need a big hard disk? Because popular applications like these are so greedy for megabytes—as are the files they create, thanks to the disk-hogging graphics that seem to find their way into every document.*

How Fast Is Fast?

It doesn't matter how quick your processor is—if you have a slow hard disk, you have a slow computer. One of the best performance upgrades you can make is to replace a sluggish old hard disk with a fast new model. But when you choose among *current* hard disks, you'll find the range from fastest to slowest remarkably small—less than 10 percentage points. If such speed differences concern you, consider the following guide to manufacturer specifications, which can give you a *rough* idea of which drives are faster than others:

- **Average seek time.** The most commonly used spec in hard disk advertisements, average seek time is the amount of time it takes for the read/write head to move from one track to another. Most drives have an average seek time ranging from 8.5 milliseconds (ms) to 16ms. Supposedly, the lower the number, the faster the hard disk—but in fact average seek time is a bit of a red herring. For example, Quantum ProDrive LPS drives have an average seek time of 16ms, yet perform faster than most drives with a 12ms average seek time.

- **Data transfer rate.** This spec measures how fast data moves from the drive to your PC's memory. For most hard disk drives, these figures range from 1.5MB to 3MB per second. A related measurement, the *burst transfer rate*, measures the rate for a small block of data to move from the drive to system memory in a single burst. These figures typically range from 4MB to 10MB per second. In theory, higher numbers should mean faster throughput—but these differences rarely show up in ordinary applications.

- **Disk rotation speed.** A better measure of data throughput is how fast the platter spins. The higher a platter's rotations per minute (RPM), the faster the data a drive is looking for passes under the read/write head, cutting access time. The speed gain is even more noticeable when the data is stored sequentially, such as with some large graphics files—the head just scoops up data at a faster rate. Until recently, a speed of 3600 RPM was the norm, but today's drives spin up to 5400 RPM. Generally, faster rotational speed adds considerably to a drive's price.

- **Buffer size and segmentation.** When a hard disk fetches data, in many cases the requested data has already been accessed recently. So it's a waste of time for the drive to find that data on the platter again, when instead it can store frequently used data in a *buffer*—a small quantity of

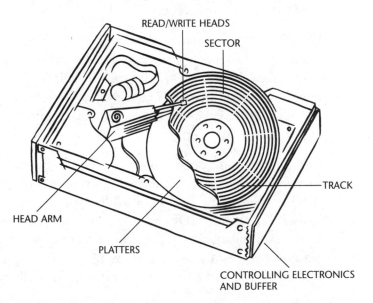

Figure 2: Inside a typical hard disk. *Coated with a thin film similar to the coating on magnetic tape, a hard disk's platters rotate at several thousand RPM. Acting on instructions from DOS, the drive's controlling electronics tell the read/write heads (there's one for every platter surface) to seek for or deposit data in specific locations. A buffer on the circuit card affixed to the drive holds often-used data.*

memory located on the drive itself. Buffer sizes range from 64K to 256K. Typically, a 256K buffer is segmented into 16 pieces, each of which holds a portion of the data you've already used or expect to use soon. As a rule, the larger and more segmented the buffer, the faster the hard disk.

What's the Best Connection?

Your computer and hard disk communicate with each other using an *interface*, or connector, located on the motherboard or on a card plugged into an expansion slot. There are two popular hard disk interface standards: Integrated Drive Electronics (IDE) and Small Computer System Interface (SCSI—pronounced "scuzzy"). The interface that's right for you depends on your system and on the type of peripherals you plan to add in the future.

Most PCs sold today come with a built-in IDE interface. If that's true of your system, your best bet is to replace or supplement the existing drive with an IDE drive, which is the easiest drive to install and set up. If your storage requirements are massive, if you need a specific SCSI device (such as a CD ROM), or if your PC has a built-in SCSI interface, then buy a SCSI hard disk.

IDE Drives and Interfaces

The advantage to buying a drive with an IDE interface is that you can usually set up a new hard disk quickly, and you don't need to install an extra expansion card in the process (see the section "Disk Drive Installation" in Chapter 8: *Upgrade It Yourself*). The downside is that IDE is slightly slower than SCSI—although you'd probably notice the difference only in multimedia applications—and you're often limited to installing two drives on one interface.

An up-and-coming spec dubbed *enhanced IDE* promises to make IDE as speedy as it is convenient, boosting performance in some applications by as much as three times. As a bonus, the new IDE standard lets you install up to four devices without special hardware. Enhanced IDE must be built into both the system and the drive for you to gain the speed benefits, so keep your eyes open when you shop. Also be aware that the technology goes by several names: Western Digital calls it Enhanced IDE, but Seagate calls it Fast ATA, while Maxtor prefers High Performance ATA.

SCSI Drives and Interfaces

Price and sometimes difficult installation make SCSI drives much less popular than IDE drives. The main advantage to SCSI is that you can hang up to seven SCSI devices—hard disks, CD ROMs, tape backups, and scanners—off of a single interface. This can be a boon if your PC is short on slots and you have the patience to make all those devices work together (a daunting task). And the selection of devices extends far beyond that of IDE, which is basically a hard disk standard.

SCSI interfaces are rarely built into PC motherboards, which means you'll have to buy a SCSI card if your new drive doesn't come bundled with one—usually a $50 to $150 expense. If you have a choice, buy a 16-bit SCSI card rather than a cheap 8-bit card, and purchase SCSI-2 drives and interfaces rather than the older SCSI-1 variety. The added performance and better compatibility will make this money well spent.

HOT TIP

Which Size?

A hard disk won't do you any good if it doesn't fit into your machine, so you need to check two additional specs before buying a drive: *form factor* and *height*. The form factor is actually the diameter of the platters—which are either 3 1/2 inches or 5 1/4 inches wide (this is *not* the measurement of the outside case; for example, a 3 1/2-inch drive actually measures 4 inches across). And there are three standard vertical measurements: full height (3 inches), half height (1 1/2 inches), and third-height (7/8 inch).

Virtually all desktop PCs, even compact systems, have at least three 3 1/2-inch *drive bays*—compartments in the PC's case where drives are installed. A small drive can be mounted in a

Disk Caches: Software or Hardware?

As you compute, your system accesses the same data over and over. Because your disk drive is the slowest component in your system, it makes sense for this frequently used data to be copied from the hard disk into an area of memory called a *disk cache*, where the data can be accessed much faster than it could be by a hard disk's read/write head.

Several manufacturers sell *hardware cache* cards (also known as *cache controllers*), which may contain several megabytes of memory dedicated to disk caching (this memory is separate and distinct from the memory buffer on the drive itself). These cards work well, but they're expensive. Unless you're setting up a network server, you're better off using *disk caching software*, which employs a portion of the main memory already installed in your system. Software caches improve performance nearly as much as hardware caches do, and a perfectly decent one—SmartDrive—comes free with both DOS and Windows. See Chapter 21: *Utilities* for more on disk caching software.

How a Hard Disk Stores Data

At the heart of a hard disk drive is a rotating platter coated with a thin magnetic film. Similar to the grooves on an LP record, concentric magnetic *tracks* are laid down on the platter by the drive's magnetic read/write head. These tracks are divided into numbered segments called *sectors,* which the hard disk uses to store the actual data (see Figure 2). This basic framework of tracks and sectors is called the *low-level* or *physical format.* The drive manufacturer almost always does the low-level formatting before shipping the drive to you or to a reseller.

However, when you buy a hard disk that's not already installed in a PC, it's seldom ready to run. On top of the physical formatting, the drive must be *partitioned* and *logically formatted,* either manually or using DOS's automatic installation utility (see "Hard Disk Installation" in Chapter 8: *Upgrade It Yourself*).

- **Partitioning.** A hard disk may be set up as a single *logical drive (*one big C:) or it may be broken up into multiple volumes—C:, D:, E:, and so on. Establishing these partitions is the first thing you do when you set up a hard disk manually. Usually, you accomplish this with DOS's FDISK or with a utility that comes with the drive.

- **Logical formatting.** To do this manually with DOS, you simply enter format c: /s (only if there's no data on the drive already, of course!). The /s makes a drive *bootable,* so when you turn on your system, DOS is loaded automatically from the C: drive. If you have multiple logical drives, you need to format each one separately (format d: and so on). Logical formatting also creates the *file allocation table* (called the *FAT*—there's one for each logical drive), which maintains vital status information in groups of sectors called *clusters.* The root directory (C:\ for drive C:) is also created; it links DOS file names to the first cluster in which the file is stored.

You don't really need to worry about the FAT or the partition table, since DOS handles them in the background. Just be aware that any error messages referring to the FAT, "allocation errors," or the partition table are serious business. Consult "Data Recovery" in Chapter 21: *Utilities* for more on this subject.

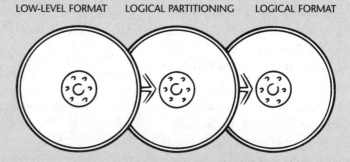

LOW-LEVEL FORMAT   LOGICAL PARTITIONING   LOGICAL FORMAT

Figure 3: The three levels of hard disk preparation. At the factory, your drive is given its low-level format, the basic framework that an operating system uses as a foundation for storing data. Logical partitioning divides the physical drive into C:, D:, and so on, or establishes one big drive. Logical formatting is the final stage in preparing a drive to store data.

large drive bay, but there's no way to stuff a big drive into a little bay. Most drives of 500MB and under are 3 1/2-inch half-height or third-height devices. At 1.2GB and beyond, expect the form factor to increase to 5 1/4 inches, and to full-height as the drive nears 2GB.

How Reliable Is It?

Just like a car, a disk drive experiences wear and tear—but unlike a car, serious repairs are usually impractical. On average, you can expect today's hard disks to last four or five years, about the life expectancy of your PC before it becomes obsolete. Some live longer; some are lemons.

A one-year warranty is de rigueur, but I strongly recommend buying a drive with more insurance than that—a few companies offer five years, which you pay for, but may well be worth the peace of mind. Several vendors have an extended warranty option that includes 24-hour replacement, which is not a bad idea. You can have all the backup tapes you want, but when your hard disk *really* dies, there's no amount of tender loving care or screaming that will bring it back to life. Replacement is the only answer—and the sooner the better.

Floppy Drives

If you just bought a PC, your system probably came with a 3 1/2-inch floppy drive that can read both 1.44MB and 720K floppy disks. But those floppies aren't the only ones on earth. There must be hundreds of millions of 5 1/4-inch 1.2MB and 360K disks running around out there, containing everything from company archives to old applications to data somebody created hours ago with an old PC.

To handle old- and new-style floppies, many people have one 1.2MB and one 1.44MB drive in their system. But compact desktops seldom have more than two drive bays that are accessible from the outside, and if you want to install a tape backup to protect your hard disk's data—as you should— you may not have room for two

Floppy disk size	Capacity
3 1/2 inches	1.44MB
	720K
	2.88MB
5 1/4 inches	1.2MB
	360K

Figure 4: *Everyone should have a 1.44MB 3 1/2-inch floppy drive (which also handles 720K disks). Old 5 1/4-inch disks abound, so you might want to get a 1.2MB/360K drive, too. The 2.88MB format hasn't taken off yet, and may never.*

HOT TIP

floppy drives. One solution is to buy a combo drive, such as the TEAC FD-505, that crams a 3^{1}/2-inch and a 5^{1}/4-inch drive into the space normally occupied by one 5^{1}/4-inch drive.

Another solution, especially if your new desktop can't accommodate 5^{1}/4-inch drives at all, is to say, "Hey, could you copy it to a 3^{1}/2, please?" when someone tries to give you a 5^{1}/4 disk—a reasonable request. Unless you want others to turn *your* disks away, don't buy IBM's 2.88MB drive. It's nice to have twice the capacity of a 1.44MB disk for big files, but few systems other than IBM's have 2.88MB drives, and standard 1.44MB drives won't read 2.88MB disks.

CD ROM Drives

Aside from games and educational software, few multimedia CD ROM titles provide a compelling reason to pick up a CD ROM drive. However, if you need to do business research and don't want to pay stiff, ongoing fees to an on-line service, a huge database on a CD ROM disk could be the answer. Even if the above applications leave you cold, rest assured more (and more interesting) CD ROM titles will be coming to a CD ROM drive near you in the near future.

CD ROM disks are *read-only* laser disks similar to audio CDs. No, you can't save data on them, but you can *read* up to 680MB off of a single disk. An increasing number of software companies are exploiting this capacity by putting their applications on CD ROM, so you can install a big program like *CorelDraw* without swapping floppy disks. And if you need lots of fonts and clip art for desktop publishing, a CD ROM drive is a necessity.

One nice aspect of CD ROM is that you hardly ever have to worry whether a certain CD ROM drive will read a specific CD ROM disk. Virtually all CD ROM drives can play ordinary audio CDs, MPC (that is, standard multimedia) disks, and disks mastered in the ISO 9660 format. Most also fully support the Photo CD standard (Kodak's format for photos converted to CDs). If you see an old funky drive that lacks

DANGER

compatibility in any of these areas, avoid it like the plague.

Speed Matters

Unlike hard disks, CD ROM drives vary considerably in the performance they deliver. And it's easier to tell from the specs what the performance will be: The numbers for average seek time and data transfer rate have real meaning, for example. However,

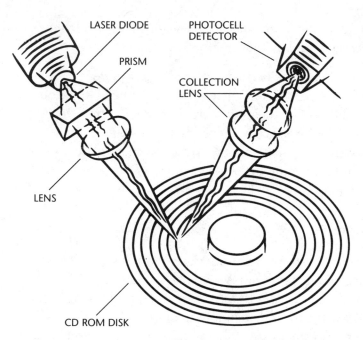

LASER DIODE

PHOTOCELL DETECTOR

PRISM

COLLECTION LENS

LENS

CD ROM DISK

Figure 5: The inner workings of CD ROM. Unlike a hard disk drive, which stores data magnetically and enables you to save or alter data, a CD ROM drive uses a laser beam and photocell detector to read data only—up to 680MB of it on a single, replaceable disk.

remember that if you use a CD ROM drive simply as storage space for clip art, fonts, and the like, performance isn't critical, and you can save money by buying a cheap drive that costs as little as $150.

HOT TIP

- **Rotational speed.** Here's the basic parameter that most affects both speed and price. You have four choices: single, double, triple, and quadruple speed. The rule of thumb is to never buy a drive with less than double-speed performance (in the $300 to $500 range), unless performance doesn't matter at all. Some triple-speed drives are only a little faster than double-speed models and cost considerably more, so check other specs (and magazine reviews) carefully. Quadruple-speed drives are great for multimedia video but are often twice the price of double-speed models.

REMEMBER

- **Data transfer rate.** This is usually directly proportional to the rotational speed (single speed equals roughly 150K per second, double speed equals 300K, and so on). However, as with hard disks, a memory buffer can increase the transfer rate significantly; buffer sizes range from 64K to 256K (the bigger the better). If you want a drive to run a multimedia video application, don't buy one with a transfer rate of less than 300 kilobytes per second, or expect jerky playback.

- **Average seek time.** As with hard disks, a CD ROM's average seek time is the amount of time it takes to locate a piece of information on disk. Instead of using several mechanical read/write heads, however, CD ROM drives use a laser beam to sweep the disk for data. Since there's only one pickup source instead of multiple read/write heads, it takes much longer to locate the desired data. Most CD ROM drives have an average seek time of 200ms to 400ms; the lower number is better, and you shouldn't accept anything worse than 350ms. Quick seek times are

REMEMBER

especially important for reference software, such as encyclopedias or telephone directories, which involve frequent random information searches.

- **CPU utilization.** This doesn't affect *drive* performance per se, but it does have an impact on overall system performance, which is what you care about anyway. Some drives require that the CPU help them do their job more than others—thus slowing down the system—although this performance hit depends on the application being run. There's no standard spec to measure this—another reason to check performance benchmarks in the monthly computer magazines *PC World* and *PC Magazine*.

Choose Your Interface

REMEMBER

CD ROM drives give you a choice of IDE or SCSI interfaces, although, unlike with hard disks, SCSI CD ROM drives are by far the most popular. Although 16-bit SCSI cards can provide up to 10 percent greater CD ROM throughput, 8-bit cards cost a lot less and are adequate for all but the most demanding multimedia applications. If you plan on sharing a SCSI interface with a hard disk, though, spend the extra bucks for a 16-bit adapter.

HOT TIP

Several CD ROM drives, including some models from Panasonic and Sony, only work with their own nonstandard interface cards. Also, many drives can plug right into certain sound boards. Buying a CD ROM drive that has an interface that's compatible with your sound board can save you money and free up the slot the CD ROM adapter would otherwise occupy. In addition, if you buy a sound card and a CD ROM drive together in a *multimedia upgrade kit*, installing these two components in the same machine will probably be easier than if you bought them individually, and you'll probably get a few cool CD ROM titles thrown in for free.

Bells and Whistles

If you've narrowed your choice down to a few drives with similar price and performance, here are a few features that might break the tie for you:

- **Ejection options.** Simply put, the more ejection options you have—an eject button, software eject, and emergency eject—the better.

- **Audio options.** For CD ROM applications that incorporate sound, you want a standard audio output into which you can plug amplified speakers. For private listening, a front-panel headphone jack and a volume control are must-haves. And if you do a lot of dubbing, standard RCA jacks that plug into your stereo are also big plusses.

- **Maintenance.** CD ROM drives and their disks are exposed to contamination from dust, smoke, and other pollutants. Maintenance features such as an automatic lens-cleaning mechanism and a dust door help protect the drive from the elements. A disk caddy is also good protection, although it's kind of a pain. If you don't like shuffling CD ROMs in and out of a single disk caddy, you can purchase additional caddies for about $10 each from retailers such as Egghead Software.

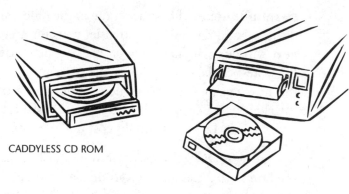

CADDYLESS CD ROM

CD ROM WITH CADDY

Figure 6: The helpful caddy. Drives that use disk caddies help protect your CD ROM disks from dust and permanent scratches. Swapping disks in and out of one caddy is tedious, though, so you may want to buy several caddies.

Alternative Storage

The problem with a hard disk drive is when it's full, it's full. For anyone who needs unlimited capacity for gobs of data—desktop publishing documents, multimedia applications, architectural drawings, whatever—removable hard disk cartridges and read/write optical disks are the answer. For life on the road, or for schlepping work between home and office, a portable hard disk drive is another interesting alternative.

Removable-Media Drives

Along with simply providing unlimited storage, high-capacity removable-media drives are popular both for keeping data secure—you can simply lock a cartridge or disk in a safe at night—and for backing up sensitive data very quickly. Removable-media drives are most practical for storing data files rather than for running applications, because even the fastest removable-media device can't match the speed of your average hard disk.

Whether you choose a drive with removable cartridges—such as the Bernoulli Box or the SyQuest/SyDOS drives—or a floptical or magneto-optical drive, remember that the more data you store, the less it will cost you per megabyte.

REMEMBER

- **Bernoulli Boxes.** These are some of the oldest and most popular removable-media devices—and the only ones that let you concatenate data from one cartridge to the next without assigning each cartridge a new drive letter. The Bernoulli drives are the fastest of the removable-media type, and along with the SyDOS drives, they are the next cheapest after magneto-optical on a cost-per-megabyte basis (including cartridges). A Bernoulli drive that uses 90MB cartridges should go for $500 or less, while a 150MB model should cost under $700.

- **SyQuest/SyDOS drives.** Removable disks made by SyQuest/SyDOS are widely used on both Macs and PCs in the desktop publishing world for transporting massive documents. Unlike the Bernoulli Box, though, each cartridge must have its own logical drive designation, which limits the total number of cartridges to 22. The SyDOS 51/4-inch drives use 44MB and 88MB cartridges, while the SyQuest PC drives use cartridges with 105MB and 270MB capacities. The cost of SyDOS drives is very similar to that of Bernoullis, with the drive speed just a nose behind.

- **Flopticals.** Like floppy drives on steroids, flopticals use laser optics to store up to 21MB of data on one 31/2-inch disk. The advantages of flopticals are a low buy-in cost ($400 and under) and the convenience of using the drive for your current library of 1.44MB and 720K disks (as well as IBM's 2.88MB disks). This makes flopticals a good solution for backups and transporting data between PCs. But compared with the other removable-media solutions, floptical disk capacity is limited, speed lags, and the cost per megabyte is high.

- **Magneto-optical (MO) drives.** These drives are the Mercedes of removable-storage devices, squeezing 128MB or 256MB of data on a 31/2-inch cartridge that slips into your pocket (51/4-inch disks can pack 1.2GB). The cartridges are virtually impervious to damage, so they're ideal for long-term storage. Moreover, MO drives have a common standard (for example, MO disks recorded on a Pinnacle drive can be read by a Sony RMO-S350 drive). MO drives are about a third slower than Bernoulli and SyDOS drives, and the cost of a drive ($1000 or more) is steep, but if you store a lot of data, MO drives offer the cheapest per-megabyte cost of the removable-media drives.

Portable Hard Disk Drives

Do you split your computing time between home and office? Does your mobile lifestyle force you to switch PCs often? Then a portable hard disk may be the best place for your data and applications. While portable hard disks aren't the fastest drives, they're truly convenient for road work, because they plug right into your parallel port.

Portables range in size from 20MB all the way up to 1.3GB. The smallest of the lot are about the size of a slice of bread and weigh less than a pound; the more capacious drives weigh in at 11 pounds and measure as large as a dictionary. About half are battery-powered, while the rest run off your PC's power source. If you plan to use a portable hard disk with a notebook PC, you definitely want one that "goes to sleep" during periods of inactivity in order to conserve battery power. Prices start as low as $300 and go as high as $3000.

HOT TIP

- **Trading speed for portability.** Portable drives' speed limit is largely imposed by the parallel port. As a rule, portable hard disks are anywhere between 20 and 50 percent slower than the average internal hard disk drive (the slowdown seems most noticeable in Windows graphics applications). In other words, when you see a portable hard disk drive advertised with an average seek time of 13ms, don't believe it—the parallel port will make the drive much slower than a desktop unit with the same spec. When you can compare one portable to another, look for a faster disk rotation speed and a segmented buffer.

REMEMBER

- **Special software.** Every portable drive comes with special software so that DOS and your PC can recognize the drive's existence. Simply put, DOS commands such as FORMAT, CHKDSK, and FDISK don't work across the parallel port interface. Moreover, the included utilities may not react as you expect—Windows may not work with the drive's disk caching software, and you may not be able to create a permanent Windows swap file (see Chapter 12: *Windows and DOS* for more on swap files). The bottom line is that you may have to relearn some basic procedures.

If the lackluster speed of portable drives sounds like something to avoid, you may want—depending on the job at hand—to purchase a fairly small drive and leave your applications on the machines you shuttle between. Then you can copy the files you're working on from the portable to the internal hard disk, and then copy them back again when you're done.

Product Directory

Hard Disk Drive Manufacturers

CMS Enhancements
2722 Michaelson Dr.
Irvine, CA 92715
800/237-2707
714/222-6000

Conner Peripherals
3081 Zanker Rd.
San Jose, CA 95134
800/526-6637 (West Coast)
800/ 230-5638 (East Coast)
408/456-4500

Core Int'l
7171 N. Federal Hwy.
Boca Raton, FL 33487
800/688-9910
407/997-6044

Maxtor Corp.
211 River Oaks Pkwy.
San Jose, CA 95134
800/262-9867
408/432-1700

Optima Technology
17526 VonKarmen
Irvine, CA 92714
800/367-3787
714/476-0515

Perisol Technology
3350 Scott Blvd. Bldg. 1201
Santa Clara, CA 95054
800/447-8226
408/738-1311

Procom Technology
2181 Dupont Dr.
Irvine, CA 92715
800/800-8600
714/852-1000

Quantum Corp.
500 McCarthy Blvd.
Milpitas, CA 95035
800/624-5545
408/894-4000

Seagate Technology
920 Disc. Dr.
Scotts Valley, CA 95066
408/438-6550

Storage Devices Inc.
6800 Orangethorpe Ave.
Buena Park, CA 90620
800/872-7341
714/562-5500

Western Digital
8105 Irvine Circle Dr.
Irvine, CA 92718
800/832-4778
714/932-4900

CD ROM Drive Manufacturers

CD Technology
766 San Aleso Ave.
Sunnyvale, CA 94086
408/752-8500

CMS Enhancements
800/237-2707
714/222-6000

Creative Labs
1901 McCarthy Blvd.
Milpitas, CA 95035
800/998-5227
408/428-6600

Hitachi Home Electronics
800/241-6558
310/537-8383

NEC Technologies
1255 Michael Dr.
Wood Dale, IL 60191
800/388-8888
708/860-9500

Panasonic
800/742-8086
201/348-7000

Philips LMS
One Philps Dr.
Knoxville, TN 37914
800/777-5674
615/521-3422

Pioneer New Media
Technologies
2265 E. 220th St.
Long Beach, CA 90810
310/952-2111

Procom Technology
800/800-8600
714/852-1000

Sony Electronics
3300 Zanker Rd.
San Jose, CA 95134
800/352-7669
408/432-0190

Storage Devices
800/872-7341
714/562-5500

Plextor
4255 Burton Dr.
Santa Clara, CA 95054
800/886-3935
408/980-1838

Toshiba America
  Information Systems
Disk Products Division
9740 Irvine Blvd.
Irvine, CA 92713
714/457-0777

Magneto-Optical Drive Manufacturers

CMS Enhancements
800/237-2707
714/222-6000

IBM
800/772-2227

Panasonic
800/742-8086
201/348-1000

Pinnacle Micro
19 Technology
Irvine, CA 92718
800/553-7070
714/727-3300

Prima Storage Solutions
3350 Scott Blvd. Bldg. #7
Santa Clara, CA 95054
408/727-2600

Procom Technology
800/800-8600
714/852-1000

Relax Technology
3101 Whipple Rd.
Union City, CA 94587
510/471-6112

Sony Electronics
800/352-7669
408/432-0190

Storage Devices
800/872-7341
714/562-5500

Removable Cartridge Drive Manufacturers

Iomega Corp.
1821 W. Iomega Way
Roy, UT 84067
800/777-6654
801/778-3712

Storage Devices
800/872-7341
714/562-5500

SyQuest/SyDOS
SyQuest Technology
47071 Baseline Pkwy.
Fremont, CA 94538
800/245-2278
510/226-4000

Portable Hard Drive Manufacturers

The BSE Company
2114 N. 4th St.
Flagstone, AZ 86004
602/527-8843

CMS Enhancements
800/237-2707
714/222-6000

Disctec Corp.
925 S. Semoraw Blvd. #114
Winter Park, FL 32792
800/553-0337
407/671-5500

Pacific Rim Systems
2655 Barrington Ct.
Hayward, CA 94545
510/782-1013

Prima Storage Solutions
408/727-2600

Relax Technology
3101 Whipple Rd.
Union City, CA 94587
510/471-6112

Storage Devices
800/872-7341
714/562-5500

Tulin Technology
2156 O'Toole Ave.
San Jose, CA 95131
408/432-9057

5 Monitors, Etc.

By TJ Byers

- Finding the right size monitor at a decent price
- Monitor controls and image quality
- Matching graphics cards and monitors
- Buying considerations for graphics cards

How important is your monitor? Ask someone who just spent 12 hours suffering in front of a crummy one. Paying extra for a monitor that's easy on the eyes makes sense—even if it costs half the price of the PC itself. And when you're talking that kind of money, it's worth getting educated about the specifications to look for when you go shopping. That's what this chapter is about, mostly.

Remember, though, that the monitor you buy won't work without a *graphics controller*, a small cluster of circuits residing either on your motherboard or (more likely) on an expansion card. The monitor itself is pretty dumb. If a monitor is the movie screen, then the graphics controller is the projector—it regulates the monitor's resolution, the number of colors displayed, and several other key factors. Your monitor won't work to its full potential unless you match controller and monitor correctly—another task you'll get some advice on here.

If you already have a PC, then buying a new graphics card will be an upgrade for you, and you should turn to the "Installing Expansion Cards" section of Chapter 8: *Upgrade It Yourself* to see what's involved. If you're buying a whole system, monitor included, use this chapter in conjunction with Chapter 2: *How to Buy a PC* to get the best deal. Just remember not to scrimp on the monitor, or your eyes will regret it.

Monitor Buyers' Guide

When Walt Disney created the classic *Fantasia*, he said to his cartoonist, "It's a color world. So let's make the most of it." The same thinking underlies software. No one even considers buying a monochrome monitor anymore; because applications now use color so effectively, you can easily get lost in a screenful of complex information without it. The price of color monitors ranges from $199 to several thousand bucks—a broad range, indeed. But most of us can expect to pay between $400 to $1000, depending on screen size.

Screen Size and Shape

REMEMBER

The bigger the screen, the less time you spend scrolling through or switching between applications, and the more time you spend working. Monitor sizes range from 14 inches to 26 inches, with prices rising sharply when you go beyond 17 inches. Note that the number of inches is actually the diagonal measurement of the CRT (for *cathode ray tube*; see Figure 2), so the screen area is always smaller than the number of inches suggests. For example, a 17-inch monitor's actual screen is seldom diagonally wider than 15$1/2$ inches.

HOT TIP

If you buy a cheap 14-inch monitor, you're cheating yourself. For one thing, unlike 14-inch models, virtually all 15-inch monitors and larger have flat screens with square corners. If you strategically tilt or swivel a flat-screen monitor on its base, you have a much better chance of eliminating reflective glare (the number one cause of eyestrain) than with a curved-screen monitor.

- **The 15-inch rule.** For most Windows applications, a 15-inch monitor is the best choice. The screen has significantly more viewing area than a 14-inch monitor—a nice bit of added elbow room for large spreadsheets or multiple applications—and the electronics are generally of higher quality. Street prices normally range from $400 to $600, with a few premium models, such as the NEC 4FGe, going for $700.

- **The 17-inch monitor: affordable luxury.** Do you frequently cut and paste between Windows programs? Do you spend time making documents or presentations look their best? Then a 17-inch monitor is right for you, offering nearly 33 percent more screen area than a 15-inch display. Once an expensive luxury, these beauties now go for under $1000, with a few dipping as low as $600.

- **The behemoths.** Monitors from 19 to 21 inches are prized by desktop publishers, who are willing to pay the high $1600 to $2500 tariff in order to get a big, sharp view of the page. Engineers and architects who use computer-aided design (CAD) software also favor the big screen. Their time is worth too much for them to waste time scrolling through large drawings, which is why expensive monitors over 21 inches are sold to this group of users.

If you choose a monitor over 15 inches, you'd better have room. Some 17-inch models measure 20 inches from screen to rear end, and weigh 50 pounds or more—enough to buckle the chassis on some compact PCs. Don't forget to calculate for the extra inches of a tilt-and-swivel stand, and make sure there's enough space for twisting and turning.

DANGER

Image Quality

Some basic specifications affecting image quality can help you narrow your choice of monitor right away. You'll find these specs here. Once you've finished this first round of elimination, go to the store and look at several prospective buys side by side (just as you'd compare, say, stereo speakers).

- **Dot pitch.** The image on a color screen is made up of tiny triads of red, green, and blue phosphor dots. *Dot pitch*—the distance in millimeters between phosphor dots of the same color—is a major factor in determining the sharpness of a monitor. Generally, the smaller the dot pitch, the sharper the

14-INCH MONITOR,
640-BY-480 RESOLUTION

15-INCH MONITOR,
800-BY-600 RESOLUTION

17-INCH MONITOR,
1024-BY-768 RESOLUTION

19-INCH MONITOR,
1280-BY-1024 RESOLUTION

Figure 1: Resolution, screen size, and image size. *The larger the monitor, the more you can see of the same image. This proportional drawing shows the smallest recommended screen size for the four standard resolutions—on each monitor, higher resolutions usually work, but text would be too small to read.*

image. As a rule of thumb, you should never consider a monitor with a dot pitch larger than .28mm. At .25mm, Trinitron CRTs (used in monitors by Sony, Seiko, and other manufacturers) have the finest commercially available dot pitch.

- **Maximum resolution.** Much as strategically arranged dots of ink produce a photographic image, *pixels* (short for *picture elements*) create the image you see on screen. The *resolution* of an image is its width and height in pixels, which are arranged and sent to the CRT by the graphics controller. The lowest resolution anyone uses is 640-by-480 pixels; the highest (outside of CAD and desktop publishing) is 1280-by-1024 pixels. High resolution enables you to see more of a spreadsheet, more applications, more of a layout, or what have you. However, high resolution on a small monitor may make text too small to read comfortably—which is why you should buy a larger monitor if you opt for higher resolution (see Figure 1).

- **Refresh rate.** This is the number of times per second the CRT's electron gun can produce a full-screen image. A faster refresh rate means less flicker—and less eye fatigue. Studies show that the minimum acceptable refresh rate is 70 screens per second (70 Hz), with 72 Hz the international standard. (This rate is sometimes dubbed "flicker free," but the flicker is still there—it's just too fast for most people to see.) Note that most quality monitors can achieve 70 Hz or better at resolutions of 1024-by-768 pixels or lower, but many downshift to a flickery 60 Hz at 1280 by 1024 or higher.

- **Horizontal scan rates.** This handy spec (the number of scan lines an electron gun can produce per second) usually tells you the maximum possible refresh rate at any given resolution (or vice versa). For example, a monitor with a horizontal

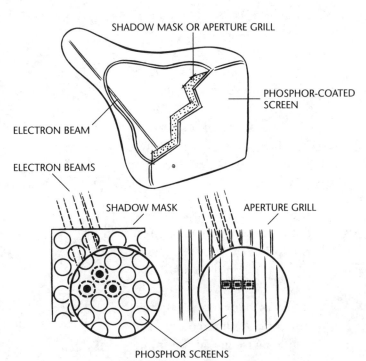

SHADOW MASK OR APERTURE GRILL

PHOSPHOR-COATED SCREEN

ELECTRON BEAM

ELECTRON BEAMS

SHADOW MASK

APERTURE GRILL

PHOSPHOR SCREENS

Figure 2: A CRT and all those dots. *Inside a monitor's CRT, an electron gun sweeps the phosphor-coated inner surface of the screen, illuminating the dots it lands on. The closer together the dots are (that is, the smaller the dot pitch), the sharper the image generally is, regardless of the resolution.*

Resolution	Refresh rate	Horizontal scan frequency
640 by 480	60 Hz	31.5 KHz
640 by 480	70 Hz	38 KHz
640 by 480	72 Hz	39.4 KHz
800 by 600	60 Hz	38 KHz
800 by 600	70 Hz	45 KHz
800 by 600	72 Hz	48 KHz Best spec for 15-inch monitors
1024 by 768	60 Hz	48 KHz
1024 by 768	70 Hz	57 KHz
1024 by 768	72 Hz	60 KHz Best spec for 17-inch monitors
1280 by 1024	60 Hz	64 KHz
1280 by 1024	70 Hz	74.5 KHz
1280 by 1024	72 Hz	76 KHz Best spec for 19-inch monitors

Figure 3: *The horizontal scan rate determines both the maximum possible resolution and the top refresh rate (the higher the refresh rate, the less eye-wearying flicker). Remember that to get the best performance from your monitor, your graphics card must match or exceed your monitor's specs.*

scan rate of 60 KHz has a maximum refresh rate of 72 Hz at a resolution of 1024-by-768 pixels (see Figure 3).

- **Vertical scan rate**. To avoid producing tiny, unreadable type, you'll probably run your monitor at less than maximum resolution. In that case, you may be able to run your monitor at refresh rates exceeding 72 Hz, for rock-steady images. For example, a monitor with a 76-KHz horizontal scan rate may produce refresh rates as high as 103 Hz at 800 by 600 resolution. The likelihood of this depends on two factors: First, the *vertical scan rate* (the speed of the refresh electronics) must meet or exceed the desired refresh rate. Second, your graphics controller must be capable of running at this speed, too (see "Graphics Cards" later in this chapter).

- **Image stability**. Any monitor worth its salt can handle several different resolutions (a monitor that can display several resolutions is called a *mulitiscan* monitor). But Windows, which permits you to switch rapidly between applications that may use wildly different resolutions, can throw some multiscan monitors for a loop—if they aren't *microprocessor* controlled. Surprisingly, the difference in price between monitors with and without a microprocessor is just tens of dollars, well worth the extra cost.

HOT TIP

DANGER

Whatever you do, don't let a fast-talking sales person sell you a monitor with interlaced scanning. While the refresh rates may look good on paper, a quick look at the screen will convince you otherwise—because it will flicker as badly as an old-time nickelodeon. Always insist on a *noninterlaced* monitor.

Controls and Adjustments

You always have to set the brightness and contrast, but many microprocessor-controlled monitors make other screen adjustments automatically. However, you may want to override these defaults, make additional adjustments, or even fiddle with the color tonality of the screen. To do this, you need the right controls.

Making It Picture Perfect

At the factory, workers carefully fine tune your monitor to produce the best possible image. But when the UPS man drops your new monitor, those adjustments can go out of whack. If your monitor has the right controls, you can readjust it yourself without having to send it to a repairperson. Here's a glossary of common controls that can help you produce the best possible image:

HOT TIP

- **Degauss** removes random color swirls caused by changes in the earth's magnetic field. To avoid putting a strain on your monitor, wait at least 10 minutes before pressing the degauss button a second time.

- **Horizontal position,** sometimes called horizontal phase, moves the image from side to side.

- **Horizontal size** increases or decreases the width of the image.

- **Keystone balance** distortion occurs when the image

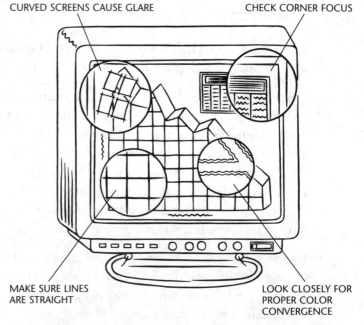

CURVED SCREENS CAUSE GLARE

CHECK CORNER FOCUS

MAKE SURE LINES ARE STRAIGHT

LOOK CLOSELY FOR PROPER COLOR CONVERGENCE

Figure 4: Monitor checkpoints. When you choose a monitor, pay special attention to focus in the corners, and make sure lines are straight all the way across the screen. These factors, along with color convergence (revealed by how tightly red, green, and blue converge to produce white) are important, because you may not be able to make corrections—problems may be inherent.

starts looking like a parallelogram instead of a rectangle. Adjust the control until the corners are square.

- **Pincushion balance** distortion occurs when one side of the image bows inward and the other side bows outward. Adjust the control until both sides are straight.

- **Pincushion/barrel** distortion is an equal amount of inward or outward bowing on both sides of the image. Adjust the control until both sides are straight.

- **Rotate** spins the image so that its edges line up parallel with the edges of the bezel. A skewed image due to shipping and handling is a common problem, so look for this control if you plan to move the monitor a lot.

HOT TIP

- **Screen temperature** affects the overall tone of the image. The commonly supported screen temperatures are: 9300 degrees Kelvin (bluish-white/outdoors), 6500 degrees Kelvin (neutral/tungsten lamp), and 5000 degrees Kelvin (ruddy/warm tungsten lamp).

- **Static convergence** corrects an annoying separation of white dots into their red, blue, and green color components. The distortion is caused by a misalignment in either the vertical or horizontal convergence, or both. You need a special test pattern to properly adjust this.

- **Trapezoid/keystone** distortion happens when the width of the image changes size from top to bottom. Adjust the control until the top width equals the bottom width.

- **Vertical position** moves the image up or down.

- **Vertical size** increases or decreases the height of the image.

All this button punching could strand you with a screen that looks nothing like what you intended. That's why most microprocessor-controlled monitors have a Recall or Reset button to bring the screen back to factory specs should you find yourself in the video twilight zone.

Color Matching

People who produce color publications often have trouble matching colors on screen to colors in print. Shining gold can transmute into straw-colored tan, vibrating red may turn to mud—and your hot color brochure may look like it was made with Crayolas. The fault is not with the monitor, the color printer, or the color prepress service bureau. The problem is in the way the eye perceives colors.

Video monitors use the additive color method: Three light sources in the primary colors of red, green, and blue are blended together to create a spectrum from pink to violet. Color printers, on the other hand, use the subtractive color method: Dyes or pigments are used to absorb certain colors and reflect others, giving the paint or ink its characteristic tint. The problem is, the two methods don't always match perfectly—especially when it comes to subtle shades.

A number of monitors—NEC's MultiSync FG series, for example—have controls that enable you to bring screen colors close to printed colors. Special color calibration systems (which attach to the surface of the monitor) do even better, but they cost a lot, and color matching is an inherently inexact science in any event. Natural light changes the way a screen looks during the day, and ink in various stages of drying changes color. Only people who have lots of experience or enlist the help of a professional printing service can expect to get consistent results (see Chapter 18: *Desktop Publishing* for more on professional color services).

Health and the Environment

Monitors produce electromagnetic emissions, which may or may not pose a serious health hazard. Monitors also require lots of AC power. Manufacturers have responded to both problems (see Chapter 11: *Health, Safety, and the Environment* for more on these topics).

- **Monitor emissions**. While studies have yet to prove that *electromagnetic radiation* (EMR) produced by monitors constitutes a health hazard, public concern has grown, prompting monitor makers to adopt the strict Swedish MPR-II emissions standard defining exposure limits. In fact, you'll be hard pressed to find a multiscan monitor that doesn't meet the standard. Nonetheless, remember that no one claims to have established "safe" limits. It's best to keep your monitor at (literally) arm's length when you compute, and—more important—make sure that no one is exposed for long periods of time to the back of a monitor, the strongest source of emissions.

HOT TIP

- **Low power.** The Environmental Protection Agency's Energy Star guidelines suggest that no monitor or PC should draw more than 30 watts of electricity when idle. The monitor industry responded by creating the DPMS (Display Power Management Signaling) standard. Essentially, DPMS defines four descending levels of power below full on, with a final level of five watts or less. A DPMS monitor can both reduce waste and cut your power bill, but remember that both the monitor and graphics controller must be DPMS compliant for the scheme to work.

Graphics Cards

Graphics cards are much cheaper than monitors—a $200 model will generally do just fine. Moreover, graphics cards typically outperform monitors, so you generally need to worry about finding a monitor that can handle your graphics card rather than the other way around (for example, many graphics cards deliver 120 Hz refresh at 1024-by-768 resolution, beyond the capability of all but a handful of very expensive monitors). Nonetheless, if you buy a cheap card from the discount bin, you can still get a card that flickers badly at the resolution you want. Accept a card that can do no less than 1280 by 1024 at 72 Hz (*without* interlacing).

REMEMBER

Almost every graphics card meets or exceeds those specs. To narrow the field further, you should consider speed first—not the refresh rate, but the speed at which a graphics card can shovel data to the screen. The number of colors a card can produce is also a consideration, although most cards provide plenty for all but the most demanding color desktop publishing. Here's how to pick the card that has the right stuff for you.

Speed

If you have a graphics controller that's more than two years old, you may be able to speed up your overall system performance significantly by upgrading. Most graphics cards today are speedy *Windows accelerators* that can shuttle information to the screen as fast as the system serves it to them. However, in ordinary Windows applications, the speed differences among currently available cards is pretty slight. The following factors are most telling in multimedia applications, where video sequences pump huge quantities of data to the screen at a time:

- **Local bus or not?** If you own a system with a VL or PCI local bus, it probably came with a local bus graphics card that's plenty fast, although an upgrade to an even faster card could help you speed up multimedia applications. Just be aware that if you have an older system without local bus slots, you can't use a local bus video card in it (see Chapter 8: *Upgrade It Yourself* for more on matching cards and busses).

- **Controller chip.** Basically, this chip *is* the graphics controller. At this writing, Tseng labs ET4000 chips seem to deliver the highest performance for the cost. Reviews of graphics cards in *PC World* and *PC Magazine* both show speed test results and tell you which cards use which chips, enabling you to determine the hot chips (and cards) to look for.

REMEMBER

- **Memory path**. Graphics boards have their own memory, often as much as 2MB (see below). The amount of data in memory that a controller chip can access at one time may affect performance significantly. Look for a card that accesses memory 32 bits at a time—or 64 bits at a time, if the cost is the same as that of a card with a 32-bit memory path. Note that many manufacturers promote cards that use VRAM (a special type of fast memory for graphics) as the hottest performers. This isn't necessarily true—the controller chip, bus type, and memory path generally have a bigger effect—but VRAM cards almost always cost more than DRAM (that is, standard memory) cards.

- **For multimedia video only**. Multimedia video sucks up so much disk space, everyone uses some kind of compression scheme to shrink the size of multimedia video files. Those files must be decompressed on the fly as the video is played, and if you have a card that does this, the decompression is *much* faster—which means the video runs much smoother. Decompression cards are available separately, but you can also buy graphics cards with decompression capabilities (such as Diamond Computer Systems' Viper Pro). Unfortunately, there are several video compression schemes (Indeo, Cinepak, Captain Crunch, MPEG Motion-JPEG, and so on), so you need to make sure the board you select can decompress the video files you want to play.

HOT TIP

Perhaps the most overlooked performance factor is a card's *Windows drivers*, small programs that come with the graphics card and enable it to work with Windows at resolutions higher than 640 by 480. A poorly written Windows driver can bog down performance and cause other problems, so always contact the manufacturer to make sure you have drivers of the most recent vintage. Usually, the company will send you the latest drivers on disk for free, or you can download new drivers from the company bulletin board service (see Chapter 20: *Communications* for instructions on downloading files).

Memory, Resolution, and Color

Like a PC's CPU, a graphics controller chip needs memory—called *video memory*—to do its job. The quantity of video memory (which is installed on the card itself) determines both the number of colors and the maximum resolution a card can produce.

REMEMBER

For example, a card with 1MB of video RAM can deliver a maximum of 256 colors at 1024-by-768 resolution—but at 640-by-480 resolution, a 24-bit graphics card with 1MB may be able to produce 16.7 million colors. Whether you actually get that many colors depends on the *DAC* (*digital-to-analog* conversion) chip. If your board has an 8-bit DAC, you get 256 colors, max. If your board has a 24-bit DAC, you get your 16.7 million colors.

How Memory Puts a Cap on Colors				
	512K	**1MB**	**2MB**	**4MB**
640 by 480	65,536	16.8 million	16.8 million	16.8 million
800 by 600	256	65,536	16.8 million	16.8 million
1024 by 768	16	256	65,536	16.8 million
1280 by 1024	4	16	256	65,536

Figure 5: At a given resolution, your graphics card can only produce so many colors, depending on the resolution and the amount of memory. Note that these numbers assume that the card has a 24-bit DAC.

The key thing to remember is that a card needs enough memory to produce the resolution and the colors you want. For example, say you wanted to preview color photographs for a color publication, and you were looking for a card that could produce 16.7 million colors at a resolution of 1024 by 768, a data-rich image that would require 4MB of video RAM to produce. Some graphics cards may advertise the ability to produce such an image—but when you open up the box, you realize the card only comes with 2MB, and you need an expensive memory upgrade to bring it to 4MB (see Chapter 8: *Upgrade It Yourself* for more on upgrading video memory).

Product Directory

Monitor Manufacturers

Aamazing Technologies
1050 W. Beacon St.
Brea, CA 92621
714/255-1688

Acer America
2641 Orchard Pkwy.
San Jose, CA 95134
800/733-2237
408/432-6200

ETC Computers
2917 Bayview Dr.
Fremont, CA 94538
510/226-6250

Goldstar Technology, Inc.
3003 N. First St.
San Jose, CA 95134
408/432-1331

IBM
800/772-2227

Idek
46711 Fremont Blvd.
Fremont, CA 94538
800/394-4335
510/249-5900

Mag Innovision
2801 S. Viejo St.
Santa Ana, CA 92704
800/827-3998
714/751-2008

Mitsubishi Electronics
5665 Plaza Dr.
Cypress, CA 90630
800/843-2515
714/220-2500

Nanao USA Corp.
23535 Telo Ave.
Torrance, CA 90505
800/800-5202
310/325-5202

NEC Technologies, Inc.
1255 Michael Dr.
Wood Dale, IL 60191
800/388-8888
708/860-9500

NSA/Hitachi
100 Lowderbrook Dr. #2400
Westwood, MA 02090
800/441-4832
617/461-8300

Optiquest, Inc.
20480 Business Pkwy.
Walnut, CA 91789
800/843-6784
909/468-3750

Panasonic
800/742-8086
201/348-1000

Philips Magnovox
One Philips Dr.
Knoxville, TN 37914
800/822-1219
615/521-4316

Relisys
320 S. Milpitas Blvd.
Milpitas, CA 95035
800/783-6333
408/945-9000

Sampo Corp. of America
5550 Peachtree Industrial
  Blvd.
Norcross, GA 30071
404/449-6220

Samsung Electronics America
  Information Systems Division
301 Mayhill St.
Saddle Brook, NJ 07662
800/726-7864
201/587-9600

Samtron Displays, Inc.
14251 E. Firestone Blvd. #101
La Marada, CA 90638
800/726-8766
310/802-8425

Seiko Instruments USA Inc.
1130 Ringwood Ct.
San Jose, CA 95131
800/553-5312
408/922-5800

Sony Corp. of America
800/352-7669
201/930-6432

TVM Professional
  Monitor Corp.
4260 E. Brickell
Ontario, CA 91761
800/822-8168
909/988-3368

ViewSonic
20480 E. Business Pkwy.
Walnut, CA 91789
800/888-8583
909/869-7976

Wyse/Amdek
3471 B First St.
San Jose, CA 95134
800/722-6335
408/473-1200

Graphics Card Manufacturers

Aamazing Technologies
714/255-1688

Actix Systems
3350 Scott Blvd. Bldg. #9
Santa Clara, CA 95054
800/927-5557
408/986-1625

ATI Technologies, Inc.
33 Commerce Valley Dr. East
Thornhill, Ontario L3C 7N6
  Canada
905/882-2600

Boca Technology Group, Inc.
21346 St. Andrews Blvd. #219
Boca Raton, FL 33433
407/997-6227

Diamond Computer Systems
1130 E. Arques Ave.
Sunnyvale, CA 94086
408/736-2000

Genoa Systems
75 E. Trimble Rd.
San Jose, CA 95131
800/934-3662
408/432-9090

Hercules Computer
  Technology
3839 Spinnaker Ct.
Fremont, CA 94538
800/532-0600
510/623-6030

Micro Express
1801 Carnegie Ave.
Santa Ana, CA 92705
800/989-9900
714/852-1400

Number Nine
  Computer Corp.
18 Hartwell Ave.
Lexington, MA 02173
800/438-6463
617/674-0009

Orchid Technology
45365 Northport Loop West
Fremont, CA 94538
800/767-2443
510/683-0300

STB Systems, Inc.
1651 N. Glenville #210
Richardson, TX 75081
800/234-4334
214/234-8750

Western Digital (Paradise)
8105 Irvine Circle Dr.
Irvine, CA 92718
800/832-4778

6 Printers and Printing

By Steve Cummings

- The basic choice: laser, ink jet, or dot matrix?
- Getting the most laser for your money
- When to buy a PostScript laser printer
- Finding the best ink jet, dot matrix, or color printer
- Printing tips for laser printers and Windows printing
- Print spoolers, printer sharing, paper tips

How do you pick the right printer out of hundreds on the market? The easy answer: Buy a Hewlett-Packard LaserJet.

If you print standard documents like letters, reports, or maybe some newsletters and forms, and as long as you don't need color or portability, choosing a LaserJet is a no-brainer. No, they didn't pay me to say that, and I'm not saying LaserJets are the very best printers at the best possible price. It's just that you can't go wrong with a LaserJet.

LaserJets produce excellent print quality and are extremely reliable. Compared to other printers, LaserJets work with more software and more add-on devices. Supplies, parts, and repair services are widely available. And even if they're not the rock-bottom cheapest printers, LaserJets are reasonably priced—you can buy the cheapest model, the LaserJet 4L, for less than $700.

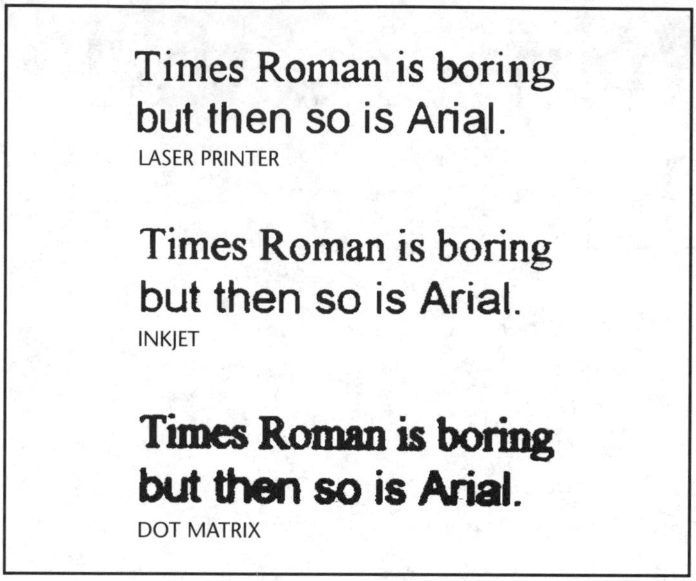

Times Roman is boring
but then so is Arial.
LASER PRINTER

Times Roman is boring
but then so is Arial.
INKJET

Times Roman is boring
but then so is Arial.
DOT MATRIX

Figure 1: Three types of output, magnified. *These enlarged samples of 10-point Times Roman and Arial text tell the story. Laser quality beats all comers, with ink jet output second and dot matrix a distant third.*

Nonetheless, laser printers can't satisfy everyone's printing needs. If you need inexpensive color, or if even the cheapest laser is too much for your budget, consider one of the many reasonable alternatives covered here. Then, when you've made your choice, turn to the "Printing Advice" and "Printer Utilities" sections at the end of this chapter to get the most out of your machine.

Which Printer Type for You?

Buy a laser printer if...	Buy an ink jet printer if...	Buy a dot matrix printer if...
You want great-looking letters, reports, or booklets	You want an economical color printer	You need to print on multipart forms
You want good to excellent speed	You can't spend more than $400 or so	You want an economical way to print on 11-by-17-inch paper
You can afford at least $500	You want excellent quality for letters and reports	You want the cheapest possible printer

Figure 2: *Laser printers may be the best general purpose choice, but ink jet and dot matrix printers can do things lasers can't.*

Laser Printers

Why do they call them *laser* printers? Because inside a tiny laser beam scans across a rotating, electrostatically charged drum to create an image of the printed page. Toner sticks to the scanned image on the drum, which in turn rolls onto the paper, where the toner is fused at about 400 degrees to create hard copy. The quality produced by this process is so good, and the cost of laser printers has fallen so low, you need a good excuse *not* to buy one.

- **Personal** lasers cost from $500 to $1000 in stores and take up about as much desk space as an open magazine, but they print slowly—between 2 and 5 *pages per minute (ppm)*—and generally hold only 100 to 200 sheets of paper at a time.

- **Desktop** lasers are faster (6 to 12 ppm) and hold more paper, so they're good for small groups or individuals who print a lot. They're also slightly bigger than personal lasers and cost between $1200 and $2500.

- **Network** lasers need to be fast—12 to 15 ppm and up—and hold plenty of paper, since they're designed to serve a LAN's-worth of people. They're big and expensive ($3000 to $20,000), with price and size varying widely according to the expected printing volume. And, of course, they come ready to hook up to a network.

- **Color** lasers are just beginning to appear. Currently, other color printing technologies offer better output for less money (see "Serious Color Printers" at the end of this chapter).

Print Quality

Now for the technical stuff. Laser print quality depends on three factors, all of which depend in turn on the basic element of a laser-printed image, that humble spec of toner known as the *dot*:

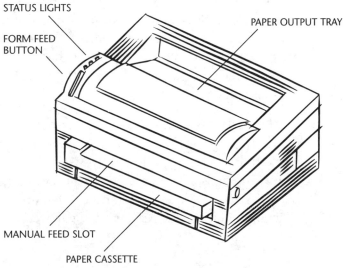

STATUS LIGHTS

FORM FEED BUTTON

PAPER OUTPUT TRAY

MANUAL FEED SLOT

PAPER CASSETTE

Figure 3: The Hewlett-Packard LaserJet 4L. *The most popular personal laser printer costs less than $700, produces excellent output, and takes up precious little desk space.*

600-DPI OUTPUT   300-DPI OUTPUT

Figure 4: The benefits of 600 dpi. *With scanned photos, the difference between 600-dpi and 300-dpi output is dramatic.*

- **Resolution** is measured in *dots per inch (dpi)*. It's the key factor determining print quality. The resolution standard for laser printers is rapidly shifting from 300 to 600 dpi. At 600 dpi, text looks considerably sharper, and when you print scanned photos, the improvement is dramatic. You can buy the lowest-priced 600-dpi LaserJet for around $800.

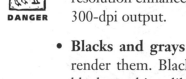

- **Resolution enhancement** simulates higher resolution by strategically sizing and offsetting dots to give fonts and line graphics smoother curves and sharper edges. ("Resolution enhancement" is a Hewlett-Packard term, but other companies offer similar technologies.) It works, but watch out for manufacturers that use resolution enhancement to claim "600-dpi quality," when in fact they're enhancing 300-dpi output.

- **Blacks and grays** must be seen in print in order to judge a printer's ability to render them. Black areas should be solid and dark—if not, large characters and block graphics alike will look weak. Ask to see printed output, and watch out for unwanted bands in solid shades or hairlines that mysteriously break up. The more shades of gray a printer can simulate, the more life-like printed photos will look. In general, the higher the resolution, the more gray shades available.

Speed

Manufacturers routinely exaggerate ppm speed ratings, but at least they're in the ball-park for text printing. When it comes to printing graphics, though, huge differences emerge even among printers that have the same ppm rating. How huge? The top-performing 8-ppm desktop printers print graphics almost three times faster than the slowest ones.

Likewise, different kinds of graphics take different amounts of time. You may encounter a rating called *gppm* (for *graphics pages per minute*), but this is absolutely useless out of context. For a meaningful comparison between two printers, you must test them with the same graphics files. Do so yourself if your dealer will let you, or check out the latest computer magazine speed tests.

REMEMBER

Paper Handling

Every printer comes with a *duty cycle* rating, a recommended maximum number of pages a printer should print each month. It's hard to tell what this number means, since each company seems to estimate duty cycles differently. Just don't make a personal laser your network printer, OK? And check these important features:

- **Paper sizes.** Desktop laser printers usually have two paper trays, so you can easily switch between legal- and letter-size paper. Personal models generally have a single tray that you can adjust to hold legal-size paper, and/or they offer a feeder slot into which you slip single sheets. Only big, relatively expensive printers such as the Compaq Pagemarq have room for 11-by-17-inch paper, useful for large spreadsheets, poster-size graphics, and the like. A few models can feed continuous, fanfold computer paper.

- **Capacity.** No one likes to fill the paper tray. Personal laser paper trays typically hold 100 or 200 sheets. Extra-cost trays give personal lasers from Epson and Panasonic a 400-sheet capacity, putting them in the same range as desktop models. Network paper trays typically hold 500 or 750 sheets; with some models, a second tray kicks in when the first one is empty.

- **Duplex printing.** A boon to the environmentally conscious, the ability to print on both sides of a page is offered only by a handful of network and desktop models (Lexmark 1039s are particularly reliable for duplex printing). Otherwise, you can always do it the boring way and flip one-sided pages back in the paper tray.

- **Envelopes.** Envelopes have long been the bane of laser printers. The laser printer's physical design makes envelope printing awkward. More often than not, you must manually change the paper path to get a single envelope through the mill. This is particularly true of personal printers. Desktop and network printers generally offer optional bulk envelope feeders that can hold up to 70 envelopes. But watch out for jams—I've never seen a laser printer digest many envelopes without one.

Fonts

Every laser printer comes with at least a handful of fonts built in, but if you use Windows, who cares? Windows makes handling fonts so easy, and the selection of fonts is so vast, the number or quality of a printer's built-in fonts shouldn't determine whether you buy it or not. Even DOS users can buy special font utilities that make built-in printer fonts of questionable value.

REMEMBER

But there are exceptions. Sending fonts from an application to a printer across a network can bog down performance, and either built-in fonts or *font cartridges*—cassette-size font libraries that plug into a socket offered by some printers—may deliver much better performance.

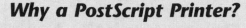

Why a PostScript Printer?

PostScript printers cost more than equivalent non-PostScript machines—often a few hundred dollars more. Most people don't need PostScript, since Windows gives unlimited access to fonts, and using PostScript can slow down graphics printouts by a factor of two or more. Don't spend the extra money unless:

- You need to print PostScript graphics or documents that other printers can't handle. EPS clip art files can only be printed by a PostScript printer (though you can easily convert them into other formats that will print on non-PostScript machines). Some programs, such as *Illustrator* and *QuarkXPress*, require a PostScript printer.

- You need to print from a Mac as well as a PC. Non-PostScript printers can be adapted to work with Macs, but going with PostScript is easier.

- You need to print PostScript files created by someone else's software or someone else's computer (to print the PostScript document, you copy the file to the printer, just as if you were copying it to a different disk).

- You need a way to print proofs of documents that will eventually be printed on a high-resolution *imagesetter* (most professional electronic publishing equipment is PostScript-based). Without a PostScript printer, you run the risk that your proofs won't look exactly like the final document.

If you opt for PostScript, be aware that some models use circuitry approved by Adobe Systems, the originator of PostScript, while others use copycat circuits. "Genuine Adobe" PostScript tends to cost a little more, but it's probably a bit more reliable.

Also note that most PostScript printers also have a LaserJet-compatible mode. Automatic switching between modes based on the current type of print job is a useful feature.

One more thing: You can get PostScript printouts without buying a PostScript printer. Programs like *ZScript* and *Freedom of the Press* enable you to print PostScript documents on any printer—albeit slowly.

Some network models offer optional hard disks that hook right to the printer and store as many fonts as you like.

PostScript printers, such as Apple LaserWriters, have at least 35 built-in PostScript Type 1 fonts. Other laser printers offer PostScript upgrades, so you can buy your printer now and pay for PostScript capability later. But remember: *Adobe Type Manager for Windows* gives *any* printer unlimited access to Type 1 fonts (see Chapter 13: *Fonts* for more on PostScript).

Compatibility

Here's one big reason LaserJets are the safe choice: They set the standard for compatibility. That means virtually every software package works with the LaserJet, which is another way of saying all those packages have a LaserJet *driver*, a little program that tells the printer what to print and where to print it.

One the other hand, drivers for Epson, Texas Instruments, Panasonic, Lexmark, Compaq, Canon and other brands aren't as common. If you don't have a driver for your printer, you have to select a LaserJet driver instead. As long as your printer claims to be "LaserJet compatible"—as most do—you have reason to hope the thing will work properly. In practice, results with text are usually good, but with graphics things may get dicey.

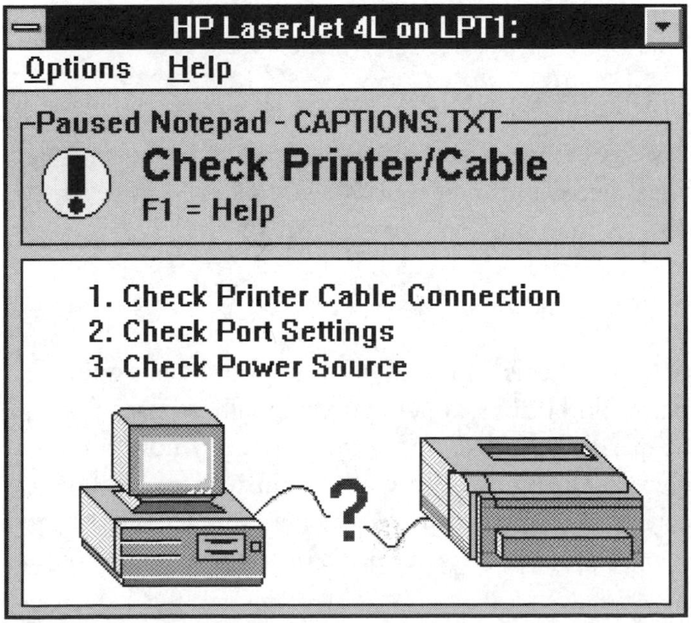

- **Windows.** The great thing about Windows is that once you install a printer through the Control Panel, every application you use under Windows will work with that printer. Windows comes with plenty of laser printer drivers, but it probably won't have one for the latest model (the one you just bought), so it's best to buy a printer that includes its own Windows driver.

Figure 5: LaserJets come with software that provides you with status reports, such as this pop-up alert box indicating a problem has occurred.

DANGER

Some models, such as Epson lasers, rely entirely on their ability to emulate the LaserJet using Windows' LaserJet driver.

- **PostScript.** Virtually every application comes with a PostScript driver, which means you can almost always access the 35 or more Type 1 fonts built into PostScript printers. Some high-end desktop publishing programs, such as *QuarkXPress*, require a PostScript printer.

- **PCL.** This is the "language" LaserJets use to render their pages, so "PCL compatible" is another way of saying "LaserJet compatible." The latest LaserJets use PCL revision 5E, but

> ## The LED Alternative
>
> A few "laser" printers actually use LEDs (light-emitting diodes) to etch the photosensitive drum. In place of a single laser, there's a stationary row of these tiny lights, one for each dot that can be printed on the page. (For an 8.5-inch-wide page at 300 dpi, that comes to 2550 LEDs.) The LEDs are like tiny flash bulbs, which fire wherever a dot of toner is required, one line of dots at a time. The drum rotates, another line flashes, and so on. The rest of the printing process works the same as it does in a laser printer.
>
> LED printers have two distinct advantages over a laser printer. Because the LEDs are fixed, they can withstand more vibration and rough handling than the delicate optics of a laser printer. Furthermore, most LED printers can achieve 300-by-1200-dpi resolution easily by printing an extra three lines as the drum advances.
>
> LED printers deliver output that's pretty much indistinguishable from (some say a little less sharp than) that of lasers. Okidata is probably more committed to this technology than any other manufacturer. The company's 300-dpi personal model, the OL 400e, costs only about $500 in stores; the 600-dpi OL 410e goes for about $650.

they also work with drivers that speak earlier versions of PCL (although the application won't be able to take advantage of all the new printer's features). However, older LaserJets and their compatibles may choke on drivers that speak PCL 5E.

Control

Check out the front panel readout and controls. Is it easy to figure out what's going on? Many printers have little displays and buttons to help you manually adjust toner density, resolution enhancement, paper feed, and so on. Better yet, a few now come with software that lets you configure such things from your PC instead of fiddling with buttons. Here again, the LaserJets excel. For example, when a LaserJet runs out of paper or encounters some other problem, a message pops up over your application letting you know what's wrong.

Memory

Laser printers need at least 1MB of RAM to print a full page of 300-dpi graphics. Printers with 600-dpi resolution require at least 2MB. Most printers come with these respective amounts already installed, but a few personal lasers don't. With many popular models, you may be able to get memory upgrades from mail-order houses for lower prices than the manufacturer offers.

PostScript laser printers need more memory, simply because you're more likely to do complex desktop publishing jobs with one. How much more depends on the number and type of fonts you plan to use at one time, but 1MB in addition to the 1MB for graphics is a good rule of thumb. With the exception of some personal PostScript models, you'll find that most PostScript printers come with enough memory for both font processing and a full page of graphics.

Some very organized companies load blank electronic forms into printer memory so that applications merely need to send form data to the printer, vastly speeding print time. Depending on the number of forms, this can hog quite a bit of RAM. Fortunately, this is really a network printer issue, and most can be upgraded to hold more than enough RAM for the job.

Operating Costs

Supply costs are similar for most laser printers: about 3 to 4 cents per page. One manufacturer, Kyocera, has cut costs significantly: You never have to replace the drum, so you pay only for toner and paper (for a cost of less than 2 cents a page).

Top Five Toner Tips

Most of the time, laser printers quietly and efficiently crank out page after page without any intervention from you. The only thing you have to maintain regularly is the toner.

1. Use print quality as your guide for knowing when to replace the cartridge. When the printer gives you a "toner low" message, you can keep right on printing as long as the pages look good.

2. When the print starts to look washed out, pull out the cartridge, rock it gently from side to side, and put it back—this may redistribute the remaining toner enough to give you many more good printouts.

3. Use remanufactured print cartridges to save money and reduce waste. They work just as well as the brand-new ones, as long as you get them from a reputable remanufacturer that guarantees its work.

4. Don't worry if the first pages you print after changing a print cartridge look too light or uneven. It takes awhile to break in a new cartridge. To speed the break-in process, try printing four or five sheets of solid black.

5. To get more pages out of a toner cartridge, turn down the print density (darkness) setting. Some new laser printers have a "draft mode" setting that basically does the same thing, which gives your proof printouts a wan look but lets you easily bump up toner density for your final copies.

Replacing toner cartridges, drums, and belts can be tricky, but perhaps the biggest trick of all is finding replacement consumables for an off-brand laser. You'll always find toner cartridges for popular LaserJet models at a nearby office supply store. And the other guys? You may have to order from the manufacturer.

Extras

Some models, such as Compaq's Pagemarq, have optional modules that turn your printer into a plain-paper, receive-only fax machine. The cheapest add-on fax device, called FaxMe, is a $159 cartridge that plugs into LaserJet font slots. TeleDisk makes an attachment that receives faxes and stores them in its own memory even when the printer is off. In the future, expect to see more models, such as the Okidata DOC-IT, that combine printing with both faxing and scanning.

Several companies sell devices that plug into various LaserJet models to increase apparent resolution. LaserMaster's WinJet, for example, boosts the apparent resolution of a 300-dpi LaserJet Series II or III to 800 dpi, and increases the LaserJet 4's from 600 dpi to 1200. This PC expansion board comes with its own special software and adds PostScript capability to your printer. It hogs close to 4MB of your PC's RAM, but it works, and print quality improvements are dramatic.

Ink Jet Printers

Ink jet printers are laser printers for the budget-conscious. Instead of transferring toner, they use tiny nozzles in a movable print head to squirt precisely aimed streams of ink onto the page. They're slower than lasers—typically turning out 2 text pages per minute—and they can't quite match laser print quality, but they cost hundreds of dollars less.

Ink jets share two laser printer limitations: Few accept anything but letter- and legal-size paper, and since there's no impact against the page, they can't print on multipart forms. But they have one important advantage over lasers: Many inexpensive models can print in color, and even upscale ink jets designed for high-volume color printing top out at around $2000. By contrast, the cheapest color laser printer costs around $8,000.

You won't find an overwhelming number of ink jet models to pick from, so comparison shopping is a little easier than with other printer technologies. The major manufacturers are Hewlett-Packard and Canon, but Lexmark, Epson, NEC, and a smattering of other vendors build ink jets, too.

Print Quality

All ink jets deliver at least 300-dpi resolution, so you can count on decent output quality no matter which model you pick. Still, you'll notice significant differences from printer to printer.

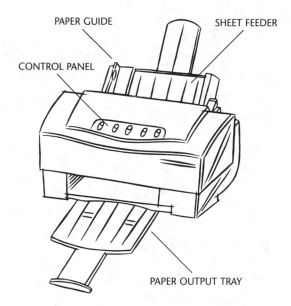

- **Resolution.** Some brands offer 360-dpi or even 600-by-300-dpi printing, delivering smaller dots and sharper edges than 300-dpi models, but still not quite laser quality. How much the ink spreads or smudges also plays a role: A little spreading makes the dots blend together for smooth edges, but too much gives a fuzzy look.

Figure 6: Low-cast color and sharp text. Offering acceptable color output for less than $600, the Canon BJC-600 uses "bubble jet" technology, a variation on the standard ink jet method.

- **Mechanical variations.** Some printers are better than others at keeping the ink jet tightly focused so it doesn't spray droplets where they're not supposed to go. Also, as the printhead travels across the page, imprecise alignment from pass to pass may cause a slight stairstepping or wavy effect, especially with inexpensive models. So check the output!

- **Color.** If you're considering a color model, ask to see several sample printouts to be sure the colors are true enough to suit you. For example, two models in the popular HP DeskJet line, the DeskJet 500C and the 310, enable you to plug in a three-color ink cartridge or a black cartridge, but not both together. With the color cartridge installed, these printers create blacks by mixing the three colors, which gives you a very dark but definitely un-black green. The DeskJet 550C costs more but gives you three colors and black at the same time.

Many ink jets still use water-soluble inks that smear easily if you touch them before they dry and can wrinkle the paper when you print dense graphics. HP DeskJets use an oil-based black ink that avoids such problems.

HOT TIP

Speed

Although the typical ink jet printer pushes out only 1 or 2 pages of text a minute, faster models are out there. The DeskJet 1200C, for instance, prints text at about 6 ppm. It costs $1500 or so, but it also does a good job with color graphics.

Paper Handling

Forget about duplex printing. As for paper capacity, you'll seldom find an ink jet that holds more than a couple hundred sheets at a time. But if you need to print decent graphics on 11-by-17 paper, you may find that an ink jet is your most cost-effective option. You can buy a Canon BJC-800, which prints in color on 11-by-17 sheets, for around $1500.

HOT TIP

Compatibility

> ### Printer Connections
>
> You hook printers to PCs in one of two ways: using a parallel cable or a serial cable. Most printers have both parallel and serial *interfaces* (a techie word for connectors), which means you can use either kind of cable, although some give you a choice of one or the other interface when you buy the printer.
>
> In almost every case you should opt for the parallel connection. Parallel communication is faster than serial, and your PC's serial ports are often taken by mice or modems, while people seldom use parallel ports for anything but printers. Some printers boost performance with *high-speed* parallel interfaces, but to take advantage of this your PC needs a high-speed parallel port, and only newer-model PCs (and many laptops) have one.
>
> If your printer needs to be more than 10 feet from your PC, the standard parallel interface cable may cause printer errors. In this case, you should either use a shielded parallel cable (which is bulky and expensive) or buy a printer with a serial interface; both are good for 50 feet or more. However, the longer a standard serial (RS-232) cable is, the slower the data rate must be to avoid trouble. An alternative is to use an RS-423 cable, which is RS-232 compatible and good for 100 feet before the data rate starts dropping off.
>
> If you have to walk that far to your printer, you should probably be generous and share the thing. *Network-ready* printers come with connectors that hook right up to the network cable.

Like lasers, ink jet printers sometimes come with their own Windows drivers, and many software applications support popular ink jet models. Most ink jets printers are compatible with the DeskJet 500, and a driver for that printer comes with Windows.

Operating Costs

The cost to print a page of black text varies wildly depending on the model. The printers with the least expensive ink are the DeskJet 1200C and the Texas Instruments TI microMarc, at 3 cents and 4 cents a page, respectively, including paper. At the high end of the scale, Canon's printers eat up about 10 cents a page.

It's easiest to find supplies or service for DeskJets. But this only applies to the "real" DeskJets, which include the original DeskJet, the Plus, the 500, the 500C, and the 550C, as well as the portable 300 and 310. All of these printers use the same ink cartridge. The guts of the DeskJet 1200C are different, and it uses different ink cartridges.

Dot Matrix Printers

Who needs 'em? Their little print heads rattle noisily across the page, knocking little metal pins against an inked ribbon to lay dots on paper. It's brutal compared to the quiet swish of a laser or ink jet, and the print quality isn't pretty.

Still, dot matrix printers have their place. If you need to print on multipart carbonless forms, only a dot matrix fills the bill. If you want an inexpensive way to print super fast or on wide paper or boxfuls of continuous-form paper, dot matrix is a must. And if you just want the cheapest printer available, well, how does less than $150 for a funky little machine grab you?

Print Quality

Sharpness depends largely on the size and accurate positioning of the print head's metal pins, but you won't see this mentioned in the ads.

- **Pins.** Instead, you'll see dot matrix printers described as 9-pin, 18-pin, or 24-pin models. In general, the more pins the better the resolution. But this isn't a given, so as always, compare actual printouts when you assess print quality.

- **Resolution.** Many 24-pin dot matrix printers offer 360-dpi resolution, 60 more dots per inch than most

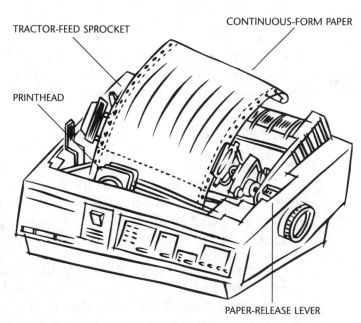

TRACTOR-FEED SPROCKET

CONTINUOUS-FORM PAPER

PRINTHEAD

PAPER-RELEASE LEVER

*Figure 7: **Still buzzing after all these years.** Shown here with its cover off, the Epson ActionPrinter 5000+ typifies low-end, 24-pin dot matrix printers.*

lasers. But don't let this fool you. The dots are bigger and the moving print head causes irregularities, so you won't get laser or even ink jet print quality, especially with graphics and small-size text. Sans serif fonts in normal body text sizes, though, often look surprisingly sharp. Most dot matrix printers come with a handful of fast-printing built-in fonts; some also have slots for their own font cartridges.

- **Color.** Dot matrix printers with multicolored ribbons are the cheapest route to color output. But they generally do so badly with graphics, you'll get more for your money if you buy a low-end ink jet with color capability.

Speed

Instead of pages per minute, dot matrix printers go by *characters per second (cps)*. Manufacturers tend to inflate cps ratings even more than ppm. Anyway, you can be sure the printer's low-quality *draft mode* will be promoted, which is usually three times faster than its *letter quality* mode, the only mode you'd want to use for printouts someone else will read.

Ppm ratings are a lot easier to comprehend than cps measurements. Here's how to make the translation: A typical line of text contains 65 to 75 characters, and there are usually 60 lines per page, for a total of about 4200 characters a page. So you divide the cps rating by 4200 and multiply that by 60 to get ppm. A 300-cps printer, for example, can usually pump out drafts at around 4 ppm.

When speed itself is a primary criterion but a rocket-fast laser printer costs too much, consider a high-end dot matrix machine. Models like the Mannesmann Tally MT691 spit out about 15 text pages a minute in draft mode and cost less than $2500.

Paper Handling

Many people buy dot matrix printers to print big spreadsheets on 16- or 17-inch-wide paper. These *wide carriage* printers generally cost at least $100 more than equivalent models that handle standard-width paper only. Note that dot matrix printers are also more adept at handling such odd printing jobs as preprinted letterhead, envelopes, and labels.

If you need a printer that will bang its way through multipart forms, check the specs. Some dot matrix models can only handle forms with three or four parts, while others grind their way through five-part forms. Also look for *paper parking*, which keeps continuous-feed paper queued up when you need to insert single sheets or envelopes one at a time. Add-on feeders for stacks of single sheets are widely available.

Compatibility

Don't worry about it. Every program works with Epson dot matrix printers, and every printer is Epson compatible. As always, it's best if your application has a driver for the printer or your printer has a driver for the application, but that only makes a difference with graphics. And who wants graphics printed with a dot matrix printer?

Noise

Noise once made dot matrix printers hard to live with. Thankfully, many now offer a "quiet mode" that makes them relatively unobtrusive—several even damp things down to 43 decibels, barely above the 41 decibels of a laser printer. Unfortunately, in quiet mode, dot matrix models typically print at about half their normal speed.

Serious Color Printers

You can use a cheap ink jet or a dot matrix printer for fun color output, or even for a chart or two in a report. But you'd never want to use those printouts for printing scanned color photos, marketing materials, or transparencies for a formal presentation. Those jobs require more serious color printers:

- **High-end color ink jets.** At $1000 to $4000, these are the least expensive options for serious color printing. The best of the lot, the Hewlett-Packard DeskJet 1200C, can serve up vivid, clear transparencies and printed handouts, and you can expect other new ink jets to match its eye-catching colors.

The Hidden Costs of Color					
	Ink jet transfer	**Thermal-wax**	**Dye sublimation**	**Solid ink**	**Laser**
Cost per page	10¢ to 50¢[1]	50¢ to 75¢	$2 and up	40¢ to 85¢[1]	40¢ to 50¢
Stock	Plain paper; clay-coated paper[2]	Coated paper; transparencies	Polyester-coated paper; transparencies	Prints well on anything	Plain paper; transparencies

[1]Depends on print density and model [2]Yields better results than plain paper

Figure 8: *Most color printers require special paper and expensive ribbons or inks, so make sure you consider the cost per page when you choose a color model.*

- **Thermal wax transfer printers.** At $3500 to $9000, thermal transfer printers produce especially vibrant color transparencies at relatively fast speeds (2 to 5 minutes per page), although photos tend to look grainy. In other words, they're good for presentation-quality flip charts and the like. The QMS ColorScript, the Seiko Colorpoint, and the CalComp thermal transfer printers all offer similar quality at comparable prices.

- **Dye sublimation printers.** At $8000 to $10,000, a dye sublimation printer such as the Kodak ColorEase is your very best choice for color printing, especially when you're reproducing photographic images. No one knows color and photographic paper like Kodak, so the Kodak ColorEase gives you particularly rich color images, perhaps the best available. These printers tend to be a little slower than comparable thermal wax models.

- **Solid ink printers.** At $7000 to $10,000, solid ink printers such as the Tektronix Phaser III are pricey, but they excel at producing crisp, clear text on plain paper.

- **Color lasers.** At $10,000 to $20,000, these printers are the least affordable, and they produce output inferior to that of dye sublimation and solid ink printers. They are somewhat faster, however.

If you can't justify the cost of a color printer, you can always take your color print file to a service bureau and have them create printouts for you. Service bureaus usually offer color duplication, too, which beats waiting for one of these printers to crank out a bunch of copies.

Should You Buy a Used Printer?

Buying a used printer is a pretty safe gamble—these machines rarely break down. As long as the printer is working well when you test it, you'll probably get many months of reliable performance from a second-hand unit. Plenty of laser printers have produced half a million pages and more without serious breakdown (let's see, that's 136 pages a day, seven days a week, for ten years).

If I was buying used, I'd be inclined to consider only models that were top sellers in their day. That gives you the best assurance that you'll be able to find supplies, parts, and service when you need them. Of course, if the price on a less popular model is really, really low, and the thing works...

To test a used printer, print maybe ten pages of sample text and graphics and give them a close inspection. Check the ports and power cord connections to make sure they're not loose, and make sure that all the front panel controls work properly.

Laser Printers

You'll do fine with most HP models, except for the original LaserJet and the LaserJet Plus (which are too big, too heavy, and print grayish blacks).

- All printers in the LaserJet III family give you resolution enhancement for sharper 300-dpi printouts. If you jump to the LaserJet 4 generation, resolution soars to 600 dpi, except with the 4L. Remember that only the bigger desktop models (the Series II, III, and 4) have slots for add-on cards like network adapters and resolution boosters like the LaserMaster WinJet board; the IIP, IIIP, 4L, and 4P lack these slots.

- After HP, I'd look for other printers that use a Canon SX, LX, EX, or PX engine (the core part of a laser printer that's responsible for actually printing the page). This includes various models from Canon (duh), QMS, and Apple. Unfortunately, the earlier Apple LaserWriters lack parallel ports, and serial port printing is slow.

- Check your test printouts for vertical lines, gray streaking, spots or streaks of black or "white" (unprinted areas). The problem may be just a bad toner cartridge or a dirty printer, but you never know.

Ink Jet Printers

DeskJets are reliable and popular, but avoid the original model, which is slower than later ones, and in some cases had a terrible thirst for ink (the Plus, the 500, and the 550 are all OK). On your test printouts, look for evidence of misalignment from one row of dots to the next. Missing dots probably only means the cartridge is old and clogged, but replace it to be sure this corrects the problem.

Dot Matrix

Brands to look for include Epson, Panasonic, NEC, and Okidata. Your sample printouts should show even coverage throughout the printout with no missing dots. Some "banding" (tiny gaps between some rows of dots) is probably inevitable, but don't buy if this symptom is pronounced. Just make sure you do the testing with a fresh ribbon—most ribbons dry out quickly with disuse. You can get some really good bargains on older Epsons, especially the 17-inch carriage models ($50 or less) which have an adjustable-width tractor feed.

HOT TIP

Printing Advice

Because printers are such durable beasts, you can get healthy-looking pages month after month without doing much but changing the toner, ribbon, or ink cartridge, and maybe dusting the innards with a lint-free cloth now and again (with lasers, you may also have to replace the drum, eventually). Nonetheless, I've pulled together a few tips about software, consumables, and printer sharing that will hopefully make your printing experience a happier one.

Speed Printing

Well, you can't really speed up your printer, but you do have some control over how quickly the printing process goes.

Most of the time, how long a printer takes to finish printing your document doesn't matter much. What's more important is how soon you can use your computer again after you start a print job, so you can get work done while the printer does its business. That's when you need a software utility called a *print spooler*, such as Windows' Print Manager or LaserTools' *PrintCache*.

On the other hand, when you want to print as fast as possible, print spoolers work against you, because they actually delay the flow of information from your application to the printer. Most spoolers have a command that lets you turn them off or, under Windows, assign a higher priority to print tasks.

HOT TIP

You can minimize print job slowdown by setting up the spooler to store the print file in RAM instead of on the hard disk. Some spoolers only use

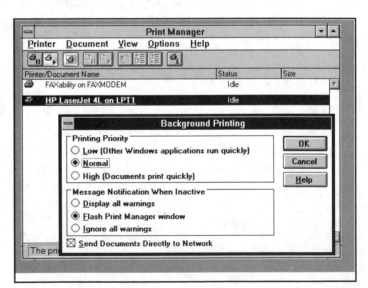

Figure 9: *Applications pass off printing jobs to Windows' Print Manager so you can get back to work sooner. The Background Printing dialogue box lets you decide whether to give printing or software applications higher priority.*

disk storage, but you can trick them by creating a RAM disk and directing the spooler to store data there (see Chapter 21: *Utilities* for more on print spoolers).

The Stuff You Print On

Here's what you need to know about paper, labels, and transparencies for lasers and ink jets. Continuous-form paper for dot matrix printers can be bought at any office supply store, and differences in paper thickness and quality don't mean much. Paper thickness seems to have little effect on whether dot matrix printers jam (which they tend to do) and you wouldn't want to print your résumé with a dot matrix, anyhow.

Paper

For everyday printing chores, ordinary 20-pound copier paper works just fine for both lasers and ink jets, and it costs only about $3 a ream (500 sheets). Expect to pay about 25 percent more for recycled stock. For a huge selection of interesting colored and patterned papers that work well in lasers, call PaperDirect (800/272-7377) for a catalog.

Regular bond paper not intended for copiers isn't so good, because it may leave too much paper dust behind in your printer. Paper that's too thick or too thin will jam (depending on the model, the acceptable range is typically between 16- and 24-pound paper). Preprinted forms or letterhead are usually OK, but they can cause trouble—unless the inks can withstand the heat, they'll melt and muck up your laser printer. Perforations may cause jams, and you should never pass stapled paper through your machine.

DANGER

With ink jet printers, although regular copier paper works well, special clay-coated papers produce noticeably better results—especially when printing in color. Clay-coated paper for printers is the same type used in glossy magazines. The heavier the weight, the greater the clay content (usually between 15 and 25 percent) and the sharper the image. Beware: Clay has a low melting temperature, and should never be used in a laser printer.

Labels

Never use ordinary label stock in a laser printer. The printer's heat can melt the glue, which can damage the printer's insides. Labels made specifically for laser printers are sold everywhere.

DANGER

HOT TIP

Laser printers can't print reliably on partly used label sheets—passing the sheet through again often leads to jams. You can minimize the risk by printing the bottom labels of the sheet first, and by straightening the sheet as much as possible. But a more reliable solution is smaller sheets of labels; you can cut your own or buy Mini-Sheets from Avery.

For ink jet printers, the main problem is that the ink tends to smear on the smooth surface of standard label paper. Special label stock for ink jets is also available, though it's a little difficult to come by.

By the way, you can buy specialized printers just for producing labels. These little units, like the one made by CoStar, are inexpensive, can print individual labels as well as large runs, and even work with Windows scalable fonts.

Transparencies

DANGER

When you print transparencies with an ink jet, the main thing to remember is to hold the transparency by the edges until it dries or it will smear. With lasers, you usually have to feed transparencies one at a time into a manual feed slot. You'll get different results with different types of transparencies, so you may have to experiment—more *character voids* (blank spaces in characters) crop up on some than on others. But the big question to ask is: Can it take the heat? The last thing you need is a melted transparency in your laser, so make sure you buy transparencies approved for laser use.

Printer Sharing and Switching

Sharing a printer or two among several PCs is seldom reason enough to install a full-blown network. Here are a couple of ways to share printers on the cheap:

- **Laser add-in boards.** Pacific Data Products, Extended Systems, and several other companies make add-in boards for LaserJets (and some other lasers) that enable you to plug multiple PCs into a single printer using standard phone wire (an inexpensive adapter connects your serial port to the wire). These boards play traffic cop with incoming print jobs, without any need for special software. Expect to pay around $100 per user.

- **Printer sharing boxes.** These external devices come in many guises. For example, Black Box sells a simple manual switch that gives two computers access to one serial printer for under $100; an autoswitching unit for six PCs and one parallel printer costs around $250. Only use units with electronic switches for laser printers, since manual types cause power spikes that can damage lasers. Some models

Top Five Windows Printing Tips

Printing under Windows is effortless once you install the printer. Here are a few tips to get the most from your printer.

1. **Get the latest driver.** Many of the printer drivers that come with Windows 3.1 are out of date. For faster printing and better handling of fonts and graphics, get the most recent one for your printer by calling the manufacturer.

2. **Install LaserTool's PrintCache.** It's a faster print spooler than Print Manager. You don't want to run two spoolers at once, though, so to turn off Print Manager, uncheck the box labeled Use Print Manager in the Control Panel's Printers dialog box.

3. **Drag-and-drop printing.** Open the File Manager and make sure the Print Manager icon is on the desktop. Find the file you want to print, click on it, and drag it toward the icon. The file icon will turn into a "bar sinister," but don't let that deter you—it will turn back into a file icon when you get to the Print Manager icon. Drop the file, and Windows opens the application that created the file and displays its Print dialog box. Click OK to print.

4. **Use Flipper to change orientation.** If you often switch back and forth between the portrait and landscape orientations, get a freeware program called *Flipper*. Whatever application you're using, you can change the page orientation instantly just by clicking on the Flipper icon—saving the hassle of paging though Print Setup dialog boxes.

5. **Printing to a file.** If you want to use a printer that isn't hooked up to your computer, you can "print" your document as a disk file. You'll need this trick if you want to print documents on high-res imagesetters at a service bureau. Open the Printers dialog box under the Control Panel and click on Add to install the driver for the printer that the file will print on (Windows won't care that the printer isn't actually hooked up). Go back to the Printers box, choose Connect, pick FILE from the Ports list, and then click OK a couple of times. At "print" time, type in a name (and path) for the disk file when Windows asks you to. Then copy the file to a disk.

also connect to multiple printers; pricier units have a *print buffer*, a chunk of memory to store print jobs so your application or spooler doesn't have to wait.

- **Resource sharers.** For under $2000, companies like Digital Products and Black Box will sell you a unit that links a half-dozen PCs to a couple of printers using standard phone wire, and you'll probably get access to a couple of modems as well. (You choose the device you want to use by entering a special command.) As an added bonus, you get to share files with other PCs, almost as if you'd installed a peer-to-peer LAN (see Chapter 22: *About Networks* for more on peer-to-peer printer sharing).

If you just want to hook up two or more printers to a single PC, you need an A/B switch. If you don't have a laser, a manual-switching unit for around $60 will do just fine. Laser-safe electronic switches start at around $200. Higher-end models come with print buffers and utilities that let you choose printers from a menu; some even switch automatically by sensing the type of file you are printing.

Printing Utilities

You'll find a wealth of printing utilities available as shareware. If you have a LaserJet or compatible, get at least one DOS shareware utility that lets you set margins, switch orientation, download and select fonts, and so on. Loads of such programs are available free or at low cost from various on-line services or from shareware vendors. For a start, try Public Software Library's disk set #27843 (800/242-4775). Also, see *4Print* and *4Book* below.

Print Formatters

These utilities print documents using layouts not available with standard software.

4Print and 4Book

These must-have DOS shareware utilities are among the best for LaserJets and compatibles. Using a small but readable font, *4Print* formats ASCII text files so two "pages" print on each side of the paper. An add-on to *4Print*, *4Book* orders the pages so you can fold the printed sheets into a booklet. Korenthal Associates, Inc., 230 W. 13th St., New York, NY 10011; 212/242-1790.

ClickBOOK

This $69.95 program makes booklets like *4Book*'s, but it also provides more options—and works with any Windows program and any Windows printer. BookMaker Corp., 625 Emerson St. #200, Palo Alto, CA 94301; 800/766-8531, 415/617-1101.

Double-Up for Windows

Double-Up is similar in concept to *4Book* and *ClickBOOK*, only it's exclusively for PostScript printers and offers many sophisticated options for professional printing—hence the $259 price. Legend Communications, Inc., 54 Rosedale Ave. West, Brampton, Ontario, Canada L6X 1K1; 800/668-7077, 905/450-1010.

PostScript Translators

Need to print PostScript files on non-PostScript printers? Read on.

ZScript

ZScript prints PostScript documents on non-PostScript printers by converting the output from the Windows PostScript printer driver. This $295 program also works with non-Windows programs running in a DOS window. It includes *SuperPrint*, a Windows print spooler that's faster and more capable than Print Manager. Zenographics, 4 Executive Cir., Irvine, CA 92714; 714/851-6352.

Transverter Pro

This $395 program converts all types of PostScript files into editable (Adobe Illustrator) EPS files, or into WMF files you can print on non-PostScript printers. TechPool Software, 1463 Warrensville Center Rd., Cleveland, OH 44121; 800/382-2256, 216/382-1234.

PostScript Printing Utilities

Getting a PostScript printer lets you print PostScript files but adds a few compatibility problems in the bargain. These utilities can solve them.

Printer Control Panel

Most PostScript printers also emulate the LaserJet and can switch between PostScript and LaserJet modes via software command. The $149 *Printer Control Panel* can automatically set the appropriate mode during a print job. This utility also prints ASCII text files on a PostScript printer—with a choice of fonts. LaserTools, 1250 45th St. #100, Emeryville, CA 94608; 800/767-8004, 510/420-8777.

PS-Plot and PSFX

PS-Plot ($85) downloads fonts, prints printer information and character set charts for installed fonts, prints ASCII files—and prints HP plotter files. *PSFX* ($175) prints from software that lacks a PostScript driver by converting from output meant for an Epson dot matrix printer. Legend Communications, Inc., 54 Rosedale Ave. West, Brampton, Ontario, Canada L6X 1K1, 800/668-7077; 905/450-1010.

Specialized Printing

Get your calendars, labels, envelopes, and name tags here.

Calendar Creator Plus for Windows

The best program available for *printing* calendars (rather than scheduling future events), *Calendar Creator Plus for Windows* also prints agendas and schedules. The DOS version is good, too. Either one costs you $59.95. Power Up!, 2655 Campus Dr. #100, San Mateo, CA 94403; 415/345-5900, 800/851-2917.

DAZzle

A $39.95 Windows envelope-printing program, *DAZzle* is probably more reliable than your word processor's envelope command, and it lets you add logos and postal bar codes. It also verifies destination ZIP code by modem and prints labels. Envelope Manager Software, 247 High St., Palo Alto, CA 94301; 800/576-3279.

Labels Unlimited for Windows

One of the best label design and printing programs costs only $79. It lets you print labels from databases and print bar codes on your labels. Spinnaker Software, 201 Broadway, 6th Floor, Cambridge, MA 02139; 800/227-5609.

Name Tag Kit

This is a DOS utility, plus supplies for printing large-type name tags. At $69.95, it beats magic markers any day. Power Up!, 2655 Campus Dr. #100, San Mateo, CA 94403; 415/345-5900, 800/851-2917.

Product Directory

Printer Manufacturers

Brother International Corp.
Business Machines Group
200 Cottontail Ln.
Somerset, NJ 08875
800/284-4357
908/356-8880

Canon Computer
  Systems, Inc.
123 E. Paularino Ave.
Costa Mesa, CA 92628
800/848-4123

Citizen America Corp.
2450 Broadway #600
Santa Monica, CA 90404
800/477-4683
310/453-0614

Compaq Computer Corp.
P.O. Box 692000
Houston, TX 77269
800/345-1518

CoStar Corp.
100 Field Point Rd.
Greenwich, CT 06830
800/426-7827
203/661-9700

Eastman Kodak Co.
901 Elm Grove Rd.
Rochester, NY 14653
800/344-0006

Epson America, Inc.
20770 Madrona Ave.
Torrance, CA 90509
800/922-8911
310/782-0770

Everex Systems, Inc.
48431 Milmont Dr.
Fremont, CA 94538
800/628-3837
510/498-1111

Hewlett-Packard
16399 W. Bernardo Dr.
San Diego, CA 92127
800/752-0900

LaserMaster
6900 Shady Oak Rd.
Eden Prairie, MN 55344
800/365-4646
612/944-9330

Lexmark Int'l, Inc.
740 New Circle Rd.
Lexington, KY 40511
800/358-5835

Mannesmann Tally Corp.
8301 S. 180th St.
Kent, WA 98032
800/843-1347
206/251-5524

Microtek Labs, Inc.
680 Knox St.
Torrance, CA 90502
800/654-4160
310/297-5000

NEC Technologies, Inc.
1414 Massachusetts Ave.
Boxborough, MA 01719
800/632-4636
508/264-8000

NewGen Systems Corp.
17580 Newhope St.
Fountain Valley, CA 92708
800/756-0556
714/641-8600

Okidata
532 Fellowship Rd.
Mount Laurel, NJ 08054
800/654-3282

Panasonic Communications
and Systems Co.
2 Panasonic Way
Secaucus, NJ 07094
800/742-8086

QMS, Inc.
1 Magnum Pass
Mobile, AL 36618
800/523-2696
205/633-4300

Qume
500 Yosemite Dr.
Milpitas, CA 95035
408/942-4000

Seiko Instuments USA
1130 Ringwood Ct.
San Jose, CA 95131
800/553-5312
408/922-5800

Seikosha America, Inc.
55 Reed St.
Southriver, NJ 08882
908/257-7890

Star Micronics America, Inc.
420 Lexington Ave. #2702
New York, NY 10170
800/447-4700
212/986-6770

Tandy/Radio Shack
One Tandy Center
Fort Worth, TX 76102
817/390-3011

Tektronik, Inc.
P.O. Box 1000
Wilsonville, OR 97070
800/835-6100

Texas Instruments
P.O. Box 202230
Austin, TX 78720
800/527-3500

Xerox
Office Document Systems
80 Linden Oaks
Rochester, NY 14695
800/832-6979

7 | Input Devices

By Scott Spanbauer

- Should you replace your current keyboard?
- Rodent alert: mice, more mice, and trackballs
- Input exotica: handwriting and voice recognition
- The ins and outs of desktop and handheld scanners

Too bad computers aren't telepathic yet. You still have to get the data in there and tell the computer what to do with it, which usually means banging away on the keyboard and whisking a mouse around your desktop. But thanks to PCs' appetite for graphics and some alternative technology, letting your fingers do the talking isn't the only way to supply your computer with the data it craves.

Scanners scoop up graphics like digital vacuum cleaners, enabling you to add photolike images to newsletters and presentations or use simple line art for letterhead or other decorative applications. Run optical character recognition (OCR) software on scanned documents, and you can produce megabytes of reasonably accurate electronic text without lifting a finger.

Then there are the more exotic technologies, such as digital photography, voice recognition, and pressure-sensitive tablets for artists. This chapter covers them all, from the mundane keyboard to PCs that respond to spoken commands. If you're in the market for any of these devices—particularly scanners—then you'll find plenty of buying tips here.

Keyboards

Your PC came with a keyboard, and you may never have given the thing a second thought since the first time you used it. In fact, switching to a better one could improve your typing efficiency and accuracy and even prevent injury. Consider these simple improvements and extras:

- **A better feel.** Don't believe your fingers can tell the difference? Then try this sometime: Walk around a superstore (or a large office) and try a bunch of different keyboards. Some keys click crisply when you press them, others feel like marshmallows, many are in between. You may well find a keyboard that feels a lot better than the one you use, and it will probably cost no more than $50. Your hands are important. Why not buy it?

- **A built-in pointer.** Hate meeces to pieces? Then consider a keyboard that includes a built-in pointing device. IBM's Lexmark division makes several popular models: The Classic Touch 101 comes with either a marble-sized trackball to the right of the [Enter] key, a slightly larger ball in the keyboard's upper-right corner, or a pointing stick that juts out between the G and H keys. The pencil-eraser-size joystick is great for program navigation once you get the hang of it.

- **Another layout.** Most typewriters place the [Caps Lock] key below [Shift], but you'll find [Caps Lock] above [Shift] on most PC keyboards, and [Ctrl] below. If you don't like your current keyboard layout, or would like to experiment, try a keyboard—such as any of Northgate's Omnikey models—that lets you swap keys. If you don't mind relabeling the keys on your current keyboard, you can swap key assignments easily using a shareware or freeware keyboard utility from CompuServe or America Online (see Chapter 21: *Utilities* for more on shareware).

HOT TIP

If you want to change layouts to something other than that for U.S. English, you can do so easily with Windows. Just go to the Main group, open Control Panel, and double-click on International. Click on Keyboard Layout in the resulting dialog box, and you get a list of alternative layouts for 18 different countries—plus the innovative

Dvorak layout, which minimizes finger movement by placing frequently used keys in the home row.

Ergonomic Keyboards

Fast typists who spend long stretches at the keyboard are prime candidates for repetitive strain injury (RSI), particularly carpal-tunnel syndrome. If you've experienced wrist or hand problems or if you're bound and determined to prevent them, you might want to look into one of several ergonomically designed keyboards.

Ergonomic keyboards break the keyboard into two angled sections—or otherwise fit the keys to your hands' natural resting position, rather than the other way around. For example, Key Tronic's FlexPro keyboard splits open in the middle, enabling you to adjust the two key groups so your hands address the keys at a more natural angle. The Kinesis Ergonomic Keyboard takes a more radical approach, dividing a standard QWERTY layout into two easily accessible wells and thumb-key sections.

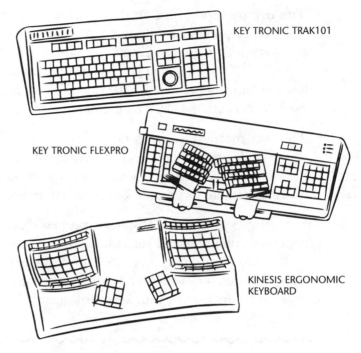

KEY TRONIC TRAK101

KEY TRONIC FLEXPRO

KINESIS ERGONOMIC KEYBOARD

Figure 1: Keyboard alternatives. *You don't have to stick with a stock keyboard. Look around and you'll find plenty of alternatives with integrated pointing devices, injury-preventive designs, and better responsiveness overall.*

Remember, though, that an ergonomic keyboard by itself is no guarantee against injury. Regular breaks and a properly configured workspace are most important. See Chapter 11: *Health, Safety, and the Environment* for some basic strategies for avoiding RSI.

Keep Those Keys Clean

You may like your current keyboard just fine, except that letters repeat when they shouldn't, don't work unless you really pound them, and generally just look filthy. No wonder—you've had your dirty hands all over that keyboard for years. Worse, you've nibbled donuts, sipped coffee, and ripped open envelopes over the thing, to the point where key mechanisms don't work like they should. Here are some quick cleaning tips:

- **The dry method.** Turn off the computer, disconnect the keyboard, turn it over, and give it a good shake. Buy a can of pressurized air (available at photo shops) and try blowing detritus out. Canned air is also good for cleaning out individual stuck keys: Pry off the offending key's cap with a pen or screwdriver, being careful not to lose any moving parts under the cap (those springs can get away easily!), and give the hole beneath the key a couple of quick blasts.

- **The wet method.** A damp rag will do—avoid abrasive cleaners or scrubbers. If you've spilled something sticky on your keyboard, as a last resort, you can even take the whole thing into the shower with you for a thorough cleansing. The water won't hurt it, but be sure the keyboard is thoroughly dry before you plug it back in.

DANGER

To prevent sticky keyboard situations to begin with, avoid eating, drinking, and smoking around your computer, and keep the keyboard covered when not in use. You can find hard plastic keyboard covers at most office supply stores, although a plain dishtowel works just as well. For unavoidably grungy settings, such as a factory floor, soft plastic membrane covers protect your keyboard against dirt as you type.

Pointing Devices

Is "pointing device" just a fancy name for a mouse? Yes, but the phrase also applies to other cursor-moving tools. *Trackballs* are basically upside-down mice—instead of moving the whole device around the desktop with your arm, you move the ball itself with your thumb or fingers. *Graphics tablets* let you point and click, too, but their real benefit is for drawing, as anyone who's tried a freehand sketch with a mouse can tell you.

A Plague of Mice

You can get RSI from using a mouse just as you can from using a keyboard, so if your mouse doesn't fit your hand well, find a model with a more comfortable shape. And try a few clicks before you buy—mouse buttons that are too stiff cause unnecessary strain, and loose buttons can be clicked accidentally (for a tutorial on mouse basics see Chapter 1: *For Beginners Only*). Here are some other criteria to help you find the best mouse:

- **Connections.** Many mice come with two connectors: a PS/2-style plug for the standard mouse port built into most systems and a 9-pin serial connector for a serial port. You can also buy mice with a bus mouse interface card, which adds to the price. If your PC has a mouse port, use it—the other two connections waste either a serial port or an expansion slot (see Chapter 8: *Upgrade It Yourself* for more on mouse installation).

HOT TIP

- **Software compatibility.** If your mouse is Microsoft Mouse compatible, you don't need to worry about it working with Windows or most DOS applications. Windows also has built-in support for Genius, Logitech, and Mouse Systems mice—but Microsoft-incompatible mice come with a *driver* (a small program that enables hardware to talk with software) for Windows anyway. To learn how to install a mouse for use with DOS, see "How to Set Up Windows and DOS" in Chapter 12.

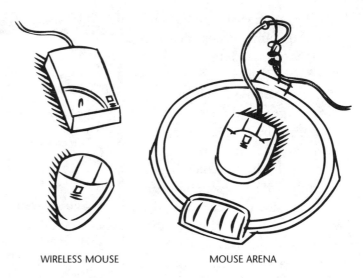

WIRELESS MOUSE   MOUSE ARENA

Figure 2: Mouse mutations. *On the left is Logitech's MouseMan Cordless, which communicates with a receiver using infrared signals. On the right is a typical mouse in the Mouse Arena, a special mouse pad with a wrist rest.*

- **Extra buttons.** Many mice have three buttons. Few applications recognize the third button, but software bundled with three-button mice solves the problem, enabling you to set up and assign application commands or command sequences to the middle button.

- **Resolution.** If you work with graphics, kern type, or perform other kinds of detailed screen work, be sure to consider mouse resolution, which varies from 150 to 500 dots per inch depending on the model. The higher the resolution, the better you'll be able to pick on-screen nits.

- **The wireless option.** Your mouse doesn't have to have a tail. Cordless mice use one of two types of transmission methods: infrared or radio frequency. Infrared mice require a direct line of sight between the mouse and its receiver unit. Radio mice work fine with under-the-desk computers, but they may conflict with a room full of similar mice. Both types of receivers require a serial port.

You can buy mice very cheap, but remember that the cheapest are usually the least comfortable and often don't last very long (the best inexpensive mouse I've seen is IBM's Easy Options mouse). Microsoft sells only one mouse—which is overpriced, comfortable, and durable—while both Logitech and Mouse Systems offer a slew of rodents, one of which should suit your fancy.

Like keyboards, mice start acting funny when they get dirty (see Chapter 10: *When Things Go Wrong* for instructions on how to clean one). One good way to prevent grungy buildup is to buy a mouse pad—it won't magically repel dirt, but you'll be less likely to set your morning donut down on it, and your mouse will perform smoother in the bargain. If you're worried about RSI, consider

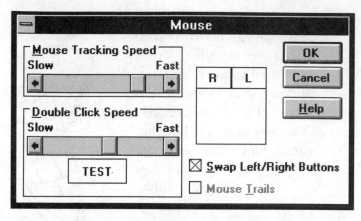

Figure 3: *The Mouse control program in Windows' Control Panel lets you set the mouse's sensitivity from skittish to sluggish and adjust the double-click speed to a comfortable rate. Attention lefties: Here's where you swap buttons.*

HOT TIP

Forminco's Mouse Arena, a raised mouse pad with a wrist rest that keeps your hand from bending upward and causing strain.

Getting on the Trackball

Why use a trackball instead of a mouse? A trackball has the advantage of using much less deskspace, but other than that, the choice is a matter of taste—some people hate trackballs, other people love 'em. Trackballs come in an even greater variety of designs than do mice, so you should really get your hands on a few before deciding which to buy.

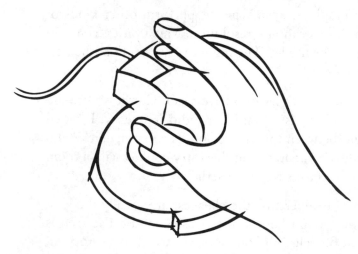

Figure 4: Move your thumb, not your arm. *Logitech's popular trackball, the TrackMan Stationary Mouse, enables you to move the cursor with your thumb while clicking or holding down buttons with your forefingers.*

All the mouse buying issues pertain to trackballs as well: hardware and software compatibility, resolutions, and extra buttons (normally they duplicate the mouse's two-button arrangement). Likewise, a trackball can hurt your hand or wrist, so a wrist rest might be a good idea. And most people agree: The bigger the ball, the easier a trackball is to use.

Clicking and dragging can be tricky with a trackball, since you have to hold down a button with one finger, then rotate the ball with another finger, your thumb, or your other hand. Most manufacturers address this problem with a *drag-lock* button, which maintains the left button in the clicked position until you punch drag-lock again. However, if you buy a trackball that's designed to be rotated with your thumb, you can usually avoid the cumbersome drag-lock solution once you get used to moving the cursor.

HOT TIP

My Graphics Pad, or Yours?

Whether you're a budding computer artist or a high-tech design professional, you need a flat input surface on which to paint or draw as you would on paper or canvas (close to it, anyway). The range in price and capability is enormous: You can pay thousands for a big, high-resolution *digitizing tablet* that's designed for use with computer-aided design (CAD) software, or under $100 for a fun *graphics pad*. Here are a few quick buying tips:

- **Size and resolution.** Graphics pads come in sizes ranging from 5 inches square (such as Acecad's inexpensive Acecat II 5x5) to much larger, with bigger pads offering higher resolution. If you plan to use the pad with a low-end paint or draw program, a small pad is fine, and even the lowest-resolution pads (500 dots per inch) will be plenty accurate. Choose a model with a cordless stylus for the most natural feel, but avoid battery-powered styli if possible, because the weight makes them harder to use and changing batteries is a pain.

REMEMBER

- **Pressure sensitivity.** Pads like Wacom's ArtZ Serial come with a pressure-sensitive stylus that lets you vary the weight of strokes much as you would when using a paintbrush or airbrush. Used with sophisticated programs like *Fractal Design Painter* or *Adobe Photoshop*, pressure-sensitive pads enable you to create faux watercolors and oils or touch up photos that could grace a magazine cover.

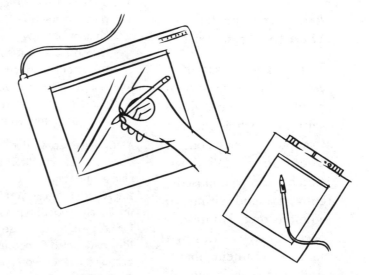

Figure 5: Top graphics pads. The Acecat II 5x5 graphics pad (right) costs less than $100 on the street and works fine in fun, artistic applications. For more precise illustrations, consider a pad such as Wacom's ArtZ Serial, which has a pressure-sensitive stylus for sophisticated brush and shading effects.

- **Connections and compatibility.** All graphics tablets are serial devices, so consider your supply of free ports before buying. As with other pointing devices, make sure the tablet comes with driver software that supports your software.

If CAD is your thing, you'll need a digitizing tablet large enough for you to trace blueprints and undertake very detailed work. Expensive tablets come with a *puck*—a transparent, circular sighting window with crosshairs that lets you work more precisely than you could with a pen. Many digitizing tablets accommodate menu templates that work with specific programs, so you can click zones on the surface of the pad to execute commands quickly.

Are Pens Mightier Than the Keyboard?

Your graphics pad may come with some sort of handwriting recognition software, such as the Pen Computing extensions to Microsoft Windows, which can supposedly convert handwriting to editable text. Hunt-and-peckers may see this as a sign of imminent liberation from the keyboard, but they shouldn't.

Talking Instead of Typing

If handwriting recognition still has a few kinks, then voice recognition is downright experimental. However, there's no dearth of products out there competing for your dollars. Voice-recognition products fall into two categories:

- **Command-and-control systems.** Microsoft's Windows Sound System, a sound card that includes limited voice recognition software, is a typical command-and-control system: You say "File, Save," into the microphone, and the software executes the command—sometimes—if you talk slowly, pause between words, and repeat yourself. The recognition software eats up processing power because it continually attempts to analyze every sound it encounters, including background noise.

- **Dictation systems.** Designed to convert continuous speech into text, dictation systems such as Dragon Systems' DragonDictate seem like the nontypist's dream come true. They generally come with large libraries of known words, often targeting specific professions. Unfortunately, even the best dictation systems have trouble understanding normal speech: For best results, you must speak slowly, clearly, and be prepared to go back and fix misrecognized words (not to mention homonyms like "there" and "their").

Many voice recognition systems require that you spend quite a bit of time "training" them to recognize your specific enunciation, which means that no one else can use the system (nor can you if you have a bad cold). In the final analysis, both types of recognition systems are best for people who can't use a keyboard, either because they're disabled or because their hands are otherwise occupied as they work.

Even after training the software to recognize your writing, you'll probably experience a 90-percent success rate at best, which means you'll spend quite a bit of time correcting errors. For now, handwriting recognition makes sense only in a few specialized applications (such as collecting data in the field using hand-held computers). However, if you have a fax modem card, note that a graphics pad is a great way to annotate faxes right on the screen—without the tedium of printing them out, scribbling on them, and scanning them before you return them to the sender (see Chapter 20: *Communications* for more on fax modems).

Scanners and Scanning

Of all the input devices covered in this chapter, a scanner may seem like the one you can most easily live without. That's too bad, because scanners are also among the most versatile peripherals you can add to your system.

Scanners aren't just for scanning art and photographs. Most come bundled with capable OCR programs that let you turn mountains of press releases, legal papers, or other printed matter into searchable, editable text. If you use a fax modem, a scanner gives you the ability to send hard copy originals. Finally, if you have a printer attached to your system, adding a scanner can turn your system into an effective (if somewhat slow) photocopier.

Scanners come in three basic varieties:

- **Hand scanners.** For a couple hundred bucks, a hand scanner will help you get started with computer graphics or desktop publishing. You can scan very long originals—the only limits are your computer's memory and the length of your scanning surface—but the width is limited to about 4 inches. To overcome this problem, hand scanner software knows how to "stitch" side-by-side scans together, though this doesn't always work too well. To get an accurate scan with a hand scanner, you must drag the scanner in a straight path at an even speed.

- **Flatbed scanners.** These provide accurate, straight scans of originals as large as $8^1/2$ by 14 inches, but they generally cost two to three times more than hand scanners. Flatbeds are better multipurpose devices because you don't have to stitch pages together for OCR, faxing, or impromptu photocopying. Most also have optional document feeders that whiz through piles of hard copy, and transparency adapters that let you scan slides and negatives.

- **Sheet-fed scanners.** Close relatives of flatbeds, sheet-fed scanners accept full pages much like a fax machine does. While sheet-fed scanners are compact and economical—and make good sense for faxing and OCR applications—flatbeds do better at producing straight, accurate scans, and let you scan books and other three-dimensional objects.

REMEMBER

Most desktop scanners connect with your computer via a SCSI interface card. If you already have a SCSI card in your PC (to hook up a CD ROM, for example), you'll save a little money if the scanner will work with it—just be sure to confirm with the manufacturer that scanner and card are compatible. Increasingly, hand scanners and even a few flatbeds connect via your PC's parallel port, which means you don't have to open up the computer and hassle with hardware conflicts (scans will be a bit slower, though).

On the software side, note that you can control scanners from *within* Windows applications, thanks to a standard known as TWAIN. Every scanner comes with a TWAIN scan control program that pops up within your application, enabling you to adjust brightness, contrast, and so on. In addition, scanners generally come with image-editing utilities to help you clean up and otherwise enhance scanned images (see Chapter 17: *Graphics Software* for more on image-editing software).

Which Scanner to Buy

All scanners cost somewhat more if you want color capability. Formerly high-ticket luxuries, color scanners are now only slightly more expensive than units that merely capture 256 shades of gray (something virtually every scanner can do). If you're on a tight budget but need color, consider a color hand scanner. Otherwise, a grayscale scanner is all you need for OCR and faxing, not to mention most desktop publishing tasks.

Much of a scanned image's quality depends on the quantity of data per dot that a scanner can capture. For example, if you scan in black and white, the scanner captures only one bit

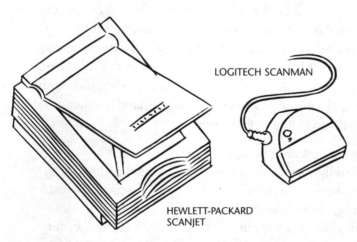

LOGITECH SCANMAN

HEWLETT-PACKARD SCANJET

Figure 6: Hand scanners vs. flatbeds. Budget-priced hand scanners are great for scanning small originals, while flatbed units let you grab large originals in one swoop and are much better for OCR applications. Both types are available in color and grayscale models.

per dot (the dot is either on or off). By comparison, Hewlett-Packard's ScanJet IIP uses 8 bits to describe each dot, for a total of 256 possible gray shades. Color scanners work in much the same way, capturing 8 bits per dot for three colors: red, green, and blue. The resulting 24-bit scan contains 16 million different colors.

Expect to pay around $500 on the street for a good flatbed grayscale scanner, and between $700 and $1000 for a color model. High-priced desktop scanners can reproduce sharp images on a broad range of printer types, thanks to high resolution (up to 1200 dots per inch) and the ability to register fine color gradations. Before you pay top dollar for the latest and greatest, though, note that the majority of scanning tasks require neither color *nor* high resolution.

REMEMBER

Color Scanning Strategies

How many colors or shades you scan depends on what you want to do with the scanned image. For example, on the 256-color display used by most PCs, a color photo scanned at 16 million colors (24 bits) looks pretty much the same as one scanned at 256 colors (8 bits)—and consumes three times the disk space. But were you to have those same images professionally printed, the 16-million color image would reveal subtle tones and detail, and the 256-color image would look crude by comparison.

Even if you produce color publications, however, you don't necessarily have to set your scanner controls to 24 bits. Reducing colors from 16 million to 65,000 (using a simple shareware image-editing program like *Paint Shop Pro*) can save you megabytes of disk space and yield an image that looks nearly as good.

HOT TIP

Tones, Resolution, and Disk Space						
Size (inches)	Number of tones	100 dpi	200 dpi	300 dpi	400 dpi	635 dpi
2 by 4	2 (line art)	9K	39K	87K	156K	393K
2 by 4	256 (color or grayscale)	78K	312K	703K	1248K	3150K
5 by 7	256	341K	1367K	3076K	5468K	13782K
2 by 4	16 million	234K	937K	2109K	3748K	9450K
5 by 7	16 million	1025K	4101K	9228K	16404K	41346K

Figure 7: *Many scanners can produce high-resolution images with millions of colors—but unless you're producing a professional publication, you're wasting disk space.*

Halftones and Scanning Resolution

Unlike displays, laser printers and even professional imagesetters are basically one-bit devices. Because they can only print black dots (or leave white spaces), these devices can't reproduce the grayscale and color data captured by the scanner—at least, not by themselves.

Borrowing a trick from traditional printing technology, programs capable of printing graphics (such as image editors, word processors, and desktop publishing applications) convert continuous-tone images into a printer-friendly format using a *halftone*.

REMEMBER

The halftoning process filters original tones, converting darker tones to larger dots, and lighter tones to smaller dots (for evidence, examine any photograph in a newspaper or magazine under a magnifying glass). The fineness of the halftone screen (called the halftone screen *frequency*) is measured in lines per inch (lpi), and the fineness of the screen depends on printer resolution. Because digital halftoning discards much of the original image's data, you can get away with a scanning resolution far lower than the output device's resolution (see Figure 8).

HOT TIP

As a rule of thumb, choose a halftone frequency that matches your printer, then scan at a resolution roughly one and a half times the halftone frequency. Scanning at a higher resolution won't hurt your final image, but it won't help it either, and it will simply chew up disk space unnecessarily. If you'd rather not do the math, get Lightsource's superior scanning program *Ofoto* (415/925-4200), which automates the entire process.

Matching Scan Resolution With Print Resolution

Printer resolution	Halftone screen frequency	Optimal scanning resolution
300 dpi (laser printer)	53 lpi	75–106 dpi
600 dpi (laser printer)	75 lpi	106–150 dpi
1270 dpi (phototypesetter)	100 lpi	141–200 dpi
2450 dpi (phototypesetter)	133 lpi	188–266 dpi

Figure 8: *Most printers use halftones to print scanned photos. The printer's resolution determines the optimal halftone screen frequency, which in turn determines the best scanning resolution. Scanning at a higher resolution simply wastes disk space.*

Don't forget that line art consists of only two colors—black and white—and therefore doesn't require halftoning to print on laser printers and phototypesetters. As a result, you'll get best results if you match scanning and printer resolution as closely as possible. For phototypesetter output, however, you may find that the quality is sufficient if you scan at half the printer's resolution.

OCR: From Hardcopy to Editable Text

You're probably surrounded by valuable data trapped in hard copy—newspaper clippings, white papers, correspondence, whatever. Someday you may need to search through that text or borrow chunks of it. When that day comes, you can spend hours fishing through files and typing away—unless you've scanned those documents and converted them to editable text using an OCR program.

OCR runs document image files produced by your scanner through a special recognition routine that—depending on the print quality of the original document—can produce text files fairly low in errors. As with other recognition technologies,

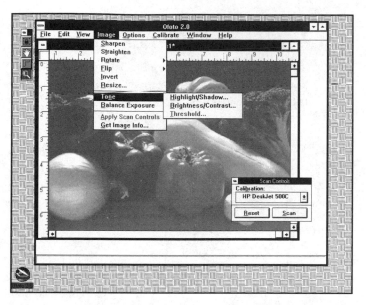

Figure 9: *Light Source's Ofoto 2.0 optimizes the scanning process whether you're a neophyte or a pro, choosing the right resolution for your target output device.*

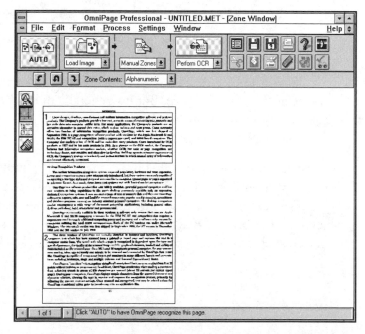

Figure 10: *There's nothing worse than trying to find a document buried in a haystack. With surprising accuracy, OCR programs such as Caere's OmniPage convert hard copy to searchable, editable computer text.*

Digital Photography

If your job is to take pictures of people or things and file them away in an employee or inventory database, you may need a digital camera instead of a scanner. Logitech's FotoMan Plus takes 8-bit pictures (256 shades of gray) just like a normal camera loaded with black-and-white film, and it even has a built-in flash and a variety of optional lenses. It stores up

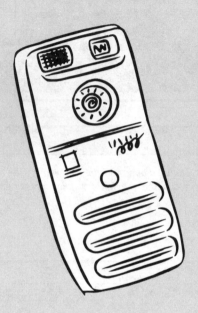

to 32 digital images in memory, which you then transfer to your computer via serial link. You can save the files in a variety of formats, including TIFF, JPEG, PCX, BMP, and EPS (see Chapter 17: *Graphics Software* for more on graphics file formats).

But what if you need color or want to use the very best photo equipment and lighting? If you have an *XA-compatible* CD ROM (most double-speed or faster models support this spec), you can take your film in for processing and get back a PhotoCD instead of an envelope of snaps. Many graphics applications support PhotoCD images, and unless you live in Outer Mongolia, there's probably a PhotoCD-capable lab nearby.

Figure 11: Digital cameras such as Logitech's FotoMan Plus cut out the middleman—the scanner—enabling you to acquire grayscale images with a minimum of fuss.

this is not an exact science. But it's generally quicker to correct errors than to type in reams of documents by hand, and storing searchable documents on disk or tape takes far less space than using a filing cabinet.

Most scanners—even handhelds—come bundled with pared-down versions of leading OCR programs, notably Caere's *Personal Pagekeeper Portfolio*, which recognizes and archives text in a database. For modest OCR needs, these bundled applications will serve admirably. If OCR is something you plan to do daily, you may need something better, such as Caere's *OmniPage 5.0* or Calera's *WordScan*.

Top Ten Scanning Tips

Getting images into your PC is easy, if you have the hard disk space. Here are a few tips to help you get the best scans with the least effort and the least wasted megabytes:

1. **Fix the original.** It's a lot easier to correct your original than it is to edit a digital image. Unless the original is a precious antique, clean up scratches, dirt, too-light lines, and the like before scanning. Use a pen, eraser, pencil—whatever works.

HOT TIPS

2. **Learn to edit images.** Teach yourself to use the scanning software. No scanner does a great scanning job using default settings. For best results, you may need to adjust brightness, contrast, and other exposure controls.

3. **Match resolutions for line art.** Scan line art at high resolutions—but not too high. Since the black-on-white pixels in a line-art scan are sent to paper or film pretty much one for one, try to match scan resolution to printer resolution. If you need to enlarge the original, do it during the scan, not later on in your application.

4. **Don't scan photos at maximum resolution.** If you're going to print them, chances are you're going to halftone them, which means you should scan at somewhere between 100 and 250 dpi, depending on your printer.

5. **Don't scan color originals at 24 bits.** You can't reproduce 16 million colors in print anyway. Try an 8-bit color scan (256 colors), or reduce the color depth of the 24-bit image using a graphics utility.

6. **Don't scan the whole thing.** You might be tempted to scan that entire color map of Central Asia into a 24-bit TIFF file, but don't—it'll take up 30MB of hard disk space. Instead, scan just the part you need.

7. **Use a scanning tray.** Hand scanners are nearly impossible to drag in a straight line. Fortunately, some genius invented the scanning tray, which holds the scanner in a straight trajectory over the original.

8. **Clean the platen.** Like copy machines, flatbed scanners must be cleaned regularly. Wipe dust, gunk, and ink stains from the scanner's platen using glass cleaner—but spray the cleaner on the towel, not on the glass.

HOT TIPS

9. **Keep hand scanners clean.** Handheld scanners don't have a platen, but they pick up dirt just like a mouse. Keep your scanning surface clean, and store the scanner in a plastic bag when not in use.

10. **Mess around.** Scanners are lots of fun, and the best way to learn to use them is to play around. Don't feel limited to photos or line art—you may not be free to use them in your publications without paying royalties anyway. Don't be afraid to scan household objects, leaves, and other bits of nature (fabrics, woods, whatever).

Product Directory

Keyboard Manufacturers

Key Tronic Corp.
P.O. Box 14687
Spokane, WA 99214
800/262-6006

Kinesis
915 118th Ave. SE
Bellevue, WA 98005
800/454-6374
206/455-9220

Lexmark Int'l
1221 Alverser Dr.
Midlothian, VA 23113
800/438-2468

Northgate Computer Systems
7075 Flying Cloud Dr.
Eden Prairie, MN 55344
800/526-2446
612/943-8181

Pointing Device Manufacturers

Acecad
2600 Garden Rd. #111
Monterey, CA 93940
408/655-1900

Kensington Microware
2855 Campus Dr.
San Mateo, CA 94403
800/535-4242
415/572-2700

Logitech
6505 Kaiser Dr.
Fremont, CA 94555
800/231-7717
510/795-8500

Microsoft Corp.
One Microsoft Way
Redmond, WA 98052-6399
800/426-9400
206/882-8080

Mouse Systems Corp.
47505 Seabridge Dr.
Fremont, CA 94538
510/656-1117

Wacom Technology Corp.
501 S.E. Columbia Shores Blvd. #300
Vancouver, WA 98661
206/750-8882

Scanner Manufacturers

AVR Technology
71 Daggett Dr.
San Jose, CA 95134
800/544-6243
408/434-1115

Calera Recognition Systems
475 Potrero Ave.
Sunnyvale, CA 94086
408/720-0999

Canon Computer Systems
2995 Redhill Ave.
Costa Mesa, CA 92626
800/848-4123
714/438-3000

Epson America, Inc.
20770 Madrona Ave.
Torrance, CA 90503
800/289-3776
310/782-0770

Envisions Solution Technology
822 Mahler Rd.
Burlingame, CA 94010
800/365-7226
415/259-8121

Hewlett-Packard
3000 Hanover St.
Palo Alto, CA 94304
800/752-0900

Logitech
800/231-7717

Microtek Lab, Inc.
3715 Doolittle Dr.
Redondo Beach, CA 90278
800/654-4160
310/297-5000

Mustek, Inc.
15225 Alton Pkwy.
Irvine, CA 92718
800/468-7835
714/453-0110

UMAX Technologies
3170 Coronado Dr.
Santa Clara, CA 95054
800/562-0311
408/982-0771

OCR Software

Caere Corp.
100 Cooper Ct.
Los Gatos, CA 95030
800/535-7226
408/395-7000

Calera Recognition Systems
408/720-0999

8 | Upgrade It Yourself

By Eric Knorr

- Upgrade basics: tools and safety tips
- The ABCs of installing expansion boards
- What kind of memory to buy and how to install it
- Installing hard disks and CD ROM drives
- Choosing and transplanting an upgrade CPU
- Superfast serial port upgrades

Once you get accustomed to your PC, you don't want to do without it. That's the real reason for you, rather than a service person, to add or replace hardware in your PC: Who wants to work around someone else's service schedule and lose the use of a PC for days? And of course, you save money when you do it yourself—for example, having a superstore add a hard disk to your system usually costs around 50 bucks.

Another reason to entrust your PC's innards to no one but you is that *you* control the quality of the components and workmanship. Most upgrades are easy to do if you have good information, something not all service people avail themselves of. And what better way to ensure that top-of-the-line parts are used than to install them yourself?

If you're new to PCs, you should give Chapter 2: *How to Buy a PC* a close look before getting too deep into this chapter. You'll find terms and concepts explained there that will help you understand what's going on here.

What Every Upgrader Should Know

PCs were designed to be upgraded by whoever owns one—that's why they have standard slots into which you plug expansion cards. You don't need a degree in rocket science, a working knowledge of hexadecimal, or the cunning to build a transistor radio out of several digital watches. A little bit of manual dexterity can help, but otherwise, we're talking cookbook stuff. As my high school geometry teacher said whenever someone screwed up, "Can you bake a cake?" In other words, follow the instructions, and you should get the right results.

Tools of the Trade

Unless you make a point of avoiding hardware stores, you probably have the necessary implements for performing almost any upgrade on hand:

One medium flat-head screwdriver

One small flat-head screwdriver

One medium Phillips screwdriver

One small Phillips screwdriver

Tweezers

Flashlight

Those are all the tools you need to get going. To avoid stripping screw heads and to give yourself a little extra torque, I also suggest buying a couple of hex nut drivers, one 3/16 inch and the other 1/4 inch. Hex screws are often used to hold down expansion cards and fasten system casings, so if you strip a hex screw head with a screwdriver, a nut driver can keep you from standing there wondering what to do.

HOT TIP

A hemostat—a locking, scissorlike pair of tongs used by surgeons—is handy for retrieving screws and other small parts that sometimes fall into inaccessible corners in your PC. If you work on an old Compaq system (they just keep going and going), you'll need two Torx wrenches, one T-10 and one T-15. Finally, a *chip puller* (available at any electronics store) helps you replace older CPUs without damaging them.

As for software, all you really need is an emergency boot disk, which you should have anyway (to learn how to create one, see "Safety Check" in the last section of Chapter 12: *Windows and DOS*). A boot disk can help you install a hard disk or get things up and running if things go wrong. I also recommend picking up a copy of *Setup Advisor*, an inexpensive Windows utility from Touchstone Software (800/531-0450), which can help you install expansion cards correctly the first time.

HOT TIP

Disassembly Without Destruction

Is this the place where you're going to read all the boring stuff about how to avoid hurting yourself or your PC as you take it apart? You bet—but I'll keep it short, and along the way I'll explain how to get your PC open and ready for work:

1. **Back up before you start.** You should back up your hard disk regularly anyway, but in the unlikely event that you accidentally disable your system while fishing around inside it, having a backup copy of your data before you start means you can restore that data to another system and minimize the downtime (see Chapter 9: *Protect Your Data*). If you're adding or changing a hard disk, you *must* do this.

DANGER

2. **Write down your hard disk setup.** Every PC comes with some kind of setup routine—your PC's manual (or manufacturer tech support) will explain how to run it. Start the routine and go directly to the section pertaining to your system's hard disks (typical headings: "Fixed Disk 1, Fixed Disk 2," and so on). Highlight the hard disk entry, press Enter, and write down all the information given about your hard disk—the capacity, cylinders, heads, sectors per track, starting cylinder for write precompensation, and anything else listed. Sometimes PCs "lose" this information, so keep it safe at all times.

REMEMBER

3. **Stop that static.** Before you handle delicate circuitry, such as an expansion board, touch your hand to a grounded object to discharge any static electricity—touching your PC's metal fan grille while your PC is still plugged in should do the trick. And I

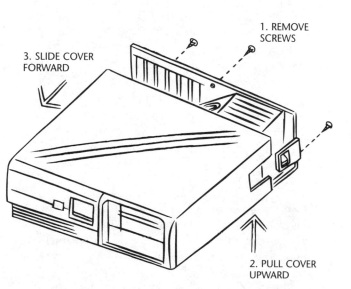

3. SLIDE COVER FORWARD

1. REMOVE SCREWS

2. PULL COVER UPWARD

Figure 1: Removing the cover. First remove the screws along the edge of the back panel of your PC (don't unscrew the fan by mistake). Then pull the cover up before you slide it forward to remove it. If the cover gets caught as you slide, don't use force or you may break a connection.

kid you not: Don't wear polyester when you work, because moving around in polyester generates static.

DANGER

4. **Power down.** Turn off your PC and monitor, but don't unplug the PC, so you can continue to discharge static if necessary. Never, never open up your PC's power supply or stick any object inside one of its vents, because there's enough current running around in there to knock you for a loop, permanently.

5. **Remove the cover carefully.** Your standard computer casing reminds me of a childproof bottle cap. You remove a few screws on the rear of your system, try to pull the cover back, and—hey, what's the problem here? For some reason, you generally need to give the cover a little yank upward before you slide it forward and remove it completely from the chassis. As you do this, don't force things if the cover snags—just reverse direction, lift up a little more, and try again. Otherwise, you may tear a wire or cable.

6. **Keep parts organized.** This usually means screws. I keep a roll of clear two-inch packing tape handy, tape related screws together, and while I'm working, stick them on the side of the chassis where they'll be handy for later reassembly.

HOT TIP

7. **Write stuff down.** This is the thread you unroll to get you back out of the labyrinth. If you panic and suddenly realize you don't know what you're doing, you can quickly put things

Save That Manual!

If you just bought your PC, then I'm getting to you at exactly the right time. The documentation that came with your machine is your ticket to doing things right. It tells you how to use your all-important system setup software, needed for any configuration changes, and should explain how to change your CMOS battery—the component in your system most likely to fail (see Chapter 10: *When Things Go Wrong*). In short, you get a lot of specific information about your model of PC that this chapter can't tell you.

Your system may also come with separate manuals for such components as your graphics card, hard disk, and modem—you accumulate this documentation every time you buy hardware. Documentation on boards and drives may be even more important than the manual for your PC itself, because the settings on such components are often both complicated and critical. If you run into trouble and the company you bought the device from has gone belly up, you may have to simply *get rid* of the mystery device if you've lost the docs.

My advice to you is not only to save the documentation, but also to do a quick inventory of the boards and drives in your system and make sure you have documentation on everything. If you don't, call the manufacturer and request a copy, and do it sooner rather than later. In the dog-eat-dog world of high tech, you never know when calling that number will result in the familiar message, "We're sorry, but that number has been disconnected."

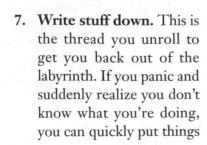

back the way they were if you've written down—even sketched with paper and pencil—how cables, expansion cards, jumpers, switches, and so on were arranged to begin with.

Everyone needs a clean, well-lighted place to work, but this goes double when you're playing ace mechanic with your PC. Nothing is more uncomfortable (or more likely to cause you to lose or drop components) than working on the cramped corner of a desk. If you don't have access to a work table, any wide, clean, flat surface with a nearby high-intensity lamp will do.

Installing Expansion Cards

The physical part of installing an expansion card—whether a graphics card, fax modem, sound card, or whatever—couldn't be easier. A single screw holds each card in place, and aside from making sure the card is inserted all the way into the expansion slot, there's not much to the whole deal (unless cables connect to the card, which may make things somewhat tricky). Here are a few general tips on installing expansion cards:

- **Run the software first.** Quality expansion cards come with diagnostic software that tells you how to set up your card before you physically install it. This software usually works well. But if you don't read the documentation, you might not realize these wonderful little programs won't work after you plug the card into a slot—which means you have to remove the card and start over. Serves you right for not reading the manual.

- **Handle with care.** Of course you shouldn't toss cards around, but you should also avoid touching them against any conductive surface. A card lying flat on a metal surface (such as the top of a power supply) could spell disaster. Your hands are somewhat conductive, too, so you should make a practice of holding cards by their edges—but *not* by their edge connectors (the part with the little gold strips that plugs into the slot).

- **Log those connections.** Before you remove boards with cables connected to them—typically, hard disk interface cards—disconnect the cables first. Before you do *that*, make a note of how the cables were connected so you don't plug something in wrong later. When you do reconnect, don't force a connector if it doesn't slip on easily—you've probably got it the wrong way around.

- **Don't lean on it, rock it.** Sometimes a card fits very tightly in a slot. If you yank too hard to remove it, you could damage the motherboard, the most important component in your PC. Rock the board an inch or so either way as you pull, and it should come loose without too much force. The same gyrations make inserting cards easier.

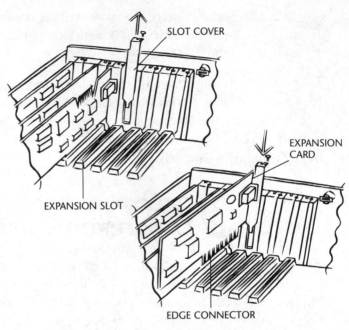

Remember that reading the manual for an expansion card before you attempt to do anything with it is not an optional undertaking. While a legitimate test of software is seeing how far you can get without even hitting the Help button,

DANGER

Figure 2: Installing an expansion card. A single screw holds a standard expansion card in place. Don't use brute force to remove or insert cards— "work" the card back and forth a little if the fit is tight. At all times, avoid touching the gold tines on the edge connector that plugs into the slot.

it's a very bad idea to approach hardware installation in the same lighthearted way. You could fry something permanently or, more likely, hang up your system temporarily if you don't go to school on the documentation first.

Matching Cards and Slots

When you shop for an expansion card, step one in narrowing down your selection is easy: The slots in your computer can only accept certain types of boards. Here are the principal standards for slots and boards:

HOT TIP

- **Industry Standard Architecture (ISA).** You'll find ISA slots in almost every PC, and the vast majority of expansion cards are ISA cards. Most ISA slots run at a poky 8 MHz (although a few systems run them as fast as 12 MHz). ISA slots and cards come in two varieties: 8-bit and 16-bit. You can plug an 8-bit card into a 16-bit slot, and sometimes you can plug a 16-bit card into an 8-bit slot, but in the latter case this will degrade the card's performance. It's best to install 8-bit cards in 8-bit slots so you have 16-bit slots free for any 16-bit cards you may want to add.

- **VESA Local (VL) bus.** VL slots are usually extensions to ISA slots that enable VL graphics cards, hard disk interfaces, and a few other devices to run at high speed— up to 33 MHz (and even 66 MHz under some circumstances). VL devices can move data 16, 32, or even 64 bits at a time instead of merely 8 or 16 bits (with the VL bus, the number of bits depends on the card and the CPU, not the length of the slot). VL bus cards will not work in standard ISA slots, but a VL bus extension won't prevent you from plugging in an ISA card.

REMEMBER

- **Personal Computer Interconnect (PCI) local bus.** The successor to the VL bus, the PCI bus tops out at 66 MHz and enables PCI cards to pump data 16, 32, or 64 bits at a time. In addition, some PCI cards (usually hard disk controllers) are *bus masters*, which means they can "take over" the PCI bus and operate even faster. PCI slots sit right alongside ISA slots, so you can take your choice of installing an ISA or a PCI card without wasting space.

- **Extended Industry Standard Architecture (EISA).** Some desktop PCs come with EISA slots, but mostly network servers have them. EISA slots come in 16-bit and 32-bit varieties, both of which can accept either EISA and ISA cards (unless you match 16-bit and 32-bit EISA slots with cards of the same type, you're wasting capacity). EISA cards run at a leisurely 8 MHz, but some are bus masters, since like PCI the EISA standard supports this feature. Generally, unless you're setting up a server, EISA cards cost too much for the added performance they give you.

- **Micro Channel Architecture (MCA).** Available only in some IBM PS/2 machines and in a handful of PCs from other vendors, MCA slots accept only MCA cards—which like EISA cards cost more and offer only a little bit better performance. You can also find a few

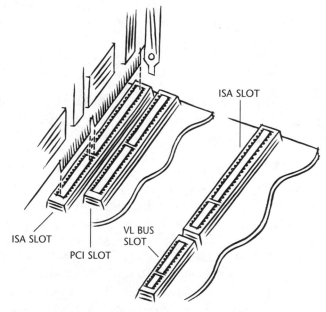

ISA SLOT

ISA SLOT

VL BUS SLOT

PCI SLOT

Figure 3: Two local bus layouts. *This diagram shows the usual positioning of VL and PCI local bus slots. VL bus slots are usually in line with the ISA slots, so either an ISA or a local bus card can occupy the same position; PCI slots run alongside ISA slots, which achieves the same economy.*

Accessing Your PC's Setup Routine

Most upgrades require that you access your PC's setup routine. Your system manual explains how to do this—if you still *have* your system manual. Well, you can always call tech support... if you can get through. If you can't, or if the manufacturer has gone out of business, try these tricks:

- **Look for a disk.** You might have lost the manual, but if you have the floppy disks that came with your system, one of them is likely to contain the setup routine. Look for SETUP.EXE or a similar file name and enter that name at the A: prompt.

- **Press the magic keys.** In most systems, the setup routine comes on disk and is built into the system BIOS, which means you can usually access it using a special key combination. Some popular permutations: Ctrl Alt Esc, Ctrl Alt Insert, and Ctrl Alt S.

- **Reboot and lean on it.** Sometimes holding down the Esc key while your system boots will return a message saying something like: "Keyboard error; would you like to configure your system?" Choose Yes and you'll bop right into the setup routine. If Esc doesn't work, reboot and try the key combinations in the preceding paragraph.

Still no luck? Well, now you know why you should stash your manual in a safe place. If you really can't raise manufacturer tech support, browse CompuServe and post some messages in the IBM forum to see if anyone has a system like yours and knows what to do. You might also try some local BBSs or user groups (see Chapter 21: *Communications* for more on accessing on-line services).

DANGER

MCA bus masters, but so what? This incompatible standard was never what it was cracked up to be, and unless you're stuck with an MCA system you have no use for MCA cards.

HOT TIP

Most systems come with both local bus and ISA slots. If you have a free local bus slot and you can find a local bus version of the card you want to buy—particularly a graphics card—you should definitely buy it instead of the ISA version. You'll get better performance—especially with graphics—for only a little more money.

Make sure you get a money-back guarantee with any card you buy—but this goes double for local bus boards. Many people have experienced compatibility problems between VL bus cards and VL bus systems, although this seems to be a problem only with older VL hardware. PCI is a newer standard and appears to have many of the same problems.

Avoiding the Four Common Card Conflicts

Life would be great if you could just plug a card in your system and have it work without a hitch. By pure luck, this sometimes happens. But more often than not, you have to *configure* the card, that is, adjust small switches or move little bits of plastic called *jumpers* to make it work properly.

Why the complication? Because your system has limited resources—not just memory and disk space, but hardware resources that enable cards and drives to interact correctly with your system and with DOS. In a correctly configured system,

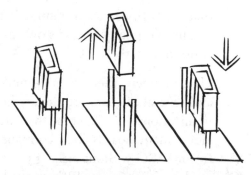

Figure 4: How jumpers work. *Here's what a typical jumper block looks like. To change your configuration, you move the jumper from one pair of pins to another or remove the jumper entirely. It all depends on what you need to do and how the manual tells you to do it.*

the cards, drives, system, and DOS all share resources in an orderly way, like children contentedly passing the fish sticks, string beans, and potatoes around the table. In a badly configured system, you've got a food fight.

Fighting for the Same IRQ

When a card installation problem occurs, it's usually a *hardware interrupt* problem. A hardware interrupt is a top-priority message from a card (or other device) to the CPU

```
 File   Utilities   Help
╔══════════════════════════ IRQ Status ══════════════════════════╗
║  IRQ  Address    Description      Detected       Handled By     ║
║  ───  ───────    ───────────      ────────       ──────────     ║
║   0   D5B4:0000  Timer Click      Yes            win386.exe      ║
║   1   0E49:1923  Keyboard;        Yes            Block Device    ║
║   2   F000:EF6F  Second 8259A     Yes            BIOS            ║
║   3   F000:EF6F  COM2: COM4:      No             BIOS            ║
║   4   F000:EF6F  COM1: COM3:      COM1:          BIOS            ║
║   5   0C3D:009F  LPT2:            InPort Mouse   Default Handlers║
║   6   0C3D:00B7  Floppy Disk      Yes            Default Handlers║
║   7   0070:06F4  LPT1:            Yes            System Area     ║
║   8   0C3D:0052  Real-Time Clock  Yes            Default Handlers║
║   9   F000:ECF3  Redirected IRQ2  Yes            BIOS            ║
║  10   F000:EF6F  <Reserved>                      BIOS            ║
║  11   F000:EF6F  <Reserved>                      BIOS            ║
║  12   F000:EF6F  <Reserved>                      BIOS            ║
║  13   F000:F070  Math Coprocessor Yes            BIOS            ║
║  14   F000:EF6F  Fixed Disk       Yes            BIOS            ║
║  15   F000:EF6F  <Reserved>                      BIOS            ║
║                          ▄ OK ▄                                 ║
╚════════════════════════════════════════════════════════════════╝
 IRQ Status: Displays current usage of hardware interrupts.
```

Figure 5: *Microsoft Diagnostics comes free with both Windows and DOS. Among other things, it shows both the usual interrupt assignments and which interrupts are currently free (indicated by a No or a blank in the Status Detected column) for use by another card. And it's sort of accurate.*

145

"I need service immediately!" Nearly every card needs to send interrupts, doing requires its own *interrupt request (IRQ)* line, which is a sort of person-e to the CPU.

ately, there are a limited number of IRQ lines (a mere 16 in every system) and several of them are already hogged by the PC itself for the keyboard, the communications (COM) ports, the parallel (LPT) ports, and so on. By the law of averages alone, many boards come configured to use the *same* IRQ. Two boards can't contend for one IRQ without making your system go haywire, which is why two devices contending for the same IRQ is called an *interrupt conflict*. If you can't even get through a card's software installation or if your system locks up soon after you turn it on, then you probably have an interrupt conflict.

REMEMBER

Interrupt conflicts are normally easy to avoid, because most cards give you a choice of IRQ settings. If decent setup software comes with the card, you just pop the disk in a floppy drive and run the installation routine. The program senses which interrupts are being used and which are available—and by process of elimination tells you which interrupt to use for the card you're installing. To assign the interrupt on the card, you usually move a match-head-size plastic jumper—here's where the tweezers come in—from one tiny pair of pins to another. Sometimes you make this change with installation software instead.

Some cards lack good installation software, so you have to check which interrupts are free some other way and consult the documentation to determine which jumper to set. In such cases, you can try running a program called Microsoft Diagnostics (MSD). This program comes with both Windows and DOS (use whichever version is most recent—probably the one in your DOS directory). Here's how to use MSD to see which interrupts are free:

1. Exit Windows if necessary, change to your DOS directory, and type `msd`.

2. From the main menu, click on IRQ Status (or type q). The IRQ numbers are in a column on the left side of the screen.

3. Check the Status Detected column. If you see No or a blank space, then that interrupt is free for use by the card you're installing.

This is the way it should work, anyway. In fact, making interrupt diagnoses using MSD isn't that accurate. Commercial programs such as *Setup Advisor* or *QA Plus* do a better job, but they're not perfect. That's why you should have documentation for every card in your system. If you know for a fact which boards are using which IRQs, then you can be sure which interrupts can be safely used by the board you're installing.

REMEMBER

Scrabbling for the Same I/O Address

IRQs aren't the only bones of contention. Sometimes, two cards try to use the same *I/O address*, an area in system memory used by cards and other devices for exchanging data with the CPU. All devices should have their own I/O address. And if they don't? Nothing, if they don't use the address at the same time—which is why I/O address conflicts are so insidious. You may not experience a system crash for some time, and then, poof!

I/O address conflicts occur most often between like devices, such as two hard disk interface cards or two graphics cards. Here again, good installation software should tell you which free I/O address you should assign a card before you plug it in. Sometimes you use a jumper to set the I/O address, but more often you set a *DIP switch* on the board or make the selection in software. DIP switches are sometimes hard to set; a small screwdriver or pen can help.

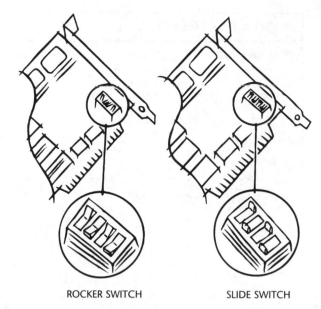

ROCKER SWITCH   SLIDE SWITCH

Figure 6: How to set a DIP switch. Often, to change a card's I/O address or other settings, you move a DIP switch—a tiny slide or rocker switch on a small switch block. If you've got big fingers, try flipping the switch with a pen.

If your installation software is too dumb to check for I/O address problems, it's probably because the manufacturer thought no one else would use that address; just hope that *another* manufacturer whose card is in your system didn't make the same assumption. You should still check the availability of I/O addresses in advance—but MSD can't help you. However, commercial programs such as *Setup Advisor* and *QA Plus* can; they sense existing I/O assignments and give you the possibilities for the current card.

The best method to avoid conflict is to write down the I/O addresses of all the cards in your system and avoid those addresses when you install new cards. This is all the more vital because you can't change I/O addresses on some cards, so you sometimes run into a situation where two cards simply can't coexist in the same system (not infrequent with two hard disk interface cards). In this case you should *shop* with the idea of finding a card that can be set to an unused I/O address.

Available DMA Channels		
DMA Channel	**Bits**	**Typical status**
0	16	Used by system
1	8	Free
2	8	Used by floppy disk controller
3	8	Free
4	16	Sometimes used by system
5	16	Free
6	16	Free
7	16	Free

Figure 7: If you're installing a card that uses DMA—say, a sound card or a hard disk interface—then you have several free channels to choose from. Note that a 16-bit card may get better performance using a 16-bit channel.

Battling Over DMA

Do you want to add a scanner or hard disk interface card? A sound card or network card? Then there's a good chance you'll be installing a device that uses *direct memory access (DMA)*, whereby a device improves performance by doing an end run around the CPU and writing directly to system memory.

Your system has eight *DMA channels*, each one a kind of data expressway to memory. Channel 0 and Channel 4 are sometimes used by the system, and the floppy drive uses Channel 2, but the rest may well be up for grabs. Sound cards almost always use DMA and by default are often configured for Channel 3. If you're installing a 16-bit card— a card with an edge connector that has two segments and entirely fills a 16-bit slot— configuring it to access Channel 5, 6, or 7 may improve performance.

HOT TIP

Two devices shouldn't use the same DMA channel, but if they do, the outcome won't be as severe as that caused by an IRQ or I/O address conflict. Instead of crashing the system, a DMA conflict usually prevents one device from completing its task while the other device takes over the channel. Nonetheless, a conflict will, at the least, hobble performance and—with so many channels to choose from—can be easily avoided.

Unfortunately, software can't reliably test your system to see which device is using which DMA channel. Here, to prevent a conflict before it happens, you simply need to know which DMA channels (if any) are being used by other cards in your system. If two devices demand the same DMA channel and can't be switched to another channel, you can usually disable one board's DMA access entirely.

Living at the Same ROM Address

Not all cards come with a ROM (read-only memory) chip containing a small program to help the card do its chores, but most video boards, network cards, and hard disk interfaces do. Your system reserves an area in memory for ROM starting addresses. Similar types of devices tend to take the same addresses and so stay away from other types of devices' territory.

Post That Configuration!

In this section you'll notice the repeated advice to "write down" the IRQs, I/O addresses, DMA channel assignments, and ROM addresses taken by your expansion cards. So where do you put that information so you won't lose it? I suggest writing it all on a small piece of paper and taping it to your power supply (be sure not to cover any ventilation holes). If you keep this little log up to date, when you install a new expansion card you'll instantly know which system resources are free.

If you do experience a conflict, you often can't relocate the ROM address, because many applications expect the device's ROM to be in a certain place, according to rules laid down in the Pleistocene Era of PCs. Along with conflicting I/O addresses, ROM address conflicts are another reason putting two similar cards in the same machine may be impossible.

The symptoms of a ROM address conflict resemble that of an interrupt conflict: Your system quickly locks up and you can't do anything with it. Keep a record of your cards' ROM addresses along with everything else.

Installing a Microsoft Mouse

Installing a mouse is one the easiest and the most frequent upgrades performed, which is why I'm explaining how to install this device first. Here, I'll be giving you specific instructions about a specific device—Microsoft Mouse, which is among the best and most popular rodents. It comes in three varieties: PS/2-style, serial, and bus (which includes a small expansion card). If your PC has a standard mouse connector on the back panel, just buy the PS/2-style mouse and plug it in.

For the mouse to work, you or some installation software needs to add a line in your CONFIG.SYS file that loads a *driver*, a small program that enables the mouse to talk to your software. To set up Windows to use the mouse, run Windows Setup (enter `setup` at the DOS prompt in your Windows directory; or select Setup in the Main program group and choose Options//Change System Settings) and select "Microsoft, or IBM PS/2" from the Mouse list. To set up a mouse for use in DOS applications, see "How to Install DOS and Windows" in Chapter 12: *Windows and DOS*.

Serial Mouse Installation

HOT TIP

If your system lacks a mouse connector but you have a free serial port, you should buy the serial version of Microsoft Mouse, which is ridiculously easy to install. However, note that if you have an internal modem, a serial port may *look* free when it isn't. Check your communications software to see which serial port is being used by the modem, and *don't* plug the mouse into it.

1. Check out the back of your machine. Your serial ports *should* be labeled COM 1 and COM 2 (or Serial Port 1 and Serial Port 2).

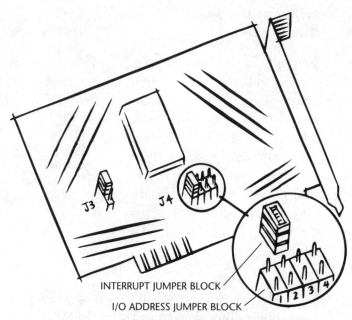

Figure 8: Installing a Microsoft Mouse interface card. *With this card, the interrupt numbers are clearly labeled. To change interrupts, just move the jumper to a different number.*

If they aren't, check your manual or turn to the illustration of common serial port types in the "Upgrading the Serial Port" section near the end of this chapter.

2. If COM 1 is free, plug your mouse into it; if it's not free, plug the mouse into COM 2.

3. If your mouse's connector and the connector on your PC are completely different and your manual says that you are in fact looking at a serial port, then you have the wrong *type* of serial port. You'll have to get a serial port adapter, available at any electronics store, to plug in your mouse.

Tell Windows and/or DOS that a mouse is present, as explained above, and that's it. If for some reason the mouse doesn't work, it's possible the COM port to which you've attached the mouse has been disabled. Start up your system's setup routine and look for anything to do with serial or COM ports. Choose the "Enable" option for the COM port in question, save the configuration, and reboot.

Bus Mouse Installation

No mouse port? All serial ports in use? Then you need to install a bus mouse—which means installing an interface card. Fortunately, Microsoft's bus mouse makes this easy.

1. Run MSD or some other diagnostic software to determine which interrupts are free (see "Avoiding the Four Common Card Conflicts" earlier in this chapter).

2. Microsoft's bus mouse card is unusual in that IRQ numbers actually appear on the card itself. Look for jumper block J4, and you'll see the numbers 2 through 5 labeling four pairs of pins. If IRQ 5 is available, for example, you simply move the jumper to the pair of pins by that number (see Figure 8).

3. Turn off your system, open it up, and find a free 8-bit ISA slot (if you don't have an 8-bit slot, a 16-bit slot will do). Remove the slot cover, insert the card all the way into the slot, and screw the card down. Replace the system cover but don't replace the cover's screws quite yet.

Now perform the same software setup you'd do with any other mouse. If the mouse doesn't work or your system hangs, MSD probably reported a free IRQ incorrectly. Check the documentation for the other boards in your system and find a free IRQ by process of elimination. Failing that, try trial and error—IRQ 5 is often a safe bet.

HOT TIP

Another possibility is that a mouse interface has already been installed in your system and you missed it—in which case you have an I/O address conflict. A few cards (notably some ATI graphics cards) come with their own mouse interface; if you have one, you didn't need to buy the bus mouse, since you could have installed a mouse in the existing port. At this point though, you might as well resolve the conflict and install the bus mouse: Just move the jumper on jumper block J3 from its current pair of pins to the other pair, reinstall the card, and put your system back together.

Upgrading Graphics

Most people replace their current graphics *controller* (the monitor's controlling elec- tronics, which may be either on a card or on the motherboard) because they want more speed, higher resolution, and less flicker. You can get all these attributes from many reasonably priced graphics cards. But remember that the *monitor* must also be able to handle less flicker and higher resolution. You can damage a monitor by trying to drive it beyond its specifications (for more on matching monitors and graphics cards, see Chapter 5: *Monitors, Etc.*).

DANGER

If you have a local bus PC, buy a local bus graphics card to get maximum perfor- mance. As with all local bus cards, however, call both the card and PC manufacturers before you buy to make sure the card actually works in your specific model system (and make sure you get a 30-day, money-back guarantee).

REMEMBER

Assuming you've got the right monitor, upgrading with either an ISA or a local bus card should be pretty easy, as long as you're planning to bump up resolution in Windows only. If you want to increase the resolution for a specific DOS application, you need to make sure the card comes with a driver for that application. That said, follow these steps:

1. Look at the back of your system to determine whether your system's existing graphics controller is on a card or on the motherboard. If the monitor isn't plugged into a card but into a connector in another location, then you have motherboard graphics. Check your PC's manual to determine how to disable your system's built-in graphics controller, and keep that information handy.

2. Don't bother running diagnostic software before you install the new card, because you'd need your old graphics controller to run it—and it probably uses the same resources as the new card does. However, you should still check the assignments of your other cards to make sure you don't cause an IRQ or I/O address conflict (you don't have to worry about ROM BIOS or DMA conflicts).

3. Turn off your system and monitor, unplug the monitor, and remove the PC's cover. Remove the old graphics card—or, if you're adding a graphics card to a system with motherboard graphics, follow the procedure to disable that circuitry (usually you move a jumper). If you're installing a local bus card, you'll need a free local bus slot. Install the card, reaffix the cover, plug the monitor into the card, and turn on your system. At this point the display should look the same as it did before.

4. Slip the installation disk that came with the graphics board into a floppy drive. Run the install routine and follow the prompts. Usually, if you want a higher resolution in Windows (and your monitor can handle it), the utility will copy the appropriate high-resolution Windows drivers to your hard disk. Then you set up the monitor to run with the least flicker at your chosen resolution (usually 70 or 72 Hz) by selecting the monitor type from a list.

5. Finally, run Windows Setup to select the video driver for your new resolution (usually to 800 by 600 or 1024 by 768). Go to the Main group and double-click on Setup. Select Options//Change System Settings and click on the Display list. Scroll to the bottom of the list and select "Other display [Requires disk from OEM]." Windows may ask you to insert a disk in drive A:, but if you've already copied the drivers to your hard disk, you can change directories and load the driver of your choice from there. Click on Restart Windows for the change to take effect.

That should be it. But if you get a bunch of squiggly lines, then you're probably trying to push your monitor beyond its specs. Quickly press Enter Alt F X Enter to exit Windows (reboot if this doesn't work). At the DOS prompt for your Windows directory, enter `setup`. To get Windows running again, go to the Display list, choose VGA, and press Enter twice to accept the configuration. Choosing VGA from the DOS version of Windows Setup is the usual way to back out of video driver problems until you decide what to do.

HOT TIP

If the first Windows driver that came with your card did not work, return to the Windows version of Setup and try one of the lower-resolution drivers that came with your card. You should also check with the card manufacturer and see if you have the latest Windows drivers—they seem to go through many bug fixes and revisions. The company will usually either mail you a disk or let you download drivers from a BBS for free (to learn how to log onto a BBS, see Chapter 20: *Communications*).

Adding Video Memory

All graphics cards come with *video memory*, a relatively small quantity of RAM in which the image on your screen is created. The more memory on the card, the more colors and the higher the resolution the card can produce. For example, 512K is enough to display 16 colors at 1024 by 768, but you need 1MB for 256 colors at that same resolution (see Chapter 5: *Monitors, Etc.* for more on resolution, colors, and memory).

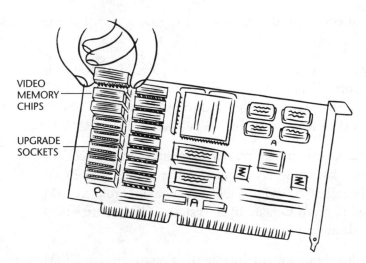

VIDEO
MEMORY
CHIPS

UPGRADE
SOCKETS

Figure 9: Video memory upgrades. Many graphics cards enable you to add memory to bump up resolution and colors. Just buy the appropriate chips as cheaply as you can, plug them in, and change video drivers to get the added capabilities. Remember to make sure your monitor can handle the upgrade.

Many cards come with a certain quantity of video memory, but they enable you to add more later. To do this, check your card's documentation and see what kind of memory chips the card uses. Buy those chips at a discount electronics store and plug them into the open sockets on the card. The documentation should explain how to tell the card that more memory has been installed (if necessary— many cards sense this automatically). When you reinstall the card and turn on your system, change drivers to take advantage of your card's new capabilities.

Installing an Internal Modem

To "install" an external modem, all you do is find a free serial port, connect the modem to it, and plug in your phone line. In your communication software's installation routine, you select the make and model of modem ("Hayes Compatible" usually works if you can't find your brand) and tell the software which serial port you've plugged your modem into (usually COM 1

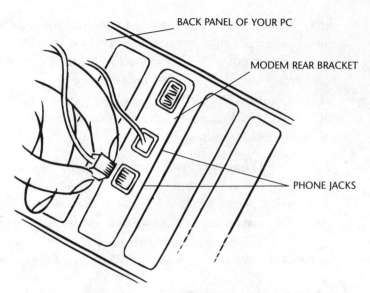

BACK PANEL OF YOUR PC

MODEM REAR BRACKET

PHONE JACKS

Figure 10: Hooking a modem to the phone lines. *Most modems come with two phone jacks—one for the phone line itself and another for your telephone. If you're using the same line for both voice and data, you need to make both connections.*

or COM 2; check "Upgrading the Serial Port" at the end of this chapter). Then you're ready to communicate.

To install an internal modem, you configure the software in the same way, but the hardware installation is quite a bit trickier:

1. First check the back of your machine and see if anything (typically, a mouse) is hanging off one of the serial ports. When adding serial devices, always start with COM 1 first—so if COM 1 is free, configure the card to use it. Usually you do this by moving a jumper. If COM 1 is not available, install the card for COM 2.

2. Before you open up your system, you can run a diagnostic program to check for free I/O addresses, but you don't have to worry about DMA assignments or ROM addresses—nor about IRQs, because the IRQ you'll be using belongs to the COM port you've already configured the card to take. In all systems, COM 1 uses IRQ 4 and COM 2 uses IRQ 3 by default.

REMEMBER

3. Next, start your PC's setup utility. Look for anything pertaining to serial or COM ports, and follow the procedure to *disable* the COM port that you've configured your modem to use. Save the configuration, exit the setup software, and turn off your machine.

4. Open your PC's cover and insert the modem into a free slot. Put your system back together, plug the phone line into the rear bracket of the modem card, run the communication software setup routine, and you're ready to roll.

Adding a Sound Card

Sound cards have a bad reputation for causing conflicts, and it's well deserved. Almost all of them use at least one IRQ, I/O address, and DMA channel—and to emulate SoundBlaster (the most popular sound card ever), some use *two* interrupts and *two* I/O addresses. Unless you've carefully noted the IRQ and I/O assignments for every other card in your PC, sound cards' hunger for hardware resources can easily cause problems. In particular, I've seen Microsoft's Windows Sound System wreak utter havoc.

DANGER

Sound cards from the major manufacturers come with diagnostic software that senses which resources are free and recommends settings for the card. Run the software before you physically install the card and configure jumpers or switches accordingly. Remember that no installation software is perfect, though, so if your PC is full of cards, knowing exactly which assignments are open may be the only way you can get the sound card to work properly.

Once you've found a home for the card in your system and run the software that installs the card's sound driver, you'll need to plug in your external speakers—and a microphone, if you want to record your own sounds (see Figure 2 in Chapter 23: *Multimedia* for a diagram of typical sound card connections). Many sound cards also have CD ROM drive interfaces, which can save you the cost and trouble of adding a separate CD ROM interface card to your system. For more on setting up a CD ROM drive and sound card simultaneously, see "Installing a CD ROM Drive" later in this chapter.

Adding Memory

The less Windows has to access the hard disk—accessing memory instead—the better the performance. That's why you shouldn't run Windows with less than 8MB of main memory, and if you run several big applications at once, 16MB can't hurt. Fortunately, standard SIMMs (Single Inline Memory Modules) are now used in nearly every system. Not only are they easy to install—they snap right into sockets on the motherboard—they're cheap. You generally pay between $35 and $50 a megabyte, though prices literally fluctuate daily.

Buying the Right SIMM

SIMMs come in several different varieties. Everything except the capacity of the SIMMs you install is determined by your PC's memory specifications, so check your manual carefully:

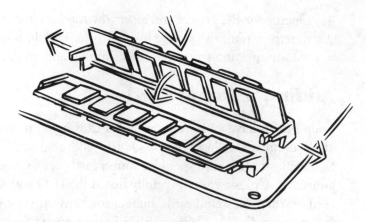

Figure 11: How to install a SIMM. *Begin by slipping the SIMM vertically into place. Then gently bend the plastic side brackets outward as you tip the SIMM over to approximately a 45-degree angle—its installed position.*

- **Number of pins.** SIMMs have either 30 pins or 72 pins. Systems with 30-pin SIMM sockets must be upgraded four SIMMs at a time. Even with eight SIMM sockets (the typical 30-pin arrangement), this greatly limits the selection of memory capacities. SIMMs with 72 pins have no such restrictions, except in Pentium systems, where 72-pin SIMMs must be added in pairs.

- **Parity.** Look in your system manual to see whether your motherboard uses *parity checking* (some systems let you switch parity checking on and off, but you should leave the setting where it is or the memory already installed may not work). Systems with parity checking and 72-pin sockets require 36-bit (also known as "x36") SIMMs; nonparity systems with 72-pin sockets take 32-bit ("x32") SIMMs. Parity systems with 30-pin sockets need 9-bit ("x9") SIMMs, while nonparity systems with 30-pin sockets take 8-bit ("x8") SIMMs.

- **Capacity.** Expect to find 30-pin SIMMs in 1MB and 4MB capacities. The 72-pin type comes in 1MB, 2MB, 4MB, 8MB, and 16MB capacities. You can usually mix and match 72-pin SIMMs of differing capacities in the same system, giving you the opportunity to install exactly the amount of memory you want.

- **Speed.** The three most common SIMM speed ratings are 60, 70, and 80 nanoseconds (ns)—the lower the number, the faster the memory and the more you pay. Just make sure the speed of the SIMM matches the memory access speed specified in your system manual. Whatever you do, don't buy a SIMM rated slower, or you're inviting memory errors that could trash your data.

DANGER

Buying memory that's rated faster than your system needs it to be won't hurt anything, you'll just waste a little money. SIMM speed ratings don't really specify how *fast* memory is, they indicate the top speed at which the SIMM can be *accessed* by a system. So you won't gain any performance by, say, installing 60ns SIMMs in a system that calls for 80ns SIMMs.

REMEMBER

Plugging in SIMMs

About the height and width of a stick of chewing gum, your average SIMM snaps into its socket fairly easily, but remember your motherboard isn't the place to use force. Break a SIMM socket, and you may well need to have your system professionally repaired. The trick is to lightly spread the delicate plastic side brackets as you extract or insert SIMMs (see Figure 11).

DANGER

Note that old-fashioned 30-pin SIMMs can lead to some maddeningly wasteful situations. For example, some older systems sold with 2MB had eight 30-pin, 256K SIMMs—so at least four of them must be discarded before you can upgrade the memory further. In this instance, you might want to add four 4MB modules and bring the system up to 17MB immediately. If instead you stopped at 8MB in 1MB SIMMs, you wouldn't be able to go beyond *that* without discarding SIMMs again.

Installing Hard Disks

Adding or replacing a hard disk can be a somewhat complicated upgrade, mainly because the drive and PC won't always talk to each other without encouragement. As with any upgrade, however, staying cool and following instructions will get you there eventually.

Here, you'll learn how to set up the two most popular types of hard disk: IDE and SCSI. The mechanical installation is much the same with both drive types, but the software setup is quite different—that's why I've dealt with the nuts-and-bolts stuff first and the specifics of installing each type of drive later. Finally, you'll learn how to set up the drive using DOS.

Note that it's cheaper and less hassle to install an IDE hard disk in a system that already has an IDE interface, and a SCSI hard disk in a system with an existing SCSI interface. Note also that if you have an old ST506 (also known as MFM) drive that you want to replace, you should upgrade to an IDE or a SCSI hard disk instead of trying to find an ST506 drive to match your current controller. This means you'll have to buy an interface card with the new drive (see Chapter 4: *Disk Drives*).

HOT TIP

REMEMBER

As noted at the beginning of this chapter, before you start you *must* write down your hard disk setup information and back up your entire hard disk, preferably to tape. The possibility of something going fatally wrong is slim, but there's no need to take even a small risk with your data. Moreover, if you're replacing a hard disk, backing up the old one and restoring the backup to the new drive is the safest and easiest way to transplant your old data to the new drive.

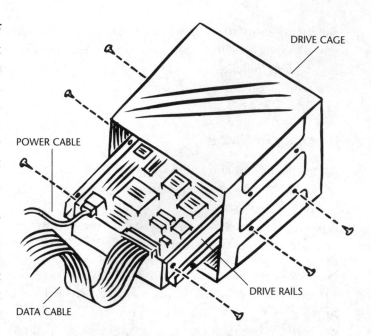

Figure 12: Mounting a hard disk. A hard disk's mechanical installation is pretty simple. When you mount a 3½-inch drive in a 5¼-inch drive bay (shown here), you need to attach drive rails first.

Mechanical Connections

The first thing you need to determine is whether you have room for your new hard disk, that is, whether you have a free *drive bay* (an empty area in your PC for mounting a drive). Some compact PCs have only two bays—one for a floppy drive and one for a hard disk—so you must replace the old hard disk if you want more disk space.

Hard disks are either 3½-inch drives or 5¼-inch drives. You can mount a 3½-inch drive in a 5¼-inch bay, but not the other way around—so if your PC has only a 3½-inch bay free, your choice of hard disks may be somewhat limited. Hard disks larger than 540MB are usually 5¼-inch drives.

Assuming you have the right hard disk for the right bay, and there's no more than one other hard disk in your system, this step-by-step guide to making all the mechanical connections should work for you:

1. Turn off your PC and open it up. To access the free drive bay, you may need to temporarily unplug and clear away the flat, gray ribbon cables that connect other drives. If so, make sure you write down exactly how those cables were hooked up so you can reconnect them later. If you're replacing a drive, remove it now.

2. If you're replacing an IDE hard disk, go to step 4. If you're adding a second IDE hard disk, you must configure the drive you want to boot from as the *master* and the other as the *slave*. You do this by moving jumpers, but *which* jumpers depends

HOT TIP

on the hard disk, so consult the documentation for both drives. When you add an IDE hard disk, it's always easiest to leave the current boot drive as the master.

3. If you're installing a SCSI drive instead, remember that every device on a SCSI *chain* (that is, the drive, the interface, and any other devices hooked to the interface) must have a unique SCSI ID number from 1 to 7. You assign these numbers by moving jumpers or flipping switches, so check the documentation. If you're going to boot from the new drive, assign it a 0; otherwise, give it a 1. Next you need to make sure the last drive on the ribbon cable has a *terminating resistor pack* (probably three small comblike components right next to the largest connector). If two or more drives will be hanging off the same SCSI interface, *remove* the terminating resistors from any drive that's not at the end of the chain.

REMEMBER

4. Slide the new hard disk into a free bay and use the four screws that came with the drive to secure it to the drive cage. If you need to install a 3 1/2-inch drive in a 5 1/4-inch bay, attach the drive rails (supplied with most 3 1/2-inch drives) before inserting it (see Figure 12).

5. Locate the flat, gray data cable that is (or was) hooked to your existing hard disk and plug it into the rear of the new drive (most hard disk ribbon cables have at least two drive connectors). If you can't remember which cable connected your hard disk, note that IDE cables have 40 wires and SCSI cables have 50 wires. (At the other end of the cable is the drive interface—IDE interfaces are usually on the motherboard, while SCSI interfaces are usually on a card.) With SCSI, the connectors on the drive and the cable are usually keyed so you can't plug the two together the wrong way around. This isn't true of many IDE drives, however. The trick is to look for the red or blue stripe on the ribbon cable and make sure it's nearest the power connector (see Figure 13).

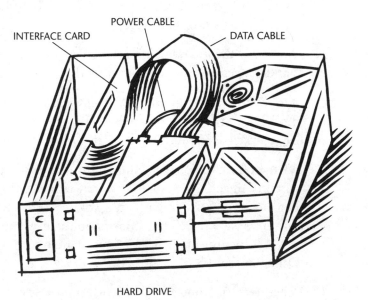

Figure 13: Installing an interface. *If the interface isn't built into the motherboard, you need to install an interface card. Seat the card in the slot nearest the hard disk, and make sure the red stripe on the data cable lines up with "pin 1" on the card's connector.*

6. Next look for an unconnected white plug at the end of a bundle of four wires sprouting from the power supply. That's a power connector, and you should plug it into the power socket on the back of the new hard disk. Power connectors are always keyed so you can't reverse them accidentally.

7. Replace you PC's cover, but don't screw it in just yet, because you may want to check a few things if you run into trouble later.

REMEMBER

This completes the mechanical connections. Remember, though, that if you need to install a SCSI drive in a system with an existing IDE drive, you'll need to add a hard disk interface card. If you plan to keep the existing IDE interface, conflicts are likely, so check to see if the two interfaces can be configured to coexist before you buy.

DANGER

The interface card should be installed in a slot near the new drive so the ribbon cable can reach. When you connect the ribbon cable to the card, it is possible to reverse the connector accidentally, so make sure "pin 1" (which should be labeled on the board) matches up with the red stripe on the cable (when in doubt, follow the documentation that came with the interface card). Avoid creasing or crushing cables, or you may break the delicate wires inside.

Setting Up an IDE Drive

Once you've plugged in the cables, you're ready to help your IDE drive and PC get acquainted. Here's how to proceed:

1. Have all of the following information about your new hard disk handy: the capacity, cylinders, heads, sectors per track, and starting cylinder for write precompensation.

2. Start your PC's setup utility (consult your manual to find out how) and find the Hard Disk or Fixed Disk entries. If you're replacing a hard disk, select the hard disk marked as number 1. If you're adding a hard disk, select number 2.

3. When you make your selection, most likely your PC's *drive table* will appear. This contains a list of drive types officially supported by your system BIOS. You'll see that each type has its own number of heads, cylinders, and so on. See if any of the types precisely match the information you wrote down about your new drive in step 1. If by some miracle you find a match, enter the drive type number, save your setup configuration, and exit the utility.

4. When you can't find a match, look for a "user definable" drive type—usually Type 0, Type 47, or Type 99. Fill in the blanks with the information about your new drive, save the configuration, and exit the utility.

5. You say your PC's setup program has no user-definable drive type? Then buy a utility such as Micro House's *EZ-Drive* or Ontrack Data Recovery's *Disk Manager*. Just boot from drive A:, swap in the utility's disk, and run the automatic installation routine. Many hard disks come with either *Disk Manager* or *EZ-Drive*, so you may want to use them instead of the drive table method to begin with.

If you can't match drive and drive type, and your drive table lacks a user-definable type, you can also choose a type with parameters as close as possible to those for your drive. If you try this, *do not* choose a drive type with greater capacity, more heads, or more cylinders, or you may damage your new hard disk.

DANGER

Setting Up a SCSI Drive

The main thing to know about setting up a SCSI hard disk is that you should not use your system setup utility to tell your PC you've installed a new drive. SCSI drives do an end run around your system BIOS and talk directly to DOS. Sometimes they accomplish this using a device driver loaded in your CONFIG.SYS file, other times with a ROM chip on the SCSI interface card. So if you're trading an IDE drive for a SCSI drive, remember to run your setup utility and set the drive to Not Installed (or a similar wording).

Many SCSI drives and interface cards come with special software that takes care of setting up the drive, including partitioning and logical formatting (see below). *CorelSCSI*, sometimes bundled but also sold separately, accomplishes this task very well. It's especially handy at resolving conflicts encountered when trying to hang several different types of SCSI devices—CD ROMs, scanners, and so on—off the same SCSI interface. Note that if your SCSI interface is not DOS INT 13H compatible, you'll have to use special software, since you won't be able to use the standard DOS partitioning method.

Partitioning and Formatting

Here's the final stage in setting up your hard disk to store data. The steps below outline the manual method for a system with one hard disk. If you go out and buy a new version of DOS, you can simply run the automatic routine described in the section "How to Install DOS and Windows" in Chapter 12. However, you'll still have to decide whether you want multiple logical drives (drives C:, D:, E:, and so on) and what size they'll be. You can get a little help here with that decision:

1. Put your DOS boot floppy in drive A: and turn on your machine. When the system boots, swap the disk containing DOS's FDISK utility into the drive and type `fdisk`.

Larger Drives, Bigger Clusters, More Waste

DOS stores data in 512-byte sectors. However, it monitors the status of those sectors (whether they're available, being used by a file, or damaged) in groups of sectors known as *clusters*. Unfortunately, DOS believes an entire cluster is in use even if a file uses only part of it. This means that DOS wastes half a cluster on average for every file on your hard disk.

This wasted space is called *slack space*. The larger the logical drive, the larger the clusters and the more slack space. For instance, a typical 340MB drive configured as one big drive C: might have 12MB in slack space. If it were set up as two 170MB drives, the slack space would be cut in half; three 113MB drives would reduce the waste to 3MB.

Some people don't mind wasting a little space for the sake of convenience, and they prefer not to mess with a bunch of small logical drives. Which route you choose is up to you, but a sensible policy is to avoid creating logical drives larger than 511.9MB. That would waste 8K per file, which may be a little much even for the most cavalier among us.

Logical drive size	Cluster size	Space wasted per 1000 files
16 to 127.9MB	2K	1MB
128 to 255.9MB	4K	2MB
256 to 511.9MB	8K	4MB
512MB to 1GB	16K	8MB

Figure 14: DOS wastes half a cluster on average for every file stored on disk. The larger the partition, the bigger the cluster—and the more space wasted.

2. Choose Create DOS Partition or Logical DOS Drive from the menu. From the subsequent menu, choose Create Primary DOS Partition.

3. DOS will ask you whether you want to use the maximum available size for a primary DOS partition and make the partition "active," that is, bootable. If you press Enter to accept this option, you'll create one big drive C:, and you're done with FDISK. Whether you do this or create several logical drives is partly a matter of taste, and partly a matter of how much disk space you're willing to squander, because larger partitions cause DOS to waste more space (see Figure 14).

4. If you answer no to creating a single partition, DOS will ask you how many megabytes you want to assign to the primary partition. If you're going to create multiple logical drives, you might as well take Figure 14 seriously and minimize the waste by creating a partition smaller than 256MB.

5. Press [Esc] to return to the Fdisk Options menu and select Set Active Partition. Enter 1 to make the primary partition bootable. This also makes the primary partition the C: logical drive.

6. Press [Esc] again and select Create Extended DOS Partition, whereupon you'll be prompted for the extended partition size. Accept the default—the space remaining on your hard disk after you created the primary partition—and press [Esc].

7. Next, you'll be prompted to create logical drives within the extended partition. Keeping in mind the space you have remaining, enter the number of megabytes for the second logical drive, and press [Esc]. If you wanted to create a third logical drive, you'd select Create DOS Partition or Logical DOS Drive, enter the number of megabytes for that drive, and so on.

A quick example may make this easier to understand. If you had a 750MB drive, one way to slice it would be: a 250MB primary partition (drive C:), a 500MB extended partition, and two 250MB logical drives (drives D: and E:) within that extended partition.

To logically format the drive, begin by booting from the A: drive. Enter `format c:/s` and ignore the warning about all data being lost, since there's no data there to begin with. This will format your primary DOS partition as bootable. To format any other partitions, enter `format d:` and so on—*without* the `/s`, since you can have only one bootable logical drive on the hard disk.

Installing a CD ROM Drive

Most CD ROM drives are SCSI devices, but there are exceptions. For example, many CD ROM drives come bundled with a sound card that doubles as a drive interface—and the drive will *only* work with that specific card. These *multimedia upgrade kits* include special installation software that generally makes setting up CD ROM drives simple. Just mount the drive, hook up the data and power cables, and—if you're hooking up a sound card—run the audio cable from the CD ROM drive to the sound card (see Figure 2 in Chapter 23: *Multimedia*). Run the installation software, and you should be OK.

If you want to use a sound card as a CD ROM interface, but you don't want to buy a kit, your choice of CD ROM drives will be limited to the drives that the sound card supports. Try to connect a sound card to a CD ROM drive that the sound card manufacturer does *not* explicitly list as compatible, and usually, you're wasting your time. Two exceptions to this rule are Adaptec's SoundMachine and Creative Labs'

DANGER

SoundBlaster 16/SCSI. Both of these sound cards can hook up with any SCSI-2 device, CD ROM or otherwise, although only the SoundMachine can support a bootable SCSI hard disk.

HOT TIP

Buy a SCSI CD ROM drive, and you'll find that setting one up is very similar to setting up a SCSI hard disk. Just remember that hard disks get the lowest SCSI ID numbers and interface cards get the highest, so you should typically assign the CD ROM drive the SCSI ID number 3, 4, or 5. Also, if you buy an external CD ROM drive, and there's another SCSI device on the chain, remember to *remove* the terminating resistor from the interface card. And of course, when you install a SCSI card, you'll have to check for the usual card conflicts described at the outset of this chapter.

If you bought the interface card and the CD ROM drive from different vendors, or if you're trying to hang several different SCSI devices off the same interface card, you may well have trouble getting everything to work together. In that case, get a copy of *CorelSCSI*, an excellent configuration utility available at most software chains for well under $100. Boot your machine from drive A:, swap in the *CorelSCSI* program disk, and let the automatic installation routine lead you step by step. Reboot your machine, and your CD ROM drive should appear as the last drive in your system.

Adding a Floppy Drive

Like the floppies they spin, floppy drives come in 3½-inch and 5¼-inch varieties, as do the drive bays in your system. No one can install a 5¼-inch drive in a 3½-inch bay without a blow torch, but as with hard disks you can easily add drive rails and mount a 3½-inch drive in a 5¼-inch bay. The difference with floppy drives is that you must install them in a bay on the front of the PC, so you can slip floppies in and out of them. Here's how to install a second floppy drive:

1. Turn off your machine and pop the hood. Look for a free externally accessible drive bay and remove its cover plate.

2. Slide the drive into the bay from the front of the PC (see Figure 15). Screw the drive (or the rails you've already mounted to the floppy drive) to the drive cage. Then secure the floppy drive's front bracket to the front panel of the system.

3. Look for the flat, gray data cable that's already connected to the first floppy drive (nine times out of ten, the other end of the cable will be plugged into the motherboard). Connect the data cable to the edge connector on the rear of the floppy

drive and plug in the white power connector (usually, you'll find a small connector specifically designed for 3^1/2-inch floppy drives).

4. Replace the system cover and turn on your PC. Start the system setup routine, and indicate the type of floppy drive you've added (1.44MB, 1.2MB, or whatever). Save the configuration, exit the routine, reboot your PC, and the drive should work.

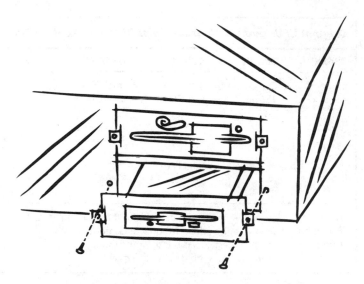

Figure 15: Mounting a floppy drive. Unlike installing a hard disk, adding a floppy drive requires that you find an externally accessible drive bay and slip the unit in from the front.

Note that unless you have four externally accessible drive bays, you won't have room for two different kinds of floppies along with an internal tape drive and an internal CD ROM drive. That's why many people have a fondness for TEAC's Combination FD-505, which integrates one 5^1/4-inch and one 3^1/2-inch floppy drive into a single compact unit.

CPU Upgrades

Nothing gives a PC a new lease on life like a new CPU. The least expensive way to perform this upgrade is usually to change the chip itself. You can do this with most 486 systems, and even with many 386 PCs. Performing the upgrade normally takes only slightly longer than opening and closing your PC's cover.

There are two other ways to replace a CPU: Buy a CPU upgrade card or replace the motherboard. Many systems—notably many IBM, Compaq, and AST machines—were designed to accommodate CPU upgrade cards from the manufacturer. These cards are expensive, however, and you're usually better off putting that money toward a new machine. Then there are the upgrade boards from such third parties as Evergreen, Kingston Technology, and LCC Computers, which are also generally pricey for the performance gained.

Original CPUs and the Upgrade Chips That Can Replace Them[1]						
386SX	**386DX**	**486SX**[2]	**486DX**[2]	**DX2**	**DX4**	**Pentium**
Cyrix 486SRx2	Cyrix 486DRx2	Intel SX2 OverDrive[3]	Intel DX2 OverDrive[3]	Intel DX4 OverDrive	Intel Pentium OverDrive	Future Intel Pentium OverDrives[4]
		Intel DX2 OverDrive[3]	Intel DX4 OverDrive	Intel Pentium OverDrive	Future Intel Pentium OverDrives[4]	
		Intel DX4 OverDrive		Future Intel Pentium OverDrives[4]		

[1]Upgrade clock speeds should be matched with those of original CPU.
[2]Pentium OverDrives can be added to some later models.
[3]Currently offers the biggest speed boost for the money.
[4]Will come in several varieties; no details yet available.

Figure 16: *This chart gives you an idea of the CPU upgrade chips available for the seven most popular system types. Note that the SX2 OverDrives and Cyrix chips lack a math coprocessor, while the other OverDrives include one. Expect SX2 and DX2 OverDrives to deliver a 30 percent to 70 percent performance increase.*

Replacing the motherboard can give you the biggest boost of all, but here price is not the only expense. You have a day's work ahead of you—disassembling your machine, unplugging and labeling cables and connectors, trying to get old hard disks to work with the new system BIOS, and so on. If you don't know what you're doing, this can be like do-it-yourself brain surgery. And if the system is old enough to warrant having its motherboard replaced, then it may well have sluggish old drives, a crummy monitor, too little memory...in other words, a full upgrade may cost more than a powerful new PC.

Almost everyone adds boards, drives, or memory. But when you think about replacing the CPU you should always ask yourself: Would I be better off spending this money on a new system? The less a CPU upgrade costs, the better.

Buying the Right Upgrade CPU

Adding or replacing the original CPU is easy, but *choosing* the right upgrade chip is hard. Check out Figure 16 to get a general sense of which upgrade chips will work in your system, and consider these additional pointers as you shop:

- **Keep expectations realistic.** Although they're nicknamed "clock doublers," SX2 and DX2 OverDrives never claimed to double real world system performance—depending on the application, expect a 30 percent to 70 percent boost (DX4 OverDrives, so-called clock triplers, do only marginally better). Cyrix avers that its

486SRx2 and 486DRx2 upgrades raise the processing speed of old 386 systems to 486 levels, but this depends on the speed of your 386. Expect a 15- to 35-percent boost in system performance.

- **Match clock speeds.** Make sure you buy an upgrade CPU that matches the speed of your system. For example, if you want a "clock doubler" for a 33-MHz 486SX system, buy either a 66-MHz SX2 OverDrive or a 66-MHz DX2 OverDrive. *Don't* install a cheaper 50-MHz OverDrive or it may malfunction and die.

  DANGER

- **Don't ignore 486DX upgrades.** Intel spent a lot of money promoting the upgradability of its 486SX systems. What the company didn't say as loudly is that most 486DX systems can also accept SX2, DX2, and DX4 OverDrives. Intel maintains a constantly updated list of 486DX systems that are certified as OverDrive compatible (call Intel's fax-back line at 800/525-3019 to see if yours is on the list).

- **Don't bother upgrading DX2s (yet).** DX4 OverDrives cost a lot and offer only a marginal improvement over DX2 performance, so save DX4 OverDrives for slower SX and DX systems (even then, you're better off with a DX2 OverDrive). Likewise, due to architectural differences between 486 and Pentium systems (and the expense of squashing Pentium technology into an upgrade chip), Pentium OverDrives that plug into 486 motherboards probably won't be very good deals.

Intel has made vague noises about next-generation Pentium OverDrives designed for upgrading both 486 and Pentium systems, but these won't see the light of day for some time. In the meantime, the best deal in upgrade processors is the DX2 OverDrive. Its math coprocessor will make little difference to those who don't use CAD applications or seldom perform statistical and financial calculations, but it costs the same as its coprocessorless sister chip, the SX2 OverDrive—under $200. A 30- to 70-percent system speedup is worth that kind of money.

HOT TIP

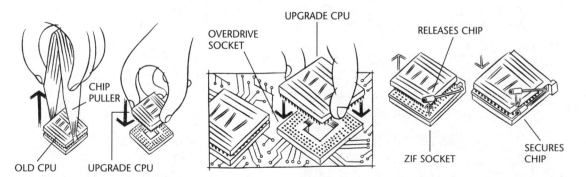

Figure 17: How to upgrade your CPU. *At left, the old-fashioned method—pull the old CPU by force with a chip puller and plug in the new one. At center, the simplest method, where you just plug the upgrade chip into a socket dedicated to the purpose. Finally, the ZIF socket makes force unnecessary.*

Plugging in the Chip

How easy is it to upgrade a CPU? That depends, not surprisingly, on the design of the original system. Here are the four methods:

- **Yank it first.** In 386DX, 486DX, and some 486SX systems, you must remove the original CPU first, because the upgrade chip plugs right into the original CPU socket. Unfortunately, these sockets weren't designed for easy CPU swapping, so you have to use force to pull the chip. I've done this successfully with a screwdriver, carefully prying the chip's edges bit by bit until it loosened, but you're best advised to use a *chip puller*, which is designed to safely extract chips (see Figure 17). You can find one at any electronics store.

- **The 386SX piggyback.** For the minority of people who will bother to upgrade old 386SX PCs, Cyrix offers its 486SRx2, which clips right on top of the 386SX CPU.

- **Open socket.** Many 486SX, DX2, and DX4 systems come with an open socket, so you can plug an OverDrive into it and leave it at that. The original CPU goes to sleep automatically.

- **Zero insertion force (ZIF) socket.** This is the elegant one-socket method. You raise a lever on the side of the ZIF socket, remove the original CPU effortlessly, drop in the upgrade chip, and snap the lever back into position to secure the chip.

Note that Cyrix upgrade chips make you go through a brief software installation routine along with adding or swapping chips. Just pop the utility in a disk drive, start the routine, and follow the steps. Also, some systems may require that you move a jumper when you change CPUs, so be sure to check your manual.

Upgrading the Serial Port

Many people prefer external modems over internal models because they're so much easier to install (and because they have those cool little lights). If you just bought a high-speed external modem and you have an old PC, your serial port may have just become the world's biggest communications bottleneck.

How can you tell? Well, the heart of a serial port is its Universal Asynchronous Receiver/Transmitter (UART) chip. To see which kind you have, type msd at the DOS prompt and type C at the main menu. At the bottom of the COM Ports screen you'll see a line that says UART Chip Used. If you see a 16550A on that line, you have a high-speed serial port and you've got nothing to worry about. If you see 8250 or 16450, bad news.

Fortunately, in most PCs, the UART chip sits in a socket and can be replaced. You can buy a 16550A UART chip from a mail-order house for about $15; just pull the old one with a chip puller and plug in the new one. If the UART isn't removable, you'll have to buy an internal modem with its own high-speed serial port if you want top-speed communications.

Product Directory

Diagnostic Utilities

QA Plus
Diagsoft, Inc.
5615 Scotts Valley Dr. #140
Scotts Valley, CA 95066
800/342-4763
408/438-8247

Setup Advisor
Touchstone Software Corp.
2130 Main St. #250
Huntington Beach, CA 92648
800/531-0450
714/969-7746

Hard Disk Installation Utilities

CorelSCSI
Corel Systems Corp.
1600 Carling Ave.
Ottawa, Ontario
  Canada K1Z 8R7
800/836-3729
613/728-8200

Disk Manager
Ontrack Data Recovery
6321 Bury Dr.
Eden Prairie, MN 55346
800/752-1333

EZ-Drive
Micro House Int'l
4900 Pearl East Cir. #101
Boulder, CO 80301
800/926-8299
303/443-3388

SCSI Card Manufacturers

Adaptec, Inc.
691 S. Milpitas Blvd.
Milpitas, CA 95035
800/959-7274
408/945-8600

Always Technology Corp.
31336 Via Colinas Dr.
Westlake Village, CA 91362
818/597-1400

Creative Labs, Inc.
1901 McCarthy Blvd.
Milpitas, CA 95035
800/998-1000

Future Domain
2801 McGaw Ave.
Irvine, CA 92714
800/879-7599
714/253-0400

CPU Upgrade Manufacturers

Cyrix Corp.
2703 N. Central Pkwy.
Richardson, TX 75080
800/462-9749
214/994-8388

Intel Corp.
End User Components Division
1900 Prairie City Rd.
Folsom, CA 95630
800/525-3019

Kingston Technology Corp.
17600 Newhope St.
Fountain Valley, CA 92708
800/835-6575
714/435-2600

LCC Computers, Inc.
2110 Matheson Blvd. East
Mississauga, Ontario
  Canada L4W 5E1
800/265-3552
416/624-6700

9 Protect Your Data

By Daniel Tynan

- The perils of PCs and how to protect yourself
- Backup software, tape drives, and proven methods
- How to inoculate your system against viruses
- Keeping your data private, safe, and sound
- Power protection: surge suppressors and UPSs
- How to successfully burglar-proof your PC

Forget what anybody else tells you. The most important part of your PC isn't your hard disk, your monitor, or those overpriced bits of silicon under the hood—it's your data. Why? Because it's the one thing you can't replace.

Yet your data is in jeopardy this very minute. Sooner or later, your hard disk will die. At any time, viruses—those lethal little programs created with evil intent—could infect your PC and turn your files to oatmeal. If your PC is in an office, careless or disgruntled employees could steal your data or use it for target practice. Thieves may walk off with your hardware; power surges and failures can wipe out hours of work; fires, floods, earthquakes, and other disasters of Biblical proportion could strike...

Feeling paranoid yet? Don't sit there worrying—do something! You can prevent many of these calamities, and recover from the rest. This chapter will show you how. Skip it at your peril.

Back It Up or Lose It All

You've probably heard this before: The best way to protect yourself against disaster is to have an up-to-date copy of your data, called a *backup*, on hand. Even if your machine goes belly up, you can transfer the backup data onto another computer's hard disk and be up and working again in no time.

REMEMBER

If you want to gamble, go to the racetrack. If you want to keep your data safe and sound, back up your hard disk. Here's how.

Backup Basics

The task is simple: You want to copy data from your hard disk to a floppy disk—or to a tape cartridge, which holds much more data but requires a tape drive (a low-cost device discussed a little later on). You want this copying stuff to be painless, with as little intervention from you as possible.

Backup software is designed to make the whole process pretty much automatic. You pick the files you want to back up, and the software starts filling up floppies (or tape cartridges), prompting you for new ones as needed.

But backing up is only half the story. Eventually, you'll need to reverse the process and restore files by copying part or all of your backup data back to your hard disk. Backup software's ability to *restore* comes in handy when:

• Your hard disk bites the dust or becomes infected by a virus

• You accidentally delete a file or directory and can't undelete it

• You need to revert to an earlier version of a file

People often forget that backup programs create a handy index of all the files in your set of backup disks or tapes. So if you accidentally delete a single file, you can just scan the index, find the file, and restore it quickly—without having to restore other data in the process.

HOT TIP

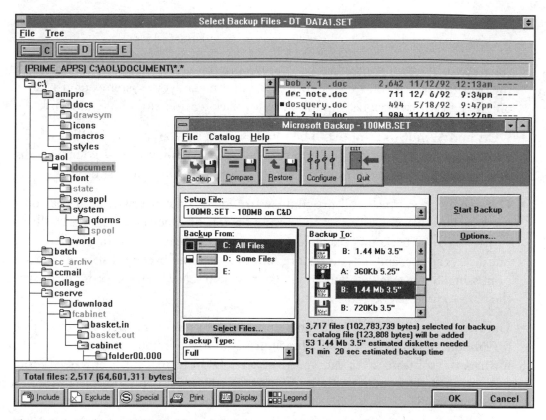

Figure 1: *A standard part of DOS, Microsoft Backup sprouts a directory tree that makes it easy to pick the files you want to back up. Unfortunately, the program doesn't support tape drives.*

Backup Software

DOS comes with two backup programs: Microsoft Backup for DOS and Microsoft Backup for Windows. The best thing about these programs is their cost (free). Is it worth peeling off another $100 for a different backup program, or should you stick with DOS's? It all depends on what you want your backup program to do. Here are the buy-or-die features you should look for, only some of which are found in DOS's backup software:

- **Easy file selection.** You should be able to choose drives, directories, and files for backing up and restoring data by clicking on a map of your hard disk called a *directory tree.* You can then refine your backup to include or exclude files by extension (like DOC), date range, attribute (such as read-only), and so on.

- **Automatic backups.** Once you've made your selections, you should be able to save them in a setup file (or *script*), which then runs automatically at a specified day and time—even when you're not around. Some programs come with prefab scripts for backing up, say, all your word processing or spreadsheet files.

HOT TIP

- **Backups while you work.** Many Windows programs let you perform backups "in the background" as you work. A nice idea, but it makes your system sluggish, so it's only practical for quick backup jobs, not for backing up your whole hard disk.

- **DOS and Windows support.** The top programs let you use the DOS version of their programs to restore a backup created under Windows, so if your hard disk dies, you won't have to reinstall Windows before restoring the rest of your data.

- **Data security.** Virtually all programs warn you against overwriting a previously used backup disk or restoring an old file on top of a newer one. Most will also verify that your backup is readable, compare backup data to the original to ferret out discrepancies, and let you restore files even if some backup disks are damaged or missing. Some even let you protect your backup sets with passwords and encrypt the data so no one else can read it.

- **Data compression.** Most programs shrink files to minimize the number of disks (or amount of tape) you'll need. How much compression you get depends on what formats the software saves data in. Most offer DOS format (uncompressed), their own compressed format, and the QIC format (the most common format for tape drive cartridges).

HOT TIP

- **High-speed backup.** The best backup programs support *Direct Memory Access (DMA)*, which means the software can read your hard disk at the same time it's storing information on floppy or cartridge, boosting backup speed. However, DMA conflicts are frequent, so the ability to turn off DMA is as important as having it.

- **Support for tape drives.** Any backup software worth its salt supports tape drives as well as floppy disks, which makes backing up big hard disks much easier.

The Three-and-a-Half Best Backup Programs

Unless your hard disk is pretty small—or unless you like swapping floppies a whole lot—you'll want a tape drive to back up your whole hard disk. Neither the DOS nor Windows version of DOS's Microsoft Backup work with tape drives. But *Central Point Backup, The Norton Backup for Windows*, and *Fastback Plus* all do, and they have more features, too. For Windows backup, I prefer *Central Point Backup* because it's a touch easier to use than *Norton Backup for Windows*. For DOS diehards, I'd give *Fastback Plus* the nod—it's the champ at moving files between systems and a no-brainer for novices.

Microsoft Backup

Though you can't use them with tape, both the DOS and Windows versions of Microsoft Backup feature a snazzy graphical directory tree and let you create your own backup scripts. If your hard disk goes down for the count and you need to

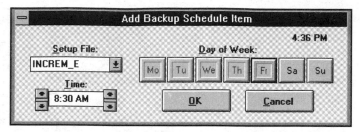

Figure 2: *Central Point makes scheduling backups so easy, even your boss may be able to do it. Simply select a backup script, click on a time and a day, and you're done.*

restore *everything*, compatible DOS and Windows versions mean you can restore files without reinstalling Windows first. But without support for DMA, Microsoft Backup is slow, and there's no way to schedule automatic backups. Even if you don't care about tape drives, it's worth saying no to Microsoft and buying a better program.

Central Point Backup

You can buy *Central Point Backup* by itself, or as a part of the *PC Tools* utility library, which comes in both DOS and Windows versions (see Chapter 21: *Utilities* for more on utility libraries). For my money *Central Point Backup* is the easiest backup package to use. It does just about everything, and it comes with scads of predefined backup scripts, as well as a slick scheduler. Built-in virus scanning means you may not have to shell out extra bucks for a separate antivirus package. Best of all, for about $50 more you can get the whole enchilada—*PC Tools*—making it the bargain of the year.

The Norton Backup for Windows

Like *Central Point Backup*, *Norton Backup for Windows* can be bought separately or as part of a bigger package (*Norton Desktop for Windows*). The two look and work pretty much alike, with some exceptions—like a button you press at installation time that automatically schedules *Norton*'s backups each day at 4 p.m., or a macro recorder for capturing and replaying keystrokes. Also, *Norton Backup*'s Share feature lets other users on a *NetWare* network back up their hard disks to your tape drive, and vice versa. On the other hand, *Norton Backup* lacks data encryption or virus scanning. The real pain? Customizing your backup schedule is a hassle.

Fastback Plus

Fastback Plus is a variation on the old good news/bad news routine. The good news: You can schedule daily modified backups as well as weekly full backups at installation time, and selecting files to back up is a snap—you pick everything from a single screen. *Fastback*'s express menus option makes backup a breeze even

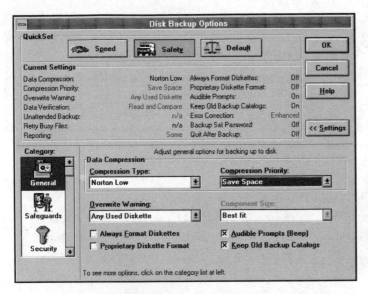

Figure 3: You can futz with Norton Backup for Windows' custom options 'til the cows come home—or simply press one of the three big buttons on top (Speed, Safety, or Default) and let Norton make the decisions for you.

for the technologically challenged. The bad news? Restoring files can be a pain, and its ASCII-only file viewer is useless for eyeballing most word processing or spreadsheet files. Still, *Fastback* packs some tasty features, like virus scanning and password protection, plus the ability to restore backups made with *Fastback*'s Mac version. It can also back up other hard disks on the network (server-based or peer-to-peer) to your tape drive, or shuffle files between desktop and laptop using a parallel cable.

Backup Hardware

Think you can back up your hard disk to floppies? Sure thing. To back up an entire 100MB, all you'd need would be 50 or 60 floppies and at least 45 minutes of your time feeding disks into the A: drive. Then you'd simply label and store all those disks. I live for this kind of scutwork, don't you?

With a tape backup drive, you can press a few keys and walk away—or better yet, schedule backups to occur when you're not around. One audio-cassette-sized 2.5-inch-by-3.25-inch tape cartridge can hold 250MB of compressed data, so few people will need to swap cartridges while backing up. And if you need to restore, you'll deal with one cartridge instead of all those floppies.

HOT TIP

The catch, of course, is that tape drives cost extra—usually around $150 for a basic model. The price rises with increased capacity and speed. If your hard disk is 80MB or smaller, you can live with floppy backups and save money. If your disk is bigger, buy a tape drive and save time and frustration.

Tape Drives for Beginners

Looking at things superficially, as I like to do, there are two kinds of tape drives: those that go inside your computer and those that go outside.

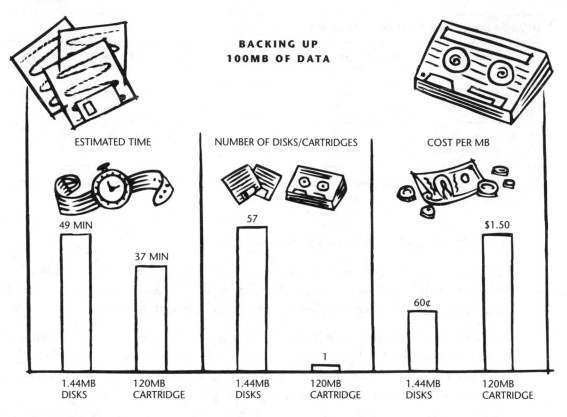

**BACKING UP
100MB OF DATA**

| ESTIMATED TIME | NUMBER OF DISKS/CARTRIDGES | COST PER MB |

49 MIN   37 MIN   57   1   60¢ $1.50

| 1.44MB DISKS | 120MB CARTRIDGE | 1.44MB DISKS | 120MB CARTRIDGE | 1.44MB DISKS | 120MB CARTRIDGE |

Figure 4: Tape backup vs. floppy stackup. *Tape backup beats floppy backup every which way but cost (if you figure in the cost of a tape drive). Best of all, you don't even have to be around when a tape drive does its stuff. Or would you rather swap 57 floppies?*

- **Internal drives** cost less than the ones that go outside. They install in an empty bay in the front of your computer, and plug into the same connectors used by your PC's floppy drives—or into a separate interface board you install in a free expansion slot.

- **External drives** are self-contained units that plug into a connector on the back of your PC. Most external drives come with an interface board, but some attach to your PC's parallel printer port—which makes them ideal for sharing among several machines, or for backing up computers that don't have room for an internal drive, such as laptops.

HOT TIP

Beyond this simple distinction, you plummet into Acronym Hell (DC2000, DC6000, IDE, SCSI...it never stops). Tape backup drives, whether internal or external, vary widely in speed, price, storage media, and the way they connect to your PC. Lucky for you I'm going to make it easy for you.

DC2000 Drives: The Tape Backups To Buy			
Tape format	**Native capacity**	**Compressed capacity[1]**	**Estimated drive price**
QIC-80	80MB or 125MB[2]	160MB or 250MB[2]	$100 to $250
QIC-3010	255MB or 340MB[2]	510MB or 680MB[2]	$300 to $400

[1]The 100-percent increase in tape capacity shown here is best case; you may get as little as 60 percent.
[2]Using extended-length tape.

Figure 5: Most people purchase inexpensive QIC-80 tape drives that attach right to the floppy disk controller. To get the maximum native or compressed capacity, buy an extended-length tape.

So You Want to Buy a Tape Drive

HOT TIP

Which kind should you get? Simple: Buy a DC2000 drive that uses either the QIC-80 or QIC-3010 tape format. The big names in tape backup are Colorado Memory Systems, Conner Peripherals, Iomega, and Mountain Network Solutions.

Personally, I like Colorado's DC2000 drives—they're cheap and work with hundreds of different PCs. But frankly, it doesn't matter much which vendor you buy from. Just make sure you find a model with the best balance of storage space, speed, and price. Here are some things to keep in mind as you shop:

- **Hardware compatibility.** Not all tape drives work with all computers. Before you plunk down any cash, call the tape drive vendor and verify that the model you want to buy will work with your PC. If you're planning to buy an internal drive, make sure it will fit inside your computer's empty drive bay. Most drives are designed to fit standard floppy bays, but some can squeeze into one-inch high "microfloppy" bays.

- **Software support.** All tape drives come with backup software, but it's generally pretty lame compared to software you can buy separately. If you buy a QIC-80 drive, you can rest assured your drive will be supported by backup software sold separately, such as the excellent *Central Point Backup*. If your tape drive uses another format, such as Conner's AccuTrak (formerly Irwin Servo), make absolutely sure that the software you buy supports it.

- **Speed.** DC2000 tape drives that hook to your system's floppy connector are generally slowest and cheapest. External models that plug into your parallel port are often just as slow but may cost twice as much. Things get faster when you buy a DC2000 model with an interface board, potentially twice as fast if it's an *accelerator* board (which means it has special speedup circuitry that adds significantly to the drive's price). SCSI models are even faster—but cost $700 and up. You don't want to pay that kind of money unless you're backing up a network.

- **Reliability.** Two clues to a tape drive's reliability are its *mean time between failure (MTBF)* rating and its warranty. The best models come with an MTBF rating of 40,000 hours or more and a two-year warranty.

Note: Buy preformatted tapes, when available. They cost more, but save the hour or two you spend formatting tapes the first time you use them.

HOT TIP

Backup Strategies

Backing up is like flossing: A little each day is more effective than a lot every six months. Nothing's more frustrating than needing to restore a file and discovering you never backed it up, or that your only backup copy is hopelessly out of date. The answer is to set up a schedule for doing backups and stick to it.

Here's the tricky part: There are actually three different kinds of backup techniques, each with its own pluses and minuses.

- **Full.** Backs up all files in whatever drives or directories you've specified. Full backups are the safest route for protecting your data but take the most time and storage space. Unless you're backing up a network server's hard disk, you'll rarely perform a full backup more than once a week.

- **Incremental.** Backs up only files that have changed since the last full or incremental backup. Incrementals are the fastest kind of backup and are best for daily backups.

- **Differential.** Backs up every file that's changed since the last time you did a full backup. Since you only need to keep the latest copy of a differential backup (as opposed to each day's incremental copy), they're easier to restore.

The most efficient backup strategy mixes regular full backups with daily incrementals or differentials, but never both. Remember: Incremental and differential backups go together like gasoline and matches. There's a chance you'll miss or overwrite a file, and attempting to restore from both kinds of backup sets would be a nightmare.

DANGER

Not everyone needs to follow the same backup strategy. The main question you need to ask is: How much data can I afford to lose? Here are some basic approaches.

The Bare Minimum

So you have a fair-size hard disk but you don't want to buy a tape drive? To cut the time spent shuffling floppies, you can ignore your program files (since you can always reinstall them from their original disks) and focus on your data.

HOT TIP

Back up all your data files once a month. To do this, you'll have to tell your backup software to copy only those files that have specific data file extensions (DOC, XLS, and so on). Better yet, store your data files in a different drive or directory (such as C:\DATA) than your program files, with data file subdirectories for word processing, spreadsheets, databases, and so on. Then you can simply tell the software to back up only those directories.

REMEMBER

Every day, do a differential or incremental backup of your modified data. You can't get away with less.

Backups by the Book

The problem with the data-file-only approach is that it could take forever (longer, if you lost the original disks) to reinstall your software if everything goes kaput. And full data-file backups a month apart are risky, since you may not discover in time that one of your backup floppies was marinated in coffee. The solution: Buy a tape drive and do a full backup of all files (programs and data) once a week, and incrementals each day. Then create two backup scripts—one for full backups, another for daily incrementals—and use the software's scheduling module to run them automatically.

The Anal-Retentive Backup

If losing even an hour's worth of data is a potential disaster, modify your backup schedule to perform several incremental backups per day. If you use Windows, you can run them in the background as you work. Most Windows backup programs won't back up a file if it's being used by another program, so you'll have to close the file before you start the backup.

Network Backup

Because LANs typically store files vital to a company's existence, they require the most tenacious backup strategy. If you're maintaining a server-based LAN, you'll want to do a full backup of the server's hard disk each night. Setting up unattended backups using a high-speed SCSI tape drive is the best way to go (see Chapter 22: *About Networks* for more on network servers).

A handful of products, such as *ARCserve* and *Network Archivist*, enable you to automatically back up all the workstations on the LAN using software on the server—but you'd better have a huge-capacity backup device, or else someone to stand around and swap tapes. For smaller, peer-to-peer LANs, Symantec's *Fastback Plus* and Artisoft's *Artisave* let you back up several hard disks on the LAN to a tape drive installed on one system.

If you plan to archive older network backup tapes, keep a written log of what files and directories you backed up, when you did it, and what tapes you used. This will make it a lot easier to find and restore older files.

HOT TIP

Storing and Labeling Backups

Doing regular backups earns you plenty of good computer karma, but it's not worth much if you misplace or mislabel your backup disks or tapes, or if your only copies are destroyed in a fire.

Rotating Media

The bunch of disks or tapes you use to back up your data is collectively called a *backup set*. Always use at least two sets and alternate between them. If one set gets damaged or lost, you can restore your data using the previous set. You'd still lose a few days' work, but it's better than starting from scratch.

REMEMBER

If you typically work with a handful of files each day, use tapes for full backups and floppies for modified ones. You probably won't need much storage space for daily backups, and you'll save the cost of buying a third tape.

HOT TIP

The E-Z Disaster-Protection Plan					
Monday	**Tuesday**	**Wednesday**	**Thursday**	**Friday**	**Monday**
Full backup (Set A)	Modified files only (Set B)	Modified files only (Set B)	Modified files only (Set B)	Modified files only (Set B)	Full backup (Set C)

Figure 6: *On Monday do your first full backup using Set A. Tuesday through Friday, use another batch of disks or tapes (Set B) to perform incremental or differential backups of modified files. The following Monday do another full backup using a third set, and move Set A into off-site storage for safekeeping. Then repeat the process, erasing and reusing Set B for modified files, and alternating between Sets A and C for full backups and off-site storage.*

Storage

Observe these three Golden Rules for storing backups:

1. Store backup disks separately from other floppies, preferably in their own disk caddy, away from dust, moisture, and smoke.

2. Keep backup sets away from phones, monitors, power supplies, and anything else that gives off a magnetic field that can erase their contents.

3. Always keep one recent full backup copy in a secure place off site.

REMEMBER

A backup set is worthless if your computer has been stolen or destroyed in a fire and you don't have another system where you can restore your data. So scout out a compatible system before disaster strikes.

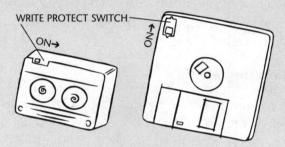

Backing Up Forever

Who wants ancient files rattling around a hard disk? No one, especially if disk space is at a premium. If you need to keep those files for history's sake, you can use backup software to archive them. Just back up the files as you normally would, use the software's *compare* option to ensure that the backups are valid, and erase the originals from your hard disk. Be sure to store archive media separately from your backup sets, and write-protect the archive disks or tapes. DC2000 minicartridges have a black plastic tab in the upper-left corner; slide the tab to the right to keep your data safe.

WRITE PROTECT SWITCH

ON→

←NO

Figure 7: *When you archive old data, remember to flick the write protect switch to keep yourself from accidentally using the disk or tape.*

Backup Labeling

Here's the most tedious part. But believe me, you don't want to sit there staring at a disk trying to remember which backup is on it. So label each backup disk and cartridge with the following:

• **The date** the disk or tape was first formatted

• **The type** of backup (full, incremental, differential)

• **The drives** or directories backed up (C: and D:, C:\DATA, etc.)

• **The date** of the backup

• **The number** of the disk or tape in the set ("Set A/Disk 5")

Why bother with the date of the first format? Because most disks and tapes wear out after about two years, and you'll want to know when to think about replacing them.

If you're religious about regular backups, you can label disks or tapes with "Daily" or "Weekly" (or the day of the week when you do it) instead of the date. Add your name or initials if your backup sets are stored in the same place as other people's sets.

Killer Viruses

A software virus is a program whose sole purpose is to wreak havoc with your system—a technoweenie's idea of a practical joke. Viruses range from annoying but harmless creatures that pop up stupid messages on your screen, to malevolent beasts that can trash all the data on your hard disk—and crash your computer so badly that it could take a techie all day to bring it to life again.

Viruses are nasty business. Once one gets into your system it can replicate, hide inside other programs, and spin off new viruses. It can lurk silently on your hard disk for months and suddenly strike when the PC's internal clock reaches a certain day (like Friday the 13th).

Fortunately, your system can't develop a virus spontaneously on its own—it can only catch one from infected floppy disks or files. In truth, most users will spend their entire lives without encountering a virus. Nevertheless, your odds of contracting a virus increase if you engage in any of the following activities:

1. You download program files from private bulletin boards

2. You exchange floppy disks with other users

3. You purchase software that has been returned to the store and repackaged

4. You share program files via electronic mail or across a LAN

You probably belong to group #2, and you probably don't know whether or not you belong to group #3. There's also a slim chance your new hard disk was infected at the factory. That's why, to be on the safe side, everyone should employ some kind of strategy for detecting and eradicating viruses.

Antivirus Software to the Rescue

Fortunately, there's a cure for these vile creatures. More than two dozen utilities detect viruses and remove them, and many cost under $50. Here's how they work.

A Brief, Disgusting Guide to Viruses

There are more than 2000 known software viruses, with new ones born every day. Essentially, there are two different types:

- **Boot sector viruses** take up residence in the part of your hard disk where the computer stores the files it needs in order to start up (the boot sector). They become active each time you turn on or reboot your computer. Boot viruses spread via infected floppy disks.

- **Program infectors** attach themselves to any file that runs a program (or part of a program), like those with the extensions EXE, COM, DLL, and DRV. They activate whenever the file is run, or install themselves as terminate-and-stay-resident (TSR) programs that hang around in your PC's memory and infect other programs. Program viruses can be contracted from floppies, electronic bulletin boards, and networks.

Some viruses attack both the boot sector and program files. There are also a few especially pernicious subspecies:

- **Stealth viruses** attempt to escape detection by undoing any changes they've made to a file's size, creation date, or other attributes (factors that usually indicate the presence of a virus).

- **Polymorphic (or self-mutating) viruses** continually change their internal code so that they look different with each infected file, making them harder to identify.

- **Trojan horse** programs pretend to be legitimate software (typically games) while secretly infiltrating files on your hard disk causing either mischief or serious damage. A Trojan horse is not a true virus because it doesn't replicate itself. Some antivirus programs detect and destroy Trojan horse programs anyway.

Detection

There are three methods antivirus utilities use to diagnose viral infection:

- **Signature search.** Every antivirus program begins by scanning your PC's memory and hard disk for hundreds of virus "signatures"—telltale strings of text that inform the utility a known virus is present. Because saboteurs constantly cook up new viruses, most antivirus software developers release regular updates of the virus signature database.

- **File snapshots.** When program files change, trouble may be afoot. Most virus scanners take mathematical snapshots of program files right after installation and sound the alarm if changes occur.

- **System watchdogs.** The best method for detecting new or unknown viruses is to look for "viruslike" behavior, such as attempts to format your hard disk or change program files.

Disinfection

Once antivirus software detects a virus, it pulls out the scalpel and goes to work. Depending on the kind of virus and the extent of its destruction, it may:

- **Remove** the virus and repair the damage

- **Delete** the file and instruct you to restore a previous version (another good reason for doing regular backups)

- **Tell you to restart** your PC and with a clean boot disk in drive A:. Many antivirus programs will create a disk (sometimes called a "rescue" or "emergency" disk) that you can use to restore your hard disk's original boot sector files. Make sure you write-protect the floppy after creating it so it doesn't also become infected.

HOT TIP

The Inoculators

Antivirus mania has hit the mainland. You'll now find antivirus utilities in communications programs, utility libraries, backup software, and data security packages—not to mention DOS. If you rarely haunt BBSs or swap floppies with other users, DOS's virus protection may be all you need.

No antivirus utility can cure every virus, and some of these vermin are specifically designed to thwart a particular antivirus program. If you belong to any of the high-risk groups listed at the beginning of this section, most virus gurus recommend using two antivirus packages—one to scan your disks when you start up your PC, and another to stay resident in memory in case of sudden attacks.

HOT TIP

```
┌─ ──────────── Verify Error ────────────┐
│  ┌──┐  C:\CONFIG.SYS              ┌─ Update ─┐
│  │  │  File has been changed.     └──────────┘
│  └──┘                             ┌─ Repair ─┐
│           From:        To:        └──────────┘
│                                   ┌─ Stop ───┐
│  Attribute:  ...A        ...A     └──────────┘
│  Time:       13:51:14    10:09:00 ┌─ Continue┐
│  Date:       10/15/1994  10/27/1994└──────────┘
│  Size:       185         185
│  Checksum    FEFB        FEFB
└──────────────────────────────────┘
```

Figure 8: *When Microsoft Anti-Virus discovers that an important file has been altered, it gives you the option of accepting the changed file and updating its mathematical portrait, repairing it, ignoring the changes, or stopping the scan to delete the file and restore a backup copy.*

A fact of life with antivirus software is the inevitable false alarm. Every time a program file changes size—when you upgrade an application, for example—the virus scanner will flag it as a virus. That's why antivirus software should be easy to turn *off.* You should

REMEMBER

also be able to use a simple command to tell the software that updated program files are OK, so they aren't flagged again and again when your disk is scanned (unless they suspiciously change again, of course). Without these features, nerve-wracking alarms will make you give up on antivirus software forever.

HOT TIP

If you ask me, the most painless antivirus package is *The Norton AntiVirus*. It automates virtually everything, from scanning at startup to loading the TSR; changing program defaults is a matter of clicking your way through a few dialog boxes, and shutting off the TSR is a snap.

But why take my word for it? Log on to CompuServe, GEnie, or some other on-line service and you'll find several cheap antivirus shareware packages you can try before you buy. Simply do a search on the keyword VIRUS, scroll through the various forums, and download to your heart's content (see Chapter 21 for more on shareware).

The Seven Warning Signs of Viruses

Has your system been infected? If you notice any of these symptoms, grab the nearest antivirus program, run a virus scan, and keep your fingers crossed:

1. Your PC is inexplicably slow

2. Files suddenly disappear from your disk

3. Program files increase in size

4. Your hard disk light flashes for no apparent reason

5. Your computer crashes repeatedly or reboots unexpectedly

6. Odd messages appear on your screen (like "your computer is now stoned")

7. The same problems occur on several computers in your office

Of course, you could have some of these problems and still not have a virus. And some of the most successful viruses show no outward signs at all. That's why, to be safe, you should run an antivirus scan every time you start your PC.

The Top Five Virus Programs

Company:	Central Point Software	McAfee Associates	Microsoft	Ontrack Computer Systems	Symantic
Product:	AntiVirus	ViruScan, Clean-Up, VShield	Anti-Virus[1]	Dr. Solomon's Anti-Virus Toolkit	The Norton AntiVirus
Checks for viruses during install	Y	N	N	Y	Y
Schedules virus scans	Y	N	N	Y	Y
Automatically scans disk at startup	Y	N[2]	N[2]	Y	Y
Scans individual directories or files	Y	Y	N	N	Y
Monitors system for viruslike activity	Y	Y	Y	N	Y
Detects and removes:					
Stealth	Y	Y	Y	Y	Y
Polymorphic	Y	Y	Y	Y	Y
Trojan horse programs	Y	Y	Y	Y	Y
Creates boot sector disk	Y	N	N	Y	Y
Scans compressed files	Y	Y[3]	N	Y[4]	Y
Scans network drives	Y	Y	Y	Y	Y
Immunizes files	Y	N	N	N	N
Minimum TSR RAM required	8K	1.5K	8K	7K	2K
Maximum TSR RAM required	46K	46K	46K	130K	40K
Virus updates via BBS	Y	Y	Y	N	Y

[1]Included with DOS.
[2]Yes if you add a line to your AUTOEXEC.BAT.
[3]PKLite and LZ executable files only.
[4]File compression utility must be in same subdirectory.

Figure 9: *Microsoft Anti-Virus comes free with DOS, but you'll probably want more than what it has to offer. Norton AntiVirus is a good bet because it has a full set of features and simplifies setting up automatic scans.*

Ten Tips for Fighting Infection

1. Start your system using a clean, write-protected boot disk, and then scan your hard disk using antivirus software in the floppy drive.

2. Set up your antivirus program to scan your most important program files (like COMMAND.COM and your word processor or spreadsheet applications) every morning when you turn on the computer.

3. Schedule weekly virus scans of all the executable files on your disk.

4. Scan any boot disks you've created and write-protect them.

5. Scan all new floppies before copying files from them to your hard disk.

6. Scan any network drives you use (better yet, have your LAN administrator scan all network drives each day).

7. Scan any program files attached to E-mail messages or downloaded from a BBS or on-line service. Most BBS sysops scan files before uploading them, but it never hurts to double-check.

8. Back up program installation disks to clean floppies and write-protect them *before* you install new software. That way, a virus can't infect your original program disks.

9. Use a memory-resident virus detector to sniff out new virus strains.

10. Update your antivirus software's virus database every three months—or sooner if you notice symptoms but your utility hasn't detected anything.

PC Security: Who Needs It?

The scariest threat to your data isn't hardware failure or software viruses, it's other humans. When you screw up—delete an important file or accidentally reformat your hard disk—you realize it immediately and can usually undo the damage. But if somebody else screws up your system, accidentally or otherwise, you may not find out until it's too late.

Do you really need to worry about security? You do if:

1. You share a computer with someone else (like a child, co-worker, or hostile spouse)

2. You keep confidential or personal files on your PC at work and you want them to stay that way

3. You maintain sensitive company files and need to prevent tampering or damage

Keeping data secure means controlling access—to your files and directories, your hard disk, or your PC itself. How much security do you need? If you're in group 1, you can probably get by with the simple techniques outlined in the section that immediately follows. If you're in group 2 or 3, you'll need to look at the options discussed in the section "More Stringent Measures."

Minimum Security PCs

Unless you're a work-at-home hermit or you keep your office door locked at all times, it's a safe bet that other people have access to your PC when you're not around. Fortunately, there are several things you can do to protect yourself against accidental damage or unwanted intrusion—and, best of all, they won't cost you a dime.

- **Use the system** lock on your desktop PC to prevent the computer from accepting keyboard input.

- **Define a system password** using your PC's setup program. For the system to load DOS, you have to type the magic word.

- **Use built-in password protection** in *Word for Windows, 1-2-3*, and other popular apps that let you limit access to certain files.

- **Password-protect your screen saver** to keep your PC secure when you escape from your desk. A password prompt comes up when anyone touches your mouse or keyboard. You can assign passwords to Windows' built-in screen saver and Berkeley Systems' *After Dark* program. **HOT TIP**

- **Log off E-mail** when you leave your desk. If you don't, anyone can read your private mail and send messages to other people in your name.

- **Make important files read-only,** so they can't be changed or deleted. There are two easy ways to do this. Switch to the directory where the file is stored and type ATTRIB *filename* +R at the DOS prompt (substituting the name of the file you want to protect for *filename*, with a space before the plus sign). Or you can use Windows' File Manager to highlight the file name, select File//Properties, and put an X next to the "Read Only" attribute. To undo this process, simply type ATTRIB *filename* -R or uncheck the Read Only box. **HOT TIP**

- **Put confidential files in hidden directories.** A hidden directory won't show up when you issue a DIR command, so only you will know it's there. To hide directories you can use the same ATTRIB command, but type the directory name followed by +H; or select the Hidden attribute in File Manager's Properties box. When you

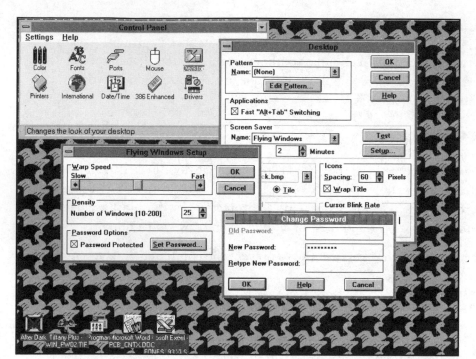

Figure 10:
Password-protecting Windows' screen saver makes it hard for other users to sneak onto your desktop when you're not around. Simply select the Desktop from Windows' Control Panel, click the screen saver Setup button, followed by Set Password. Then type in the secret word.

want to view the directory in File Manager, select View//By File Type and check the box next to Show Hidden/System Files.

Naturally, you need to find the right balance between security precautions and ease of use. You wouldn't want to lock every door in your house, and you don't want to hide every file on your disk.

More Stringent Measures

A skilled PC sneak can easily find his or her way around most of the simple techniques discussed above. To protect against deliberate damage, you'll need to spend a little money on one (or more) of the kinds of products listed here.

Floppy Drive Locks

A drive lock will keep potential vandals from booting up your system with a floppy disk to bypass the password protection on your hard disk. These devices slide into your floppy drive and lock with the turn of a key. Drive locks cost from $13 to $50; see the end of the chapter for a list of manufacturers.

Data Encryption Software

Even hidden and password-protected files can be read using a utility like *The Norton Utilities*. Data encryption software scrambles your files so that no one can read them—at least until you issue the password (called a *key*) that unlocks their secrets. Encryption is particularly useful for:

- Sending confidential files via electronic mail, where privacy is less than assured

- Protecting sensitive company data on notebook PCs, lest the little machines fall into the wrong hands

Most encryption programs use a *public/private* key approach. To send your best friend Ted a scrambled file, you'd run the file through an encryption program and assign it a key that Ted provided (the public key). Ted would then unscramble the file using a private key that only he knows. The same is true in reverse—for Ted to send you an encrypted file, he'd have to know your public key. Sort of like two halves of the same password.

Serious encryption programs—the ones, like Information Security Corp.'s *SecretAgent*, that employ CIA-level encryption algorithms such as DES or RSA—are complex, expensive, and often so calculation-intensive that you'd need a special encryption chip in order to use them. Unless you're James Bond, you can get by with cheaper, simpler alternatives such as PC Guardian's *Encryption Plus* and CMG Products' *PC Padlock*. (*Encryption Plus* ships with all new Compaq notebooks.) These programs cost less than $50 and use a single key. *PC Tools* and *The Norton Utilities* also include capable encryption programs.

The Password Is...

Even the best data security system is only as secure as the passwords you choose. Here are some quick do's and don'ts in selecting passwords:

Do

- Use passwords of seven characters or more

- Change passwords every three months or so

- Store a written copy of your password in a safe place, such as a locked drawer—away from the computer

Don't

- Use your name, or that of your spouse, child, or pet

- Use "password" or "mypassword"

- Use your phone number, street address, or other easily accessible personal information

- Write your password on a Post-it note stuck to your desk, or file it in your Rolodex under *P*

HOT TIP

If all you want to do is scramble files on your hard disk, you can use *PKZip 2.04G's* built-in encryption switch. For $47 this popular shareware package lets you assign a password to compressed files. But remember: If you forget the password, there's no way to decompress the file.

Access Control Products

If your job is to safeguard the PCs for an entire department or organization, you may want to roll out the heavy artillery: access control software. These top-to-bottom security utilities let you assign different levels of security for each user, and they are usually designed to work on a LAN.

With access control software, you can password-protect just about anything, from floppy drives to individual directories, files, and applications. You can even lock out potentially damaging DOS commands, such as DEL or FORMAT, or design a menu system that prevents access to DOS completely. You can also encrypt data, create an audit trail of attempts at unauthorized entry, and assign a single password to whole groups of protected applications.

For more information about keeping your data secure, contact the National Computer Security Association. The NCSA provides its members with an electronic BBS, a newsletter, training services, a research library, and more. Membership fees start at $55 for individuals and $125 for corporations. NCSA, Attention: Jonathan Wheat, 10 S. Courthouse Ave., Carlisle, PA 17013; 717/258-1816, 717/243-8642 (fax).

Removable Storage Devices

The best way to keep your data safe is to store it on removable media and keep it under lock and key at night. A handful of storage devices let you take the data and leave the drive behind—and can even double as backup devices. These include complete hard disks that slip in and out like totable car radios, special cartridges such as the 150MB units used by Bernoulli Boxes, and magneto-optical drives that use 256MB disks that can fit in a shirt pocket. The trade-off? Most are slower than hard disks, and all are more expensive.

Access Control Software: Try and Break This!

Company:	Fisher Int'l	Mergent Int'l	PC Dynamics	PC Guardian	SafetyNet
Product:	Watchdog for Windows Personal Edition	PC/DACS	Menu Works Total Security	Data Security Plus	Stoplight ELS
Number of users	unlimited	unlimited	99	3	16
Controls access to:					
Hard disk	Y	Y	Y	Y	Y
Floppy drives	N[1]	Y	Y	N	Y
Keyboard	Y	N	Y	Y	Y
DOS commands	Y	Y	Y	Y	Y
Directories and files	N[1]	Y	Y	Y[3]	Y
Applications	Y	Y	Y	Y[3]	Y
Menu-based shell	N[2]	Y	Y	N	Y[3]
Antivirus utility	N[1]	Y	Y	Y	N[4]
Data encryption	Y	Y	Y	Y	N[4]
Creates audit trail	Y	Y	Y	Y[3]	Y
Single sign-on	Y	Y[3]	N	Y[3]	N[4]

[1] Available in full Watchdog package.
[2] Uses Windows' Program Manager.
[3] Extra-cost option.
[4] Available with full Stoplight package.

Figure 11: *When all else fails, these heavy-duty access control programs can protect any PC from being tampered with.*

~~~~~~

Avoid Power Struggles

Too much AC power surging from the wall socket can cause hard disk data errors, as well as damage your modem, motherboard, and other system components. Not enough juice can instantly shut down your PC, obliterating any data you haven't saved. AC power can be affected by faulty wiring, blackouts and brownouts, and lightning storms. Fortunately, there are dozens of devices designed to sit between your PC and the wall socket, smoothing out power problems. They fall roughly into three camps:

- **Surge suppressors** protect against power *spikes* and *surges*—sudden increases in voltage passing to your computer. Because spikes can cause catastrophic damage, every user needs a good surge suppressor. The simplest models are power strips with sockets for plugging in your PC, monitor, and other devices.

- **Line conditioners** (sometimes also called *voltage regulators*) protect against power sags, which account for more than 80 percent of all power problems. Most also defend your system against surges and interference generated by other electronic devices. If you live in an area where brownouts are frequent or the lights flicker every time you crank on the air conditioner, you'll want a line conditioner.

- **Uninterruptible power supplies** (UPSs) are battery-powered boxes that give you enough juice to safely shut down your system in case of a total blackout. They also protect against power surges and are a must for LAN servers and other PCs where critical data is constantly updated.

DANGER Some UPS vendors claim their products will protect your system when lightning strikes. But do you really want to find out? To be safe, turn off and unplug your PC, printer, and modem during electrical storms.

Power Shopping

You don't have to be an electronics whiz to figure out which suppressor, line conditioner, or UPS to buy. But you will need an idea of what PC devices you'll be plugging into it, and how much power they consume.

Surge Suppressors

Most people go to their local hardware store and buy a cheapo power strip. Pay a bit more for a power strip with surge suppression, and you'll be protected against surges and spikes. Prices start at around $20, but plan on paying about $50 for a good one. Here's what to look for:

- **Energy dissipation.** A suppressor's ability to dissipate power surges is rated in *joules*. Generally, the higher the joule rating, the more likely your suppressor will filter out power problems. But joule ratings can vary depending on the manufacturer. A more reliable measure is Underwriters Laboratories specification 1449, which gauges the maximum surge power the device will let through. The rating is expressed in peak volts, so lower numbers are better—the best suppressors have a UL 1449 rating of 330 volts.

- **Power control features.** Better surge suppressors provide LEDs that alert you to problems on the line. Some models are designed to sit under your monitor and let you turn everything on and off with a single switch. Others let you plug in phones and other devices as well as computer equipment. All of these features boost the quality (and cost) of the model.

Line Conditioners

Line conditioners use a special ferromagnetic transformer to maintain a steady flow of power, so you can keep computing even when the lights dim. As with surge suppressors, you'll want to get a model that comes with enough outlets and protects against voltage spikes as well as power sags. Prices range from $130 for an LC with two outlets to more than $500 for one with 14 sockets.

- **Capacity.** The main question is how much of a power load the LC can handle. Unfortunately, some vendors measure an LC's capacity in wattage, while others do it in volt-amps (VA). Here's the quick way to figure out how big an LC you need:

1. Make a list of everything you plan to plug into the line conditioner.

2. On the back of each device you should find a metal plate listing its maximum power needs in amps (1A = 1 amp). Write down all the amp figures and add them up. For example:

System unit (1.0A) + Monitor (1.5A) = 2.5 amps

3. Multiply the total amps by 120. This gives you your VA rating.

VA rating = 2.5A x 120 = 300 VA

4. To translate this figure into wattage, take the VA rating and multiply that by the device's power factor (which indicates how much of the juice flowing to the machine provides useful energy). With PCs the power factor is typically .6 (or 60 percent).

Wattage rating = 300 x .6 = 180 watts

Most PCs have VA ratings between 300 and 400, which means wattage ratings from 180 to 240. You'll need to add in the VA or wattage figures for your printer, external tape drive, and any other peripherals you plan to add. Then buy a line conditioner with 20 to 25 percent more capacity than you currently need, to leave room for adding new devices.

Uninterruptible Power Supplies

UPSs are designed with one thing in mind—to let you save data and exit applications gracefully during a total power failure. There are several types of UPSs, but most fit into two genres: *standby* models, where there's a lag of a few milliseconds between the moment everything goes dark and the instant the battery kicks in; and *on-line* UPSs, where there is no time lag. Prices range from $140 for individual PCs to several thousand dollars for units that can handle multiple network servers.

REMEMBER

- **Capacity**. Figuring out what capacity UPS to get involves the same mathematical process as line conditioners do. Fortunately, UPS vendors make life simpler by measuring everything in VA units. Some have even done the math for you, providing VA ratings for popular brands of PCs. But don't factor a printer into your UPS plans; printers suck huge amounts of power, and an interrupted print job is no disaster.

- **Shutdown time.** The capacity of your UPS also determines how much time you'll have before shutdown. At full load (when your system's power needs match the capacity of the UPS) you'll get at least 5 minutes of power. At half load you could get 20 minutes or more.

- **Power features.** Some UPSs come with built-in line conditioning, providing full blackout and brownout protection. Others feature their own lighting systems, so you can see your keyboard in the dark. On-line UPSs provide a continuous power source, minimizing the chance of data loss due to a power glitch. More advanced models have built-in hardware and software that automate shutdowns during unattended operations, such as overnight backups of a LAN.

Almost every UPS vendor carries a full line of surge suppressors and line conditioners; for information about specific products, contact the manufacturers listed at the end of this chapter.

REMEMBER

Whether you're buying a suppressor, line conditioner, or UPS, a five-year warranty (or better) is your best indication of product quality. The best products boast lifetime warranties and insurance policies against damage caused by power problems.

Power Insurance: How Much Time Are You Buying?

	\multicolumn{6}{c}{Volt-Amp Rating of Uninterruptible Power Supply}					
	250	400	450	600	900	1250
Your Power Load (in VA)	\multicolumn{6}{c}{Typical UPS Run Times (in minutes)}					
75	29	72	88	105	155	210
100	23	47	65	79	110	160
150	14	30	41	54	83	115
200	8	19	32	41	65	92
250	5	13	24	31	47	75
300	-	9	18	22	40	64
350	-	7	14	17	35	54
400	-	5	11	13	29	46
450	-	-	8	10	24	40
500	-	-	-	7	20	34
600	-	-	-	5	15	25
700	-	-	-	-	13	22
800	-	-	-	-	11	17
900	-	-	-	-	10	13
1200	-	-	-	-	-	9

Source: American Power Conversion

Figure 12: *Buying a UPS with a higher volt-amp rating gives you more juice when the lights go out—so you can keep on working, even in the dark.*

Burglar-Proof Your PC

Today's PCs are smaller and more portable than ever—which makes them prime candidates for theft. Short of strapping your PC to a pit bull, the best solution is an antitheft device. Some devices work like car alarms, guaranteed to deafen, if not deter, would-be burglars; others are the PC equivalent of The Club, designed to make pilfering your PC more trouble than it's worth.

Most antitheft devices make you attach brackets to your desktop CPU, monitor, keyboard, and printer, then feed a steel cable through each bracket and into a padlock. With laptops and notebooks, you plug the cable into a special slot or a port in the back of the machine and then loop it around something heavy, like the desk. Other devices put your computer inside a box that attaches to your desk with heavy-duty adhesives. Both kinds can be a hassle to dismantle when you need to pop the PC's hood and install a new device, or simply move the machine—but not as much of a hassle as replacing your computer.

- **Anchor Pad** offers a variety of antitheft devices, ranging from simple cables that loop between your computer and peripherals to reinforced steel cabinets for housing your PC. Anchor Pad Products, Ivie Industries, 800/626-2467.

- **CMG's Locking Station** is aimed at those who use a notebook in the office as well as on the road. This lockbox attaches to your desk with super-adhesive, two-sided tape, and provides small openings for hooking up an external monitor, keyboard, and other peripherals. When you want to take the machine on the road, you unlock a steel drawer and slide it out. CMG Computer Products, 800/880-9980.

- **The Elert Personal Portable Alarm** straps to your desktop PC, laptop, or even your briefcase. Once the motion detector alarm is tripped, the battery-powered unit emits a 107dB shriek, and keeps shrieking until you enter a three-digit code on its keypad—or until it runs out of juice (about two-and-a-half hours later). Quorum International, 312/471-2659.

- **Kablit Security System** attaches to your portable or desktop PC using existing system screws or powerful glues. Secure-It, 800/451-7592.

- **Kensington Microware's MicroSaver** is a portable cable system designed to keep people from walking away with your laptop. The locking device fits into an existing security slot in Apple PowerBooks, AST PowerExecs, Compaq LTEs, and Toshiba T1800 and T4500 laptops. Kensington Microware Ltd., 800/535-4242.

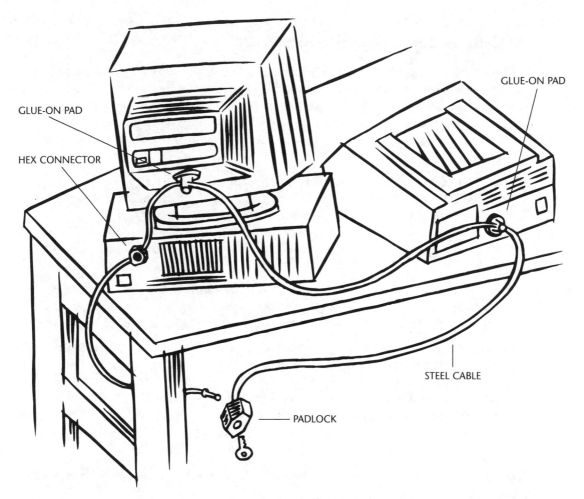

GLUE-ON PAD

GLUE-ON PAD

HEX CONNECTOR

STEEL CABLE

PADLOCK

Figure 13: *With this typical $50 security system, you attach brackets to your PC and its expensive friends and string together the whole deal with steel cable. One look at this setup and most burglars will head straight for your VCR.*

- **The SonicPro 128B** looks like an inexpensive pocket calculator—until you try moving it and get 110dB of earsplitting noise. The 128B adheres to your desktop or laptop with heavy-duty double-sided tape. An internal silicon chip lets you program the alarm's sensitivity, duration, and delay, as well as set up two user ID numbers. Each unit requires four AAA batteries and comes with a three-year $5000 theft-protection policy. SonicPro International, 800/848-0300.

PC Insurance: Are You Covered?

Homeowners' and renters' insurance policies typically have a $5000 liability limit on hardware and software, and they rarely cover damage from power surges and other common computer ills—not to mention losses outside the home (like your notebook PC getting stolen at the airport). If you use your PC to run a home business, your homeowner's policy may not cover you at all. The following agencies offer separate policies that specifically cover your computer:

The Computer Insurance Agency	Data Security Insurance	Safeware
6150 Old Millersport Rd. NE	4800 Riverbend Rd.	The Insurance Agency
Pleasantville, OH 43148	Boulder, CO 80301	2929 N. High St.
800/722-0385	800/822-0901	Columbus, OH 43202-0211
614/263-5100	303/442-0900	800/848-3469
		614/262-0559

These companies provide the full replacement value for hardware and software up to the amount of coverage, including losses from power surges, lightning, viruses, and theft of your notebook on the road. Annual premiums range from $50 to $130, depending on the policy.

Regardless of what insurance you get, remember to keep good records of all equipment and software purchased, including serial numbers and date purchased, as well as all invoices, canceled checks, and credit statements. Be sure to register your software, too (some policies won't cover the loss of programs that aren't registered). Finally, take photos or videotape of your equipment to help substantiate your claim.

HOT TIP

Product Directory

Access Control Software

Data Security Plus
PC Guardian Security Products
1133 E. Francisco Blvd., Suite D
San Rafael, CA 94901
800/288-8126
415/459-1162

Menu Works Total Security
PC Dynamics, Inc.
31332 Via Colinas #102
Westlake Village, CA 91362
800/888-1741
818/889-1741

PC/DACS
Mergent International
70 Inwood Rd.
Rocky Hills, CT 06067
203/257-4223

StopLight
Safetynet, Inc.
55 Bleeker St.
Millburn, NJ 07041
800/851-0188
201/467-1024

Watchdog for Windows, Personal Edition
Fischer International
Systems Corp.
4073 Merchantile Ave.
Naples, FL 33942
800/237-4510
813/643-1500

Backup Software

ARCserve
Cheyenne Software, Inc.
3 Expressway Plaza
Roslyn Heights, NY 11577
800/243-9462
516/484-5110

Central Point Backup
Central Point Software
15520 NW Greenbrier Pkwy.
 #200
Beaverton, OR 97006-9937
800/964-6896
503/690-8090

Network Archivist
Palindrome Corp.
600 E. Diehl Rd.
Naperville, IL 60563
800/288-4912
708/505-3300

The Norton Backup for Windows 3.0
Fastback Plus
Symantec Corp.
10201 Torre Ave.
Cupertino, CA 95014-2132
800/441-7234
408/252-3570

Antivirus Software

Central Point AntiVirus
Central Point Software
800/964-6896

Clean-Up
ViruScan
Vshield
McAfee Associates
2710 Walsh Ave. #200
Santa Clara, CA 95051-0963
408/988-3832

Dr. Solomon's Anti-Virus Toolkit
Ontrack Computer
 Systems, Inc
6321 Bury Dr. #16–19
Eden Prairie, MN 55346
800/752-1333
612/937-1107

The Norton AntiVirus
Symantec Corp.
800/441-7234

Data Encryption Utilities

Encryption Plus
PC Guardian Security Products
800/288-8126

PC Padlock
CMG Computer Products
P.O. Box 160310
Austin, TX 78716
800/880-9980
512/329-8220

PKZip 2.04G
PKWare
9025 N. Deerwood Dr.
Brown Deer, WI 53223
414/354-8699

SecretAgent
Information Security Corp.
1141 Lake Cook Rd., Suite D
Deerfield, IL 60015
800/843-1132
708/405-0500

Locks

Anchor Pad Data Security System

Ivie Industries
18700 Beach Blvd. #205
Huntington Beach, CA 92648
800/626-2467
714/842-2378

Disk Drive Lock

Secure-It
18 Maple Ct.
East Longmeadow, MA 01208
800/451-7592
413/525-7039

Disk Lock

Doss Industries
214 California Dr.
Burlingame, CA 94010
415/347-2301

Lockette

Z-Lock Manufacturing Co.
P.O. Box 949
Redondo Beach, CA 90277
310/372-4842

PC Guardian Floppy Drive Locks

PC Guardian Security Products
800/288-8126

SlotLock

Z-Lock Manufacturing Co.
310/372-4842

Surge Suppressors/UPSs

American Power Conversion
P.O. Box 278
132 Fairgrounds Rd.
West Kingston, RI 02892
800/800-4APC
401/789-5735

Best Power Technology
P.O. Box 280
Necedah, WI 54646
800/356-5794
608/565-7200

Curtis Manufacturing
30 Fitzgerald Dr.
Jaffrey, NH 03452
800/955-5544
603/532-4123

Tripp Lite
500 N. Orleans
Chicago, IL 60610-4188
312/329-1391

Tape Backup Hardware

Colorado Memory Systems
800 S. Taft Ave.
Loveland, CO 80537
800/451-0897 x172
303/669-8000

Conner Peripherals
36 Skyline Dr.
Lake Mary, FL 32746
800/526-6637
407/263-3500

Iomega Corp.
1821 W. Iomega Way
Roy, UT 84067
800/777-6179
801/778-1000

Mountain Network Solutions
360 El Pueblo Rd.
Scotts Valley, CA 95066
800/458-0300
408/438-6650

10 When Things Go Wrong

By Eric Knorr

- Common DOS error messages and remedies
- Windows problems and what to do about them
- The basics of software data recovery
- Elementary hardware troubleshooting

When your PC does something unsociable, like give you a rude message or refuse to cough up the location of some vital file, it's usually because you accidentally clicked the wrong button or typed in the wrong command. That happens to the best of us, and "recovering" from this sort or error is quite easy.

But sometimes the problem is more serious—or worse, mysterious. Windows may make a habit of crashing, so that you have to reboot and abandon unsaved data every time. Or you may experience the ultimate terror: You turn on your PC and DOS tells you your hard disk isn't there.

Solutions exist for these sorts of predicaments, even the big ones. That's what you'll find in this chapter: common remedies for common ailments. However, the number of PC problems is exceeded only by the number of causes, and trained professionals are often stumped by puzzles that seemed simple at first. This chapter doesn't even come close to covering every possibility. As a quick reference, though, it may help.

This chapter should be used in conjunction with the previous one, Chapter 9: *Protect Your Data*. There you'll find out all about the best disaster protection—creating regular backup copies of your data. If you have a recent backup, lightning can fry your PC, and you needn't worry about anything except your insurance coverage. Chapter 9 also explains how to tell if you're under attack by a computer virus, and how to eradicate the thing.

Note that you'll find a separate section on communications problems at the end of Chapter 20: *Communications*, which may come in especially handy if you have diffculties with modem communications under Windows. Also note that solving network problems is not in the scope of this chapter or this book. Let network professionals deal with those headaches—that's what they're paid for.

Simple DOS Error Messages

Usually, these very common messages mean that you screwed up a little on a procedure, no harm done. They're arranged from most to least common (more or less). If you're unfamiliar with any of the terms discussed below, turn to Chapter 12: *Windows and DOS*.

Bad command or filename

This message usually means you just mistyped a command. Or you tried to run a program by entering the name of an EXE, COM, or BAT file missing from both the current directory and your path (see Appendix A for more on the PATH statement).

File not found

If you enter a DOS command along with the name of a file you want to do something with, and you misspell the file name or the file isn't in the directory specified by the command, you get this message.

File cannot be copied onto itself

This is the closest DOS comes to having a sense of humor. If you use the COPY command followed by a file name and forget to enter the destination for the file copy, this message appears.

`Overwrite [file name] (Yes/No/All)?`

If you try to copy or move a file into a directory containing a file of the same name, DOS asks you if you really want to overwrite, that is, completely obliterate, the file in the directory. Usually, you enter y for Yes (or a for All when overwriting a group of files) only when you want to store a new version of a file and you don't care about the old version. Just make sure which version is which, because there's no way to recover overwritten files. If you're not sure, or you accidentally gave two files the same name, enter n for No and give one of the files a different name.

DANGER

`Syntax error`, `Invalid parameter`, or `Required parameter missing`

These messages indicate that you've entered some portion of a multi-part DOS command improperly. To figure out where you went wrong, consult Chapter 12's Cookbook, DOS's Help, or Appendix C.

`Invalid switch`

A *switch* is a character (preceded by a slash) that modifies a DOS command. For example, entering `format a:/s` would create a boot disk in the A: drive. If you entered `format a:/x` by mistake, you'd get this message.

`Insufficient disk space`

Most of the time this message appears when you try to copy more files onto a floppy than will fit. But in rare circumstances you may get this message when you try to save a file on your hard disk. If you're really low on hard disk space, you'll have to delete unnecessary files in order to save the file. If this message is a surprise and there should be plenty of space, this message may be a sign that your PC is infected by a virus (see Chapter 9: *Protect Your Data* for more on viruses).

DANGER

`Not ready reading drive A`
`Abort, Retry, Fail?`

Most of the time you get this message because you tried to access a floppy drive that didn't have a floppy disk in it (the drive letter could just as easily be B). In that case, just press a for Abort. However, sometimes you change to drive A:, remove the floppy disk before changing back to another drive, and accidentally enter a command. At that point, you get this message no matter what until you put the floppy disk back in the drive and press a. (In rare cases, you may get this message because the floppy disk is damaged; see "Data Recovery" later in this chapter.)

```
Non-System disk or disk error
Replace and strike any key when ready
```

You almost always get this message because you accidentally left a floppy disk in drive A: when you started or rebooted your PC. You don't need to "replace" anything—just remove the disk and press any key, and your system will boot normally.

Windows Problems

Windows has more social graces than DOS. For example, when you try to access an empty floppy drive, you get a dialog box explaining that there's no disk in the drive and that you should insert a disk and try again. In fact, most Windows messages are self-explanatory dialog boxes that pop up to confirm various actions you perform with the File Manager (for more on those messages, see Chapter 12's Cookbook).

Otherwise, Windows messages generally indicate something has gone wrong. Worse, depending on your hardware, what applications you're using, or some mysterious combination of the two, Windows may crash without any warning at all. This section gives you some of the common causes for these malfunctions and some simple advice on how you may be able to prevent them. One rule of thumb: Make sure there's at least 8MB of RAM in your system, and you'll vastly decrease the likelihood of Windows problems. If you have any less than 4MB, Windows won't like it, and neither will you.

DANGER

Crashes and Cures

Major Windows problems—the ones that cause you to lose unsaved data—fall roughly into two categories:

- **General Protection Faults.** Commonly known as the GPFs, these are the most dreaded Windows messages. At the least, a GPF indicates the application you've been working in is about to crash and that you should save all data right away. At the worst, it means that Windows itself is about to come tumbling down like a house of cards, taking all running applications with it. (Note that GPFs are often accompanied by a message saying that so-and-so application "violated system integrity." Don't believe it—Windows often blames the wrong software.)

REMEMBER

- **Freezes.** Sometimes the application you're using *freezes* or *hangs*, which means that it stops responding to all mouse or keyboard input. Your only recourse is to press Ctrl Alt Del, which should bring up a full screen explaining that your application has stopped responding to the system and that you have a choice of pressing [Esc] (which usually does nothing), [Enter] (which shuts down the application), or [Ctrl][Alt][Del] again (which reboots your system).

Always try [Esc] first—by some miracle, your application might start working again. When that doesn't do anything, press [Ctrl][Alt][Del] again and choose [Enter] to close the frozen application. If the application doesn't close and your screen is still frozen, as a last ditch effort to keep Windows running you might try pressing [Alt][Tab] to see if you can switch to another application, so you can at least save data in other apps—this works in rare cases. More likely, you'll be left with the last resort: pressing [Ctrl][Alt][Del] twice to reboot your PC.

HOT TIP

Sometimes a kind of deep freeze occurs, where [Ctrl][Alt][Del] does nothing at all. In that situation, you need to press your PC's reset button (if it has one) or turn off your PC and turn it on again.

If crashes happen once in a blue moon, you probably don't need to worry—it's just part of the cost of using Windows. But crashes on a regular basis are unacceptable. Although there are probably hundreds of reasons for GPFs and freezes, a few seem more likely than others. Try the following procedures, and if you're lucky, Windows may stop misbehaving.

Replace the Video Driver

Most people use Windows at a resolution higher than 640 by 480, the standard VGA resolution (see Chapter 5: *Monitors, Etc.* to learn about the mysteries of graphics cards). To accomplish this, all graphics cards come with a Windows *driver*—a small program enabling software and hardware to communicate—that must be installed through a simple procedure. Unfortunately, Windows drivers are often poorly written and are a common cause of Windows crashes.

REMEMBER

To see if your Windows driver is the culprit, try using Windows at ordinary VGA resolution for a while. Follow this procedure:

1. In the Main group, double click on Setup.

2. Pull down the Options menu and select Change System Settings.

3. Drop down the scrolling Display list, select VGA, and click OK.

4. Click the Current button and accept Windows' suggestion to reboot.

When Windows comes up again, you may have to adjust your monitor to center the image properly, and your Windows desktop will very likely be smaller. But if the driver was the problem, Windows will stop crashing.

HOT TIP

Windows drivers are revised regularly. If you have a problem driver, a later version is probably available from the graphics card manufacturer. Most companies will send you an update on disk for free, or you can download one from the company's BBS (see Chapter 20: *Communications* for file download procedures). To install it, follow the same procedure described above, but select "Other display [Requires disk from OEM]" instead. Put the replacement driver in drive A: and click OK.

If the new driver still has problems (or causes other ones!), you can always send the board back if it's still under warranty. Alternatively, if you want to use your board at a resolution higher than VGA, you can choose Super VGA [800x600, 16 colors] from Setup's Display list and see if that works. A working driver from the graphics card manufacturer is always preferable, though, because it will probably give you much better performance than Windows' generic Super VGA driver.

Look for Hardware Conflicts

If Windows crashes all over the place, a hardware conflict is very likely behind it. In Chapter 8: *Upgrade It Yourself*, you'll find a complete discussion of the four most common hardware conflicts, all of them caused by incorrect settings on expansion cards. Use the troubleshooting advice there to see if you can track down what's causing problems.

Don't Run DOS Programs Under Windows

Running a DOS application under Windows is always a little risky, and ill-behaved DOS programs are a frequent cause of Windows crashes. Run two DOS programs at once, and you're really pushing it. The best policy is to replace your DOS application with a Windows one.

REMEMBER

However, chucking your DOS app isn't always practical—DOS modem communications are inherently faster, and there are several excellent DOS database programs out there. If you must run a DOS application under Windows, shut it down when you're not using it to decrease the chances of trouble.

Purge Redundant Utilities

Windows comes with two memory managers. HIMEM.SYS is necessary for Windows to run—when you install Windows, this program is set up to take care of extended memory automatically. EMM386.EXE gives old DOS applications such as

When Windows Won't Start

If you try to start Windows, and you go bouncing right back to the DOS prompt, very likely you have a bad (or wrong) Windows video driver. From your Windows directory, type setup. A screen will appear listing various system settings. Go to the Display setting, press Enter and select VGA from the scrolling list. Press Enter and you'll be back at the DOS prompt.

Enter win and Windows should now start. Doublecheck your graphics card manual to make sure you didn't select the wrong Windows video driver. If you followed the correct procedure, call the manufacturer and see if you can get a replacement driver.

1-2-3 access to expanded memory outside of Windows (see the "Memory Optimizers" section of Chapter 21: *Utilities* for an introduction to the types of memory).

Third-party memory managers such as *QEMM-386* conflict with HIMEM.SYS and EMM386.EXE, so if by some chance your CONFIG.SYS is loading another memory manager *along with* HIMEM.SYS or EMM386.EXE, delete the CONFIG.SYS line that loads the other memory manager.

HOT TIP

Also, because both DOS *and* Windows come with HIMEM.SYS and EMM386.EXE, make sure your CONFIG.SYS file isn't loading duplicate copies of these programs. If your version of DOS is more recent than your version of Windows, edit your CONFIG.SYS file so that it loads HIMEM.SYS (and EMM386.EXE, if necessary) from your DOS directory rather than from your Windows directory.

By the same token, make sure your system isn't loading duplicate *disk caching* programs (which speed performance by copying frequently used data from disk to RAM for faster access). Most people opt for SmartDrive, a disk caching utility that comes free with both DOS and Windows. Disk caching programs are generally loaded from your AUTOEXEC.BAT file, but sometimes an INSTALL line in your CONFIG.SYS file does the job. Check both files for redundant disk caches; only one copy of a single disk caching program should be loaded (see Appendix A for more on editing AUTOEXEC.BAT and CONFIG.SYS).

Scan Your Hard Disk for Errors

Damaged data or program files cause crashes. See the "Data Recovery" section of this chapter to learn how to diagnose and repair hard disk data errors.

Check for System BIOS Problems

The Basic Input/Output System (BIOS) is a the vital ROM chip in your PC that handles all sorts of low-level operations (loading DOS when you turn on your PC, for one). BIOSs that are older than three or four years—or even new, buggy BIOSs—may have trouble with Windows. Open up your PC and look for a pair of large chips (sometimes one chip, occasionally four) labeled BIOS. Write down the company name, revision number (if any), and date. Then check with the PC manufacturer's tech support to see if any problems have been reported with the BIOS.

Most systems copy their BIOS into memory, which in rare cases can cause problems with Windows. Start your PC's setup utility, look for a Shadow RAM entry, and set it to Off (see Chapter 8: *Upgrade It Yourself* for instructions on how to start your PC's setup program).

Try a Few Tricks

Here's a mixed bag of tricks that may get Windows running smoothly again. No guarantees here, folks, but you never know:

HOT TIPS

- In your CONFIG.SYS file, make sure FILES= is followed by the number 30 at a minimum. Raising it higher—say, to FILES=60 or so—uses a significant bit of memory, so if this doesn't work set FILES= back to 30.

- If it doesn't already, the SHELL= line in your CONFIG.SYS file should read SHELL=C:\DOS\COMMAND.COM /E:2408 /P.

- Look for the STACKS= command in your CONFIG.SYS file. The value should be 9,256 at least. If it is, try STACKS=9,512. For a real memory waster, try STACKS=64,512. Restore the setting to STACKS=9,256 if this trick has no effect.

- In your SYSTEM.INI file, go to the [386Enh] section and add the line EMMExclude=A000-EFFF. If *that* doesn't work, remove the line and add SystemROMBreakpoint=OFF. If that doesn't work, try adding this line: VirtualHDIRQ=OFF.

Disable Suspect Programs

DOS programs aren't the only mischief makers. If you tried the above measures and nothing worked, a program that alters both Windows and its applications, such as *Norton Desktop for Windows* or *PC Tools for Windows*, may be causing trouble. Both these programs come with excellent uninstall utilities. If all else fails, install them and see if going back to ordinary Windows helps.

Another offender is *Adobe Type Manager (ATM)*, the popular font program that enables you to use PostScript fonts with your applications. To see whether *ATM* is giving you grief, double-click on its Control Panel (marked by a script "A" and usually located in the Main group). Click the Off radio button and reboot your PC.

If your problems disappear, then you know that some conflict between *ATM* and another program was the cause.

Also watch out for applications older than two or three years—they may not be compatible with Windows 3.1, the current version.

Check Your Fax Driver

Sending and receiving faxes using Windows fax software can be a buggy affair. For example, Intel's *Faxability* software uses a driver that hangs around in expanded memory outside of Windows and has been known to cause GPFs. To see if your fax driver is the cause, insert `rem` before the line that loads your fax driver in your AUTOEXEC.BAT or CONFIG.SYS file. Save the file and reboot your system. If the crashes abate, your fax driver is the culprit. Check with the fax software company to see if a later version of the software is available, or see if the company's tech support has any troubleshooting suggestions. Also make sure that your fax software has been correctly **HOT TIP** installed for your make and model of fax modem.

Reinstall Windows

Sometimes Windows' initialization files (WIN.INI, SYSTEM.INI, and so on) become so cluttered—usually by Windows applications that changed these files heedlessly on installation—that Windows becomes unstable. Or perhaps one of Windows' program files has been damaged. Either way, as a last resort, you can reinstall Windows using the original Windows disks.

This can leave you in a bit of a fix, however, because the Windows applications you've already installed may require certain settings in your INI files—which means you may have to reinstall your apps as well! To avoid this, do the following:

1. Copy all your INI and GRP files to another directory (call it \WINTEMP) before you reinstall Windows.

2. Now do it—reinstall Windows. Put Disk 1 in drive A:, type `setup`, and follow the prompts just as you did when you first installed it. Accept the suggestion to install Windows in the existing Windows directory.

3. After reinstallation, copy all your GRP and INI files (except WIN.INI and SYSTEM.INI) from \WINTEMP back to your Windows directory.

Now start Windows. Because you restored the GRP files, your program groups should be arranged just the way you had them. Mess around with a few applications for a while and see if Windows is behaving itself. If so, you may have fixed the problem, whatever it was.

To restore more old settings, begin by exiting to DOS and giving the clean WIN.INI file in your Windows directory a new name (WIN.CLN, whatever). Then copy the WIN.INI file from \WINTEMP back to the Windows directory. If Windows starts crashing again, exit to DOS, delete WIN.INI, and rename WIN.CLN back to WIN.INI. Note that if you go with the clean WIN.INI file, you'll have to restore file associations, font installations, and other settings manually.

Nonlethal Windows Difficulties

Here's a grab bag of Windows dilemmas that are usually more annoying than fatal. For advice on problems with Windows communications, turn to the troubleshooting section at the end of Chapter 20: *Communications*. For TrueType or PostScript Type 1 fonts problems, see Chapter 13: *Fonts*.

Out of Memory

Yes, Windows' message "Insufficient Memory to Complete this Operation" could mean you should get more RAM—remember that you need 8MB to run Windows comfortably. However, this message could also mean you have too little *base* memory (memory under 640K). Try running a memory optimizer, such as DOS's MemMaker, and see if that helps.

REMEMBER

If it doesn't, try reducing the number of windows you have open. As they work, some people just keep opening documents in separate windows, until Windows doesn't have room to open any more—at which point thay get the message telling them Windows has no more to spare.

If you get the Insufficient Memory message when you try to run a DOS app, you may need to alter that app's configuration (see "Trouble With DOS Applications" below).

Application Execution Error

You get a dialog box by this name when you try and fail to start a program. It almost always indicates that you improperly installed an application, or that you accidentally deleted or moved one of its files. Run the installation routine again from beginning to end. If you still get this message, there may be something wrong with the app's program disks.

Mouse Mischief

First, make sure you've followed the correct mouse installation procedure outlined in Chapter 8: *Upgrade It Yourself*. Also check that your mouse is Microsoft compatible, or at least has a driver for Windows that's been installed properly using Windows' Setup program.

Troubleshooting 101

Crashes and other problems are often caused by hardware drivers that conflict with each other. To see what might be causing problems for you, hold down F8 as your system boots. This gives you the option to accept or reject each line in your CONFIG.SYS and AUTOEXEC.BAT files, the configuration files in which drivers are loaded. Without any special drivers, your CONFIG.SYS and AUTOEXEC.BAT files should look something like this:

CONFIG.SYS

```
device=c:\dos\himem.sys
device=c:\dos\emm386.exe ram
buffers=15,0
files=30
dos=umb
lastdrive=H
fcbs=4,0
devicehigh=C:\dos\setver.exe
dos=high
stacks=9,256
```

AUTOEXEC.BAT

```
lh c:\dos\smartdrv.exe /x
@echo off
prompt $p$g
path C:\windows;c:\dos
set temp=c:\dos
```

Do you see any lines in addition to the DEVICE or LH lines listed above? If so, try saying No to one of them using the F8 trick as your system boots. If things run smoothly thereafter, then you've just isolated the problem and you need a new driver (or you need to specially configure it using advice from the manual or manufacturer tech support). If rejecting the driver makes no difference, reboot and say No to another driver—and so on until you (hopefully) find the problem. If this procedure doesn't work, you may well be experiencing a hardware conflict (see the section "Installing Expansion Boards" in Chapter 8: *Upgrade It Yourself*).

If you see a mouse pointer on screen and it won't move, load your MOUSE.INI file (found in your Windows directory) into Notepad or DOS's Edit. Find the MouseType= entry. If your mouse is plugged into a mouse port, make sure this entry reads MouseType=PS2. If it's hooked to your first serial port (COM1), the line should read MouseType=Serial1; if it's plugged into COM2, the line should read MouseType=Serial2. For a bus mouse, make sure the line says MouseType=Bus.

HOT TIP

If you use DOS applications under Windows and you lose the mouse pointer when you switch from a DOS to a Windows application, you very likely have a bad video driver. Call your graphics card manufacturer for a replacement.

If your mouse won't run outside of Windows, don't blame Windows—you need to load a separate driver for your mouse to work with DOS applications. See the "Installing DOS and Windows" section of Chapter 12: *Windows and DOS* for more information.

Printing Problems

Most printing problems under Windows are due to a bad driver—or installation of the wrong driver. For example, when you install Windows and it asks you what kind of printer you have, don't select one that's "close." Choose the Unlisted option, and load the correct Windows driver from the driver disk included with your printer.

That is, if your printer has a Windows driver. Some, such as Epson laser printers, don't have a Windows driver, and you must install a LaserJet driver instead. On the other end of the spectrum, current LaserJets require that you run a full installation routine in order to use all printer features. The moral: Check your printer manual to make sure.

HOT TIP

In some cases the Windows driver that came with your printer may be bad. If you've followed your printer's installation instructions carefully, and the printer still won't work properly, double click the Printer icon in the Control Panel, click the Add button, and check the list of printer drivers to see if you can find your printer there. If so, try that driver instead of the one that came with your printer. As a last resort, try the Generic/Text Only driver for the time being until you can get a good driver (or good advice) from the printer manufacturer.

If you have trouble printing large files, make sure the drive containing the directory where Windows keeps its temporary files (usually C:\WINDOWS\TEMP) has at least 5MB of free disk space. If not, you need to do some housecleaning anyway, or get a new drive—with only 5MB free, you'll see an "Insufficient disk space" message soon enough.

Trouble With DOS Applications

As noted before, some DOS applications simply won't behave under Windows. However, nearly all DOS programs need a little configuration help. That's what Windows PIF (Program Information File) Editor is for—consult the "DOS Under Windows" section in Chapter 12 for basic instructions on how to use the PIF Editor.

However, a few glitches can't be helped by editing a DOS program's PIF file. Here's a fairly common one: Sometimes you switch from a Windows app to a windowed DOS app, and a bunch of random capital letters and caret (^) characters appear on the screen when you start typing. The cure? Just tap the Ctrl and Alt keys a couple of times. This restores DOS's keyboard status byte and makes the problem go away.

HOT TIP

Weird Screen Stuff

Yes, it's that old troublemaker, your Windows video driver again. If you get random dots in paint or draw programs, or if garbage appears around some fonts, your Windows video driver is probably to blame. Get a replacement.

Data Recovery

Along with backing up your hard disk, scanning your hard disk for errors should be part of your regular routine. Most data errors are small, but some can threaten the health of all data on your hard disk—like when you turn on your PC and get the message "Bad or Missing Command Interpreter," "Bad Partition Table," "Disk Boot Failure," or "Invalid Partition Table."

DOS comes with a capable data recovery program called ScanDisk that's fine for detecting and fixing the easy stuff, such as lost clusters or cross-linked files. However, you're best advised to get one of the following programs for maximum protection and recovery: *The Norton Utilities, Norton Desktop for Windows, PC Tools Pro,* or *PC Tools for Windows* (see Chapter 21: *Utilities* for more information on data recovery).

On installation, all of these four programs offer to create a "rescue" or "emergency" floppy disk that vastly increases the chance of successful recovery should you experience catastrophic hard disk problems. Basically, if you boot from drive A: and follow the prompts presented by the emergency routine, you have a good chance of rescuing most of your data. You can manually create a rescue disk with DOS, but your chances of full recovery won't be as good (see "Safety Check" in Chapter 12).

HOT TIP

All of these programs help you recover from data accidents, such as mistakenly formatting a disk or deleting a file. Figure 1 outlines the procedures to follow no matter what program you use.

Six Routes to Data Recovery

Problem	Norton Utilities	Norton Desktop for Windows	PC Tools Pro	PC Tools for Windows	DOS	DOS Under Windows
Deleted file	UnErase	Click on UnErase under Tools menu	UnDel	Click on Undelete in WinShield folder	UNDELETE	Click on Undelete icon in MS Tools
Deleted subdirectory	UnErase	Click on UnErase under Tools menu	UnDel	Click on Undelete in WinShield folder	N/A	Click on Undelete icon in MS Tools
Formatted disk	UnFormat[1]	UnFormat[1]	UnFormat[2]	UnFormat[2]	UNFORMAT[3]	N/A
Lost clusters	Run Norton Disk Doctor	Click on Norton Disk Doctor under Tools Menu	Run DiskFix	Run DiskFix	RunScanDisk	N/A
Cross-linked files	Run Norton Disk Doctor	Click on Norton Disk Doctor under Tools Menu	Run DiskFix	Run DiskFix	RunScanDisk	N/A
Corrupted FAT or root	Run Norton[1] Disk Doctor	Click on Norton Disk Doctor under Tools Menu[1]	Run DiskFix[2]	Run DiskFix[2]	Run ScanDisk[4]	N/A

[1]Use Rescue Disk if drive C:.
[2]Use Emergency Disk if drive C:.
[3]If drive C:, must use boot disk and run UNFORMAT from a floppy.
[4]Not recommended; if you try it, you'll need to insert a copy of ScanDisk in drive A:.

Figure 1: *If you've accidentally formatted drive C:, or if your hard disk won't boot, the best thing to do is boot from drive A: using a Rescue Disk or Emergency Disk (prepared with Norton or PC Tools, respectively). Failing that, boot from a DOS system disk and then swap in a floppy containing either Norton Disk Doctor, PC Tools' DiskFix, or DOS's ScanDisk.*

Hardware Problems

Sometimes hardware simply wears out or breaks. There's nothing you can do about that except call manufacturer tech support. However, many hardware problems have relatively simple solutions—especially because flipping the wrong setting on an expansion card or making a wrong choice in your PC's setup program is often the cause. In Chapter 8: *Upgrade It Yourself*, you'll find out how to avoid these kinds of self-imposed problems.

Nonetheless, you're liable to experience a bona fide malfunction sometime in the life of your PC. The problems discussed in this section are relatively common occurrences with pretty easy solutions.

What! No Drive C:?

One day you turn on your PC. Instead of the usual friendly beep, you get an ominous message: "Invalid Drive Specification," "General Failure Reading Drive C:," or something equally terrifying. Panic! Dread! Does this mean everything on drive C: is lost?

Probably not. Follow these steps in order, and you may well get your hard disk running again. Before you try these procedures, boot from your A: drive and see if you can access your C: drive. If you can, before you do anything else, run one of the data recovery programs discussed earlier in this chapter. Then back up all data not already stored on backup disks or tape.

1. **Run setup.** If you have an IDE hard disk, start your system's setup routine (see Chapter 8 if you don't know how). Look for Hard Disk 1, Fixed Disk 1, or a similar entry. If you see the word None, or something similarly negative, then your system's CMOS battery may be failing and you've lost your system configuration. Change None to the correct drive type, save the configuration, and reboot. Don't turn off your machine until you change the battery. (If you don't know the drive type, call the manufacturer's tech support. You may need to crack open your PC and copy down the drive's model number so that a support person can help you. Then replace your PC's battery, as described later in this chapter.)

2. **Check your CONFIG.SYS file.** If you have a SCSI hard disk, you may have a line in your CONFIG.SYS file that enables your drive to run. And if you've installed new software lately, it may have scrambled your CONFIG.SYS file badly enough so that the drive won't operate. Check your documentation to see exactly how the hard disk DEVICE line in you CONFIG.SYS file should read. Then

boot from a floppy, create a CONFIG.SYS file on the floppy containing the proper line, and reboot. If you can access drive C:, edit the CONFIG.SYS file on drive C: using DOS's Edit so that the DEVICE line is back to the way it should be.

3. **Check the connections.** Turn off your PC, open it up, and reseat all of the cables—yes, unplug them and plug them in again. This ensures nothing has come loose and scrapes away corrosion that may have accumulated on contacts, a common problem. If your drive hooks up to a card, unplug the card from its expansion slot and plug it in again, all the way into the slot. Turn on your machine and see if it works.

4. **Leave it on.** Keep your system running for 30 minutes to an hour. Then reboot and see if it works. If the drive is old and the machine was cold overnight, components inside the drive may have contracted enough to throw the hard disk slightly out of alignment. Once warm, the hardware may work again. If the warmup trick works, this is a good that your drive needs replacing.

If none of these strategies works, and you haven't backed up your data in while (something you're sure to regret at this point), then it's time to bring in the professionals. Three such services are Group One Electronics (818/993-4575), Ontrack Data Recovery (800/752-1333), and Workman and Associates (818/791-7979).

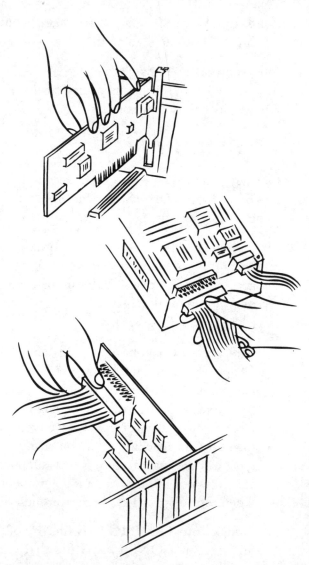

Figure 2: *Is a loose connection screwing up your hard disk? Plug and unplug cables, and if your hard disk works, poor contact was the problem.*

Keeping It Clean

Over time, your PC collects dust in the worst possible place—on the inside. Dust is a problem because it causes heat buildup in the components it covers, which can reduce the lifespan of those parts. It may also clog your PC's vents and make the cooling fan less efficient. Every once in awhile, when you open your PC, come armed with a dustbuster. Vacuum every horizontal surface inside your PC and give the vents special attention.

By the same token, a dirty mouse will give you poor control over the cursor. To clean one, follow the procedure shown in Figure 3.

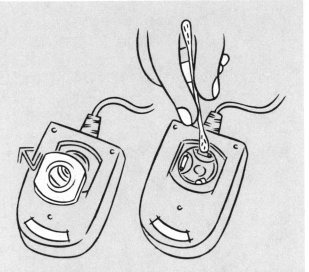

Figure 3: *Here's how you clean a mouse. Remember to use alcohol on the cotton swab as you wipe the rollers. The ball inside the mouse should be cleaned with lukewarm, soapy water and dried thoroughly.*

Battery Replacement

A dying CMOS battery—a surprisingly common problem—can wreck havoc with your system. The symptoms? Your PC loses its setup information which may prevent it from booting when you turn it on. Replacing a CMOS battery is usually pretty easy. Just check your system manual and look for the battery on the motherboard; replacements are available at most electronics stores (such as Radio Shack). Figure 4 gives you a look at the most popular battery types.

Figure 4: *A dead or dying CMOS battery can keep your system from booting. Here's what the three most popular battery types look like.*

11

~~~~~~

Health, Safety, and the Environment

By Anita Amirrezvani and Robert Luhn

- Avoid your monitor's radiation
- Protect your hands from cumulative trauma
- Create an ergonomic workstation
- Save paper and the environment
- Reduce power consumption and costs
- Find a happy home for orphan PCs

Living well is an art, and so is using computers. Most of this book focuses on the intricacies of choosing hardware and using software, but in this chapter we show you how to minimize your PC's negative effects both on yourself and on the environment.

If your workstation is poorly designed, using a PC can tire you, hurt you, or even result in debilitating physical ailments. The worst computer-related problems, like carpal tunnel syndrome and tendinitis, can cause severe pain in the hands and arms, requiring physical therapy or surgery and long absences from work. This chapter explains how to avoid such health hazards.

Then we turn to another pressing problem: the environment. Your personal computer may seem sleek and benignly high-tech, but it contributes to our environmental woes by gobbling up power, paper, and other resources. Fortunately, it's pretty easy to use your PC in an environmentally sound way, and you can save money in the bargain. This chapter shows you how.

Health and Safety Guide

Is there more to safe, comfortable computing than following your mother's admonition to "sit up straight"? You bet. Good posture can mitigate back problems, but it won't help your eyes, nor will it save your wrists or hands from painful injury. Read on for some down-to-earth advice about protecting your whole body from the perils of the information factory.

Monitors: Preventing Eyestrain and Fatigue

We are a nation of viewers. The average American watches TV for an astonishing 6 hours per day; PC workers may spend even longer in front of a monitor. All that computer work can cause physical discomfort—blurry vision, headaches, fatigue, or muscle strain—if ergonomic considerations are ignored. Here are the key factors to keep in mind when using your monitor:

- **Make sure lighting is indirect.** Place your PC at a right angle to windows so the sun doesn't shine from behind or directly into your eyes. You may also need curtains or blinds to control light throughout the day.

- **Control artificial lighting.** Standard office lighting is too bright for computing. To decrease lighting levels, you can buy overhead lighting with *parabolic louvers*, honeycomblike baffles that help diffuse light. If you're stuck with direct overhead lighting, arrange your work area so the computer is positioned between rows of overhead lights. If fluorescent lights are too bright, simply remove every other tube. With overall lighting levels lower, you may want to add bright task lighting, such as a desk lamp, to make it easy to read printed materials.

HOT TIP

- **Avoid glare.** Buy a monitor with a tilt-and-swivel capability so you can turn it away from glare. Glare screens, which mount on the front of a monitor, can be a big help. There are three types: mesh, plastic, or glass. Mesh screens are the least expensive, while glass filters are best at keeping the image sharp as they reduce glare. All types tend to darken your monitor, so you'll need to make appropriate adjustments in screen contrast and other lighting. Experiment with several types of glare screens from companies such as ACCO, I-Protect, NoRad, Kantek, and OCLI to determine what works best in your work environment.

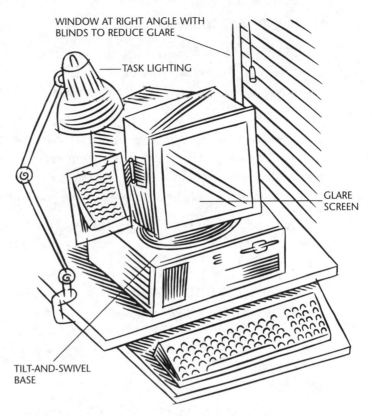

- **Avoid fuzziness.** Your monitor should always display characters that are crisp and sharp. If you notice blurring or distortion that can't be eliminated with the brightness and contrast controls, you may need a new monitor, or you may need to adjust hidden controls. A handy utility called *DisplayMate* can help you identify and fix monitor problems.

Figure 1: How to reduce eye fatigue. Set your workstation up like this, and you can cut eyestrain significantly. One factor you may not be able to control is overhead lighting—if it's too strong, you might consider loosening a couple of fluorescent tubes.

- **Avoid flicker.** Monitor flicker is caused by a slow refresh rate (the number of times the monitor repaints the screen per second). Sometimes flicker is undetectable, but it can still fatigue your eyes after a few hours. Look for a monitor and graphics card with a refresh rate of at least 70 Hz. Remember to check the refresh rate at all the resolutions you plan to use, since vendors use a lower refresh rate at higher resolutions. Whatever you do, never buy a monitor that uses interlaced scanning at your preferred resolution—this causes the worst flicker of all.

DANGER

Staying Out of the Rays

The jury is still out on whether the low-frequency radiation emitted by monitors causes higher miscarriage or cancer rates. If you want to limit your exposure to ELF (extremely low frequency) or VLF (very low frequency) electromagnetic fields, here are your options:

- **Check your work environment.** The strongest emissions come from the *back* of a monitor. Make sure you're not surrounded by an army of monitors directing their rays at you from their backs and sides. Also, since rays weaken with distance, try to keep your torso at least 2 feet away from your monitor.

- **Buy a specialized screen.** Many glare screens or hoods partially block the electro-magenetic fields emitted by your monitor. However, these are not as effective as MPR II monitors.

- **Purchase an MPR II monitor.** MPR II monitors meet the Swedish government's standard for reduced low-frequency emissions, a much tougher standard than is common in the U.S. Most major manufacturers sell monitors that meet MPR II standards, and the additional cost (if any) is usually minimal.

HOT TIP

Eye Care

The eye loves variety, but PC users usually spend most of their time focusing on a single object at close range. Here's how to reduce fatigue:

- **Look away from your PC often,** preferably into the distance. Blink frequently to moisten your eyes. To relax, close your eyes and cover them for a few moments with your palms.

- **Buy an antistatic** cleaner or screen to help repel the dust that gathers on your monitor, which can irritate your eyes.

- **Get regular checkups** to ensure the health of your eyes, and keep your doctor informed about your working conditions. A growing number of optometrists understand the special problems of computer users and offer special glasses for those who do a lot of screen work and have poor vision.

HOT TIP

Keyboards: Protecting Hands and Arms

The hand is a small miracle, precise enough to do the most intricate brain surgery or chisel a diamond out of a rock. But it also has limits. Any task involving awkward twisting, bending, repetition, or a fixed position—whether it's driving a screw, cutting meat, or typing in data—can cause serious discomfort and even physiological damage.

Millions of Americans now work on computers, which explains the increasing prevalence of a group of occupational hazards called repetitive strain injuries (RSIs). Some 185,000 Americans were diagnosed with RSIs in 1990, compared to only 45,000 in 1986. These injuries cause pain in the muscles, nerves, or tendons, and they can be disabling or even crippling. Some victims aren't able to hold their children, drive a car, or even lift a coffee cup.

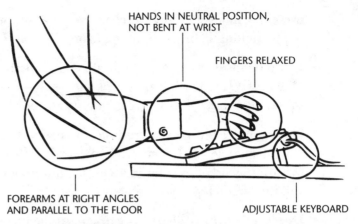

HANDS IN NEUTRAL POSITION, NOT BENT AT WRIST

FINGERS RELAXED

FOREARMS AT RIGHT ANGLES AND PARALLEL TO THE FLOOR

ADJUSTABLE KEYBOARD

Figure 2: Keyboard common sense. *A good typing angle and an adjustable keyboard reduce wear and tear on the wrists and hands. Note that wrist rests are not a cure-all; if they make your hands bend at all, they can actually hurt.*

Computer users suffer from several common RSIs, which usually affect the hand, wrist, or arm. Many professionals call these *cumulative trauma disorders* because they take time to appear, and they worsen if left untreated. See a doctor immediately if you feel any pain in the arms, wrists, or hands; and follow these precautionary measures to help avoid symptoms altogether:

- **Adjust your keyboard to fit your body.** Your wrists should always be in a neutral position. To accomplish this, position your keyboard at a height that allows your wrists to remain straight. Many keyboards have feet that let you make adjustments for maximum comfort; some bizarre variations on the standard keyboard design may also suit you. Wrist rests—cushions that you place between you and your keyboard—can also help keep your wrists relaxed (as long as you don't use them *while* you type), but they're not for everyone. Resting your wrists and bending your hands upward can result in prolonged pressure or bending that can cause RSIs.

REMEMBER

DANGER

- **Rest to avoid injury.** Most health professionals recommend a break every 2 hours—or if your work is keyboard-intensive, every 45 minutes. Even while you're working, take advantage of opportunities to relax, such as while your PC is loading a program or recalculating a spreadsheet. Some workers rest their forearms on padded armrests to chill out.

- **Work more efficiently.** Learn your program's shortcut keys so you can navigate through your files with fewer keystrokes. If you use the same text frequently, such as your name and address, create boilerplate files to avoid retyping the same information. Automate any frequent program tasks with macros. Finally, consider alternatives to typing, such as making a telephone call instead of sending E-mail, or using a scanner with optical character recognition rather than keying in data (see the "Scanning It In" section of Chapter 7: *Input Devices* for more on OCR).

- **Get a headset.** Keep your body aligned properly by using a headset instead of the phone. If you type while on the phone, use a speakerphone or a headset rather than squeezing the receiver between your head and shoulder.

- **Do simple exercises to reduce muscular tension.** Rotate your shoulders or make big circles with your arms to get circulation going. Massage your hands and forearms, gently flex your wrists up and down, or clench your fists for a few seconds and then stretch out your fingers.

DANGER

- **Don't wait for problems to worsen.** At the first sign of discomfort in your hands, wrists, or arms, contact a medical professional. Waiting could cost you your livelihood.

In the future, users will be able to interact with computers by talking. But until then, new keyboards may provide a solution if you're uncomfortable with standard designs. Some are radically different than typical keyboards and require learning a new way to type. Combined with exercises and a well-designed workstation, however, they may help keep debilitating RSIs at bay (for more on alternative keyboards, see the "Keyboards" section of Chapter 7: *Input Devices*).

Workstations: Saving Your Back and Neck

If we were all built the same, workstation design would be simple. But since human anatomy is so varied, each workstation needs to be individually tailored. That's the single most important factor in preventing musculoskeletal problems such as back, neck, or arm pain.

When you use your PC, your neck should be straight, your shoulders relaxed, your elbows by your sides, your forearms and thighs approximatly parallel to the floor, and your wrists neutral, not twisted or bent. Here are some tips for positioning your equipment in order to maintain good working posture and reduce physical stress:

REMEMBER

- **Position your monitor.** Make sure the top of your monitor is at eye level, or slightly below, to maintain a straight back and neck. If the monitor is too low, put a book underneath it, buy a stand, or raise the shelf if you have an adjustable workstation.

- **Purchase a document stand.** If you frequently refer to documents as you use your PC, maintain your alignment by positioning a stand at approximately the same height and distance as your monitor.

- **Position your keyboard.** Along with placing your keyboard so your wrists are relaxed and straight, when accessing faraway keys remember to move your entire hand rather than twisting your wrists. You should also keep commonly used accessories like your telephone, Rolodex, or reference books within easy reach.

- **Don't ignore your legs.** The space underneath your desk is just as important as what's on top. Remove obstructions near your legs or feet; you don't want your thighs jammed against the desk or to be unable to stretch your legs.

- **Compensate for older desks.** Older desks are usually too high for computing. If you can't buy a new workstation, try raising your chair or adding a keyboard drawer. A footrest can take pressure off your knees and back; even a phone book or a ream of paper can do the trick.

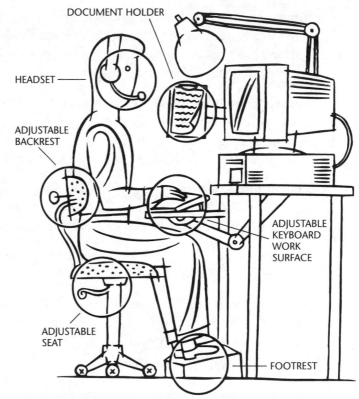

Figure 3: The well-designed workstation. *Yes, sitting up straight helps, but so does the right hardware. An adjustable chair and keyboard drawer help you tailor your workstation to fit your body. For your neck's sake, keep the top of your monitor's display area at eye level or a bit below.*

HOT TIP

I Think, Therefore I Sit

Your chair is critical. For proper positioning of your hands on the keyboard, the chair should adjust easily up or down. *Pneumatic lift* is recommended so you can raise or lower your chair without getting up. The seat itself should be adjustable and padded; it's best if the front is rounded to take pressure off the backs of your knees.

- **Support your back.** The best chairs for computing have an adjustable backrest, with plenty of support for your lower back. If your chair doesn't offer enough support, buy a lumbar support cushion to help out.

- **Move the chair instead of your body.** If your chair swivels, you won't have to twist your body to reach things. The chair should also be on wheels so you can travel with the chair instead of bending or twisting. Five-legged chairs are recommended for improved stability.

- **Test various chairs to get the perfect fit.** Since most large corporations buy several types of chairs, ask your facilities manager if you can test the options. If you're buying for yourself, look for a store that specializes in ergonomically designed chairs. If you need to cut costs, buy a cheap desk rather than compromise on the chair.

- **Try standing.** Some people feel that standing reduces pressure on the back. In that case, put the PC on a stand on the floor and adjust shelving or work surfaces to accommodate the monitor and keyboard at appropriate heights.

- **Exercise often.** Try to follow a regular exercise program that utilizes different muscles than those you use at work.

If you work in an office, unless you're lucky your boss is probably ignorant about ergonomics. The *VDT Trainer's Kit* can help educate your co-workers (*VDT* stands for *video display terminal*, an old-fashioned term for a computer keyboard and monitor). This excellent resource contains slides and written materials developed by the University of California that are useful for educating employees about computing health and safety issues. Also highly recommended is the annual product directory published in the September/October issue of *VDT News*, a comprehensive source for ergonomic products.

A Guide to Green Computing

When it comes to protecting the environment, most people focus on the big threats (oil spills, ozone holes) and the small but poignant victims (snail darters, baby seals). But the innocent-looking PC on your desk also contributes to our eco woes.

Your PC uses maybe three or four times the energy of a 75-watt light bulb. Multiply that by the 42 million computers in the U.S., and you have a significant energy drain. And you don't even want to think about the millions of trees it takes to supply laser printers and copiers with tons of paper.

It's not a pretty picture. But the computer industry is finally starting to think green. It's producing chips using less ozone-eating CFCs. And many companies offer PCs, printers, and monitors that comply with the U.S. government's Energy Star guidelines, which suggest standards for lower energy consumption using devices that power down automatically when idle.

PC users can do their part, too, and reduce office expenses at the same time. For example, AT&T owns 7000 photocopiers that put out 46 million copies a month. By asking employees to duplex documents—copy on both sides of a sheet—the company expects to save $400,000 a year. What you do today and buy tomorrow can have a similar (if smaller) impact in your office and at home.

Saving Trees

In the world of waste, paper is king. Nearly 40 percent of the waste in American landfills is

Combined enErgy consumption of all U.S. PCs and peripherals each year

14.4 billion kilowatt hours, or the annual output of three-and-a-half nuclear power plants

The amount of paper consumed by photocopiers and laser printers in one year

14 million tons of paper, or 238 million trees

Figure 4: PCs, lasers, and copiers: conspicuous consumers. Why go green? Because this huge waste of resources could be cut dramatically if everyone followed a few conservation measures.

paper, and a chunk of it came out of printers and photocopiers. You can keep paper out of the trash heap, save a few trees, and trim your budget with a few simple steps:

- **Think before you print.** Avoid unnecessary drafts by fully proofing documents on screen. Run spelling checkers to catch errors. If you're fiddling with images, use the program's "thumbnail" option to print out multiple pages on a single sheet of paper. For drafts and working documents, use programs such as *4Print*, *MicroText*, or *ClickBook*, which print two or four pages on each side of a sheet. **HOT TIP**

- **Cut unnecessary pages.** Eliminate cover pages, activity reports, and test pages issued by your fax machine and laser printer. Abolish unnecessary office forms, and redesign multipage forms into double-sided single-page ones.

- **Go duplex happy.** Most photocopiers and some network laser printers can print on both sides of a sheet automatically. You can also duplex manually on almost any laser printer; to avoid jams, let the paper cool before you flip it over and put it

HOT TIP

through. If you must print on only one side, keep bins by your printers, copiers, and plain paper fax machines to hold discarded pages. Use them for scratch paper and print memos, drafts, and other internal documents on the blank side.

- **Close the recycling loop.** Buy recycled paper products that contain *postconsumer* waste. Major paper vendors from James River to Weyerhauser offer bright white paper with 10 percent to 30 percent postconsumer materials that are indistinguishable from virgin stock. Make sure that the waste is postconsumer: Don't be fooled by "contains waste paper" or "meets EPA guidelines" labels. Recycled paper works well in lasers, photocopiers, and plain paper fax machines, as shown by large-scale tests conducted by the federal government, Pitney Bowes, Kodak, and others.

- **Set up a paper recycling program.** To keep things simple, standardize on one copier/laser and one letterhead paper. Ask employees to recycle white paper only, since it's easier to identify and is valued by recyclers. Some recyclers may even pay you for your used white paper; if nothing else, you'll lower your garbage bills.

HOT TIP

The Less-Paper Office

Despite what optimists may tell you, the paperless office hasn't arrived. But we're getting there—bit by bit—as electronic communications proliferate. If you use your network and the phone lines effectively, you'll save both paper and power:

- **Post it online.** Use E-mail to the limit, and set up an internal electronic bulletin board to post memos and other announcements. Keep frequently accessed information on line, such as catalogs, Rolodexes, employee handbooks, schedules, and customer lists. For example, California's Pacific Gas & Electric keeps templates on a server so managers can "publish" their reports electronically.

- **Fax first, courier last.** A fax board is an efficient way to send and receive faxes. Although a pain to set up, you can read faxes on screen, delete the ones you don't want, and print only the ones you do. You can also send (but not receive) text-only faxes via MCI Mail, America Online, and other online services. If you must use a fax machine, get a plain-paper unit instead of a thermal one—it can use recycled (and recyclable) paper.

- **Network your office to the max.** Individual printers and fax modems eat energy and your budget. Instead, hook up a few fast printers and fax modems to your network server, and let everyone access them from his or her PC (see Chapter 22: *About Networks*).

Less Power to the PC

Your PC and laser printer are hot machines—in every sense of the word. Pacific Gas & Electric estimates that for every 100 watts consumed by office equipment, you'll expend another 30 watts for air conditioning. What can you do now to save energy with the hardware you already have? Plenty:

- **Turn it off!** You shouldn't switch your hardware off and on like a blender, but you shouldn't leave your PC, monitor, and printer on day and night, either. At the very least, turn your equipment on in the morning and off at the end of the day. If you're away from your desk for more than 3 hours, snap off your CRT and printer. The savings can be huge: In an office with 150 PCs, just turning off the color monitors at night could save a company as much as $17,000 in annual electricity costs.
HOT TIP

- **Buy smart.** Laptop computers are nearly as powerful as their desktop cousins—and they use a tenth of the power. Smaller monitors use less power than big ones, and LCDs (like those on laptops) use the least power of all. A 300-dot-per-inch ink jet is enough printer for most people—and it draws about a tenth the energy of a laser printer.

- **Internal beats external.** Buying a modem or CD ROM player? Internal units are not only cheaper, they're also more efficient, because they use your PC's power supply instead of a wall socket. When you shop for comparable products, check out the power requirements, too—buy the 20-watt fax modem instead of the 40-watt unit.

Buying Tomorrow's Green Machines

Time to buy new hardware? Make a commitment to the environment by purchasing Energy Star PCs and peripherals. The Environmental Protection Agency has convinced hundreds of hardware vendors to produce these power-saving products. Most Energy Star devices use a "sleep mode" to cut power use to the bone after a period of inactivity. Buying an Energy Star desktop PC may save you about $100 per PC per year in energy costs.

Energy Star PCs and peripherals cost a bit more than conventional hardware. But prices will keep dropping now that the federal government—the world's biggest computer customer—is required by law to buy Energy Star products.

Figure 5: Wearing the green. *The Energy Star logo on a piece of hardware indicates the device uses no more than 30 watts (45 watts for certain printers) when idle.*

Under Energy Star guidelines, no component (PC, monitor, or printer) can use more than 30 watts when in an idle state, or 45 watts for color and 15-page-per-minute printers. Beyond this, Energy Star products vary wildly in their actual power use. Two things will affect your electricity bill: the energy consumption in active mode and in sleep mode.

Since the EPA has no plans to test Energy Star machines, you'll want to compare the power specs on every component you shop for. Your task will be easier when the Computer Business and Equipment Manufacturing Association issues a universal testing standard. Only then are manufacturers' power ratings likely to be based on exactly the same tests. Other key points to consider:

- **Keep expectations realistic.** Energy Star PCs are only guaranteed to meet EPA power specs in their advertised factory configuration. If you add a power-hungry video board or hard disk, it will gobble more power. Today's Energy Star systems aren't super energy savers, though the next generation of PCs will be. One glimpse of at the future: IBM's pricey PS/E line, which relies on a tiny power supply, accommodates low-power PCMCIA cards, and needs no fan.

DANGER

- **Make sure it's compatible.** Beware of mixing and matching Energy Star components: Some power-saving monitors work only with the systems they were designed for. Fortunately, the Video Electronics Standards Association has established a power signal standard called DPMS so that all complying components will be compatible. In the meantime, check the compatibility of different brands before you mix them. The EPA's Energy Star product database, available free of charge, includes compatibility information.

- **Check printer specs.** Energy Star laser printers are designed to power down automatically. Some let you select the interval from a control panel or via software; others shut down after a fixed time. Check how long it takes a printer to "wake up"—30 seconds should be tops. And though you may see ink jet printers bearing the Energy Star logo, remember that most ink jets on the market—except faster color units—already use less than 30 watts.

- **Consider retrofitting.** Want your old hardware to get green? The MonitorMiser and the Wattless VDU Power Saver can automatically shut down your monitor after a set period of time. Or plug your PC and monitor into a smart power strip like the Smartbar, which is more complicated to use but lets you specify shutdown intervals via software.

The Three Rs and the PC

Future PCs may be easier to recycle, but what about that ancient LaserJet, that tottering XT? Remember the environmental mantra: "reduce, reuse, *then* recycle." Some tips from the field:

- **Old PC, new job.** If your old AT or XT is still running, put it to good use. Give it to your kids, the local school, or a charity. Have secretaries and interns use old PCs for word processing and spreadsheets. Ancient PCs can function as modem and print servers on a network; they can even be used as voicemail systems.

Going to Sleep and Waking Up

You don't need to buy a complete Energy Star system to save power. Some Energy Star monitors work with existing PCs by powering down automatically when signaled by a screen saver (Acer, Nanao, and Sony offer monitors with this capability). If your PC has an older graphics card, it will probably require updated drivers to support Energy Star monitors.

By the same token, you can also use older monitors with some Energy Star PCs. Austin Computer Systems offers a PC that automatically shuts off non–Energy Star monitors after a user-specified period of time.

When Energy Star systems take a catnap, make sure the sleep isn't too deep. Check whether your PC will wake up and respond to incoming fax or modem transmissions—or network E-mail, backups, and so on. AST's Bravo PCs can; so will a new generation of motherboards from such manufacturers as Elitegroup.

- **New lease on your laser.** With a modem-in-a-cartridge from Moonlight Computer Products or Practical Peripherals, creaky LaserJet IIs and IIIs can become receive-only fax machines. The output is sharp, and your new "fax" can use recycled (and recyclable) paper. Another fax alternative: the FaxPak box from Teledisk Systems, which can store up to 40 pages even when your PC is off.

- **Refill and reuse.** Don't toss that used toner cartridge—laser printer and photocopier vendors (such as HP, Lexmark, and Xerox) will take them back, postage paid. The old cartridges are ground up and turned into new ones. You can also stretch your budget by either selling your depleted cartridges to third-party suppliers or having them refilled (for $30 less than a new cartridge) and sent back.

- **Don't bury that dead PC.** You *can* recycle hardware if you look around. For example, Compaq accept its old laptop batteries and reclaims the metals. HP's Support Materials Organization has been taking back old LaserJets and HP computers for years. If your vendor won't take back a dead PC, printer, or monitor, consider other options: The Computer Recycling Center in Mountain View, California, refurbishes dead hardware and donates it to local schools, while the National Cristina

Foundation in Greenwich, Connecticut, and the East-West Foundation in Boston, Massachusetts donate reconditioned hardware to charity. Reclaimers such as Ecology Plus in San Jose, California, will take (in large quantities) just about any dead computer equipment. Check your area for similar organizations.

Consumer Caveat: Recycled Cartridges

When it comes to recycling toner cartridges, green computing has its opportunists. Some "drill and fill" companies do just that—dump new toner into an old cartridge, which can leak and damage your printer. Make sure the cartridge is *remanufactured*—disassembled, worn parts replaced, and new toner poured in (a toner cartridge can only be refilled a few times). Also confirm that using remanufactured cartridges doesn't invalidate your printer warranty.

Finally, a note about the future. Thanks to strict European disposal laws, U.S. vendors are now designing PCs that will be easier to disassemble and recycle. IBM and HP, for example, already make some PC and printer shells out of a single plastic that's easier to reclaim; other vendors use a snap-apart design instead of cumbersome adhesives and permanent fasteners. Future PCs won't be biodegradable, but they'll be more recyclable than many other industrial products.

Product and Resource Directory

Monitor Accessories

ACCO USA
770 S. Acco Plaza
Wheeling, IL 60090
800/222-6462

I-Protect
6151 W. Century Blvd. #916
Los Angeles, CA 90045
310/215-1664

Kantek
15 Main St.
East Rockaway, NY 11518
800/536-3212

NoRad
1160 E. Sandhill Ave.
Carson, CA 90746
800/262-3260

OCLI
2789 Northpoint Pkwy.
Santa Rosa, CA 95407
707/545-6440

Power-Saving Products

FaxPak
TeleDisk Systems
2401 Marinship Way #300
Sausalito, CA 94965
800/669-3700

MonitorMiser
Technology Marketing
  Partners
535 Del Rey Ave.
Sunnyvale, CA 94086
415/940-7800

PrinterFax
Moonlight Computer Products
5965 Pacific Center Blvd. #711
San Diego, CA 92121
619/625-0300

Fax Me
Practical Peripherals
375 Conejo Ridge Ave.
Thousand Oaks, CA 91361
805/497-4774

Smartbar
Sequence Electronics
150 Rosamond St.
Carlton Place, Ontario,
Canada K7C 1V2
800/663-1833
613/257-4773

Wattless VDU Power Saver
Ergonomics Inc.
P.O. Box 964
655 2nd St. Pike
Southampton, PA 18966
215/357-5124

Paper-Saving Printer Utilities

4Print
Korenthal Associates
511 Ave. of the Americas #400
New York, NY 10011
212/242-1790

ClickBook
Bookmaker Corp.
2470 El Camino Real #108
Palo Alto, CA 94306
415/354-8161

MicroText
OsoSoft
1472 Sixth St.
Los Osos, CA 93402
805/528-1759

Organizations

Campaign for VDT Safety
9 to 5: National Association
  of Working Women
614 Superior Ave. NW
Cleveland, OH 44113
216/566-9308

Computer Recycling Center
1245 Terra Bella Ave.
Mountain View, CA 94043
415/428-3700

East-West Foundation
55 Temple Pl.
Boston, MA 02111
617/542-1234

Ecology Plus
1701 Rogers Ave., Unit F
San Jose, CA 95112
408/452-7717

Energy Star Program
Environmental Protection
  Agency
Global Change Division
Washington, DC 20460
202/233-9114
202/233-9659 (fax-back service)

HP/Support Materials
  Organization
8000 Foothill Blvd.
Roseville, CA 95678
916/785-7124

National Cristina Foundation
591 W. Putnam Ave.
Greenwich, CT 06830-6095
203/622-6000

Repetitive Motion Institute
Valley Health Center
750 S. Bascom Ave.
San Jose, CA 95128
408/299-8016

Silicon Valley Toxics Coalition
760 N. First St.
San Jose, CA 95112
408/287-6707

VDT Coalition
Labor Occupational
  Health Program
University of California
2515 Channing Way, 2nd Fl.
Berkeley, CA 94720
510/642-5507

VDT Eye Clinic
University of California
Optometric Eye Center
200 Minor Hall
Berkeley, CA 94720
510/642-1399

Publications

Recycled Papers:
The Essential Guide
The MIT Press
55 Hayward St.
Cambridge, MA 02142
800/356-0343
617/625-8569

Solving the Puzzle of
VDT Viewing Problems
National Lighting Bureau
2101 L St. NW #300
Washington, DC 20037
202/457-8437

VDT Trainer's Kit
Labor Occupational
  Safety & Health
University of California,
  Los Angeles
1001 Gayley Ave., 2nd Fl.
Los Angeles, CA 90024
310/794-0383

VDT News
(September/October
annual product directory)
P.O. Box 1799
Grand Central Station
New York, NY 10163
212/517-2802

12

Windows and DOS

By Robert Lauriston

- Windows and DOS for absolute beginners
- A reference for everyday Windows and DOS tasks
- How to set up DOS and Windows on a new hard disk
- The regular maintenance that your PC needs to stay in shape
- Windows' mini-applications, from Paintbrush to Write
- How to set up DOS applications under Windows

When you sit down at your computer, you know what you want to do—write a letter, log some checks, play a game—but something always seems to get in the way. Actually, two things get in the way: DOS and Windows.

You can't easily avoid these two obstacles, either. Without DOS, the *operating system* software that keeps your hardware humming, your PC would be a useless tangle of circuitry. Without Windows, you couldn't use Windows applications—and from word processors to electronic address books, Windows applications almost always let you do more in less time with fewer headaches than old-fashioned DOS applications do.

Where Windows is sometimes awkward to use, DOS can be infuriating. Sad to say, you should really learn a little about both. This chapter is devoted to teaching you most of what you need to know about Windows and DOS—enough to get your work done and stay out of trouble. If you already know your way around, and you want to learn (or remember) how to do something specific, turn to the Cookbook later in this chapter, or to Appendix C: *Important Stuff DOS's Help Doesn't Tell You.*

Why Both Windows and DOS?

DOS provides the basic services for computing, sort of like a building's foundation provides power and plumbing hookups. Just as you can't make dinner, take a hot shower, or zone out in front of the TV in an unfinished building, you can't do much on a PC without an application. Run a DOS application (say, *WordPerfect 5.1*), and you've built a small, single-family home on the foundation. Run Windows, and you've built an apartment building where several applications can live at the same time, sharing DOS's basic services plus the added amenities that Windows provides.

Windows supplies its applications with a common *user interface*—the mosaic of words, buttons, arrows, and bars that determines how an application looks and works. This means Windows applications tend to look and work alike, so if you know how to use one or two Windows applications, you can often learn a new one quickly, because it will have many similar menus and commands.

Windows' unified way of working has other benefits. Not only can you run several applications at one time (and shuttle between, say, a spreadsheet and word processor), you can also copy data from one application to another pretty easily. And when you buy a new printer or other piece of hardware, a simple installation procedure ensures that most every Windows application you use from then on will work with that hardware.

These conventions make life easier, but no matter what anyone tells you, the real reason to use Windows is for its applications. Programs like *Excel* and *Word for Windows* are far from perfect, but they're about as good as software gets.

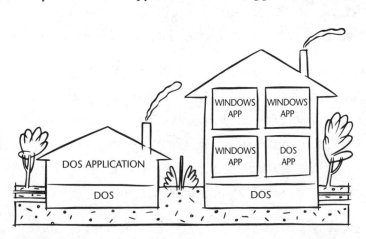

Why Windows Is Better Than DOS Alone. *Like single-family homes, DOS applications stand apart—each one has a different "look," and it takes a while to get from one to another. Windows applications are more like apartment units: Get familiar with one and you can learn your way around another easily, and next door is only a step away.*

〜〜〜〜〜〜〜〜〜〜〜〜〜〜〜〜〜〜〜〜〜〜〜〜〜

The 10-Minute Windows Tour

Windows itself is an *environment*, a place where you work in applications and switch between them, as well as organize the data you create with them. This tour will acquaint you with this environment, and prepare you for the everyday tasks covered in the special Cookbook section later in this chapter.

Windows can be a little confusing when you're just starting out. The easiest way to learn is just to dig in and begin learning Windows' basic conventions, which are pretty much consistent for both Windows and its applications. There are two main attractions on this tour:

- **The Program Manager** is the place where you start applications and arrange them in groups so you can find them easily.

- **The File Manager** is the place where you copy, move, and otherwise manipulate files, the basic units of data in both Windows and DOS.

We'll stop the bus when we get to the File Manager and have a good look, because the File Manager clearly shows how Windows and DOS keep your files organized. Understand this simple arrangement, and you'll find it easy to perform most Windows and DOS tasks.

This tour assumes that both Windows and DOS have already been installed on your PC. In the unlikely event that they haven't been, you can find out how to do it yourself in the section following the Cookbook, "How to Install DOS and Windows." This tour also requires a mouse. If you haven't installed one, turn to Chapter 8: *Upgrade It Yourself* for detailed instructions.

The Tour Starts Here

When you turn on your PC, it may go directly into Windows, or you may land in DOS itself—it all depends on how someone (or the company that sold you the computer) has set up your PC. You'll know if you're in DOS because all you'll see is a blank screen plus something called the *DOS prompt*, which looks like this:

```
C:\>
```

This prompt is where you type in the commands that tell DOS to do your bidding. You can find out more about DOS later in this chapter. For now, simply type cd\windows and press the Enter key. Then type win and press Enter. Your hard disk will whir for a bit, and Windows will start. If you're using Windows for the first time, this is what you'll see:

This window is the Program Manager. You use it both to start and to organize applications.

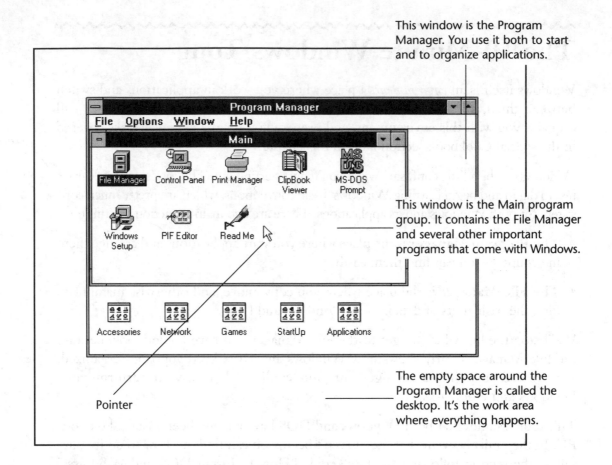

This window is the Main program group. It contains the File Manager and several other important programs that come with Windows.

Pointer

The empty space around the Program Manager is called the desktop. It's the work area where everything happens.

This is Program Manager's menu bar. Move the mouse pointer so the tip of the arrow rests on Help.

Click, that is, tap the mouse's left button, on the word "Help" to drop down the Help menu.

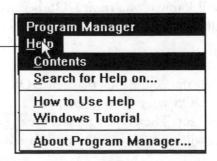

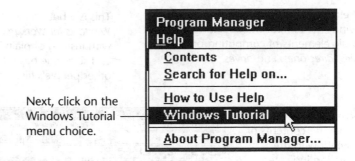

Next, click on the
Windows Tutorial
menu choice.

Choosing Windows Tutorial from
the Help menu starts this interactive
introduction to Windows and
mouse basics. Follow the instructions
on screen to run the tutorial now,
or press the [Esc] key to skip the
tutorial and continue with this tour.

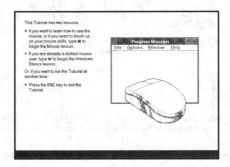

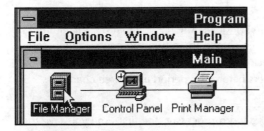

Now move the mouse pointer to the File Manager
icon and *double-click*, that is, tap the mouse's
left button twice, quickly. If nothing happens,
try again, faster.

After you double-click the File Manager icon, you'll see the
pointer turn into an hourglass for a split second. This is
Windows' way of telling you to wait. Get used to it.

Welcome to the File Manager. This is Windows' tool for manipulating the basic elements of computing on a PC: *files, directories,* and *drives.*

This is a button bar. You'll see this one only if you have *Windows for Workgroups,* which many new PCs come with instead of plain Windows. If you're on a network and someone has set things up right, you can access other people's files and applications using these buttons.

Scroll arrows steadily move the contents of a window in the direction indicated. Just put the pointer on the desired arrow and hold down the left mouse button.

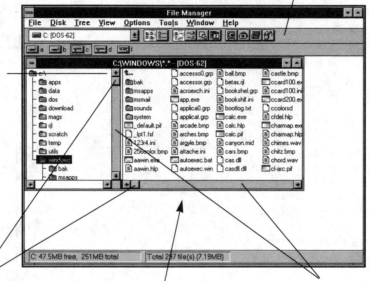

Scroll boxes provide the fastest way to scroll. Move the pointer to one, hold down the left mouse button, and drag the button along the scroll bar in the desired direction.

These are *scroll bars.* You use them to view information you can't currently see on screen. All Windows applications have them.

Rules for Naming Files

Take a good look at the files in the *directory window.* In Windows, the *file names* always fall immediately to the right of the file icon. You'll see that the file names are in two segments—one before and one after a period. For some ungodly reason, back in ancient PC history someone decided that file names can have no more than eight characters before the period and three characters after (the second segment is known as the *file extension*).

When you create a data file in an application, such as a word processor, the first time you save the file (that is, copy it to your hard disk for safekeeping) you have to give it a file name. Unfortunately, nearly every application proclaims its ownership of the file you name by adding its own extension—DOC for a *Word for Windows* file, for example.

This leaves you a measly eight characters with which to create a descriptive name for a file. For example, as I write this, the name of the file I'm working in is CH12AED2.DOC, which means "Chapter 12A, edit revision 2" to me, but *only* to me. That's the effect of being strapped for characters: To track their files, people create code names that no one else can decipher.

This is a *program file,* which contains the programming code applications are made of. Program file icons look like little windows.

These are *data files.* They contain information you or someone else has created using an application. They look like little pages—a good way to think about them, because (as you'll see) you store files as you do paper documents. The File Manager represents data files it recognizes as pages with printing on them.

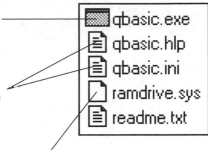

When the File Manager can't figure out which application created a file, it represents the file as a blank page.

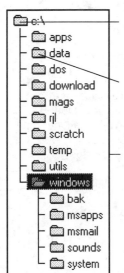

This is the *root* directory. All the other directories branch from it. The files most important to the basic functioning of your system live here.

This is a *directory* (sometimes called a *subdirectory*). It looks like a file folder, and just like the real thing you use it to store files and other folders. Double-click on any directory, and all files as well as any directories inside it appear. In a given directory, each file must have a different name.

This display of directories, which shows where each directory is in relation to the others, is called the *directory tree,* so named because the lines showing directory locations branch like the limbs of a tree.

This is the *path.* It shows the name of the directory on the directory tree that you've highlighted with your pointer.

These are your PC's *drives.* Usually, A: is your floppy disk drive, B: is your second floppy drive (if you have one), and C: is your hard disk. To complicate matters, a single hard disk may be divided into several *logical drives* (or *volumes*) instead of one big C:, you have C:, D:, E:, and so on, each with its own root directory, subdirectories, and files. Drive letters D: and beyond may also refer to other actual hard disks, CD ROM drives, network drives, or other devices (see Chapter 4: *Disk Drives*).

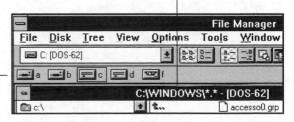

With all this attention to File Manager, what happened to Program Manager? It's still there. If you had X-ray specs, you could see it—*behind* File Manager. Click File Manager's minimize button...

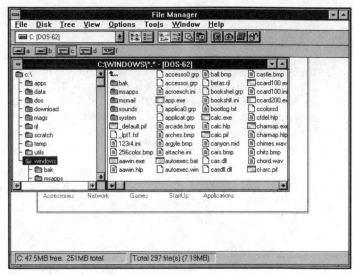

Minimize button   Maximize button

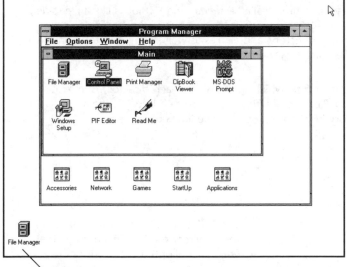

Application icon

...to shrink File Manager into an icon on the desktop. Double-click that icon, and File Manager returns to its previous size.

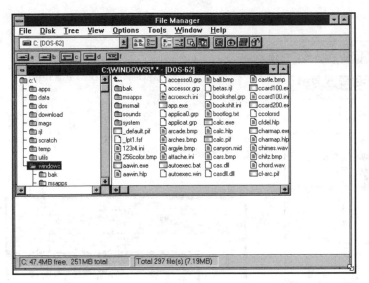

You can see both File and Program Manager at once by changing the size of File Manager's window. Position the pointer over the window's lower-right corner. When it changes to a double-arrow shape, click...

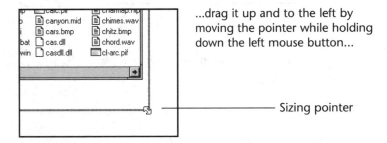

...drag it up and to the left by moving the pointer while holding down the left mouse button...

Sizing pointer

...and then let go. Now you can see Program Manager peeking out from behind File Manager. To bring it to the front, just click on it.

Title bar

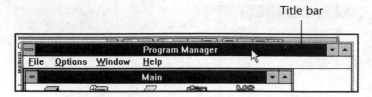

Now move the Program Manager by clicking on its title bar and dragging down and to the right.

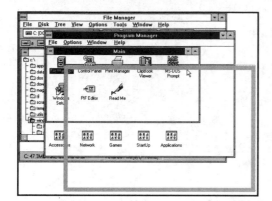

When the outline is in the right spot, let go of the mouse...

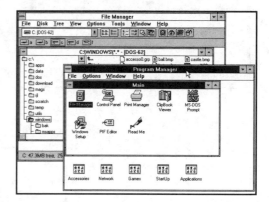

...to drop the window in place.

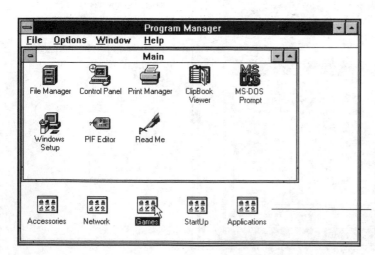

These are Program Manager's program group icons. Each program group is a kind of expandable cubbyhole in which you can store similar applications. Try double-clicking on the Games program group icon.

Although the icon for the Games group is *within* Program Manager's window, it behaves just as the File Manager icon did when you double-clicked on it on the desktop. The Games icon turns into a window—or rather, in Windows lingo, the window *restores* itself to the same size it was last time it was open.

Drag the upper-left corner of the Games group window down and to the right to make the window smaller.

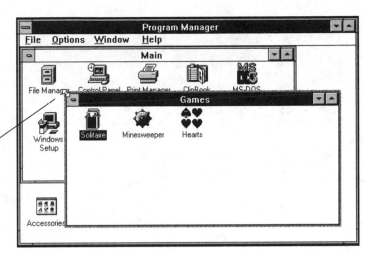

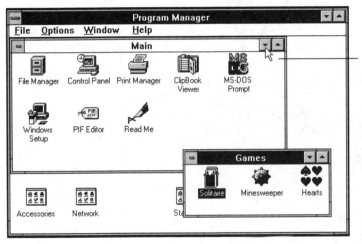

Now click on the Main group window's Minimize button to reduce it to an icon.

Double-click on the Accessories group to restore it, then...

—...click on its Maximize button...

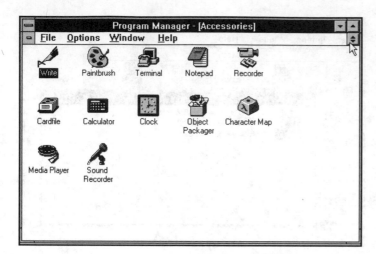

...to make the Accessories group window fill the Program Manager window. There are a few useful little programs here, which are discussed at the end of this chapter in the section "All That Windows Stuff."

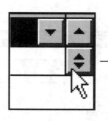

To return the Accessories window to its previous size, click its Restore button...

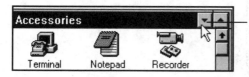

...and then click its Minimize button to reduce it to an icon.

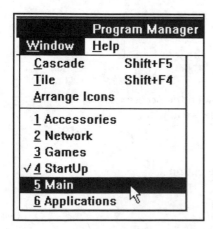

You can also switch between program groups using menu commands. Choose Main from the Window menu to switch to the Main group.

Then double-click on the Control Panel icon to open it.

Inside the Control Panel window, you'll find yet more useful programs, several of which you'll learn how to use later in this chapter. For now, double-click on the Desktop icon.

Welcome to a typical dialog box. You'll find dialog boxes like this one—with the same types of buttons, boxes, and so on—throughout Windows and its applications. You use dialog boxes to set options for programs and commands; the Desktop dialog box lets you change Windows' appearance and behavior.

Check boxes work like on/off switches. If you click this one, the check mark disappears. Click again, and it reappears.

List boxes work like option buttons, only you make your choice from a drop-down list.

Option buttons work like a car radio—only one button in a set can be on.

Command buttons are in every dialog box. Cancel and OK are universal. None of the selections you make take effect until you click OK.

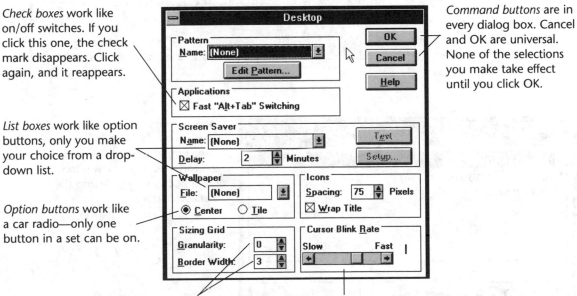

Text boxes let you type in data. The little up and down arrows are spinners—they let you enter numeric data by "spinning" numbers up or down, like setting a digital clock.

Sliders are used to set options with a continuously variable range, like blink speed, sound volume, or brightness.

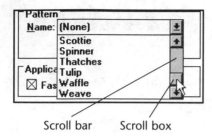

Scroll bar   Scroll box

Try changing the desktop Pattern. Click on the list box arrow to drop down the list, drag the scroll box to the bottom of the scroll bar, and click on Weave. (The Wallpaper box should read [None]; if it doesn't, change it.) Click on OK to close the dialog box, and the Weave pattern will appear on the desktop.

With Program Manager, File Manager, and the Control Panel all open, the desktop is getting pretty cluttered. As you open additional programs, switching between them by clicking one with the mouse becomes impractical. Instead, double-click on an empty part of the desktop or press Control Esc to display the Task List.

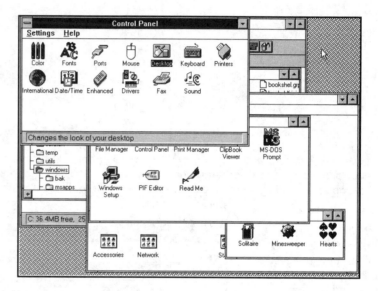

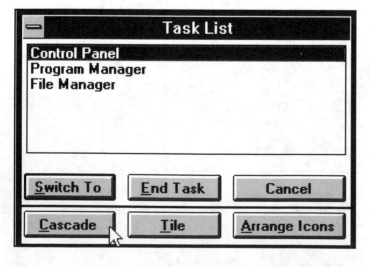

You can switch to any running program by double-clicking on its name in the Task List. If you wish, you can rearrange the windows into a neat stack by clicking the Cascade button.

Control menu box

When you finish working in a
program, close it by double-clicking
its control menu box.

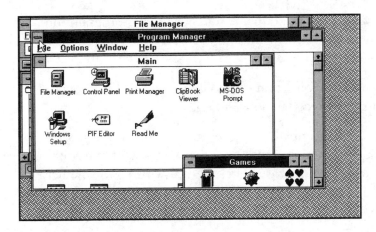

When you finish working in
Windows, double-click on the
Program Manager's control menu
box to exit. Remember, when you
turn off your PC, *always* exit
Windows first.

DANGER

So long!

The Minimum DOS You Must Know

If Windows is so great, why do you need to know about DOS at all? After all, as you'll see in the Cookbook, Windows offers an easier way of doing almost everything you'd need to do with DOS. Here are four reasons you may need to get acquainted with DOS anyway:

1. **You can't afford Windows.** If you inherited an old 286 or 386 PC and you can't afford to buy a new one, you may not have adequate computing power to run Windows. That means you have to use old-fashioned DOS applications, and you need to learn DOS itself pretty well.

2. **You need to run one or two DOS programs.** A number of vital programs do not work with Windows. Neither do many games. To run these DOS programs, you need to know a few DOS basics.

3. **Sometimes using DOS is easier.** Doing things in Windows gets a little convoluted at times, so it's less hassle to do certain jobs in DOS.

4. **Things go wrong.** DOS wasn't originally designed to support Windows, so sometimes Windows gets shaky, or simply refuses to work at all. At times like these you may have to go down into the basement and deal with DOS whether you like it or not. While you might be able to avoid #1, #2, and #3, you need to be ready for this one—unless you have a PC expert on call.

Everything a typical PC user is likely to need to do in DOS is covered in the Cookbook later in this chapter. To follow those instructions, it helps to have a basic explanation of how to work with DOS. So, here goes!

DOS Prompt Basics

How do you get to the DOS prompt, the place where you tell DOS what to do? If your machine hasn't been set up to go directly into Windows, the DOS prompt is the only thing you'll see when you turn on your PC. If you're in Windows, switch to the Program Manager, then choose Exit from the File menu and click OK. If you're in a DOS application, you'll have to figure out how to exit that application and get to DOS.

Great. Now you're in DOS, your PC's basement. It's hard to see down here. Instead of Windows' pretty wallpaper patterns, you get a little sign glowing alone in the dark: the "C:\>" prompt mentioned at the beginning of the Windows tour. (If your prompt *doesn't* look like this, type `prompt $p$g` and press the (Enter) key.)

Loosely translated, DOS is saying, "Ready for orders, master." To tell DOS to do something, you type a *command*, and then press the (Enter) key.

Displaying The Contents of The Current Directory

Let's start with the first DOS command everyone learns, the DIR command. This command displays a list of all file names and any directory names in your *current directory* ("C:\>" means you are currently in drive C:'s root directory). Type `dir`, and those three letters will appear to the right of the DOS prompt, like this:

```
C:\>dir
```

Press (Enter), and you'll see a directory listing that looks more or less like this (exactly what you see depends on what's stored on your hard drive):

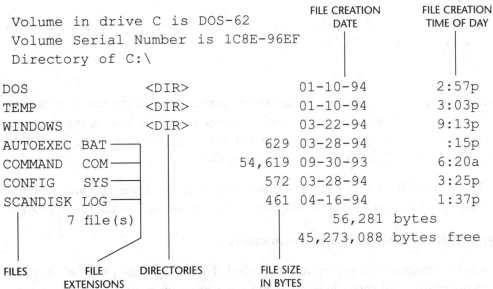

```
C:\>dir
                                    FILE CREATION      FILE CREATION
                                        DATE            TIME OF DAY
   Volume in drive C is DOS-62
   Volume Serial Number is 1C8E-96EF
   Directory of C:\

DOS               <DIR>             01-10-94            2:57p
TEMP              <DIR>             01-10-94            3:03p
WINDOWS           <DIR>             03-22-94            9:13p
AUTOEXEC  BAT              629      03-28-94             :15p
COMMAND   COM           54,619      09-30-93            6:20a
CONFIG    SYS              572      03-28-94            3:25p
SCANDISK  LOG              461      04-16-94            1:37p
         7 file(s)                  56,281 bytes
                                45,273,088 bytes free

FILES      FILE      DIRECTORIES    FILE SIZE
        EXTENSIONS                  IN BYTES
```

Typing a DOS command and pressing (Enter) is commonly referred to as *entering* a command—when someone tells you to "enter" a DOS command, they mean "type it and press (Enter)." Same thing if someone tells you to "do" a command, as in "do a DIR." **REMEMBER**

You can modify the behavior of most DOS commands by adding *switches* to them. For example, try adding the /OD switch to the DIR command to display the files sorted by date:

```
C:\>dir /od
 Volume in drive C is DOS-62
 Volume Serial Number is 1C8E-96EF
 Directory of C:\

COMMAND   COM              54,619 09-30-93          6:20a
DOS              <DIR>             01-10-94          2:57p
TEMP             <DIR>             01-10-94          3:03p
WINDOWS          <DIR>             03-22-94          9:13p
CONFIG    SYS                 572 03-28-94          3:25p
AUTOEXEC  BAT                 629 03-28-94          6:15p
SCANDISK  LOG         461 04-16-94          1:37p
        7 file(s)                     56,281 bytes
                            45,273,088 bytes free
```

Changing Directories

Now let's try the CD (change directory) command: Enter `cd\dos` and the DOS prompt will change from C:\> to:

```
C:\DOS>
```

This indicates that you've changed your current directory from the root directory to the DOS directory. In so doing, you've taken a step along one limb of the directory tree, just as you could do by clicking on a different directory in Windows' File Manager. You just can't see what you're doing in DOS.

Enter `dir`, and you'll see a list of all files in the DOS directory. Enter `cd\` and the DOS prompt changes back to C:\>, indicating that you've moved back to the root directory.

Adding Paths or File Names to Commands

Paths, which are simply directory names preceded by a backslash, can be added to DOS commands to indicate where an action performed by a command should happen. For example, you can do a DIR on the DOS directory without leaving the root directory. Just type `dir`, a space, and the DOS directory's path, `c:\dos`. The root directory's DOS prompt, plus what you've typed, should look like this. Don't forget the space:

```
C:\>dir c:\dos
```

Press (Enter) and you'll see the same directory listing you saw when you entered DIR in the DOS directory.

Now let's see if a *specific file* named FORMAT.COM is in the DOS directory. Enter the same path as before, followed by a backslash and the file name. What you've entered, plus the resulting partial directory listing, should look like this:

```
C:\>dir c:\dos\format.com

 Volume in drive C is DOS-62
 Volume Serial Number is 1C8E-96EF
 Directory of C:\DOS

FORMAT     COM             22,916 09-30-93         6:20a
        1 file(s)                    56,281 bytes
                              45,273,088 bytes free
```

That's really all the DOS you need to know to follow the instructions in the rest of this chapter. If you want to learn more, go through the Cookbook and experiment with the commands it describes, and read Appendix C: *Important Stuff DOS's Help Doesn't Tell You.*

Windows and DOS Cookbook

You seldom need more than a handful of mouse clicks or commands to get Windows or DOS to do most of what you need it to do. If you'd like to learn how to perform common tasks in a hurry, and maybe learn a few handy tricks besides, then you've come to the right place.

This Cookbook explains step by step how to perform 18 file, disk, and application tasks in both Windows and DOS. Why in both, since Windows usually offers an easier way of doing anything DOS can do? Because even if you'd love to avoid the DOS prompt, you'll probably find yourself there sooner or later, either to run old software or to fix problems.

Beginners who find any part of this Cookbook confusing should turn to the brief introduction to Windows and DOS at the beginning of this chapter. If you're more advanced, and you can't find what you're looking for here, turn to the end of this chapter for more tips, or check out the various appendixes for detailed advice on customizing and configuring DOS and Windows.

File Tasks

Disk Tasks

Application Tasks

~~~~~~

To see what files are in a directory...

You need to see where a file is located before you open it in an application, move it, or otherwise manipulate it. Files live in directories, so that's where you look for them.

Do this in Windows:

1. Start the File Manager.

2. Click View on the File Manager's menu bar, and select the Tree and Directory option.

3. In the directory tree display (the left window), click on the directory folder you think contains the files you want. The files in that directory will appear in the right window.

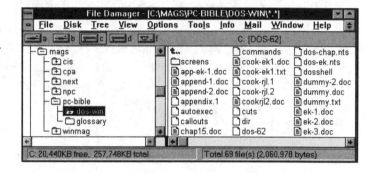

4. If there are more files in the directory than File Manager can show all at once, select View//Directory Only to omit the directory tree and see more files. You can also scroll, of course, or—for the biggest possible view—maximize the File Manager itself by clicking on the up arrow in the upper-right corner. (If there's still a small directory window within the maximized File Manager, then maximize that window in the same way.)

By default, File Manager displays only file names. If you want more information, select View//All File Details to display file size, the date and time the file was last saved, and the file attributes (select a file, choose File//Properties, and click on the Help button in the dialog box for more information on file attributes). Or select View//Partial Details, and check the boxes for only those details you want to see on screen.

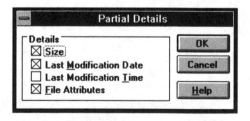

By default, File Manager displays files in alphabetical order. If you want to change that, pick one of the Sort options from the View menu. The most useful option is Sort by Type, which groups files by their extensions—so if you want to quickly scroll through just the DOC files, for example, you'll find them all in one segment of the directory list.

Do this in DOS:

The DOS prompt tells you which directory you are in—C:\WINDOWS> would be your Windows directory, for example. (If you just see C>, add the line `prompt $p$g` to your AUTOEXEC.BAT file; see Appendix A: *Tuning CONFIG.SYS and AUTOEXEC.BAT* for more information.) To see what files are in your current directory, enter:

`dir`

A list will scroll by showing the name and size of every file in the directory, along with the date and time it was last edited. To get a list of all files, sorted alphabetically (/o) one screenful at a time (/p), enter:

`dir /o/p`

To list all files, grouped by extension and then sorted alphabetically by name (/oen), one screenful at a time (/p), enter:

`dir /oen/p`

To list all files sorted by date (/od), enter:

`dir /od`

To list only those files with the TXT extension, enter:

`dir *.txt`

To see all files starting with the letter *d,* enter:

`dir d*`

To list files in a directory other than the current one, enter the full directory path name. For example, to see all the 1-2-3 data files in C:\WORK, you would enter:

`dir c:\work\*.wk?`

For more on the wildcards * and ?, see "To select multiple files..." a little later in this Cookbook.

Danger Zone: Hidden Files

Normally, neither DOS nor Windows lists *hidden* files, which are special files that DOS, Windows, and some applications need to operate properly. There's a reason for hidden files' invisibility: If you rename, delete, or move them, you may lose data, crash your system, or both! The most likely reason you'd want to see hidden files is to discover how much disk space they're taking up. To reveal hidden files with the File Manager, select View//By File Type and check the Hidden Files check box; hidden files will be marked by an exclamation mark icon. To reveal them in a DOS directory listing, type `dir` followed by a space and `/a`, then press Enter.

To move from one directory to another...

The file you want to do something with often resides in a directory other than the one you're in—so you need to look in another directory to find the file.

Do this in Windows:

In the File Manager:

1. Check the first letter on the title bar to make sure you're on the drive you want to be on. If not, click on the appropriate drive icon (just below the title bar) to change drives.

2. Select the View//Tree and Directory command.

3. Use the scroll bar in the middle of the File Manager window to scroll through the tree in the left Window until you find the folder icon for the directory you want. If you prefer, you can navigate using the keyboard's up and down cursor keys.

4. To display a directory's contents in the right window, click on its folder in the left window. If a directory folder appears in the right window and you want to display its contents, double-click on it.

If you select Tree//Indicate Expandable Branches, you'll note that all directories containing other directories have a plus sign on them. When you click on a folder to display its subsidiary directories, the folder opens and the plus sign turns into a minus sign. To reveal all the subdirectories on the drive without having to open folders, select Tree//Expand All.

In the File//Open and File//Save dialog boxes found in most Windows applications:

1. Select another drive from the Drives list if the dialog box displays the wrong drive.

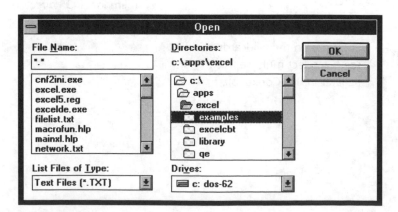

2. Instead of a full tree display, Windows' dialog boxes give you just the path for the current directory, both as text (C:\APPS\EXCEL in the example) and as a hierarchy of folder icons. Files are displayed in the left window.

3. To move to a different subdirectory, double-click on the folder icons. For example, to switch to C:\DOS, you'd double-click on C:\ to display the directories in the root directory, then double-click on the DOS folder.

Do this in DOS:

Use the CD (for "change directory") command followed by the name of the destination directory to move from one directory to another. For example, to move to a different directory on the current drive (say, the DOS directory), enter:

```
cd\dos
```

To move to a directory on another drive—say, from C:\ to A:\DATA—you need to switch to the other drive before using the CD command:

```
a:
cd\data
```

To move to the root directory of the current drive, enter:

```
cd\
```

To move up one level—that is, from the current directory to the directory immediately above it on the directory tree—enter:

```
cd..
```

To move from one directory to another directory lower down on the same branch of the tree, just leave out the backslash. For example, to move from the Windows directory (C:\WINDOWS) to the Windows system directory (C:\WINDOWS\SYSTEM), enter:

```
cd system
```

To move between two subdirectories with the same parent directory—for example, from C:\WINDOWS\SYSTEM to C:\WINDOWS\MSAPPS—enter:

```
cd..\msapps
```

To copy or move files or directories...

Copying and moving files and directories are part of routine disk housekeeping. There are a million reasons to perform either task—to copy files from your hard disk to a floppy so someone else can use them, to move files from a working directory to one that contains finished work, and so forth.

Do this in Windows:

1. Start the File Manager, and select Tree and Directory from the View menu.

2. If only one directory window in the File Manager is open, select Window//New Window, then press [Shift][F4] to tile the two windows vertically.

3. In the left directory window, click the *source directory*, that is, the directory *from which* you want to copy or move a file.

4. In the right directory window, click the *target directory*, that is, the directory *to which* you want to copy or move a file.

5. Select the file(s) that you want to move or copy (see "To select multiple files..." later in this Cookbook).

6. To *move* the file between one hard disk directory and another, hold down the left mouse button, drag the file from the source directory to the target directory, and release the mouse button to *drop* the file, completing the action. To move the file between a hard disk directory and a floppy, hold down the [Alt] key as you drag and drop.

7. To *copy* the file between one hard disk directory and another, hold down both the left mouse button *and* the [Ctrl] key, drag the file from the source directory to the target directory, and release the button to drop the file. To copy a file between your hard disk and a floppy, simply drag and drop without using the [Ctrl] key.

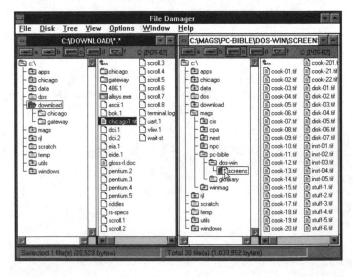

The procedure for moving and copying directories is identical to the one for files. Moreover, you can drop files or directories anywhere in a directory or on a folder in the tree display. You can even drop a file or directory on one of the drive icons at the top of the window—a handy method for copying files to floppy disks in your A: or B: drive.

Do this in DOS:

Use the COPY, XCOPY, or MOVE commands (the XCOPY command makes copying directories easier). As usual in DOS, you need to type not only the file name but at least one full directory path name to move or copy a file.

To copy a file named LETTER1.DOC *from* your current directory to a directory named \CORRESP on your C: drive, enter:

```
copy letter1.doc c:\corresp
```

To copy a file named LETTER1.DOC to your current directory *from* a directory named \CORRESP on your C: drive, enter:

```
copy c:\corresp\letter1.doc
```

To move LETTER1.DOC rather than copy it, simply substitute the MOVE command for the COPY command, as in:

```
move c:\corresp\letter1.doc
```

To copy the entire contents of your C:\WORK directory to a floppy, enter:

```
copy c:\work a:\
```

To copy a group of directories in one pass, you need to use XCOPY. For example, to copy C:\1994 and all the directories beneath it to W:\BACKUP, you would enter:

```
xcopy c:\1994 w:\backup\1994 /s/e/v
```

To copy all files with the DOC extension from your current directory to a floppy, enter:

```
copy *.doc a:
```

The /s switch specifies that all directories under C:\1994 containing files will be copied, the /e switch specifies that empty directories will also be copied, and the /v switch makes DOS verify that everything was copied correctly. Note that with XCOPY, you always need to enter the complete path for the source and target directories.

Danger Zone:
Overwrite Confirmation

If you copy or move a file from one directory to another, and there's a file in the target directory that has the same name, both Windows File Manager and DOS ask you whether you want to *replace* the file in the target directory, that is, if you want to overwrite the file in the target directory with the file of the same name from the source directory. If you don't want this to happen, you need to rename one of the files before proceeding (see "To rename files or directories..." in this Cookbook).

To select multiple files...

If you need to do the same thing (move, copy, delete, and so on) to a group of files or directories, you can often avoid time-wasting repetition by selecting all the files first and entering the command once.

Do this in Windows:

1. Start the File Manager and go to the directory containing the files you want to select.

2. To select several adjacent files (or directories) from the directory list, click the first file, hold down the (Shift) key, and then click the last file.

3. To select files (or directories) scattered throughout the list, click the first file, hold down (Ctrl), and click each additional file.

For other selection options—such as selecting all files in a directory—choose Select Files from File Manager's File menu and use DOS wildcards, described in the next paragraph.

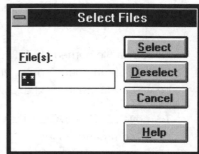

Do this in DOS:

Use *wildcards*, which are special characters that stand in for actual characters in a file name similar to the way jokers substitute for real cards in card games. The asterisk (*) represents multiple characters, while the question mark (?) represents a single character. Here are a few common examples using DOS's COPY command:

copy *.*	all files
copy *.doc	all files with the extension .DOC
copy d*.*	all files starting with *d*
copy ??	all files with one- or two-character names
copy a??c	all files with four-character names that begin with *a* and end with *c* (a24c, azbc, aaac, and so on)
copy ??.w*	all files with one- or two-character names and extensions starting with *w*

DANGER Note that DOS ignores any characters it finds after an asterisk (the period excepted). For example, if you mistakenly entered *w.*, DOS would read it as *.* without the w.

To create a directory...

It's faster and easier to find files if you arrange them in directories. You may also need to create directories for programs that don't install automatically.

Do this in Windows:

1. Start the File Manager and select the View//Tree and Directory command.

2. In the directory tree window, click on the directory folder in which you want to create the new directory. To create a directory at the topmost level (that is, in the root directory), press the [Home] key to jump to the top of the tree, and click on the folder labeled only by the drive letter.

3. Select File//Create Directory.

4. Type the name you want to give the new directory and click OK.

Create Directory
Current Directory: C:\UTIL
Name: `pkzip`
OK
Cancel
Help

Do this in DOS:

1. Change to the directory in which you want to create the new directory.

2. Enter md followed by a space and the name of the new directory. For example, to create the directory C:\WORK\AUGUST95, enter:

```
c:
cd\work
md august95
```

Feeling confident? Then you can create the directory from anywhere, without changing directories first, by entering:

```
md c:\work\august95
```

To delete files or directories...

Old, useless copies of files often confuse matters and always take up disk space unnecessarily. The general rule: If you don't need it, delete it.

Do this in Windows:

1. Start the File Manager, and select the file or directory you want to delete.

2. Press the Delete key, then click the Yes button (or Yes to All button, if you're deleting multiple files or directories).

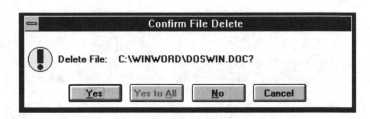

The way File Manager asks for confirmation every time you delete a file can be annoying. You can avoid that by selecting Confirmation on the File Manager's Options menu and unchecking File Delete in the resulting dialog box. While you're at it, you might as well eliminate other pointless interruptions by unchecking Mouse Action and Disk Commands. Deleting an entire directory is destruction on a mass

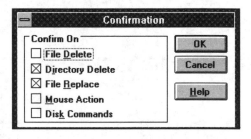

scale, so you may want to leave that confirmation option checked. The same goes for File Replace, which helps prevent the common mistake of copying an old version of a file over a new one.

Do this in DOS:

Deleting is about as straightforward as things get in DOS: Just enter DEL followed by a space and the file name. As usual, you need to include the path name if the file isn't in the current directory, along with wildcards if you want to delete multiple files. For example, to delete all TMP files in your C:\DOS directory, you'd enter:

```
del c:\dos\*.tmp
```

Now, here's a simple yet dangerous variation:

```
del c:\dos
```

In plain English, that means "delete everything in my DOS directory" (del c:\dos*.* is an explicit way of saying the same thing using wildcards). If you actually try to enter this command, DOS is smart enough to come back at you with, "All files in directory will be deleted! Are you sure (Y/N)?" Good thing, too, since you'd have trouble running your computer without DOS.

To get rid of entire directories, use the DELTREE command, which is even simpler—and more dangerous. It removes the specified directory, all directories beneath it, and all of their files. For example, to get rid of the C:\TEMP directory, enter:

```
deltree c:\temp
```

Fortunately, as with wholesale attempts at deleting files, DOS asks you to confirm DELTREE operations. To bypass the confirmation—say, when you want to delete all the files and directories on a floppy—add the /y switch, as in:

```
deltree /y a:\
```

If DELTREE makes you nervous, you can use DOS's RD (for "remove directory") command instead. Enter rd followed by a space and the directory name, and the directory will disappear—but only if it's completely empty of files.

~~~~~~

To rename files or directories...

The usual reason you need to rename a file or directory is to correct a typing mistake you made when you orginally named it. But there are a zillion other reasons—for example, to preserve an earlier version of a file.

Do this in Windows:

1. Start the File Manager and select the file or directory you want to rename.

2. Select File//Rename.

3. Type the new file or directory name, then click OK.

Using wildcards, you can also easily change the extension for a group of files in a directory. For example, to give any file in a directory with a TXT extension a DOC extension instead:

1. Choose Select Files from the File Manager's File menu.

2. Enter `*.txt` in the File(s): box.

3. Select File//Rename, enter `*.doc` in the To: box, and click OK.

```
┌──────────────────────────────── Rename ─────────────────────────────┐
│ ─                                                                    │
│ Current Directory: C:\SCRATCH                         ┌──────────┐   │
│                                                       │    OK    │   │
│ From:    │ 102.TXT AAPL.TXT MESA.TXT PGP.TXT │        └──────────┘   │
│                                                       ┌──────────┐   │
│ To:      │ *.doc                             │        │  Cancel  │   │
│                                                       └──────────┘   │
│                                                       ┌──────────┐   │
│                                                       │   Help   │   │
│                                                       └──────────┘   │
└─────────────────────────────────────────────────────────────────────┘
```

Do this in DOS:

To change a file's name, use the REN (for "rename") command followed by a space, the old file name, a space, and the new file name. For example, to change DRAFT.MAR to FINAL.DOC, enter:

```
ren draft.mar final.doc
```

To give a group of files with the same extension a different extension, use a wildcard. For example, to give all files with the SET extension the BAK extension, enter:

```
ren *.set *.bak
```

To change a directory name, you use the MOVE command, strangely enough. For example, to change C:\DATA\CIRREMT to C:\DATA\CURRENT, you'd enter:

```
move c:\cirremt current
```

You cannot use wildcards to rename multiple directories.

Danger Zone: Renaming Directories

Renaming program directories can cause big problems. Some programs expect to find files in certain places, and won't run properly, if at all, when you rename the directory in which they're stored. Unless you really know what you're doing, you should only rename directories that contain data files.

To find a file...

Unless you're better organized than anyone else, you'll occasionally forget where you saved a file.

Do this in Windows:

1. Start the File Manager. If it doesn't display the contents of the drive you want to search, click the desired drive icon. (You can only search one drive at a time.)

2. To search the entire drive, press the [Home] key to move to the top of the tree. To search only a particular directory, click on it.

3. Pick Search from the File Menu.

4. In the Search dialog box, type the name of the file you want to find after Search For:, or approximate the name with wildcards (for example, MO*.XL? to find all *Excel* data files that

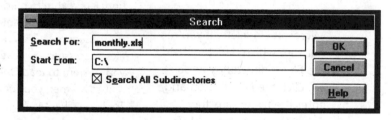

start with *mo*; see "To select multiple files..." for more on wildcards).

5. If you want to search only the current directory but *not* its subdirectories, uncheck Search All Subdirectories. Otherwise, leave it checked and click OK.

Do this in DOS:

Get a utility (such as one included in the excellent utility libraries *The Norton Utilities* and *PC Tools Pro*), because DOS itself has no facility for finding files. Or send $5 and the coupon from your DOS User's Guide to Microsoft to receive the company's DOS Shell, which includes a file search command and many other useful features for manipulating files in DOS.

To recover accidentally deleted files or directories...

Sooner or later, all of us accidentally delete a file or directory. Fortunately, you can almost always recover files (and usually directories) easily.

Do this in Windows:

1. Start the File Manager and select the directory that contained the deleted file or directory.

2. Select File//Undelete to start Microsoft Undelete. If you're not sure which directory held the file or directory you deleted, click the Find button and enter the file or directory name (or the name as close as you remember it, with wildcards).

Danger Zone: When You Delete by Mistake

If you delete a file or directory by accident, don't do anything else before you use either Windows' or DOS's undelete feature! The data is on disk, waiting to be recovered, but only if it's not overwritten by something else you do subsequently—such as copy or move a file. To recover files successfully a greater percentage of the time, set up your system to load Delete Sentry or Delete Tracker automatically when you turn on your machine (see "Recovery Tools" in Chapter 21: *Utilities*).

3. Scroll through the Microsoft Undelete list and click on each file or directory you want to recover. Notice that in place of the file or directory name's first character, a question mark may appear instead.

4. Click the Undelete button and replace the question marks with the first character of each file or directory name as prompted. If you don't know the missing character, pick whatever makes the most sense.

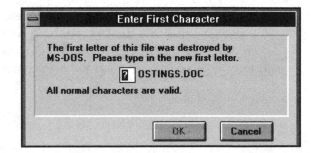

If you recovered a file or files in steps 1 through 4, you're done. If you just recovered a directory or directories, you're only half done, because recovering a directory does not automatically recover its files. Continue with the following steps to undelete a directory's files:

5. Click the Drive/Dir button.

6. Select the recovered directory from the Directories list in the Drives and Directories dialog box, then click OK.

7. Return to step 3.

Do this in DOS:

1. Change to the directory in which you deleted the files (DOS only recovers files, not directories) and enter `undelete`.

2. Undelete will show you the names of the recoverable files one at a time. For each one, press `y` to undelete it or `n` to skip it. If prompted, enter the missing first character of each file you choose to undelete. If you don't know the missing character, pick whatever makes the most sense.

To format a floppy...

You need to format a floppy disk before you can use it. Formatting lays down the basic informa-tion necessary for storing files.

Do this in Windows:

1. Insert the floppy disk.

2. Start the File Manager and select the Disk//Format Disk command.

3. Pick from the Disk In list the drive containing the floppy disk you want to format.

4. Adjust the Capacity setting if you're for-matting a low-density disk (that is, a 720K disk in a 3^1/$_2$-inch floppy drive or a 360K disk in a 5^1/$_4$-inch floppy drive).

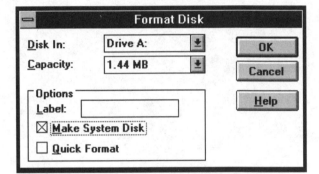

5. If you'd like a descriptive name for the disk to appear on File Manager's title bar, type up to 11 characters in the Label field.

6. Check Make System Disk only if you want to be able to boot your PC from the floppy.

7. Check Quick Format to quickly erase files from an already-formatted floppy.

8. Click OK to start formatting.

Danger Zone: Unformat Alert

If you're safety-minded, DOS has a big advantage over Windows—the ability to save unformat information, which makes it much easier to recover data from an accidentally formatted disk. Just add the /u switch to any of the varia-tions on DOS's FORMAT command on the opposite page. The only downside is that you lose a little bit of disk space in your quest for safety.

Do this in DOS:

Insert the floppy disk. Then enter one of the following commands. If the floppy is in the B: drive, substitute B: for A: in the command.

To format a brand-new floppy, enter:
```
format a:
```

To erase all files from an already-formatted floppy, enter:
```
format a: /q
```

To format a 720K floppy in a $3^1/2$-inch drive, enter:
```
format a: /f:720
```

To format a 360K floppy in a $5^1/4$-inch drive, enter:
```
format a: /4
```

To create a system disk that you can boot your PC from, add /s to any of the above variations on the format command, as in:
```
format a: /s
```

Whenever you format a disk, DOS will prompt you to enter a descriptive label after it finishes formatting. If you don't want to bother, just press [Enter].

To recover data from an accidentally formatted disk...

Hey, everybody makes mistakes. If you accidentally format a floppy or hard disk, you may be able to recover the data using DOS's Unformat utility.

Do this in Windows:

Go to the DOS prompt by exiting Windows or double-clicking on the MS-DOS Prompt icon in the Program Manager's Main group. Then follow the DOS instructions below.

Do this in DOS:

If you accidentally formatted drive C:, start at step 1. If you accidentally formatted a floppy disk or another hard disk, skip to step 4.

Danger Zone: Emergency Disks

The best way to recover from an accidental format—especially if you just formatted drive C: by mistake—is by using an emergency disk you've already created with a good commercial utility package such as *The Norton Utilities* or *PC Tools Pro*. If disaster strikes, you just stick the disk in drive A:, turn on your machine, and follow the instructions. You'll have a much better chance at recovering your data than if you use DOS's UNFORMAT command alone (see the "Recovery Tools" section of Chapter 21: *Utilities*).

1. Put your emergency disk in drive A: and turn on your PC. If you don't have an emergency disk, you're in trouble. If you know someone who uses the same version of DOS that you do, have them make you a boot disk and copy UNFORMAT.COM from their DOS directory onto the floppy (see the section "Safety Check" later in this chapter). Then continue with the following instructions.

2. Insert the boot disk in drive A:.

3. Press Ctrl Alt Delete to reboot. When you see the A:\> prompt, go to step 4.

4. Enter the command unformat c: (if you're unformatting a floppy or another hard disk, replace C: with the letter for that drive).

5. When prompted, press Enter. If DOS finds the unformatting data it's looking for, it will ask if you want to "update the system area" (that is, unformat the disk). If you see this prompt, press y and you're done.

6. If DOS *can't* find the unformatting data it's looking for, you'll see a prompt like this: "If you want to search for the MIRROR image file through the entire hard drive press y, or press n to cancel the UNFORMAT command" (DOS erroneously says "hard drive" even if it's working on a floppy). In plain English, you're screwed. If you see this, press y anyway.

7. Once DOS is satisfied that what it's looking for is not on the disk, you'll see another prompt asking, "Are you sure you want to do this?" Press y again, and DOS will recover what it can. Generally you won't get back any files that were in the root directory, and any subdirectories will be renamed arbitrarily: SUBDIR.1, SUBDIR.2, and so on.

To copy a floppy disk...

Sometimes you need to duplicate an entire floppy disk, either to make a backup copy or to give a copy to someone else.

Do this in Windows:

1. Start the File Manager and select Disk//Copy Disk.

2. If you have only one floppy drive, or one 3^1/2-inch and one 5^1/4-inch floppy drive, insert the disk you want to copy into the drive and set both Source In and Destination In to that drive letter.

3. Click OK. When you see the "Insert source disk" prompt, click OK again.

4. When prompted to "Insert destination disk," remove the disk you're copying from, insert the disk you want to copy to, and click OK. Any files already on the second disk will be erased.

DANGER

If you have two 3^1/2-inch or two 5^1/4-inch drives, Insert the disk you want to copy in drive A: and the disk you want to copy to in drive B:. Set Source In to A:, Destination In to B:, and click OK.

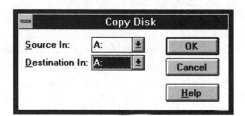

Do this in DOS:

1. Insert the disk you want to copy into the drive, and then enter the command: `diskcopy a: a:` (or `diskcopy b: b:`, as appropriate)

2. When you see the prompt, "Insert SOURCE diskette... Press any key to continue," press the space bar.

3. When you see the prompt, "Insert TARGET diskette... Press any key to continue," remove the disk you're copying from, insert the disk you want to copy to, and press the space bar.

In some cases you may have to repeat steps 2 and 3 several times, swapping the source and target disks in and out of the drive, before DISKCOPY is finished.

~~~~~~

To install an application...

Before you can use an application, you have to install it on your hard disk. This takes some time, but usually all you need to do is follow prompts once you get started.

Do this in Windows:

1. Start the File Manager and click on the A: (or B:, if appropriate) drive icon.

2. If you see any files named README, READ.ME, README.TXT, README.WRI, or something similar, they may contain important information about installation. If their file icons show up as documents (pages with four horizontal lines), double-click to open and read them. If they show up as generic blank pages, drag them into Notepad. Print out the file and look for any instructions you should follow during installation.

3. Double-click on the installation program (usually SETUP.EXE; check the application's manual). An installation routine will start that should lead you through the whole process step by step. If you opt for custom installation and you're not sure which options to leave in or leave out, check the manual—don't guess!

Do this in DOS:

1. Change to the A: (or B:, if appropriate) drive.

2. Enter the command:
```
dir read*
```

3. If the directory listing shows a README file with the extension BAT, COM, or EXE, check to see if there are any last minute changes to the installation instructions (if any) by entering the command:
```
readme
```

4. If the directory listing shows a file with a name like README.TXT, READ.ME, or README.1ST, use MORE to read the file, as in:
```
more < readme.1st
```

5. Enter the command to start the program's installation utility (usually `install` or `setup`), you'll probably be led step by step through an installation routine. However, in some cases, DOS programs need to be installed manually. It's easy: Just create a directory and copy the files from A:. For example, to install a hypothetical DOS utility called MemTest, you would enter the following:

```
md utils\memtest
cd utils\memtest
copy a: *.*
```

Note also that some programs are distributed in compressed files that must be decompressed manually before you can run the program. For more on compression schemes and compression utilities, see the section "Shareware and Freeware Utilities" in Chapter 21: *Utilities*.

Danger Zone: Installation Headaches

Some poorly designed installation routines work only if you run them from the A: drive. That's a problem if the program is on a disk that you can only read in the B: drive. You can usually work around this obstacle by removing any disks from the A: drive and entering `subst a: b:\` before you start installing—but make sure you do this only *after* you've exited Windows, or you're cruising for a Windows crash. When you're through installing the application, enter `subst a: /d` to return drive A: to normal.

Think twice before letting applications install themselves in the directories suggested by the installation routine. Your hard drive will be more manageable if you install applications in directories two levels down from the root. For example, you could put all your major applications under \APPS, games under \GAMES, utilities under \UTILS, and so on (see "How to Organize a Hard Disk" later in this chapter).

To start an application...

You have to start an application before you can use it.

Do this in Windows:

Choose one of these four methods:

1. Double-click on the program's icon in the Program Manager.

2. Double-click on the program's EXE or COM file in the File Manager.

3. Double-click on one of the program's documents in the File Manager. This will start the application and open the document automatically.

4. Choose Run from the File menu in either the Program Manager or the File Manager, type in the program's startup command (click on Browse if you need to find the program's EXE or COM file), and click OK.

A whole bunch of Windows utilities offer still more ways to start programs. You'll find them in the "Windows Fixers" section of Chapter 21.

Do this in DOS:

There are three basic ways to start applications in DOS. Which one you choose depends primarily on whether or not the program is in your *path*, which is a list of directories following the PATH command in your AUTOEXEC.BAT file (see Appendix A: *Tuning CONFIG.SYS and AUTOEXEC.BAT*).

If the program's directory is in your path, just type the name of its EXE file without the extension. For example, you might enter q to start Quattro Pro, or wp to start *WordPerfect*.

If the program's directory is not in your path, type the full path and name of the EXE file. Start with the drive letter if it's not on your current drive, as in:

```
c:\qpro\q
```

for Quattro Pro, or

```
c:\apps\wp51\wp
```

for *WordPerfect*. Alternatively, you can change to the program's directory, then enter the command to start it, as in:

```
cd\qpro
q
```

pen a file...

...r (usually) to print a file, you need to open it.

Do this in Windows:

Normally, you choose Open from your application's File menu, select the file, and click OK.

If the application isn't running (or if you just want a change from the usual routine), try double-clicking on the file's icon in the File Manager. This way of opening a file works only if a *file association* has already been set up, so that Windows knows by the file's extension which application the file should be opened in. Most Windows applications establish these associations on installation—but some don't, and you may want to change associations anyway (so TXT files open in your word processor instead of Notepad, for example). To set up or change an association, do this:

1. Select a file with the extension whose association you want to create or change. (You can't define an association for files with no extension.)

2. Select File//Associate.

3. Scroll through the Associate With list until you find the program you want files with the extension to open in.

4. If the desired program isn't on the list, click the Browse button, select the program's EXE file from the directory display, and click OK.

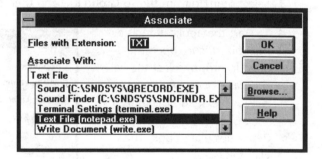

You can also try opening a file by selecting it in the File Manager, dragging the file across the desktop, and dropping the file on an application's minimized icon. The advantage to the drag-and-drop method is that Windows will open (or try to open) the file in the application no matter what file associations have been set up. Unfortunately, this method doesn't work with all programs.

Do this in DOS:

You can instruct most DOS applications to load a file as they start up. The following examples assume that the applications in question are listed in your path:

To start *WordPerfect* and open the file MAR95.TAX in the C:\DATA\REPORTS directory, enter:

```
cd \data\reports
wp mar95.tax
```

for Quattro Pro, or

```
cd\apps\wp51
wp
```

for *WordPerfect*.

~~~~~~

To run programs automatically at startup...

If you use the same applications day after day, nothing beats having them start up automatically when you turn on your PC so you don't have to start them all manually.

Do this in Windows:

1. Open Program Manager and select the icon for the program you want to launch automatically every time you start Windows.

2. Pick Copy from the Program Manager's File menu.

3. Select StartUp from the To Group list, and then click OK.

4. To start the application as a minimized icon, open the StartUp group, select the program's icon, and press Alt-Enter. Check Run Minimized in the resulting Program Item Properties dialog box. Then click OK.

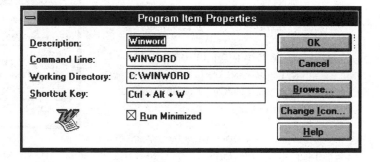

To start Windows automatically when you turn on your PC, follow the DOS instructions below.

Do this in DOS:

To start a program automatically when you turn on your computer, make it the last line of your AUTOEXEC.BAT (see Appendix A: *Tuning CONFIG.SYS* and *AUTOEXEC.BAT*). For example, to start Windows automatically, enter this as your AUTOEXEC.BAT file's last line

```
win :
```

The colon (:) turns off the flashy Windows logo display, which gets old fast.

To start 1-2-3 release 3.1 and open the file 1995EST.WK3 in the F:\TAXES\ directory, enter:

```
cd f:\taxes
123 f:1995est.wk3
```

To edit AUTOEXEC.BAT in the MS-DOS Editor, enter:

```
edit c:\autoexec.bat
```

~~~~~~

To print a file...

In Windows, you "print" not only to get a hard copy of a document, but also to send faxes via fax modem.

Do this in Windows:

Almost every Windows application has a File//Print command. You just set any options you want (like a page range) in the resulting dialog box and then click OK.

If you want to open a document, print it, and close it again, you need to select the document in the File Manager, choose Print from the File menu, and click OK. Alternatively, if the Print Manager is minimized on the desktop, you can drag the document's icon out of the File Manager and drop it on the Print Manager icon. However, this drag-and-drop move doesn't work with all programs.

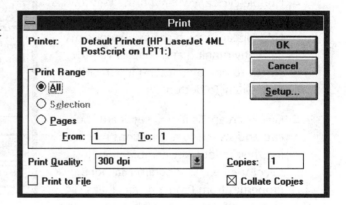

Do this in DOS:

There's no consistent way to print documents in DOS—some programs use File//Print, but there are many other alternatives. Check the application's on-line help or manual.

If you want to print a plain text file, you can copy it to the printer port. For example, to print a copy of your AUTOEXEC.BAT file, enter:

```
copy autoexec.bat lpt1
```

To switch between applications...

DOS was designed to run just one application at a time. Windows is expressly designed to let you run multiple applications at the same time so that, for example, you don't have to close your word processor to read your E-mail.

Do this in Windows:

There are five ways to move from one application to another in Windows:

1. If the application you're working in isn't maximized, one of the best ways to switch applications is to simply click on any part of another application window.

2. Pressing Alt Tab takes you back to the last program you left—a fast way to switch back and forth between two programs.

3. Hold down Alt and press Tab repeatedly, and you can cycle through all the applications currently running.

4. Double-click anywhere on the Windows desktop (or press Ctrl Esc), and the Task Lisk appears, which shows all programs currently running and enables you to switch to one by selecting it and clicking the Switch To button.

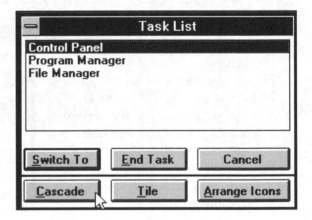

5. Give each application a keyboard shortcut, and switch to applications by entering their unique key combination. Just select the item in Program Manager, pick Properties from Program Manager's File menu, and enter the combination in the Shortcut Key box.

Do this in DOS:

DOS has no task-switching utility. That was a feature of the DOS Shell, found in DOS versions 5.0 and 6.0, but it was dropped from 6.2. If you want task-switching without Windows, use a third-party utility like *WordPerfect Office*'s Shell or *PC Tools*' Desktop.

How to Install DOS and Windows

These days, DOS and Windows almost always come preloaded on new PCs, so you may never have the pleasure of installing them from scratch. In the event circumstances force you to confront this daunting task, be reassured—despite what DOS old-timers might tell you, with the automatic setup routine in current versions of DOS 6.2 and Windows 3.1, it's not all that hard. Here's a quick guide. *(Warning: If you're trying to get your hard disk running after a system crash, don't follow these instructions. Instead, see Chapter 10: When Things Go Wrong.)*

DANGER

When installing DOS and Windows, it's a good idea to start in the morning on a weekday. The process takes a couple of hours (at least), and if you run into trouble you'll want to be able to contact Microsoft or your vendor's tech support.

Step 1: Set Up DOS

If you've just bought a new PC, hook the thing together, make sure there's no disk (or cardboard drive protector) in the A: drive, and flick the On switch (see Chapter 1: *For Beginners Only*). If you see a DOS prompt (C> or C:\>), or if Windows starts up, stop now—DOS is already there and you can skip the following procedure. If nothing happens, turn off the machine and follow the steps below:

1. Find DOS's Disk 1, slip it in your A: drive, and turn on your PC. When you see the "Welcome to Setup" message, press (Enter) to continue.

2. The next screen will have "Configure unallocated disk space" highlighted. Press (Enter) to accept this option. After a pause the system will reboot automatically. The next screen offers a message that DOS's Setup routine is *formatting* the drive, that is, laying down the basic information that enables DOS to store data on a disk. This can take a while—a percentage indicator lets you know how much is left to go.

3. Next, Setup displays Date/Time, Country, and Keyboard Layout options. If the date or time is wrong, reset it. Ignore the other options unless you don't work in English, or you want to use a non-U.S. keyboard. Press (Enter) to continue.

4. Press (Enter) again to accept C:\DOS as your DOS directory. Insert Disks 2 and 3 as prompted. When Setup tells you that DOS is installed, remove Disk 3 and press (Enter) to reboot the system.

Note that some systems come with special versions of DOS whose setup routines vary slightly from the above procedure. Also note that if you're simply upgrading DOS versions—say, from 6.0 to 6.2—the procedure is similar. You just won't get the "Configure unallocated disk space" message; nor will DOS format your drive, which is a good thing, since that would destroy all the data already on your disk.

Step 2: Install Disk Compression (Optional)

DOS includes its own disk compression utility, which nearly doubles the amount of space on your hard disk (see Chapter 21: *Utilities* for more on disk compression). The more data there is on your hard drive, the longer it takes to install a disk compression

HOT TIP

utility. If you're going to do it, this is the best time.

> ## Boots, Reboots, and Cold Boots
>
> What does a PC do when it *boots*? Immediately after you turn on your PC and it performs its self-test, it looks for an operating system to load into memory. The first place your PC looks is the A: drive (see "Safety Check" later in this chapter to learn how to create a boot disk). If no disk is there, the machine turns to drive C:, unless you've specifically changed your PC's configuration in some weird way. If drive C: has been formatted as a DOS *system disk*—DOS sets it up this way automatically on installation—your PC will load DOS into memory and beep to tell you things are up and running. In other words, your PC will have *booted* from the C: drive.
>
> Sometimes, you need to *reboot* your system to put a configuration change into effect, or to get out of a bad situation where your system freezes, or hangs—that is, just sits there, unable to accept input from the mouse or keyboard. Rebooting destroys any unsaved data, making it a method of last resort if you're trying to get out of a bad situation. To reboot, press [Ctrl][Alt][Del] simultaneously: Your system will perform an abbreviated self-test, and then load DOS.
>
> When things get so messed up that even [Ctrl][Alt][Del] doesn't do anything, you need to either push the reset button on the front of your PC (if it has one), or turn your system off, then on. Old-timers sometimes call the latter a "cold boot."

Microsoft has changed DOS's compression utility twice recently, so check the documentation for your particular DOS version to learn the procedure for installing compression. Two things will happen for sure:

1. You'll be warned to back up your data almost immediately. Don't bother if you have a new hard disk, since it merely contains the version of DOS you just installed.

REMEMBER

2. Before compressing, DOS will automatically run ScanDisk, a utility program that checks for errors on your hard disk. If by chance you see any error messages, follow the prompts to correct the problems. If ScanDisk can't fix them, write down exactly what ScanDisk has reported and call the manufacturer's technical support immediately.

Compression routines take time to do their stuff. Be prepared to wait several minutes even if you have a new, nearly empty hard disk. If you have a big, full hard disk, take a long lunch.

Step 3: Run ScanDisk

If you didn't install disk compression, run ScanDisk immediately after setting up DOS (just type `scandisk` at the DOS prompt). It's always possible that your drive has problems that could make installing and configuring the rest of your software pointless, and you can trust ScanDisk to ferret them out. *Do not skip or abort ScanDisk's surface scan*, although it takes awhile. This routine tests for physical damage to your disk and locks out any damaged areas so that no data will be written there and lost to the ozone.

Step 4: Set Up Windows

Setting up Windows is as easy as setting up DOS. It just involves swapping a few more disks.

1. Slip Windows' Disk 1 into your A: drive and enter `a:setup` at the DOS prompt. Press Enter to pass the first screen.

2. Press Enter again to use Express Setup, and press Enter yet again to accept C:\ WINDOWS as your Windows directory. For the moment, accept the configuration options on the next screen by pressing, you guessed it, Enter.

3. When Setup starts copying files, swap disks as instructed. There are about 10MB of files, so it takes a few minutes. Enter your name and company in the on-screen form, then follow the prompts to set up your printer. (If you wish, you can skip this step for now and set up your printer later using Windows' Control Panel.)

4. Next, Setup will search your DOS directory for applications. If it asks if C:\DOS\EDIT.COM is the MS-DOS Editor, click OK. When Setup is finished, click on the Reboot button to restart your computer.

DOS comes with several utilities (including Microsoft's Backup and Anti-Virus) that you'll want to install under Windows. To do so, enter `dos\setup /e` at the prompt. Press Enter twice to accept C:\DOS and C:\WINDOWS as the relevant directories.

Step 5: Install Device Drivers

If you have a CD ROM drive, fax board, sound board, or other device that needs a *device driver*—a little program that enables the hardware to work—you'll need to install the driver now. Usually, such hardware comes with a disk that installs the

Double Trouble: CONFIG.SYS and AUTOEXEC.BAT

When people moan and groan about PCs, it's usually to complain about all the adjustments necessary to ensure that things work right, especially when new hardware or software is installed. And where do they make those adjustments? Mostly in two key files, both of which are created by DOS on installation, and which kick into action as soon as you turn on or reboot your system:

- **CONFIG.SYS** is an ordinary text file containing some of the nastiest-looking gibberish you're likely to see—DOS commands at their most obscure. Many of the text lines in this file load device drivers into memory, where these little programs must reside in order for certain PC components to function. Others arrange memory in some (hopefully) beneficial way or set certain DOS options, such as the maximum number of files you can open at one time.

- **AUTOEXEC.BAT** is a text file, too, but it's also a mini-program called a *batch file*—basically, a string of DOS commands you save in a file and "play back" later (AUTOEXEC.BAT is the only batch file that executes automatically when your system boots). AUTOEXEC.BAT typically contains a PROMPT command that modifies the DOS prompt to tell you which directory you're in, a PATH command specifying which directories DOS should look inside when you enter something at the DOS prompt, and commands to start programs right after you flip on your PC—Windows, for example.

Both CONFIG.SYS and AUTOEXEC.BAT live in the root directory of the disk your PC normally boots from (almost always drive C:). To edit either file using DOS's simple text editor, enter `edit c:\config.sys` or `edit c:\autoexec.bat`. Under Windows, pick Run from Program Manager's File menu and enter `sysedit`—both files (plus WIN.INI and SYSTEM.INI, two Windows configuration files that are a whole other story) will pop up at once in separate windows, ready to edit. For more information, turn to Appendix A: *Tuning CONFIG.SYS and AUTOEXEC.BAT.*

driver automatically, but even so you often need to make manual adjustments to your AUTOEXEC.BAT or CONFIG.SYS file (see Appendix A: *Tuning AUTOEXEC.BAT and CONFIG.SYS* for instructions on installing drivers).

Step 6: Set Up a Mouse to Work With DOS (Optional)

When you install Windows, it sets things up automatically so, if you've physically installed a mouse, it will work. But if you want to use a mouse with DOS applications, you may need to install a mouse driver in your AUTOEXEC.BAT. Drivers and instructions for installing them come with higher-priced mice. If you have a cheapo clone mouse with no software, you can use Windows' mouse driver with DOS applications—but you have to install it manually.

If Windows is running, exit it. Insert the Windows installation disk with the file MOUSE.CO_ in drive A:. (For Windows 3.1, that's Disk 4 if you bought Windows with 1.44MB disks, Disk 5 with 1.2MB disks, or Disk A with 720K disks). Then type this at the DOS prompt:

```
expand a:mouse.co_ c:\windows\mouse.com
```

and press Enter. Now add this line to your AUTOEXEC.BAT file:

HOT TIP

```
c:\windows\mouse.com
```

Step 7: Optimize Memory

DOS's MemMaker utility modifies your CONFIG.SYS and AUTOEXEC.BAT files to make more efficient use of RAM. This has two benefits: Performance improves, and you can run more and bigger programs (see Chapter 21: *Utilities* for more on memory optimizers).

1. If Windows is running, exit, then at the DOS prompt enter `memmaker`. When prompted, choose Express and press Enter.

2. Setup will ask if you use applications that require EMS. Answer Yes only if you sometimes need to run DOS applications outside of Windows, and if those applications in fact need EMS (check the manual to see if EMS is required). If you're not sure, choose No—the EMS option takes up an important segment of memory, and if you find you need EMS you can run MemMaker again at any time to add it.

3. MemMaker will reboot your machine several times as it tests different memory settings. When it's finished, it will ask if your system appears to be working okay. If it is, answer Yes, and MemMaker is done.

If things aren't working right, MemMaker will undo its changes. If your system stops working entirely, boot from a floppy, then enter `c:\dos \memmaker /undo`.

HOT TIP

Setting NumLock at Startup

Even though you can change the setting with a single keystroke, some people go crazy when their PC starts up with Num Lock on, because they prefer to use the numeric keypad for moving the cursor instead of entering numbers. Other folks' think that Num Lock should be on and stay on—which is usually, but not always, the default. Most PCs enable you to use a setup utility to toggle Num Lock on or off when your PC starts. If your PC doesn't offer this option, you can accomplish the same end by adding one of these lines to your CONFIG.SYS file: `numlock=on` or `numlock=off`.

How to Organize a Hard Disk

REMEMBER

While DOS and Windows pretty much install themselves, they don't give you any help in organizing the contents of your hard disk. You can save yourself a lot of confusion later if you figure out how you want to arrange your directories *before* you install your applications or start creating documents.

A well-organized disk starts with an uncluttered root directory (the topmost directory, usually C:\). I've been using variations on this basic top-level plan for years, never creating more than a dozen or so directories in the root so its contents always fit in a single DOS screen or File Manager window.

Segregate Data and Applications

When you install an application, nine times out of ten it will suggest creating its directory (containing all its program files) right in the root directory. It's easier to navigate your drive if you create a directory called C:\APPS and change installation routines' defaults so that the application directories go there (as in C:\APPS\EXCEL).

For programs that create data files on their own—a spreadsheet, word processor, fax program, and so on—create matching subdirectories in another directory called C:\DATA. With data and program files completely separate, you can easily set up your backup program to back up only data files on a regular basis (to learn about backups, see Chapter 9: *Protect Your Data*).

HOT TIP

Organize by Project

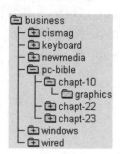

How you organize your business documents depends on what kind of work you do, but you'll be able to find what you need faster if you create a new directory for each project you work on. For example, as a writer it makes the most sense for me to create a directory for each magazine I write for. Each magazine's directory contains a separate subdirectory for each article. Sometimes I create additional directories, say to get lots of test data or graphics files out of the way of my word processing documents.

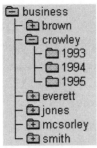

Here's a setup that might make sense for an accountant: Create a directory for each client, then create a new subdirectory for each year's files. Depending on your application, it might make more sense to use dates in file names instead of subdirectories.

If you track clients or projects using account numbers, using the same numbers on your hard drive may make sense. This example is from some attorneys I know: The first level is the four-digit client

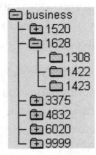

number, the second level is a four-digit case number. This approach means temps and people sharing computers don't get confused about where to look for files relating to a particular case.

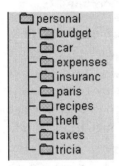

When you're using your employer's computer, it's a good practice to keep your personal files separate from business stuff. That way it will be easier to pack up and move if you change jobs or want to transfer the files to a home computer. Similarly, on your home computer you might want to create separate directories for each business you're involved in (for example, putting work you bring home from the office in one directory and stuff related to your spouse's self-employment in another).

A Place for "Little" Programs

Everyone ends up collecting handy little utility programs over time, so it's a good idea to create a \UTILS directory and keep them organized from the outset. Store your one-file utilities and batch files there and add \UTILS to your DOS path, and you'll be able to run any utility from the DOS prompt (see Appendix *"Tuning CONFIG.SYS and AUTOEXEC.BAT"* for more on the PATH statement). Multiple-file utilities

are best stored in separate subdirectories for easier upgrading or purging as they become obsolete. Use batch files in the \UTILS directory to start the utilities in subdirectories, and you won't need to add each utility directory to your path (see Appendix D: *Batch Files*).

Temporary Holding Areas

HOT TIP

It's a good idea to create directories in which to hold files temporarily, before you know where they should go or after it makes sense to care. For example, all my communications programs dump incoming files into a directory called \DOWNLOAD, which serves as a kind of in-box. A directory called \SCRATCH contains files I don't need to keep but don't feel absolutely safe about deleting yet either.

HOT TIP

All by themselves applications often create temporary files, which are supposed to be deleted automatically but often aren't. Whenever possible, I set up applications so that they create their temporary files in \TEMP. To prevent abandoned temp files left by crashed or buggy programs from cluttering up my hard disk, I have a line in my AUTOEXEC.BAT that deletes everything in \TEMP whenever I boot my PC.

REMEMBER

None of these strategies is likely to be a perfect fit for you, but the basic ideas should help you figure out your own plan of attack. One thing's for sure: Don't accept the default way that applications organize data, which is to store all files created by an application in a single directory, often intermingled with program files. Eventually you'll end up with a zillion documents and a very slow-scrolling directory. Trying to figure out what you have to keep and what you can purge or your archive will be a huge headache.

Safety Check

An entire chapter of this book—Chapter 9: *Protect Your Data*—covers the whole gamut of ways in which you can keep your data from disaster. Here, you'll find a practical guide to safeguarding your system right from the start using the utilities that come with DOS. These precautions fall into two categories: The ones you set up once and forget, and the ones that require a routine maintenance schedule.

One-Time Protective Measures

Here are four things you should do as soon as you've set up your hard disk. They don't take long, and they'll save you grief in the end.

Increase Virus Protection With VSafe

DOS's memory-resident VSafe utility watches for signs of virus activity and pops up a warning if it detects anything suspicious. To install it, add the command `lh vsafe` to your AUTOEXEC.BAT file.

Program Item Properties		
Description:	VSafe Manager	OK
Command Line:	C:\DOS\MWAVTSR.EXE	Cancel
Working Directory:	C:\DOS	Browse...
Shortcut Key:	None	Change Icon...
☐ Run Minimized		Help

Coming Soon: Windows 4

As this book goes to press, Microsoft is testing its first major upgrade to Windows since version 3.1. From what Microsoft says, Windows 4 will make Windows considerably easier to use. A new desktop will integrate the functions now split between the Program Manager, File Manager, Task List, and Control Panel. Files will be able to have long, plain-English names that include spaces and a mix of upper- and lower-case letters. The new Plug-and-Play architecture will make installing network cards, modems, drives, and other peripherals hassle-free. As in Windows for Workgroups, networking will be built right in.

Perhaps most important, you'll no longer need to go through DOS to get to Windows—you'll boot straight to the desktop. Installing Windows 4 will happen all in one step, and you won't have to learn anything about DOS, because there will be no DOS to learn about. And Windows 4 will run all the apps you currently own, on the same hardware, only faster and more reliably.

At least, that's what it says in Microsoft's press release. Sounds great, but will they really be able to deliver? Who knows, but they've certainly set themselves a tough challenge.

Enter Windows 4. *This new version of Windows remakes Windows' look entirely.*

To prevent VSafe from interfering with Windows, you must also create a VSafe program item in your StartUp group. Pick New from the Program Manager's File menu and choose Program Item. In the Program Item Properties dialog box enter `VSafe Manager` after Description, `c:\dos\mwavtsr.exe` after Command Line, and `c:\dos` after Working Directory. Leave Shortcut Key and Run Minimized blank.

REMEMBER

Guard Against Accidental Deletes

DOS includes two utilities designed to improve the effectiveness of Windows' and DOS's Undelete: Delete Sentry and Delete Tracker. Of the two, Delete Sentry is much more effective—it actually moves "deleted" files to a hidden directory for safekeeping. Delete Sentry takes up about 15K of RAM and up to 7 percent of your hard drive (unless otherwise configured). To turn on Delete Sentry, add the line `lh undelete /s` to your AUTOEXEC.BAT file.

If you wish, you can configure Delete Sentry's settings by running the Windows version of Undelete (choose Undelete from File Manager's File menu) and choosing Options//Configure Delete Protection.

Create an Emergency Boot Disk

After a bad disk crash, virus infection, or hardware failure, you may find that your PC will no longer boot. If that unpleasant situation should ever arise you'll need an emergency boot floppy. Why not take a couple of minutes to make one right now? (The utility libraries *PC Tools* and *Norton Utilities* come with their own emergency disks, but you may still need to boot from a floppy to use them; see Chapter 21: *Utilities*.)

To prepare an emergency disk, put a new or blank disk in drive A:, make it bootable (enter `format a: /s` or select Disk//Make System Disk in File Manager), and label it Emergency Disk. Then copy the following files from your DOS directory to Drive A:

EDIT.COM
EDIT.HLP
FDISK.EXE
FORMAT.COM
MSD.EXE
QBASIC.EXE
SCANDISK.EXE
SYS.COM
UNDELETE.EXE
UNFORMAT.COM

If you use a separate antivirus utility, copy its files to the floppy as well. Otherwise, copy the DOS version of Microsoft Anti-Virus to the floppy:

MSAV.EXE
MSAV.HLP
MSAVHELP.OVL
MSAVIRUS.LST

HOT TIP

Scan the floppy for viruses to make sure it's clean, then write-protect it. That way, if your system is infected by a virus, the little bugger won't infect your emergency boot disk. Keep the emergency disk with your backup tapes or disks.

Create an Emergency Restore Disk

Restoring is the other half of backing up your hard disk regularly, which is the only ironclad insurance against data disaster. When you lose data—perhaps *everything* on your hard disk—you need to restore that data to the hard disk from your latest backup disks or tapes.

To do this, you need a floppy disk containing the DOS version of your backup program's restore utility. (Why the DOS version if you're a Windows user? Because otherwise, if you lost everything on your hard disk, you'd have to reinstall Windows manually before you restored anything.) Some backup programs include such disks, but DOS's Microsoft Backup doesn't. To create an Emergency Restore disk manually, copy the following files onto it:

MSBACKDB.OVL
MSBACKDR.OVL
MSBACKFB.OVL
MSBACKFR.OVL
MSBACKUP.EXE
MSBACKUP.HLP
MSBACKUP.OVL
MSBCONFG.HLP
MSBCONFG.OVL

Regular Maintenance Checklist

To keep your hard drive in good shape and your data secure, you should perform four maintenance tasks regularly:

1. Check for viruses.

2. Check the drive for data errors.

3. Back up your files.

4. Defragment the drive.

You're best advised to do these tasks in the above order. You *must* check for data errors *before* you defragment your hard disk, so you can correct any disk problems that might otherwise cause the defragging software to trash your disk (see Chapter 21: *Utilities* for a complete explanation of data recovery and disk defragmenting). You should also back up before running Microsoft Defragmenter or any similar disk utility, since on rare occasions something may go wrong and ruin some files. And you want to scan for viruses first because you don't want to back up infected files.

DANGER

If you have *The Norton Utilities* or *PC Tools Pro*, you have versions of the above utilities that are better than DOS's, and you should use them. Otherwise, use Microsoft's Anti-Virus, ScanDisk, and Defragmenter (all of which come with DOS), and the backup software that came with your tape drive. If you don't have a tape drive, you can use Microsoft Backup. Here's a basic how-to guide to these four important utilities.

Check for Viruses With Microsoft Anti-Virus

REMEMBER

Worst case, a computer virus infection can corrupt data or even erase your entire hard drive. DOS includes both DOS and Windows versions of Microsoft Anti-Virus to detect and remove those parasites. Remember that the most common way of getting infected is by floppy disk, so if you always scan floppies the first time you use them or after lending them to someone else, you'll greatly reduce your chances of catching a virus. Here's how you use Anti-Virus for Windows:

1. Start Microsoft Anti-Virus by double-clicking on the "doctor" icon in the Program Manager's Microsoft Tools group.

2. Click on the icon(s) for the drive(s) you want to check.

3. Click the Detect button.

4. If the program pops up a Virus Found dialog box, click the Clean button.

Here's how you run the program from the DOS prompt. To check all hard drives, enter:

```
msav /a
```

To check a floppy in drive A:, enter:

```
msav a:
```

Neither the Windows nor DOS version of Microsoft Anti-Virus is much good unless you keep it up to date, since otherwise they may not catch new viruses specifically designed to fool them. To get an update of virus "signatures" that Anti-Virus will check for, use a modem and communications software to download the latest files from Microsoft's bulletin board system (503/531-8100).

Check Your Hard Disk With ScanDisk

Crashes and other software glitches can create errors in your drive's file structure. ScanDisk searches for such errors and fixes them. Moreover, regularly running its *surface scan* routine, which checks for physical disk defects, can prevent major disk problems before they happen.

1. Exit all applications (including Windows).

2. If you use a disk cache other than DOS's SmartDrive, or another memory-resident utility that affects disk operations, reboot without it. That is, hold down [F8] as your system boots, which will give you the option to accept or reject each line in your CONFIG.SYS and AUTOEXEC.BAT files. Reject any lines that load the offending utilities.

3. Switch to the drive you want to test, and then enter `scandisk/autofix/surface`.

4. If ScanDisk detects any problems, it will offer to create an undo disk before fixing them. You can skip this step by selecting Skip Undo from the menu. The advantage of creating an undo disk is that in the unlikely event ScanDisk's attempt to repair the drive makes things worse, you'll be able to restore the drive to its pre-ScanDisked condition.

5. When ScanDisk has finished, it will display a screen reporting what it did: either "ScanDisk did not find any problems," or a description of the errors it fixed. When you see this screen, select Exit.

6. Depending on what kind of problems ScanDisk encounters, it may create some files in the root directory with names like FILE0000.CHK, FILE0001.CHK, and so on. If you lost some files in a disk crash and don't have backup copies, examine these files with DOS's Edit

Checking for Data Errors With CHKDSK

If you have a version of DOS that predates version 6.2, you don't have ScanDisk. Instead, your version of DOS came with the relatively crude CHKDSK, which can detect and fix only a few simple problems. Here's how it works:

1. Exit all applications (including Windows).

2. Enter `chkdsk c:/f` at the DOS prompt. (To check and fix another drive, replace `c:` with the appropriate drive letter.)

3. If CHKDSK detects a problem it can correct, you'll see the prompt "Convert lost chains to files?" If you lost some files in a disk crash and don't have backup copies, press `y`. Otherwise, press `n`.

4. If you told CHKDSK to convert those chains to files, after the utility finishes running you'll find one or more files in the root directory of the drive with names like FILE0000.CHK, FILE0001.CHK, and so on. Inspect those files with DOS's EDIT or Windows' Notepad to see if they contain some or all of the data you lost.

Using CHKDSK is a last resort, because it's not so hot at handling some problems and can even occasionally make things worse. Remember that the data recovery programs in the popular utility libraries *The Norton Utilities* and *PC Tools Pro* are better than *either* ScanDisk or CHKDSK.

or Windows' Notepad to see if they contain any of your lost data. Otherwise, enter `del *.chk` to delete them.

Back Up Your Hard Drive With Microsoft Backup

Microsoft Backup can only back up to floppies. This being the case, consider buying a tape drive and a program that can back up to tape (such as *Central Point Backup*) instead. Floppy disks aren't a very practical backup medium for today's hard drives. Even with data compression, a 1.44MB disk can only hold around 2MB of data, so you might need a hundred floppies to back up an entire 200MB hard drive, and you'd spend an hour and a half swapping disks.

If you really want to use this turkey, have a big stack of floppies ready. The DOS and Windows versions of Microsoft Backup are nearly identical, so the same instructions work for both. If you're using DOS 4.0 or an older version, see the DOS command-line instructions below.

1. Start Backup in Windows by double-clicking on the "safe" icon in Program Manager's Microsoft Tools group. In DOS, enter `msbackup` at the DOS prompt. The first time you run Backup, you need to configure it. It will check your system, let you choose which drive you want to back up to, and then do a test backup to make sure it works reliably.

2. Click on the Backup button.

3. If you want to back up all the files on the drive, select Full from the Backup Type menu. If you want to back up only those files that have changed since the last backup, select Incremental instead (see Chapter 9: *Protect Your Data* for more on backup strategies).

4. Click (in DOS) or double-click (in Windows) on the icon for the drive you want to back up.

5. After Backup finishes scanning the drive, it will display

Backing Up With DOS 4 and Earlier Versions

DOS 4 and earlier versions don't have a menu-driven backup program, only a rudimentary command-line utility. Here's the basic drill:

- **Full backup.** Back up all files on drive C: to A:, automatically formatting new, unformatted disks as necessary:

  ```
  backup c:\*.* a: /s/f
  ```

- **Incremental backup.** Back up only those files that have changed since the last backup, appending them to the last disk of the backup set:

  ```
  backup c:\*.* a: /s/m/a/f
  ```

an estimate of the number of floppies required for the backup. If you have enough disks, click Start Backup.

6. Before you insert each disk, mark it with the date and its backup set disk number (for example, 10/15/94-1, 10/15/94-2, and so on).

7. When Backup is finished, select Quit. The Exit Backup dialog box will appear. If Save Settings is checked, click to uncheck it. Then click OK to finish exiting.

Defragmenting Your Drive With DEFRAG

Regular defragging can keep your disk performance from degrading as DOS spreads files around the drive. Microsoft Defragmenter isn't the greatest program for this, but it gets the job done—and using it is easy. Exit all applications, including Windows, and then enter this command:

```
defrag c: /f /sne
```

Defragging can take a long time if you have a lot of files on your drive. You might want to start it running before you go to lunch.

DOS and Windows Alternatives

Not everybody uses DOS or Windows. Someone who doesn't might try to persuade you that you'd be better off with something else—and there's a remote possibility they might even be right. Here's a look at the major alternatives.

- **IBM PC-DOS 6.3.** Since IBM has rights to the source code for MS-DOS (that is, the DOS discussed throughout this book), PC-DOS is pretty much guaranteed not to have compatibility problems. The biggest advantages to PC-DOS are the name-brand utilities IBM bundles, which are significantly better than the limited versions sold by Microsoft. For example, its disk compression can squeeze more into a given space, and its backup program works with tape drives.

- **IBM OS/2 2.1.** This replacement for both DOS and Windows can run most Windows apps, but IBM is constantly playing catch-up as Microsoft introduces new technology, so the latest and greatest stuff may not run until the next upgrade. Still, if you try Windows and find it can't run all your applications reliably, you might give OS/2 a try. It's cheap, and IBM offers a money-back guarantee. You'll need at least 8MB of RAM, preferably 16MB.

- **Windows NT.** Like OS/2, Microsoft's next-generation operating system can run most Windows apps, though it's not so great at running DOS apps. If and when applications appear that take advantage of NT's capabilities, it might be worth considering, but currently it's mostly useful running on a network server (see Chapter 22: *About Networks* for more on NT).

All That Windows Stuff

Windows comes with a couple of dozen little and not-so-little applications, and DOS adds a few more. What is all that stuff? Here's a quick look and a few tips about how to get more out of those that are worth your trouble—and a few cautions about those that aren't.

Main Group

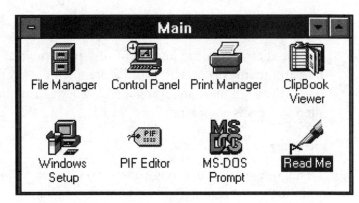

Here's where you'll find the most vital programs for using and configuring Windows. You'll use File Manager all the time.

- **File Manager.** Use this for all those everyday tasks involving files, directories, and disks. See the "Windows and DOS Cookbook" to learn to perform all the most common File Manager tasks.

- **Control Panel.** Set most of Windows' options and configure device drivers here (see the "Control Panel" section below).

- **Print Manager.** Lets you cancel or reorder print jobs that started within applications.

- **Clipbook Viewer.** You can share data with other users on a Windows for Workgroups LAN by copying it to a page in the Viewer. (The regular Windows counterpart, the Clipboard Viewer, isn't good for much.)

- **Windows Setup.** After initial installation, Windows Setup is mostly used for changing video modes (see Chapter 5: *Monitors, Etc.* for more on this topic). It includes a menu-driven utility for deleting unused Windows components so you can use the disk space for other things.

- **PIF Editor.** Use this to control how Windows handles specific DOS applications (see the section "DOS Under Windows" later in this chapter).

- **MS-DOS Prompt.** Brings up a C:\> prompt where you can enter most DOS commands or start DOS applications.

- **Read Me.** Opens a Windows Write file containing late-breaking information about your version of Windows.

Accessories Group

If all the applications in this group were suddenly erased by an act of god, you probably wouldn't miss them that much. The Notepad, which enables you to edit unformatted text files fast, is far and away the most useful application here.

- **Write.** If your word processing needs are very simple—no fancy stuff like multiple columns, footnotes, or mail merge—you might get by with this basic word processor. You can insert graphics; format text with a variety of fonts; set tabs, line spacing, and justification; and define headers or footers with automatic page numbers. Look in your Windows directory for some informative WRI files. Since every copy of Windows includes Write, it's a handy format for exchanging documents between people who use different (or unknown) word processors.

- **Paintbrush.** If you've never used a paint program before, you might find Paintbrush a lot of fun, but it's not a serious graphics tool (see Chapter 17: *Graphics Software* for a look at some real paint programs).

- **Terminal.** In a pinch, you can get by with this bare-bones communications program. But once you're on line, why not download something better? Many shareware programs are better than this laggard program (see the "Shareware and Freeware" section of Chapter 21: *Utilities*).

- **Notepad.** Windows' text editor is an indispensable tool for editing Windows configuration files (INI, SET, and so on). For other uses, Notepad has one big limitation: It can't open files much bigger than 50K. (You can always use Write to edit text files that won't fit in Notepad. To open a document that's not a straight text (TXT) or Write (WRI) file and preserve the original formatting, choose No Conversion when opening.)

- **Recorder.** Windows' Recorder can automate repetitive tasks for applications that don't have their own macros, or for tasks involving more than one app. It's pretty limited—all you can do is store a series of actions (including mouse moves) in a Windows REC file, and "play them back" by pressing a shortcut-key combination you specify. You can't edit REC files, so if you make a mistake you have to start over from scratch.

- **Cardfile.** A sorry excuse for an electronic Rolodex, but with one saving grace: You can link document files to cards and use Cardfile's index feature to organize them by assigning descriptions and keywords.

- **Calculator.** One of Windows' best little programs. You can increase this handy tool's number-crunching abilities by choosing View//Scientific. Expand Calculator's power further by pressing Ctrl-s to open the Statistics Box.

- **Clock.** Displays an always-visible digital or analog clock on the screen.

- **Object Packager.** An esoteric tool you'll probably never need.

- **Character Map.** Helps you find special characters (proper fractions, bullets, and so on) and paste them into other applications. Choose the font you want from the Font list box, double-click on the character you need, click the Copy button, switch back to your document, and choose Edit//Paste.

- **Media Player.** Depending on what multimedia hardware you have in your system, this will play sound, MIDI music, digital video, animation, and other kinds of files.

- **Sound Recorder.** Records sound to disk (see Chapter 23: *Multimedia* for instructions on how to use it).

Games Group

Nothing to knock your socks off here, but playing one of these games is still better than twiddling your thumbs while on hold with Microsoft's tech support.

- **Solitaire** is notoriously addictive to people who were enamored of the card game to begin with.

- **Minesweeper** is a more serious challenge. The object is to uncover all mines in the shortest possible time without getting blown up.

- **Hearts,** which comes only with Windows for Workgroups, lets you challenge other users across a network.

Network Group

These goodies come only with Windows for Workgroups.

- **Network Setup.** Don't mess with it unless you're the network administrator.

- **Mail.** Starts the Microsoft Mail electronic mail program.

- **Schedule+.** A group scheduler designed to be used with Mail.

- **Remote Access.** Lets you connect to a properly equipped Windows for Workgroups LAN via modem.

Microsoft Tools Group

DOS creates this program group for the Windows versions of its bundled utilities. For more details, see the previous section, "Safety Check."

Anti-Virus. This utility checks for viruses and removes them.

Backup. Creates a backup version of your hard disk's data, but only on floppy disk, not on tape.

Undelete. Resurrects accidentally deleted files, but works best when DOS's Delete Sentry has been installed.

Application Group

When you run Windows Setup's Options//Set Up Applications command, it puts the applications you select in the Application group.

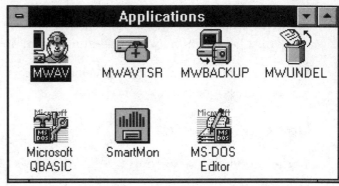

During Windows Express Setup installation, it creates icons for Microsoft Anti-Virus, Backup, and Undelete. All of these are duplicates of the icons DOS puts in the Microsoft Tools group, so you can delete them here. Just select the icons one by one, and pick Delete from the Program Manager's File menu each time.

You can also delete MS-DOS Editor, since you'll use Notepad under Windows for editing unformatted text (TXT) files. MWAVTSR is Windows' name for VSafe; change this icon's clunky name to VSafe Manager and drag it into your StartUp group (see the previous section, "Safety Check," for more information). If you're not short of RAM, drop SmartMon (SmartDrive Monitor) into the StartUp group as well (see "Windows Tips" for more information).

Now you can delete the Applications group and organize your applications in a much more logical way. The "Windows Tips" section later in this chapter offers several suggestions for customizing Windows the way you want it.

Control Panel

Though it's within the Main program group, the Control Panel contains several applications and works like a program group in itself (except that when you run one of its applications you need to close that app before you can start another). When you need to

customize or configure Windows, you can do most of what you need to do with the Control Panel's mini-applications.

- **Color** lets you play interior decorator with the color of borders, backgrounds, buttons, and text in Windows and its applications.

- **Fonts** is where you add or remove Windows TrueType fonts or set TrueType options (see the section "Using TrueType" in Chapter 13: *Fonts*).

- **Ports** enables you to change settings for your PC's serial (COM) and parallel (LPT) ports without using DOS's clunky MODE command (see Chapter 8: *Upgrade It Yourself* for more on configuring ports).

HOT TIP

- **Mouse** is the first place you should go if you're a left-handed mouse user—it lets you switch the selection button from left to right. Also, if the mouse feels sluggish, you can change the Tracking Speed to make it more responsive.

- **Desktop** enables you to change Windows' appearance in other ways—choosing a "wallpaper" pattern for the desktop, selecting a screen saver, and so on.

- **Keyboard** has one purpose: To let you set the speed at which characters are repeated when you hold down a key.

- **Printer** is where you install printers, as well as change the default printer that Windows prints to—a good place to switch between printing to a fax-modem and an actual printer, for example.

- **International** enables you to change the keyboard layout for computing in a language other than English or in a country other than the United States.

- **Date/Time** is simply for setting your PC's clock.

- **MIDI Mapper** is for assigning synthesized sounds if you plan to hook a keyboard to your a sound card (see the section "Sound Hardware" in Chapter 23: *Multimedia*).

- **ODBC** is an obscure tool for setting up databases under Windows. You'll probably never use it.

- **386 Enhanced** enables you to fine tune Windows to run multiple applications efficiently (turn to the "Windows Tips" section later in this chapter for advice on 386 Enhanced).

- **Drivers** needn't be messed with most of the time. Mostly, you'll need this little program for configuring and deinstalling multimedia hardware.

- **Sound** is only useful if you have sound card. Here, you can tie sound effects to various system events, such as opening a window or exiting Windows.

DOS Under Windows

One of the main reasons for Windows' popularity is its ability to run your old DOS applications. You can run them either full-screen, so they look just the way they do without Windows, or (usually) in a window on the desktop. Full-screen, DOS applications generally run quite a bit faster.

You can start most DOS applications under Windows the same way you do in DOS—just open the MS-DOS Prompt window in the Main group and enter the application's start-up command—but DOS apps often work better if you use a Program Information File (PIF) to make a few adjustments. When you install Windows, it searches your drive for applications and creates PIFs for those it recognizes. Recent DOS applications usually come with a PIF—look for it in the program's directory or installation disks.

Using the PIF Editor

If you need to create or modify a PIF, use the PIF Editor in the Program Manager's Main group. Here's how to use the PIF editor:

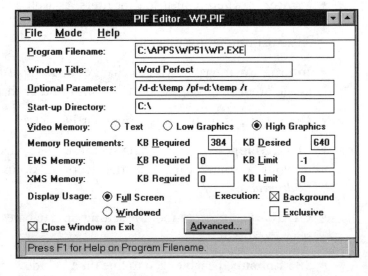

- **Program Filename** should contain the full path and name of the command you use to start the program.

- **Window Title's** contents are displayed on the title bar when you run the program in a window.

- **Optional Parameters** is for any parameters you would type after the command at the DOS prompt (such as a file to load at start-up).

- **Start-up Directory** specifies the directory where the program should look by default when you open or save a file. Try entering the directory containing the program's data files (which should be different than the directory where the program itself resides; see "How to Organize a Hard Disk" earlier in this chapter). If the program doesn't work, go back into the PIF Editor, open the program's PIF file, and enter the name of the program's own directory instead.

- **Video Memory** defaults to Text; choose High if the program uses graphics (the DOS version of *Harvard Graphics* does, for example).

- **Memory Requirements, EMS Memory, and XMS Memory** tell Windows how much of the various kinds of memory the program needs. In most cases, you can leave these boxes blank; the PIF Editor automatically inserts 640K in the KB Desired box, which is as it should be. However, to give applications that use expanded or extended memory as much room as they want, you may want to enter -1 in the appropriate KB Limit box.

HOT TIP

- **Windowed**, if selected, causes the application to start in a window instead of full-screen.

- **Background** should be checked if you want the application to keep running when you switch to Windows or another application—otherwise it's suspended until you switch back.

- **Exclusive** does the opposite of Background: When you start or switch to the application, Windows and all other apps are suspended. This option is mostly useful with programs that have trouble running under Windows or that interfere with other applications.

HOT TIP

Press the Advanced button, and you'll get an extra dialog-box-full of settings. There's little you need to know about here, with one exception: Allow Close When Active. Checking it lets you close DOS applications using Windows desktop controls instead of having to switch to the app and exit. Just be careful not to close a DOS app with unsaved documents.

Bringing DOS Apps Into the Family

HOT TIP

To switch DOS applications between full-screen and window mode, press [Alt][Enter]. You can change the font size used in the window display by dropping down the Control menu (click on the button in the upper-left corner of the window), picking Fonts, and choosing from ten different sizes.

You can cut and paste text between Windows and DOS applications, or between two DOS applications running under Windows. If you're running the DOS application full screen, press [Alt][Enter] to switch it to a window display. To copy, choose Edit//Mark from the Control menu, use the mouse to select a rectangle of text of the screen, and press [Enter]. To paste into a DOS application, position the cursor where you want the text to appear in the DOS app's document, then choose Edit//Paste from the Control menu.

Windows Tips

It takes awhile to learn how to use Windows to its best advantage. That is, unless someone lets you in on a few tricks. Here are some of my favorites, loosely divided into three groups: speed tips that help you get your work done faster, smart tips for organizing and customizing the Windows environment, and shortcuts for quick mouse and keyboard work.

HOT TIPS

Speed Tips

Even on a powerful PC, you can experience frustrating delays under Windows. If you don't like waiting even a second or two, give these four tips a try.

Boost Disk Speed With SmartDrive

Windows and DOS come with a *disk caching* program called SmartDrive, which (like all disk caches) moves frequently used data from disk to memory, where your applications can access that data faster. For maximum speed, SmartDrive has an option called *write caching*. Unfortunately, a system crash with write caching turned on can sometimes seriously trash your hard disk, so to be safe you should normally leave write caching turned off.

However, sometimes write caching is worth the risk. You'll get a big speed boost when working with lots of small files—say, cleaning out your E-mail or copying stuff between disks. So here's a convenient way to set things up so you can turn on write caching temporarily, when you need it most.

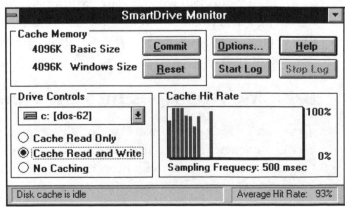

First—if it's not already in your Application group—you'll need to create a program item for SmartDrive Monitor, a small program for adjusting SmartDrive's features. Open the Application group, select New from Program Manager's File menu, choose Program Item, and enter `c:\dos\smartmon.exe` after Command Line. Choose the drive(s) you want to turn write caching on for from the Drive Controls menu, and then click Cache Read and Write. Don't forget to click Cache Read Only when you're ready to go back to safety mode.

Speed Up DOS Task Switching With the Control Panel

You can get a performance boost, particularly when switching between DOS applications, by changing Windows' virtual memory settings. First, defragment your hard drive (see "Regular Maintenance Checklist" in the "Safety Check" section earlier in this chapter). Then go to the Main group, open the Control Panel, double-click on the 386 Enhanced icon, click the Virtual Memory button, and click Change.

Windows will find the drive with the most free space and usually recommends creating a *permanent* swap file two to three times larger than the amount of RAM in your system. Usually you should just accept the recommendation. However, disk space allocated to the swap file won't be available for storing data, so if space is at a premium, you may want to reduce the size of the swap file by typing in a smaller number. Click OK, and Windows will create the

HOT TIPS

swap file. Click OK to continue, then Restart Windows to complete the process. Checking the Use 32-bit Disk Access box can make things even faster, though not all drives are compatible with this mode.

Get Applications Fast in Windows

If you define a shortcut key for a program item in the Program Manager, you can start it or switch to it by pressing a key combination, even if you can't see the icon on screen.

Program Item Properties

Description:	File Damager Alt-Shift-F
Command Line:	WINFILE.EXE
Working Directory:	
Shortcut Key:	Shift + Alt + F

☐ Run Minimized

OK
Cancel
Browse...
Change Icon...
Help

Select the program item and press Alt Enter to edit its properties. Click in the Shortcut Key field, and then press the key combination you want to use (Ctrl Alt, Ctrl Shift, Shift Alt, or Ctrl Shift Alt, plus a character). As you can see here, I usually type the shortcut after the program's description, so it appears in the program-item icon's label. Next time you want to switch to the program, just press its shortcut key.

To *start* an app with its shortcut key, first you need to switch back to the Program Manager. Unfortunately, there's no obvious way to define a shortcut for Program Manager itself. The trick is to create a program item for Program Manager (enter `progman.exe` after Command Line) in your StartUp group, and define a shortcut for it.

Use Alt Tab for Quick App Switching

If you press it once, Alt Tab takes you back to the app you just left. That makes it a very efficient way to switch back and forth between two applications.

You can also hold down Alt and press Tab repeatedly, which makes the names of the currently running programs pop up on screen. When you see the one you want, let go of Alt to switch to it. This eliminates the delays that would otherwise result from Windows displaying the applications as you switched. This trick can really save time, particularly when you're switching between full-screen DOS applications.

Smart Tips

One of the best things about Windows is that it's pretty easy to adapt to your working style, and to the kinds of tasks you have to perform. Want easy access to all your applications? Worried about your PC's clock running slow? Read on for the answers to these questions and more.

HOT TIPS

Customize Program Manager

Program Manager's defaults are pretty silly—if you leave it set the way it came out of the box, you can end up spending a lot of time switching between program group windows and scrolling them to find the icons you need.

The first step to getting Program Manager under control is to turn off Auto Arrange and Save Settings on Exit on the Options menu. Once you've arranged Program Manager the way you like it, save it manually using the hidden Save Now command: Just press Shift Alt F4 .

While you might have 50 or more applications, utilities, and games on your hard drive, chances are you use only a handful every day. To get the most out of Program Manager, why not create a new program group to hold those key applications, and make it big enough so that you can see all of them at once? Then put the applications you seldom use into a few logically named groups (Utilities, Games, and so on). To move program-item icons between groups, just drag and drop. If you never use a particular icon or group, select it, and then press Del to get rid of it.

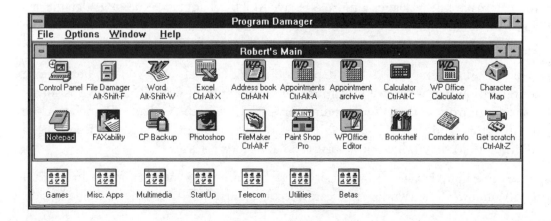

HOT TIPS

Once you've organized your groups, adjust their window size and position, using Window//Arrange Icons as necessary to neatly organize the icons. Minimize all the group windows except your core-application group, then save your settings. Here's how my Program Manager looks:

Most of the applications I use in the course of an average week are right here where I can get at them. A few are in the StartUp folder, so they start automatically when I run Windows. I moved the rest of my core applications into other program groups once I memorized the shortcut keys I use to start them. (I created the joke title bar by changing the Description field for the Program Manager item in my StartUp group.)

Clean Up After Program Setup Utilities

Lots of application installation utilities insist on creating a new program group, even if they only have one program item. To keep your Program Manager neat, clean up after these arrogant setup utilities by dragging their icons into the appropriate groups, and then deleting the unnecessary new group.

Add Documents to Program Manager

Program Manager holds not just programs but documents as well, such as the Read Me that comes with Windows (a Write document). You can create an icon for a data file by dragging it out of the File Manager and dropping it in the appropriate Program Manager group.

If you install a read-only file in Program Manager, it can serve as a template, since you'll be forced to save it under a new name. To make a file read-only, select it in File Manager, choose File//Properties or press Alt Enter, check Read Only, and click OK.

Customize File Manager

You can make File Manager a more effective tool by changing some of its default settings. First, shut off Save Settings on Exit on the Options bar. When you have File Manager set to your liking, save it manually by pressing Shift Alt F4.

Which Winfile setup works best depends on what kind of work you do, but here's a configuration that works well for me. The default view of C:\WINDOWS is silly—you seldom work in the Windows directory—so I use Tree//Collapse Branch to close the directory, and select C:\. Then I choose Tree//Indicate Expandable Branches to add the "+" to show which directories contain subdirectories.

Since most File Manager drag-and-drop tasks require two windows for the drop part, I used Window//New Window to create a second, and Shift F4 to tile them side by side.

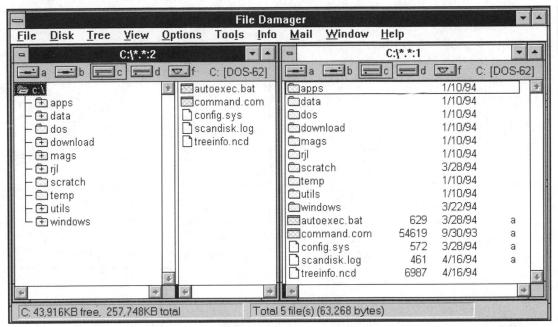

I set the right window to View//Directory Only and View//Partial Details (showing everything but the time, so the screen's not quite so cluttered), and I set the left window to View//Tree and Directory and View//Files, then saved my settings.

This gives me a display that can be used for a wide variety of tasks with a minimum of fiddling around.

Make Directory Icons in File Manager

If you work with a particular directory a lot, you can create an icon for it in the File Manager. Select the directory, choose Window//New Window, choose View//Directory Only, and click the window's minimize button to reduce it to an icon. Rearrange your File Manager windows, put the icon where you want it, and then press Shift Alt F4 to save the settings. When you perform drag-and-drop operations, you can drop right on the minimized window without opening it.

HOT TIPS

Customize Windows' Desktop

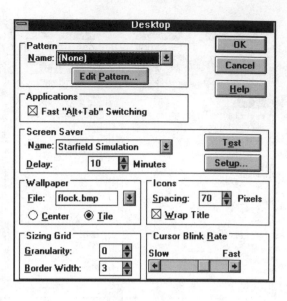

You can use Desktop in the Control Panel to change the way Windows' desktop looks. Here's a quick tour of the Desktop dialog box:

- **Pattern** textures the desktop by covering it with what you could think of as tiles, each with the same 64-pixel square pattern (*pixels* are the dots that make up the image on screen). Pick a pattern from the list or create your own by clicking the Edit Pattern button. (Note that Wallpaper must be set to None or you won't see the pattern.)

- **Wallpaper** is similar, except that the tiles' pattern is the graphic of your choice (as long as it's in the BMP file format). For larger graphics, click the Center option button to center a single image in the center of the desktop.

- **Spacing** controls the horizontal spacing of icons on the desktop and in the Program Manager. The setting indicates the number of pixels between the center of one icon and the next. Use a smaller setting and turn on the Wrap Title option, and you can fit more icons in the same space.

- **Granularity,** when set above 0, turns on an invisible grid that icons and application windows will snap to when moved or resized, which will make your desktop look tidier.

- **Border Width** changes the thickness of window borders. Setting this to its maximum value of 50 makes Windows look quite bizarre.

Set the Clock and Calendar

It's not unusual for PCs' clocks to run a little slow. To adjust the clock in Windows, open the Control Panel, double-click the Date/Time icon, set the time, and click OK. To change the default time display, for example to use 24-hour military time (17:35 instead of 5:35 p.m.), double-click on the International icon.

Generally, setting the date and time in Windows will change your system's clock permanently, but on some systems the clock will go back to its old setting when you turn off the system. In such cases, you'll have to change the clock using your PC's setup utility.

Display the Tiniest Clock

It's easy to make Windows' Clock visible all the time: Just choose Always on Top from its Control menu.

To keep the clock from getting in the way, choose Settings//No Title. 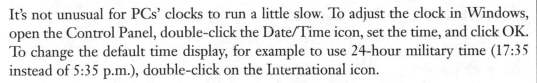 Next, drag the clock's border until it's as small as you can stand it, then click in the middle of the window and drag the clock to the top of your screen, a couple of inches from the right edge. That's about the least-used spot on the desktop. If you ever want to change the clock's settings, just double-click on it to restore the title bar and menus.

Windows Shortcuts

Doing what you want to do with the least hassle isn't always obvious in Windows. This quick reference will help you out, whether you want to teach your mouse a few tricks or you prefer keeping your hands on the keyboard.

Windows Mouse Tricks

General

Pop up Task List	Double-click on desktop
Close window	Double-click Control menu
Maximize window	Double-click on title bar

Program Manager

Create new program item	[Alt]–double-click on blank area of group window
Change program item or group properties	[Alt]–double-click on icon
Save current Program Manager settings	[Shift]-click on File//Exit Windows

File Manager

Move file(s) from one disk to another	[Alt]-drag and drop
Copy files from one directory to another on same disk	[Ctrl]-drag and drop
Copy files to another disk	Drag and drop on drive icon
Open new directory window	Double-click on drive icon
Expand to show all directories	[Shift]-click drive icon
Split window to show files and directories	Drag split bar from left edge of window
Tile windows side by side	Hold [Shift] while clicking Window//Tile

Windows Keyboard Shortcuts

General

Pop up Task List	`Ctrl` `Esc`
Close document window	`Ctrl` `F4`
Close application window	`Alt` `F4`
Switch document windows	`Ctrl` `Tab`
Switch application windows	`Alt` `Tab`

Program Manager

Change program item or group properties	`Alt` `Enter`
Switch to another program group	`Ctrl` `Tab`
Close current group window	`Ctrl` `F4`
Select another program item	Tap first letter of icon label
Save current Program Manager settings	`Alt` `Shift` `F4`
Close Program Manager (and exit Windows)	`Alt` `F4`

File Manager

Move to root directory in tree view	`Home`
Move up one level in tree view	`Ctrl` `←`
Select adjacent files/directories	Hold `Shift` and use cursor keys
Select nonadjacent files/directories	Press `Shift` `F8` use `Spacebar` to tag items
Select all	`Ctrl` `/`
Deselect all	`Ctrl` `\`
Run program (or open file) minimized	`Shift` `Enter`
Change directory windows	`Ctrl` `Tab`
Switch current directory window to another drive	`Ctrl`-[*drive letter*]
Open new directory window	`Tab`, select drive icon, `Enter`
Tile windows side by side	`Shift` `F4`

~~~~~~

DOS Shortcuts

When working at the DOS prompt, there are several shortcuts you can use to avoid having to retype commands. Remember that you have to have *entered* the command for DOS to duplicate what you typed. Note that [←Backspace] and [Del] work as they usually do, and by default typing overwrites characters from the last command.

DOS Prompt Tricks	
Recall last command	[F3]
Recall one character from last command	[→]
Recall series of characters from last command	[F2], then first character *after* the portion you want to recall
Skip characters in last command	[F4], then first character *after* the portion you want to skip
Insert characters, then recall rest of last command	[Ins], type characters, then [F3]

You can really save time with these shortcuts. For example, if you just entered `md data\wp` to create a new directory, you could then simply type `c` and press [F3] to get the command `cd data\wp`. Or if you just entered `dir c:\windows\*.ini`, you could press [F2], type two periods, and add `cfg` to get `dir  c:\windows\*.cfg`.

Even Better DOS Shortcuts

If you find yourself doing a lot of this kind of thing, you might want to add the DOS utility DOSKEY to your AUTOEXEC.BAT file (just add a line containing the program name; see Appendix A: *Tuning CONFIG.SYS and AUTOEXEC.BAT*). Once DOSKEY is loaded, you can use the up arrow key to scroll through the last several commands you entered. When you find the one you want to modify, you can edit it with wordprocessor-like commands. The right and left arrows move back and forth, Ctrl-right and Ctrl-left move a word at a time, and Ins toggles between insert and overstrike modes.

DOSKEY Shortcuts	
Scroll through command history	Up/down arrow
Display command history as menu	F7
Choose command to edit from menu	F9
Search for command	Type beginning of command, then F8
Move cursor left or right	← or →
Move left or right one word	Ctrl ← or Ctrl →
Move to beginning or end	Home or End
Toggle between overstrike and insert modes	Ins
Delete character to left or right of cursor	←Backspace or Del
Delete everything to left or right of cursor	Ctrl Home or End
New, blank DOS prompt	End

13 | Fonts

By Daniel Will-Harris

- Font fundamentals
- Tips for using type
- Using TrueType and PostScript with Windows
- A gallery of great typefaces and type combinations
- Font utilities: managers, converters, editors, and effects
- The top font companies and their specialties

You see type every day, all around you. In your lifetime you've seen billions of letters and millions of words, yet you might never have actually noticed the typefaces they were created in. That's how it should be, for the most part.

- **Type is an unconscious persuader.** Type attracts attention, sets the style and tone of a document, colors how readers interpret the words, and defines the feeling of the page.

- **Type is your personality on paper.** Typefaces have personality. Change your typeface and you go from casual to formal, silly to serious, staid to stylish, old-fashioned to modern.

- **Type is power.** Type has an effect on people even if they don't consciously notice it. You can use this power to your advantage to attract attention, strengthen your message, and improve your image, or you can overlook it and work against yourself—saying one message with your text while conveying another with your type.

- **Type is image.** You'd dress your best if you were going to an important meeting, and your documents need to be well dressed, too. Type can reinforce both your company's image and your personal image. If you use a typeface consistently enough, people will start to associate you with it. Without knowing why, they might find themselves thinking of you when they see that typeface.

- **Type is important.** The right typeface can encourage people to read your message. The wrong typeface or bad typography can make your message go unread. Presented with two documents side by side, one well written but ugly, and the other rambling but attractive, which do you think people will choose to read?

- **Type is communication.** Communication means relaying information about our logic and emotions to others. The better you learn to communicate, the better others will know you, and the better you'll know yourself because logic, emotion, and about 98 percent water are what you're made of.

- **Type is easy.** Windows takes away all the hassle from using fonts. You see fonts on screen exactly as they'll print. You install fonts once (a virtually automatic process), and they're available for all your Windows programs. Even if you're a DOS diehard, you're in luck: A growing number of utilities let you easily use fonts with popular DOS applications.

Type Terms and Fundamentals

Fonts are the electronic files that contain *typefaces*. A single typeface is made up of the upper- and lowercase letters of the alphabet, the numbers zero through nine, punctuation marks, and special characters—all in a particular style, such as Times New Roman or Arial (both standard fonts that come with Windows). If the font is *scalable*—and most fonts are these days—you can use your application to change its size, from tiny to big enough to see across the street.

Type size is always measured in *points*. There are approximately 72 points per inch. Body text, such as the text you're reading, is generally set from 10 to 12 point. Subheads should generally be between 14 and 18 point. Headings range from 24 to 72 point, or larger for special effects.

`Monospaced (Courier)`   Proportionally spaced (Times)

Type can either be *monospaced* or *proportionally spaced*. Typewriter type, and certain fonts such as Courier and Letter Gothic, are monospaced—each letter has the same width whether it's an *i* or a *W*. Typeset-quality fonts, such as Times Roman and Arial, are proportionally spaced—each letter is just the width of the character (you can fit four *i*'s in the space of one *W*).

Serif (Bodoni Bold Condensed)   Sans serif (Futura Book)

Typefaces fall into one of two camps: serif and sans serif. A serif is the small crossbar (or finishing stroke, or doohickey) that ends the main stroke of letters. Sans (French for "without") serif typefaces don't have serifs.

Regular   *Italic*   **Bold**   ***Bold Italic***
(the Times family)

Typefaces generally come in several *weights*, such as Regular, Italic, Bold, and Bold Italic. Different weights of the same typeface are called a *family*. Each of these weights are contained in a single font file. Faces designed for headings and headlines may have only one weight, but body text faces usually have four, with professional fonts offering as many as 16 or so, from very light to extra black. Body text families should have three weights, but some inexpensive packages fool you and give you only one or two weights, making the fonts much less versatile and useful than they should be.

DANGER

Body type   𝔇𝔦𝔰𝔭𝔩𝔞𝔶 𝔗𝔶𝔭𝔢 DISPLAY TYPE

Type can be broken down into two more categories: *body* and *display*. Body typefaces, such as the one you're reading right now, are designed to be read for paragraphs or pages, but they can also be used for display text. Most body faces have serifs. Display text is larger type designed specifically for headings and headlines, that is, to be used for only a few words at a time. For the most part, display faces shouldn't be used for body text because they're too difficult to read in smaller sizes.

REMEMBER

```
┌─────────────────────────────────┐
│ the space between the lines ◄─── leading │
│ the space between the lines             │
└─────────────────────────────────┘
```

The space between lines of text is called leading because in the days when metal type was used, the space between lines was achieved by using thin strips of lead hammered to a precise thickness. The general rule for determining leading is to add 20 percent to the type size—for example, if you have 10 point text, you should have 12 point leading. It's not unusual to add more leading, but you never want to use less because it can make type much more difficult to read.

WAVE   WAVE

Unkerned   Kerned

Kerning involves moving letters closer together or farther apart so that they *appear* evenly spaced, which in turn makes them easier to read. Most fonts include *kerning* pairs (To, Tr, We, and so on) that adjust their spacing automatically when typed consecutively. The kerning pairs included in a font are usually all you need for body text, but sometimes you need to kern large text manually. However, the quality of today's fonts and kerning pairs is high enough so that manual intervention is rarely necessary.

QQertazn   fi, ff, æ   ぐ ✿ ❏ ▼ ✗ ✧ ★ → ✄

Swash characters   Ligatures   Ornaments

The most expensive and professional fonts have special "expert" sets that include true small caps and old-style numbers. They can also include *special swash characters, ligatures* (special typographic characters that combine two letters into one, such as fi or ff), and matching *ornaments*. Also known as dingbats or pi fonts, ornament fonts are made up of pictures rather than alphabets. Because they're pictures, they don't fall into the regular body/display, serif/sans categories and are in a fun and useful class by themselves.

Two Rules for Using Type

There are entire books about using type (I've written several). People spend their whole lives studying the practice. But here's what it's all about:

1. Type is on the page to serve the text. It should make the words easy to read and provide a suitable background. *Type* should not overpower the *text*.

2. There are no *good* and *bad* typefaces, there are *appropriate* and *inappropriate* typefaces. Think about your reader and the feeling you want to convey, then choose a typeface that fits.

Simplistic? Maybe so. But if everyone followed these two rules, you would have read more things in your life, and understood better what you did read.

Top Ten Type Tips

1. Body text should be between 10 and 12 point; 11 is best when printing to a laser printer. Use the same typeface, type size, and leading for *all* your body copy.

2. Use enough leading (or line spacing) in body text. Always add at least 1 or 2 points to the type size. Example: If you're using 10 point type, use 12 point leading.

3. Don't make your lines too short or too long. Optimum size: more than 30 characters and less than 70 characters.

4. Make paragraph beginnings clear. Use *either* an indent or block style for paragraphs. Don't use both. And don't use neither, either.

5. Use only one space after a period, not two.

6. Don't justify text unless you have to. If you justify text you must use hyphenation.

7. Don't underline *anything,* especially not headlines or subheads since lines would separate the headlines and subheads from the text with which they belong. Use italics instead of underlines.

8. Don't set long blocks of text in italics, bold, or all caps because they're harder to read.

9. Use subheads liberally to help readers find what they're looking for.

10. Leave more space above headlines and subheads than below them.

Fonts and Font Formats

Fonts can be built into the printer, built into cartridges that plug into the printer, or installed on your hard disk and then sent to the printer (called *downloadable* fonts). Built-in fonts and cartridges have a speed advantage but offer a limited number of typeface choices. Downloadable fonts are now the most popular because they offer the widest choice of typefaces, and because downloading—particularly under Windows— has become virtually automatic.

Font rasterizers—programs that manage the preparation and downloading of fonts— have revolutionized font handling. When you start up the TrueType rasterizer built into Windows, or the optional *ATM* (*Adobe Type Manager*) rasterizer, you don't even know that it's there. You just choose fonts in any size and see them on screen almost exactly as they'll appear on paper. Font management under Windows is especially easy, because Windows rasterizers automatically make their services available to every Windows application.

TrueType vs. PostScript Type 1

You have a choice of several font rasterizers for Windows, but the vast majority of people either stick with Windows' TrueType rasterizer or use *ATM*, which comes free with many applications and font packs. The key difference between the two? The TrueType rasterizer can use only TrueType fonts, while *ATM* can use only PostScript Type 1 fonts.

Both TrueType and PostScript Type 1 are fully scalable font formats, which means the rasterizer can change the height and proportional width of any TrueType or PostScript Type 1 font. Type 1 was the first scalable font format for personal computers and was designed to work with PostScript, a powerful computer language for describing pages to printers. In the old days, the only practical way to get PostScript fonts was to buy a PostScript printer, which had both the rasterizer and (usually 35) fonts built in.

But those days are long gone. You can now choose from a huge number of Type 1 or TrueType fonts and install them under Windows easily.

Which Should You Use?

First, you need to know that font *quality* is *not* based on font format. There are good TrueType fonts and bad TrueType fonts. There are good Type 1 fonts and bad Type 1 fonts. The format itself is just a particular way to *describe* what the font looks like—what's important is the design of the typeface itself and how carefully it was *digitized* (turned into an electronic font). TrueType and Type 1 each have their own advantages and disadvantages:

- **Cost.** The TrueType rasterizer is built into Windows, while *ATM* is a separate piece of software (which is now included free with all new Adobe type packages). As for the fonts, the TrueType variety tends to be less expensive, with Microsoft, Bitstream, and Agfa offering professional-quality fonts in some of their lowest-cost packages.

- **Speed.** PostScript Type 1 fonts can be noticeably slower on screen, especially with programs that manipulate type, such as *CorelDraw*. Also, Type 1 fonts can actually take more time and memory to print on PostScript printers than TrueType fonts do.

- **Selection.** More typefaces are available in Type 1 format than in any other, although converting from Type 1 to TrueType (or vice versa) is easy.

- **Compatibility.** PostScript Type 1 fonts used to be the more popular, and many service bureaus still prefer files prepared with Type 1 fonts (although this is becoming less of an issue). A few high-end programs, notably *Adobe Illustrator*, do not support TrueType fonts, and *QuarkXPress* won't display rotated TrueType fonts, though they will print.

- **Font embedding.** You can *embed* TrueType fonts in documents, so when you share files, recipients can display and print those typefaces without having to install the fonts on their machine. Type 1 fonts can't be embedded.

- **Multiple Master support.** *ATM* supports special new Multiple Master Type 1 fonts that give you infinitesimal control over weight, width, and "optical size"—a boon for people serious about type. (TrueType GX, a new version of TrueType, can do similar things, but it's currently available only on the Mac.)

- **Quirks.** TrueType typefaces with extremely complex designs do not always display or print correctly.

As you can tell, it rarely matters what font format you use. Most Windows users will find TrueType fastest and easiest. Graphic designers will also want PostScript Type 1 for its huge font selection and robust handling of complex typefaces.

HOT TIP

Best of all, these two font formats can work together, side by side. Not just in the same document, but in the same line of text. You don't even have to know what format your font is in: You just choose it from the font list and it appears on screen, ready to be printed. Finally, a program called *FontMonger* allows you to convert between several popular font formats easily.

Using TrueType

Windows comes standard with 14 fonts, including four weights of Times New Roman, a classic serif face; four weights of Arial, a modern sans serif; and four weights of Courier, a typewriter (or "monospaced") font. Although these are carefully designed fonts, they have as much personality as an IRS form, which isn't surprising, since they're quite similar to the typefaces found there.

Adding New Fonts

Adding TrueType fonts could-n't be easier (well, it could be easier if someone else did it for you, but otherwise this is about as easy as it gets):

1. Open the Main group in the Program Manager, start the Control Panel, and double-click on the Fonts icon.

2. Click on Add. If the fonts are on a floppy disk, choose Drives (or click in the box below it) and select the drive with the disk containing your fonts.

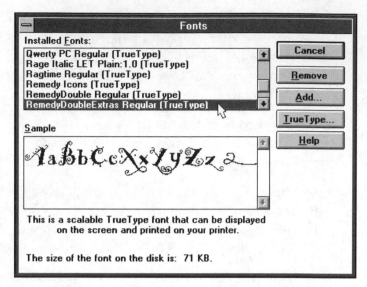

Figure 1: *The TrueType font manager is part and parcel of Windows 3.1. To install TrueType fonts, just double-click on the Fonts icon in the Control Panel.*

3. A list of font names will appear. Click on the ones you want, and then click OK. The fonts will be copied to your \WINDOWS\SYSTEM directory and installed into Windows. If your fonts are already on the hard disk, you can install them without Windows copying them. But I recommend that you just let Windows copy the fonts and be done with it—they're easier to manage when they're all in a single directory. Trust me on this.

When you're finished, click on the Close button. That's it. Once installed, the fonts are available to all Windows applications and will print on all printers.

TrueType Embedding

With PostScript Type 1 fonts, if you want to share a document with someone, and he or she doesn't have the same fonts, the document will reformat and look *wrong* on his or her machine. With TrueType, you can keep that formatting intact by *embedding* fonts in a document so the fonts travel with it.

There are four levels of embedding, each of which is coded into the font itself:

- **None** means you're out of luck.

- **Print/Preview** enables you to create a document you can view and print but not edit.

- **Editable** gives you a document you can edit—but the fonts are active only for that particular document.

- **Installable** actually installs the font on the system for use by all programs.

Very few fonts are installable, because few companies like giving away their fonts. The fonts that ship with Windows are, as are those in the very first Microsoft *TrueType Font Pack*. Certain programs—notably Microsoft's *TrueType Font Assistant*, which ships with the Microsoft *TrueType Font Pack #2*—can specifically tell you how a font can (or can't) be embedded.

Not all applications support font embedding. If a program does, you'll see a check box in the Save or Save As dialog box (in *Word for Windows 6* it's under the Options button) that says something like "Embed or Include Fonts."

Making Sure Big Type Prints

If you're working with very complex TrueType fonts in very large sizes (over 72 points), you might find that the fonts display but do not print. That is because Windows' rasterizer has two different ways of filling characters: a fast way for small sizes and a slower method for very large sizes. Sometimes Windows can't decide which method to use and refuses to print certain characters or even the whole font. And if a font is improperly made, it may not display *or* print.

If you have this problem, you can change the point where Windows' rasterizer switches fill methods by adding the following line to the [TrueType] section of your WIN.INI file: `OUTLINETHRESHOLD=70`

Start at 70, but if Windows suddenly starts drawing fonts slower, carefully raise the value (the default value is 127)—but not too far or you'll end up with *more* missing characters. Certain incorrectly produced TrueType fonts may print in a distorted manner at smaller sizes using low settings; if so, set the number higher.

TrueType Fonts for PostScript Printers

When you print a TrueType font on a PostScript printer, Windows normally converts that font into PostScript format as you print. But Windows gives you several options on exactly how it does this.

Run the Windows Control Panel and choose Printers, then select a PostScript printer. Click on Setup, Options, Advanced. The first box lets you specify how TrueType fonts are sent to PostScript printers. Choose Adobe Type 1. It's the best way to get good-looking fonts at small sizes *and* decent print speed.

A few PostScript printers, such as those from Apple and LaserMaster, come with TrueType support. If your printer has it, you'll find the option to enable it in one of your Printer Setup dialog boxes. Do it to get the best performance.

Using PostScript Type 1

If you don't own *ATM* already, consider a low-cost font package from Adobe, such as the *Adobe Type Set Value Pack* or *Wild Type*. These packages not only cost less than *ATM* by itself (which runs about $75 in stores), but they also contain a number of fascinating fonts, plus a selection (Times Roman, Helvetica, Courier, and so on) very similar to that included with Windows.

HOT TIP

Installing Fonts Using ATM

Unlike the TrueType rasterizer, *ATM* needs to be installed, which takes about five minutes. To install Type 1 fonts:

1. Run the ATM Control Panel from the Program Manager.

2. Click on the Add button. Choose the drive and directory where the fonts are located.

3. Select the fonts you want to install. Make sure to check the directory listed in the "Target Directory for PostScript Outline Fonts" and the "Target Directory for Font Metric Files" boxes. This is where your fonts will be copied to.

4. ATM likes to give PFM (Type 1 width-information) files their own directory, but this doesn't really accomplish anything except make it more difficult to reinstall fonts. I suggest you put both your PFM and actual font outline files (which

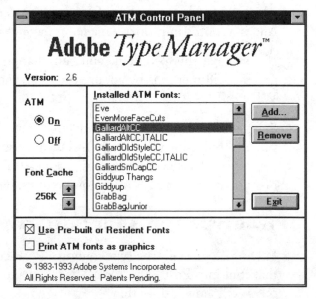

Figure 2: Adobe Type Manager (ATM) installs like any other Windows application—just run the install routine using Program Manager's File//Run. As with TrueType, you seldom need to fuss with it unless you're adding fonts.

HOT TIP

end in .PFB) in the same directory. I also suggest that you put all your Type 1 fonts into a single directory.

5. If you use a PostScript printer, make sure that the "Install as autodownload fonts for the PostScript driver" check box has an x in it. If you don't do this, you may get Courier from the printer rather than the font you see on screen.

DANGER

6. Click on the Add button to install the fonts.

Multiple Master Fine Tuning

How much control does *ATM* offer over Multiple Master fonts? Sanvito script, for example, gives you 380 different weights to choose from! At times such differences are invisible, but the ability to choose *just* the weight you want can be tremendously useful. "Just a little lighter" or "just a little darker" is now a typographic possibility.

Because scalable typefaces can be printed any size, people have had little choice but to use the same design at 6 points as at 72 points. Now, Multiple Master

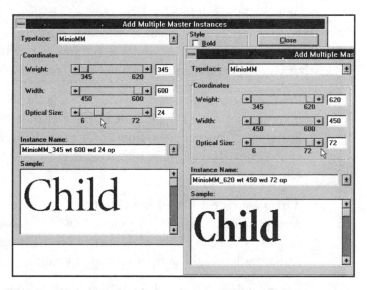

Figure 3: With Adobe Type Manager, you can tweak a Multiple Master Type 1 font ad infinitum using fine controls over weight, width, and optical size.

technology enables you to touch up a typeface in every size from largest to smallest, in the same manner traditional typography once allowed. With *ATM*, you make these adjustments in the Add Multiple Master Instances dialog box.

ATM Type 1 Fonts and PostScript Printers

It's rare to have trouble using *ATM* Type 1 fonts with a LaserJet. But strangely, using Type 1 fonts with PostScript printers can cause problems. Sometimes, when you select a printer, you won't see all the fonts you know you've installed using *ATM*, because Windows' PostScript driver can't tell the difference between *ATM* fonts and those fonts built into the PostScript printer itself.

If you install a PostScript printer *after* you install the fonts in *ATM*, the fonts are not listed with that printer, so Windows thinks they aren't available. To correct this, go into the *ATM* control panel, select all the fonts and choose Remove, and then re-install them. They'll now be added to all the PostScript printers on the system.

Built-In Printer Fonts

There are so many disk-based TrueType and PostScript Type 1 fonts available, no printer could possibly have as many fonts built in. The one advantage built-in fonts provide is better performance, which is most apparent on PostScript printers. The disadvantage is that these fonts don't automatically have matching screen fonts, so what you see on screen may not be what comes out of your printer.

- **PostScript** printers (and cartridges) contain what's called the "PostScript 35," a ubiquitous set of 35 Type 1 fonts. They include: four weights each of Avant Garde, Bookman, Century Schoolbook, Courier, Helvetica, Helvetica Narrow, Palatino, and Times Roman, plus one weight each of Symbol, Zapf Chancery, and Zapf Dingbats.

- **The LaserJet 4** has 54 built-in TrueType fonts— four weights each of: Albertus, Antique Olive, Arial, Clarendon, Coronet, Courier, Garamond Antiqua, Letter Gothic, Omega, Times CG, Times New Roman, Univers, Univers Condensed, and a single weight of Symbol and Wingding.

Any application that can drive a PostScript printer should come with its own set of screen fonts to match the PostScript 35. LaserJet owners can request matching screen fonts when they return the registration card for the printer. You're given a choice between TrueType or IntelliFonts. Choose TrueType.

Fonts can also reside on font cartridges that slip into a slot in the printer. Cartridge fonts used to be more popular because they provided convenience and speed, but their limited font availability and high price have made them less attractive than TrueType or Type 1 fonts. The one place they're still useful is in network settings where downloading any fonts can be slow.

Type Gallery

The next six pages of typeface samples showcase some of the most popular body and display faces, along with some of the ones I find most interesting. In the first two pages, I've suggested some combinations of serif and sans-serif typefaces. To see which go together, look at the small letter in a circle under the typeface name. A *white* letter inside a *black* circle indicates a sans-serif matching typeface—to pair it with a matching serif typeface, look for a face marked by the same letter in *black* inside a *white* circle. For example , Gill Sans has a G (white letter inside a black circle) which means it's a sans serif matching face. Goudy Old Style, Cantoria and Cheltenham have G (black lettter in a white circle) which means they match Gill Sans. If there is no letter, then the face is best used by itself.

Amerigo *Bitstream* Ⓕ	ABCDEFGHIJKLMNOPQRSTUVWXYZ abcdefghijklmnopqrstuvwxyz 01234567890
Bembo Aldine 401 Ⓜ	ABCDEFGHIJKLMNOPQRSTUVWXYZ abcdefghijklmnopqrstuvwxyz 01234567890
Bernhard Modern Ⓚ	ABCDEFGHIJKLMNOPQRSTUVWXYZ abcdefghijklmnopqrstuvwxyz 01234567890
Bodoni Ⓕ	**ABCDEFGHIJKLMNOPQRSTUVWXYZ** **abcdefghijklmnopqrstuvwxyz 01234567890**
Cheltenham *Bitstream* Ⓖ	ABCDEFGHIJKLMNOPQRSTUVWXYZ abcdefghijklmnopqrstuvwxyz 01234567890
ITC Charter	ABCDEFGHIJKLMNOPQRSTUVWXYZ abcdefghijklmnopqrstuvwxyz 01234567890
Electra Ⓖ	ABCDEFGHIJKLMNOPQRSTUVWXYZ abcdefghijklmnopqrstuvwxyz 01234567890
Cantoria Ⓖ	ABCDEFGHIJKLMNOPQRSTUVWXYZ abcdefghijklmnopqrstuvwxyz 01234567890
Futura Light Ⓕ	ABCDEFGHIJKLMNOPQRSTUVWXYZ abcdefghijklmnopqrstuvwxyz 01234567890
ITC Galliard	ABCDEFGHIJKLMNOPQRSTUVWXYZ abcdefghijklmnopqrstuvwxyz 01234567890
Gill Sans *Humanist 521* Ⓖ	ABCDEFGHIJKLMNOPQRSTUVWXYZ abcdefghijklmnopqrstuvwxyz 01234567890
Goudy Old Style Ⓖ	ABCDEFGHIJKLMNOPQRSTUVWXYZ abcdefghijklmnopqrstuvwxyz 01234567890
ITC Highlander Ⓗ	**ABCDEFGHIJKLMNOPQRSTUVWXYZ** abcdefghijklmnopqrstuvwxyz 01234567890
Hiroshige	ABCDEFGHIJKLMNOPQRSTUVWXYZ abcdefghijklmnopqrstuvwxyz 01234567890
Joanna Ⓚ	ABCDEFGHIJKLMNOPQRSTUVWXYZ abcdefghijklmnopqrstuvwxyz 01234567890

ITC Kabel ⓚ	ABCDEFGHIJKLMNOPQRSTUVWXYZ abcdefghijklmnopqrstuvwxyz 01234567890
ITC Legacy Serif ⓛ	ABCDEFGHIJKLMNOPQRSTUVWXYZ abcdefghijklmnopqrstuvwxyz 01234567890
ITC Legacy Sans ⓛ	ABCDEFGHIJKLMNOPQRSTUVWXYZ abcdefghijklmnopqrstuvwxyz 01234567890
Melior *Zapf Elliptical* ⓜ	ABCDEFGHIJKLMNOPQRSTUVWXYZ abcdefghijklmnopqrstuvwxyz 01234567890
Minion *Adobe* ⓜ	ABCDEFGHIJKLMNOPQRSTUVWXYZ abcdefghijklmnopqrstuvwxyz 01234567890
Myriad *Adobe* ⓜ	ABCDEFGHIJKLMNOPQRSTUVWXYZ abcdefghijklmnopqrstuvwxyz 01234567890
Optima *Zapf Humanist* ⓞ	ABCDEFGHIJKLMNOPQRSTUVWXYZ abcdefghijklmnopqrstuvwxyz 01234567890
Palatino *Zapf* *Calligraphic* ⓞ	ABCDEFGHIJKLMNOPQRSTUVWXYZ abcdefghijklmnopqrstuvwxyz 01234567890
Perpetua *Lapiday 333*	ABCDEFGHIJKLMNOPQRSTUVWXYZ abcdefghijklmnopqrstuvwxyz 01234567890
Serifa 55	ABCDEFGHIJKLMNOPQRSTUVWXYZ abcdefghijklmnopqrstuvwxyz 01234567890
Shannon *Agfa*	ABCDEFGHIJKLMNOPQRSTUVWXYZ abcdefghijklmnopqrstuvwxyz 01234567890
Silica *Stone* *Foundry*	ABCDEFGHIJKLMNOPQRSTUVWXYZ abcdefghijklmnopqrstuvwxyz 01234567890
ITC Souvenir ⓗ	ABCDEFGHIJKLMNOPQRSTUVWXYZ abcdefghijklmnopqrstuvwxyz 01234567890
Weiss ⓞ	ABCDEFGHIJKLMNOPQRSTUVWXYZ abcdefghijklmnopqrstuvwxyz 01234567890
Amethyst Script *FontHaus*	*Script Faces ABCDEFGH abcdefgh 0123456789*

Caflish Script *Adobe*	Script Faces ABCDEFGH abcdefgh 0123456789
Carpenter *Image Club*	Script Faces ABCDEFGH abcdefgh 0123456789
Erazure *FontHaus*	Script Faces ABCDEFGH abcdefgh 0123456789
Liberty	Script Faces ABCDEFGH abcdefgh 0123456789
Lucida Handwriting *Microsoft*	Script Faces ABCDEFGH abcdefgh 0123456789
Marguerita *Letraset*	Script Faces ABCDEFGH abcdefgh 0123456789
Marigold	Script Faces ABCDEFGH abcdefgh 0123456789
Mistral	Script Faces ABCDEFGH abcdefgh 0123456789
Motion *Emigre*	Script Faces ABCDEFGH abcdefgh 0123456789
Ovidius *FontHaus*	Script Faces ABCDEFGH abcdefgh 0123456789
Party *Letraset*	Script Faces ABCDEFGH abcdefgh 0123456789
Poetica *Adobe*	Script Faces ABCDEFGH abcdefgh 0123456789
Pristina *Letraset*	Script Faces ABCDEFGH abcdefgh 0123456789
Sanvito *Adobe*	Script Faces ABCDEFGH abcdefgh 0123456789
Shelley	Script Faces ABCDEFGH abcdefgh 0123456789

Spring *LetterPerfect*	*Script Faces ABCDEFGH abcdefgh 0123456789*
Al Oz Brush *Al*	Display Faces ABCDEFGHIJKLMNOPQRSTUVWXYZ abcdefghijklmnopqrstuvwxyz 01234567890
ITC Anna	DISPLAY FACES ABCDEFGHIJKLMNOPQRSTUVWXYZ 01234567890
ITC Beesknees	ABCDEFGHIJKLMNOPQRSTUVWXYZ
Bernhard Bold Condensed	Display Faces ABCDEFGHIJKLMNOPQRSTUVWXYZ abcdefghijklmnopqrstuvwxyz 01234567890
Bernhard Fashion (alt) *ImageClub*	Display Faces ABCDEFGHIJKLMNOPQRSTUVWXYZ abcdefghijklmnopqrstuvwxyz 01234567890
Bizarro II *Precision Type*	ABCDEFGHIJKLMNOPQRST
Bodega Serif Black *FontBureau*	Display Faces ABCDEFGHIJKLMNOPQRSTUVWXYZ abcdefghijklmnopqrstuvwxyz 01234567890
Bremen *Bitstream FontBureau*	ABCDEFGHIJKLMNOPQRSTUVWXYZ
Castellar *Monotype*	ABCDEFGHIJKLMNOPQRSTUVW
Celestia *FontHaus*	ABCDEFGHIJKLMNOPQRSTUVW
Citation *Letraset*	ABCDEFGHIJKLMNOPQRSTUVW
Copperplate Gothic	DISPLAY FACES ABCDEFGHIJKLMNOPQRSTUVWXYZ ABCDEFGHIJKLMNOPQRSTUVWXYZ 01234567890
Esposition *Handcrafted*	Display Faces ABCDEFGHIJKLMNOPQRSTUVWXYZ abcdefghijklmnopqrstuvwxyz 01234567890
Fajita Picante *Image Club*	DISPLAY FACES ABCDEFGHIJKLMNOPQRSTUVWXYZ ABCDEFGHIJKLMNOPQRSTUVWXYZ 01234567890

Futura Extra Black	**Display Faces ABCDEFGHIJKLMNOPQRSTUVWXYZ abcdefghijklmnopqrstuvwxyz 01234567890**
Harting *Precision*	ABCDEFGHIJKLMNOPQRSTUVWXYZ
Herculanum	ABCDEFGHIJKLMNOPQRSTUVWXYZ
Oz Handicraft *Bitstream*	Display Faces ABCDEFGHIJKLMNOPQRSTUVWXYZ abcdefghijklmnopqrstuvwxyz 01234567890
Jensen Aribique *FontHaus*	ABCDEFGHIJKLMNOPQRSTUVWXYZ
Lilith Initials *FontHaus*	ABCDEFGHIJKLMNOPQ
Lo-Type	*Display Faces ABCDEFGHIJKLMNOPQRSTUVWXYZ abcdefghijklmnopqrstuvwxyz 01234567890*
Metropolis *FontHaus*	**Display Faces ABCDEFGHIJKLMNOPQRSTUVWXYZ abcdefghijklmnopqrstuvwxyz 01234567890**
Mighty Special *FontBank*	ABCDEFGHIJKLMNOPQRST
Paisley Two Alternate *Image Club*	Display Faces ABCDEFGHIJKLMNOPQRSTUVWXYZ abcdefghijklmnopqrstuvwxyz 01234567890
Poster Solid & Inline *Handcrafted*	**ABCDEFGHIJKLMNOPQRSTUVWXYZ**
Rasta Rattin Frattin *Precision*	ABCDEFGHIJKLMNOPQRSTUVWXYZ
Remedy *Emigre*	Display Faces ABCDEFGHIJKLMNOPQRSTUVWXYZ abcdefghijklmnopqrstuvwxyz 01234567890
Searsucker *Agfa*	ABCDEFGHIJKLMNOP
Shades *Agfa*	**ABCDEFGHIJKLMNOP**

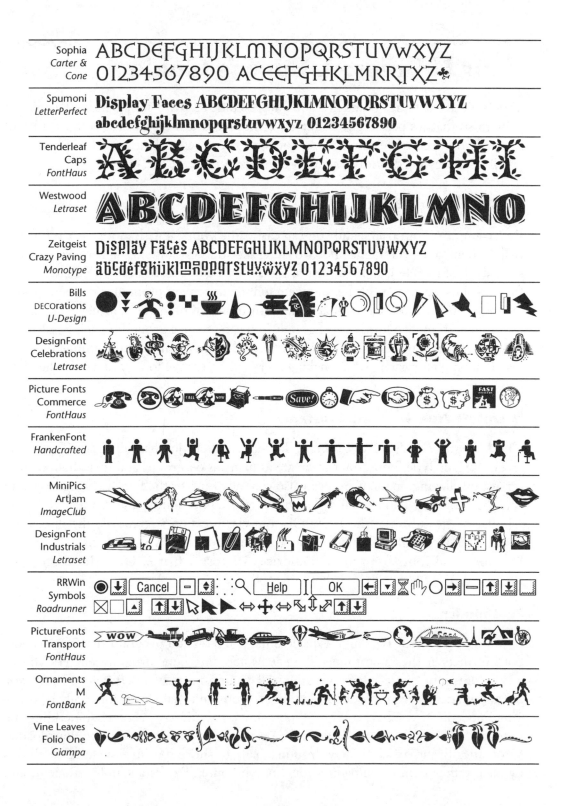

Sophia *Carter & Cone*	ABCDEFGHIJKLMNOPQRSTUVWXYZ 0123456789O ACEEFGHKLMRRTXZ❧
Spumoni *LetterPerfect*	Display Faces ABCDEFGHIJKLMNOPQRSTUVWXYZ abcdefghijklmnopqrstuvwxyz 0123456789O
Tenderleaf Caps *FontHaus*	ABCDEFGHI
Westwood *Letraset*	ABCDEFGHIJKLMNO
Zeitgeist Crazy Paving *Monotype*	Display Faces ABCDEFGHIJKLMNOPQRSTUVWXYZ abcdefghijklmnopqrstuvwxyz 0123456789O
Bills DECOrations *U-Design*	
DesignFont Celebrations *Letraset*	
Picture Fonts Commerce *FontHaus*	
FrankenFont *Handcrafted*	
MiniPics ArtJam *ImageClub*	
DesignFont Industrials *Letraset*	
RRWin Symbols *Roadrunner*	
PictureFonts Transport *FontHaus*	
Ornaments M *FontBank*	
Vine Leaves Folio One *Giampa*	

Font Utilities: A Buyer's Guide

Typefaces are artistic. Fonts are software. Windows' own font handling is robust enough so that it's possible you may never need a font utility. But if you use a lot of fonts, if you need to customize your fonts, or if you're working with DOS software, you'll definitely need at least one font utility program.

Font Managers

Buy a couple of font packs, and you can easily find yourself with more than 100 fonts. Install them, and you might find two things: Windows runs slower because it has to keep track of them all, and your list of fonts seems endless. You can eliminate both of these problems with one of the following font management programs; these programs let you create groups of fonts that you can turn on and off quickly, rather than having to install and remove fonts one at a time. You can create a group for each family, or a group for correspondence or newsletters. This helps limit the number of fonts installed on your system, while making it easy to access the fonts you need, when you need them.

Microsoft TrueType Font Assistant

The *Microsoft TrueType Font Assistant* does an excellent job handling TrueType fonts and only TrueType fonts. You can create as many as 64 groups and turn them on and off just by clicking on them. You can also view any font, or the fonts in any group, and sort them by font name, serif style, width, font embedability, and "similar to." The "similar to" feature uses the PANOSE font classification system (see the discussion about *FontWorks* that follows for more information on PANOSE) that's built into Windows and fonts from most foundries. Microsoft Corp., One Microsoft Way, Redmond, WA 98052; 800/426-9400.

FontMinder

If you use both TrueType and Type 1 fonts, you'll want a program that can manage both formats at the same time—like *FontMinder 2.0*. This program enables you to group fonts into "packs" that you can install or uninstall easily. Better yet, *FontMinder 2.0* automatically groups fonts by families, so you can install an entire family by dragging one icon. If you have a lot of Type 1 fonts, *FontMinder* becomes something of a necessity rather than a convenience: You can select which fonts will be downloaded automatically and which to download manually to shorten print time (and do all this by pack rather than downloading fonts one by one). This is a simple, efficient, and valuable tool for anyone who has to deal with a lot of fonts. Ares, 561 Pilgrim Dr., Ste. D, Foster City, CA 94404; 800/783-2737, 415/578-9090.

FontHandler

FontHandler lets you work with both TrueType and Type 1 fonts. When you start the program it provides an excellent font viewer that lets you see any font in the text of your choice. The Keyboard Manager gives you quick access to upper-ASCII characters, so rather

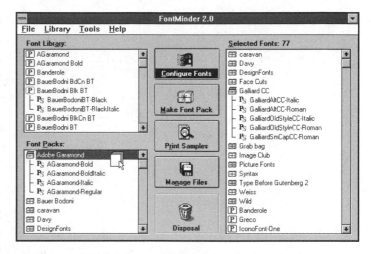

Figure 4: *FontMinder's drag-and-drop font handling lets you create TrueType and PostScript Type 1 font groupings easily. The program even groups families automatically for easy installation.*

than typing NumLock-Alt-0162 to get a cent sign (¢), you can remap the character to, for example, Control-Shift-c/. *FontHandler* also allows you to create groups so that you can more easily install or uninstall fonts, and it works with both TrueType and Type 1 fonts. The grouping system is similar to but more complex than *FontMinder*'s. Qualitype, 29209 Northwestern Hwy. #611, Southfield, MI 48034; 800/950-2921, 313/822-2921.

Figure 5: *FontMonger converts to and from dozens of font formats. You can also edit character sets and even create fonts from scratch.*

Font Converters and Editors

These utilities aren't just for font fanatics. As more documents include a wider variety of fonts, sooner or later you'll need to convert fonts between formats, tweak big headlines, or add special characters. Here are a few of my favorite tools for these jobs.

FontMonger

If you have Type 1 fonts that you need in TrueType format,

or TrueType fonts that you want in Type 1 format, you can accomplish either (or both) by using Ares' *FontMonger*. You can also convert from IntelliFont, NimbusQ, Corel wfn, or LaserMaster lxo, and convert to Type 1, Type 3, TrueType, NimbusQ, TrueType for Mac, Type 1 for Mac, Type 3 for Mac, or Type 1 for NeXT. What's more, you can edit characters, reassign characters on the keyboard, put characters from one font into another, and change font names. You can even create your own fonts from scratch. A must-have for anyone serious about type, *FontMonger* does all of this with a remarkably easy to use interface. Ares, 561 Pilgrim Dr., Ste. D, Foster City, CA 94404; 800/783-2737, 415/578-9090.

FontFiddler

Most fonts these days come with adequate kerning, but if you're a real perfectionist, or if you set a lot of display type, consider *FontFiddler*. This exceptional kerning editor lets you do more than kern by pairs: You can work with real words and kern them visually. The program comes with a long list of words designed to point out the most important pairs—make the words "look right" and you've automatically built the kerning. It's visual, intuitive, and terrific. It's also great for changing font names, or changing weight assignments to more easily build the kind of "families" you want (say Futura light with medium as bold, instead of extra black). This one program works with both Type 1 and TrueType fonts and it does a great job of custom kerning. Ares, 561 Pilgrim Dr., Ste. D, Foster City, CA 94404; 800/783-2737, 415/578-9090.

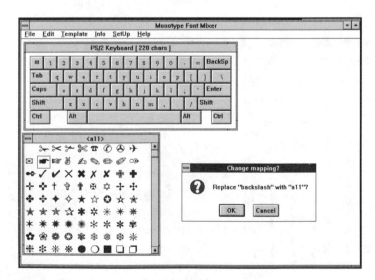

Figure 6: *Font Mixer lets you customize the character sets of PostScript Type 1 fonts.*

Font Mixer

Monotype's *Font Mixer* does one thing, but it does it well—it lets you rearrange and mix the characters from Type 1 fonts. You could, for example, take your favorite dingbats and place them on keys you might not otherwise use (such as { or }), or simply move typographic quote characters from their upper-ASCII positions (which normally require Alt-keystrokes to access) to the keys on your keyboard. *Font Mixer* only works with Type 1 fonts, but unlike *FontMonger*, it doesn't alter the fonts' original hinting. Monotype, 150 S. Wacker Dr., Chicago, IL 60606; 800/666-6897, 312/939-0378.

Font Generators

Feeling creative? Or are you stuck working with a document file that contains fonts you don't have? These two utilities make generating new fonts a snap.

FontWorks

Most of the time, if you receive a document file that has fonts you lack, Windows substitutes Times or Helvetica, the for-

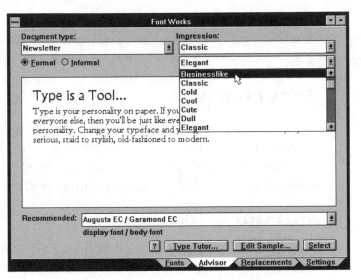

Figure 7: *Even if you receive documents from someone else's computer— FontWorks ensures they will look as close as possible to the original. Also included are an on-screen type tutorial, and this interactive Advisor which tells you the best fonts to use.*

matting goes haywire, and what you see bears little resemblance to the original. *FontWorks* solves that problem by using the PANOSE font classification system and a revolutionary new "synthetic" font engine to create duplicates of the missing fonts instantly. So if someone sends you a file set in Goudy Old Style and you don't have it, you will as soon you open the file. The program comes with "definitions" for more than 150 popular typefaces, including *true* (not generic) italics. Also included is a font management and grouping feature for both TrueType and Type 1 fonts.

FontWorks also includes the Advisor, which suggests appropriate font groups in response to questions you answer about your document's readers, the impression you want to create, and so on. Finally, you get the Type Tutor, an on-line typography tutorial that lets you learn and try basic and advanced type techniques. I created the Advisor and wrote the Type Tutor, so *naturally* I think they're good, and I hope you'll agree. ElseWare, 101 Stewart St. #700, Seattle, WA 98101; 206/448-9600.

Font Chameleon

Like *FontWorks, Chameleon* uses a synthetic-font technology to create fonts—not from traditional outline information, but from small descriptor files, which are more compact and flexible. The program doesn't replace missing fonts or provide tutorials, but it does give you impressive control over font design—with an extremely simple interface. The most impressive feature is its ability to "morph" between two existing faces (say Bodoni and Optima) and generate a whole new typeface design in a completely nontechnical way. *Chameleon* gives you unprecedented design control. Ares, 561 Pilgrim Dr., Ste. D, Foster City, CA 94404; 800/783-2737, 415/578-9090.

Font Effects

You don't have to use type as it is. You can add to it, take it apart, make it glow, fill it with marble, and do countless other things to turn letters into art. Although there are programs specifically designed to add special effects to text, you can also use illustration and paint or photo programs to make your fonts even flashier.

TrueEffects for Windows

TrueEffects lets you fill your fonts with a variety of interesting patterns ranging from a simple crosshatch to a wood grain, to a classic "sunset" of horizontal lines, to a "fog" effect that looks like airbrushing. You can create outlines and drop shadows and fill fonts with various shades of gray. The convenient thing about this program is that you don't have to do anything special to use these effects. Once you "create" an effect from the program, Windows considers the font to be like any other font—so all you have to do is choose it from your font list. The effects appear on screen just as they'll print on the page. Note: The effects don't work in certain programs, such as *CorelDraw*, which use their own font-handling routines. MicroLogic, 1351 Ocean Ave., Emeryville, CA 94608; 800/888-9078, 510/652-5464.

WordArt

Microsoft's original *WordArt* program was awful but the latest version uses any TrueType font and allows you to set type in arcs or circles, rotate type, or fill type with shades of gray or simple patterns, create outlined text, or add drop shadows. The program is simple to use, but limited, and comes bundled with various Microsoft programs, including *Word for Windows* and *Publisher*. It uses Object Linking and Embedding (OLE) so you can edit *WordArt* graphics at any time by double-clicking on them. Microsoft Corp., One Microsoft Way, Redmond, WA 98052; 800/426-9400.

Fonts for DOS

Believe it or not, fonts are getting easier to handle under DOS. These utilities all let you use scalable TrueType or PostScript Type 1 fonts with DOS programs and make font installation easy.

Whichever DOS font solution you choose, stick with Windows-compatible fonts, since you'll probably move to that environment eventually. For example, while Speedo fonts may be fastest, only Bitstream sells them, and they aren't readily compatible with Windows. I recommend TrueType as your first choice, then PostScript Type 1. Avoid other formats if possible.

HOT TIP

TrueType for WordPerfect

If you use *WordPerfect 5.0* or *5.1 for DOS*, LaserTools has the font solution for you: *TrueType for WordPerfect* (which includes 101 TrueType fonts and more special effects). The company also offers *FaceLift* for Bitstream and Speedo fonts; *Fonts on the Fly* for Agfa and the IntelliFont format; and *PrimeType* for Type 1 fonts. LaserTools products are known for their solid reliability and performance. Printing times are surprisingly fast. LaserTools, 1250 45th St., Emeryville, CA 94608; 800/767-8004, 510/420-8777.

TrueType for DOS

Microsoft Word and *Microsoft Works* users will want to look at MicroLogic's *TrueType for DOS*. This program also works with *WordPerfect*, *LetterPerfect*, and *PlanPerfect*, and not only provides complete access to TrueType, but adds dazzling special effects as well. MicroLogic also offers *MoreFonts for WordPerfect 6*, which contains 145 TrueType fonts (which obviously work with Windows too). Users of *WordPerfect for Windows 5.1* or *5.2* should also consider MicroLogic's *MoreFonts* because it greatly improves the font handling of these programs. MicroLogic, 1351 Ocean Ave, Emeryville, CA 94608; 800/888-9078, 510/652-5464.

Font References

If you're looking for a very complete listing of typefaces, you have several choices. *The Electronic Type Catalog* from Bantam/ITC ($34.95; 800/634-9325) gives you almost 700 pages of classic faces, plus new releases from major foundries up to 1990. The ITC Directory of new typefaces ($150 per year; 800/634-9325, 212/289-9125) is a three-ring binder with quarterly updates showing the very latest from large and small foundries. The FontShop's encyclopedia binder displays all of its more than 5000 fonts and is updated regularly ($49.95; 800/36-FONTS, 416/348-9837).

Font Sources

Here's where you find the fonts themselves. Fonts from these foundries can be purchased directly, or they can sometimes be purchased at retail outlets or from mail-order firms. Many of the foundries are also represented by FontHaus, FontShop, Monotype, and FontBank Online. Unless otherwise noted, fonts are available in both TrueType and PostScript Type 1 formats.

CD ROMs are being used more often for delivering fonts. CDs come in two basic formats: unlocked and locked. On an unlocked CD, all the fonts are available as soon as you buy the disc. On locked CDs, only a certain number of fonts are available with the purchase of the disc; the others must be unlocked. This is usually accomplished using a telephone and a credit card. You're given special codes that then give you access to the fonts you purchased by phone.

Adobe arguably has the largest digital type library available, with over 1200 fonts (Type 1 only, of course). These fonts cover all the classic faces, as well as many new designs, always of the highest quality and usually at the highest price. Adobe has an ever-growing collection of "original" faces including the incredibly popular Lithos and Tekton. Many "expert sets" are available. A locked CD ROM is available. Adobe Systems, Inc., 1585 Charleston Rd., Box 7900, Mountain View, CA 94039; 800/83-FONTS, 415/961-4400.

Agfa has a large type library on the Mac, but its PC offerings are more limited. The company offers two excellent, low-cost TrueType packages: *Desktop Styles* and *The Discovery TrueType Pack* (which includes an on-line guide to type). Agfa, 200 Ballardvale St., Wilmington, MA 01886; 508/658-5600.

Alphabets is known for its fine revivals of designs. The fonts are carefully rendered and priced at around $79.95 per family. Alphabets, Box 5448, Evanston, IL 60204; 800/326-4083, 708/328-2733; 73306,2703 (CompuServe).

Bitstream has an enormous library of the highest-quality fonts with an increasing number of original designs—including delightful fonts based on *Star Trek* and *The Flintstones*. Bitstream was started by type designers, so its digitizations are extremely true to the original designs. Bitstream's latest product is "500 fonts on CD," which contains 500 fonts in both Type 1 and TrueType formats and sells for $49.95. These are top-quality fonts at an unbelievable (but true) price. Bitstream's fonts are available in Type 1, TrueType, and Speedo formats. Bitstream, 215 First St., Cambridge, MA 02142; 800/522-FONT, 617/497-6222.

Carter and Cone, two of the founders of Bitstream, now run their own digital type foundry. Matthew Carter is the eminent type designer of Snell Roundhand, Bell Centennial, ITC Galliard, and Bitstream Charter. C&C's first release was an expanded Galliard family, including expert characters, old style figures, alternate and swash characters, and fractions and small caps. The company has released two new display faces, Mantinia and Sophia. Carter & Cone Type, Inc., 2155 Massachusetts Ave., Cambridge, MA 02140; 800/952-2129, 617/576-0398.

Casady & Green offers a low-cost eclectic collection of 120 fonts, including calligraphic faces. It also has a line of fonts that have Eastern European and Cyrillic characters. Casady & Green, 22734 Portola Dr., Salinas, CA 93908; 408/484-9228.

Castle Systems. Jason Castle is a type designer who specializes in sensitively reviving classic faces, as well as creating new ones, including Xavier (which has a feeling similar to Lithos but includes wonderful lowercase letters as well). Castle's fonts are special because of his attention to details—they're subtle and fine. Castle Systems, 1306 Lincoln Ave., San Rafael, CA 94901; 415/459-6495; 71601,1014 (CompuServe); CastleSys (America Online).

CompuServe DTP Forum (go dtp) is not a foundry, but it is a good place to find a wealth of shareware fonts, which range in quality from professional to abysmal. As with all shareware products, you can try before you buy. Prices range between $5 and $25.

Corel isn't a font foundry, yet the unlocked CD ROM that ships with *CorelDraw* is a complete type library in itself, containing almost 750 fonts, most of them from Bitstream. It's an amazing value. Corel, 1600 Carling Ave., Ottawa, Ontario, Canada K1Z 8R7; 800/836-3729, 613/728-8200.

David Rackowski is a symphonic composer who likes to digitize wild display faces in his spare time. His faces are well-drawn and are available through FontHaus and Precision Type.

Digital Typeface Corporation, a subsidiary of LaserMaster (which makes high-speed, high-res printers and add-ons), publishes three volumes of fonts through this subsidiary. Digital Typeface Corp., 6900 Shady Oak Rd., Eden Prairie, MN 55344; 612/943-8920.

Elfring, first name Gary, creates "keycap" fonts for manuals and the like. You build keycaps by typing several letters. For example, if you want the Alt key, you'd type "(ALT)". A Bar Code Font Pak with 3/9, 2/5, 2/5 interleaved, 128, UPC-A, and Postal bar codes costs $125. Gary Elfring, P.O. Box 61, Wasco, IL 60183; 708/377-3520, 708/377-3520 (fax).

Emigre's Zuzana Licko is known for her cutting-edge typefaces. All the faces in this company's library are unique. The latest faces are more mainstream but still have a completely original attitude. Emigre, 4475 D St., Sacramento, CA 95819; 800/944-9021, 916/451-4344.

FontBank Online sells *extremely* low cost packages and now also sells fonts by many different designers 24-hours a day on CompuServe (go fontbank). It specializes in revival display faces and sells a BigFont CD ROM containing 2000 fonts for $349, which instantly gives you a huge and varied library for a reasonable price. FontBank, 2620 Central St., Evanston, IL 60201; 708/328-7370; 75300,632 (CompuServe); FontBank (America Online)

FontHaus specializes in selling fonts from foundries and designers—usually at a discount. It currently offers about 5000 fonts, at 40 to 50 percent off retail. Its specialty is a large selection of exclusive fonts from designers around the world. The company also publishes an attractive type catalog/magazine called *x-height*. FontHaus now sells fonts on CompuServe (go fonthaus). FontHaus, 1375 Kings Hwy. E. Fairfield, CT 06430; 800/942-9110, 203/846-3087.

FontShop is a one-stop shop for fonts, carrying over 5000 fonts from more than 25 foundries (large and small). Its $50 encyclopedic type catalog is a great resource. FontShop has its own line of very new and original faces called FontFont. A locked CD ROM is also available. FontShop, 40 Wellington St. W., Toronto, Ontario, Canada M5V 1E8; 800/36-FONTS, 416/348-9837.

Image Club offers over 750 fonts, many of them unique, and all at reasonable prices. The company releases a new package each season, and its newest faces are especially appealing and unusual. Image Club also has an unlocked CD ROM of Type 1 fonts. Image Club, 729 24th Ave. SE, Calgary, Alberta, Canada T2G 1P5; 800/661-9410, 403/262-8008.

IQ Engineering is known for high-quality font cartridges that pack a large number of fonts. IQ also sells the *SuperType Master Library*, an excellent, low-cost TrueType font package. IQ Engineering, Box 60955, Sunnyvale, CA 94088; 408/733-1161.

Handcraftedfonts specializes in new faces that have an Art Deco look. Founder Jonathan Macagba's Poster and Exposition faces are fresh, yet they effectively and beautifully evoke the Vienna Secession and turn-of-the-century designs. Custom type services are also available. Jonathan Macagba, 849 N. Fifth St., Philadelphia, PA 19123; 215/829-1558.

Judith Sutcliff's company is called "The Electric Typographer," but I think of her work more as "The Electronic Calligrapher." Her calligraphic faces are unique, elegant, exquisite, and look as if they were handwritten. The Electric Typographer, 2216 Cliff Dr., Santa Barbara, CA 93109; 805/966-7563.

Lanston Type Company is a unique library of digital typefaces that contain all the quirks and idiosyncrasies that made the faces famous, and versions of some fonts with both short and long descenders. Very special: Goudy Initials, dramatically illuminated initial caps. Giampa TextWare Corp., 1340 E. Pender St., Vancouver, British Columbia, Canada V5L 1V8; 800/663-8760, 604/253-0815.

Letraset may sound familiar if you've ever used "press-on" type. Now many of these unique faces are available for the PC. Letraset's library also includes a number of new designs and picture fonts. Nielsen & Bainbridge, 40 Eisenhower Dr., Paramus, NJ 07652; 800/343-TYPE, 201/845-6100.

LetterPerfect's Garrett Boge started one of the first small foundries and specializes in all original faces that tend to look more hand-drawn than computer generated. LetterPerfect also does custom font design work. LetterPerfect, Box 785, Gig Harbor, WA 98335; 800/929-1951, 206/851-5158.

Linotype-Hell might sound like a particularly bad state of mind, but actually it's a fine old type foundry where the originals of many popular typefaces were developed. Most of the fonts in Adobe's library come from Linotype-Hell. However, LH releases many fonts itself, long before Adobe licenses them, and it'll sell individual fonts as well as families. Many expert sets are available, as are locked and unlocked CD ROMs. Linotype-Hell's fonts are available in Type 1 format only. Linotype-Hell, 425 Oser Ave., Hauppauge, NY 11788; 800/842-9721, 800/668-0770 (Canada).

Microsoft not only built TrueType into Windows 3.1, but it also offers several high-quality sets of TrueType fonts. Microsoft Corp., One Microsoft Way, Redmond, WA 98052; 800/426-9400.

Monotype created half of Microsoft's first TrueType font pack, so it has considerable TrueType experience, but it has a large library of Type 1 fonts as well. It has a well-respected library and the most original versions of Gill Sans, plus many other classic faces. A locked CD ROM is a terrific deal because it includes the unlocking of any eight fonts in the Monotype Library. Monotype, 150 S. Wacker Dr., Chicago, IL 60606; 800/MONOTYPE, 312/939-0378.

Precision Type sells fonts from all major foundries and many smaller ones, plus most of the utilities listed here, for substantially less than list price—averaging about 40 percent off. It's a veritable one-stop shop for fonts and utilities. The $6.95 *Reference Guide* is a terrific resource, showing samples of thousands of fonts. Precision Type, 47 Mall Dr., Commack, NY 11725; 800/248-3668, 516/864-0167.

Quadrat's David Vereschagin has created a family of highly readable sans serif type-faces called *Clear Prairie Dawn*, as well as several new display face families. Quadrat, 50 Alexander St., Toronto, Ontario, Canada M4Y 1B6; 416/960-0606.

Roadrunner's Liz Swoope couldn't find "keycap" fonts that she found clean and easy to read, so she created her own. These keycaps are modern and businesslike and make computer documentation easier to follow. The keyboard layout is mnemonic and logical. Roadrunner, P.O. Box 21635, Baton Rouge, LA 70894; 800/414-4268, 504/346-0019.

U-Design's Bill Tchakirides has designed a whole slew of fascinating little picture faces with an emphasis on Art Deco. They're charming and reasonably priced. U-Design, 270 Farmington Ave, Hartford, CT 06105; 800/945-3468, 203/278-3003 (fax).

URW invented one of the first systems for creating digital fonts and now has a large library of Type 1 type. URW offers *TypeWorks*, an unlocked CD ROM containing 600 Type 1 fonts. *TypeWorks* includes many faces from ITC, each available in five differ-ent "styles"—outline, inline, relief, drop shadow, and rounded—3000 fonts in all. URW, 4 Manchester St., Nashua, NH 03060; 603/882-7445.

14 Word Processing

By George Campbell

- Windows word processing basics
- The step-by-step guide to great documents
- Reviews of Ami Pro, Word, and WordPerfect
- Over 100 tips on how to use the top word processors

Word processors are more than glorified typewriters. In fact, the best are more like desktop publishing programs, only with chunks of graphics, spreadsheet, and communications software thrown in. Are you ready for a word processor that takes up 30MB of hard disk space?

If this sounds like overkill, remember that few people bother with a boring page of text unless you shove it under their nose. Want people to actually *read* your documents? Then it might not be a bad idea to start learning your way around the huge rack of tools word processors offer.

This chapter will get you acquainted with these tools, so you can produce better-looking pages with less hassle—and learn a few secrets that simply make day-to-day word crunching a whole lot easier. Finally, you'll get quick reviews of the top packages, along with some hot tips for using each one.

Anatomy of a Word Processor

Let's start with a very quick tour of the most popular Windows word processor, Microsoft's *Word for Windows.* All the basic components discussed below are shared by the other two Windows word processors worth considering—Lotus' Ami Pro and WordPerfect Corporation's *WordPerfect for Windows*—along with the latest version of *WordPerfect for DOS.* (*Microsoft Word for DOS* works differently and will be covered later in this chapter.)

You'll find title, menu, and scroll bars in almost any Windows program, and all three Windows word processors adopt the usual Windows conventions (pressing [Alt] gets you to the menu bar, for example). But Windows word processors have other key components in common:

HOT TIP

- **Button bars,** sometimes called *toolbars* or *icon bars*, provide fast access to common commands. They take up so little room, you should leave them on screen at all times—it's quicker to click on a command button with your mouse than to dig around in menus You get a choice of several button bars, some tailored to specific tasks (for example, the lower button bar in *Word for Windows* is for formatting only).

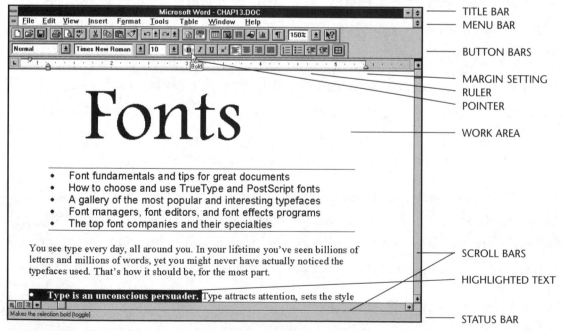

Figure 1: *Do all Windows word processors look alike? Not really, but they all have the same key parts shown in this Word for Windows editing screen.*

- **The ruler** does more than show you how wide your page is. If you click a little margin icon with your mouse and move it as you hold down the left mouse button, you can adjust the margin for a paragraph or for a whole document. Setting tabs is as easy as clicking on the ruler.

HOT TIP

- **The work area** gives you various views of your document, including a *draft mode* for fast typing and scrolling, and a slower *layout view* that more closely approximates the look of the final page. You also get a *full-page* view that usually renders text unreadable. Not surprisingly, you'll find these options under the View menu.

- **The insertion point** looks like a large capital I, which you can move around freely with the mouse. But as soon as you click the mouse button—whoop, there it is—the cursor jumps to wherever you've put the insertion point and you can type in text right there. The insertion point turns into the mighty pointer when you move it out of the work area and pass it over button bars, menus, scroll bars, rulers, and dialog boxes.

- **Status bars** indicate the current page number, whether or not you've pressed Caps Lock or Ins (to toggle into overwrite mode), and other relatively mundane stuff. The status bars in *Ami Pro* and *WordPerfect for Windows* also show the current typeface and font size.

From Outline to Printout

Here's a recipe for cooking up any document. It mostly applies to Windows word processors, but much of it will also be useful to people who use DOS programs. Some tips are for beginners only, but even old hands will probably find a few shortcuts that beat doing things the old-fashioned, hard way.

Thinking It Through

No one needs an outline to write a quick letter. However, I used an outline to write this chapter, and you should too for any document that runs more than a couple of pages—it's better than revising at the last minute because you forgot something crucial. Happily, every major word processor has an outline mode that makes creating outlines easy. Type in the main points, press Tab to indent to sublevels, and the program will number outline items automatically. When you add, delete, or move items, the outline renumbers itself.

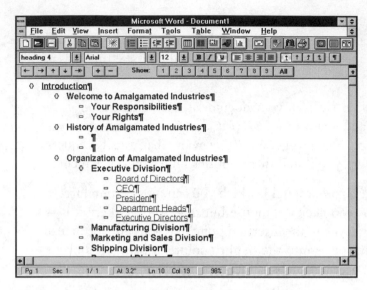

Figure 2: Collapsible outliners like this one in Word for Windows help you think through long documents so you don't forget what you're doing.

Best of all, you can start typing the actual text right into the outline and build your document block by block. You can hide that text by contracting the outline to view headings only, and expand it to see the text again (sort of like pulling a 3-by-5 card from a file). When you reorganize outline headings, the text beneath follows obediently along. Some programs, such as Microsoft's *Word for Windows*, can use an outline to create a table of contents automatically.

Templates and Document Design

We're not talking art here. When you open a new word processing document, some very basic "design" decisions have been made for you: standard margins, half-inch tab settings, a typeface for body text, and so on. The program stores these settings in a special kind of file called a *template*. Unless you specify otherwise, a simple *default* template automatically attaches itself to every new document, controlling its basic look.

HOT TIP

You might want to accept the default template, but chances are you shouldn't. Why? Because your word processor has templates for all occasions: letters, memos, invoices, fax cover sheets, business cards, you name it. With most Windows word processors, when you pick New from the File menu, you get a handy list of all alternate templates. You'll even find sophisticated templates with page layouts for newsletters and snazzy reports.

Figure 3: *Want to see what the whole enchilada looks like? Thumbnail views of a document, such as this one in WordPerfect 6.0 for DOS, can help you design a long document from top to bottom.*

Say you load a letter template. You'll see places for the address, the salutation, and so on blocked out with the correct margins. If it's an *automated* template, boxes will pop up prompting you for addresses and so on, so you can enter the data much like you would when filling out a form. You can simply save the finished letter as a document, or customize the template (include your own address, change margins or typefaces, add a letterhead), cutting out even more work the next time you use it. You can also create

HOT TIP

your own templates from scratch and save them under their own names, which will then show up on the File//New template list.

Typing It In

You're ready to type in your document's priceless prose. Nothing could be simpler, really. But a bit of advice may save some time.

- Just type in the text and worry about choosing fonts, changing margins, and doing other formatting stuff later. Compulsive formatting as you type interrupts thinking and slows writing.

HOT TIPS

- Indenting with spaces is never a good idea, and extra spaces are a downright nuisance when you begin formatting. If you need more than one space, use the Tab key instead.

- You already know this one: Keep your pinkie off the Enter key, except at the ends of paragraphs. Start a new paragraph and increase the right margin if you want shorter lines.

Getting Help

So you opened the manual, turned to the tutorial, and went through every function step by step until you learned the program backwards and forwards. Yeah, right. Well, at least you ran the on-line tutorial, didn't you? Hmm. Maybe you flipped through the Getting Started booklet? Well, here's a list of things to try when you get stuck:

1. If you're using a command or working in a dialog box, press F1 or click the help button for assistance with the task at hand.

2. Press F1 in the main editing screen to open the Help window. Click on Search and enter the topic you want help with. Try a few different wordings if you come up empty-handed at first.

3. Open the Help window. Click on Index or Table of Contents and browse through the list to find what you need.

4. Check your manual's index.

5. Call the company's customer support number.

6. Using a modem and communications software, log onto the company's bulletin board service and leave your question in the appropriate area. Allow at least 24 hours for a response (for more information on hooking up by modem, see Chapter 20: *Communications*).

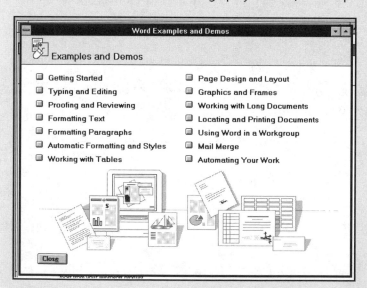

Attention users of *WordPerfect 5.1* (or earlier versions): The latest word processors offer special help for the millions of people hooked on pre-6.0 DOS versions of *WordPerfect*. Check the Help menu and look for a *WordPerfect* option. The DOS and Windows versions of *WordPerfect 6.0* go a step further and actually accept most 5.1 command keystrokes.

Figure 4: If you're stuck, your program's help system may offer a mini tutorial that will help you do exactly what you're trying to do. To learn your program better, try running a tutorial when you're not in trouble sometime.

- No matter what you write, you enter the same words again and again—your name, your company, whatever. All major DOS and Windows word processors have a *glossary* for stockpiling repeating words and phrases, which you can then plop into your document just by typing an abbreviation and pressing a key. Surprisingly few people bother with glossaries, but believe me, they can save a ton of keystrokes.

HOT TIPS

Power Word Crunching

It's editing time. A few tricks can really help, no matter which word processor you use.

Getting Around

You already know that pointing and clicking with your mouse is faster than using the cursor keys. But what if the place you want to go in your document is off the screen? You can scroll or page up or down to get there, but if your destination lies more than a couple of pages away, these methods are quicker:

- Use your program's search tools (try the Edit menu) to find any unique word you can remember that is at or near your destination.

HOT TIPS

- With Windows word processors, use Go To on the Edit menu to jump to specific pages. And don't forget Ctrl Home and Ctrl End, which take you to the beginning and end of a document, respectively.

- Use *bookmarks*, which let you mark one or more locations in your document and return to them in a flash. Click where you want the bookmark to go, pick the Bookmark command (its location varies depending on the program), and enter a bookmark name. To find the bookmark, click Go To and enter the bookmark name again. Insert one every time you leave off editing a document you plan to return to later.

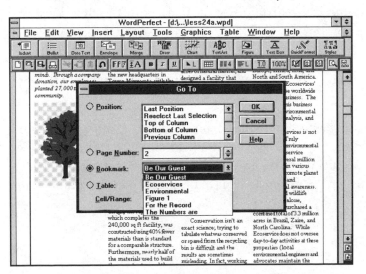

Figure 5: Bookmark features like those in WordPerfect 6.0 for Windows let you leap around large documents like a long jumper.

Quick Selection

Select it first. That's good advice for almost anything you do with any program. For example, rather than using Backspace, it's almost always faster to hold down the left mouse button, drag the mouse to highlight the offending text, and zap it with the Del key. These text selection shortcuts work in all Windows word processors:

HOT TIPS

- To select a word, double-click on it.

- To select a sentence, hold Ctrl and click the left mouse button.

- To select a paragraph, triple-click anywhere inside it.

- To select a block of text fast, click on the beginning of the block, then hold down the Shift key and click at the end of the block.

REMEMBER

Beyond this, each Windows word processor has its own mouse shortcuts for selecting lines, paragraphs, and so on. Search for "selecting text" in your Help index and learn those shortcuts! As you edit, turn on your program's display of paragraph markers. If you accidentally delete a paragraph marker, you may lose the formatting you applied to that paragraph.

Moving and Copying

Here's the fun part. It's called *drag and drop*. You start, as usual, by selecting text.

HOT TIPS

- To move the highlighted text, put your cursor on it a second time. Hold down the left mouse button and *drag* the little insertion marker to the new location. Let go of the mouse button and the selected text will *drop* in and replace the insertion point.

- To copy the selected text, do exactly the same thing, but hold down the Ctrl key as you do it.

You can pick Cut, Copy, and Paste commands from your program's Edit menu to accomplish the same things, but that's no fun at all. In any case, remember that using mouse or keyboard shortcuts is always faster and easier than picking commands from menus. You'll find many keyboard shortcuts listed right on your program's pull-down menus.

Figure 6: *Most Windows menus are also cheat sheets. On this Edit menu, note the quick keyboard shortcuts for common editing tasks.*

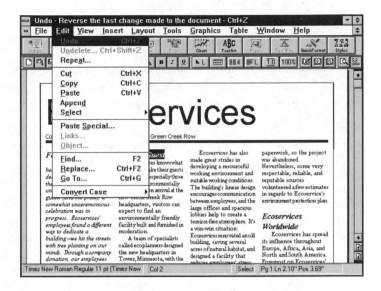

Fast Formatting

Even if you use a template, you may decide to change the whole document's margins or tabs. Maybe you'll indent a paragraph here and there, and certainly you'll want to boldface or italicize *something*. These touches fall into the broad category of formatting, which different word processors tend to handle in different ways. Before we get into some broad advice, here's a quick tour of some formatting terms and procedures:

- **Character attributes** refer to **boldfacing**, *italicizing*, and <u>underlining</u>, as well as the typeface and its size (this is 11-point Janson). With some word processors, you can also adjust such attributes as the spacing between letters (called *kerning*; see Chapter 13: *Fonts* for more on type fundamentals).

- **Justification** can be
left,
center,
or right,
whereas *justified text* simply means that each full line of text is of equal length—the spaces between the words adjust themselves so that the text is flush with both the left *and* right margins of the page. You're reading justified text.

- **Headers and footers** are words and/or numbers (such as your name and the page number) that you want to appear at the top or bottom of every page in a document.

Stop Repeating Yourself—Use Macros

Whenever you find yourself entering the same sequence of commands more than a couple of times, consider creating a *macro,* a string of commands (or commands plus text) that you can save and call up again with a couple of keystrokes. The easy way to create macros is to "record" them. Here's how:

1. Find your program's macro recording command and click on it.

2. Perform the actions you want to record.

3. Turn off recording.

Easy, huh? Depending on the program, you'll be prompted to give the macro a name either when you begin or when you end recording. Then assign a keystroke combination to call up the macro. Choose something easy to remember, like Ctrl A for a macro that inserts your address. If you want to get really fancy, most programs let you add new buttons to their toolbars that execute macros you've created.

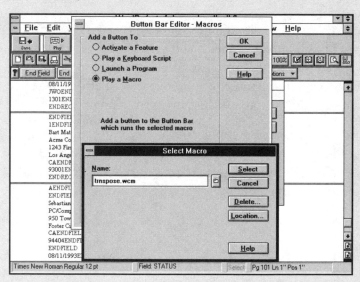

Figure 7: *WordPerfect for Windows lets you edit its Button Bar to include custom buttons that run macros you've created yourself.*

All word processors come with a set of prewritten macros. Learn what they do, and use them when it makes sense. You can also modify macros (how you do this varies from program to program), but doing so may involve editing a very long string of commands. You can even build very powerful macros without recording at all, assembling them command by command in a macro editing mode—but that's programming, and who wants to learn how to do *that?*

- **Columns** are just what you think they are. Many documents can be enhanced by using columns to shorten lines for better readability, such as newsletters. Each word processor handles columns differently. Most do a good job with them, though some programs make it more difficult than others to create columns in sections of documents.

- **Line spacing** can simply mean double or single spacing, but when you get down to finer increments, it's called *leading*. Most word processors can adjust leading to a fraction of a *point* (there are 72 points to an inch).

Of course, every program has lots more formatting goodies. In Windows word processors, you'll find the most common formatting commands have been turned into buttons that stay on screen all the time. It's always faster to use buttons than to pull down menus, but it's often faster still to select text with a mouse and then use a keyboard shortcut—Ctrl B for boldface, Ctrl I for italics, and Ctrl U for underlining are pretty much universal, for example.

HOT TIP

With Windows programs, you can see the results of your formatting efforts on screen all the time. If you plan to bind your final document, you can even set up different margins for alternating pages and check the results with a two-page preview.

Formatting With Styles

Styles are the biggest formatting time-savers ever invented. Each program handles them a bit differently, but here's a basic idea of how they work:

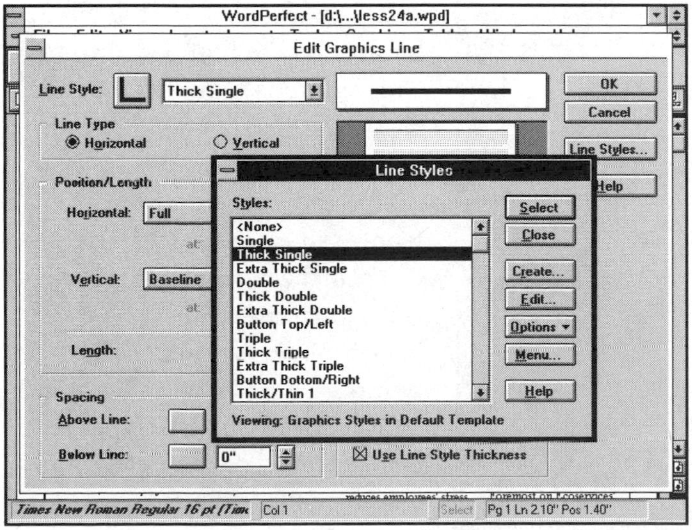

REMEMBER

Say you're working on a document and decide to use 18-point Arial bold headings. Why choose the font, set the size, and boldface the headings every time? Instead, you can save those settings under a style name, which you can pick from a list (or summon with a keyboard shortcut) and apply to text later. In that way, you can create a complete set of styles for your document.

Figure 8: *As shown here in WordPerfect 6.0 for Windows, you can even use styles to format graphical elements like lines.*

Styles can be *global* (available in all documents) or *local* (attached to a specific document). When you create a list of styles for a document, save that document as a template (called a *style sheet* by some programs) so all that formatting will be easily available when you create a similar document. After all, the templates included with your word processor are little more than lists of styles.

REMEMBER

There's little excuse for *not* using styles. Whenever you use the same formatting more than once, store the formatting as a style. With long documents you may save hours rather than minutes.

Getting Graphical

These days, a page with nothing but text on it may not get anyone's attention, even if your prose is Pulitzer material. And if it's not, why not *show* what you have trouble *describing*? All word processors let you import or create graphics. Once you learn how, you can say "See Figure 1" instead of fumbling with words.

Tables Are Graphics, Too

Guess what? Your word processor is also a primitive spreadsheet. Not only can you build a table in which rows and columns of information line up nicely, but you can also use simple functions to add up numbers and do other calculations. Useful stuff, since "graphics" in documents are most often tables. It sure beats the heck out of lining up numbers with the ⟨Tab⟩ key.

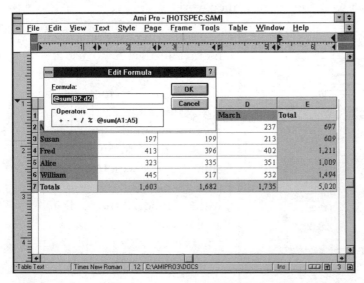

With Windows word processors, you just click on the table button, set the number of rows and columns you need, and adjust the size of the grid with your mouse. Then type in data to fill the cells, or import it from a spreadsheet. You can control the formatting of the cell contents—to make numbers line up on their decimal points, for example—and choose from several types of table borders, or even play with background shading.

Figure 9: *Is it a spreadsheet or a word processor? The numbers in this Ami Professional table add themselves up and look good at the same time.*

Charting the Numbers

Does your table of numbers show a trend over time, such as revenues from month to month? Then chances are it will work better as a bar chart or a line chart. If you've got a stack of percentages, then a pie chart is in order. How do you create these graphics with a *word processor*?

The specifics vary from program to program, but it's generally best to start with a table. Then you select (or copy) the table, click on the chart button, and watch the program draw a

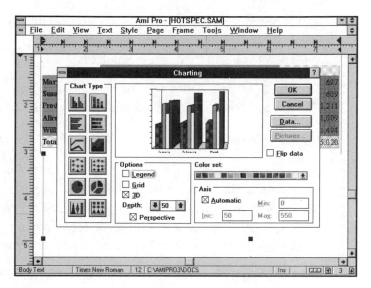

Figure 10: *It slices, it dices, and it does charts, too. It took about two seconds to get from the table in the previous figure to the bar chart preview here.*

bar chart automatically. You can choose from a few other chart types, add labels and legends, opt for a 3-D look, and make all kinds of picky modifications. Go ahead—go wild (see Chapter 16: *Presentations* for charting tips and basics*)*.

Getting the Picture

Now we are talking about art: scanned photos for newsletters, illustrations for technical documents, and clip art to liven things up (your chosen word processor has many cute little drawings on file somewhere, and you can buy more). Unless you have talent, or you're doing something simple, draw stuff from scratch only if you have to—even though all Windows word processors come with their own very capable drawing programs (see Chapter 17 for more on drawing software).

Here's a quick step-by-step procedure using a piece of clip art to create your own custom letterhead that might even save you money:

1. Click at the top of the page where you want the graphic to go.

2. Insert the clip art by picking its file name from a list in a dialog box (how you call up this box varies from program to program).

3. Notice the eight little black boxes, or *handles*, surrounding the graphic. Click and drag one of the corner handles to resize the graphic; to crop it, hold down the (Shift) key as you drag. To move it, simply drag and drop it, just like with text. Fish around some menus, and you'll quickly figure out how to flip, stretch, squash, or box the graphic, or edit it with drawing tools.

4. Type your (or your company's) name, address, and phone number next to the graphic in a nice font that everyone else in the world *isn't* using (see Chapter 13: *Fonts* for a gallery of great typefaces).

5. If people say it looks ugly, believe them and try again (or get professional help). If you get compliments from strangers, save it and use it as your letter template.

Using Text as Graphics

Sometimes text can be the most powerful graphic element of all. For instance, instead of using the piece of clip art in the preceding letterhead example, you might want to use the company name alone. If the font itself isn't interesting enough for a logo, you can always modify the text in a full-fledged drawing program and import it as a graphic when you're done (see Chapter 17: *Graphics Software).*

HOT TIP

Or here's an easier trick: Make the capital letters in the company name a couple of points larger than the other letters. Draw a box around the text (using a "frame" or "border" tool, depending on the program). Change the box's background to black and the text color to white, and you get:

AirFlow Design Studio

Voilà! Instant logo. Not a bad special effect if you don't overuse it.

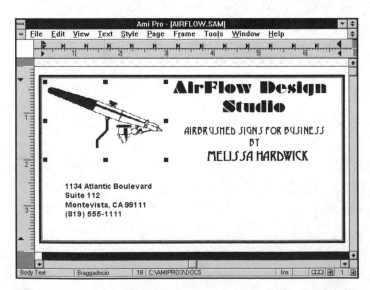

Figure 11: *You can drag images around just like text, and use the surrounding handles (those little black boxes) to resize them.*

Linking Up With Other Programs

Though word processors can imitate spreadsheets, drawing programs, and so on, they don't compare to the genuine articles. Fortunately, under Windows, you can easily incorporate data from other programs, and even create "live" links between your document and files created by other programs.

Say you want to take a table you've already created in your spreadsheet program and insert it into a word processing document. In Windows-speak, this table (it could be a picture, a chart, or anything else created by another Windows program) is called an *object*.

1. Switch to your spreadsheet program, highlight the table, and type Ctrl C to copy it.

2. Return to your word processing document, click on the place where you want to insert the object, and select Paste Special from the Edit menu.

3. The spreadsheet table you copied will appear in the document. If you want to change the object, double-click on it and you'll automatically switch back to the spreadsheet program, where the table will be loaded and ready to edit.

This works with most, but not all, Windows programs. If working with data from other programs is important, consider buying all your major applications from the same publisher. Software publishers spend extra time designing close links among their own programs, and you can get a huge discount when you buy them together in "suites" or boxed sets.

Finding Your Goofs

Of the three tools included with word processors to correct or improve your prose, only spell checkers are much use. Don't take electronic thesauruses or grammar checkers too seriously.

- **Spell checkers** should always, always be run before you print, even if you're the world's greatest typist and you won every spelling bee in elementary school. Other than that obvious advice, there's not much to say about spell checkers, except that the usual 300,000 words these things hold isn't as much as it sounds, and spell checkers routinely flag correctly spelled words. That's why you should add words you use often to your spell checker's custom dictionary, keep *Webster's* nearby at all times, and remember that a spell check is no substitute for a good proofreading job.

- **Thesauruses** (electronic or otherwise) can be dangerous weapons in the wrong hands. Simple words are best. But if you really can't find the right word, your word processor's thesaurus *might* serve up a reasonable alternative to the wrong one. Mine just offered *option, choice, selection, course,* and *discretion* in place of *alternative. Course? Discretion?* Oh well. Keep a copy of *Roget's Thesaurus* handy, too.

- **Grammar checkers** are bad jokes. In my experience, they're wrong more often than they're right, so anyone who accepts all the corrections suggested by a grammar checker is in big trouble. They also supply flaky "readability" ratings that you're best advised to ignore. Use a grammar checker only under these conditions: You already know good grammar from bad, and you have taken the time to customize it to catch only the things it's best at catching, such as overlong sentences.

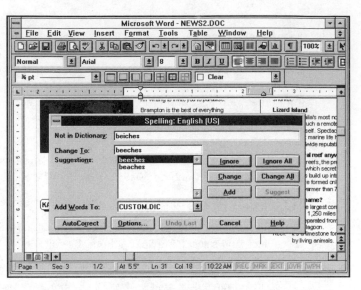

Figure 12: *How to run a spell check is obvious in any word processor. Like other programs, Word for Windows makes it easy for you to add words to a custom dictionary and change the spelling of a word throughout a document.*

Quick, Print It!

How fast a document prints is usually the function of the printer more than anything else. But these tips may help speed things along, especially with Windows programs:

- The fewer the fonts or graphics, the faster the printing.

- Use a print spooler, a special utility that takes over the print job from your word processor so you can stop waiting and go back to editing documents. All the current Windows programs

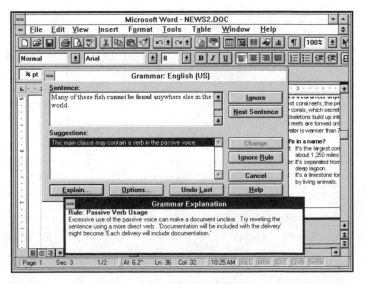

Figure 13: *Amazing—Word for Windows' grammar checker actually got it right! All grammar checkers (including this one) seem to get it wrong more often, which can be dangerous for the grammar-impaired.*

Form Letters and Addresses: Making the Merge

Everyone needs to send nearly identical letters to a list of people at least once in their life. If the only real differences between the letters are the names and addresses, and the addressee information is already stored in a database, don't bother typing it again and again into copies of the same document. Use *mail merge* instead, and automatically drop those names and addresses in every form letter copy.

When you create your document, instead of typing in a name and address, you insert *field names*, which are markers for the various parts of the database record (see Chapter 19: *Databases*). Normally, the program will help you with this part by offering a list of field names to pick from. You include punctuation and formatting, just as if the field names were normal text. Then, when you perform the merge, the word processor pours the appropriate information from the database into the document.

Conditional mail merge commands let you further customize your merged documents—such as the ability to automatically include one paragraph if a recipient is from California and another if he or she is from Utah. Most word processors let you do that and more. You'll generally find the mail merge command under the File menu.

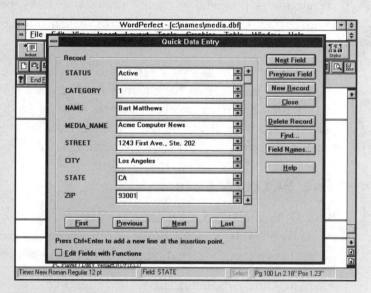

Figure 14: *Mail merge sounds scary, but once you set up the form letter, it's easy. As this WordPerfect for Windows screen shows, you don't even need a database program to set up your own database of names and addresses.*

include their own print spoolers, and Windows itself includes a print spooler called Print Manager that runs by default.

- If you need to print several documents but you don't want to hang around while it's happening, make sure your printer has plenty of paper and *batch print* your documents by selecting several files to print back to back.

Picking the Best Program

Not many people like learning new software if they don't have to, so most people pick one word processor and stick with it for years. There's an economic advantage here: The price of upgrading (that is, of buying the latest version of a program you already own) is about half that of buying software cold.

Being *able* to upgrade is one of the best reasons to buy a Windows word processor rather than an old-fashioned DOS one. The DOS versions of *WordPerfect* and *Word* are almost as powerful as their Windows versions, but they're dead ends. Neither WordPerfect Corporation nor Microsoft plans any major upgrades to their DOS word processors.

REMEMBER

Windows runs best on a 486 or Pentium system, so the only reason to buy a DOS word processor is because you have wimpy hardware: a low-powered 386 PC (25 MHz or less) or an old 286. In that case, choose *Word for DOS*—you could even live with its performance on a 286. The latest version of *WordPerfect for DOS* requires nearly as much horsepower as the Windows version.

HOT TIP

The Bottom Line

Both DOS and Windows word processors list for about $500, but nobody pays that much. You can buy any of the major programs for around $250, and if you own an earlier version, you'll be happy to learn that upgrades average approximately $130.

All these word processors, particularly the Windows ones, have more features than you'll probably ever use. The key to choosing the right program is to find one that's strong in the area you're most concerned with—which is why I've rated the programs for you, area by area, according to how powerful a program's features are and how easy they are to use. My opinion: *Word for Windows* is best overall, with *WordPerfect for Windows* close behind.

Word Processors Rated on a Four-Point Scale

	Ami Professional 3.01	Word 6.0 for DOS	Word 6.0 for Windows	WordPerfect 6.0 for DOS	WordPerfect 6.0 for Windows
Page display	4	1	4	3	3
Outlining	3	3	4	3	3
Glossary	2	3	4	0*	3
Editing	3	3	4	3	4
Formatting	4	3	4	4	4
Columns	3	2	3	4	4
Fonts	3	2	3	4	4
Styles	3	2	3	4	4
Layout	4	2	3	3	3
Long documents	3	3	4	4	4
Graphics tools	4	1	3	3	4
Tables	3	2	3	4	4
Charting	3	0*	4	0*	4
Drawing	3	0*	4	0*	4
Frames for text and graphics	4	1	3	2	2
Proofing	4	3	4	4	4
Printing	4	1	4	3	4
Learning tools	2	3	4	3	3
Macros	3	3	4	3	3
Customizing	3	2	4	4	4
Mail merge	3	2	4	4	4
Group work	2	2	3	4	4
Integration with other programs	3	2	4	3	3

* Feature not included

Figure 15: *These five word processors are rated not just according to the number of features, but also on how easy they are to use. The overall winner? Word for Windows, followed by WordPerfect for Windows.*

Ami Professional

The first time you run *Ami Professional*, you feel like you already know how to use it. The screen display and command icons seem natural, and as you learn more, you'll find you can make surprisingly quick work of complicated page layouts.

Ami Pro's logical menus and icon bars let you branch easily, so you don't get overwhelmed with features. As with the other Windows programs, you get horizontal and vertical rulers, plenty of keystroke shortcuts, and the ability to drag icon bars to wherever you're working for fast command access. But unlike *WordPerfect* and *Word for Windows*, *Ami Pro* lacks *shortcut* menus, brief command lists tailored to the task at hand that pop up when you click the right mouse button. In *Ami Pro*, you get one of three generic dialog boxes instead.

Ami Pro focuses on helping you create well-designed pages. Frames for text and graphics are easy to manipulate, and the program's editing screens are close to the final appearance of printouts. You can even control brightness and contrast for scanned photos. But in its current version, *Ami Pro* doesn't provide a "thumbnail" view of several pages, as *Word* and *Wordperfect* do.

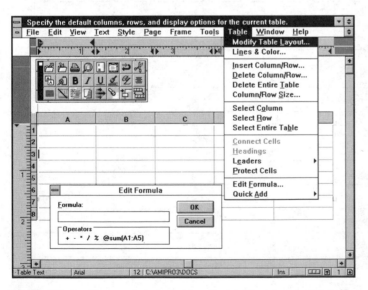

Network users won't find very powerful annotation or long-document tools, which are needed for work groups. Academic users will miss cross-referencing tools. You can't print files in batches, and managing files could be smoother. Too bad. The interface is so lovable, and the graphics and formatting so capable, this was my favorite word processor until the latest versions of *WordPerfect* and *Word for Windows* came out. With luck, the next release will bring *Ami Pro* up to par.

Figure 16: As with many tasks in Ami Pro, the intuitive interface makes creating and editing tables easy.

Ami Pro Tips

The key to *Ami Pro*'s interface is its extensive set of icon bars, which the program terms "SmartIcon sets." Each set is tailored to a specific task: editing, graphics, proofing, and so on. A list of SmartIcon sets appears when you click on the small blue icon at the right end of the status bar; you can switch sets by picking from the list or by cycling through the bars with the "Next icon set" icon, at the far right in every set. To find out what any SmartIcon does, click the icon with the right mouse button and read the description in the title bar.

HOT TIPS

Typing and Editing

- Unlike other programs, *Ami Pro* puts its search and replace commands in the same dialog box. To search, you select Edit//Find and Replace, enter the text to find *only* in the Find field, and then click the Find button. This feature is pretty clumsy, especially since there's no command to repeat searches.

- When working with small fonts, select View//Enlarged to make the text bigger.

- If you don't like drag and drop (some people find it's too easy to accidentally move text), turn it off: Select Tools//User Setup, and click the Disable Drag and Drop check box.

Formatting

- Want to modify the page layout? Click the right mouse button anywhere in the page margin and pop up the Modify Page Layout dialog box.

- To modify a style—such as the body text style for a whole document—place your cursor on text formatted in that style and click the right mouse button. A dialog box will appear, enabling you to change character attributes, indentation, and so on.

- To copy formatting from one block of text to another, click on the source block, then press Ctrl T for fast format. Your mouse pointer will change to a brush. Hold down the left mouse button and drag the brush across any other text in the document. Release the button to apply the formatting.

HOT TIPS

- The easiest way to specify a new style for a paragraph is to put the cursor in that paragraph, click on the leftmost button in the status bar, and pick a new style from the pop-up list.

- Want a style to adopt the same attributes as the paragraph where your cursor is? Select Style//Define Style and answer Yes. Then select Style//Save as a Style Sheet (*Ami Pro*'s name for a template) to make the change permanent.

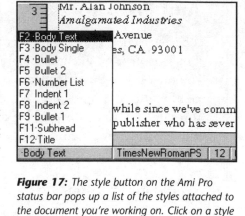

Figure 17: *The style button on the Ami Pro status bar pops up a list of the styles attached to the document you're working on. Click on a style to apply it to the current paragraph—or press a function key if you prefer.*

Graphics

- When you import a graphic, *Ami Pro* automatically wraps a frame around it. However, it's usually more efficient to insert a frame (select Frame//Create Frame), size it, select it by clicking on it, and *then* import the graphic into the frame using File//Import Picture.

- To enter text in a frame, double-click inside it. To change a frame's layout, right-click on the frame to bring up the Modify Frame Layout dialog box.

- To create a drawing, first insert, size, and select the frame, and then choose Tools//Drawing. To create the image, use the tools in the SmartIcon set that appears. If you add text to a drawing, you can rotate that text with the Draw//Rotate command or the rotate button on the drawing icon bar.

- When you create a data chart, first highlight the table containing the data, then select Tools//Charting. If the data isn't in your document already, select the same command—a window for the data will appear and you'll be prompted to enter the numbers on the fly.

Figure 18: *Ami Pro's frame layout dialog box is typical of the program's dialog boxes, which let you set all options for an object in one place.*

HOT TIPS

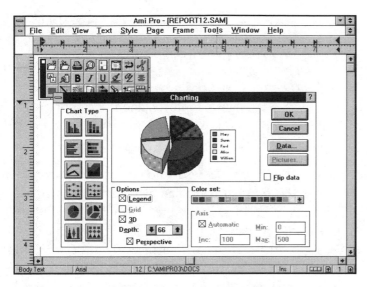

Figure 19: *Ami Pro offers a dozen chart types to choose from, and you can add 3-D effects to any of them.*

- Use the Tools//Drawing command to add your own text or modify parts of the chart. Each element of the chart is a separate drawing object.

Printing

- Printing envelopes is easy. Load the letter containing the address you want to use and select File//Print Envelope. *Ami Pro* will scan your letter looking for an address. When it finds it, the Print Envelope dialog box will appear. Specify the envelope size and whether you want to print a return address, and click OK to print the envelope.

Macros

- To create and edit automated style sheets, you need to access the SmartFields menu—and the only way to do that is by running a special macro. Select Tools//Macros//Playback, and a dialog box listing all available macros will appear. Scroll through the list until you reach the *smartfld.smm* macro and double-click on it. The SmartFields menu, containing all the tools, will add itself to the menu bar.

- To create a custom icon that runs a macro, begin by selecting Tools//SmartIcons. Select an icon from the Available Icon list, click Edit Icon, choose the macro you want to assign, and click OK. Pull down the list of SmartIcon sets and choose the one on which you want the new icon to appear. Drag the new icon from the list on the left and drop it into the SmartIcon set on the right. Click Save Set, and then click OK.

〜〜〜〜〜〜〜〜〜〜〜〜〜〜〜〜〜〜〜〜〜〜〜〜〜〜

Microsoft Word for Windows

Called *WinWord* for short, *Word for Windows* is the best word processor you can buy. It has a huge list of features that you can access with handy toolbars, and it has shortcut menus that pop up at the click of a right mouse button. As with *Ami Pro*, you can get up and running with this word processor in a hurry.

Very clever automation is what sets *WinWord* apart. One of the coolest features is AutoFormat, which can analyze a raw draft and turn it into an attractive document with a single command. *WinWord* even AutoFormats and AutoSizes tables, adding shading and borders and adjusting column widths and row heights. Slow typists will appreciate AutoText, *WinWord*'s glossary feature, which inserts words when you type their first few letters and press F3. And for the compulsive among us, there's AutoCorrect, which fixes common spelling and punctutation errors as you type.

Some of *WinWord*'s dialog boxes look like stacks of file folders, enabling you to control several sets of related options at once, without getting confused. Other boxes show previews of changes you're considering so you don't have to experiment in your document. If you make a mistake, it can be undone using the Undo command—in fact, you can Undo up to 100 previous edits.

While not quite as powerful as *WordPerfect for Windows*, *WinWord* is much easier to handle. Like the other Windows-based word processors, *WinWord* takes up a huge amount of disk space (26MB in its full installation), but that's just the penalty you pay for nearly unlimited control over the appearance of your documents.

Figure 20: *Word for Windows' multiple toolbars and clever automatic features help make it the best word processor ever.*

Word for Windows Tips

WinWord offers toolbar access to most features, and clicking the right mouse button on just about anything pops up a shortcut menu tailored to the task at hand. Best of all, though, are *WinWord*'s automatic features. For example, to format a document automatically, just select Format//AutoFormat when you're done typing in text. *WinWord* will analyze your document, looking for headings, addresses, and so on—and then make its own formatting suggestions. Just click the Style Gallery button to preview the suggested styles, and accept or reject them one by one.

Typing and Editing

- When selecting text for copying or moving, simply click once anywhere in the word, then drag. *WinWord* will automatically select the entire word. The same trick works for sentences. (See Figure 25 for more text selection shortcuts.)

- Use AutoText to enter text you type frequently. Type the text once, select it, and click the AutoText button on the toolbar. *WinWord* will automatically assign an abbreviated name to the text. From then on, when you want to retype this block of text, you can just type the abbreviation and then press F3. *WinWord* will fill in the rest automatically.

- To add commonly mistyped words with their corrections to the AutoCorrect feature, which fixes misspelled words as you type, just click the AutoCorrect button during a spell check.

Formatting

- To view the formatting for a block of text, drag the question mark icon over the text and then click to see a detailed description of all the formatting.

- In multicolumn documents, you can change the width of individual columns quickly by dragging the column markers on the ruler.

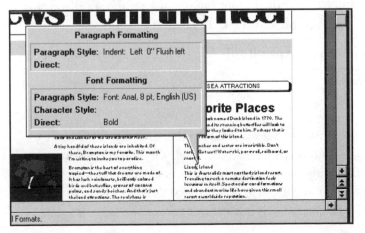

Figure 21: *For a detailed description of formatting for a block of text, just click the right mouse button and check this Word for Windows dialog box.*

HOT TIPS

- To apply formatting like boldfacing or italics to a word in your document, you don't need to select the entire word. Simply click anywhere in the word and use the formatting command. *WinWord* automatically chooses the whole word for formatting.

- To view multiple pages at once, click the thumbnail icon on the toolbar, then drag over the grid to select the number of pages you want to view. You can even edit in this mode.

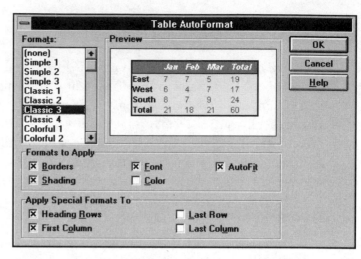

Figure 22: *Predesigned formatting options, like these for a Word for Windows table, are among the program's most powerful tools, unmatched by any other word processor.*

- To copy formats from one location to another, use the Format Painter feature. Select text containing the format you want, and then click the toolbar's paintbrush icon. Move the mouse pointer where you want to apply the same formatting and drag over the text to be reformatted. If you want to copy formatting to several locations, double-click the paintbrush icon instead.

- To insert a large dropped capital letter at the beginning of a paragraph, position the cursor at the beginning of the paragraph and select Format//Drop Cap.

- You're typing in boldface and want to turn it off? Ctrl Spacebar always takes you back to the normal style.

Graphics

- *WinWord* actually lets you create *callouts* (text labels that use lines to point out various elements in a figure or text). To create a callout, click the paintbrush icon on the main toolbar. Then, in the drawing toolbar that appears at the bottom of the screen, click the callout icon. Point at the place you want to describe, then drag the box to a blank location on the screen. Type your callout text in the box.

- You can draw lines, boxes, and other graphics anywhere on the page. To do this, click the paintbrush icon to display the drawing tools toolbar. Use those tools to create graphics objects, even right on top of text.

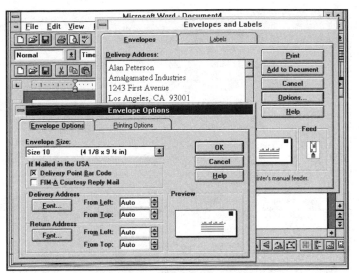

Automation and Customization

- When you select Tools// Macro//Record, the dialog box lets you assign your macro to a toolbar, a menu, or a keystroke. You can also decide whether to make the macro available in all documents, just the current document, or in all documents that have the same template.

- *WinWord* lets you add *fields*, which can include commands, text pulled from other files, the current date and time, and much more. To insert a field in your document, select Insert//Field and choose from Categories and Field Names.

Figure 23: Printing envelopes, once a chore in most programs, is simple in Word for Windows. This dialog box shows you exactly what you'll get.

- To customize your *WinWord* keyboard, select Tools//Customize and then click on the Keyboard file folder. In the dialog box, you'll find scores of ways to change key assignments for one document, for a single template, or globally. To restore your keyboard to its original settings, click the Reset All button, answer Yes in the confirmation box, and then click Close.

Microsoft Word for DOS

Allergic to Windows? Stuck with a low-powered PC? Then have a look at the DOS version of *Microsoft Word*. Though less powerful than the Windows word processors— or *WordPerfect 6.0 for DOS—Word for DOS* is still a capable program and runs much faster.

Word has the same problem all DOS word processors do, *WordPerfect 6.0* excepted: You can't really see what the final page will look like, except in a noneditable preview display. You may not care, though, if you work on manuscripts, legal papers, or other documents that don't require fonts or fancy formatting.

Word has a logical menu structure and a surprising number of features, and you can even use TrueType fonts with ease. Still, this is a Windows world, and it's unlikely that this program will be updated again. In the long run, you're better off buying a Windows word processor and hardware powerful enough to use it.

Figure 24: Word for DOS won't give you a clear view of the page when you're editing, but for users stuck with low-end PCs, it's the best choice.

Word for DOS Tips

HOT TIPS

Word may be an old-fashioned DOS word processor at heart, but it still borrows heavily from the Windows programs. The menu bar matches *Word for Windows'*, and you'll find many of the same features and conventions, including drag and drop, a Ribbon for formatting, and the usual keyboard shortcuts for boldface, italics, and so on.

Typing and Editing

• For frequently typed text, create glossary entries. Select the text you want to store, then choose Edit//Glossary. In the dialog box, type an easy-to-remember abbreviation in the Glossary Name field and then click Define. Later, when you need to retype that text, just type the abbreviation and press F3 .

Word Mouse Shortcuts		
To Select	**Position Mouse Pointer**	**Mouse Action**
Word	In word	Double-click
Sentence	In sentence	Ctrl -click
Line	In left margin next to line	Click
Paragraph	In left margin next to paragraph	Double-click
Entire Document	In left margin	Ctrl -click

Figure 25: These shortcuts for selecting text work both in Word for DOS and Word for Windows.

Formatting

- Instead of templates, *Word* offers style sheets, which are simply lists of styles without the pop-up data entry windows and other automated features of, say, *Ami Pro* style sheets. To attach an existing style sheet to your current document, select Format//Attach Style Sheet, and then pick a style sheet from a list.

- To apply a paragraph style fast, click anywhere in the paragraph and pick the style from the style list.

- To create a new style, format a block of text exactly as you want the new style to look. Select the text, then pick Format//Record Style from the main menu. In the dialog box, type a two-letter code for the style; select whether the new style should apply to characters, paragraphs, or sections of the document; then add a description. Pull down the list of style names and click on one of the names in the list. Finish up by clicking OK.

- If you want to create a new style sheet, create a set of named styles (see last tip) first, then select Format//Define Styles. Select the styles you want to save from the list, click on File//Save As, and choose Style Sheet. Give the style sheet a new name in the dialog box and then click OK.

- Need to replace formatting throughout a document? Leave the text fields in the Replace dialog box blank; click the Replace Formatting Only button; and then click the button to search for character, paragraph, or style formatting. Check the appropriate boxes to specify the formatting to find, then click the Replace With button and check off the substitute formatting. Click OK to start.

- To view your document as it will appear on the printed page, select File//Print Preview or press Ctrl F9. (You can't edit in this mode.)

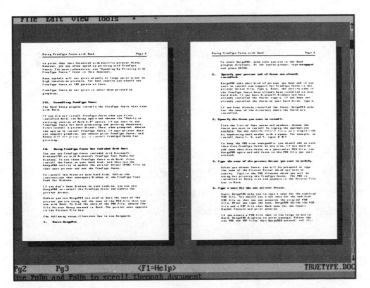

Figure 26: *You can't edit while in Word for DOS's print preview mode, and the display is very slow, but at least you get a decent look before printing.*

HOT TIPS

Graphics

- The easiest way to insert a table in a document is to select a point in text and click the pound sign (#) on the Ribbon. To add a row to the end of a table, move the cursor to the last cell, and then press [Tab]. To adjust column width, use your mouse to drag the T-shaped markers on the ruler.

- To insert a graphic, select Insert//Picture and pick the graphics file from the list in the dialog box. You can't size the graphic with the mouse, so you'll need to select options for alignment, size of image, and size of the space above and below the image from the dialog box.

- Once inserted in a document, a graphic is represented as an empty box with a file name inside. To have a look at graphics before you insert them, click Preview while in the Picture dialog box.

- To add borders to your image, click inside the box or on the image's file name. Then select Format//Borders and choose a border style, line type, and background shading.

Printing

- Need to print just part of a document? Select File//Print. In the Page Range box, choose the Selection option, enter the first and last pages you want to print, and click OK.

- To print in the background while you continue to work, select File//Print, then click the Queue button. Turn on the Use Print Queue check box and then click OK.

Macros

- You can create most macros by selecting Tools//Record Macro. In the dialog box, give the macro a name and then tab to the Macro Keys box and enter the shortcut key you want to use. Select OK. You'll see the letters MR (for macro record) on the status bar at the bottom of the screen. Type the text or execute the commands you want to record (you can't use mouse actions), and select Tools//Stop Recorder to finish.

- You can run macros the same way you retrieve glossary entries. Just type the name of the macro in your document and press [F3].

- Create a macro named AUTOEXEC, and it will run automatically when you start *Word 6.0*—great for setting things up just the way you like them.

WordPerfect for Windows

WordPerfect for Windows is the most powerful word processor ever written. It has more features than any one person could possibly use—30MB worth in its full installation. Sheer size makes it strong in every area, from editing, to formatting, to graphics, to proofing. But unless you spend a little time customizing *WordPerfect*'s interface to simplify it, you may find yourself swamped by all the options presented every time you select a command.

Fortunately, *WordPerfect for Windows* is also the most customizable program. You can hide or move any of the button bars, and you can change the buttons on all of them except the Power Bar, which contains the commands that are used most often. Throughout the program, you're coached through complex operations, such as mail merges and envelope printing, so you can learn as you work.

The charting and drawing modules are the best—you can even wrap text around the contour of a graphic. When you're working with graphics, a palette of image tools appears, letting you manipulate the image without leaving your editing screen. You can also scan images directly into graphics frames in a document. And with dozens of formulas to choose from, *WordPerfect for Windows*' tables are closer to real spreadsheets than are those of any other word processor.

I rate *WordPerfect for Windows* slightly behind *WinWord* because it's harder to learn, and because you should spend time setting it up the way you like it. But if you want the word processor with the maximum number of features and the most customizable interface—plus excellent customer support—choose *WordPerfect for Windows*.

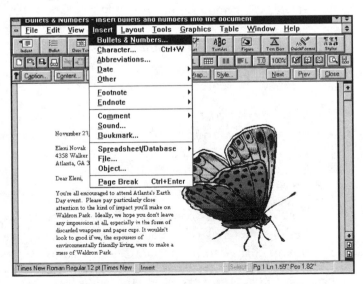

Figure 27: *Is this word processing or rocket science? The most powerful word processor of all, WordPerfect for Windows is also the most complex.*

WordPerfect for Windows Tips

HOT TIPS

As with *WinWord*, pressing the right mouse button prompts a shortcut menu relating to the object you've selected, and button bars give you options galore. Don't be intimidated by all the options in this program. Study your manual and look for ways to make the program work *your* way. If you can conceive of a way to change the program, you can probably do it. (The Windows and DOS versions of *WordPerfect* work almost identically, so see the next section for more tips.)

Typing and Editing

- For somewhat faster text entry and scrolling, select View//Draft Mode. Your text will still appear in the correct fonts, but you won't see headers, footers, or footnotes.

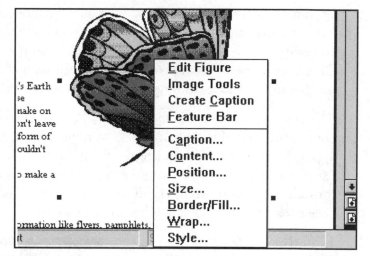

- To select text quickly with the mouse, move the pointer into the left margin. Click once to select a sentence or double-click to select an entire paragraph. If you click and drag in the margin, you'll select text

Figure 28: *Menus with all the appropriate options appear when you right-click on any object.*

sentence by sentence. Double-click and drag to select whole paragraphs at a time.

- Use *WordPerfect 6.0's* QuickMark feature to mark a position you'll need to return to frequently. To mark the current cursor location as a QuickMark, press Ctrl Q. Then, anytime you need to move to that location, just press Ctrl F.

Formatting

- To avoid having formatting changes affect an entire document, make sure you highlight a block of text *before* formatting. Otherwise, you may see the entire document change to boldfaced text, for example.

- Use QuickFormat to apply the same formatting to several blocks of text in your document. Select a block of text that you've already formatted, then click the QuickFormat button on the Button Bar. Move the paint roller mouse pointer to the

HOT TIPS

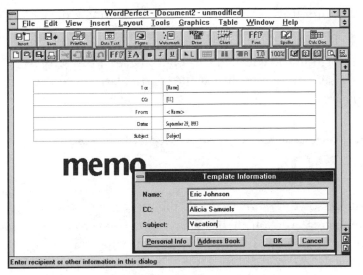

Figure 29: *WordPerfect's prefab templates help you create complex documents in a hurry. Dozens are supplied with the program.*

text you want to reformat and click and drag it over the text. When you're done, click the Quick-Format button again.

- If styles don't seem to be working correctly, formatting too little or too much text, turn on the Auto Code Placement option in the File//Setup//Environment dialog box.

- To create your own templates, select Options in the File//Template dialog box, and then use the blank document and the Template Feature Bar at the top of the screen to customize your template as much as you want.

Graphics

- To create contoured text that follows a curve in the drawing program, first enter the text into the drawing. Then, use the drawing program's curve tool to draw the contour you want. Hold down as you click on both the curve and the text, and then use the Arrange//Effects//Contour Text command.

Printing

- For best results, select the Windows Printer Driver in the File//Select Printer dialog box.

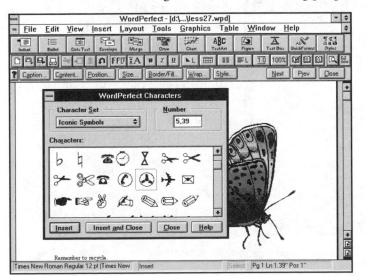

Figure 30: *WordPerfect offers a wide range of special, foreign, and symbolic characters, all of which print in very high quality—a unique feature.*

HOT TIPS

- Use the native *WordPerfect 6.0* printer drivers only when you are printing a document created with the DOS version of the program.

- Be sure to enable background printing if you need to continue to work while printing is in progress. Otherwise, you may wait a while, particularly if you're printing a long, complex document.

WordPerfect for DOS

WordPerfect 6.0 for DOS is the successor to *WordPerfect 5.1*, the most popular word processor ever written. Like the current version of *Word for DOS*, *WordPerfect 5.1* worked fine with low-powered hardware, but it only showed you what the page looked like in a noneditable preview. *WordPerfect 6.0* for DOS is a complete departure from 5.1—in fact, it looks and acts much like *WordPerfect for Windows*, with an editing mode that displays fonts and graphics.

Other Windows-like features include scalable fonts, adjustable screen magnification, and flexible button bars that provide access to hundreds of commands. A much improved mail merge and macro language, plus an outliner and grammar checker, are further enhancements.

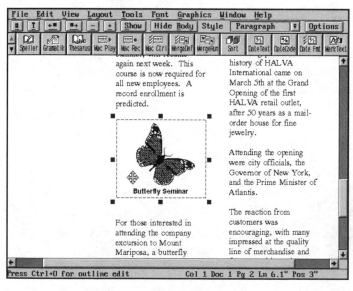

Charting and drawing excepted, *WordPerfect for DOS* has all the hot features of *WordPerfect for Windows*, including the huge set of formatting tools. You also get bookmarks for quick access to different parts of a document, outstanding envelope and label printing (with barcodes), E-mail and faxing from within any document, and workgroup tools like annotations and redlining. And users of previous *WordPerfect* versions can employ most of their old keystrokes.

Figure 31: *WordPerfect 6.0 for DOS is a dead ringer for the Windows version—you can even size graphics on the screen. It also has the same hardware requirements, so why not buy the Windows version?*

So what's wrong with this picture? For one thing, just like *WordPerfect for Windows*, all of the program's power is right in your face unless you customize the interface. More significantly, unless you have a fast 486 PC (or you switch to the faster "text mode"), this baby is just as slow as the Windows version. So buy the Windows version instead. You'll get more features, plus all the advantages of Windows.

WordPerfect for DOS Tips

Like the Windows version, WordPerfect for DOS has so many options, it's worth spending time customizing the thing, a process that requires digging around in the manual.

HOT TIPS

Here's one place to start. The program has several button bars, each with two rows of buttons. For some reason the button that calls up a menu *of other* bars is buried in the second row. To move this button to the first position on the first row, choose View//Button Bar Setup//Edit, and use the Move command to relocate the button. (Note: The DOS and Windows versions of WordPerfect 6.0 work almost identically, so for more tips, check out the previous section.)

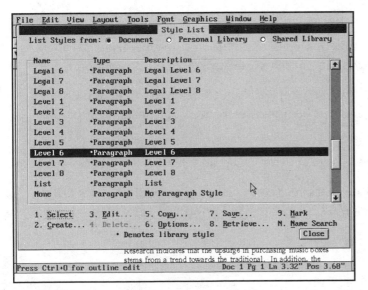

Figure 32: *Like the Windows version, the DOS version of WordPerfect gives you a mind-boggling array of style options.*

Typing and Editing

- When you're just typing, select View//Text Mode to switch to the much faster text display.

- If you accidentally delete a block of text, you can restore it by pressing Esc R. To restore the previous deletion, press Esc P instead.

- If you make a formatting error or give some other command you regret, press Ctrl Z to undo your action.

Formatting

- Styles can include text. For example, you could create a style for a bulleted list that contained not only a bullet and an indent, but a heading as well.

- To apply a style to text, highlight the text and then press $\boxed{\text{Alt}}\boxed{\text{F8}}$ or click the styles icon on the button bar. Pick the style you want from the list that appears.

- Want to establish a new default font for new documents? Begin by selecting Layout//Document. In the resulting dialog box, select Initial Font. Choose the font you want to use for most text in your documents, and then turn on the All New Documents option before clicking OK.

- To return a block of text to basic formatting, highlight the text, click the Styles button on the button bar, and choose None.

- When creating styles, it's always fastest to format a block of text the way you want it, and then select the Create from Current option in the Create Style dialog box.

Graphics

- To edit an image, double-click on it to pop up the Edit Graphics Box dialog box.

- To wrap text around the contours of a graphic, right-click on the image and then choose the Contour Text Flow option in the Text Flows Around Box option list.

- To draw lines in text, select Graphics//Graphics Line//Create to call up the Create Graphics Line dialog box. Lines can be moved or resized by clicking on the line and using sizing handles.

- To add a border to an entire page, select Layout//Page and then select Page Borders.

- For a unique look, try the Watermark feature to place a lightened graphics file in the background. Select Layout//Header/Footer//Watermark, and then choose Watermark A or Watermark B.

Printing

- Fonts built into your printer print fastest. Check the Type area in the Font dialog box to see which fonts are built in.

- For fast draft printing, turn off graphics printing. Select File//Print and set the Graphics Quality option to Do Not Print in the Print//Fax dialog box.

- To print in the background, press $\boxed{\text{F5}}$ to start the File Manager. Mark the files you want to print with an asterisk (*), and then click the Print button.

HOT TIPS

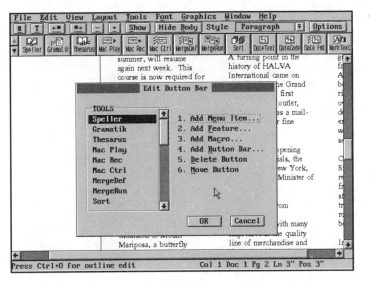

Figure 33: *WordPerfect's button bars can be rearranged to suit your working style. It only takes seconds in this dialog box.*

- Before printing any complex document, use the File//Print Preview command and click on the Thumbnail icon on the button bar to see several pages at once and check for layout problems.

- To create a mail merge data file, use a table. Select Tools//Merge//Define//Data [Table] to call up the Merge Codes dialog box. There, select Create a Table with Field Names. The rest is automatic.

Macros

- To record a macro press Ctrl F10. Type a file name for the macro, assign it to a keystroke, and then click OK. Type your text and give any commands you want to record. When you're done, press Ctrl F10 again.

- To assign a macro to a button bar icon, select View//Button Bar Setup//Edit. In the dialog box, select Add Macro and then double-click on the macro's file name.

Product Directory

Ami Professional 3.01
Lotus Development Corp.
55 Cambridge Pkwy.
Cambridge, MA 02142
800/872-3287
617/577-8500

Microsoft Word for DOS
Microsoft Word
for Windows
Microsoft Corp.
One Microsoft Way
Redmond, WA 98052
800/426-9400
206/882-8080

WordPerfect 6.0 for DOS
WordPerfect 6.0
for Windows
Word Perfect Corp.
1555 N. Technology Way
Orem, UT 84057
800/526-5198
801/225-5000

15

~~~~~~~~~~~~~~~~~~~~~~~~~~~~~~~~~~~~~

Spreadsheets

By Richard Scoville

- Spreadsheet basics, from cells to graphs
- How to build a spreadsheet template
- How to create a database spreadsheet
- Avoiding common spreadsheet mistakes
- Advice on the top six spreadsheet programs

Crunch, crunch. What's that noise? It's the sound of 27 bazillion spreadsheets out there crunching numbers, doing everything from abscissas to zymosis. A hoard of PC laborers whack away at the electronic rock pile using spreadsheet programs from Lotus, Microsoft, and Borland. The worksheets these hard workers create boil down to just two basic types:

- **Templates** are what most people think of as spreadsheets—kind of custom calculators that you plug numbers into. You could use a template to automate an expense voucher or a sales report. Or you might use a template for a budget, where you try out alternative sets of data to gauge their effect on the bottom line.

- **Lists** are for record keeping—accounts receivable, vehicle maintenance records, sales receipts, whatever. A list is actually a database: You can use it for reference and just print it out, but more likely you'll want to use the program's database features to select items from the list, calculate group totals and other statistics, and generate graphs (see Chapter 19 for more on database basics).

The trick to using spreadsheet software isn't getting started—the basics are simple enough so that most people can be up and running (well, jogging) in an hour or two. The problem is that most people who use spreadsheet programs exploit only a tiny fraction of the power these tools have to offer—or worse, use them to produce inaccurate results.

This chapter can help. No matter what spreadsheet program you use (or plan to use), I'll show you how to create useful, error-free templates, and set up lists right the first time so you can rearrange data the way you want it. I'll also compare the quality and capabilities of today's popular spreadsheet programs—*1-2-3*, *Excel*, and *Quattro Pro*—and help you decide which one is best for solving your problems. Along the way, you'll get some timesaving tips for the program of your choice.

Spreadsheets for Beginners

Using a spreadsheet is a bit like working in a machine shop. The software provides you with components—cells, functions, and so on—along with tools in the form of commands. Your job is to use the tools to assemble the components into a custom calculation machine—a template or list *worksheet* (the name for a document created by a spreadsheet program).

Today's spreadsheet programs are remarkably similar—in the way they look, in the way they operate, and in the range of their analytical gizmos. In every program, the worksheets have multiple *pages*, each of which has a little exposed tab so you can flip to it easily with a mouse. Your basic worksheet page has these essential parts, which you'll recognize even if you've never seen one before:

- **Rows,** identified with numbers down the left edge of the worksheet

- **Columns,** identified with letters across the top edge

- **Cells,** the boxes created by the intersection of rows and columns, which contain the worksheet's data and formulas

WORKSHEET   FORMULA BAR   MENU   TOOLBARS

ROW AND
COLUMN
HEADINGS

FRAME

CELL POINTER

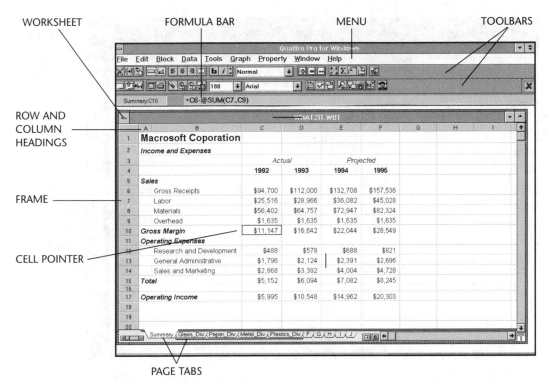

PAGE TABS

Figure 1: *Like all spreadsheet programs, Quattro Pro for Windows shows the address and contents of the active cell in its formula bar. In this case, cell A10 contains a formula that takes the Gross Receipts value from cell C6 and subtracts the sum of the direct costs in cells C7, C8, and C9.*

The *cell pointer* is the spreadsheet's cursor; it highlights the worksheet's *active cell* (the one into which you type numbers or text). The *formula bar* displays the contents of the active cell along with its *address*, which is a combination of the cell's column letter and row number (B8, for example).

The Toolbox

A worksheet's rows and columns are just a grid, the pegboard into which you plug your calculation machine's components—your data and the formulas you create that manipulate it. You need tools to help you fashion a worksheet, and in every spreadsheet program, you'll find the following:

- **Functions and operators** to make formulas work—to sum or average columns of numbers, to find the rate of return on an investment, and a lot more

- **Formatting tools** for turning worksheets into attractive reports

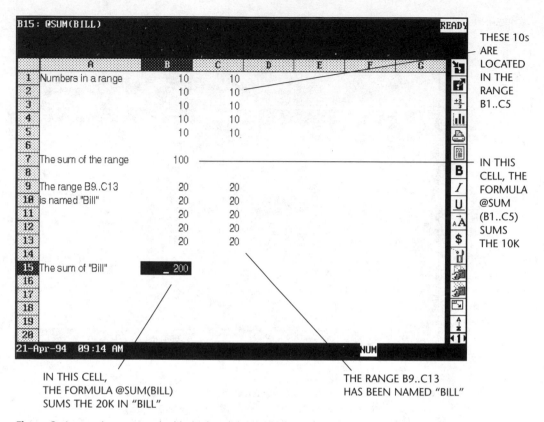

Figure 2: *A range is a rectangular block of worksheet cells that you might want to calculate with or perform some action on. It's a good idea to give ranges meaningful names to make your formulas easier to interpret.*

- **Graphs** that turn data into bar charts, line charts, pie charts, and so on

- **Macros** for automating repetitive operations

- **Database** features for managing, summarizing, and viewing lists

- **Analytical tools** for more specialized applications

You can access almost all of the above by pulling down menus (the names lie in a neat little row in the *menu bar* at the top of the screen). But most of the commands you need are at the ready, represented by little icon buttons on the *toolbar* right beneath the menu bar.

In most programs, you can even customize the toolbar so your favorite commands are always available at a single mouse click. If you ever forget what an icon does, just drag the cursor over it, and an explanatory message will appear on the *status line*, a handy little readout at the bottom of the screen.

Ranges and Range Names

A *range* is a rectangular block of cells that contains something you want to work on: perhaps a set of numbers that you want to sum or a group of labels that you want to print in italics. A range may be as small as a single cell or as large as the entire worksheet. A *range address* is composed of the addresses of two of its opposing corner cells, for example B1..C5 (in *Excel*, ranges use colons instead, as in B1:C5). You often use these addresses in formulas.

In general, working with ranges is a two-step process:

1. **Select the range** first, either by dragging with the mouse or holding down the Shift key while you use the arrow keys (in 1-2-3 for DOS, you hold down the F4 key).

2. **Do something**—click a button on the toolbar, drag the range to a new location, click on the right mouse button to choose a menu option, whatever.

Cell and range addresses are hard to remember—worse, they change when you move things around in the worksheet (see "Copying and Moving" later in this chapter). So it's best to *name* ranges that you will use often in commands and formulas. Thereafter, you can substitute the name for the cell addresses in formulas, as shown in Figure 2. The more ambitious and complex your worksheets, the more important it is to make systematic use of range names to keep things orderly and sensible.

HOT TIP

Cell Values: Formulas vs. Data

The cells of a spreadsheet contain either *data*—simple numbers or text—or *formulas*, which perform calculations on the data cells. The *value* of a cell is simply "how much it's worth." If a cell contains the number 2, then that's its value; if a cell contains a formula, then the cell value depends on the value of the cells to which it refers.

Formulas and What They're Made Of

How do you create a formula? Whatever spreadsheet program you use, you can construct simple formulas almost automatically. You just choose the cell where you want to place the formula, pick a function from a menu or toolbar, and select the cells you want included in the calculation. For example, the formula =SUM(D3:D43), which adds together the values in cells D3 through D43, takes exactly three mouse clicks in Microsoft's *Excel*.

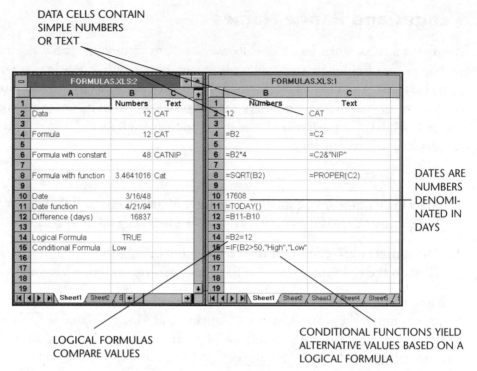

DATA CELLS CONTAIN SIMPLE NUMBERS OR TEXT

DATES ARE NUMBERS DENOMINATED IN DAYS

LOGICAL FORMULAS COMPARE VALUES

CONDITIONAL FUNCTIONS YIELD ALTERNATIVE VALUES BASED ON A LOGICAL FORMULA

Figure 3: *Two views of the same Excel worksheet: The left window shows the values of the cells; the right window reveals the underlying formulas and data. The formula in cell B8 uses a numeric function to calculate the square root of the value in B2; C8 uses a string function to capitalize the initial character of the label in C2.*

Formulas have four possible components:

- **Cell or range addresses** for the cells containing the numbers you want to crunch (D3:D43 in the preceding example)

- **Constants,** numbers or text enclosed in quotes that don't change in the course of a calculation

- **Functions,** which are like prepackaged formulas (SUM in the preceding example)

- **Operators,** such as +, −, >, <, and so on, which bind the cell addresses, functions, and constants together into a formula

Functions make formulas shorter and easier to write, and spreadsheet programs come with hundreds of them. Take the simplest function, SUM. Instead of entering =SUM(D3:D43), you'd have to use the + operator and 41 cell addresses (D3+D4+D5 and so on, all the way to D43). Functions are designed to relieve you of such drudgery.

A worksheet may contain many formulas, but all you see on screen normally are formula *results*—after all, those results are the reason for creating worksheets to begin with. In all spreadsheets, you can execute a command to view all formulas (which looks like a mess). If you want to view a formula in a single cell, place your cell pointer on that cell and the formula will appear in the formula bar at the top of the screen.

REMEMBER

Data and Formula Types

Whether data or formulas, the stuff you enter into cells comes in three basic varieties: *numeric*, *string* (or text), and *logical*—plus *dates*, which are actually a special kind of number.

- **Numeric** data is simply the numbers you enter in lists or calculations. Numeric formulas use numeric operators (+, –, *, and / for addition, subtraction, multiplication, and division, respectively) and numeric functions, such as SUM or AVERAGE, which compute numeric values.

- **String** data is text, often used to label a row or column. There's only one operator for strings—the & sign, which pastes two strings together into a larger one—but there are several string functions. How do you "calculate" text? Consider a formula containing the UPPER function, which turns text uppercase. If Cell C2 contains the label "cat," the formula UPPER(C2&"nip") has the value "CATNIP."

- **Logical** formulas can be created in any program, but only *Excel* has a logical data type, which simply includes the logical values TRUE and FALSE (in *Quattro* and *1-2-3*, logical formulas have numeric values: 1 means true, 0 means false). These values usually exist only as answers to true-or-false comparisons in logical formulas, all of which employ *logical operators* (=, >, <, and so on) as well as *Boolean operators* (AND, OR, and NOT). For example, the formula A1=25 is true when a number in cell A1 is equal to 25; the formula A1>=20#AND#A1<30 is true when the number is between 21 and 29. Logical formulas go well beyond simple comparisons and commonly work hand in hand with the conditional function IF. For example, the formula =IF(A1>400,A1-400,0) subtracts 400 from the value in A1 only when that value exceeds 400.

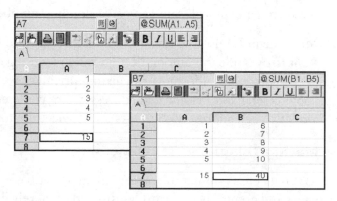

Figure 4: *When you copy formulas, their cell referents adjust to their new location. Cell A7 contains a simple SUM function that adds the numbers in the range A1..A5. Copy the formula to B7, and it sums B1..B5.*

- **Dates** have a special format, but they're really ordinary numbers, which means you can use them in calculations. A spreadsheet may *display* 3/16/48 but it *thinks* of that date (my birthday) as the 17,608th day of the century. To find out my age in days, if you're interested, you'd use the formula =TODAY()-17608 to calculate the number of days elapsed from 3/16/48 to today. The most recent Windows spreadsheets include a greatly expanded set of functions for performing such date calculations.

Copying and Moving

When you get right down to it, the most powerful tool that a spreadsheet program provides is the ability to quickly copy or move cell values and formulas. In the Windows spreadsheets, you can use the ever-popular *drag and drop* procedure to accomplish this.

Drag and drop works like this: To move cell contents, you hold down the left mouse button and highlight the cells in question by dragging the cell pointer across them. Then you bring the pointer back to the edge of the area you just highlighted, until it turns into a little arrow. Hold down the left button again, *drag* the arrow to where you want to move the cell contents, and release the button to *drop* the contents there. If you hold down the Ctrl key at the same time, you copy the cell contents instead of moving them.

HOT TIP

Copying: Shifty Formulas

When you copy data values, you simply duplicate numbers or labels from one cell to another. But when you copy a formula, rather than getting an exact duplicate, you get a *similar* formula that's appropriate to its new location. For example, as shown in Figure 4, if you copy a formula in cell A7 that sums the numbers in column A cell B7, the formula copy will sum the corresponding numbers in column B.

REMEMBER

Most formulas use such *relative* cell addresses. However, in certain situations you'll want to override this automatic adjustment by using an *absolute* cell address. For example, if you copied a formula calculating pricing for several products, you'd want every copy to refer to the same cell address where you'd entered the markup rate. To make a relative cell address absolute, you just select the formula and press F4.

HOT TIP

Moving Things Can Be Dangerous!

Moving cells is similar to copying them, but it has a very different effect on the worksheet and especially on formulas. Instead of merely duplicating a cell entry, it relocates a cell and eliminates the destination cell in the process. The effect on formulas can be devastating. Here's what can go wrong:

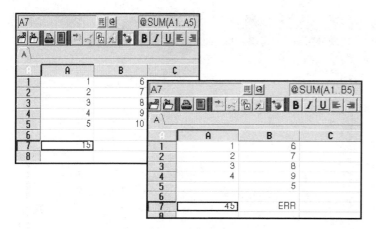

Figure 5: When you move cells that a formula refers to, the formula changes to track its movement. In this Quattro spreadsheet, cell A5 has been moved to B5. The formula in A7 that referred to it has changed: Instead of @SUM(A1..A5), it now reads @SUM(A1..B5), and the formula in B7 that referred to B5 now displays an error message.

- When you move a cell that lies at the corner of a range, you change the size of the range, so a formula that refers to that range can end up referring to the wrong set of values.

DANGER

- When you move a cell onto one that a formula refers to, the formula ends up displaying an error message because you've destroyed one of the data cells it needs for its calculations.

These hazards mean that it's usually better to copy cells containing data rather than move them, and then go back and carefully delete the original cells.

HOT TIP

Cell Formatting

Think of the cell format as the packaging of the cell value. You can manipulate the format of a cell separately from its contents. For instance, every spreadsheet enables you to copy formatting from one cell or range to another without disturbing the contents of the destination cell or range. And to save time, all the major spreadsheet programs provide convenient push-button access to common formatting features.

- **Alignment.** You can left-, center-, or right-justify a label within its cell, and in the Windows spreadsheets you can align numeric data and formulas as well. In addition, the Windows programs let you wrap text within a cell. Most spreadsheets also let you center a label within a range of cells—perfect for creating report titles.

HOT TIP

- **Number format.** For clear reports, it's important that numbers appear with the proper decimal places, commas, currency symbol, and so on. All spreadsheets offer a basic selection of number formats, and *Quattro Pro for Windows* and *Excel* make an advanced art out of them by letting you create your own customized formats.

- **Fonts and text attributes.** The DOS spreadsheets all provide fonts to enable you to print your work in a variety of typefaces and sizes. And of course, the Windows spreadsheets have access to any Windows font. To add emphasis, you can print your cell entries boldfaced, underlined, italicized, and so on, and you can even change

HOT TIP

the color of the on-screen text to distinguish formulas and data cells.

- **Cell shading and border lines.** How about hot pink cells in a fish-scale motif, edged with a Baroque gilt frame? Doable, even if it's not you. At the least, you can emphasize current totals in your humdrum reports by letting them appear in a lightly gray-shaded row. Or you can make a tidy line across the worksheet to separate the total formulas from the data cells.

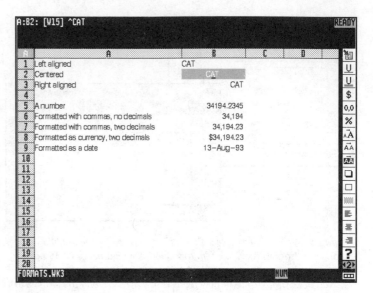

Figure 6: *Aligning labels in Windows spreadsheets is easy, but in 1-2-3 and Quattro for DOS, it's accomplished with label prefixes. In cell B2, the caret label prefix centers the label within the width of the column.*

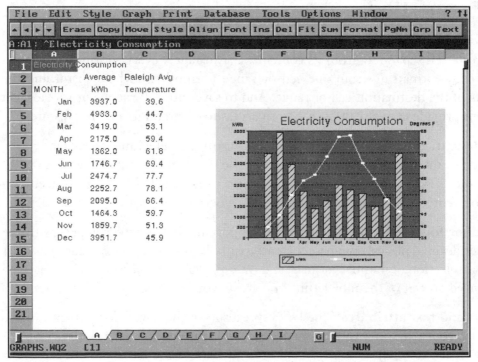

Figure 7: *This Quattro for DOS bar graph is tied to the data values shown at left. One series (B4..B15) produces the bars showing average monthly electricity consumption in a Southeastern home; the other (C4..C15) produces the line showing the average monthly temperature.*

Bar Chart

Show changes in a "countable" quantity over time

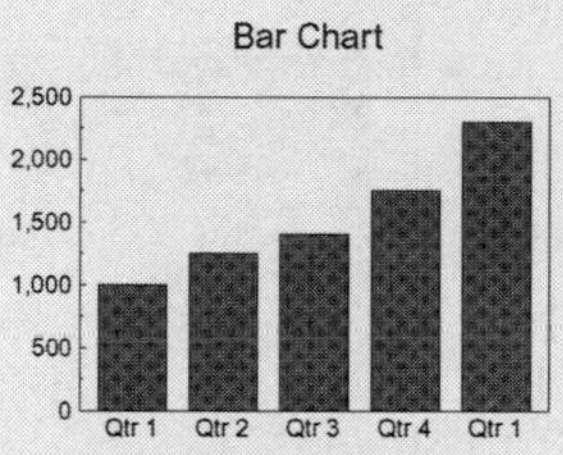

Line Chart

Show changes in a continuous variable or index over time

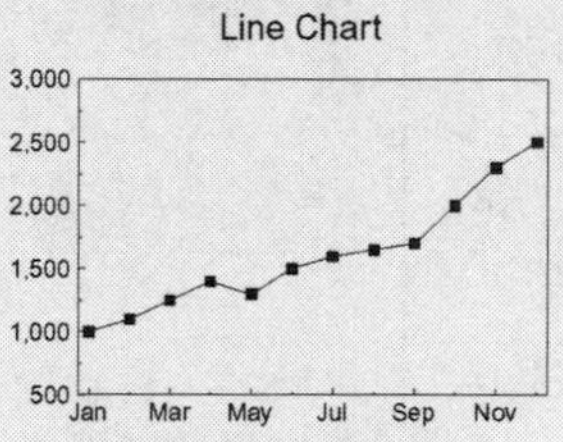

Column Chart

Compare quantities across categories

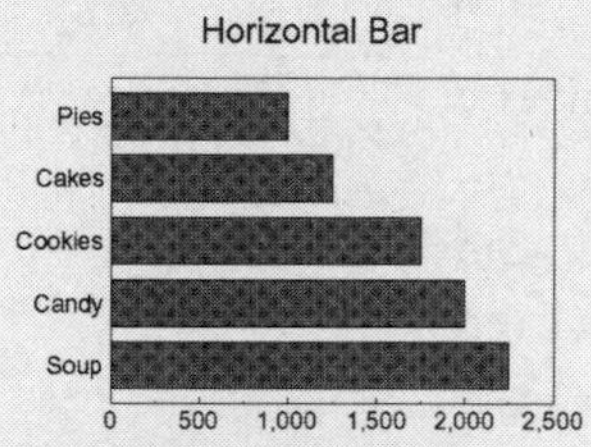

Pie Chart

Show simple proportions

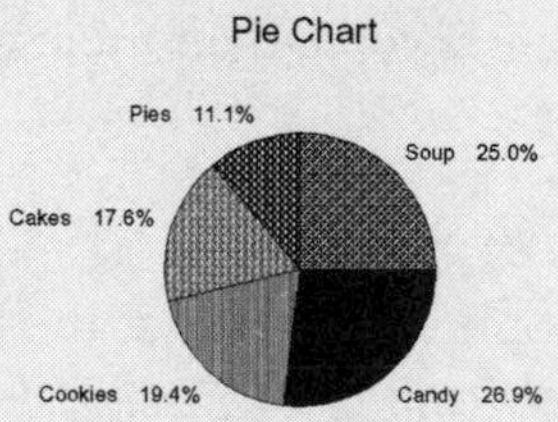

Scatter Diagram

Show the relationship between two variables

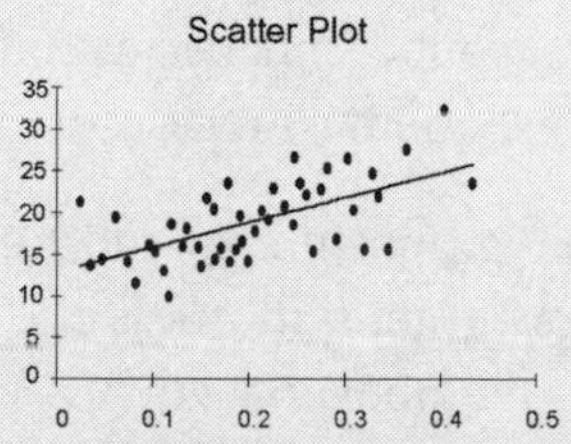

Radar Chart

Compare entities across several dimensions

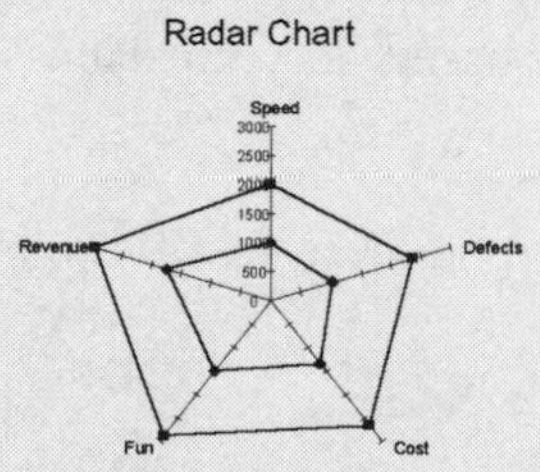

Figure 8: Chart gallery
Most spreadsheets come with a full range of graphs, each one designed to express a different type of data relationship.

You can store cell format settings under named *styles*, then apply the same formatting to a new range by invoking the style. Styles speed things up a lot. You can even save styles and pass them to anyone with the same spreadsheet program—a good way for a company to give worksheets a consistent look.

HOT TIP

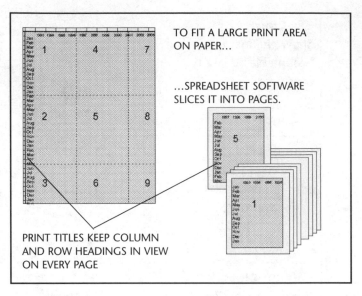

TO FIT A LARGE PRINT AREA ON PAPER...

...SPREADSHEET SOFTWARE SLICES IT INTO PAGES.

PRINT TITLES KEEP COLUMN AND ROW HEADINGS IN VIEW ON EVERY PAGE

Windows spreadsheets all provide some form of "automatic," "intelligent," "speedy" formatting. It's none of the above. Usually, you end up with a mess that you'll spend more time on than you would have spent formatting the

DANGER

Figure 9: *When you print a big worksheet, your spreadsheet slices it up into multiple pages automatically. To repeat the column and row headings on every page, you need to tell the program which rows and columns contain those headings before you print.*

worksheet from scratch. Automatic formatting makes the product reps look great at trade shows, but in real life it's worse than useless. Just do it yourself.

Graphs

HOT TIP

There are two kinds of people in the world: those who enjoy staring at tables full of numbers in search of The Meaning of Life, and those who would rather glance at a well-designed graph, get the gist, and get on with it. Your spreadsheet's graph module lets you satisfy the latter group. And because the graphs reflect up-to-the-moment changes in data, you can use them to try out various "what-if" scenarios.

It's easy to whip up a basic graph in a spreadsheet. You just highlight a range, pick a toll bar option, and the program will guess the graph you want to create, complete with labels created from the labels on your worksheet. To make things even easier, *Excel*'s "Graph Wizard and *Quattro Pro for Windows*" Graph Expert offer step-by-step help for setting up a chart based on your data.

Printing

Printing a small worksheet is simple. If you're using a DOS spreadsheet, you must define a range to print, but Windows spreadsheets even select a range for you. Just run your program's print preview command, check the page layout, adjust the margins, maybe set up a page header and footer, and go. If your worksheet is slightly larger than a single page, you can use your program's auto-compression feature to shrink the worksheet to fit.

However, if your worksheet is really big, then shrinking is not an option, and you must produce a multipage report. The problem is making sure that each page looks right, with labels in both the top row and the left column to identify the values in the cells. To do this, you need to tell the program which rows and columns to use as print titles, so it can duplicate them on every page of the report. Every spreadsheet offers a way for you to do this.

Macros

A *macro* is a prerecorded series of spreadsheet actions, which you "play back" to automate some repetitious operation. In the DOS programs, the individual macro commands (called *macro statements*) represent the actual keystrokes you would use to carry out actions at the keyboard. For example, in *1-2-3*, the sequence of command options that widens the current column to 25 spaces is /Worksheet Column Set-Width 25, which you can execute by pressing the keys /, W, C, S, 2, 5, and then Enter. The macro statement that executes the same operation is /WCS25~ (the ~ symbol represents the Enter key).

In the Windows spreadsheets, where mouse clicks take the place of most menu commands, the commands of the macro languages describe actions instead of keystrokes. For example, the *Excel 5.0* macro statement to set the current column width to 25 is Selection.ColumnWidth = 25.

Depending on the program, you create a macro either by entering macro statements directly into a worksheet or by using the program's *macro recorder*, which records the macro statements as you carry out actions on the worksheet. It's useful to think of three distinct types of macros, each with its own purpose:

- **Construction macros** automate the routine tasks of setting up or manipulating any worksheet. Thus, you might create a macro to convert all the labels in a column to uppercase. Since construction macros are all-purpose tools, you'll want to store them independent of any individual worksheet, using the program's *macro library* feature so you can use them with any worksheet.

- **Production macros** automate the routine tasks associated with an individual worksheet, such as preparing and printing a multirange report or managing data entry. They are stored within the individual worksheet rather than in a macro library. They're meant to be used by experienced users, who simply want to speed up repetitive operations.

- **Application macros** are designed to automate a worksheet for use by an unskilled user. Writing application macros is definitely a professional skill, not to be attempted by the spreadsheet dabbler. Application macros typically provide a customized interface, extensive error-checking, and custom help—all the accoutrements of a well-built application.

HOT TIP

In all macros, statements often refer to actions that occur in specific ranges of the worksheet. In order to write macros that function reliably, you *must* use range names to refer to any cell or range addresses that the macro must deal with.

Lists (That Is, Databases)

Most people use spreadsheets for record keeping, and when you organize those records into a list, it's called a *database*—a set of facts about people (employees, customers), things (inventory items, assets), or events (financial transactions, sales calls). Storing and retrieving big lists containing thousands of records is a task for a database program like *Paradox* or *Access* (see Chapter 19: *Databases*). But if you want to *analyze* shorter lists of similar facts, a spreadsheet program is the right tool for the job.

First, some jargon. In a spreadsheet database, *fields* are columns and *records* are rows, while a *table* is a cell range. The first row of a table contains unique *field headings* that identify the contents of that column. If there's more than one table at a time involved in a database, then you have a *relational* database.

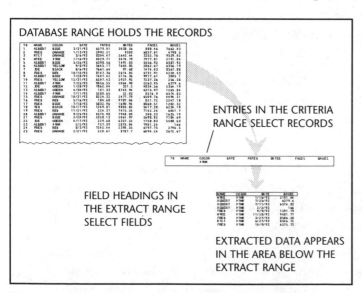

Figure 10: *In a spreadsheet database query, the criteria range selects records from the database range, and the query command copies the records to the extract range, where they're ready to examine or print.*

Sorting, Selecting, and Summarizing

Every spreadsheet program gives you several basic sets of tools for organizing, extracting, and summarizing lists of data.

- **Sorting** lets you rearrange records (rows) in a table according to the entries in one or more of the columns. For example, if a table has ID, Name, and Date columns, and the list is currently ordered by ID number, you could quickly reorder the list by name using a sort command and identifying the Name column as the *sort key*.

  HOT TIP

- **Queries** select subsets of records and fields. In the classic spreadsheet query scheme, you designate the database table as the *input range*. Then you define a *criteria range* that consists of at least two rows: The first is a copy of the table's field headings; the others contain values (for example, a specific date under the Date heading) or numeric ranges (say, >1000 under the Sales heading) for which you plan to find matching records. Next, you set up a one-row *extract* (or *output*) range containing headings for the fields that you want to appear in your answer. Enter the command to *extract* the results, and the program starts by erasing everything on your spreadsheet below the output range, so be careful. Then it finds the records

  DANGER

Importing Data

Nobody likes to type in data from scratch. You have three likely outside sources for data that already exists electronically:

- **Other spreadsheets.** Basically, any spreadsheet program can use data from any other spreadsheet program. The question is how many steps you have to go through to get it. For example, you can open a *1-2-3* worksheet file in *Excel* just as you would one of *Excel*'s own worksheets. But to open an *Excel* file in a DOS version of *1-2-3*, you'd need to use *1-2-3*'s file import routine first.

- **Text and word processing files.** You can load a plain text file of tabular data into any spreadsheet, as long as the file contains delimited data, with each record on a separate row and with commas between the field values and quotes around the text values. The numbers or words will generally line up nicely, though you'll probably need to clean up the headings. Under Windows, you'll get similar results if you copy or cut a table from a word processor and paste it into a Windows spreadsheet.

- **Database files.** *1-2-3* release 3.4 and *1-2-3 for Windows* provide direct access to database files using the Data Lens feature, which lets you query an external table as if it were an input range in your spreadsheet. *Quattro Pro for Windows* and *Excel* provide accessory programs that tap into an external database, select records, and pump the results into your worksheet.

in the database that meet the criteria and copies their field values into the area below the output range.

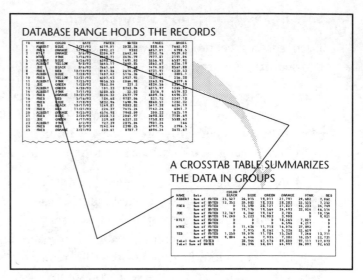

DATABASE RANGE HOLDS THE RECORDS

A CROSSTAB TABLE SUMMARIZES THE DATA IN GROUPS

Figure 11: *A crosstab table summarizes records from a database table according to the categories that appear in one or more fields. This example shows summary sales figures for two products, organized by color and sales rep.*

- **Summarizing** involves such actions as counting the number of records that meet various criteria or producing a subtotal of a group of records. The most basic tools provided for this purpose are the *database statistical functions* DSUM, DCOUNT, and so on. With these functions, you could find out the number of inventory items that fell below a certain level one month, sales totals for people in a certain region, you name it. The sky's the limit.

Slicing and Dicing With Crosstabs

Database statistical functions often require a lot of fussing. To provide an easier and more flexible way to summarize data, the Windows spreadsheets offer *crosstab* tables. Crosstabs enable you to quickly set up a table of subtotals or other summary statistics based on one, two, or more fields, in various configurations. The Windows spreadsheets offer plenty of on-line help to get you started with crosstab tables.

Building a Template Worksheet

Template worksheets are for playing the "what-if?" game and for automating printed paper forms. In this section, you'll learn how to create a template version of that old pain in the butt, the travel expense voucher. This example explains how to do it with the most popular Windows spreadsheet, *Excel*, but most of the tips here are transferable to other Windows spreadsheets.

Here's the scenario: You work as a U.S. rep for McBlast Brothers Pyrotechnic Emporium. You want to create an expense form that does running totals, complete with the personal vehicle cents-per-mile calculation.

Entering Labels

Your first step is to enter the labels that will give your template its basic shape, as in Figure 12. Select File//New, put the cell pointer on cell A1, type `McBlast Bros. Inc. Travel Expense Voucher`, and press (Enter). Notice that the label you just entered is much longer than the cell you put it in. That's OK—labels, unlike numbers, can spill out onto adjacent cells.

	A1	↓		McBlast Bros. Inc. Travel Expense Voucher			
	A	**B**	**C**	**D**	**E**	**F**	**G**
1	McBlast Bros. Inc. Travel Expense Voucher						
2							
3	Name:			Date:		Mileage:	
4		MON	TUE	WED	THU	FRI	
5	Date						
6	Location						TOTAL
7	Hotel						
8	Breakfast						
9	Lunch						
10	Supper						
11	Airline						
12	Taxi						
13	Tips						
14							
15	Vehicle Miles						
16	TOTAL						

Figure 12: *The first step in building a template is to enter the labels and establish the basic structure for your new worksheet.*

Repeat the process as you enter `Name:` in A3. Now for a small shortcut: Put the cell pointer on A5, type `Date`, and instead of pressing (Enter), press the right arrow key. You've entered the label and moved to the next cell all in one step.

HOT TIP

 — AUTOFILL HANDLE

If you need a set of labels that fall into some common patterns (MON, TUE, WED..., January, February..., and so on), *Excel* can help. Put the cell pointer on B4 and enter MON. In the lower-right corner of the cell, you'll notice a tiny square, called the Autofill handle. Move your pointer over it until the pointer becomes a black plus sign, hold down the left mouse button, and drag the plus sign across four cells to the right. *Excel* obligingly fills in the remaining days of the week.

HOT TIP

Building and Checking Formulas

REMEMBER

Let me say this real loud, so you'll be sure to hear me: *Never, ever sign your name to a piece of paper printed out of one of your spreadsheets without making sure that the results are correct.*

Spreadsheets make it easy to do complex calculations—and even easier to do them incorrectly. The most important way to prevent errors is to avoid using real data as you construct the formulas. Instead, enter dummy data values that make it easier to spot errors. Later, once you're sure the formulas are working properly, erase the dummy values and enter the real ones.

Sums and Copies

The formulas in the expense voucher are so simple, entering dummy values may seem a little obsessive—but hey, this is spreadsheets, not poetry class. Start by entering the dummy data value .1 into cell G3. Then enter 1 into cell B7, grab the Autofill handle, and drag the black plus sign all the way across to F7 to copy the number 1 into those cells. Voilà! You've just entered the dummy data for five days' hotel expenses.

	A	B	C	D	E	F	G
1	McBlast Bros. Inc. Travel Expense Voucher						
2							
3	Name:			Date:		Mileage:	0.1
4		MON	TUE	WED	THU	FRI	
5	Date						
6	Location						TOTAL
7	Hotel	1	1	1	1	1	5
8	Breakfast	1	1	1	1	1	5
9	Lunch	1	1	1	1	1	5
10	Supper	1	1	1	1	1	5
11	Airline	1	1	1	1	1	5
12	Taxi	1	1	1	1	1	5
13	Tips	1	1	1	1	1	5
14							
15	Vehicle Mi	1	1	1	1	1	5
16	TOTAL	7.1	7.1	7.1	7.1	7.1	35.5
17							

Figure 13: *The formulas in B16:G16 all include an absolute reference to the mileage rate in cell G3. For example, the formula in the cell surrounded by the cell pointer reads =SUM(B7:B13)+B15*G3.*

 HOT TIP Now it's time to use the SUM function in a formula to add those values up. Put the cell pointer on G7 and click the Autosum button on the toolbar. All by itself, *Excel* enters =SUM in G7 and guesses that you want to add B7 through F7. Click the Autosum button again, and *Excel* displays the result: 5.

AUTOSUM BUTTON   Every expense item needs a similar formula and its own set of dummy values. Select the range B7:G7, and you'll notice that the Autofill handle moves to the lower-right corner of G7. Drag the handle down to G13, and the whole range B7:G13 will be filled in, dummy values, formulas, and all.

To fill in the Vehicle Mileage row, select B13:G13, move the pointer to the edge of the range until you see an arrow, hold down both the left mouse button and the Ctrl key, drag the selection down to row 15, and release the left mouse button. In every case, note that each SUM formula in column G refers to its own row.

Absolute Cell Addresses

To build the formulas for the overall total, select B16 and enter =SUM(B7:B13) +B15*G3 (remember to select the cells or ranges with the cell pointer and let *Excel* enter the addresses for you). The total in B16 will be 7.1. Let's see, 7 ones is 7, and 1 mile times 10 cents per mile is .1, so it looks OK.

DANGER

Congratulations! You've just entered your first erroneous formula. Don't believe it? Then try copying the formula in B16 into C16:G16 using the Autofill handle, and check the results. Although the original formula was correct, the copies you made have adjusted all their cell references, *including* your mileage factor. The formula in C16, for example, multiplies C15 times H3 instead of G3. H3 is empty, so the mileage component of C16 ends up as zero.

What to do? You need to make the reference to cell G3 absolute, so it won't change when you make copies. Select cell B16, then click the mouse pointer on the formula bar on the G3, and press F4. Press Enter. The formula now reads =SUM(B7:B13)+B15*G3. Copy it again into C16:G16 and note that all the results are now correct.

Inserting a Row

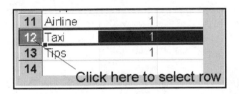
Click here to select row

Let's say you forgot to create a row to track car rental fees. Click on the row number 12 at the left edge of the worksheet frame to select the entire row. Now choose Insert//Rows to add a blank row, and notice that everything below row 11 just moved down one row.

REMEMBER

Notice also that all the formulas in the TOTAL row (now row 17) have adjusted to accommodate the new row you inserted. Every spreadsheet has this feature, or else you'd spend all your time fixing formulas whenever you adjusted your worksheet.

To complete the basic template, enter Rental Car into cell 12, and copy a set of 1's and the row formula (from column G) into the new row.

Formatting Your Template

Your labels are in place, the formulas are correct, and you've even got some fake data in there—but your template doesn't look too snazzy. You don't need to work too hard to dress it up a little. You apply most formatting either by clicking buttons on the Formatting

B17		=SUM(B7:B14)+B16*G3					
	A	B	C	D	E	F	G
1	McBlast Bros. Inc. Travel Expense Voucher						
2							
3	Name:			Date:		Mileage:	$0.100
4		MON	TUE	WED	THU	FRI	
5	Date						
6	Location						TOTAL
7	Hotel	1.00	1.00	1.00	1.00	1.00	$4.00
8	Breakfast	1.00	1.00	1.00	1.00	1.00	$4.00
9	Lunch	1.00	1.00	1.00	1.00	1.00	$4.00
10	Supper	1.00	1.00	1.00	1.00	1.00	$4.00
11	Airline	1.00	1.00	1.00	1.00	1.00	$4.00
12	Rental Car	1.00	1.00	1.00	1.00	1.00	$4.00
13	Taxi	1.00	1.00	1.00	1.00	1.00	$4.00
14	Tips	1.00	1.00	1.00	1.00	1.00	$4.00
15							
16	Vehicle Miles	1	1	1	1	1	5
17	TOTAL	$8.10	$8.10	$8.10	$8.10	$8.10	$32.50
18							

Figure 14: *Formatting makes worksheets more appealing and helps decrease the probability of careless errors. Shading data cells, for example, can distinguish those cells from formula cells.*

toolbar, or by picking something from a menu that pops up when you click the right mouse button.

Set the Column Width and Row Height

Before getting fancy, you need to adjust the width of column A so you can see all the labels. Move your pointer to the line that divides columns A and B at the top of the worksheet frame. When the pointer turns into a two-way arrow, drag the line to widen the column. Move the pointer to the left side of the worksheet frame, and use a similar procedure to widen row 4 and narrow rows 2 and 15.

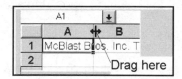

Aligning Cell Entries

Hey, look at your labels—they're all over the place. To align a label to the right, try selecting cell A3 and clicking the Right-align button on the toolbar. Repeat the process for cells D3 and F3.

RIGHT-ALIGN BUTTON

To center all the labels on row 4, select the whole row, then click the Center-align button on the toolbar. Next, center the title in cell A1 across the top of the spreadsheet. Select A1:G1, and click the Center-across-columns button.

CENTER-ACROSS-COLUMNS BUTTON

Font and Colors

Boldface the title by selecting A1 and clicking on the bold button. Now make it bigger: Click the Font Size scroll button on the Formatting toolbar, and select 12 from the drop-down list. To italicize the daily column headings, select row 4 again, and click the italic button.

 BOLD BUTTON    ITALIC BUTTON

Now shade the data cells to distinguish them from cells that contain formulas. To select all of the data cells at once, start by selecting B3:C3; then press and hold the Ctrl key, and select E3, G3, B5:F14, and B16:F16. Right-click anywhere inside the selected cells (D10, for instance), select Format Cells from the menu, click the Patterns tab, and choose a light gray in the Cell Shading box. Click OK.

Number Formats

Go for a neat, conventional appearance for dollar amounts: two decimals, dollar signs on the row and column totals, and a comma between the thousands and hundreds places.

Select B7:F14, right-click, and choose Format Cells from the menu. Click the Number tab, then click Number in the Category box. In the Format Codes box, click #,##0.00_);(#,##0.00). (The weird notation shows what the numbers will look like—don't worry about it.) Click OK, and notice the tidy appearance of your dummy data.

Now do the formulas using toolbar shortcuts: Select G7:G17, press and hold the Ctrl key, and select B17:F17. Click the currency style button to get the dollar signs, and adjust the number of decimals using decimal tools.

 CURRENCY STYLE BUTTON    DECIMAL BUTTONS

Finally, use the currency and decimal buttons to give cell G3 a dollar sign and *three* decimal places.

Lines

How about a couple of lines to separate the major sections of the template? Select A6:G6, right-click, and choose Format//Cells. Click on the Borders tab in the dialog box, click Bottom in the Border Box, and click OK. Repeat the procedure to create the line between rows 16 and 17.

Prepare to Print

You're almost done. All that remains is to clear out the dummy data values, set up the page for printing, and save the finished template. To clear the dummy values, select all the 1's, and press Del.

Now for the page setup. Select File//Page Setup and click the Margins tab. In the Center on Page box, click Horizontally. Click the Header/Footer tab, click the scroll button beside Header, and choose an appropriate heading from the list. Do the same for the Footer. Click the Sheet tab, and deselect Gridlines in the Print box. Click OK to return to the worksheet.

REMEMBER

Finally, name the worksheet page and save the file. Double-click on the notebook page tab at the bottom of the worksheet. In the dialog box, type Expense Voucher in the Name field. Then select File//Save As. Click the scroll button next to Save File As Type and choose Template. Enter a name like EXPENSES and click OK. Later, when you load the template, fill it out, and click the Save button, the Save As dialog box will pop up—which will keep you from overwriting the original template and ensure that you give a unique name to each expense report you fill out.

Avoid the Big Mistake—and Keep Your Job!

Worksheets that crank out wrong answers are worse than useless—they're dangerous, because you usually can't tell what's wrong unless you check the formulas carefully. Follow these six rules, and you (and your job) will be protected against the most common mistakes in speadsheetdom:

1. **Never erase with spaces.** If you try to clear out a cell's contents by pressing the space bar and then Enter, certain statistical functions in *1-2-3* and *Quattro*—notably @AVG, @COUNT, @STD, and @VAR—give invalid answers. Why? Because in those instances, a cell containing a space is treated as the number zero instead of as a blank cell.

2. **Point, don't type.** When you build formulas, it's more accurate to select cells and ranges and let the spreadsheet enter the addresses for you, instead of typing the addresses yourself. If the spreadsheet is big, give important cells meaningful range names. Then, as you build formulas, press F3 to select the names from a list rather than typing addresses.

3. **Never move data cells.** When you move a cell containing numbers or text, any formulas that refer to that cell change to reflect the cell's new position. For instance, if cell A1 contains the formula @SUM(B1..B50), and you move B1 to B2, the formula will change to @SUM(B2..B50). Thereafter, anything you enter into B1 will not be included in the sum. To keep your formulas intact, copy instead of move.

4. **Build formulas using dummy data.** Never build complex formulas based on real data values—it's too easy to miss careless errors in formulas. Instead, fill in the data cells with dummy values—1's, 10's, 100's, anything that makes it easy to spot mistakes.

5. **Make data cells look different.** Use your spreadsheet's formatting tools to distinguish data cells from formula cells. This will keep you from carelessly overwriting formulas with data, which may break a chain of calculations and create a hard-to-detect error.

6. **Never sign off on a spreadsheet you don't understand.** Don't employ a spreadsheet's exotic analytical tools and simply assume the answers are true. Get professional advice, double-check your setup and your formulas, test your model with a textbook example—do whatever it takes to make sure your results are correct.

Building a Database Worksheet

If you plan to accumulate data in your worksheet over time (as opposed to filling in a simple form), then you'll probably want to set up a spreadsheet database. A database worksheet will give you the reports you need, thanks to the crosstab and extract features of your program.

The example that follows uses a tiny personnel database that lists the department and location of a small group of employees. You'll learn how to create two database reports: One lists the employees from a selected department or location, along with their total salaries and hire dates. The other is a crosstab that summarizes the total salaries for each department and location.

I've selected *Quattro Pro for Windows* 5.0 for this task, because it uses the classic criteria-and-extract query system, and because it has a state-of-the-art crosstab feature. Later, I'll cover *Excel*'s filter and pivot table features, along with *1-2-3 for Windows*' snazzy Query Objects.

Setting Up a Table

Like all Windows spreadsheets, *Quattro Pro for Windows*' worksheets have multiple pages. To freely edit and format everything without worrying about messing up other areas, create your table of data on one sheet and the reports—queries and crosstabs—on separate sheets. In this example, we'll put the database (also known as the input range) on the first sheet of the workbook, the query report (which contains both the criteria and extract ranges) on the second sheet, and the crosstab table on the third sheet.

HOT TIP

Here's how to lay the groundwork. Open a new worksheet, right-click on page tab A at the bottom of the sheet, and when the dialog box appears, type `Employees` in the Page Name box, and then click OK. Enter the field headings shown in A1..F1 in the top window of Figure 15, select them, and click the bold and center buttons on the toolbar. Name sheet B `Dept_Repo` and sheet C `Dept_By_Loc`, and then click on Employees to return to the top sheet.

Dept_Repo:E5	@DCOUNT(DATABASE,0,CRITERIA)							

	A	B	C	D	E	F	G	H	I
1	SSN	Employee	Location	Department	Salary	Date_Hired			
2	801-99-4394	Manuel	Charlotte	TRAIN	$80,056	10/06/87			
3	324-73-0119	Helm	Charlotte	TRAIN	$77,730	07/19/85			
4	216-77-0522	Dylan	Raleigh	SALES	$73,952	11/29/89			
5	239-37-6483	Fogerty	Charlotte	SALES	$64,306	01/17/90			
6	771-38-7240	Danko	Raleigh	TRAIN	$92,058	11/03/92			
7	145-60-2806	Clifford	Raleigh	SALES	$58,752	02/09/86			
8	264-00-2799	Hudson	Raleigh	TRAIN	$70,488	10/31/88			
9									

Employees / Dept_Repo / Dept_By_Loc / D / E / F / G / H / I / J / K / L / M /

	A	B	C	D	E	F	G	H
1	Location	Department	Salary					
2		TRAIN						
3								
4								
5			Number of Employees:		4			
6			Total Salaries:		$320,332			
7			Last Hired:		11/03/92			
8								
9	Employee	Location	Department	Salary	Date_Hired			
10	Manuel	Charlotte	TRAIN	$80,056	10/06/87			
11	Helm	Charlotte	TRAIN	$77,730	07/19/85			
12	Danko	Raleigh	TRAIN	$92,058	11/03/92			
13	Hudson	Raleigh	TRAIN	$70,488	10/31/88			
14								
15								
16								

Employees \ Dept_Repo / Dept_By_Loc / D / E / F / G / H / I / J / K / L / M /

Figure 15: *Multipage worksheets are great for creating databases. In this Quattro Pro for Windows worksheet, the data is on the page called Employees, and the query-based report is on Dept_Repo.*

Designating Field Types

Now it's time to designate the type of data you'll put into each field in the table. Right-click in the worksheet frame to select column A and click Block Properties to display the Active Block dialog box. Click Data Entry Input, select Labels Only in the Data Entry Constraints box, and click OK. Repeat the procedure to restrict entries in column F to dates only, and before you click OK, click Numeric Format, choose Date format and Long Date International. (Note that the preceding steps are not necessary in *Excel* or *1-2-3 for Windows*, which automatically interpret social security numbers as labels and dates as dates as you enter them.) Now right-click column E, set its Numeric Format to Currency, and enter 0 as the number of decimals.

	A	B
1	SSN	Empl
2		

CLICK HERE TO SELECT COLUMN A

Now (sigh) enter the data shown in A2..F8 in the top pane of Figure 15. It's dull, I know, but somebody's got to do it.

Range Names for Easy Reference

Finally, to make it easier to set up reports and work with your database later, create some range names: one called Database to identify the entire table of data, and a set of range names to identify the individual fields (for instance, you want cell A2 to have the range name SSN, B2 will be Employee, and so on). Select A1..F8, then right-click in the selection and choose Create Name from the menu. Enter `Database` in the Name box, and click OK. Now select A1..F1, and execute the command Block//Names//Labels. Click Down in the Directions box, and click OK. *Quattro Pro for Windows* uses the labels in A1..F1 to create names for the adjacent cells, thus neatly creating your field range names.

Building a Query Report

The quickest way to build the query report is to copy information from the database table. To put both sheets on screen at the same time for easy copying, create a split-screen: Find the pane splitter at the lower-right corner of the spreadsheet window, and drag it a little more than halfway up the screen. Then click the Dept_Repo page tab in the bottom pane.

Employee	Location	Department	Salary	Date_Hired
Manuel	Charlotte	TRAIN	$80,056	10/06/87
Helm	Charlotte	TRAIN	$77,730	07/19/85
Danko	Raleigh	TRAIN	$92,058	11/03/92
Hudson	Raleigh	TRAIN	$70,488	10/31/88
		Number of Employees:		4
		Total Salaries:	$320,332	
		Last Hired:		11/03/92

Figure 16: This report was printed from the report area shown in the bottom panel of Figure 15. Note that the arrangement of the printout is different than that of the spreadsheet itself.

DRAG HERE TO SPLIT THE SCREEN

Creating Labels and Lines

Use Edit//Copy and Edit//Paste to copy field headings from the top of the database table (row 1 of Employees) to the positions shown in rows 1 and 9 of the Dept_Repo sheet in the bottom pane of Figure 15. Then add the lines to separate the list of records from the summary values: Select A5..E5 in Dept_Repo, right-click in the selection, choose Block Properties from the menu, and click on Line Drawing to view the lines dialog box. Then click on the top edge of the Line Segments example, and click OK. Now select A9..E9, and follow a similar procedure to put a line on the bottom edge of those cells.

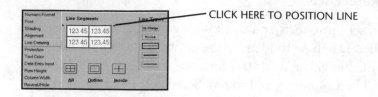

CLICK HERE TO POSITION LINE

Range Names and Formulas

Now it's time to create range names to identify the criteria and extract ranges. Select A1..C2 in Dept_Repo, right-click in the selection, select Create Name, enter `Criteria`, in the Name box, and click OK. Use the same procedure to assign the name Extract to A9..E9.

Now enter the labels for the query results: `Number of Employees:` in C5; `Total Salaries:` in C6, and `Last Hired:` in C7. In the cells that will hold the results themselves, enter the summary formulas in E5..E7, as shown in Figure 17. The formula in E5 uses the database statistical function @DCOUNT to calculate the number of records in the database that meet the current criteria value. The @DSUM function in E6 sums the values from the fourth column of the database (that's the Salary field, not Department, because *Quattro Pro for Windows* counts the leftmost column as zero). @DMAX finds the highest number—in this case, the latest date—in the fifth column. Format the cells as shown in the bottom half of Figure 15.

Cell	Formula
E5	@DCOUNT(DATABASE,0,CRITERIA)
E6	@DSUM(DATABASE,4,CRITERIA)
E7	@DMAX(DATABASE,5,CRITERIA)

Figure 17: Database statistical formulas summarize selected values from the database table.

Extracting the List

Now you're ready to extract a list of records from the table. First, enter a criterion value into the Department field of the criteria range: Type `TRAIN` in cell B2 of Dept_Repo to select the employees from that department. Now, execute the command Data//Query. In the dialog box, click in the Database Block field and press F3. This keystroke displays the Block Names dialog box. Select Database from the list and click OK, and the range name appears as the Database Block. Repeat the procedure to designate Criteria as the Criteria Table and Extract as the Output Block. Click

Question	Criterion	Comment
Which employees work in Charlotte?	Enter `Charlotte` in A2	A simple match.
Which employees had salaries greater than $70,000?	Enter `+SALARY>70000` in cell C2	This one uses a formula to select values in a range. Note that the formula refers to the field range named Salary.
Which employees in the Training department had salaries greater than $80,000?	Enter `TRAIN` in cell B2 and `+ SALARY>80000` in cell C2	In order to be selected, a record must meet both of these criteria.
Which employees were hired after 1/1/90?	Enter `+DATE_HIRED>@DATE(90,1,1)` in cell A2	Because formulas refer specifically to field range names, you can place them in any criteria range cell.

Figure 18: *Go ahead, try your hand at database querying. Enter these criteria in the criteria range in the Dept_Repo query report sheet. Remember to clear your old criteria before trying the next one.*

Extract, and *Quattro Pro for Windows* copies all of the TRAIN department records into the area below the Extract range. Click Close to close the dialog box.

After you've changed the criterion to select another set of records, you'll be able to extract them without returning to the Data Query dialog box. Just press F7 anytime to reexecute the Extract command.   **HOT TIP**

Printing the List

All this work is not going to do you any good if you don't put it on paper so the boss can admire it, right? To print the report shown in Figure 16, first select the range A9..E13 in Dept_Repo. Then press and hold Ctrl and select A5..E7. When you print a multiple selection like this, *Quattro Pro for Windows* prints the first block you select first, the second block second, and so on. Execute the command File//Print Preview to see what it's going to look like on paper. If you like what you see, click the printer button on the toolbar to send it to the printer.   **HOT TIP**

Asking Questions With Criteria

The whole reason for setting up a database is so you can easily and flexibly select groups of records that answer interesting questions. Figure 18 offers some obvious examples. To try them out, enter the criteria as shown, and press F7 to extract the records. Remember to clear the old criterion (use the Delete key) before trying out the new one.

Creating a Crosstab Report

The crosstab report shown in Figure 19, named Dept_By_Loc, occupies the third sheet. It shows the total salaries of employees in each location by department—a summary that would be next to impossible to get from the Dept_Repo query sheet.

	A	B	C	D	E
1	Total Salary by Department and Location				
2					
3		SALES	TRAIN		
5	Charlotte	$64,306	$157,786		
6	Raleigh	$132,704	$162,546		
7					
8					
9					

Figure 19: *This Quattro Pro for Windows crosstab report, based on the database in Figure 15, shows the sum of the salaries by department and location.*

The Data Modeling Desktop

Quattro Pro for Windows employs an accessory program, the Data Modeling Desktop, to generate and manipulate crosstab tables. The procedure involves launching the Desktop and sending the database data to it. Once you've arranged the crosstab report using the Desktop, you send the results back to *Quattro Pro for Windows* for printing or graphing.

Before you go to the Desktop, be sure to save your worksheet so that the data model you create will contain links to a named file; that way, *Quattro Pro for Windows* will be able to match up the worksheet and the data model when you open them later. Execute the command File//Save As and enter a file name such as LISTDEM1. Click OK.

To create the crosstab report, execute the command Data//Data Modeling Desktop. The Send Data dialog box appears with the Cell Blocks to Send field selected. Press F3, select Database from the Block Names dialog, and click OK. Then edit the Cell for Returned Data field to read Dept_By_Loc:A3. Click Hot in the Data Exchange Method box, and click OK. *Quattro Pro for Windows* launches the Desktop and loads the database table into it.

Arranging the Crosstab Fields

The Data Modeling Desktop shows a few rows of the database at the bottom of the window and an empty crosstab report at the top. To arrange the crosstab report, drag the desired field headings from the database into position on the blank report area. For instance, to designate Location as the source of the crosstab row headings, drag the Location field heading as shown in Figure 20. Then drag the Department heading into the top of the table, and drag Salary into the data area—the largest blank area on screen.

The coolest thing about the Data Modeling Desktop is how easily you can rearrange the crosstab table to achieve the results you need. For example, suppose you wanted to see the average salary for each location and department, instead of the total. Right-click in the upper-left corner of the table, and two dialog boxes appear—one lets you format the data values, the other lets you choose the calculation you want inside the crosstab cells. If you want to change the arrangement of the row and column headings, simply drag the headings around the edge of the table.

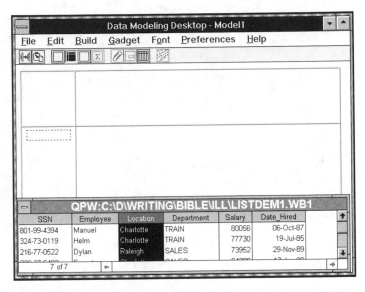

Figure 20: *To set up a crosstab report using Quattro Pro for Windows' Data Modeling Desktop, you drag the field names from the database table and position them on the crosstab table.*

Sending the Table Back to Quattro

Before you return with your crosstab table to *Quattro Pro for Windows*, be sure to save the data model in the Data Modeling Desktop. Execute the command File//Save As, enter a file name such as LISTDEMO, and click OK.

Let's say that at this point, the crosstab appears pretty much as you want it to appear in the spreadsheet. Select it by clicking in the clear space just to the left of the column headings. Then execute the command Edit, Copy to Quattro. Select Hot Link in the dialog box, and click OK.

Formatting the Table

All that's left is to format the table so that it looks like Figure 19. First, hide row 4 by right-clicking on the row number in the worksheet frame and selecting Block Properties. In the resulting dialog box, click Reveal/Hide, then click Rows

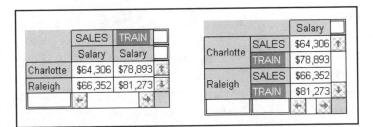

Figure 21: *To rearrange the row and column headings in Quattro Pro for Windows' crosstab tables, all you need to do is drag the row and column headings to a new position.*

and Hide, and click OK. Right-click on cell A3, select Block Properties, choose Numeric Format, click Hidden, and click OK. Enter `Total Salary by Department and Location` into cell A1, and use the bold button to make it bold. Bold the row and column headings. Then select B5..C6 and set its numeric format to Currency with zero decimals. Adjust the column widths as necessary.

And that's it!

Graphing a Crosstab

Since it's usually a lot easier to interpret a graph than a table of raw numbers, let's prepare a bar graph of the crosstab results.

Start by selecting the cells that contain the numbers you want to graph—B5..C6 in the Dept_By_Loc sheet. Then click on the graph button on the toolbar and drag the rectangular shape on the worksheet to size the graph, which will print as part of the worksheet. Release the mouse, and the graph appears.

 GRAPH BUTTON

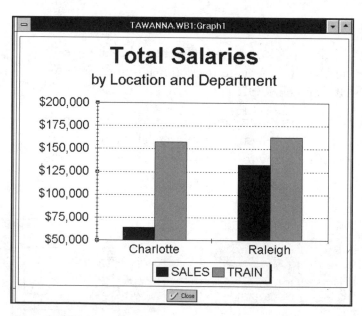

Next, you need to add labels to the graph's horizontal axis, and to create a legend so you can tell which bars are which. Click on the graph to make sure it's selected, then execute the command Graph//Series and click in the X-Axis field in the resulting dialog box. To enter the axis range, just select A5..A6 in the worksheet. Now click in the Legend field and select B3..C3. Click OK, and you'll see that the labels and legend have been added to the graph.

Figure 22: *This bar graph is based on the crosstab results shown in Figure 19. It took a little editing to make it look like this, but you create the basic graph just by selecting the crosstab's range and clicking the graph button.*

To remind you what the graph is about, you need a title. Select Graph//Titles, and in the resulting dialog box, enter

`Total Salaries` in the Main Title field, and enter `by Location and Department` in the Subtitle field. Then click OK.

Finally, you need to adjust the scaling of the vertical axis that shows salaries. Double-click on the graph, and you'll find yourself in a graph window with special menus and tools. Right-click on the vertical axis, and choose Y-Axis Properties. Choose Numeric Format and set it to Currency with zero decimals. Then choose Scale. In the High field, enter `200000`. Enter `50000` in the Low field, `25000` in the Increment field, and 5 in the Number of Minors field. Click OK, and your graph looks like Figure 22.

While you're at it, notice that you can right-click on any object in the graph window to get a pop-up menu that lets you change the properties of that object. For example, you could right-click on a series of bars and change their color or shading; you could right-click on the legend and change its font, and so on. To print a full-page version of the graph, execute the command File//Print in the graph window and follow the prompts you find there.

HOT TIP

Click Close to return to the worksheet, and you'll see your graph embedded on the worksheet as a graphic object. To move it around, drag it; to change its size and shape, click on the graph to select it, then drag one of the eight selection points along the edge of the graph object.

HOT TIP

Choosing the Right Spreadsheet

Let's cut to the chase—*Excel* 5.0 is the best spreadsheet you can buy. It has the coolest interface, it comes with the most features, and it's the most popular program. So you should run out and buy a copy, right? Well, maybe. Remember, you and maybe everyone in your organization is going to invest a lot of time (to say nothing of money) learning and using the thing.

Basically, any Windows spreadsheet can handle the jobs that most users want to do—in fact, even if you crunch numbers for a living, you'll probably only use a fraction of the features included. You shouldn't really care which program has the most gadgets, *as long as it has the particular gadgets you need.* I'll mention the key features of each program as I go, but you should also check out the feature chart at the end of this chapter to compare stuff point by point.

REMEMBER

A word about the DOS programs covered at the end of this chapter. Unless you're using a PC that can't handle Windows, there's absolutely no reason to purchase one of these programs. They simply lack the latest and greatest features offered by the

Windows versions. So even if you have wimpy hardware, you're probably better off biting the bullet, upgrading your system, and doing the Windows thing.

Excel

Excel comes with a bigger arsenal of tools than any other spreadsheet. But what's most remarkable about this program is the way it *works*. True, many of the conveniences in *Excel* can be found in other Windows spreadsheets, but you'll find more here, better implemented. Consider these interface highlights:

- **Autofill.** *Excel*'s ability to fill in cells automatically is an incredible time saver. If you know what you're doing, you can use the left mouse button (along with various key combinations) to drag the Autofill handle and fill or copy cell contents. If you're not sure what you want, drag with the right mouse button and choose options from a pop-up menu.

- **Right-click to change anything.** Select a range and click on it with the right mouse button, and you can clear it, copy it, move it, delete it, insert cells there, or change the properties of the cells or their entries. To edit a chart, right-click on its components, and pick from the menus.

HOT TIP

- **In-cell editing.** Both *Excel* and *1-2-3 for Windows* let you edit cell entries without having to move your gaze to the formula bar. Just double-click on the cell entry, and edit away. You'd be amazed how this one feature makes the program much easier to learn for complete novices.

- **Tear-off palettes.** A slick set of toolbar buttons controls cell and text colors, cell shading, and borders. Each button is accompanied by a scroll button. When you click the scroll

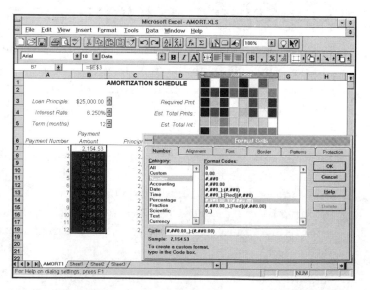

Figure 23: *Excel's interface is the state of the art. For example, Excel's dialog boxes sort options into neatly organized folders, and you can tear off palettes (such as Font Colors) and move them near where you're working.*

button for cell color, for example, you get a palette of colors that you can drag into the spreadsheet and leave floating around to use again and again.

- **Wizards.** A lot of the stuff today's spreadsheets do is complicated. That's why *Excel* has Wizards, which are tutorial dialog boxes that step you through what would otherwise be tortuous procedures. For example, *Excel*'s Chart Wizard helps you set up a graph by prompting you to select the data, choose a chart type, fill in titles and axis labels, and so on. Other Wizards aid in importing text data, creating pivot tables, consolidating worksheets, and performing other multistep tasks.

- **Drawing layer.** *Excel*'s fine set of drawing tools enables you to put rectangles, circles, polygons, arrows, lines, and freehand shapes right on top of a worksheet or chart. *Excel*'s drag and drop feature provides a quick way to duplicate shapes, and if you press [Alt] as you draw and size objects, *Excel* precisely aligns them with the worksheet grid.

Formatting

As with the other Windows spreadsheets, you can format cell entries by choosing options from the menus that pop up when you right-click on something or by clicking on toolbar buttons (which most users prefer to do). Unique among the applications, *Excel* lets you format text within a cell selectively—you can boldface a single word in a title, for instance.

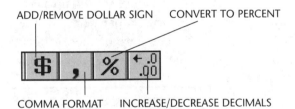

ADD/REMOVE DOLLAR SIGN   CONVERT TO PERCENT

COMMA FORMAT   INCREASE/DECREASE DECIMALS

A set of four toolbar buttons provides most of the routine numeric formats. For standard accounting formats and so on, turn to the menus; once you master the notation, you can even build your own (say, numbers that change color if they go above or below a certain value). To quickly duplicate a cell format, try the Format Painter: Just select a cell that's got the look you want, click the tool, and then select the cells you want to change to match.

FORMAT PAINTER BUTTON

Advanced Analysis and Arrays

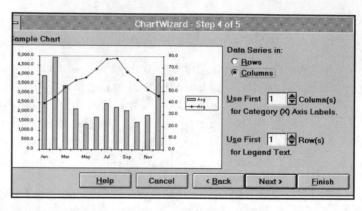

Excel is not alone in offering a whole slew of statistical functions—everything from forecasting and regression to analysis of variance and nonparametric descriptive statistics. (Sounds impressive, eh?) For engineers, there's Fourier analysis, Bessel functions, and so on, while finan-

Figure 24: *Excel's Wizards, such as the Chart Wizard shown here, are handy tutorial dialog boxes that step you through complicated procedures.*

cial analysts will find their own trove of goodies. You also get a solver for analyzing systems on nonlinear equations and a sampling add-in that generates random numbers. In short, more stuff than you could ever use.

Excel's least understood, least used, and most elegant feature, *arrays*, let a single formula do the work of many. Check Figure 25, and I'll give you the lowdown on how this supremely useful feature works. Note that column A is a list of employees, while column B shows their department assignments.

If you wanted to find out the number of employees in the TRAIN department, you could do it with a database statistical function, but that would require setting up a criteria range just for that formula. The array formula in the formula bar performs the same calculation all in one cell: {=SUM((B2:B15=D3)*1)}. The core of the formula, (B2:B15=D3), compares each label in B2:B15 with the label in D3, TRAIN—that's the equivalent of 14 separate logical formulas! Multiplying the result by one converts the TRUE logical values to the numeric value 1; the sum function adds up the ones to yield the value shown in cell E3. To enter an array formula, always press Ctrl Shift Enter, and *Excel* will mark the array with

REMEMBER its characteristic brackets.

	A	B	C	D	E
	E3		▼	{=SUM((B2:B15=D3)*1)}	
	A	B	C	D	E
1	Employee	Department			
2	Aldo	TRAIN		Department	Number
3	Frodo	SALES		TRAIN	3
4	Jerusco	MARKET		SALES	6
5	Mambo	TRAIN		MARKET	5
6	Kalko	SALES			
7	Iago	MARKET			
8	Credo	SALES			
9	Gumbo	SALES			
10	Heraldo	TRAIN			
11	Numero	MARKET			
12	Bilbo	SALES			
13	Elbo	SALES			
14	Limbo	MARKET			
15	Dumbo	MARKET			

Figure 25: *Arrays, one of Excel's least understood but most powerful features, allows one formula to do the work of many.*

	REGION	AREA	SALESPERSON	AMOUNT
2	East	1	Credo	$770,954
3	East	1	Bilbo	$716,367
4	East	1	Aldo	$1,175,695
5	East	2	Dumbo	$657,968
6	East	2	Elbo	$1,118,476
7	South	3	Frodo	$757,044
8	South	3	Gumbo	$603,946
9	South	4	Iago	$1,147,580
10	South	4	Heraldo	$572,454
11	South	4	Jerusco	$1,289,933
12	West	5	Kalko	$910,373
13	West	5	Limbo	$647,508
14	West	6	Mambo	$650,784
15	West	6	Obligato	$570,176
16	West	6	Numero	$991,389

	A REGION	B AREA	C SALESPERSON	D AMOUNT	E
2	East	1	Credo	$770,954	
3	East	1	Bilbo	$716,367	
4	East	1	Aldo	$1,175,695	
5	East	2	Dumbo	$657,968	
6	East	2	Elbo	$1,118,476	
7	East Total			$4,439,460	
8	South	3	Frodo	$757,044	
9	South	3	Gumbo	$603,946	
10	South	4	Iago	$1,147,580	
11	South	4	Heraldo	$572,454	
12	South	4	Jerusco	$1,289,933	
13	South Total			$4,370,957	
14	West	5	Kalko	$910,373	
15	West	5	Limbo	$647,598	
16	West	6	Mambo	$650,784	
17	West	6	Obligato	$570,176	
18	West	6	Numero	$991,389	
19	West Total			$3,770,320	
20	Grand Total			$12,580,737	
21					

	A REGION	B AREA	C SALESPERSON	D AMOUNT
7	East Total			$4,439,460
13	South Total			$4,370,957
19	West Total			$3,770,320
20	Grand Total			$12,580,737

Figure 26: *The left view shows a portion of the raw data; the middle shows the effect of Excel's automatic subtotal feature, which inserts subtotal formulas and outline structure. The right worksheet shows the collapsed outline view.*

Outlines, Subtotals, and Auto-Consolidation

Worksheets often grow to an ungainly size, and outlines enable you to consolidate your view of them. Set up outlines yourself, (using Data//Group//Outline) or you can let *Excel* create them with its subtotal command, which takes a database and automatically adds outline structure and subtotal formulas. Figure 26 illustrates the process: The left view shows the original list of data, sorted by REGION and AREA. The middle view shows what happens when you execute the Data//Subtotals command—one of the new subtotal formulas is on display, as is the outline control panel at left. Click on the 2 at the top of the control panel, and the worksheet collapses into the consolidated view at right.

HOT TIP

Auto-consolidation is similar to subtotaling, only it consolidates several worksheets into a single file. The classic application for this is budgeting. Suppose you've sent out a template to each location in your company, and each manager has filled in projected expenses for the coming budget period. Auto-consolidation combines all those separate templates into one worksheet, matching up the row and column labels as it goes. Thus the worksheet you received from Denver might list "Telephone" on row 16, while the one from Portland ended up with "Telephone" on row 22. Auto-consolidate matches the labels and adds the values from those rows to the "Telephone" row in the consolidation sheet.

Data From Elsewhere

Importing data from text sources is usually a pain, especially since a surprising number of people must still deal with text files culled from mini or mainframe sources. But *Excel* makes the process pretty easy. Open a text file, and the Import Wizard helps you along: First, you specify whether the data is in delimited or fixed-width format (if the latter, *Excel* makes it easy to determine and specify the width of the fields). Then you

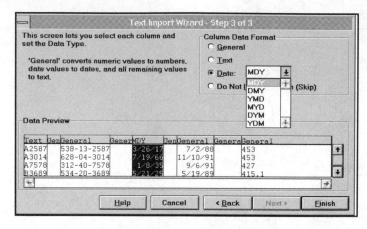

Figure 27: *That perennial pain in the spreadsheeter's neck, importing text data, is made easy with Excel's new Text Import Wizard.*

specify whether the data in each column is numeric, text, or date. And that's it—instant worksheet.

If your data resides in a PC database such as *dBASE* or *Paradox*, or on a database server such as Oracle or some other SQL database, the new Microsoft Query add-in program can tap into it. Query, which ships with *Excel* but can work with other Microsoft products such as *Word*, uses an interface similar to Microsoft's *Access* to let you view the data in external tables, set up relational queries, and then paste or hot-link the results back into *Excel*) see Chapter 19: *Databases* for more on *Access*.

Querying With Filters

The traditional spreadsheet database query procedure I described earlier in this chapter using *Quattro Pro for Windows* is a little on the cumbersome side. *Excel* offers an approach that's radically simple.

Take the personnel list in Figure 28. If you want to see just the employees hired since December, 1991, put the cell pointer anwhere in the table and select Data//Filter//Autofilter. *Excel* automatically finds the field headings in the top row and places a scroll button next to each one. Now click on the Date Hired heading and choose Custom from the pop-up menu. *Excel* scans the column and places an ordered list of actual data values in the dialog box, so you can pick precisely the value you need.

HOT TIP

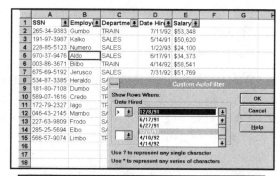

Figure 28: *Instead of conventional spreadsheet queries, Excel uses Filters. When you click on the scroll button next to a field heading, you get the dialog box shown here, which lets you select records.*

Click OK in the dialog box, and you get the result shown at the bottom of Figure 28—a list that displays just the selected values. Were you to use *Excel*'s SUBTOTAL function to summarize the filtered list (cells E17:E18), it would conveniently skip the hidden rows to produce a sum, average, or whatever, of only the selected records.

HOT TIP

Pivot Tables

In *Excel*, pivot tables perform the same function as crosstabs, and setting one up is similar to creating a crosstab with *Quattro Pro for Windows*—except that you don't have to switch to an add-in program to do it. Instead, you launch the Pivot Table Wizard and let *Excel* walk you through the process.

A typical pivot table, along with the Query and Pivot toolbar, appears in Figure 29. The table sums volume and sales values across sales reps and displays the results by region, product, and quarter. And that's only the beginning: The table is interactive, so you can quickly reorganize it to look for patterns in the data.

For instance, in B1 you can see that all regions are represented in the table. Click on the scroll button next to B1, and you can select just one region—*Excel* will serve up that region's shampoo and soap numbers. Double-click on one of the field heading buttons (Product, Data, or Qtr), and you can change the statistics used for calculations, the numeric format, and so on. Want to summarize the data by volume, or on a date field? *Excel* lets you group the values easily—to show how many salespeople had sales volumes within a certain range, or whatever. The list of possibilities goes on and on.

Macros

For its macros, *Excel* employs a programming language called Visual Basic for Applications, used in several Microsoft products. Macros are stored on special workbook pages called *modules*. Each module may include several separate macros, which are called *procedures*. Usually, you create a procedure by recording a sequence of actions first, and then you edit the recorded commands.

	A	B	C	D	E	F
1	Region	(All)				
2						
3			Qtr			
4	Product	Data	1	2	Grand Total	
5	Shampoo	Sum of Volume	11,346	12,484	23,830	
6		Sum of Sales	$1,117,596	$1,194,108	$2,311,704	
7	Soap	Sum of Volume	32,921	35,533	68,454	
8		Sum of Sales	$3,361,071	$3,477,031	$6,838,102	
9	Total Sum of Volume		44,267	48,017	92,284	
10	Total Sum of Sales		$4,478,667	$4,671,139	$9,149,806	
11						
12			Query and Pivot			
13						
14						
15						

Figure 29: *Pivot tables in Excel perform the same function as crosstabs in other programs. They let you slice and dice a database worksheet in just about any way imaginable.*

To create a macro, you use the following procedure: Execute Tools// Record//Macro//Record New Macro, enter a name in the Macro Name field, and click OK to turn on the recorder. A toolbar appears with a single button to stop recording.

THE BUTTON THAT CREATES BUTTONS

What's Missing?

Precious little. The only important missing item that I can think of is *1-2-3 for Windows'* Version Manager, a super-useful tool for comparing sets of "what-if" scenarios. Microsoft never lets a feature go unchallenged, though, so you can anticipate some kind of version management in the next *Excel* release.

1-2-3 for Windows

This full-service Windows spreadsheet offers great formatting and graph features, its own easy-to-use database system, and the Version Manager, which takes "what-iffing" to a new level of sophistication. You also get multipage worksheets (up to 256 pages), movable toolbars, and mini-menus of editing and formatting options that pop up when you click the right mouse button. Other highlights of *1-2-3 for Windows 4.0*'s interface include:

- **1-2-3 for DOS compatibility.** To ease the transition for those millions of *1-2-3 for DOS* users, *1-2-3 for Windows* provides its Classic menu system. Press the slash

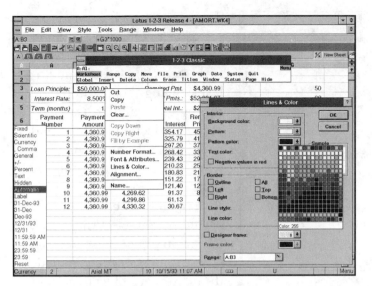

Figure 30: *1-2-3 for Windows offers right-mouse-button menus, a status bar at the bottom that you can use for quick formatting, and a Classic menu system that works just like 1-2-3 for DOS.*

key, and you get a dialog box that dutifully imitates the old-fashioned *1-2-3* menu system. Such keystroke compatibility also means that old *1-2-3* for DOS macros run fine in *1-2-3 for Windows*.

- **Formatting with the status bar.** Located at the bottom of the screen, the status bar doubles as a menu for formatting cells. Click on a displayed setting, and you get a quick pop-up menu of additional selections.

- **Customizable toolbars.** The bad news about *1-2-3 for Windows'* toolbars is that you can display only one at a time, and the mix of buttons isn't always that logical. The good news is that you can easily customize toolbars to hold just the buttons you want.

Formatting

When it comes to creating pretty spreadsheet reports, *1-2-3 for Windows* has the widest range of decorative devices. But when it comes to formatting numeric values, it runs a poor third to *Excel* and *Quattro Pro for Windows* because it won't let you create custom formats. As partial compensation, *1-2-3 for Windows* does provide a great array of fill patterns and frames for ranges and objects, and it's the only spreadsheet that lets you rotate text in a cell. You'll probably want to right-click and pop up the formatting menu rather than use the toolbars, which are pretty confusing.

Query Objects

Forget about old-fashioned input, criteria, and output ranges. In their place, *1-2-3 for Windows* offers Query Objects, which display the records and fields you've selected. You can drag a query object (like the one in the bottom half of Figure 31) anywhere on the worksheet, and then reference the cells inside it for formulas and calculations.

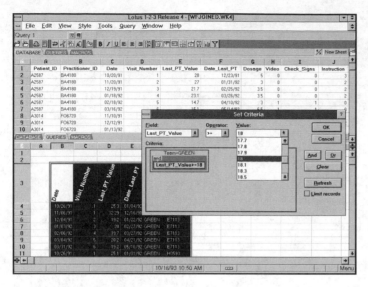

Figure 31: *In place of the usual query system, 1-2-3 for Windows offers Query Objects, which float on the worksheet surface. Selecting records is easy with the Set Criteria dialog box.*

To create a query, you indicate the table (or tables) you want to query and the fields you want from them. The ensuing multi-level dialog boxes step you through specifying the data range, selecting fields, and building a selection statement. Click the OK button, and the selected fields and records appear in the query object; whenever you select the object, the main menu displays the Query option so you can modify it. A query object can join data from separate tables, even if they're from different sources.

1-2-3 for Windows' access to external databases is built into the worksheet, rather than being relegated to an accessory program. It's complicated to use, but it's also very flexible, precisely because it allows you to mix and match data from various sources—say, to combine data from a spreadsheet range, a *Paradox* table, and a *dBASE* database, all in one query.

Version Manager

The "what-if" game—you know, changing data values in a spreadsheet to see the effect—is the reason that spreadsheets were invented. *1-2-3 for Windows'* Version Manager raises the level of play to new heights.

The Version Manager lets you create alternative sets of values (or formulas) for selected ranges and store them with descriptive names and comments. You can play "what-if" on a micro level and swap versions into individual ranges, or you can use the Version Manager Index to combine a set of versions into a named *scenario*. Scenarios let you play "what-if" at a whole new level, as you swap entire sets of versions at once.

Take a look at the simple income statement in Figure 32. The range B3..E3 is named "Sales," and the sales figures you see in that range have been stored under the version named "Last Year." Depending on events, sales for next year might be very different. For instance, if a Korean competitor finishes its new plant, sales might decline; a scenario called "Korean Plant" might use the values 2300, 2200, 2100, and 2000 in

B3..E3. Along with the values, Version Manager automatically records the user's ID and the date for each version.

The Version Manager Index helps you think bigger, because it lets you organize versions into scenarios. For instance, your "Most Likely" scenario might combine the Five Percent version for Sales, the Cost of Living version for Salaries, the Big Project version for R&D, and so on. The Index lets you view scenarios and versions by various criteria, such as range name, author, version name, and date. To cap it all off, a set of functions lets you cull important values and labels from the scenarios to use in worksheet formulas or macros.

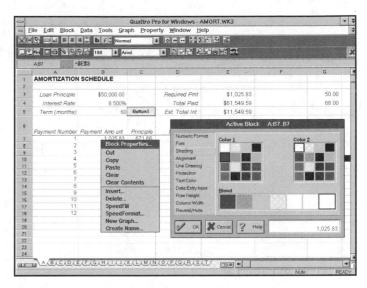

Figure 32: *1-2-3 for Windows' most innovative new feature is the Version Manager, which lets you play the "what-if" game at a whole new level of sophistication.*

What's Missing?

Benchmarked against *Excel*, *1-2-3 for Windows* comes up short in a number of crucial areas. Query Objects work well enough, but for data management, you can't beat *Excel*'s combination of pivot tables, automatic subtotals, and automatic worksheet consolidation. A major annoyance with *1-2-3 for Windows* is that you can't group worksheet pages, a handy feature for organizing projects that both *Excel* and *Quattro Pro for Windows* offer. *1-2-3 for Windows* also lacks arrays, and its macro language is no match for Visual Basic.

Quattro Pro for Windows

It's got great graphics, an attractive interface, compatibility with *1-2-3* for DOS, and solid analytical capability. But sad to say, *Quattro Pro for Windows 5.0* is a day late and a dollar short because it lacks many of the latest innovations in *Excel* and *1-2-3 for Windows*. Graphics excepted, there's no compelling reason to select *Quattro Pro for Windows* over the other two.

Quattro Pro for Windows' cheerful interface offers the usual gizmos: toolbars, autofill, multipage worksheets with tabs, and right-mouse-button access to mini-menus (all were *Quattro Pro for Windows* firsts). And it incorporates some small but handy touches, such as parentheses in formulas that change from red to green so you can check whether they're all accounted for. Some other high points:

- **Worksheet organization.** You can group worksheet pages together, either temporarily or permanently, and then edit and format them as a unit. The last page of a workbook holds graphs and custom dialog boxes, which appear as icons that you can drag around, organize, edit, or incorporate into a presentation-style "slide show."

- **Experts.** *Quattro Pro for Windows'* answer to *Excel*'s Wizards, Experts takes you through complex operations like building graphs, consolidating worksheets, and analytical procedures.

- **Customizable everything.** Like *1-2-3 for Windows* and *Excel*, *Quattro Pro for Windows* has toolbars that you can customize. However, because *Quattro Pro for Windows'* toolbars are actually a specialized kind of dialog box, you can also include sliders, radio buttons, text boxes, and so on; link them to cells in the spreadsheet; and use them to control your worksheets. The result is a quick system for creating simple spreadsheet applications.

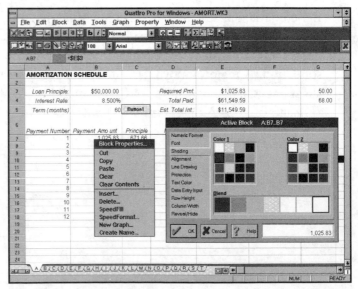

HOT TIP

Figure 33: *Click on any object, and a menu tailored to the task pops up—a convenience that originated with Quattro Pro for Windows. The menus are more consistent here than in any other Windows spreadsheet.*

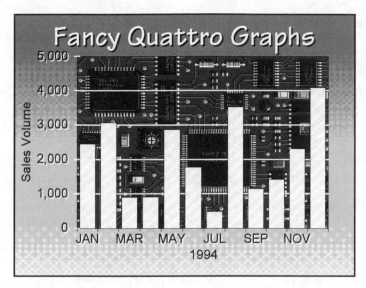

Figure 34: *Buy Quattro Pro for Windows, and you may not need a separate presentation graphics program. This program can produce flashier charts than any other spreadsheet.*

Great Graphs

If you need to present your data in the flashiest manner possible, *Quattro Pro for Windows* is the undisputed champ. You can paste scanned photos on graph surfaces, use graduated shading for text, annotate graphs with little drawings, and generally have a grand old time. *Quattro Pro for Windows* includes an Expert, comparable to *Excel*'s Chart Wizard, to help lay out graphs.

Create a graph, and on the last page of your *Quattro Pro for Windows* workbook, an icon appears. This is a great way to keep graphs organized, especially if you have lots of them to produce. Double-click on a graph icon, and you can edit the graph with a full set of charting and drawing tools. You can even organize images on the graph page into a slide show, complete with text charts, a light table to organize the images, and transition effects. In all, the graphics features of *Quattro Pro for Windows* approach those of a presentation graphics program.

Arrays, Analysis, and Scenarios

Most of *Quattro Pro for Windows*' analysis and database features play catch-up with the latest and greatest in *Excel* and *1-2-3 for Windows*. For example, the list of advanced analytical functions is roughly comparable to that of the other two. The program also has array formulas, although they lack the depth of *Excel*'s arrays.

Like *1-2-3 for Windows*, *Quattro Pro for Windows* lets you swap in groups of values and try various scenarios on for size. There's an Expert to help with this, but because *Quattro Pro for Windows*' scenarios lack the multilevel organization of *1-2-3 for Windows*, you'd be better off turning to the latter if you want to "what if" with a group of people on a network.

Databases Inside and Out

Quattro Pro for Windows' reliance on the old criteria-and-extract method of data management seems old hat. And although the Data Modeling Desktop lets you analyze data with a degree of sophistication similar to that of *Excel's* pivot tables, the Desktop is klunkier, because it's not integrated into the program.

HOT TIP

Quattro Pro for Windows includes an accessory called the Database Desktop that's modeled after Borland's *Paradox for Windows* database. If you're a *Paradox* user, this is a neat way to query external databases and incorporate the data into your spreadsheets.

What's Missing?

The biggest things missing from *Quattro Pro for Windows 5.0* are database features to match the competition. You won't find anything approaching *1-2-3 for Windows'* Query Objects or *Excel's* Filters, which truly make spreadsheet data management more efficient. Less important (but strange, considering the program's extensive graphics capabilities) is *Quattro Pro for Windows'* lack of a drawing layer. Creating fancy graphs is nice, but I'd like to be able to annotate worksheets more easily.

Quattro Pro for DOS

You have now entered the DOS zone. The interface of version 5.0 of *Quattro Pro* for DOS looks and feels about as close to Windows as you can get without Windows—which is to say that after using the Windows version for awhile, it's excruciating. Nonetheless, if you must do it in DOS, I recommend this program over any version of *1-2-3* for DOS, mostly because the menus are much more organized.

Like *Quattro Pro for Windows*, the DOS version has multipage worksheets with tabs, which means you can organize your stuff much more easily than you can in the DOS versions of *1-2-3*. In fact, many of *Quattro Pro* for DOS's features are terrific compared to those of the DOS *1-2-3* versions, but that's not saying much compared to the Windows spreadsheets:

- **Graphics.** Well, it's the only spreadsheet that does bubble charts, and it has the best graph editing of any DOS spreadsheet, but *Quattro Pro* for DOS lacks most of the flashy tricks that make its Windows cousin such a star in this area.

- **Workspace save.** You can save the entire workspace, including multiple worksheet files with their window positions, and then restore the entire constellation with a single command.

- **Worksheet organization.** *Quattro Pro* for DOS enables you to break worksheet pages into groups, to aid in editing and formatting sections of your worksheet. A consolidation feature helps you take your old single-page worksheets and arrange them into multipage files.

Quattro Pro for DOS lets you use your mouse to select ranges, execute commands, change column widths, and so on. But, at the risk of belaboring the point, why buy an imitation Windows program when

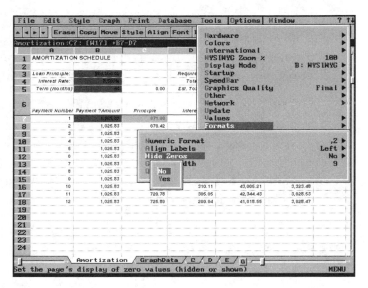

Figure 35: Quattro Pro for DOS has multipage worksheets and a Windows-like interface. If you're stuck with DOS, it's the only way to go.

you can get the real thing? You'll miss a lot, from drag and drop, to autofill, to those cute right-mouse-button menus. There's simply no reason to plow through menus when you could be pointing and clicking.

1-2-3 for DOS

I'll make it easy for you: Don't buy *1-2-3* for DOS, either version 2.4 or 3.4. If you have a bunch of old *1-2-3* for DOS spreadsheets you can't bear to part with, that's still no excuse— any Windows spreadsheet (not to mention *Quattro Pro for DOS*) can handle them, and *1-2-3 for Windows* will even run your old macros flawlessly (well, almost).

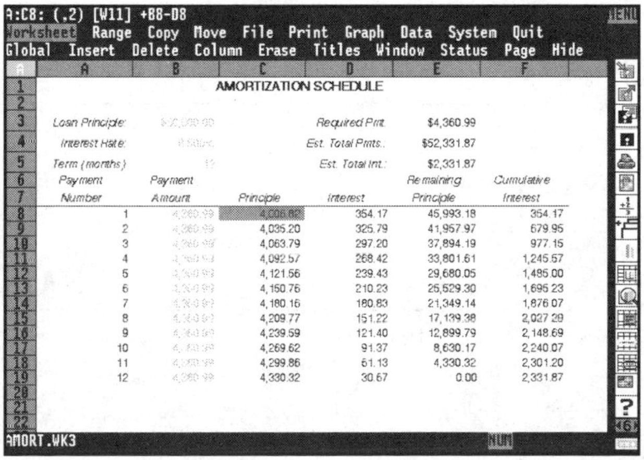

One of the big problems with the DOS versions of *1-2-3* is that they've been "enhanced" over the years (the interface dates from 1983, if you're

Figure 36. 1-2-3 for DOS pastes a few toolbars on top of its time-honored interface, but make no mistake, this is the most confusing menu system in the business.

interested), so it's hard even for experienced users to remember where to find the commands they need. A few new toolbars and dialog boxes help alleviate the confusion to some degree, offering quick access to common commands and consolidated settings for printing, graphics, and other multistep tasks.

An add-in program known as WYSIWYG (for "what you see is what you get") has been grafted onto the *1-2-3* for DOS versions to provide access to formatting, printing features, and enhanced graphics. To give you a sense of the problems lurking here, consider the printing systems—plural, that's right: one for WYSIWYG, one for the program itself. The two are wholly unrelated to each another; changing the settings under one has no effect on the other. Get the picture? Stay away!

The Top Six Spreadsheets From Best To Worst						
	Microsoft Excel 5.0	**1-2-3 for Windows 4.0**	**Quattro Pro for Windows 5.0**	**Quattro Pro for DOS 5.0**	**1-2-3 for DOS release 3.4**	**1-2-3 for DOS release 2.4**
Interface						
In-cell editing	Y	Y	N	N	N	N
Toolbars	Y	Y	Y	Y[1]	Y[1]	Y[1]
Drag-and-drop move or copy	Y	Y	Y	N	N	N
Definable autofill series	Y	Y	N	N	N	N
3-D worksheet structure	Y	Y	Y	Y	Y[1]	N
Analytics						
Data modeling	Y	Y[1]	Y	N	N	N
Worksheet consolidation	Y	Y	Y	Y	Y[1]	Y[1]
Automated scenario management	Y[1]	Y	Y	N	N	N
(continued next page)						

Figure 37: *This table compares only a small subset of spreadsheet features, but the ones listed are key. Excel covers the bases best—and it's also the easiest spreadsheet to use. Another clear message: Don't buy a DOS spreadsheet unless you have to.*

(Figure 38 continued)

The Top Six Spreadsheets From Best To Worst

	Microsoft Excel 5.0	1-2-3 for Windows 4.0	Quattro Pro for Windows 5.0	Quattro Pro for DOS 5.0	1-2-3 for DOS release 3.4	1-2-3 for DOS release 2.4
Analytics						
Statistical tools	Y	Y	Y	Y[1]	Y[1]	Y[1]
Analytical functions	Y	Y	Y	Y	Y[1]	Y[1]
Array formulas	Y	N	Y	N	N	N
Presentation						
Drawing	Y	Y	Y[1]	Y[1]	N	N
User-defined number formats	Y	N	Y	Y	N	N
Format painter tool	Y	Y	N	N	N	N
Slide shows	Y	N	Y	N	N	N
List Management						
Collapsible outlines	Y	N	N	N	N	N
List querying	Y	Y	Y[1]	Y[1]	Y	Y[1]
External database access	Y	Y	Y[1]	Y[1]	Y	N
Automatic subtotals	Y	N	N	N	N	N
Calculated query output fields	N	Y	N	N	Y	N
Importing text data	Y	Y[1]	Y[1]	Y[1]	Y[1]	Y[1]
Customizing						
User-defined functions	Y	N	N	N	N	N
On-screen controls	Y	N	Y	N	N	N

[1]Feature poorly or only partly implemented

Product Directory

1-2-3 for Windows
1-2-3 release 3.4
1-2-3 release 2.4
Lotus Development Corp.
55 Cambridge Pkwy.
Cambridge, MA 02142
800/343-5414
617/577-8500

Excel 5.0
Microsoft Corp.
One Microsoft Way
Redmond, WA 98052
800/426-9400
206/882-8080

Quattro Pro for Windows
Quattro Pro for DOS
WordPerfect Corp.
1555 N. Technology Way
Orem, UT 84057
800/451-5151

16 Presentations

By Steve Sagman

- Five steps to creating a presentation
- Tips for choosing and using presentation software
- Specialized charting, from org charts to maps
- The big screen: slides, overheads and projection

Long after Ross Perot has faded from memory, his handful of home-made charts will live on. Those simple graphs enabled millions to understand what the deficit was and why it was important.

Good visuals can make or break any presentation. But unless your message is mainly rhetorical, you not only need graphs, but also outlinelike word charts to lead your audience (and you) through your material. Plus you need handouts to give people something to think about later.

Presentation software is designed precisely to handle all these tasks. If you need a single chart for a report, use a spreadsheet program; if you need a picture or two, use paint or draw software. But if you plan to *present* information using 35mm slides, flip charts, overhead transparencies, or even animation with sound, then you've come to the right chapter.

Presentations Step by Step

Few people do dog-and-pony shows for a living. Presentation software developers know this, and they focus on creating programs that you can learn in a hurry so you can produce visual aids quickly yet not be embarrassed by the results.

All the top Windows presentation programs take pretty much the same tack. What distinguishes them as *presentation* programs, as opposed to programs that merely create charts, are automated features that ensure that each *slide* (sometimes called a *page*) fits in with the presentation as a whole. Here's how you build a presentation using any Windows presentation software.

Step 1: Choose a Design

All presentation programs come with a set of *templates* or *masters* that establish an overall design that applies to every slide in a presentation. Most templates include:

- **A background** with color shading and graphics for 35mm slides, or simple black-and-white graphics for transparencies

- **One or two fonts** in a couple of weights, sizes, and/or colors

- **A color scheme** that ensures graphs, fonts, and the background are complementary

- **Layouts** with placeholders for titles, subtitles, bullet points, and graphics

Each template contains a half-dozen or more slide layouts. Some layouts have placeholders for graphs, others for words only, but every slide has a place for a title to summarize the slide's message. You can edit layouts and backgrounds with graphics tools (change the color, add a logo, whatever) and, if you're willing to spend the time, you can create backgrounds from scratch.

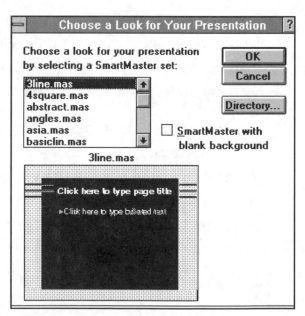

Figure 1: *Most presentation programs offer a whole gallery of presentation templates and display a preview of the choice you're about to make.*

Most programs give you a big selection of templates to choose from so that you can set the right tone for your audience—funky for a grassroots political organization, stately for the town planning board. You simply preview templates on screen and decide which seems best for the occasion. Later, when you've finished creating your presentation and you want to pitch the same message to a different audience, you can select a different template and instantly change the *look* of every slide without changing the content.

HOT TIP

Step 2: Organize Information

Once you choose a template, it's time to work on the content. You've got a choice here. You can:

- Throw words and graphs onto slides until you've exhausted all you have to say and organize the slides later, as most people do.

- Massage your ideas in an outline first, and *then* do the slides.

The advantage to working with an outline first is that you can enter all the slide titles and bullet points on one screen and edit or reshuffle that text very easily. Remember, though, that an outline is just one *view* of a presentation: Switch to slide view, and you'll see the text you've entered, neatly laid out on a series of slides.

REMEMBER

This works both ways, so if you enter text in the slide view first, each slide's title will appear as a main heading on the outline, while bulleted points will appear as subsidiary items. While in outline mode, you can move bulleted items from one slide to another and reorder slides by dragging slide titles up and down the list.

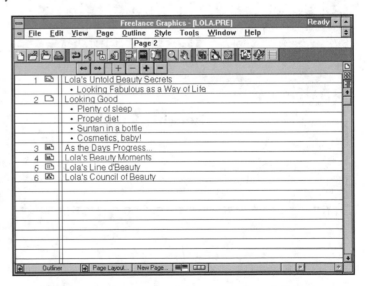

Figure 2: *Outline mode isn't pretty, but many people use it for brainstorming. You can view the entire outline, or you can "collapse" it down to the slide titles alone.*

REMEMBER

Whether you start with an outline or not, make sure that each slide tells a single story—and not all stories are best told with words. If you plan on using a graph on one slide, you probably need only a slide title and the graph itself.

Step 3: Create Slides

The first step in creating a slide is to choose the slide layout. You get layouts for word charts, several more for graphs, and a few that combine text and graphs.

HOT TIP

Graphs (officially known as data charts) should be used sparingly in most presentations. True, a bar chart or a pie chart is easier to understand than a cryptic table of numbers, but unless you're dealing with a knowledgeable audience hungry for data, you don't want to bombard people with graphs. Use graphs to support only the most important points in your presentation.

- **Title slides** start presentations or begin presentation segments. Along with the background, they typically include the name of the organization you're addressing, the topic, and maybe a logo—but nothing more.

Figure 3: *Though just a few words on a background, title slides are worth spending some time on, since they help set the tone for a presentation.*

Figure 4: *So what happened to the graphs? In fact, most presentations are made up of bullet charts like this one.*

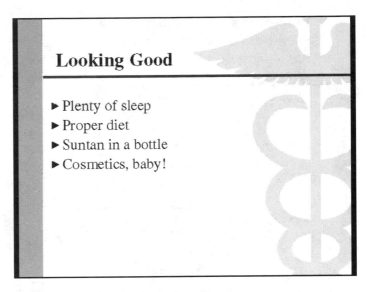

Bullet charts, also known as *word charts*, make up the bulk of most presentations. They help you and your audience remember what you're talking about. They're also handy for reviewing key points.

Figure 5: *Bar charts compare values from one time interval to another, while line charts emphasize trends. Bar/line charts like this one can show how a trend tracks against changing quantities.*

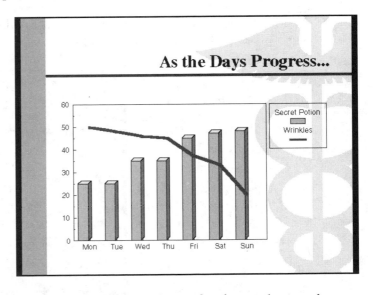

- **Bar charts** compare quantities at evenly spaced time intervals—by week, month, quarter, year, and so on. They emphasize each interval's *data point*, the individual numeric value represented by the bar height. ("Here's the revenue from our LA outlet in June, July, and August.")

- **Line charts** show continuous change over time. They emphasize trends rather than the individual data points that make up the line. ("Costs have gone through the roof over the last six months.")

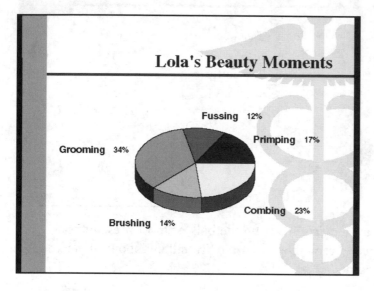

Figure 6: *Pie charts are great for showing percentages, or any breakdown of values that make up a whole.*

- **Pie charts** break down any total quantity into individual slices. ("Here's our share of the market compared with our competitors.")

Figure 7: *Keep table charts simple and easy to interpret, whether you use a handful of numbers or a few blocks of text.*

Lola's Line d'Beauty

Product	Restorative Effect
Eau de la Peanut	Natural Essence Replenitive
La Melone	Enhances vigor
Tears of the Heart	Reinvigorates passions once lost

- **Table charts** line up text or numbers in rows and columns. Use numbers in a table when the results are so dramatic that a data chart isn't needed. Use text in a table to dramatize a comparison such as pros and cons.

Figure 8: Although it's easy to create organization charts like this one with a presentation program, you need a specialized program (covered later in this chapter) to create big, complicated org charts.

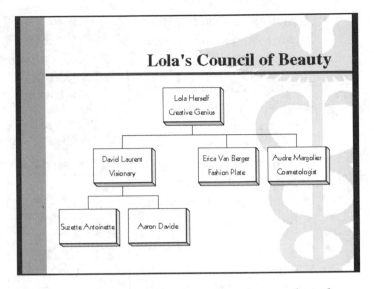

- **Organization charts** are tree-structure diagrams that show the pecking order of people, departments, or divisions. You fill in the blanks, and the program automatically creates boxes with lines drawn between them.

When you request a graph, most presentation graphics programs open a special data entry window. Here's where you type in the numbers—just click OK when you're done, and the program turns the numbers into a graph. If the data is in a word processor, spreadsheet, or database program, you can copy the numbers into the data window and avoid retyping. You can even set up a link between two Windows applications that will update a data chart when the numbers change in the original program.

Step 4: Enhance Slides

The consistent look enforced by design templates makes your presentation look custom designed. To soften up your audience even more, you can easily add a motif to the template background—your audience's company logo, say—so it shows up on every slide.

HOT TIP

For these and other modifications, check out your program's drawing tools. You won't find as rich a set of features as true draw programs offer, but you still get:

- **Line drawing tools** that let you stretch straight lines from point to point, add arrowheads, or manipulate curved or freehand lines ad infinitum

- **Shape drawing tools** for squares, circles, triangles, trapezoids, and so on, all of which you can size and stretch easily

- **Text tools** for adding text in any available font or size anywhere on a slide

- **Editing commands** to move, size, rotate, blend, or skew graphic objects (you should also be able to fill objects with shaded color and group objects so you can easily manipulate several of them at a time)

- **Clip art,** that is, predrawn symbols or cartoonlike images that you can size and position easily

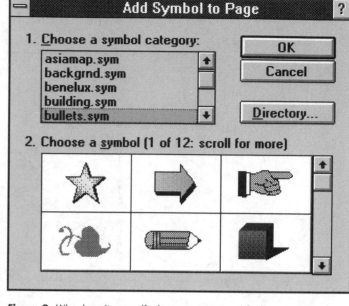

The best programs deliver a full palette of drawing tools

Figure 9: Why draw it yourself when you can copy it? All presentation programs come with clip art you can use to liven things up.

HOT TIP

and commands. What if you don't have the time or the talent to use them? Then use clip art. Every presentation program comes with a clip art library containing hundreds of symbols and images. Audiences love this stuff, especially when it enhances the meaning of a slide and makes a presentation more fun.

Of course, you won't find your company logo in a clip art library. If you need it for a presentation but you don't want to draw it, you can always scan it and import the image into your presentation (for more on scanners, see Chapter 7: *Input Devices*). Along with such scanned image file formats as PCX and TIF, presentation programs accept graphics and text in many other file formats, giving you a wide array of outside sources for graphic enhancements.

Step 5: Create the Output

With the design, content, and enhancement complete, you're ready to turn your presentation into something tangible.

- **Overhead transparencies.** You can print quality black-and-white transparencies for overhead projectors using any laser or ink jet printer. If you created the presentation in color, the program will automatically translate those hues to shades of gray. With a color printer, even an inexpensive ink jet, you'll get decent color quality and quite a bit more impact. If you don't have a color printer, you can always hire a service bureau (see below) to produce color transparencies. Some people have a bunch of transparencies with color logos and borders printed at once; then they print the presentation content on top with a laser printer.

- **35mm slides.** For vibrant colors and crisp images, nothing beats 35mm slides. But unless you buy an expensive device called a *film recorder* to make your own slides, you'll have to rely on an outside service bureau. Typically, you send your finished presentation to the service bureau via modem and receive the finished slides by Fed Ex a couple of days later (see "Slides and Service Bureaus" at the end of this chapter).

- **Flip charts.** Good for small groups, flip charts are bound hard copies of slides that you put on a little stand and flip through as you talk. Most presenters print their flip charts in color and pass out black-and-white handouts. Flip charts have one big advantage: You don't have to mess with a projector, fool with the shades, or turn out the lights.

HOT TIP

- **Electronic presentations.** Many mobile presenters like on-screen presentations best for small groups. No muss, no fuss, no projector: Just bring your color laptop and a few handouts. Most of the time, you simply page through full-screen versions of your slides and maybe add some eye-grabbing transitions from slide to slide. But depending on how fancy you want to get, you can also add animation, sound, and even video clips.

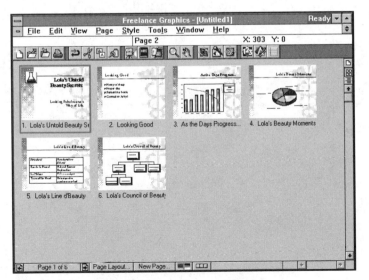

- **Handouts.** These are basically paper copies of the slides you've created. Decide how many slides you want to appear on each page, and whether you want to add blank lines so your audience can take notes. Then print away. Remember to make enough photocopies for everybody.

REMEMBER

- **Speaker notes.** These are notes for your eyes only. Just type in the things you want to say beneath each slide and print out the pages.

Figure 10: Here's "slide sorter" mode. In this bird's-eye view, you can check the slides one last time and reorganize them just by clicking and dragging. You can even copy slides from one presentation to another.

Top Ten Presentation Tips

1. **Observe the Rule of Threes.** This old cliché about public speaking has more than a grain of truth. Follow it, and you'll never lose your audience:

    A.   Tell them what you're going to tell them.

    B.   Tell them.

    C.   Tell them what you just told them.

2. **One message per slide.** Don't get bollixed up in multiple messages. Every bullet point in a word chart should relate to the issue at hand. Use more than one graph per slide for comparative purposes only. Let the sequence of slides reveal the story.

3. **Use the slide title to summarize.** To reinforce a slide's message, use "Product X Outpaces Competition" rather than "Sales of Product X."

4. **Keep bullet points short.** Because most presentations are text, concise, simple phrases are key. Write headlines, not paragraphs—the fewer the words, the stronger your point. The same goes for slide titles.

5. **No more than a dozen bars** in a bar chart. If you need to show more data, break down the data into separate charts.

6. **No more than six lines** in a line chart—fewer if the lines cross.

7. **No more than six slices** in a pie chart. If the numbers break down further, then total the rest in an "all others" slice, with a separate pie to show the "all others" breakdown if necessary.

8. **Arrange pie slices from largest to smallest,** and *explode* (that is, detach) the slice you want to draw attention to.

9. **Always use handouts.** If your audience takes them along, there's no better way to keep your message alive. And they're a great fallback if the projector breaks. Handouts also help people (especially the nearsighted) follow along.

10. **Practice, practice, practice.** It's the secret to any good presentation. Nervous? If possible, practice in the room where you'll be giving the presentation.

Freelance Graphics for Windows

Freelance Graphics for Windows doesn't dump a set of presentation tools in your lap. Instead, it coddles you every step of the way, from choosing a template, to selecting a slide type, to filling in data for graphs. An animated tutorial gets you up and running fast, and if you get stuck, clicking on a nearby Tips or Explain button pops up helpful information. No kidding: This may be the easiest–to–use application ever written.

Smart Templates

Called "SmartMaster Sets" in *Freelance* lingo, templates include a background design, a color palette, font selections, and 11 different slide layouts. The dozens of SmartMaster Sets that come with *Freelance* are the best in the business—you won't find more distinctive or interesting designs anywhere. Better yet, they're incredibly easy to work with.

- **"Click here..." blocks.** These blocks appear on every slide layout. Click on a block labeled "Click here to add a chart," for example, and *Freelance* guides you through choosing a chart type and entering data, and it replaces the block with the finished chart. "Click here..." blocks for text pop up a text-editing window, while "Click here..." blocks for symbols summon the well-organized symbols library. How can you go wrong?

- **Editing layouts.** Everyone seems to like the same SmartMaster Sets, so you may want to be original and change yours. To add a symbol to every slide, for example, open a new file, choose a SmartMaster set, and select Basic Layout. Press (Shift)(F9) to switch into Edit Page Layouts mode. Click on the light bulb icon in the drawing tools palette, choose your symbol, click OK, and then press (Shift)(F9) again. The graphic will appear on every

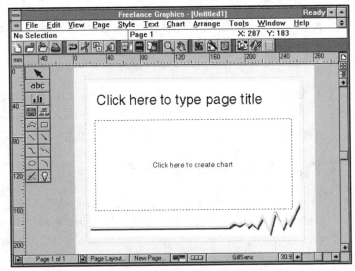

Figure 11: *"Click here," and Freelance leads you through every step. When you're done with a slide, a button on the status bar (bottom) calls up the next slide layout, while a palette of drawing tools (left) makes enhancements easy.*

slide except the title slide. Changing a template's background colors is even easier: Select Background from the Page menu, choose the new colors, and make sure you click on Entire presentation in the dialog box.

HOT TIP

Push-Button Shortcuts

Even if you have a fast PC, it takes time for changes to take effect. To save those seconds,

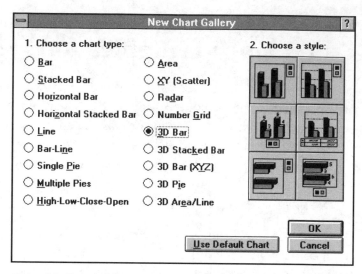

Figure 12: *Typical of Freelance's friendliness, this dialog box leads you through the charting process one step at a time.*

nearly every *Freelance* dialog box has a Preview button, so you can sneak a peek at what you want to try *before* you do it. Here's some other *Freelance* advice:

HOT TIPS

- **When in doubt, double-click.** Double-clicking on any object in a slide—a symbol, a title, a bar in a bar chart—opens a window or a dialog box that enables you to change that object's attributes. Double-click on text, for example, and the Paragraph Styles box appears; double-click on anything but a bar in a bar chart, and the data window opens. And so on.

- **If still in doubt, right-click.** A pop-up menu always appears when you click on an object with the right mouse button. Most options bring up familiar dialog boxes, but you usually get other choices as well.

- **One-click black and white.** A button on *Freelance*'s status bar (at the bottom of the screen) switches a color presentation to black and white and back again. So if you print slides on a laser printer, you can see what you'll get.

The Power Trade-Off

Freelance is easy in part because it has fewer options, particularly when it comes to charting. Compared with either *Harvard Graphics* or *PowerPoint*, you'll find fewer chart types, and chart formatting is limited: While you can "explode" a pie chart slice, for example, you can't adjust the distance between the slice and the pie. Worse, you can't position chart legends wherever you want them.

Such limitations are the trade-off for being able to learn this program and crank out your first presentation in a couple of hours or less. If you give occasional presentations and don't want to waste time learning the fine points, you can produce acceptable output with *Freelance* faster than with any other program.

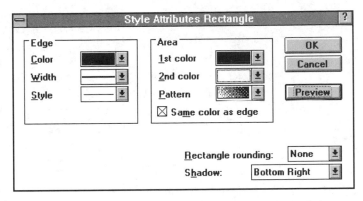

Figure 13: *Use the right mouse button to click on a graph, a symbol, or a piece of text, and Freelance pops up a mini menu of appropriate options. Pick an option (Attributes, in this case) and you get a handy little dialog box.*

Harvard Graphics for Windows

Nobody does charts like *Harvard Graphics for Windows*. You'll find many more chart formatting options than *Freelance* offers, along with considerably more drawing power for enhancing slides. All this, and *Harvard* is nearly as easy to learn and use as *Freelance*, too. If you give presentations regularly, this program's added power will definitely come in handy.

Although *Harvard's* templates lack the design flair of *Freelance's*, they help you format presentations from top to bottom in much the same way. Just as with *Freelance*, you select a template when you start a new presentation, but *Harvard* also lets you check out a template's individual slide layouts before you make up your mind. Some other *Harvard* highlights:

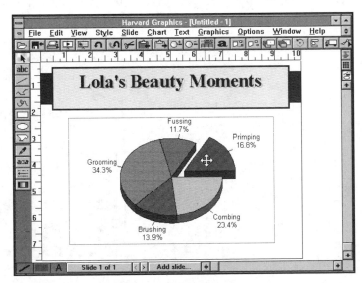

Figure 14: *Unlike Freelance, Harvard Graphics lets you edit charts at will. To detach a pie slice, for example, you just click and drag.*

- **Charting with all the extras.** For serious charting, Harvard tops them all. For example, to cut a slice from a pie chart, you click on it and drag it as far as you like from the rest of the pie. To move a legend to any location, clicking and dragging will do the trick, too. Want to get fancy and

HOT TIP

HOT TIP

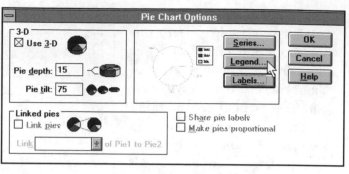

Figure 15: Harvard's dialog boxes don't just tell you, they show you. Put your pointer on a button, and the affected portion of the chart is highlighted.

fill a bar in a bar chart with a scanned photo? Just select the bar and import the graphic. If you can imagine it, you can probably do it with *Harvard*.

- **The usual conveniences, and more.** Clicking on any object with the right mouse button has the same effect as double-clicking the left button in *Freelance*—a dialog box appears with all the options for that object. Also, many dialog boxes include a little picture of the object you're editing, so if you're not sure what a "series" is, for example, dragging your pointer over the Series button will show you.

- **Drawing power.** *Harvard* comes with a sophisticated drawing program called Harvard F/X. As the name suggests, along with the usual drawing tools, you get a whole range of effects—you can rotate objects, make them glow, or even have them cast reflections.

- **Network conferencing.** Like all presentation programs, *Harvard* will do a "slide show" on your monitor. But the program is unique in its support for electronic presentations over the network. Up to 64 users can view the same ScreenShow simultaneously (and "chat" with each other from the keyboard as it runs), perfect for training or broadcasting information.

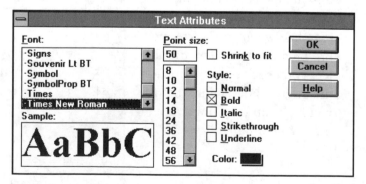

Figure 16: To summon a dialog box with all the options, such as this one for text attributes, just click on any object with the right mouse button.

The main drawback to *Harvard* is that it may cost you more than either *Freelance* or *PowerPoint*. Lotus and Microsoft sell tempting software "suites" that include a spreadsheet, a word processor, E-mail, and presentation software, all for less than $500. Software Publishing has no such suite deals. For about $250, you get *Harvard*, period.

That's no problem if you just want a presentation program—especially since *Harvard* is the leader when it comes to features. If it's harder to learn than *Freelance*, that's mostly due to a bigger toolbox, something frequent presenters can appreciate.

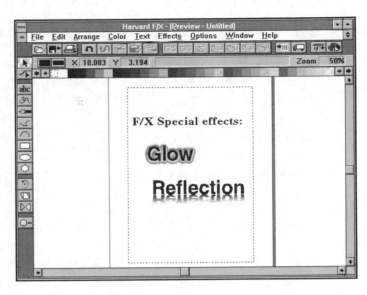

Figure 17: *When the Harvard F/X drawing program is active, an extended drawing toolbar appears, and you get a readout of drawing coordinates for professional-quality drawing precision.*

Microsoft PowerPoint

Think of *PowerPoint* as the presentation component of the *Microsoft Office* suite. Many of the ingenious interface touches found in the latest versions of *Word for Windows* and *Excel* show up here, too—quick text selection tricks, tutorial-style help as you work, shortcut menus that pop up when you click the right mouse button, and more. If you already use another Microsoft application, you'll quickly get the hang of *PowerPoint*. If you don't, it's still easy to learn, though not quite as easy as *Freelance*.

PowerPoint uses the same charting module as *Excel*. It has more charting power than *Freelance*, but not as much as *Harvard*, and creating charts is the toughest part about using the program. When it comes to creating and organizing a presentation, however, the program does very well. For example, PowerPoint is the only program with a slide sorter view that shows you transition effects between slides. Other good features include:

- **Wizards.** Like other Microsoft applications, *PowerPoint* offers Wizards, which are friendly dialog boxes that lead you through a process step by step. In *PowerPoint*, they hand you a prewritten presentation that you customize with your own facts and figures.

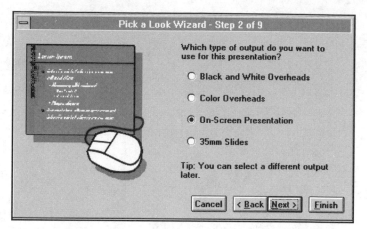

Figure 18: PowerPoint's Wizard dialog boxes coach you through every stage of creating a presentation, offering useful tips along the way.

- **AutoLayouts.** AutoLayouts are similar to the "Click here..." page layouts that make *Freelance* so easy to use. Choose a basic bullet chart from the set of 21 AutoLayouts, for example, and just click on a block to enter text, which automatically adopts the formatting built into the layout.

HOT TIP

- **Embeddable fonts.** Here's a nifty capability that only *PowerPoint* has. Normally, if you create a presentation with certain fonts on one PC and do a screen show on another PC that lacks those fonts, the second system will use substitute fonts that don't work as well. *PowerPoint* lets you *embed* Windows TrueType fonts so they travel with the presentation, no matter what PC you use for the screen show.

- **Better organization charts.** *PowerPoint* has the best organization charts of any presentation program, enabling you to create multilevel, tree-structured diagrams with ease.

- **Text effects.** Like *Word for Windows* and *Publisher*, *PowerPoint* comes with WordArt, which lets you rotate text, enhance it with drop shadows, fill it with patterns, and so on. For technical presentations, you get the same equation editor included with *Word*.

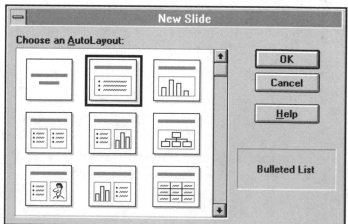

Figure 19: Each PowerPoint template includes 21 AutoLayouts, more prefab layouts for text and charts than any other presentation program offers.

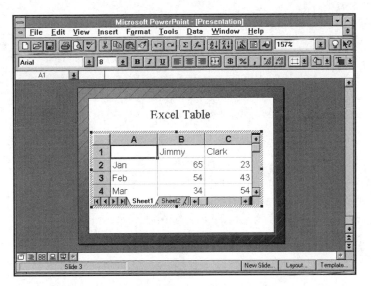

Figure 20: *PowerPoint is so closely linked to other Microsoft products, you can actually pop up another application within PowerPoint, as this Excel spreadsheet shows.*

- **Integration with other Microsoft applications.** Like *Freelance*, *PowerPoint* comes with buttons that call up other applications in the suite—so you can switch to your spreadsheet, create a table, and drag it into a presentation, for example. But *PowerPoint* goes a step further. Click on the *Excel* button, for instance, and you can edit a table using *Excel* commands without leaving *PowerPoint*. As you work, *Excel*'s toolbars and menus replace *PowerPoint*'s, then retreat

HOT TIP

when you're done. Later, just double-click on the table, and *Excel* will pop up within *PowerPoint* again.

As should be clear by now, if you already use *Word* or *Excel*, go with *PowerPoint*. Shared terminology, menus, procedures, and dialog boxes mean you'll feel like you already know how to use the program, and tight integration gives you the full power of other applications as you create your presentation. Yes, *Freelance* is a little easier, and *Harvard* has better charting, but *PowerPoint* manages to split the difference between the two pretty well.

Other Windows Presenters

Here's a quick look at several other Windows presentation programs. Pay special attention to *WordPerfect Presentations*, especially if you use *WordPerfect for Windows*.

- **Aldus Persuasion.** Though as powerful as the market leaders, *Persuasion* isn't as easy to use. It takes more brainwork to get the same job done in this program, and some important conveniences are lacking—it won't convert color presentations to black and white with a single click, for example. It's still a very popular program on the Mac, though, so people moving from Mac to PC may find it convenient.

- **CorelChart.** This is the charting component of *CorelDraw*, the most popular drawing program. You can't easily create consistent backgrounds, and you won't find outline or slide sorter views. But CorelChart produces stunning charts, complete with such niceties as image- and texture-filled backgrounds and bars. You can even perform spreadsheetlike calculations on its data sheet, and create sophisticated 3-D charts with perspective. If you want superb graphs for a report, consider using CorelChart.

- **Charisma.** Like *Persuasion*, *Charisma* is a presentation package strong on power but short on ease of use. Unless you buy a technical graphics program like *Stanford Graphics*, you won't find more flexibility or sophistication. An upcoming version promises to have an outliner and the ability to produce electronic presentations, so make sure you check it out.

- **WordPerfect Presentations.** If you use *WordPerfect for Windows* to crunch words, then *WordPerfect Presentations for Windows* may be your best bet. You'll find many of the same clever features: shortcut menus that pop up when you right-click, button bars that change depending on what you're doing, and an extensive help system. The program has both outline and slide sorter views, along with a unique split-screen view that shows how changing data affects a chart. You can even use the program to scan images directly into a presentation slide and then edit those images. This package is no slouch when it comes to charting and drawing, either, so put it on your short list of packages to consider.

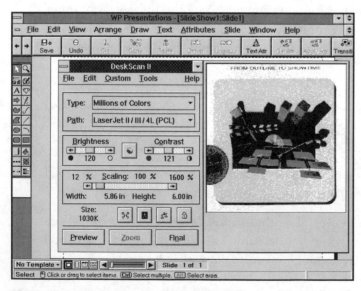

Figure 21: *WordPerfect Presentations for Windows is an excellent choice for users of WordPerfect for Windows, the word processor.*

If You Must Do It in DOS

Windows presentation programs give you a continuous view of the way your slides will look as you create them. DOS programs don't. Instead, you need to switch to a preview mode, where you can't make changes. That fact alone means you should resort to DOS presentation programs only if your PC absolutely refuses to run Windows. If so, consider the DOS versions of *Harvard Graphics*, *Freelance Graphics*, and—best of all—*WordPerfect Presentations*.

REMEMBER

Harvard Graphics

Harvard Graphics was the top DOS charting package for years. The reason? Its fill-in-the-blanks approach to creating charts is so easy, you can create single slides fast, without learning much about the program.

The latest version offers several Windows-like presentation features—you can apply a common background to several slides at a time, for example. But each chart you create is stored in a separate file, and *Harvard* offers no outliner or slide sorter. The real strength of this program is its high-quality charting, plus a drawing module that gives you a big helping of fancy effects, such as the ability to convert text to graphic shapes and fill those shapes with shaded color.

Still, *Harvard Graphics for Windows* outpaces the DOS version in every area. Moreover, the DOS version is a dead end, since Software Publishing Corporation has announced there will be no further upgrades.

Freelance Graphics

Lotus's *Freelance Graphics* has always been the number two DOS package, right behind *Harvard*. It has plenty of drawing features, and the charts work just fine, but many people find it much more difficult to use than *Harvard*.

As usual with DOS, it's hard to manage presentations as a whole. Compared with *Harvard*, the DOS version of *Freelance* has only two basic advantages: slightly tighter integration with the DOS version of *1-2-3*, and an outliner you can use to enter slide text (though you can't use it to reorder slides once they're done).

WordPerfect Presentations for DOS

If you must do it in DOS, then this is the software to use. *WordPerfect Presentations for DOS* brings the presentation finesse of a Windows program—templates, outliner, slide sorter, and so on—to DOS, along with a user interface that mimics *WordPerfect Presentations for Windows*. The DOS version has other things in common with the Windows version: You can edit scanned photos, add sound files to presentations, and work with a split-screen view of both a chart and its data sheet. If *WordPerfect* is your word processor, you'll find this program very easy to learn.

The Charting Specialists

Beyond the realm of everyday presentations lie specialized packages that help you present scientific, statistical, process, and organizational data. Here are some of the most popular programs in each category.

Scientific and Statistical

Even *Harvard Graphics* runs out of gas when you need to do surface modeling, three-variable scatter plots, error-bar graphs, and other charts favored by the pocket-protector set. These two are the leaders:

- **DeltaGraph Professional for Windows.** DeltaPoint's hugely powerful charting package also offers presentation management features. Its data sheet includes dozens of formulas, so you can crunch numbers without exiting the program. *DeltaGraph* is not especially easy to use, though.

- **Stanford Graphics.** Created with the technical presenter in mind, Visual Numerics' *Stanford Graphics* excels at power charting and data analysis, offering 167 business, statistical, scientific, and custom charts. This Windows program also includes an outliner, design templates, and speaker's notes, along with simple screen show effects.

Flowcharts and Org Charts

Flowcharts describe processes. Organization charts describe structures. Both use simple geometric symbols and connecting lines to do the job. As with presentation programs, the flowchart and org chart packages worth buying run under Windows.

- **ABC Flowcharter,** from Micrografx, takes the grief out of connecting arrows and boxes. You can create multidimensional flowcharts that show processes within processes, so when you give an electronic presentation, you can just click on a symbol and see the subprocess underneath.

- **OrgPlus for Windows,** from Banner Blue Software, can create charts with up to 32,000 members. To add an employee to an organization, you choose the level

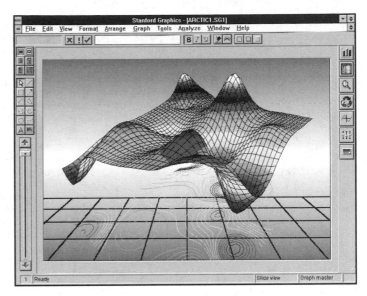

Figure 23: *If you don't know what this Stanford Graphics chart means, then you probably don't need a technical charting program.*

and branch and then enter the text. To rearrange the structure, you simply drag boxes around. Templates of organization structures help you get started, and when you polish things off, you can incorporate scanned employee pictures. A command called Make Fit automatically sizes charts so they fit on the printed page. *OrgPlus* even lets you embed an organization chart in another Windows application.

- **Windows OrgChart** is a fine alternative from Micrografx, with org chart features similar to those offered by *OrgPlus for Windows.*

Don't overlook the organization charts offered by most presentation programs. They can't handle complexity the way these products can, but they're easy to use—and you get an org chart slide formatted to fit in your presentation.

Mapping Software

Every presentation program comes with a few clip art maps to liven up slides. But if you want to tie data to maps for analysis—say, to show market share by region—then you need mapping software.

Databases often include location-dependent information, so it's not surprising that the best mapping programs work with most database software or come with a database program built right in. As you update the database, the map changes dynamically. You can even use mapping software as a conventional database. To find all contacts within a certain distance, for example, you could click a spot on screen and pop up a list.

If the mapping software runs under Windows, you can easily copy a map into a Windows presentation. If the mapping software runs under DOS, make sure it can export a graphics file that you can import into your presentation software. Here are some packages I recommend:

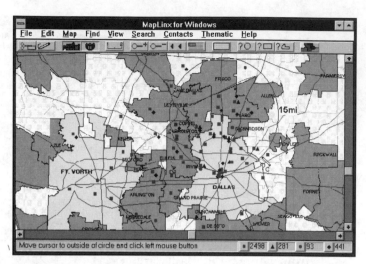

Figure 24: *Mapping software isn't just for show. This MapLinx display ties a huge hunk of data to the map, so you can see the effect of changing statistics in a database.*

- **MapLinx for Windows.** This Windows program can display data from *Act!* and *dBASE* on U.S. maps, and it lets you perform queries by drawing on the screen. It's the easiest of the mapping programs to use and can do just about anything the average business person would ask of it, as long as international maps aren't required.

- **MapInfo.** This program has lots of features, but it requires some learning time. It's a full geographic relational database, with database querying, viewing, and editing features. It can also shade regions in maps to represent statistical information, and it can size symbols according to numeric data (a larger oil barrel on a state that produces more oil, for example). *MapInfo* is the software to buy if analyzing and displaying location-dependent data is an important part of what you do.

Slides and Service Bureaus

When you're pitching to a big audience, nothing beats the quality of 35mm slides. But unless you're a professional presenter, don't bother paying the big bucks for your own 35mm slide-making equipment. But don't buy an inexpensive film recorder, either, because you'll get slides that fall short of professional quality. Instead, send your finished presentation files to an outside service bureau.

Service bureaus take a file you've sent by mail, messenger, or modem and produce superb 35mm slides with their own professional equipment. They ship finished slides by overnight delivery, so if you submit your file by the daily deadline, you should have your slides the next morning. The cost usually ranges from $4 to $10 per slide. Local bureaus sometimes offer same-day service, but expect to pay three to four times the price for each slide.

The top presentation programs make sending files to a service bureau a no-brainer. All you need is a modem. *Harvard* and *Freelance*, for example, create files specifically for the Autographix slide service. With a couple of mouse clicks, you dial Autographix's 800 number, and off goes the file. *PowerPoint* has a similar automated feature for sending files to Genigraphics.

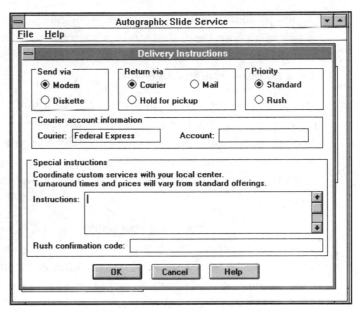

Figure 25: *Just fire up your modem and check a few options in this Harvard Graphics for Windows dialog box, and your presentation will be sent electronically to the Autographix slide service bureau.*

Note that if your presentation is especially long or has lots of graphics or scanned images, you should check with the service first to see if sending it by modem is practical. **HOT TIP**

Smaller, local service bureaus can do a fine job with your presentations, too. Before you send a rush job to a local slide house, though, request any special information about generating slides using your presentation software. Many service bureaus will be happy to provide you with tips to prevent problems that could muck up your slides. **HOT TIP**

Big-Screen Electronic Presentations

Video projectors and color LCD panels offer an attractive alternative to 35mm slides. They can't match the crisp text and vivid colors of 35mm film, but they're not bad when the lights are low. Moreover, you get these benefits:

• You avoid the cost of generating 35mm slides

• The presentation can be edited up to the last minute

• You can include sound, animation, and video clips and branch off into further explanatory screens if your audience has questions. (Try *that* with slides.)

Video projectors, such as those made by Sony or Barco, are fine when you are giving a talk in a room that's designed for such things. You'll probably find a computer projection system hanging from the ceiling of the auditorium or conference room. In that case, you just plug in and begin.

But your next pitch is far more likely to be a BYOS (Bring-Your-Own-System) affair, and you're not going to lug a video projector everywhere you go (especially since you're already carrying a laptop with your presentation on its hard disk). Instead, slip a color LCD panel into your bag and place it on an ordinary overhead projector when you arrive at your destination. Then plug your laptop into the panel, and you're ready to go.

LCD panels use the same technology as the displays in laptop computers. And if you've seen the latest laptop color displays, you know the color quality is pretty impressive. At $4000 or $5000 a pop, color, active-matrix LCD panels are no bargain, but for the frequent presenter who never knows what the next location will bring, an LCD panel can recoup its cost quickly in convenience and quality. The leading LCD models come from InFocus Systems (PanelBooks), nView (ViewFrame or Media Pro), Proxima (Ovation), and Sharp (the QA series). The panel you buy should have:

- **A large screen.** The larger the screen, the more light can pass through, which means a brighter image. That's important, since you'll never get an image as bright as a slide to begin with.

- **Lots of colors.** The best panels offer 16.7 million, which makes a huge difference with scanned color photos and video clips. If your presentations are all text, a smaller color palette will suffice.

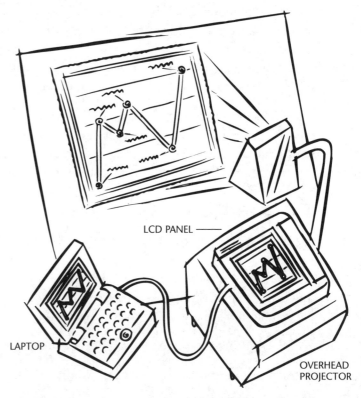

Figure 26: Put an LCD panel on an overhead projector, hook up your laptop, and you can project an electronic presentation on the wall, complete with animation and video clips.

- **A sharp image.** Make sure the panel is an *active-matrix* LCD for the best image quality.

- **A carrying case.** If your panel of choice doesn't come with a case, remember to buy one as an accessory. Make sure the case is sturdy—these panels tend to be a little delicate.

- **Easy-to-use controls.** The best LCD panels have controls for color, sharpness, and contrast on both the panel and the handheld remote control.

I highly recommend buying a panel with a remote—otherwise you'll have to scurry back to the laptop when you change slides. The less your audience is distracted by the technology, the more it's focused on your presentation.

HOT TIP

Product Directory

Presentation Software

Aldus Persuasion
Aldus Corp.
411 First Ave. South
Seattle, WA 98104
206/622-5500

Charisma
Micrografx Corp.
1303 Arapaho Rd.
Richardson, TX 75081
800/733-3729
214/234-1769

CorelDraw
Corel Corp.
1600 Carling Ave.
Ottawa, Ontario
Canada K1Z 8R7
800/772-6735
613/728-3733

Freelance Graphics
Freelance Graphics for Windows
Lotus Development Corp.
55 Cambridge Pkwy.
Cambridge, MA 02142
800/343-5414
617/577-8500

Harvard Graphics
Harvard Graphics for Windows
Software Publishing Corp.
3165 Kifer Rd.
Santa Clara, CA 95051
800/336-8360
408/986-8000

PowerPoint
Microsoft Corp.
1 Microsoft Way
Redmond, WA 98052-6399
800/227-4679
206/882-8080

WordPerfect Presentations
WordPerfect Presentations for Windows
WordPerfect Corp.
1555 N. Technology Way
Orem, UT 84057
800/526-5198
801/225-5000

Specialized Charting Software

ABC Flowcharter
Windows OrgChart
Micrografx Corp.
800/733-3729

DeltaGraph
DeltaPoint
2 Harris Ct. Ste. B1
Monterey, CA 93940
800/446-6955
408/648-4000

MapInfo

MapInfo Corp.
1 Global View
Troy, NY 11280
800/327-8627
518/285-6000

MapLinx for Windows

MapLinx Corp.
P.O. Box 690
Buffalo, NY 14207
800/352-3414
214/231-1400

OrgPlus for Windows

Banner Blue Software
P.O. Box 7865
Fremont, CA 94537
510/794-6850

Stanford Graphics

Visual Numerics
9990 Richmond Ave. # 400
Houston, TX 77042
800/729-4723
713/954-6424

Slide Services

Autographix
21 North Ave.
Burlington, MA 01803
800/548-8558

Genigraphics
Two Corporate Dr. #340
Shelton, CT 06484
800/638-7348

LCD Panel Manufacturers

InFocus Systems
7770 S.W. Mohawk St.
Tualatin, OR 97062
800/327-7231
503/692-4968

nView Corp.
860 Omni Blvd.
Newport News, VA 23606
800/736-8439

Proxima Corp.
6610 Nancy Ridge Dr.
San Diego, CA 92121
800/447-7694

Sharp Electronics Corp.
Sharp Plaza
Mahwah, NJ 07430
201/529-9636

17 Graphics Software

By Rick Altman

- The two types of graphics: vector vs. bit mapped
- CorelDraw, the hottest drawing package ever
- Other drawing programs: Illustrator, Visio, and AutoCAD
- Image edit and paint: Photoshop, Picture Publisher, and more
- Advice on assembling a graphics tool kit
- An overview of clip art and digitized stock photos
- Tips on printing color graphics
- A short course in graphics file formats

The best piece of advice I can give you about graphics software is this: Don't be so wowed by the special effects used by professional artists that you miss the great stuff anyone can do. True, programs like *CorelDraw* and *Photoshop* can create effects that would have required a $60,000 workstation a few years ago. But the cool thing is that you can easily use these same tools to spice up faxes, reports, and flyers with simple type manipulations and precooked clip art.

To create the following types of artwork, you don't have to be an expert—in fact, you don't even need the slightest ability to draw:

Figure 1: *This logo, produced with high-quality vector curves, has seen plenty of action since being placed into electronic service.*

- Full-color illustrations

- Logos

- Fancy headlines

- Photorealistic images

- Surrealistic images

- Charts, graphs, and pictograms

- Slide shows

- Animation sequences

- High-quality drawings from low-resolution originals

Once you create a piece of art, you can easily modify it and use it again and again. For example, my wife Rebecca and I hired a designer to produce a logo that would serve both of our writing and consulting businesses. Figure 1 shows the final work.

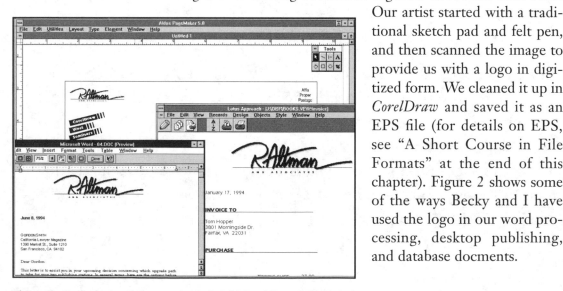

Our artist started with a traditional sketch pad and felt pen, and then scanned the image to provide us with a logo in digitized form. We cleaned it up in *CorelDraw* and saved it as an EPS file (for details on EPS, see "A Short Course in File Formats" at the end of this chapter). Figure 2 shows some of the ways Becky and I have used the logo in our word processing, desktop publishing, and database docments.

Figure 2: *Here's the logo being recycled in PageMaker, Microsoft Word, and Lotus Approach documents.*

Vector vs. Bit-Mapped Graphics

Graphics programs produce art in one of two ways: They generate curves, circles, lines, and rectangles based on mathematical formulas called *algorithms*; or they produce dots. That's it—geometric shapes or dots.

Programs that use the algorithm method are called *drawing programs*, and the geometric shapes they produce are called *vector* (or sometimes *object-oriented*) *graphics*. When you create a circle in a drawing program, that circle knows it's a circle. It understands that it has X and Y coordinates, a radius, a circumference, an outline, and an interior color. You can easily change the size or colors of the circle without compromising its integrity; it still knows that it is supposed to be a circle.

Programs that enable you to manipulate images dot by dot are called *paint programs* or *image editors*, and the artwork created by them is known as *bit-mapped graphics* (the term *bit-mapped* refers to the way the images are stored; one bit or group of bits in memory describes each dot in the picture). When you create a circle with a paint program, the circle is nothing more than a collection of dots, each with a specific color. You have to be very careful about altering its shape or size, because it doesn't know it's supposed to be a circle—it contains no information that might return it to a circle-like shape.

Is It a Bit Map or a Vector Graphic?	
How It Was Created	**Type of Graphic**
Scanned from an original photograph	Bit map
Scanned and then sent through an auto-tracing program	Started as a bit map but was converted into a vector graphic
Created from scratch in CorelDraw	Vector graphic
Created in Fractal Design Painter, Picture Publisher, or Photoshop	Bit map
A composite of a graphic created in CorelDraw and a scanned photo used as a background	Has both bit map and vector elements (that's allowed)

Figure 3: *This table gives you an idea of which software produces which type of graphic. Illustrators almost always use vector programs, while people who edit scanned images usually stick with bit-mapped graphics software.*

The Rewards of Vector Graphics

Vector drawing programs have the following advantages over bit-mapped graphics software:

- **High resolution.** When you print from vector drawing software, the objects in your drawing will print at the highest possible resolution. The software essentially tells the printer: "Print this object according to the vectors and mathematics I have established, and make the dots as close together as you possibly can."

- **Small files.** It takes less room to store a picture as a set of shapes than as a collection of individual dots.

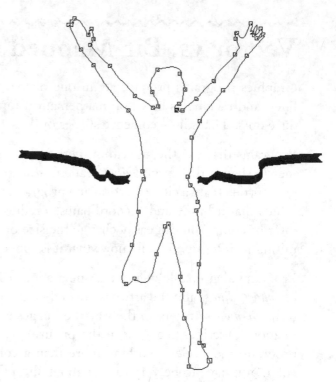

Figure 4: In drawing programs, you can change the shape of an image by dragging the nodes, also known as control points.

- **Fast printing and screen drawing.** Because the amount of data is smaller, vector drawing software transfers information faster to the monitor and to the printer.

- **Easy editing.** Vector art consists of curves, nodes, cusps, and other control points that determine the shapes of objects. These control points can be manipulated with ease.

- **Excellent control.** Figure 5 shows the difference between trying to draw a smooth arc in freehand mode and using the curve tool of a drawing program. Ironically, the ugly curve on top took me twice as long to draw as the clean one below.

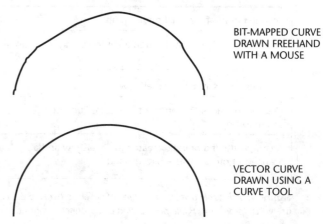

BIT-MAPPED CURVE DRAWN FREEHAND WITH A MOUSE

VECTOR CURVE DRAWN USING A CURVE TOOL

Figure 5: Using vector graphics, you can draw accurate, easily manipulated shapes fast. The perfect curve at bottom took only an instant to create.

The Pleasures of Bit-Mapped Graphics

Paint programs have the following advantages:

- **Editing down to the dot.** While there are no mathematical control points that describe bit-mapped images, you can control the dots themselves. You can zoom in on a person's eyebrow and pluck a few hairs that look too long, just by erasing the dots that make up the hairs.

- **Lifelike realism.** With control over every dot that makes up an image, you can imitate life at a level beyond vector programs. An image editor, coupled with a good scanner, allows you to start the image-creation process with an actual photograph.

For the most part, freehand illustration is now done almost entirely in vector formats, while image editing uses bit-mapped formats. Increasingly, however, artists are combining the best of both types of graphics in the same work.

It's Corel's World—We Just Live in It

CorelDraw holds an estimated 70 percent of the drawing market—all the other programs combined make up the other 30 percent. Along with being a a terrific Windows drawing program, *CorelDraw* has the added appeal of coming with a bunch of auxiliary programs. You get modules for editing bit-mapped images, creating charts, building slide shows, creating animated sequences, and—with the recent acquisition of *Ventura Publisher*—producing books, catalogs, and other complex documents (for more on *Ventura*, see Chapter 18: *Desktop Publishing*).

The question is: Which of this stuff is valuable and which isn't? Figure 6, which is based on comments by people at my *CorelDraw* seminars about which modules they actually use, sums it up.

As with all software that produces vector art, *CorelDraw* allows you to work with refined curves and other geometric shapes to produce precise effects. Its powerful typographic engine makes it easy for the accomplished artist to create logos and other text-based work, while its vast clip art library helps the artistically challenged. In fact, my ongoing *CorelDraw* seminars tell us that over 65 percent of all users of the software *do not* have a professional background in illustration and design.

Inside CorelDraw: From Drawing to Page Layout

Software Module	What It Does	How Good Is It?
Draw	The main module, used for all vector-based drawing and illustration	A great program: easy to use, yet remarkably powerful
Photo-Paint	The image-editing module, used for creating and manipulating bit-mapped art	Well designed, medium powered
Chart	The charting module, for creating two- and three-dimensional charts and graphs	Only a tiny percentage of people find much value in it
Show	The presentation module, for creating slide shows, self-running demos, and other computer-based presentations	Almost nobody uses it
Move	The animation module, for creating simple motion pictures	Almost nobody uses it
Trace	The auto-tracing module, for converting scanned images and other bit-mapped art into vector art	Worthwhile
Mosaic	The image-cataloging module, for creating libraries of illustrations and images	Worthwhile
Ventura Publisher	Page layout program	Worthwhile, but not available in versions prior to CorelDraw 5.0
Clip Art	12,000 images	A great value
Fonts	750 typefaces from Bitstream and ITC	Also a great value

Figure 6: *At seminars, surveys show that while the impressive CorelDraw bundle fulfills its marketing requirements, few users are thrilled by the ancillary programs.*

Is *CorelDraw* really that easy to use? Despite the huge number of features packed into the program, the answer is decidedly yes. The menus make sense, the screen icons seem at home, and most of the functions and dialog boxes invite you to try them before forcing you to retreat to the manual.

The CorelDraw Interface

CorelDraw's interface is notable not for its gee-whiz qualities but for its consistency and simplicity. It doesn't alter its appearance as you change modes or perform different operations.

The program's toolbar provides controls for selecting and shaping objects; editing the nodes and paths of objects; zooming in and out; creating lines, curves, rectangles, ovals, and text; and changing the outline and the interior fill of an object. Regardless of where you are in the program or what you're doing, you can always count on the toolbar to offer you those choices.

Along with the toolbar, you get *roll-up* dialog boxes, which are handy if you make continual and repeated changes to an object. You can move the roll-ups to any point on the screen, and they remain visible as you edit until you close them.

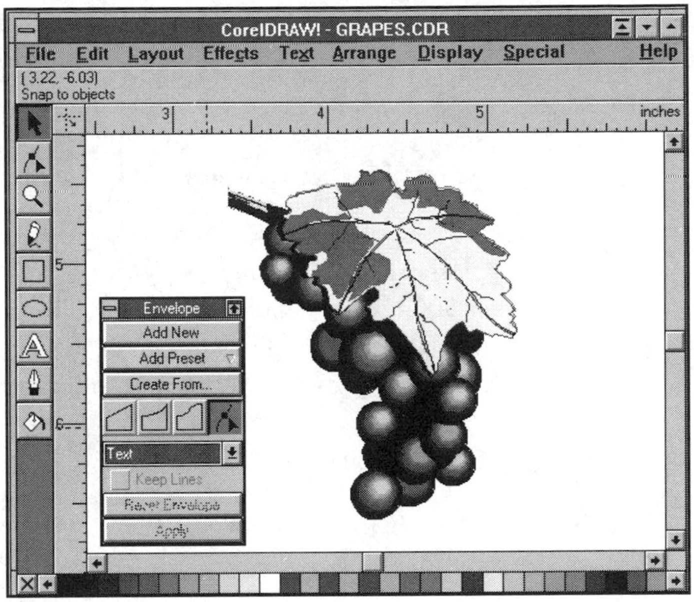

Figure 7: CorelDraw's roll-up dialog boxes stay on the screen as long as you want them, providing convenient access to special editing commands.

Under the Hood

Beneath its pretty face, *CorelDraw* packs a wallop of features. It sports an amazing array of tools, including those for:

- Creating elaborate fill patterns

- Super-flexible line widths, colors, patterns, and endings

- Automatic blending, whereby one shape turns into another

- Simulated perspective and dimension

- Calligraphic effects and support for pressure-sensitive drawing pads

- Layering and grouping objects for easy manipulation of drawing elements

- Full-color modeling, using all of the standard palettes, such as CMYK, Pantone, TruMatch, RGB, and HSB (see "The Color Conundrum" later in this chapter)

Cut-Rate Corel

Corel Corporation takes an unusual approach to marketing its software. When it introduces a new version, it doesn't discontinue the previous one—it cuts the price. Right now you have your choice of version 5.0 of *CorelDraw*, released in 1994; version 4.0, released in 1993; or version 3.0, released in 1992. Version 3.0 can be found for little more than $100 at discount software outlets, which is quite a bargain, considering all the clip art and fonts that come with it. Both CD ROM versions and floppy disk versions are available, but the CD ROM versions are cheaper.

- Styles you can use to copy formatting and design from one object to others

- Dozens of fast keys, shortcuts, and controls for precision movement and duplication of objects

- Automatic text flow across pages and inside or around objects

The *CorelDraw* user community regularly contributes to the software's overall value. User groups have been formed everywhere, and an international user conference attracts over 500 users annually from all over the world. There's also a monthly magazine, a newsletter, and an annual design contest that receives thousands of entries. All of these are excellent sources of tips on using the program.

CorelDraw Tips

Here are a few obvious and not-so-obvious tips that may help you get started using *CorelDraw*:

HOT TIPS

- A quick way to zoom in on a drawing by a factor of two is to set your right mouse button for 2x Zoom using the Special//Preferences menu—then all you have to do is click the right mouse button once.

- If you've moved your rulers in *CorelDraw*, you can (Shift)-double-click on the place where they meet to return them both to their default positions.

- To pick up where you left off editing a drawing, with the roll-ups you used last still in the same places, select View//Roll-Ups, and choose Save On Exit from the Start-Up settings drop-down box. (Avoid selecting All Roll-Ups Arranged; this option eats up lots of memory.)

- Normally, *CorelDraw* keeps track of your last four actions, so you can go backwards four steps by choosing Edit//Undo four times. If you want to be able to backtrack more than four times, choose Preferences from the Special menu and up the number of Undo Levels. The maximum is 99, but be forewarned that a high value will eat memory.

- Using *CorelDraw*'s cloning option (from the Edit menu) lets you make copies of an object that change to reflect any edits you make to the original object.

Other Drawing Programs

CorelDraw isn't the only game in town. Here are four of the most interesting illustration programs out there, including a couple that handle special functions better than *CorelDraw* can.

Adobe Illustrator: For High-Minded Artists

More than any other program, *Adobe Illustrator* helped define the field of electronic illustration and design. This program will have particular appeal if you use a PostScript printer, work in four-color reproduction, or need to communicate with Mac users. As you would expect from the developers of PostScript, Adobe Systems designed *Illustrator* to work well with PostScript fonts. But Adobe has taken its bias to an extreme: *Illustrator* doesn't support TrueType fonts at all (see Chapter 13: *Fonts* for more on TrueType).

Illustrator's files are Macintosh *binary compatible*, a fancy phrase that means an *Illustrator* file produced on a Mac will be in the exact same format as one produced under Windows. In addition, *Illustrator* supports more *color models* (professional color reproduction schemes; see "The Color Conundrum" at the end of this chapter) than any other package.

The program's tools cater to the professional designer who likes to follow a whim or an inspiration rather than a grid. It lacks many of the automatic tools and functions of its counterparts, but if you're producing a sketch from your own imagination or vision, that's not as important. If you need to replicate a precision drawing, you're likely to be frustrated by the program's lack of response and interaction.

Visio: A New Way of Looking at Graphics

Shapeware's *Visio* sits halfway between a standard graphics program and a collection of clip art. While programs like *Illustrator* and *Corel* provide you with exceptionally flexible tools for creating graphics from scratch, *Visio* is based on the assumption that most of us don't have the time, skill, or inclination to work that way. Instead, it provides sets of graphic elements that you combine to create practical drawings such as maps, house plans, office setups, and so on.

Visio cleverly divides its graphic elements into categories. To use the program, you simply call up the elements you need. What could be simpler? No wonder *Visio* has perhaps the fastest-growing following of any graphics program on the market.

Canvas: For the Budget-Minded

Canvas for Windows is the most Spartan of draw programs, with small libraries of typefaces and clip art. However, if your habit is to get in and out of a drawing project quickly, you'll love some of the automated tools that *Canvas* provides. Perspectives, extrusions, dimension lines, built-in bit-map editing—all can be done very quickly and conveniently.

Canvas is very friendly about allowing you to do stuff, but not at all friendly when you want to redo it. Many of its controls don't allow you to revisit objects and make changes. *CorelDraw*, for instance, allows you to extrude a string of text and later edit it, but Canvas requires that you first convert the text to curves, or break apart the object to which a special effect has been applied. Once done, the effect is no longer "live" and can't be modified—you have to start over.

Canvas is also not very adept with text, offering no support for imported text and lacking many basic typographical controls that are now considered standard. This adds strength to the argument that *Canvas* is a program for those who want to work expediently on simple projects.

AutoCAD: For Architects and Engineers

The drawing programs discussed so far have one thing in common—or should I say, *lack* one thing in common. They basically live in a two-dimensional world, in which three dimensions are only an illusion. *CorelDraw* offers some 3-D special effects, but to truly work in three dimensions, you need CAD (computer-aided design) software—an essential tool for draftspeople, architects, and technical illustrators.

Like most CAD programs, *AutoCAD* enables objects to "remember" their width, height, and depth. But *AutoCAD* isn't just any CAD program: It owns the lion's share of the CAD market, with nationwide authorized training centers and hundreds of add-on programs created by third parties. You pay dearly for *AutoCAD*'s power—typically thousands of dollars instead of hundreds. What does this buy you? For starters, you get hundreds of drawing layers, each of which lets you isolate parts of a drawing—the plumbing of a house, for instance—so you can work on them independently. You also get accuracy down to a hair's breadth.

The precision drawing tools themselves would be overkill for most illustrators, but they're just the ticket for draftspeople who need to copy objects in a circular array or extrude complex 3-D shapes from a surface. The program also has *auto-dimensioning*, where dimensions (in centimeters, feet, whatever you like) change precisely as you scale objects. You can even maintain a vast library of custom objects for use in other renderings, or tie *AutoCAD* drawings to external databases to track the cost of building materials or mechanical parts.

Image-Editing and Paint Software

Hold on to your hat—this chapter turns on a dime right here. When it comes to the other major category of graphics software—paint and image-editing programs—you need to stop thinking in terms of vectors, mathematics, and objects that know their own identities and properties.

Think of dots. Lots and lots of little dots. When you get down to it, that's all a photograph is. And when you scan a photo into your computer, or when you create a photorealistic image with your software, you're working with thousands, perhaps millions, of little dots. That's why scanned images require so much disk space, and that's why printing a photograph correctly is tricky—manipulating and controlling all those dots is a tall order.

Here, I've selected the most sophisticated image-editing and paint programs, all of which offer precision controls for handling full-color and gray-scale images. You've probably seen the gee-whiz effects—transplanting one person's head onto another, turning a sunny day into a blizzard, and so on. However, the most valuable features are the controls that enable you to render and print images with the highest possible fidelity. That's not as impressive as head transplants, but output quality is where the buck stops, every time.

REMEMBER

Adobe Photoshop

Photoshop originated as a custom program used by the image magicians at Industrial Light and Magic, George Lucas's special effects studio. Once adapted to personal computers (first to the Macintosh, then to the PC), it instantly defined the state of the art for professional image editing, with controls that would rival those of any darkroom.

Drop That Mouse!

Mice are great for dragging things around. But when you want to move a graphic just an itsy-bitsy distance, use your keyboard's arrow keys instead—it's a much easier way to nudge than using rodent power. In *Photoshop*, each nudge moves the selection one pixel. In *CorelDraw*, each nudge moves the selection .01 inch (but you can adjust that value in the Preferences dialog box of the Special menu).

To use *Photoshop*, you need a hot rod of a Windows system: a fast 486 or a Pentium processor, at least 8MB of RAM (16MB is much better), and hundreds of megabytes of hard disk storage. A 24-bit graphics card is helpful as well. The more hardware you can throw at *Photoshop*, the happier you'll be.

Typically you start by scanning a photograph (you can run your scanner directly from within *Photoshop*). Once you have your image on screen, the fun begins. *Photoshop* provides a variety of paint and editing tools, such as a pencil, an airbrush, a paintbrush, a smudge, and a blur. To work on an image, you select a portion of it using one of the program's selection tools. Forget the resolution of the image you're working on? Just hold down the [Alt] key as you click on the file size number in the lower left corner of the main window.

HOT TIP

You can save a particular selection within a drawing to an *alpha channel*, a sort of subfile for holding selections. You can work with up to 16 alpha channels, applying different effects to each, then recombining them. To reduce the size of *Photoshop* files, save the alpha channels as a separate Multichannel file: Select Image//Calculate// Duplicate, then delete the alpha channels from one of the files and delete the RGB channel from the other.

What makes *Photoshop* especially exciting as a graphics tool is the mini-industry that has sprung up around the program to create *filters*, which are customized special effects that produce an astonishing array of transformations. Depending on the filter you apply, you can transfigure a regular color image into a stained glass window, a pointillist painting, a charcoal drawing, a jigsaw puzzle—whatever strikes your fancy.

Picture Publisher

Frequently bundled with scanners, Micrografx's *Picture Publisher* has many of the same image-editing features found in *Photoshop*. In addition, this Windows program offers a variety of features that make working on images faster and more convenient. One such feature is FastBits, which lets you work on one portion of an image without having to load the whole image into memory. Another is an image browser that lets you search for the picture you want by keyword and review thumbnails of images on screen.

Figure 8: *You can drag Picture Publisher's floating palette of image-editing tools anywhere on screen. Pick a tool, and the palette branches to further selections.*

An especially innovative feature of *Picture Publisher* is the *object layer*, which lets you isolate a particular part of an image and apply functions such as rotation, sizing, and transparency to that portion of the image without affecting the rest.

Fractal Design Painter

Fractal Design Painter's claim to fame is the set of tools it provides for *creating* images, as opposed to tools for simply editing scanned ones. Watch a skilled artist use this Windows program with a *graphics tablet* (a touch-sensitive pad that you draw on with a stylus), and you'll swear you're watching someone paint. You can choose from a rich palette of tools: pencils, charcoals, chalks, inks, brushes, crayons, markers, and so on. What's amazing about *Painter* is the degree to which the tools simulate real painting effects; the "paint" bleeds and is absorbed into the "paper" just like the real thing.

Figure 9: *Fractal Design Painter comes closer to simulating actual painting—not to mention airbrushing or drawing with chalk or charcoal—than any other PC software.*

Two more features add to the illusion of reality. First, when you use *Painter* with a pressure-sensitive tablet, you can control the heaviness of your strokes by bearing down or easing off on the stylus—just as with real art tools. Second, *Painter* lets you select and control the properties of the drawing surface itself by determining the texture and absorbency of your digital "paper." Actually, we're not just talking about paper here, but also glass, stone, metal—even materials that don't exist in reality.

A Graphics Tool Kit

In addition to drawing, paint, or image-editing software, every digital artist needs a toolbox of special-purpose utilities, such as screen-capture programs, file-conversion programs, and image-cataloging programs.

Screen-Capture Utilities

There are dozens of ways to *capture* images—that is, to grab them right off the screen and save them in a file. A quick-and-dirty way that usually works in Windows is to press Print Screen, which copies an image of the entire screen. Then go to your destination—any Windows program that can accept a BMP file, which is most of them—and select Paste from the Edit menu. (To capture only the active window, press Alt Print Screen instead.)

HOT TIP

The Print Screen method's results are often funky, so if you want something better, the best utility available is *Collage*, which provides both an image-capturing module and an image-management module. Collage Capture enables you to isolate the portions of the screen you want to grab and offers a wealth of file formats in which to save your images. With Collage Image Manager, you can transform color images to grayscale, reduce the number of colors or shades you save (fewer means a smaller file), and create thumbnail catalogs of your screen captures. You can also convert files between a variety of formats.

Image- and File-Conversion Utilities

While utilities like *Collage* can do simple file conversions, more difficult conversions require industrial-strength software. One sort of conversion is changing a bit-mapped image into a vector drawing; another is converting an uneditable PostScript file into another format that can be opened and edited (see "A Short Course in File Formats" at the end of this chapter).

Remember that bit maps are dumb—nothing but a collection of dots—and vectors are smart, because they comprise objects that have known properties and mathematical relationships. So to convert a bit-mapped image into a vector graphic, you need software that's pretty smart, too. None of the programs that perform "auto tracing" are smart enough to deliver you from the often tedious ritual of cleaning up the results of a conversion, but they give you a great head start. *Adobe Streamline* is renowned as the one program equipped with the most options, controls, filters, and so on. And then there's good old *CorelDraw* again—it includes a tracing module that performs quite well with simple images.

Two ambitious programs, Techpool's *Transverter Pro* and Zenographics' *ZScript*, take on the task of converting Encapsulated PostScript (EPS) files into other vector formats. These programs interpret the PostScript instructions, draw the image in memory, and then save it in another format, such as the Windows Metafile (WMF) format used by all Windows drawing programs.

The Joy of Clip Media

The original intention of clip media (clip art drawings and digitized stock photos) was to provide nonartists with collections of art to use in their own publications. When you say *clip art*, most people think of the cheesy 1950s-style commercial drawings used in newsletters and newspaper ads. Of course, there's plenty of that on the market, much of it simply scanned from precomputer clip art collections. But as these examples show, there's also some beautiful clip art available—not just drawings but also patterns, textures, and scanned photographs.

REMEMBER

Photographic images aside, the better-quality clip art illustrations come in EPS format. Clip art in bit-mapped format is hard to use because you can't scale it without losing quality. You're better off avoiding such collections.

For stock photos, Kodak's Photo CD format has quickly become a standard. Agencies that license stock photos are rushing to convert their massive collections to Photo CD, and already you can find tens of thousands of images on the market. An important thing to note about stock photo collections is that your license to use them is usually more restrictive than the wide-open policies that apply to regular clip art. Even though you've bought a stock photo collection, you may not be able to use a particular photo in a commercial publication without paying a separate licensing fee—so read the fine print.

DANGER

Predictably, Corel Corporation also has a hand in clip media. All *CorelDraw* versions contain massive quantities of clip art. And Corel also sells a rapidly growing collection of photos on CD.

Figure 10: Clip art from the Art Parts collection (714/771-6754).

Figure 11: Clip art from Image Club's DigitArt collection, Volume 29 (403/262-8008).

Figure 12: Clip art from 3G Graphics' Images with Impact collection (206/774-3518).

The Color Conundrum

So you've created your masterpiece on screen. Now what? If you own a color ink jet or laser printer and you want to get good color output, your mission is simple: Mix and match colors until they look good to you, and then call it a day. But all other users better queue up, as there are numerous land mines in the exciting, complex, and scary world of color printing.

If your image is to be printed on a printing press, you need to create a piece of film, or a *separation*, for each color. For regular four-color printing, that means four pieces of film: one for cyan, one for magenta, one for yellow, and one for black. This system of four inks is known as *CMYK* (black is represented by K because in traditional printing the black component was applied first and therefore was referred to as the *key* color).

All of the major page layout and graphics programs allow you to create color separations (see Chapter 18: *Desktop Publishing*). But being able to *produce* separations is only the beginning of the battle for good color.

The real difficulty is in *controlling* color. Not only does your monitor use a different color system (the RGB system, which builds colors by combining grids of red, green, and blue glowing phosphors) than the CMYK system used by the print shop, but matching combinations of colors viewed on a monitor with colors printed on paper requires clearing a variety of hurdles. In the end, it's a process of trial and error, in which plain experience—seeing actual results, then adjusting on the next round—is the best guide. It's a process even the pros constantly struggle to master.

If four-color printing isn't needed, there's an easier system called *spot color*. At most art stores, you can buy a Pantone swatch book, which is simply a thick fan of printed samples of different shades of color, each numbered as a standardized PMS (*Pantone Matching System*) color. Inside any graphics program, you can specify PMS colors and rest assured that no matter where you go to get your picture printed, the colors you see in the swatch book will match the printed piece exactly. The drawback with spot colors is that you're limited to producing images with just a few colors—you can't show the subtle hues of a landscape or a face.

A Short Course In File Formats

No graphics program is an island. After you've created a picture, you usually need to export it somewhere: into a page layout program, a word processor, or perhaps another graphics program. There are two ways to export a graphic. The simplest method is to copy it to the Windows Clipboard, then switch to a different application and paste it in (see "A Graphics Tool Kit" earlier in this chapter). That works fine for some illustrations. But for complex graphics, you need to export the graphic into a separate file, then bring the file into another program using an import procedure.

Before you can decide what file format to use, you need to know whether the illustration in question is a bit-mapped image or a vector graphic. (If you're not sure, refer to Figure 3.) Then have a look at your program's File menu to see what file formats are supported. The Open and Save dialog boxes should list several of them; if your program has Import or Export dialog boxes, you'll find more formats listed there.

Rules of Thumb for Bit Maps

If you're exporting scanned photos, paintings, screen shots, or other bit-mapped images, you have several choices of file formats:

- **PCX** originated with an ancient little program from Zsoft called *Paintbrush*. The PCX format is the most versatile, since just about every image program in the world can save in PCX. Also, PCX files can be compressed dramatically, making them a decent choice for projects that might have to go on the road.

- **BMP** is Windows own bit-mapped graphics format. It's the least sophisticated and is quite popular for simple images like screen shots or screen icons that contain relatively few colors or shades.

- **TIFF** stands for Tagged Image File Format. This format is capable of handling the high color demands of professional-grade photos. If you have to cart your images to or from a Macintosh, or if you want to touch up a scanned photo or drop an image into a professional illustration, the TIFF format will answer the call every time. It's your best bet for bit maps.

HOT TIP

Although a TIFF file should hold intact as much bit-mapped information as you'll ever need, there's one nagging question: Which TIFF file? In fact, there are several different varieties—including six different file compression schemes—and no graphics program supports them all. Although it squanders disk space, saving a TIFF file without compression ensures that the file can be used by the widest range of other programs.

Rules of Thumb for Vector Graphics

You've got more choices when exporting vector graphics. The players in this game are: AI, CGM, DXF, EPS, GEM, WMF, and WPG. Many of these are specialty formats, used in very particular situations; others are dinosaurs that are ready for extinction. Here's a brief rundown:

- **Illustrator Format (AI).** Use this format if you intend to bring an object into *Adobe Illustrator* or across to the Mac and into an application that accepts *Illustrator* files. Otherwise, there are better ways to export vector graphics.

- **Computer Graphics Metafile (CGM).** Use CGM only if you employ a slide service that specifically asks you to use this format. Otherwise, forget it—it's too quirky for general file exchange between applications.

- **AutoCAD (DXF).** Use this format to prepare a graphic for incorporation into a CAD project.

- **Encapsulated PostScript (EPS).** Use this format for all serious work destined ultimately for a PostScript printer.

- **Digital Research GEM (GEM).** Use this format to export graphics to an old GEM version of *Ventura Publisher*—but only if that program will be printing to a non-PostScript printer.

- **Windows Metafile (WMF).** Use this format for all non-PostScript projects within Windows.

- **WordPerfect (WPG).** Use this format for graphics destined for non-Windows versions of *WordPerfect*.

Let's cut to the chase. There is no better way to export a graphic than as an EPS file. Done, end of discussion, class dismissed. It is the cleanest, most reliable, and most robust format that the graphics industry knows. All the other formats are at the mercy of the quality of the import filter used by the receiving application.

But there is the one big catch with EPS: You need a PostScript printer or an imagesetter in order to take advantage of it. If you do not have either of these devices, then your best bet is probably the WMF format. Note my carefully chosen words here: *Most* programs will *probably* do a good job at importing *many* graphics as WMF files. "Most, probably, many"—nothing is sure outside the bounds of Encapsulated PostScript. The only way to be sure is to experiment with different formats.

HOT TIP

Product Directory

***Adobe Illustrator
  for Windows***
***Adobe Photoshop
  for Windows***
Adobe Streamline
Adobe Systems Corp.
P.O. Box 7900
Mountain View, CA 94039
415/961-4400

AutoCAD
Autodesk, Inc.
2320 Marinship Way
Sausalito, CA 94965
800/228-3601
415/331-0356

Canvas for Windows
Deneba Software
7400 S.W. 87th Ave.
Miami, FL 33173
800/622-6827

***Collage Capture and
  Image Manager***
Inner Media, Inc.
60 Plain Rd.
Hollis, NH 03049
603/465-3216.

CorelDraw
Corel Systems Corp.
1600 Carling Ave.
Ottawa, Ontario
K1Z 8R7 Canada
800/836-3729
613/728-8200

Fractal Design Painter
Fractal Design Corp.
335 Spreckels Dr., Ste. F
Aptos, CA 95003
408/688-8800

Picture Publisher
Micrografx, Inc.
1303 Arapaho
Richardson, TX 75081
800/426-9400

Visio
Shapeware Corp.
1601 5th Ave. #800
Seattle, WA 98101
800/446-3335
206/467-6723

18 Desktop Publishing

By Steve Cummings

- Picking the right program for the right project
- The equipment and software you need to start
- Tips for designing professional-looking documents
- PageMaker, Quark, and Ventura reviews and tips
- Great inexpensive page layout software
- Forms and database publishing software

Word processing programs do so much nowadays, who needs desktop publishing software? *WordPerfect*, *Microsoft Word*, and *Ami Pro* can all handle graphics and fairly complicated layouts, so you can create professional-looking reports, proposals, announcements, booklets, you name it.

But desktop publishing software still has a few tricks up its sleeve. Here's where you may find it more useful than Windows word processing software:

- **Complex layouts.** When you need to place multiple graphics just where you want them on a page, or flow text across discontinuous areas, desktop publishing software does the job better than word processing software. And even though you can design fairly fancy newsletters with a word processor, many people find that desktop publishing programs simplify the process.

- **Precise typographic control.** People who know what they're doing with type need hairbreadth control over font sizes, type placement, and spacing between letters and lines. In this area, desktop publishing programs have a slight edge over today's word processors.

- **Color printing.** Word processors can print color text and graphics, but desktop publishing software offers much more control, especially with background colors and color photos.

- **Document management.** Word processors are catching up fast, but desktop publishing programs still make the better choice for really complex, book-length projects. They provide more sophisticated indexing and cross-referencing features, and they supply more special help for assembling huge documents from many component files.

How many of the above features you get depends on the kind of program you buy. Most desktop publishing software falls into one of these two categories:

- **Professional page layout packages.** *PageMaker*, *Ventura Publisher*, *QuarkXPress*, and *FrameMaker* provide the tools that professional publishers need—and they're generally priced that way. Go with this group if you'll be earning any substantial part of your living from desktop publishing, if your work involves extremely complex designs or book-length projects, or if you plan to use something better than a laser printer to produce final copies.

- **Light-duty packages.** *Microsoft Publisher*, *PagePlus*, and several other packages cost much less than the major Windows word processors and generally provide better control over type, flowing text, and graphics. They make good sense for flyers and even some newsletters, but for complex layouts or technical manuals, go with the high-priced spread.

What do all these programs have in common? At their core, they are electronic paste-up tables where you import and combine text from a word processor with drawings from a graphics program, scanned photos from an image editor, and so on. This chapter will help you pick the right desktop publishing package—and get you started using it with lots of tips on design and electronic page layout.

TO PUBLISH...		YOU NEED...
BUSINESS PROPOSAL OR FORMAL REPORT	→	HIGH-END WORD PROCESSOR; LASER PRINTER OUTPUT
DEPARTMENTAL, SCHOOL, OR CHURCH NEWSLETTER	→	LOW-END DTP SOFTWARE; LASER PRINTER OUTPUT
PROFESSIONAL-QUALITY NEWSLETTER	→	HIGH-END DTP SOFTWARE; SERVICE BUREAU OUTPUT
SIMPLE ADVERTISING FLYER	→	LOW-END DTP SOFTWARE; LASER PRINTER OUTPUT
COLOR BROCHURE	→	HIGH-END DTP SOFTWARE OR ILLUSTRATION SOFTWARE; COLOR SEPARATIONS BY A SERVICE BUREAU
PAMPHLETS, SIMPLE MANUALS	→	WORD PROCESSOR; LASER PRINTER OR SERVICE BUREAU OUTPUT
NOVELS	→	WORD PROCESSOR; SERVICE BUREAU OUTPUT
NONFICTION BOOKS, TECHNICAL MANUALS	→	HIGH-END DTP SOFTWARE; SERVICE BUREAU OUTPUT

Figure 1: The bigger the audience for your document, the more likely you'll choose a serious desktop publishing package and have a service bureau produce your output.

What You Need for Desktop Publishing

Serious page design projects call for a high-powered array of hardware and software. You can get by with less for a short, monthly newsletter or advertising flyer, but if you skimp, expect frustration!

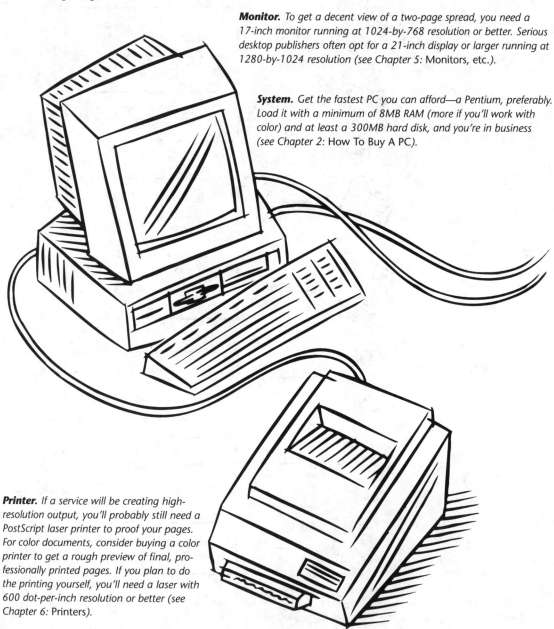

Monitor. *To get a decent view of a two-page spread, you need a 17-inch monitor running at 1024-by-768 resolution or better. Serious desktop publishers often opt for a 21-inch display or larger running at 1280-by-1024 resolution (see Chapter 5: Monitors, etc.).*

System. *Get the fastest PC you can afford—a Pentium, preferably. Load it with a minimum of 8MB RAM (more if you'll work with color) and at least a 300MB hard disk, and you're in business (see Chapter 2: How To Buy A PC).*

Printer. *If a service will be creating high-resolution output, you'll probably still need a PostScript laser printer to proof your pages. For color documents, consider buying a color printer to get a rough preview of final, professionally printed pages. If you plan to do the printing yourself, you'll need a laser with 600 dot-per-inch resolution or better (see Chapter 6: Printers).*

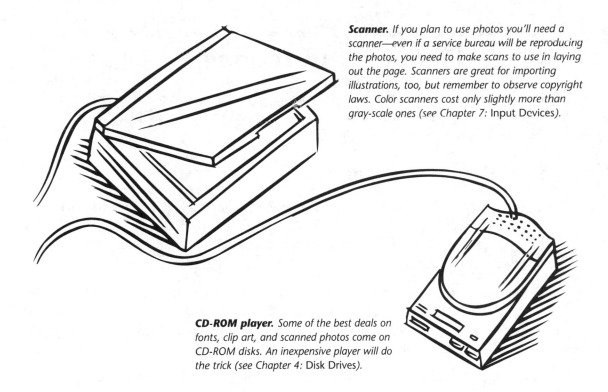

Scanner. *If you plan to use photos you'll need a scanner—even if a service bureau will be reproducing the photos, you need to make scans to use in laying out the page. Scanners are great for importing illustrations, too, but remember to observe copyright laws. Color scanners cost only slightly more than gray-scale ones (see Chapter 7:* Input Devices*).*

CD-ROM player. *Some of the best deals on fonts, clip art, and scanned photos come on CD-ROM disks. An inexpensive player will do the trick (see Chapter 4:* Disk Drives*).*

Software	Why You Need It and What You Need to Know
Desktop publishing program	The basic tool for assembling a document from many different elements
Word processor	You can type short pieces directly into your desktop publishing software, but you need more editing power for most projects.
Font collection	You don't need to fill up an entire hard disk with fonts, but you do need a varied library with examples from all the major font families.
Font utilities	Get a program like FontMinder to manage your font collection, and consider a kerning editor such as LetrTuck.
Clip art collection	Clip art consists of predrawn pictures that you can plug into documents to liven things up. You can buy clip art libraries and scanned photographs on CD ROM.
Graphics editors	You need a program for editing scanned images (in such formats as TIFF or PCX) and creating line drawings (like EPS, CGM, and WMF files). CorelDraw can handle either variety.
Graphics librarians and conversion utilities	To keep track of all your pictures on disk, get a program that catalogs them as little "thumbnail" images. You also need software to convert images from one file format to another, particularly between the various "flavors" of TIFF files. HiJaak Pro and DoDOT handle both chores.

From Planning to Proofing

Creating a document with desktop publishing software tests your skills as a manager, a graphics artist, and a technician. Here are the major tasks you'll face, along with a few ideas on how to cope with them.

Planning Your Document

Your primary goal is to communicate a message to your readers. Before you start work on a new project, identify your audience and define that core message explicitly. Everything about the design should help your reader get the message. Some general tips to get you started:

HOT TIP

- **Steal from the pros.** Pay attention to the daily barrage of print materials you see. What do you like, what catches your attention, and what do you actually read? How have people dealt effectively with material similar to yours? Don't be afraid to imitate designs that work.

- **Form and content go hand in hand.** The obvious rule of thumb is to create a design that draws attention to the important points you want to communicate. On the other hand, you must often adapt content to design—you can't get too wordy on a single-sheet flyer, to take an obvious example.

- **Consider all aspects of your design.** Most people think of design as a combination of layout, pictures, color, and type. But don't forget to consider the size of the publication as well, not to mention the kind of paper it will be printed on—factors often determined by your budget.

- **Factor in technical considerations.** How will the document be printed, folded, collated, bound, and distributed? The answers affect everything from the kinds of images you select to the width of the margins. Make sure you talk to your print shop at the earliest possible stage.

HOT TIP

- **Sketch preliminary designs on paper.** Computers are great for laying out pages, but nothing beats a pencil and paper for brainstorming. Show your sketches to people and get their reactions before you forge ahead.

Collecting Content

Although they all have their own tools for typing text and drawing simple graphics, desktop publishing programs mainly function as a place to assemble text and images

When Someone Else Does the Printing

If you plan to invest in desktop publishing software, you'll probably want someone else to do the printing most of the time. There's a world of difference in quality between what a desktop laser printer and a photocopier can produce, and what professional equipment can do. The key difference? Professional services produce a high-resolution (1200 dots per inch and up) film or high-gloss paper version of your document for printing. Here's one way of categorizing the professional services available:

- Service bureaus. You give them the document file, they produce the film or repro paper—and maybe print your document in low volume, too. Generally, service bureaus produce only black-and-white output and defer to professional printers for high-volume work. They may also double as copy shops.

- Prepress services. Fine-tuning color layouts, cleaning up photographs, and creating color separations are often jobs best left to professionals—largely because judging how the actual printed page will differ from your carefully crafted layout is a science in itself. Prepress services tackle these jobs, along with producing final film or repro. They may also handle other tasks, such as high-resolution color scanning with a scanner you can't afford.

- Professional printers. You send them the film, they print pages in any volume you want. Printers also do some prepress work, such as "stripping" photos into a film or repro version of the typeset page. The trend is toward providing more and more prepress capability, so the right printer may eliminate the need for a prepress service. If you want a printer that can turn around changes fast and produce high-quality results consistently, make sure you check references and take a close look at past publications.

from a variety of sources. Typically, the text has already been written in a word processing program, while the graphics have been created with a paint program, a draw program, or with a scanner.

Whether you or someone else prepares the material, keep in mind that it must be stored in a file format that your desktop publishing program can import. All Windows desktop publishing packages can read *Word* or *WordPerfect* files, for example, but some can't import old-fashioned *WordStar* files.

REMEMBER

Laying Out Pages

With a clear plan in mind and some text and graphics to work with, you can start creating your document's layout. Inside your desktop publishing software, you set up for the job by selecting the printer and choosing a page size and orientation (tall or wide, portrait or landscape).

The layout process proper begins when you block out headlines, body text, and graphic elements in a mock-up of the document. To accommodate items that repeat throughout, most desktop publishing programs provide master pages, which hold items you want repeated throughout your document. Position a heading, rule, or logo on a master page, and it will automatically appear on every page (or every other page, if you like).

Templates: The Easy Route to Good Designs

Here's the best time-saving tip I know: When you're just starting out in desktop publishing, don't design from scratch. Instead, use the professionally designed document *templates* that come with your desktop publishing software.

A template is a sample document that's already been laid out using dummy text and graphics. Delete the sample information, replace it with your own, and you've got a finished document that will communicate your message in an attractive package.

Though many of the templates that come with programs are pretty good, they're liable to look familiar. Independent companies sell additional templates—check *Publish* magazine for current ads. You might also hire a skilled desktop publisher to create custom templates into which you pour your own text and graphics, modifying the look as needed.

Top Five Basic Layout Tips

When you begin creating your own designs, be aware that you'll make mistakes, at least in the eyes of experienced designers. If you observe the guidelines that follow, however, you'll avoid some of the worst boo-boos that would mark you as an obvious amateur. For in-depth instruction, additional suggestions, sample designs—and a good idea of when to break the rules—consult the books and magazines listed in the "Other Resources" section at the end of this chapter.

1. **Stick to the fundamental layout.** Use standard margins, the same number of columns, and so on. You can inject variety by placing an element (such as a photo) across two or more columns, but the edges of every item should align with existing column boundaries.

2. **Use plenty of white space (blank areas).** Clutter and crowding make any message hard to see and put off your readers. Think of white space as another design element and use it deliberately, just as you would text and pictures.

3. **Give readers navigational aids in long documents.** Set aside space for page numbers, chapter titles and numbers, and even section descriptions at the top or bottom of every page.

4. **The larger the type, the wider the column.** Optimum column width depends on the size of your type, and vice versa. To judge for yourself, test your design using *dummy* (sample) text in the font you've chosen.

5. **Avoid bumping headlines.** In a multicolumn design, don't place headlines beside each other in adjacent columns. By the same token, avoid tombstoning, which is when photos or other boxy elements line up side by side across a page or a spread.

Top Five Text Layout Tips

Type is the most important factor in determining the character of your document. All of Chapter 13 is devoted to fonts and how to use them—choosing fonts for headlines and body text, adjusting *leading* (the space between lines of text), and so on. These tips are more general in nature and are meant to be employed *after* you've made some basic type decisions:

1. **Use subheadings liberally.** Give your readers guidance—and frequent breathers. Be sure the headline styles you use for each subdivision level (major headings, sub-heads, and so on) clearly reflect their relative importance and are consistent throughout your document.

2. **Break up long paragraphs**. Two- and three-sentence paragraphs may not please your tenth-grade English teacher, but readers will stay with you longer. Of course, if you're working with someone else's text, this may be beyond your control.

3. **Use bullets for text lists.** Dots or other symbols in front of a block of text help lead readers through bits of information. You'll find bullets all over this book, because they make information easier to absorb.

4. **Use numbers to show steps.** Number your lists (instead of using bullets) if the order is critical, if you need to refer to items in text, or if you're doing Top Five lists.

5. **Use style sheets.** For quick text formatting, nothing beats style sheets—lists of text styles that you create and later apply with a couple of mouse clicks. In most desktop publishing programs, style sheets work like this: You format a block of text (say, an 18-point bold Braggadocio headline), pick Style New (or a similar option) from a menu, and give the style a name like Headline 1. It will then appear on the list of styles. To apply that style, you highlight the desired text, pull down the list, and click on Headline 1.

Color and Graphics

Color costs time and money. If you have a minimum of either, consider using *spot color*, an easy way to liven up almost any layout. Spot color refers to solid blocks or blobs of color—or text passages—printed all in one hue. Spot colors can reproduce well even with a relatively inexpensive color printer (see the section "Serious Color Printers" in Chapter 6: *Printers*).

Process colors are used to reproduce photographs or blended colors by overlaying tiny dots of cyan (a light blue), magenta, yellow, and black (any color can be derived from some combination of these four hues). Creating *color separations* involves breaking down graphics into overlays in these four colors, which are then recombined to create the process colors. All professional desktop publishing programs handle color separations, but you may prefer to use a prepress service to make sure things look good in print.

Top Five Graphics Tips

Once you've imported a graphic, you can use your desktop publishing software to resize it, *crop* it (so that only part of the picture shows), or add effects like slanting or distortion. Inevitably, you'll have to adjust your software's special graphics settings to get top-quality printouts of scanned images or color graphics. You can also add decorations such as *rules* (graphic lines), boxes, and borders with the software's own tools.

HOT TIPS

1. **Stick with one kind of illustration.** When either a photo or an artistic rendering can do the job, choose one and use it exclusively throughout your document if possible. If you opt for the latter, avoid mixing artistic styles.

2. **Choose visuals for a reason.** Don't throw in illustrations for their own sake. Clip art is fine, but only if the pictures you select truly complement the text or crystallize some aspect of the message you're trying to convey.

3. **Make sure you can print it right.** Many a printed page has been ruined by poor reproduction. A terrific color photo may seem like a great idea, but not if your printer or print service can't do it justice. Test-print graphics to make sure you won't be surprised by the final product.

Figure 2: *Characters like these from the Wingdings font that comes with Windows can make nice graphical accents for a text-heavy layout.*

HOT TIPS

4. **If you can't find the perfect graphic, use type.** In fact, always ask yourself if type might do the job better. Examples include attention-grabbing headlines, *pull quotes* (brief excerpts from the text, printed in a large, snazzy font), *drop caps* (large, bold letters at the beginning of text blocks), or an individual letter, number, or symbol enlarged for its visual appeal.

5. **Keep it simple with bars and lines.** Ordinary straight lines and solid bars make great accents, as long as you don't overuse them. Experiment with different thicknesses, and try combining lines in groups.

Proofing and Final Output

Though you can catch lots of mistakes on the screen, you need to print proof copies during the design process to check your work adequately. Before you sign off on the document, it's essential to print a last test copy and give it to at least one other person for a microscopic proofreading.

Once you've fixed all the remaining typos and layout errors, it's time to produce the final document. What you do now depends on the output method you've chosen:

- **Do-it-yourself.** If you're producing a short-run, informally distributed document such an in-house report, you just print one clean copy on your laser printer and photocopy the rest. For volume reproduction, send the original to a professional copy shop.

- **Professional-quality black and white.** This generally means 1200 dots per inch and up, and that requires an imagesetter instead of a personal printer. If you don't have an imagesetter, you still need to set up your software as if you did. Under Windows, double-click on Printer in the Control Panel, select Add, and choose the imagesetter make and model (if you don't find it, choose PostScript Printer). Return to your desktop publishing software and select the option in your Print dialog box for "printing" to a disk file. Take this file to a service bureau (or send it by modem), and the bureau will create a high-resolution film version of your document for use with commercial printing presses.

HOT TIP

- **Printing in color.** Most people use a commercial printing service for color publications. Why? Because "affordable" (that is, under $20,000!) color printers are too slow to print in high volume and can't match the quality output produced by commercial machines (see the section "Serious Color Printers" in Chapter 6: *Printers*). To prepare your color document for commercial printing, you (or a prepress service) need to create color separations. If you're using spot colors, this means using your

Professional Touches: Traps and Bleeds

When you work with color, special care is required, whether you do the fine-tuning yourself or you pay a prepress service to do it for you. Part of the reason for precision is that in the printing process, each color is printed one on top of the other, in separate passes—and the colors don't always line up exactly right.

Trapped   **Off a little**

Figure 3: *The example on the right shows what can happen if you don't trap.*

NEWSLETTER BLUES

NGVMII VVHF JV

A Bucket Full of Beale Street

Mshfa dfjcvnjjzfn nxc fj fzkhfjfhz cxkjch xaeafjxdsd. Mshfa dfjcvnjjzfn nxc fjfzkhfjfhz cxkjchxa e afjxdsd. Mshfa nx c fjfzkhfjfhz cxkjc hxa eafjxdsd. Mshfa dfjcvnjjzfn nxcfjfzkhfjfhz cxkjchxae afjxdsd. Mshfa dfjcvnjjzfn n xcfjfzkhfjfhz Mshfa dfjcvnjjzfn nxcf jfzkhfjfhz cxkjchxaeafjxdsd. Mshfa dfjcvn jjzfn cxkjc hxaeafjxdsd. Mshfa dfj cvn jjzfn nxcfjfzkh fjfhz cxkjchx aeafjx dsd. Mshfa dfjcvnjjzfn nxc fj fzkhfjfhz cxkjch xaeafjxdsd. Mshfa dfjcvnjjzfn nxc fjfzkhfjfhz cxkjchxa e afjxdsd. Mshfa nx c fjfzkhfjfhz cxkjc hxa eafjxdsd. Mshfa dfjcvnjjzfn nxcfjfzkhfjfhz cxkjchxae afjxdsd. Mshfa dfjcvnjjzfn n xcfjfzkhfjfhz Mshfa dfjcvnjjzfn n cvn jjzfn nxcfjfzkh fjfhz cxkjchx xcf jfzkhfjfhz

Mshfa dfjcvnjjzfn nxc fj fzkhfjfhz cxkjch xaeafjxdsd. Mshfa dfjcvnjjzfn nxc fjfzkhfjfhz cxkjchxa e afjxdsd. Mshfa nx c fjfzkhfjfhz cxkjc hxa eafjxdsd. Mshfa dfjcvnjjzfn nxcfjfzkhfjfhz cxkjchxae afjxdsd. Mshfa dfjcvnjjzfn n xcfjfzkhfjfhz Mshfa dfjcvnjjzfn nxcf jfzkhfjfhz cxkjchxaeafjxdsd. Mshfa dfjcvn jjzfn cxkjc hxaeafjxdsd. Mshfa dfj cvn jjzfn nxcfjfzkh fjfhz cxkjchx aeafjx dsd. Mshfa dfjcvnjjzfn nxc fj fzkhfjfhz cxkjch xaeafjxdsd. Mshfa dfjcvnjjzfn nxc fjfzkhfjfhz cxkjchxa e afjxdsd. Mshfa nx c fjfzkhfjfhz cxkjc hxa eafjxdsd. Mshfa dfjcvnjjzfn nxcfjfzkhfjfhz cxkjchxae afjxdsd. Mshfa dfjcvnjjzfn n xcfjfzkhfjfhz Mshfa dfjcvnjjzfn n cvn jjzfn nxcfjfzkh fjfhz cxkjchx xcf jfzkhfjfhz

Traps and bleeds are two time-honored techniques for avoiding problems with colors and tints. When two colored items are supposed to print with their edges just touching, a *trap* is used to prevent any unsightly gaps between them by overlapping the items slightly. A *bleed* is a shaded or colored block printed over the edge of the page area, where the final page will be cut by the print shop. The overhang is necessary to ensure that the block prints all the way to the edge.

Figure 4: *The gray bar at the top of the page is called a bleed because it prints beyond the page edge. This ensures that even if the page is trimmed poorly, the bar won't fall short and leave an unsightly gap.*

desktop publishing software to create special files so a color imagesetter can print a separate sheet for each color ink. With process colors, you'll set things up so four sheets (cyan, magenta, yellow, and black) will be printed for each page.

HOT TIP

By the way, it's often a good idea to combine desktop publishing (for text and computer-generated graphics) with traditional printing technology (for photographs). On the final, camera-ready copy, you leave empty spaces where the photos go, and the commercial printer strips them in. Conventional photographic techniques may not be as flexible as manipulating scanned photos, but you usually get better results, and often with less hassle.

Picking the Right Professional Package

To decide which of the top four professional programs is right for the job, you need to define exactly what the job is. If you're laying out fancy brochures with lots of color, you need sophisticated design tools such as you get with *QuarkXPress* and *PageMaker*. If you're producing books or manuals, you want the long-document features of *Ventura* or *FrameMaker*—they do the best job of automatic numbering, indexing, cross-referencing, and helping you assemble book-type documents from individual chapters. *PageMaker* is probably the best compromise for both design-intensive and book-length projects.

Beyond these generalities, here are some specific differences among the packages that may help you choose:

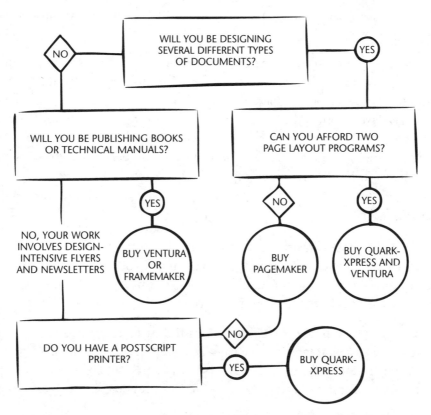

Figure 5: *QuarkXPress is the best design tool, while Ventura and FrameMaker are tops for handling long documents. That leaves PageMaker as the best compromise package.*

- **Master pages.** *Ventura* lacks master pages for holding items that appear on every page. Instead, you define "repeating frames," which are a little more awkward. *PageMaker* enables you to create only two master pages (left and right) per document, while you can set up loads of master pages with *QuarkXPress*—a nice feature when you create documents that have distinctly different sections.

- **Style sheets.** Basic specs can be important (such as the smallest and largest allowable type sizes), but pay special attention to the way style sheets work. With *PageMaker*'s system, which lets you base a new style on an existing one, you can change a whole set of styles with one command. In *Ventura*, each style is independent, so you have to alter them individually.

- **Graphics tools.** *QuarkXPress* and *PageMaker* offer the most built-in special effects for imported photos, while *QuarkXPress* gives you the broadest range of drawing tools (that is, except for *CorelDraw*, which is a separate program that's bundled with *Ventura*). *QuarkXPress* also makes it easiest to assign colors to elements in a layout, and it offers the best tools for matching the colors you assign to those used by professional printers.

- **Placing text and graphics.** The conventional method for positioning elements on the page is provided by using *frames*. A frame is a stretchable outline (usually a rectangle) that you size on the page with your mouse, and then pour text or graphics into. *PageMaker* works a little differently: It relies on a "pasteboard" metaphor, in which you simply place units of text and graphics directly on the page, without defining frames for them first. Once attached to the page, however, you can move the outlines of these elements to reposition or resize them.

PageMaker

PageMaker is the most versatile of the high-end desktop publishing packages, balancing sophisticated layout capabilities with competent handling of long documents. It's not the best product you can buy in either category, but it stays competitive across the board, making it the best general-purpose tool.

One of the great advantages of *PageMaker* is that it feels natural. The screen looks much like a real paste-up table, with a page or spread in the middle of a big workspace. You can place chunks of text and graphics on the pasteboard area where they stay accessible as you move from page to page—just as they would on a real table.

Good for Design-Intensive Layouts...

For complex layouts, *PageMaker* gives you fine control over the placement, rotation, and slant of text and graphics elements, and it boasts many professional-level features for adding color, handling color images, and preparing files for output at a service bureau. As with *QuarkXPress*, you can make layout changes (such as positioning, sizing, and rotating) to any selected element from a convenient "floating" window, instead of going through tiresome menu choices. Still, *PageMaker* requires tedious manual procedures for some common design chores that *QuarkXPress* handles in a single step.

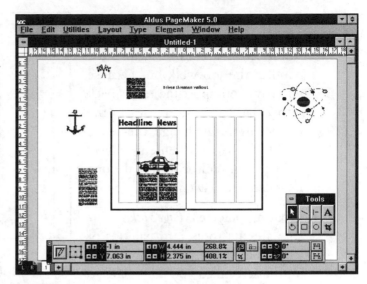

Figure 6: *As you lay out text and graphics, you'll like the hands-on feel of PageMaker's simulated paste-up table. Here, various graphics and snippets of text sit on the pasteboard, ready to move onto the document itself when needed.*

...and for Long Documents

When it comes to books and such, *PageMaker*'s ability to combine shorter files into a complete publication—along with its automatic generation of indexes and tables of contents—can serve you well. Yet *PageMaker* lacks key tools: It can't automatically renumber figures and references; it won't move graphics or captions so they maintain their relative position to a location in the body text; and to store a copy of a complete document on another disk, you have to find and copy all of the files yourself.

So much for the bad news. Other significant features include:

- **Easy customization.** You can plug in little software modules, called Aldus Additions, for specific tasks such as numbering lines of text or evening the length of two side-by-side columns. Additions appear on a submenu of the Utilities menu and function as part of *PageMaker*, albeit with some rough edges.

- **Good text editing.** With *PageMaker*'s "story editor," you edit a document's text in a separate window. It's not a word processor, but it's the strongest text editor among the professional desktop publishing programs.

- **Separate table editor.** *PageMaker* offers a separate program (not an Addition) for creating tables. It handles the job well, but because you have to import the tables back into PageMaker and return to the table editor to change them, it's decidedly less convenient than a built-in table editor such as the one included with *Ventura*.

- **Floating palettes.** *PageMaker* consolidates its tools into palettes of icons that you can drag anywhere on the screen, so you don't have to move the mouse far to reach them.

Figure 7: *In PageMaker, to align objects by their centers rather than by their edges, you need to position a guide (the line marked by arrows) and manually line up the objects by their center handles (those small black boxes).*

PageMaker Tips

PageMaker's interface is well designed for the most part, but these tips should help you skirt the rough edges:

HOT TIPS

- To change the default settings for all new *PageMaker* documents, start by closing any open documents. Then make your choices from any of the available menu items or dialog boxes (margins, fonts, and so on). To set text and graphics defaults for a particular publication, open it, make sure that no text or graphics objects are selected, and then make the menu and dialog choices you want.

- *PageMaker* lacks a command to align two or more objects automatically. Instead, you need to drag a *guide* (a nonprinting line for aligning objects) onto the page from either the left ruler or the top ruler (depending on whether you want to align objects vertically or horizontally). Then choose Snap to guides from the Layout menu, and drag the objects near the guide until they jump into place. Aligning the centers of two objects takes more work: You place the guide, zoom in, and use the middle handles on the objects' frames to eyeball the placement.

- To create an outline around a graphic image, don't use the rectangle tool—use the Addition called Create keyline. Like all Additions, you'll find it on the Aldus Additions submenu on the Utilities menu. *Keylines* are boxes that indicate the exact location of photographs that will be reproduced by conventional commercial printing techniques. If you really want a keyline, not an outline, delete the graphic when you're done.

- When a word or phrase containing an ordinary slash (such as and/or) falls at the end of a line, *PageMaker* is apt to break the word at the slash. To keep the phrase intact, delete the ordinary slash and type ⌈Ctrl⌉⌈Shift⌉⌈/⌉ instead.

- Be sure you've assigned the correct style to a paragraph before you change the font of particular words or phrases. When you change the style of a paragraph of body text, such attributes as boldface or italics will stay in place, but font changes—and *reverse* text (white on black)—are gone for good.

PageMaker Add-Ons

Here are some of the best tools I've found for adding punch to *PageMaker*. All add to *PageMaker*'s graphics and layout capabilities except *Sonar Bookends*, which offers much-needed indexing capabilities for long documents:

- **PMproKit.** This $149 set of seven type and layout utilities enables you to edit kerning pairs, set up columns of varying widths automatically, and generate rulers that you can place in a document temporarily to measure things. I especially like the feature that automatically sets tab stops based on the longest stretch of text in each column—great for quick tables. EDCO Services, 4107 Gunn Hwy., Tampa, FL 33624; 813/962-7800, 800/523-TYPE.

- **Sonar Bookends.** This automated indexing tool costs only $99.95 and works with *PageMaker*, *QuarkXPress*, and many other Windows programs (but not *Ventura Publisher*). It can generate a list of every word in a document with its corresponding page number, or simply base the index on a list of words and phrases you supply. You can exclude certain words, find and index proper nouns only, use wildcards and conditional searches, and include or ignore nonalphabetic characters. Virginia Systems, 5509 West Bay Ct., Midlothian, VA 23112; 804/739-3200.

- **Fraemz Proportional Borders.** An $89 set of pretty borders you can import into *PageMaker* documents. Shadetree Marketing, 5515 N. 7th St. #5-144, Phoenix, AZ 85014; 800/678-8848.

- **Watermark for PageMaker.** For $89, *Watermark* gives you extra control over vector (draw-type) graphics placed in *PageMaker*, enabling you to change gray-scale and color settings for best-quality printing. As the name suggests, you can also lighten a graphic to the point that it prints "behind" the other items on the page—sort of like a watermark. TechPool Software, 1463 Warrensville Center Rd., Cleveland, OH 44121; 800/925-6998, 216/291-1922.

QuarkXPress

QuarkXPress is the best desktop publishing program for the professional graphics artist. For precision layout of short publications, especially in color, there's no better choice. *QuarkXPress* has the most extensive collection of design tools, an easy system for accessing them, and sophisticated features for preparing color documents for printing. And a huge assortment of third-party add-on programs makes the potential power of the program even greater.

On the other hand, *QuarkXPress* is lousy for books and manuals, unless you supplement it with a bunch of expensive add-ons. And forget *QuarkXPress* for low-budget, do-it-yourself publishing. The program won't work with non-PostScript printers, not even Hewlett-Packard LaserJets.

A Star Designer

QuarkXPress beats the other programs at the page design game by the sheer number of tricks it can do. You see this even at the most basic level of layout control. For example, the ability to create many separate master pages in a single document frees you from rigid left-and-right page formats and lets you fool around with variations easily. *QuarkXPress* also lets you shuffle the order of your pages after you've laid them out.

When you're working on the details, *QuarkXPress* gives you precision control over graphics layout and typography, offering lots of classy effects. I especially like the fact that you can lock frames in place so they stay put—in other programs, it's easy to move one frame accidentally when you're trying to select a nearby frame instead. You can even draw elliptical or polygonal frames for imported graphics, a unique feature. In fact, you can put text inside one of these shapes and have it automatically wrap to the boundaries of the frame.

Figure 8: *QuarkXPress is the best desktop publishing program for laying out short, graphics-intensive documents, especially if they use color. You can even create elliptical or polygonal frames and have text wrap to fit automatically.*

Floating Palettes and Hot Color

QuarkXPress puts most of its features at your fingertips with a system of movable icon palettes. *PageMaker* has this too, but *QuarkXPress* still has the most comprehensive palette system. For example, only *QuarkXPress* lets you color text, borders, or whatever by dragging the color from a palette and plopping it down on the item.

QuarkXPress has a wealth of built-in features for preparing color documents for professional printing. Compared to the other programs, *QuarkXPress* lets you pick from more color models (systems for designating colors used by professional printers), and has the best, most flexible trapping controls (see "Professional Touches: Traps and Bleeds" earlier in this chapter).

QuarkXPress Tips

QuarkXPress's page graphics and page layout features are unsurpassed. Here are a few ways to take advantage of some less obvious features:

- To copy the formatting of one paragraph to another, start by clicking in the paragraph you want to change. Then hold down Shift Alt while you click on the paragraph that you're copying from. *QuarkXPress* not only copies the named style (as defined in the style sheet), but it also copies any modifications you made to formatting (such as new margins, tabs, and so on). The process also preserves any special character formatting in the target paragraph, such as boldfacing or font changes.

- All professional desktop publishing programs let you group objects—but with *QuarkXPress* you can also group groups. For example, if you want to move two pictures and their captions as a unit, first group each caption with its picture by holding down the Shift key, selecting the caption and picture, and pressing Ctrl G. Then group the pair of picture-and-caption groups the same way. After the move, if you want to adjust the position of one picture, you can ungroup the pair without worrying about disturbing the relative positions of the captions and their pictures.

- Locking a frame keeps you from moving it accidentally, but you can still move it on purpose: Type in the new coordinates in the Item Specifications box or the Measurements palette instead of dragging the object with the mouse.

- To wrap text manually around an irregular graphic, select the graphic's Picture Box, choose Runaround from the Item menu, and pick Manual Image from the Mode list. To speed up your work as you do this, hold down the spacebar while you adjust the polygonal boundary of the runaround. Otherwise, *QuarkXPress* reflows the text every time you change the boundary, costing you lots of time. Release the spacebar whenever you want *QuarkXPress* to reflow the text so you can check the results.

- If you're printing draft copies of a color document on your desktop printer, be sure to have *QuarkXPress* print the colors as shades of gray by checking the Print Colors as Grays check box in the Print dialog box. Otherwise, all the colors will turn out pitch black.

- *QuarkXPress* lets you rotate a picture's frame and the image inside it independently. The rotation tool on the Measurements palette is a bit awkward, so it's best to select the frame, enter the rotation degrees in the Item Specifications dialog box, and then do the same for the image. If you want a slanty frame for a straight-up-and-down image, rotate the two by equal but opposite amounts (say, one at 32 degrees and the other at –32 degrees).

QuarkXPress Add-Ons

Quark designed *QuarkXPress* so other software developers could build plug-in software modules called XTensions. Some XTensions are little utilities that speed up common tasks, while others add completely new features. For instance, you can fill the most glaring gaps in *QuarkXPress*'s handling of long and business-type documents with XTensions that create tables, indexes, and tables of contents.

At the moment, more than 50 XTensions are already out there. A clearinghouse called XChange sells them all. XChange publishes a catalog that describes them in detail, and you're going to want this booklet: Call 800/788-7557 to get a copy. Here's a sampling of what's available:

- **X'Spec** enables you to copy such characteristics as typeface, type size, tracking, and color from one stretch of text and apply it to any other text.

- **Bureau Manager** extracts the technical information you need when you send a document to a service bureau for imagesetting, and it copies all the required files and fonts used by the document.

- **PrintMaster** increases your control over printing. You can make the output larger or smaller than normal, print sections on a page, print discontinuous pages in a single print job, and so on.

- **MakeZone** helps manage the layout process for publications that have different versions for different audiences (such as newspapers that print a slightly different edition for each region they serve).

- **Tableworks** lets you create sophisticated tables, while preserving the ability to use *QuarkXPress*'s standard typographic and color controls.

Ventura Publisher

When it comes to laying out long documents like books and manuals, *Ventura Publisher* does a fabulous job. Bundled with the *CorelDraw* package, *Ventura*'s main strength is in assembling documents, so it relies primarily on *Corel*'s many fine tools for graphic design (see Chapter 17: *Graphics Software*). If, like many people, you believe that *Corel* is indispensable for desktop publishing, you may find that this one-two combination is all you need—you even get a database publishing module and a whopping 600 fonts.

The obvious problem with this bundle is that *Corel* and *Ventura* are still two separate programs, so you sometimes have to go through extra steps to access design tools that are built right in to *QuarkXPress* and *PageMaker*. Also, neither *Corel* nor *Ventura* have the professional prepress features of *QuarkXPress*.

The Long-Document King

The typical book-type document is built of multiple, shorter sections. *Ventura* expects this kind of chapter-by-chapter organization, and it's set up to combine multiple chapter files (perhaps written by different authors) into one big manuscript. Whenever you change anything, *Ventura* automatically renumbers chapters, pages, lists, figures, and footnotes, and keeps cross-references (like "see page 293") up to date. *Ventura* does tables and mathematical equations, and naturally, it generates tables of contents and indexes, too.

Side-by-Side Paragraphs

A little feature called side-by-side paragraphs is hard to explain, but it's why I won't part with *Ventura*. You know how many books and technical manuals have side heads, those headings in the margin beside a paragraph? Well, in *PageMaker* and *QuarkXPress*, you have to type in those headings in a separate box, not in the main body of the text. If the body text changes, you have to reposition the little box manually.

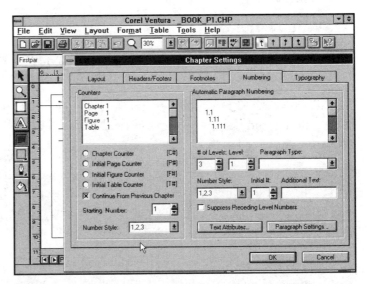

Figure 9: *Ventura Publisher comes with CorelDraw, the top graphics program, and has a similar button bar (top) and toolbox (left). This dialog box shows a Ventura strength: extensive numbering options for technical documents.*

In *Ventura*, side heads can stay part of the main text. Once you set up the side head style, a couple of clicks move the heading off into the margin and bring the next paragraph up beside it. In a big book, with lots of margin headings, this is *much* quicker than setting up all those little boxes.

All Those Files

Ventura's big advantage for long documents is the way it handles files. (Well, I see it as an advantage, but I have to warn you that other people hate the *Ventura* file system.) No other desktop publishing program makes it so easy to assemble material from multiple sources, allowing ongoing work on the original files while layout progresses.

Here's the deal. Though *Ventura*'s page display looks similar to those of other programs, *Ventura* documents don't actually contain the text and graphics you've pasted up—just a list of the files that contain them. The files remain as separate entities in their original formats, which means you can make changes to those files using the programs that originally created them. The next time you open the document in *Ventura*, those changes appear automatically.

What About Fancy Designs?

Ventura is flexible enough to handle free-form layouts capably, but hard-core graphics artists will chafe under some of its limitations. For instance, *Ventura* doesn't do bleeds. It does come with an advanced color separation utility for service bureau work, but you can't use it to make accurate color proofs on your own printer.

Ventura Tips

When it comes to headers, footers, and graphic elements, *Ventura* could do better. Most of these tips help you cope with those problems:

- Press Ctrl X to return to the last dialog box you used, or to redo the last menu command. Learn this tip—it really saves time.

- *Ventura*'s Headers & Footers command works well in most situations, but you can build more complex headers and footers—with graphical elements, for example— using repeating frames to replace or supplement *Ventura*'s automatically generated header and footer frames. Create a new frame, then choose Repeating Frame from the Frame menu and specify whether you want the frame to appear on all pages or only on right or left pages. Don't forget: You can turn a repeating frame off on any given page by choosing Hide This Repeating Frame in the Repeating Frame dialog box.

HOT TIPS

- Headers and footers can't be saved in a style sheet. To avoid having to create them from scratch each time—say, for each chapter in a book—create and save "template" chapters with the headers and footers you might want to use again. In the File Manager, locate the set of files for the document you've just created (there will be from two to six files, all with the same name, and with CHP, CAP, CIF, FRM, VGR, and VPO extensions). Use the Copy command to repeatedly duplicate this entire set of files, once for each chapter in your book (copy the whole set to CHAP1.*, CHAP2.*, and so on). Then, still in the File Manager, use the Properties command (on the File menu) to set the attributes of all the files in the original template to Read-Only. Back in *Ventura*, you can open the copies and go to work. If you later decide to add more chapters to your book, just make new copies of the template, but remember to turn off the Read-Only attribute.

- To speed up the screen display in documents that include imported images, hide those pictures while you're working on the layout. To hide them all, uncheck Show All Pictures in the View menu. To hide a particular picture, select it first, and then turn off Show This Picture.

- To place a line or box graphic created with *Ventura*'s drawing tools in a precise location, start by creating a frame, positioning it exactly where the graphic should be using the Sizing and Scaling dialog box to type in the left side and top side coordinates. Deselect the frame. Now draw your line or box on top of the frame (switching to Enlarged View can't hurt), and then delete the frame.

Ventura Add-Ons

Whatever you think of *Ventura*'s way of handling a document's constituent files, it's easy to find fault with the program's limited file management. Many of the utilities covered here fill in those gaps:

- **VP Roundup, VP Width Manager, VP File Groomer.** If I had to pick one *Ventura* add-on, it would be *VP Roundup*. It lets you catalog, copy, and delete entire chapters (with all their component files), manage style sheets, and modify a group of paragraph tags all at once. With *VP Width Manager*, you can sort, rename, and renumber typefaces; copy typefaces from one *Ventura* width table to another; and edit character widths and lists of kerning pairs. *VP File Groomer* fixes typographic no-nos in imported text files, removing unnecessary spaces and tabs, automatically typesetting fractions so they look like this (3/4) instead of this (3/4), converting hyphens to dashes, and so on. All three programs together cost $69. Skookum Software, 1301 Ryan St., Victoria BC, Canada V8T 4Y8.

- **Venturian.** A classy, $119 Windows-based disk librarian for *Ventura* documents and their component files, *Venturian* lets you move or copy any one file, all the files in a chapter, or a complete publication, while ensuring that *Ventura* can still find all the files in the new location. If you want, *Venturian* will compress the files automatically so that no matter where you decompress them, everything still works right. Electronic Publishing Services, 15370 W. Cherrywood Ln., Libertyville, IL 60048; 708/918-7750.

- **vp*ULTRA.** Even though it's a DOS program, $169 *vp*Ultra* is probably the best utility for managing *Ventura* style sheets, and it works well with the Windows version of *Ventura*. You can compare style sheets, view summary information on specific tags, copy tags from one style sheet to another, and find and delete tags that you're not using (useless tags tend to proliferate in *Ventura*, making it hard to find the ones you really need). SNA, 2200 N.W. Corporate Blvd. #404, Boca Raton, FL 33431; 800/628-6442, 407/241-0308.

- **MasterHelp.** If you're already skilled at making paper documents with *Ventura*, *MasterHelp* will help you branch out into electronic publishing. This pricey product ($995) converts *Ventura* documents into Windows help files, with the same kinds of hypertext links and graphical buttons you see when you call up the Help screen in any Windows program. But since the Windows help system can be used independently, you can also create electronic reference works on any topic you like. Performance Software, 575 Southlake Blvd., Richmond, VA 23236; 804/794-1012.

- **Index!** *Ventura*'s built-in indexing feature requires a lot of manual labor. *Index!* automates the process by searching through a document's text files, inserting the proper code whenever it finds a term you want indexed. Even though you must verify each reference, this $79 shareware program saves you lots of time. Trinity Software, P. O. Box 3610, Manassas, VA 22110; 703/791-2576.

FrameMaker

Take a look at *FrameMaker* if you publish books, manuals, or technical documentation. Even more than *Ventura*, *FrameMaker* offers an incredibly rich array of features for building long and complex documents, such as automated cross-referencing, or text that changes automatically to suit various versions of the same document. *FrameMaker* even does side-by-side paragraphs, long a *Ventura* exclusive. The program also does a decent job with free-form layouts such as newsletters, and it separates process colors without add-on software.

The main problem with *FrameMaker* is its interface. Although it has an icon toolbar that lets you access some commands easily with a mouse, unconventional terminology in some of the menus and dialog boxes may leave you befuddled. There are jillions of keyboard shortcuts, but the bad news is that most of them are cumbersome and difficult to remember.

FrameMaker has extensive workgroup publishing features, including version comparison and revision control. Versions of the program are available for Windows, Macintosh, and UNIX, and you can transfer files back and forth between them without special translation steps. Uniquely, *FrameMaker* also includes built-in hypertext features for creating and viewing electronic documents.

FrameMaker Tips

Here are some tips to help you cope with *FrameMaker*'s awkward aspects, as well as take advantage of its unique features:

HOT TIPS

- Normally, when you click on a drawing tool in *FrameMaker*'s Tools palette, you can use it only once—after that, the standard arrow pointer reappears. To keep using the same drawing tool, press Shift as you click on the Tools palette.

- *FrameMaker* automatically places each math equation in its own frame, but the frame is usually much larger than the equation itself. When you're through building the equation, select Shrink-Wrap Equation from the Equations menu in the Equations palette. You can use this trick to wrap a frame tightly around any object—just click on the frame or any of its objects, and press Esc M P.

- If you're laying out a book and you want each chapter to start on an odd-numbered page, choose Document from the Format menu, and then select Make Page Count Even in the drop-down list labeled Before Saving & Printing. If the document doesn't already end on an even-numbered page, *FrameMaker* automatically adds a blank page so that it will.

- You can search for text within a marker (such as an index entry or cross-reference) by using the Find button in the Find/Change dialog box. But don't try a search-and-replace operation using the Change button—you'll wind up replacing the marker itself with the new text. Instead, after you've found the right marker, choose Marker on the Special menu to display the marker text, and edit it there.

FrameMaker Add-Ons

Because *FrameMaker* is less popular than the other professional desktop publishing programs, you'll find fewer add-ons out there. Here are some of the best:

- **FrameViewer.** For $49.95 per installation, this program lets employees or customers view and print *FrameMaker* documents—and navigate hypertext links—

without owning a copy of *FrameMaker* itself. Frame Technology Corp., 1010 Rincon Cir., San Jose, CA 95131; 408/433-3311.

- **EndNote Plus.** This $249 program maintains a database of bibliographic references. It automatically culls in-text citations from documents, reformats them to match a chosen style, correlates them with entries in the database, and prepares a bibliography at the end of the document. Niles and Associates, 2000 Hearst St. #200, Berkeley, CA 94709; 510/649-8176.

- **Bidirectional MML Filter, MasterEditor.** The $229 *MML Filter* converts *FrameMaker* documents into ASCII text that can be edited in another program, then reconverted to *FrameMaker* format. With *MasterEditor* ($299), you can conduct search-and-replace changes on multiple *FrameMaker* files without having to open the files and issue commands. Frank Stearns Associates, 14307 N.E. 16th St., Vancouver, WA 98684; 206/892-3970.

Desktop Publishing Lite

If laying out pages with a mouse isn't something you do every day, then you probably don't need a product like *QuarkXPress* or *PageMaker.* You can turn out fancy-looking newsletters and brochures with software that costs hundreds of dollars less. And the kicker is that the low-end desktop publishing packages are easier to use than the big guns.

Besides the fact that you don't have to learn as many features, the features themselves are often presented more sensibly—the Windows products tend to work the way you expect Windows software to work, whereas the expensive desktop publishing programs are often idiosyncratic. Another big plus is that the templates thrown in with these programs tend to look better than the ones you get with the top-of-the-line packages, so you have less design work to do.

REMEMBER

You can find low-end desktop publishing software in both DOS and Windows flavors, but unless you have wimpy hardware (a 386 or less), buy a Windows program. For desktop publishing, Windows' advantages are especially compelling: typefaces that work with all your programs, a set-it-up-once way of configuring your printer and graphics card, and easy data exchange between programs.

The Trade-Offs

Of course, inexpensive publishing programs can't offer all the features of the high-priced models. If a word processor isn't enough for your publishing needs, you'd better be sure that your new desktop publishing program will go the distance. Here's where the low-priced programs fall short:

T he initial "t" in this sentence is a drop cap.

Figure 10: *Even such relatively simple typographics as a drop cap can be hard to create in a light-duty desktop publishing program.*

- **Typographic precision.** Low-end desktop publishing programs give you only a moderate degree of control over the size, spacing, and exact location of text.

- **Color output.** The only low-end program that can create color separations is *PagePlus*.

- **Long-document capabilities.** If you're printing a manual or book on a limited budget, a good word processor like *Word* or *Ami Pro* makes a better choice. With one exception (*PFS:Publisher*), low-cost desktop publishing programs can't generate indexes or tables of contents automatically, and they can't track page number references and the like within your text.

- **Miscellany.** Some of these programs can't print *crop marks*, the right-angle lines that tell the printshop where to cut the paper (if you're going to print on 8$^1/2$-by-11-inch paper, this won't matter). Most can't automatically create drop caps, those large initial characters at the beginning of paragraphs.

Which Light-Duty Program to Buy?

Microsoft Publisher is the best of the litter. (It's also the most expensive, by at least $100.) Version 2 covers the basics well, offering capable, easy-to-use facilities for laying out pages, formatting text, and adding graphics and special text effects. You also get style sheets for quick text formatting and an automatic table-maker.

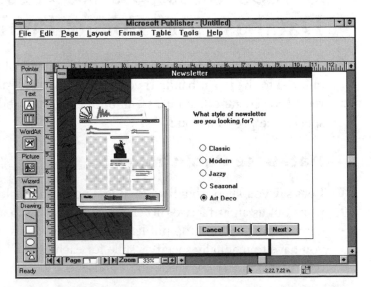

Figure 11: *Microsoft Publisher's PageWizards ask you questions about form, style, and content, and then translate your answers into attractive layouts.*

For beginning or occasional desktop publishers, *Publisher*'s PageWizards are a definite plus. After you choose the type of document you want to design—newsletter, brochure, business card, whatever—the PageWizard asks you a series of questions about the particulars. Once you've filled in all the blanks, it does the dirty work for you—voilà, an instant custom layout. This program is really, really easy.

Negatives on *Microsoft Publisher*? The biggies are no long-document features and no color seperations. As for annoyances, I could do without all the cute graphics that turn up throughout this program.

PagePlus, the poor person's substitute for *QuarkXPress*, is the best choice for apprentice graphic artists. Besides plenty of basic page layout talent, it includes a respectable set of illustration tools, with loads of special effects like tints and patterns. And *PagePlus* is the only inexpensive desktop publishing package that can make color seperations. If you're willing to live with some serious gaps and a rather quirky interface, this $60 program could stand in for *QuarkXPress* and *CorelDraw*, saving you hundreds of dollars.

If you don't need the graphics tools in *PagePlus* and don't want to fork over the cash for *Microsoft Publisher*, then check out any of the other Windows-based programs: *PFS:Publisher*, and *Express Publisher for Windows*. *PFS:Publisher* is the one low-end product that makes tables of contents and indexes automatically, so it's worth considering for simple, book-length projects.

Database and Forms Publishing

Why use a general-purpose desktop publishing tool when you can get one specially tailored to the job at hand? If you need to turn dull database output into an attractive report, or create office forms—in both electronic and paper versions—then try these specialized programs on for size.

Database Publishing

Let's say you keep a big list of names and addresses in a database, which you'd like to print out as an attractive directory. Most database packages can't do it. Try it with a general-purpose desktop publishing program, and you'll waste gobs of time, because you have to manually specify a style for each field in every record. Here's where database publishing software can be a godsend.

BrioPublish, *InfoPublisher*, and *Ventura's Database Publisher* work in concert with the major desktop publishing packages—*FrameMaker*, *PageMaker*, and *Ventura* respectively (*Ventura's Database Publisher* is now included in the *Ventura* package; it also works with *PageMaker*). These programs understand that database files have a repetitive structure, so you can pick a style for each field of the database, and every record will adopt those styles automatically. You can also work with multiple database files at the same time.

Forms Software

One common design task that most of us ordinary, aesthetically impaired mortals can handle is laying out a business form. It's possible to design forms with a standard desktop publishing package, but the job goes much quicker with specialized forms programs that have special tools for grids and *combs* (stacked rectangles of equal height). You can cheat, too—all these programs come with tons of sample forms that you can use as is or modify to taste.

Understand, though, that most forms programs do a lot more than design blank forms. They let you (or your company's order entry clerk) fill out the forms on the screen—and then print out the completed form and automatically store the entries in your favorite database program. Most also let you scan in existing paper forms and convert them to electronic facsimiles.

PerForm Pro Plus, *WindForm*, and *JetForm* lead in this category. For designing paper forms from scratch, any of them will do the job well. For converting from existing paper forms, your best choice is *WindForm OCR*, which can interpret the text as well as the boxes and blanks on scanned forms. All three are Windows applications; forms programs for DOS exist, but you should stick with Windows for the usual reasons.

Qty.	Description	Unit Cost	Total
		Sales Tax	
		Total	

Figure 12: *Forms programs make it easy to create combs— stacks of boxes like this one—and other fill-in-the-blanks elements.*

Other Resources

The further you get into desktop publishing, the more you become aware of the craft—the fine points of printing, layout, typography, and so on. Fortunately, there's no shortage of books and periodicals available to bulk up your expertise. Here are a few of the publications I've found most useful over the years:

Books

The Visual Display of Quantitative Information, $40
(how to prepare effective charts and graphs)
Graphics Press
P.O. Box 430
Cheshire, CT 06410
203/272-9187

Desktop Publishing Secrets, $27.95
(loads of practical tips on the mechanics of
desktop publishing)
Everyone's Guide to Successful Publications, $28
The Non-Designer's Design Book, $14.95
Peachpit Press
2414 Sixth St.
Berkeley, CA 94710
800/283-9444
510/548-4393

The Gray Book, $24.95
(tips for effective black-and-white publications)
Looking Good in Print, $24.95
Ventana Press
P.O. Box 2468
Chapel Hill, NC 27515
919/942-0220

Periodicals

Publish
Integrated Media Inc.
501 Second St.
San Francisco, CA 94107
800/274-5616
415/243-0600

Seybold Report on Desktop Publishing
Seybold Publications
P.O. Box 644
Media, PA 19063
215/565-2480

Technique
10 Post Office Sq. #600S
Boston MA 02109

Product Directory

Aldus PageMaker
InfoPublisher
Aldus Corp.
411 First Ave. South
Seattle, WA 98104
800/333-6687
206/628-2320

CorelDraw
Corel Corp.
1600 Carling Ave.
Ottawa, Ontario
K1Z 8R7, Canada
800/722-6735
613/728-8200

DoDOT
Halcyon Software, Inc.
1590 La Pradera Dr.
Campbell, CA 95008
408/378-9898

FontMinder
Ares Software Corp.
565 Pilgrim Dr.
Suiter City, CA 94404
415/578-9090
415/578-9090

FrameMaker
Frame Technology Corp.
1010 Rincon Cir.
San Jose, CA 95131
408/433-3311

HiJaak Pro
Inset Systems
71 Commerce Dr.
Brookfield, CT 06804-3405
203/740-2400

JetForm
JetForm Corp.
Watermill Center
800 South St. #305
Waltham, MA 02154
800/267-9976
617/647-7700

LetrTuck
EDCO Services, Inc.
4107 Gunn Hwy.
Tampa, FL 33624
813/962-7800
800/523-TYPE

Microsoft Publisher
Microsoft Corp.
One Microsoft Way
Redmond, WA 98052
800/426-9400
06/882-8080

PagePlus
Serif, Inc.
P.O. Box 803
Nashua, NH 03061
603/889-865050

PerForm Pro Plus
Delrina Technology Inc.
895 Don Mills Rd. #240
San Jose, CA 95119
800/268-6082
408/363-2345

PFS:Publisher
Express Publisher
for Windows
Spinnaker Software Corp.
201 Broadway
Cambridge, MA 02139
800/323-8088

Publish-It! for Windows
Timeworks, Inc.
625 Academy Dr.
Northbrook, IL 60062
800/323-7744
708/559-1300

QuarkXPress
Quark Inc.
1800 Grant St.
Denver, CO 80203
800/788-7835
303/894-8888

Ventura Publisher
Corel Corp.
800/722-6735
613/728-8200

WindForm
WindForm OCR
Graphics Development
  International
20A Pimentel Ct., Ste. B
Novato, CA 94949
415/382-6600
415/382-6600

19 Databases

By Celeste Robinson

- What database software is good for
- The basics of designing a database
- How to pick the right database software
- Tips for the most popular database programs
- Contact managers and textbases

You know that list of names, addresses, and phone numbers you swear you'll organize "someday"? Maybe it's in the back of your appointment book, or maybe you've entered it in a word processor or spreadsheet. Well, that list is a database, and you can make much better use of it in a database program.

Whenever you have a hunk of data that's likely to grow, and you need to extract meaningful information from it, a database program is probably the best tool for the job. Database software comes in two basic varieties:

- **Personal data managers** are inexpensive, easy-to-use programs designed to hold *your own* data, from a contact list, to a bunch of research documents, to an electronic card catalogue for your treasured CD collection. These programs keep everything filed away properly and enable you to retrieve just the information you want.

- **Programmable data managers** such as Paradox or dBASE IV are designed to hold shared data and lots of it: product inventory, customer purchase orders, you name it. You can spend months mastering these programs—or you can invest just a few hours and learn enough to create a reliable electronic filing system, to retrieve essential information fast, and even to run nicely formatted reports based on the data you've stored.

In this chapter, you'll find a guide for picking the right database software, along with plenty of tips on how to use the major programmable and personal data managers. You'll also learn how to set up a database that's easy to use and maintain, no matter how fast you think it will grow.

Why Bother With Database Software?

Database software is worthwhile any time you need to *store* and *retrieve* data—particularly large quantities of it—in list form. For example, maintaining a list of auto show attendees would be a classic job for database software. However, if the primary task was to *analyze* a fairly small quantity of data—say, to predict next year's turnout based on current car sales and attendance at previous shows—then a spreadsheet would make more sense, and you should turn to Chapter 15.

To give you a better idea of what database software can do, consider that humble list of names, addresses, and numbers. Use a database program to manage it, and you get:

- **Recyclable data.** If you stored your list in a word processing file, it would just sit there in the same format until you changed it manually. Enter information into a database, and you can quickly create address book pages, mailing labels, invitations, personalized letters, whatever you like.

- **Automatic filing.** Every time you need to add a name and phone number to your file, simply press [Enter] and let your database program do the filing—alphabeti cally, or in any order you choose.

- **Idiot-proof typing.** Database software can be set up so you can't enter a six-digit phone number, or "YN" instead of "NY" for New York. Also, it can expedite things by automatically putting slashes and dashes in phone numbers, or by filling in addresses for you as soon as you enter a company name.

- **Instant answers.** Want a list of all the Joneses you know in Manhattan? Just enter `Jones` and `212`. Can't remember what you talked to Geometrics about? If you took notes, a database can find them for you. Need to call Kowalski? Her number will probably pop up before you finish typing her name.

- **Quick calculations.** Maybe you bill by the hour, or you just want a record of how much you rack up in long-distance phone charges. If you've set up the database correctly, you can get a running total, and print an invoice at the end of the month if you like.

Now imagine offering these benefits to an officeful of people using a programmable data manager to handle thousands of names, numbers, and addresses. Each name could be linked with data on products purchased, dollars spent, late charges due, and so on. You could create financial statements and custom reports by product, customer, region, whatever. How much you can do all depends on the product you choose, and the time you want to spend learning and using it.

Databases 101 (Required)

Unfortunately, there's no way to talk about database software unless you learn some basic terminology. I'll try and make this as quick and painless as possible. Every database program has:

- **Data files** for storing information

- **Forms** for entering and viewing data

- **Queries** for finding information

- **Reports** that summarize data in various ways

- **Automation tools** to make specific tasks easier

The basic ideas are pretty simple, but some database programs muddy the water with slight variations on the lingo. As I explain each term, I'll give you its popular variations, too.

Data Files

Data files organize related information in rows and columns. Most database programs display data files as *tables*, and many manuals call data files just that. More often, they're simply referred to as *files*.

- **Fields** are pigeonholes. They're the basic elements of a data file. Each one holds a specific kind of information, such as a street address or a dollar amount. The contents of each field—what you put in the pigeonhole—is called a *field value*.

- **Records** are collections of pigeonholes that relate to a single entity: a person, an event, a place, a financial transaction, whatever. You can think of records as rows of fields in a table, though not every program lets you view records this way. A single record in a contact database would include fields for a person's name, address, telephone number, and so on.

When you set up a database, you label each field with a descriptive *field name*. You also need to pick a *data type* for each field, which means you can enter into that field only one type of information. Common data types include text, numbers, dates, notes, graphics, and references to fields in other files.

What Is a Database, Anyway?

The word *database* wins the prize for being the most confusing term of all. At any one time it may mean:

- A single data file

- A group of related data files

- A database program

Throughout this chapter, I use the term "database" to refer only to a single data file or to a group of related data files. Why is "file" singular *and* plural? Because a database is any collection of related information. For example, a database could be a single data file of musicians' names. Or it could be that file plus a related one listing the albums those musicians have recorded, plus another listing the songs they've written, plus another listing the bands they've played in, and so on.

Forms

Database *forms* usually show you one record at a time. You use blank forms to enter records, and you can use the "forms view" provided by most database programs to flip

FIELD NAMES ───────

SELECTED RECORD ───

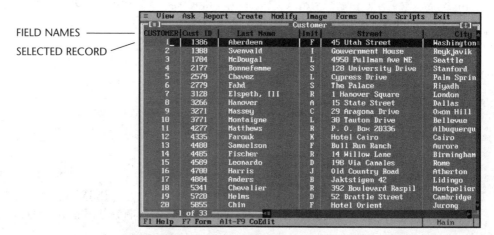

Figure 1: *Here's what a data file looks like in Paradox's table view.*

through records, just like paging through a stack of paper forms. Many database programs enable you to design attractive custom forms, and still others offer form templates that you can modify, but you might be able to make do with the simple forms that all programs create automatically based on the fields in your database. Forms are sometimes called *layouts* or *views*.

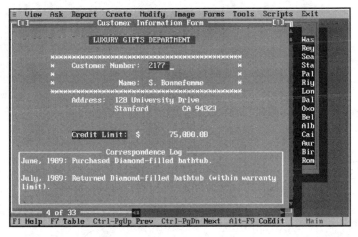

Figure 2: *This Paradox form includes fields from both the customer file and the correspondence file.*

Forms generally show most (if not all) of the field names and values in each record. Depending on the software you choose, you may be able to include fields from other data files, too. Many programs also enable you to create *lookup tables* or *pick lists*, which give you lists of field values to choose from so you don't have to type (or remember) as much. With some programs, you can design very fancy forms—with shaded push-buttons that pop up lists, scanned product photos instead of descriptions, and so on.

Queries

A database *query* is just what it sounds like: a question you ask about your data. Most database programs let you formulate queries using a technique called *query by example*, where you just check off the fields you want in your query, enter the field values, and run the query to find all records that match the criteria. For example, if you wanted to find all the deadbeats in Illinois, you'd enter Y in the Late field, IL in the State field, and instantly know who in that state *shouldn't* get the good-customer discount.

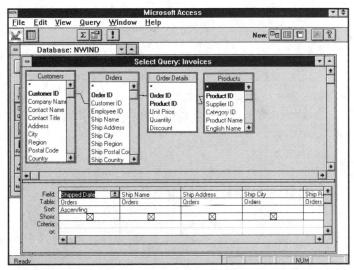

Figure 3: *To set up a multifile query with Microsoft Access, you drag the fields you want to see in the query results into the query-by-example grid at the bottom of the screen.*

Querying can get complicated, almost like a language unto itself. To fetch the records of all clients who owe you more than $100 and who are more than a month late paying up, you have to learn to use *logical operators* (AND, OR, <, >, and so on). Some queries summarize data instead of retrieving records (say, the number of customers overdue), while others change data when they find certain field values. A few programs don't use the term "query"—instead, you *find* or *filter* data to call up the records you want.

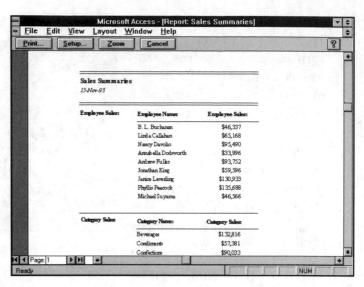

Figure 4: *Being able to create reports like this Access sales summary is one of the chief benefits of database software when you're managing lots of data.*

Reports

Reports can be as simple as a printout of a single record or a list of records retrieved according to a couple of criteria and printed in basic table format. More often, reports take planning, especially with industrial-strength programmable databases that are the backbone of an office or department.

For example, to get a printout of how a whole sales force did in November, by product and salesperson, you need to decide in advance how the columns of figures will line up, where to put headings and subtotals, and so on (see Figure 4). Programmable data managers generally include *report generators* that let you define report criteria with a menu, and move output anywhere you like by "painting" fields on a report preview screen.

Automation Tools

Here's where personal and programmable data managers differ most. Personal data managers sometimes have no automation tools at all, and when they do, those tools are generally much less potent than what the programmables offer.

- **Scripts and macros** are as automated as personal data managers get. Both are lists of commands and keystrokes you perform often—say, to run a certain type of query or report. Defining these two terms gets tricky, since different database programs mean different things by them. In some cases, you simply "record" keystroke sequences to create a script or macro; in others, you may edit lists of commands. Nearly all programs let you run scripts or macros by picking them from a list, but with some you can also set up easy-to-use buttons to run automatic sequences.

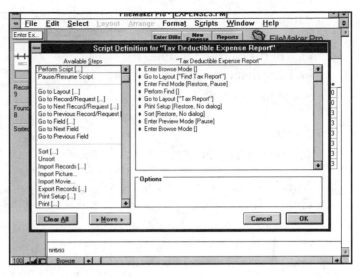

Figure 5: *This stack of commands looks intimidating, but it only took a few minutes to create it by pointing and clicking through FileMaker Pro's ScriptMaker.*

- **Programming languages** such as dBASE are what make programmable data managers programmable. These languages enable programmers to create *database applications*, which are complete custom programs intended for specific tasks—billing for a chiropractor's office, order entry for a huge clothing retailer, you name it. Often, programmers create turnkey applications where users just pick items from custom menus without having to know a thing about database software.

- **Application generators** fall midway between scripts and hard-core programming. You point and click your way through menus while the application generator writes the programming code. Step by step, you're asked how you'd like to construct the application: the array of menu choices, the criteria for push-button queries, the format for canned reports, the layout for forms, and so on. Programs written by application generators alone generally work for pretty basic jobs, but programmers sometimes use them as a starting point and then add to or customize the code.

Database Design Basics

Some database programs are better for certain jobs than others, so you can't pick the right product unless you figure out exactly what the job involves. To that end, here's a very basic guide to designing and setting up a simple database. It begins by sketching out a database design and follows up with some tips that can help you build a database with any program. Along the way, you'll get an idea of the software features to look for that can make managing your data easier.

Step 1: Choosing Fields

This is mostly common sense. Grab a piece of paper, jot down the information you want in each record, and break that information down into separate fields. At this point, you need to keep only one thing in mind: how you might want to *sort* your records—in alphabetical order, by ZIP code, whatever. Any piece of information you want to sort by must be kept in a field by itself.

REMEMBER

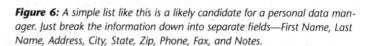

Figure 6: *A simple list like this is a likely candidate for a personal data manager. Just break the information down into separate fields—First Name, Last Name, Address, City, State, Zip, Phone, Fax, and Notes.*

For example, Name, Address, City, State, Zip, Phone, and Fax may seem like sensible fields for a contact database. Think again: If you want to sort your records alphabetically by last name—so you can print out phone book pages in order, for example—you'll need separate fields for First Name and Last Name.

REMEMBER

Note that when you're *searching* for data instead of *sorting*, that data doesn't necessarily need to be in a separate field. Most programs let you run queries that search the *contents* of fields and retrieve records based on what they find there. For example, if you want all the records for people who live on Terrace Drive, you can retrieve those records without having to keep street names and numbers in separate fields.

Step 2: Creating a Data File

Whichever database software you buy, the first step after you install the program is to create a data file. Every program leads you through the same basic routine, the core of which is entering the field names one by one. Whether you do this in a dialog box, in a blank form, or in some other place depends on the database program you've chosen (see Step 6 for more on forms).

Choosing Data Types

As you enter each field name, you'll be offered a choice of data types to help ensure that you (or someone else) enter the right data in the right field. Almost every program offers the following data types:

- **Alphanumeric** or **text** fields for holding strings of numbers or letters

- **Number** fields for values you may want to perform calculations with

- **Date** and **time** fields

- **Currency** fields for holding dollar amounts

- **Memo** fields for entering free-form text, such as notes

You may find other data types, too, such as *logical* fields (Yes/No, True/False, Male/Female), *counters* for automatically incrementing number fields (for customer orders, invoices, and other records that need unique identifiers), *graphics* fields to store pictures, or *binary* fields for holding sound or other information.

When you choose a field's data type, make sure you consider what a field's value is really used for. For instance, you would choose an alphanumeric rather than a number data type for a ZIP code field, because no one makes calculations with ZIP code numbers—and many programs automatically drop the leading zeros in number fields.

HOT TIP

And while you can store dates in alphanumeric fields, choosing a date data type is better because it prevents you from accidentally entering impossible dates, and it ensures that all dates appear in the same format, no matter how they're entered.

Setting Field Lengths

Some fields—mostly alphanumeric ones—need a length to go along with their name and type. Be generous when you choose a maximum number of characters—but not too generous. For example, say you have

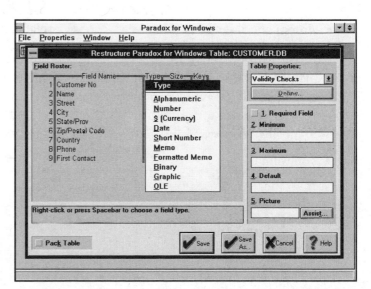

Figure 7: *In this Paradox for Windows dialog box, you get a wide choice of data types when you set up or change fields. Note the special field types for formatted memos, graphics files, and so on.*

only one contact with a very long address like 1234567 West Avenida de las Estrellas Mail Stop 9876. Pick a field length that will accommodate the rest of the addresses you need to enter, and abbreviate the one that won't fit. Sticking with shorter fields makes it easier to design forms and reports, saves disk space, and can make your database run faster.

HOT TIP

Step 3: One File or Two? (Or More?)

A simple list of contacts can be handled easily by any personal data manager. Each person's name has a finite number of associated details—an address, a phone number, an area for notes—and each field holds a single piece of information. But what happens when you take the same contact list and decide to add a dated call report for every phone call you make to each person?

You could keep these call reports in one big field, but then you couldn't do such things as sort the reports by date, or print out a list of all the calls you made on Thursday last week. In this situation, it makes sense to keep your data in two files:

• **A master file** of names, addresses, and phone numbers

• **A related file** of call reports, where each report is stored in its own record

This arrangement requires a *relational* database program, which will enable you to store information in two or more files, and combine data from fields in different files for queries and reports. Anytime you have a "list of lists"—of contacts and call reports, alumni and donations, whatever—choose a relational database program.

REMEMBER

Along with giving you more sorting options, using a relational database program to manage "lists of lists" can keep you from having to type in the same information over and over. Take an invoicing system as another example. Typically, you'd set it up like this:

• **A master file** containing customer information

• **A related file** of all your products

• **Two related files** of invoices and like-item info

```
Coco Mitchinson
525 Thornton Ave.
Highland  IL  60000
312-123-4567

11/15/93  Met Coco at the big show. She has her own dancewear business.
1/06/93   Spoke with Coco on the phone. She might be able to meet with me
          at the spring conference. Call back in late March.
3/20/93   Talked to Coco on the phone. We will meet in Miami next month.

Ray Donaldson
1775 Terrace Drive
Venice CA  90291
213/555-0987

10/31/93  Met Ray at club. He has a surf shop where he sells a good volume
          of beachy exercise clothes.
12/15/92  Invited Ray to holiday gathering at office.
```

Figure 8: In this "list of lists," you have a list of dated call notes for each person on the contact list. This situation requires separate files, which means you need a relational database.

Why this arrangement? For one thing, invoices always have unique numbers, so you need a separate invoice file containing a numbered record for each invoice. Unless you want to type in product descriptions and prices from scratch every time you make a sale, you'll want a second file for all your products so you can add product information to the invoice by scrolling through a list or entering a product number. With a master file for customers, you can add customer information to orders in much the same way.

All programmable databases—such as *Access*, *Paradox*, and *dBASE*—are relational. Most personal databases are not relational, but you'll find some exceptions, such as Lotus's *Approach*. Other personal products, such as Ace Software's *AceFile*, let you juggle multiple files, but in ways more limited than with true relational databases, which let you combine information from several different files any way you like. As you read on, decide how much relational capability you need, and check the database software sections later in this chapter to see which programs will work for you.

Relational vs. Flat File

At the beginning of this chapter, I said that database programs can be divided into two groups: personal and programmable. Well, I wasn't really giving you the whole story. In truth, people commonly use another way of categorizing databases:

- **Flat filers** for working with one file of information at a time

- **Relational database managers** that let you store information in separate files and grab related pieces to use together as you like

There's one problem with this distinction: Flat filers are a vanishing breed. Today, even low-cost personal data managers such as *FileMaker Pro* frequently offer "pseudo-relational" capabilities—for example, the ability to create lookup tables of field values in another file, such as a list of product numbers or employee names.

Database nerds argue endlessly over which products do or do not qualify as relational, but the bottom line is this: Programmable data managers usually give you all the relational power you could ever need, whereas personal data managers offer much less relational capability. So if you opt for a personal program, you need to examine the product carefully to see if it can link files the way you want them linked.

Step 4: Indexing Files

Just as indexes in books help you find information quickly, indexes for data files help database programs look up records fast. Indexes contain copies of the contents of important fields in every record—Last Name and First Name, say. Run a query to find everyone with the last name Franklin, for instance, and the software searches the index first, where it finds a few Franklins, and then calls up the actual records themselves. This method is far faster than searching the entire data file for Franklin matches.

You should index files when you set them up, provided your program will let you—some personal database programs don't bother with indexing, while all programmable database programs have it. With some programmables, such as *Access* and *Paradox*, you create keys by indexing on a field (or a combination of fields) that serves as a unique identifier for each record, such as a customer number. Along with the key, you can index on other frequently searched fields.

Step 5: Linking Data Files

REMEMBER

The trick to creating a relational database is to construct files so one can be connected with another. Here's the basic rule: If you want to use two files together, they need to have at least one field in common.

Take those two separate files for contacts and call reports. If you wanted to find out who you called in California on a certain date, you'd need to run a query that checked field values in both files. How would you do this? Well, you couldn't, unless you'd set up the files so they had a common field. In this case, you could simply add a Contact # field to both the contacts file *and* the call reports file, as shown here:

Fields in contacts file	Fields in call reports file
Contact #	Contact #
Last Name	Date
First Name	Report Notes
Address	
City	
State	
Zip	
Phone Number	
Fax Number	

The Contact # field enables you to *join* the two files, which is the first thing you do in preparation for a relational query or report. How you join files varies from program to program—some (such as *dBASE IV*) make you specify the linking fields and execute a join command, while others join files automatically using common fields.

Some relational programs let you link files using keys only. The unique values in key fields prevent you from accidentally matching up the wrong records between files. For example, when you set up the call reports file, the key would be a *combination* of the Contact # and Date fields. (You might call any number of contacts on a given date, and you might call a contact on several different days, but the unique record you're looking for contains notes about what you said to a certain contact on a certain date.)

DANGER

When you want to link files, using fields with unique ID numbers—instead of real data, such as Last Name and First Name—is almost always a good idea. Otherwise, if your contacts file had two John Smiths, the program wouldn't know which call report was associated with which person. Unique ID numbers prevent such confusion, especially when you link more than two data files.

HOT TIP

Data Relationships

There are three types of relationships possible between data files. Why you should care about this will become clear in a minute.

- **One to one.** This type of relationship exists when only one record can be matched to a single record in another file. For example, the relationship between the call reports file and the contacts file is *one to one*, because there will always be only one contact for each call report.

- **One to many.** Looking at it from the other direction, the relationship between the contacts file and the call reports file is *one to many*, because there can be several call reports for each contact.

- **Many to many.** This kind of relationship occurs when there can be more than one record with the same value in the linking field on both sides of a relationship. If you had an order file that was keyed on Contact # and Order #, there would be a many-to-many relationship between this file and the above call history file, using Contact # as the linking field.

So why worry about these relationships? For one thing, some programs can't handle many-to-many relationships. Beyond that, you need to understand a database concept called *referential integrity*. This term can mean different things in different programs, but it always involves protecting the values that link records.

For example, say you changed a record's contact number in a contact file. Because Contact # is the linking field, you'd immediately lose that record's links to all its call report records in the other file, unless you changed *their* contact numbers to match. Ideally, a program that has referential integrity should detect this kind of change and automatically make the same change for you in the linked records.

DANGER

Some relational programs can detect what kind of relationship exists between two files (based on their key fields) and automatically provide some kind of referential integrity if there is a one-to-one or a one-to-many link in place. In other cases, you must turn on the feature manually, or choose from among different referential integrity options—for example, you may decide it's safer to simply prevent any changes to the Contact #.

Step 6: Creating the "Front End"

The *front end* of a database is what the user sees when he or she enters data, runs reports, executes queries, and so on. At their most complex, front ends are applications in themselves and can take hundreds of hours to create using a database programming language. They often include menus tailored to specific tasks—from booking airline reservations to tracking sales leads—along with canned reports and queries that run at the click of a mouse.

> ## When to Break the Rules
>
> In theory, it's easy to decide when you should break down information into separate files and use a relational database. As a rule, if you find yourself entering the same kind of details more than once in the same record (Date1, Date2, Date3), then you need separate files. But sometimes it makes sense to break this rule. The following cases are examples:
>
> - **A small number of repeating details in each record.** Say you have a file of sales leads, and you have no more than two or three contacts at any one company. You could set up two files, one containing companies, and a related one containing the people you contact, but that would probably be overkill. Instead, set up a few name fields (Name 1, Name 2, Name 3) and avoid the extra work.
>
> - **Repeating details in just a few records.** The phone numbers in an address book are a perfect example. Though you might have a friend or two with a dozen numbers (home, office, car, fax, and so on), you wouldn't set up a separate file of phone numbers. Instead, it would make sense to have two or three phone number fields, and maybe keep the extra numbers in a notes field.
>
> If you think you'll have more than a few repeating details and it makes sense to store those details—product orders, call reports, whatever—in their own records, then you need a relational database.

At their simplest, front ends are merely forms for entering data and executing queries. All database programs come with default forms that you can customize. With Windows database software, you can usually dress up forms easily with fonts, shaded boxes, and the like. Many programs come with a bunch of well-designed forms for specific tasks, so if you're lucky, you'll find a form ready made for the job at hand.

HOT TIP

There's more to designing a form than including all the right fields and arranging them nicely. Database programs come with a number of tools that help speed data entry and guard against error:

- **Lookup tables** or **pick lists** give you a choice of field values and *only* those values— handy for making sure only valid customers, part numbers, and the like are entered.

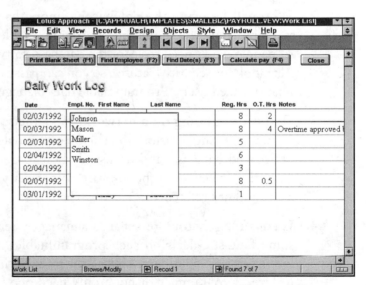

Order File Fields	Customer File Fields	Salesperson File Fields
Order #	Customer #	Salesperson #
Date	Name	Name
Customer #	Address	Commission
Salesperson #	City	Territory
Ship Via	State	
	Zip	
	Phone Number	

Line Item File Fields	Inventory File Fields
Order #	Item #
Item #	Description
Quantity	Cost
Price	Quantity On Hand

Figure 9: *To link these five data files—and avoid having to retype customer and item information for each order—each file needs at least one field (marked by the # sign) in common with another file.*

- **Formats** specify how values should be displayed—the number of decimal places for dollar amounts, the format for dates, upper- or lowercase for text, and so on.

- **Incrementing number** or **counter fields** automatically assign unique identification numbers to records.

- **Ranges** establish upper and lower limits for number fields.

- **Templates** or **masks** add special characters automatically, such as hyphens in phone numbers.

- **Calculated fields** do computations automatically when you enter numbers.

- **Sound effects** alert you with beeps or other alarms if you try to make an incorrect entry.

Figure 10: *This predesigned Lotus Approach form pops up a list of valid employee names when you click in the Employee Number field.*

DANGER

Why should you insist that values are entered uniformly? Say you want to sort all the records in a database by country. Unless your form has enforced a consistent way to enter data in the Country field, you'll end up with separate groups of records for "US," "USA," and "U.S." Worse, entering invalid data could create an *orphan record* that would be left out of queries, reports, and links with other files. No search for customers who bought a certain product will call up a customer record in which the product's ID number was entered incorrectly.

Finding the Right Data Manager

If you've gotten this far, you're at least beginning to get the idea of the features you might need in a database program. Ask yourself these basic questions to narrow down your choice further:

1. **How much relational capability do I need?** If you'll be linking more than two data files at a time, or if you think your database will steadily increase in size and complexity, then you should probably head straight for the section on programmable data managers. If you'll be managing simple lists, then see if one of the personal data managers will do.

2. **Who will be using the database?** If more than a couple of people will be using it, then maybe you should buy a program that lets you create a custom front end, so people won't need to learn the database software in order to use the database. Also look for security features, so you can password-protect certain data files from unauthorized users. Programmable data managers excel in both these areas.

3. **Will it be running on a network?** If so, then you may have limited say over the software-buying decision. In general, only a database professional should set up a networked database, and it's usually best to get a good database consultant and have him or her select the software. Whatever you do, always remember to check a consultant's references.

4. **Is cost a big factor?** Personal data managers tend to be cheaper, but you can find some fantastic deals on such programmables as *Access* and *Paradox*. The most important cost consideration isn't the price of the software, but whether you need to hire a programmer or not. You'll need one for big projects like a full-fledged accounting system, or for almost anything that runs on a network.

5. **Does the database already exist?** If so, then be sure to select a database program that can use the existing data files. Almost all programs can handle *dBASE* and ASCII (plain text) files, but beyond that, it's hit or miss. Products that demand you

SQL, the Database Esperanto

SQL (*Structured Query Language*)—pronounced "sequel"—is a universal programming language for querying that originated on mainframes. Most programmable database programs speak SQL. And a whole other class of SQL database programs for network servers—including *Microsoft SQL Server, Sybase SQL Server, Oracle, Interbase,* and *DB2*—are designed for programmers who create applications for large organizations. I haven't covered these SQL server products, because they lack a real user interface and should be installed and maintained only by professionals who know client/server databases.

Why should you bother with SQL? You shouldn't, unless you work in an organization with a network that has a SQL database program running on a server. If so, and you use a programmable database program, you may be able to send SQL queries to the server and have the query results show up in your own database program. Often, you don't even need to know SQL to run the query. You just create your query in the usual way, and your program generates the SQL commands behind the scenes.

SQL databases often hold huge quantities of data, so being able to query your company's SQL database may open up a whole new world of valuable information. Theoretically, any database program that can create a SQL query can retrieve data from any SQL database—but this is hardly the case in reality. Only certain data managers can converse with certain SQL databases, and unless a programmer has set things up so you can run SQL queries, you're probably out of luck. If your data manager speaks SQL, however, and there's valuable stuff in the SQL database, it's worth lobbying for the ability to link up.

run foreign files through a separate conversion process are less convenient than those that access those files directly.

6. **Will you use the database for mailings?** Creating and aligning mailing labels is a pain with any software. If you use your database as a mailing list, look for a program that has Avery label layouts.

HOT TIP

7. **Do you plan on doing lots of data analysis?** Then find a program that lets you create graphs, so you don't need to export data to a spreadsheet in order to analyze things graphically. *AceFile, Access,* and *Paradox for Windows* all provide this capability. These three packages also offer *crosstabs*, which are matrix-style reports that analyze databases on the combination of two fields—sales dollars by product *and* salesperson, for example.

8. **Do you want nicely formatted reports?** Of course you do. Programs that provide *style sheets* make sophisticated formatting easiest.

REMEMBER

HOT TIP

Murphy's Law of databases says they always end up being more complicated than you think they'll be. If you buy a data manager with limited or nonexistent relational capabilities, and you want it for anything beyond the simplest of tasks, make sure you find one that can convert its data files into *dBASE, Paradox, 1-2-3,* or ASCII format. That way, if you upgrade to a more powerful product later, you'll be able to use those data files with little trouble.

Programmable Database Software

Welcome to the Land of the Giants. With these heavy-duty data managers, you can craft easy-to-use applications for specific jobs and relate files in virtually unlimited ways. The applications you create will ensure that people enter data correctly and efficiently, while links between files save time—update one file, and the software updates related files simultaneously.

If you don't think you'll need to create applications, then you probably don't need a programmable. *Approach*, the most powerful of the personal data managers, can probably give you all the relational power you need without the hassle of learning a programming language. For more on *Approach*, see the section after this chapter on personal database software.

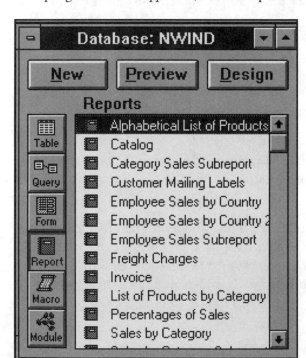

Figure 11: Unlike other programmable data managers, Access stores all the elements of a database in a single file, so you can use descriptive file names for tables, forms, reports, and so on.

The best heavy-duty programmables for ordinary people (as opposed to programmers) are *Access* and *Paradox for Windows.* No, you won't learn these Windows programs overnight, but they make quick queries a snap, and you can produce classy-looking reports easily.

Access

Access is part of Microsoft's family of Windows products. It has lots of clever on-line help, and you'll need it, because this program takes some time to learn (for example, how to key tables isn't obvious, and you must key tables before you

can join them). To summarize
this sprawling program's more
interesting features:

- **Relationships between files "stay put"** so you don't have to constantly say how you want files joined for forms, reports, and queries.

- **Wizards,** sort of animated flowcharts, step you through creating forms and reports and offer lots of options for field layouts and styles (fonts, borders, and so on) along the way. Wizards are my favorite part of *Access*.

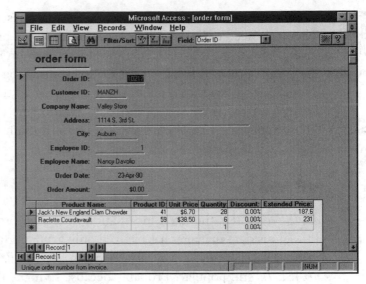

Figure 12: *Start with an existing query, and Access lets you easily create a multitable form like this one.*

- **Cue Cards** suggest what you should do next throughout the program when you click on them.

- **Direct access to lots of file formats,** including *dBASE III+* and *IV, FoxPro 2.0* and *2.5, Paradox 3.0* and *3.5, Btrieve, Microsoft SQL Server, Sybase SQL Server,* and *Oracle RDBMS.*

- **Visual Basic,** the *Access* programming language, enables programmers to create custom applications in a familiar language.

Access keeps all the various elements of a particular *database* project (data, forms, reports, queries, macros, applications) in one big file called a database. This is different from most other programs, where each of these elements has its own separate file. One advantage to this arrangement is that you're not prey to DOS's dumb rules for naming files.

Queries are *Access*'s strong suit. Just click on the Query button in the database window, and up pops the Select Query dialog box. Choose the tables you want to relate, and if you've keyed your tables correctly, *Access* will relate them graphically—with stretchy lines connecting key fields in different tables. Then drag the fields you want shown in the query results to the table at the bottom of the screen, add any query criteria, and run the query.

HOT TIP

REMEMBER

When you create a form or report, it's often easiest to start with a query—especially when you need to link more than two tables in the process. To create a form linked to several tables, go to the Database window, click on the Form icon, and then click on the New button to bring up the New Form dialog box. In the box labeled Select a Table/Query, choose the query you want to use as the basis for the form, and click on FormWizards. When Access prompts you for the type of Wizard you want, choose

HOT TIP

Main/Subform. The Wizard will lead you through the rest of the process, and style sheets will help give the results a polished look.

dBASE IV

dBASE IV 2.0 is the latest incarnation of a *DOS* program from the dinosaur days of PCs. This data manager has evolved only grudgingly. It lacks many features common to newer programs—many of which can access *dBASE* data files directly. So why is *dBASE IV* still popular? Probably because so many custom applications out there are written in the *dBASE* programming language. Instead of creating new applications from scratch, people prefer to use *dBASE IV* to revise their old ones.

REMEMBER

dBASE IV is basically the *dBASE* programming language wrapped in a collection of menus called the Control Center—the first thing you see when you start up the program. Select an option from the Control Center, and *dBASE IV* enters a string of *dBASE* programming commands behind the scenes. In fact, everything you do with *dBASE IV* is accomplished through executing *dBASE* commands, whether you use the Control Center, enter commands yourself, or run a *dBASE* program file.

```
Catalog   Tools   Exit                                        3:17:53 pm
                        dBASE IV CONTROL CENTER
                      CATALOG: C:\DBASE\UNTITLED.CAT

    Data       Queries      Forms      Reports     Labels    Applications
 <create>     <create>    <create>    <create>    <create>     <create>

 ACTIONS      CUSTCONT    CUSTCONT    ACTIONS     LABELS
 CONTACTS                             COURSECT
 COURSES                              NAMELIST
 CUSTOMER
 NAMES


 File:         New file
 Description:  Press ENTER on <create> to create a new file

   Help:F1  Use:←┘  Data:F2  Design:Shift-F2  Quick Report:Shift-F9  Menus:F10
```

Figure 13: *dBASE IV's Control Center keeps you from having to deal with the dBASE programming language. But as interfaces go, the Control Center is way behind the times.*

If you're new to *dBASE*, use the Control Center. Few people start by learning the language and typing *dBASE* commands at the program's infamous "dot prompt." The dot prompt is *dBASE*'s equivalent to the DOS prompt: spare and unforgiving. But as you get more experienced, you'll probably find that it's quicker to use the dot prompt than to poke through the menus, especially if you plan to create or modify applications.

```
 Records   Organize   Fields   Go To   Exit
┌────────┬──────────────┬──────────────┬──────────────────────────┐
│ IDNUM  │ FIRST        │ LAST         │ ADDRESS                  │
├────────┼──────────────┼──────────────┼──────────────────────────┤
│ 2345   │ Audrey       │ Palmer       │ 1729 Technology Drive    │
│ 93452  │ Eric         │ Johnson      │ 3412 Felix Lane, #234    │
│ 5822   │ Scott        │ Barkley      │ 1234 Mansion Way         │
│ 5823   │ Sharron      │ Jones        │ 1232 Forest Lane,        │
│ 5678   │ Cindy        │ Almond       │ 123 Claven St.           │
│        │              │              │                          │
└────────┴──────────────┴──────────────┴──────────────────────────┘
 Browse  C:\dbiii\STAFF      Rec 1/6      File         Num
```

Figure 14: *Offering a bare-bones, tabular view of your data, dBASE IV's Browse window is the place where you add or change records.*

You get to the dot prompt by pressing Alt E and selecting Exit to dot prompt from the Exit menu. At the dot prompt, *dBASE* normally keeps a list of the last 20 commands in something called a "history buffer." You can flip through previously executed commands by pressing the up arrow, and you can reexecute a command just by pressing Enter. To return to the Control Center from the dot prompt, press F2.

HOT TIP

To *browse* a data file (the *dBASE* term for looking at records in a tabular format), select Display or just press F2 with the file name highlighted. You can also browse a data file from the dot prompt: Enter `use` followed by the data file name and then enter `browse`. Either method opens the Browse window, where you can add records or change them. The quickest way to move between fields is with Tab or Shift Tab instead of with the arrow keys. When you're finished, press Esc to close the window and save your changes.

With the Quick Report command, you can create a simple list-style report easily. In the Control Center, highlight the name of the file on which you want to base your report and press Shift F9. Then choose Begin printing or View report on screen.

HOT TIP

FoxPro (for DOS and Windows)

I always think of *FoxPro* as a faster, better *dBASE*. It works with *dBASE* database files, its programming language grew out of the dBASE language, and like *dBASE IV*, it's geared more toward application developers than end users. Both the DOS and Windows versions of *FoxPro 2.5* have these key characteristics:

- **Speed.** *FoxPro* has always been known for its super performance, meaning it can find information and reorganize it in a jiffy.

- **dBASE compatibility.** *FoxPro* can read files from *dBASE III+* and *dBASE IV*, and its programming language is an extended version of the dBASE language.

- **Compatible Mac version.**
Along with DOS and
Windows versions, *FoxPro
2.5* comes in a Mac version,
as well as one for UNIX
(the most popular mini-
computer operating sys-
tem). All these flavors share
applications and data with
each other, and they work
in much the same way.

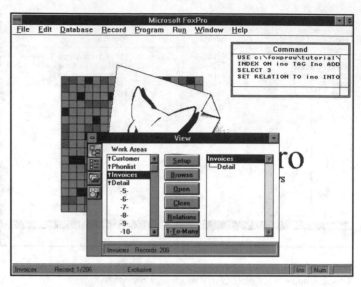

When you first start *FoxPro*,
you don't see much on the
screen—just the friendly fox
on his checkerboard, a menu
bar, and a window labeled
Command. This should be a

Figure 15: *Like dBASE, FoxPro for Windows is mainly a developer's tool. You can enter commands using the menus or directly in the Command window.*

hint that, like *dBASE IV*, FoxPro relies on programming commands for everything,
whether you type them directly into the Command window or generate them by picking options from *FoxPro*'s menus.

Like *dBASE*'s dot prompt, the
Command window lets you reexecute commands without having
to type them in. Just move the
cursor to the window, scroll
through the list until the cursor
is on the command you want to
use again, and press [Enter].
FoxPro will execute the command
and add it to the end of the list.

HOT TIP

FoxPro's Expression Builder
helps you assemble and check
expressions used with *filters*
(*FoxPro*'s name for queries) or
programming commands. An
expression is made up of such
elements as logical operators and

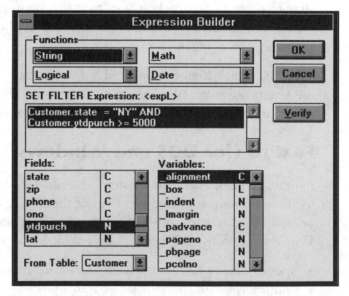

Figure 16: *Using FoxPro for Windows' Expression Builder, you can type query criteria directly into the SET FILTER Expression box, or you can choose menu options and have FoxPro enter the criteria for you.*

field names, which become part of the filter or command being executed. With the Expression Builder's SET FILTER command, *FoxPro* looks for records that match the expression you've entered.

To print a quick listing of records, or to create a basic report design that you can embellish however you like, choose File//New and select Report from the New dialog box. When the report design window opens, choose Report//Quick Report, and select a table (if one isn't already in use). Then select the default field layout in the Quick Report dialog box.

HOT TIP

Paradox for Windows

Paradox for Windows 4.5 offers more hand-holding than most programmable database programs, making it suitable for both serious application developers and ordinary users who aren't afraid to roll up their sleeves and dig in. Here are some of this program's key features:

- **The Object Inspector.** Click the right mouse button on almost any database element, and a menu pops up listing all the things you can do.

HOT TIP

- **The SpeedBar.** Like *Access, Paradox for Windows* has a row of icons at the top of the screen that enables you to execute common commands fast.

- **Flexible data access.** Direct access to *Paradox for DOS* or *dBASE* tables, along with *Sybase SQL Server, Microsoft SQL Server, Oracle,* and *Interbase* data, ensures that you'll be able to use existing databases.

- **ObjectPAL.** *Paradox for Windows'* programming language enables you to attach a code to database objects easily, without having to write big programs.

Note that being a *Paradox for DOS* expert does not make you a *Paradox for Windows* expert. In fact, you feel as if you're

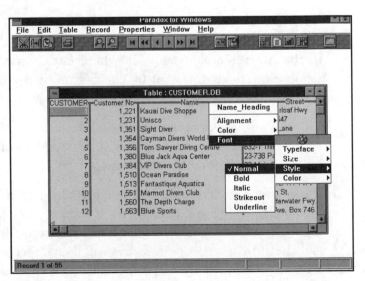

Figure 17: *Just point to an object and click on it with the right mouse button, and Paradox for Windows pops up all the options for changing an object's properties, as this series of formatting menus shows.*

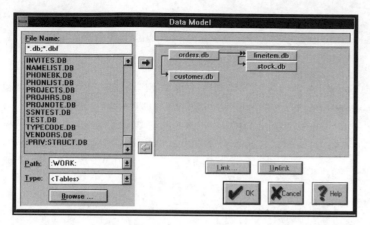

learning a whole new program, especially since none of your old *Paradox for DOS* forms, reports, queries, or applications will work. If you have a lot invested in *Paradox for DOS* applications, you might not want to switch. Otherwise, it's worth it, because the Windows version is easier to use and produces better reports.

Figure 18: *Relating tables for an order entry form is easy with Paradox's Data Model dialog box. Choose the table file names, click on the master table, drag the mouse to the subsidiary tables, and in most cases you're done.*

With *Paradox for Windows*, if you've keyed your tables properly, you can easily relate them in a form or report. For a form, choose File//New//Form to open the Data Model dialog box. In the File Name list, double-click on each table you want to relate. To draw the actual relationships, click on the master table first, and then drag the mouse pointer to the subsidiary tables. Usually, *Paradox* links the tables automatically, based on the key fields; if it can't, a dialog box will open and you'll have to pick the linking fields manually.

To create a query, click on the SpeedBar's Open Query icon. Select the table (or tables) you want to query, and you'll see a list of all the possible fields you can display in the Answer table (the place where *Paradox for Windows* shows query results). Choose the fields you want by clicking on their adjacent check boxes, and add any selection criteria you wish. Then press F8 to view the query results.

HOT TIP

To print a single *Paradox for Windows* record, you simply open a Form window and click on the SpeedBar's print icon. Click on the same icon when a Table window is open, and you'll print out all the records in the table.

HOT TIP

If you want a real report rather than just a listing, and you've spent some time designing an attractive form, Paradox has a feature you'll love. Choose File//Open//Form, highlight the form's name, select Report from the drop-down menu under Open As, and click OK. *Paradox for Windows* will then do its best to turn your form design into a report design (to dress up reports further, you also get style sheets). This process works in reverse, so you can select a report and turn it into a form just as easily.

Paradox for DOS

Paradox is my favorite programmable data manager for DOS. The current version is chock full of bells and whistles for programmers, but it still enables ordinary users to handle related tables without too much sweat. Outstanding features include:

- **Instant scripts** that record your keystrokes for an easy way to create simple applications without programming

- **Graphs and crosstabs** for sophisticated data analysis

- **Extensive query-by-example** capabilities for *updating* data as well as finding information

On the downside, you can't design forms and reports as pretty as those produced by Windows database programs, and you have to plow through menus to add things like table lookups and special field formatting—no magic dialog boxes here. Nonetheless, if you must do it in DOS and you're a user rather than a programmer, *Paradox for DOS* is the best relational data manager you can buy. It offers a decent development environment for programmers, too.

Paradox for DOS lets you use a mouse, of course, but it also offers lots of keyboard shortcuts. These can be especially handy when you're updating or adding records in the program's Co-Edit mode. To get into Co-Edit, select View from the menu bar, choose the table whose records you want to change, and press Alt F9 . Use these tricks to speed things along:

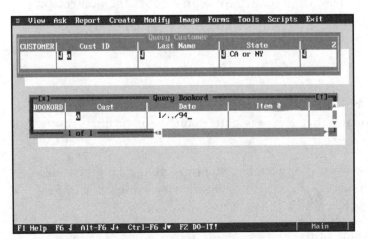

- To empty a field, use Ctrl Backspace .

- To copy a value from the same field in the previous record, press Ctrl D .

HOT TIP

- To edit a value without erasing it first, type Ctrl F or Alt F5 to go into Field View.

Figure 19: *The original query-by-example database, Paradox for DOS enables you to simply check off the fields you want to see displayed in query results.*

- To undo your last change to a table in Co-Edit, or to undo as many changes as you like in Edit mode, press Ctrl U.

- To print an Instant Report of the table you're viewing, type Alt F7 .

Queries are simple with *Paradox for DOS*, in part because you don't need to worry about whether you've keyed your tables correctly in order to run queries that involve multiple tables. Just pull down the Ask menu, choose the tables you want included in the query, and check off the fields you want displayed in *Paradox*'s query Answer table. Press F2 (*Paradox*'s all-purpose DO IT! key), and up pops the results.

Reports involving multiple tables are a lot more complicated, especially if you want to report on subsets of records. You need to design and save the report first (a procedure too complicated to go into here) and then run a query on the same tables using the same fields. When the query results appear in the Answer table, select Tools//Copy//Report//DifferentTable, choose the same master file name and the name of the report you just saved, copy it to the R report for the Answer table, and press Alt F7 to print the report. Reports like these are a lot of work, so make sure

you save your keystrokes using *Paradox for DOS*'s script feature. That way you'll be able to run the script and create the same report automatically next time.

Other Programmable Databases

The following data managers are either less popular, less capable, or harder to use than the programmables previously discussed. None of these programs would be my first choice if I were starting a database from scratch. As with *dBASE*, the best reason to use one of these programs is because you need to modify existing applications written in its programming language.

R:base

Although not nearly as popular as *dBASE*, *R:base* has been around almost as long. The main difference between the two is that *R:base* is better suited for ordinary users. Here's what I like best about *R:base*:

- **Relating files is a snap.** When you create a table, you can link it to another table just by setting up the key fields so they include the master table's key. *R:base* prompts you through the process.

- **Great documentation.** It's some of the best I've come across. My favorite part is the first chapter of the Reference manual, which gives a great lesson in relational database design.

- **Creating multitable forms and reports is easy.** As long as you have the key fields for your tables defined properly, that is. I wasn't able to figure out how to do this without the manuals.

Of course, *R:base* has the homely look of all the DOS databases. One way around this is to get *Crystal Reports* for *R:base*. With this add-on program you can design reports for *R:base* data using Windows, and you can set up icons to print the reports with the click of a mouse.

DataEase

Despite its friendly name, *DataEase* has never done it for me. Maybe it's the way it immediately prompts you for your name and a password. Or it might be the documentation that's so fabulously detailed I always have trouble figuring out which part to turn to. Anyway, here are the program's key characteristics:

- **Application oriented.** *DataEase* forces you to organize all the elements of a project in a database, which you have to "log on" to before you begin work.

- **Forms oriented.** Instead of defining a data file or table structure directly, you design a form, and *DataEase* creates the table behind the scenes.

- **Easy integration of queries and reports.** You can go through the menus to create a report that includes a query for certain data, or you can write commands to do the same thing using the *DataEase Query Language* (DQL).

- **Long file names.** *DataEase* does away with DOS's eight-plus-three character limit, enabling you to create meaningful file names.

To relate data files with *DataEase*, you fill out a special form that defines how the files are to be linked. Once a relationship is defined, it stays in place. You can then design forms for viewing and editing data that include *subforms* of related information from other files. An add-on, *SQL Connect*, enables you to access SQL database products from Oracle, Microsoft, Sybase, and IBM.

DataEase for Windows

The Windows version of *DataEase* has all the power of the DOS version. In addition, you get these significant improvements:

- **Lots of built-in style sheets.** It's easy to get good-looking forms and reports without spending lots of time on the details.

- **Query by model.** You can select data for a form or report, and sort, group, or summarize the info all from the same dialog box—which shows the links between files graphically.

- **Menu documents.** This unique type of document essentially is a blank form you can place action buttons on to create applications without programming.

Some things that should be easy with *DataEase for Windows* aren't—such as setting up data validation, which requires that you type in formulas once you get past the basics. This isn't helped by second-rate documentation and a user interface that sometimes leaves you wondering what you were trying to do in the first place.

The program comes in yet another permutation, *DataEase Express for Windows*, which is essentially the Windows version of *DataEase* without the DQL programming language. I left this program out of this section because it focuses on creating applications for groups of users, rather than managing personal data.

Personal Database Software

What makes a database program "personal"? In a word, simplicity. Most take little time to learn and offer limited relational capabilities at best. In exchange for the easy ride, you sacrifice some features you'd expect to find in *any* database software. For example, several personal database programs won't let you enter or change data when you view records in a tabular format, forcing you to switch to a form to update records.

Two personal programs offer unusually strong relational capabilities: *Approach* and *Alpha Four*. The other personal data managers can't play in this league, but several break the single-file limit in interesting ways:

- **FileMaker Pro** enables you to add repeating details to a master record.

- **AceFile** allows you to merge two files.

- **FileMaker Pro, Q&A,** and **Professional File** let you do lookups between data files.

You may be able to link files a little, but you won't find anything resembling a programming language in any of these products. However, this doesn't mean you're stuck doing repetitive tasks. Most offer some way to automate things, whether you use *AceFile*'s macro recorder, *FileMaker Pro*'s *ScriptMaker,* or the application-building tools offered by *Q&A* and *Professional File*.

FileMaker Pro is the best light-duty program (with *AceFile* close behind), while *Approach*'s combination of relational muscle and point-and-click operation is tough to beat. But remember that these are general-purpose programs. If you spend most of your day wired to the phone, and you just need a program that can track your calls, turn to the next section in this chapter. If you want to organize a database of text documents, check out the concluding section, "Textbases," instead.

AceFile

AceFile is a great little Windows program that directly accesses *dBASE* files. On the surface, it seems like a simple tool for entering lists and calling up records, but it has a few tricks up its sleeve. With *AceFile*, you can:

- **Relate data files** to display linked records

- **Join two data files** to create a new file

- **Crosstabulate and graph** data

- **Record macros**

Here's how the pseudo-relational stuff works. Basically, you link two data files at a time on their indexed fields so you can browse the files together in table view. Just select Query//Relate... and enter the file and linking field names in the Relationship Control dialog box. Then, if you highlight a product number in a customer order file,

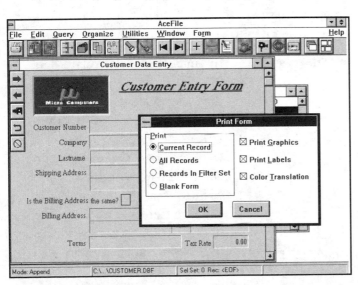

for example, *AceFile* highlights the records with the same product number in the related file. You can also Join two files to create a third file and run reports based on it.

With *AceFile*, you can only add records or edit them with a form, but at least you can simply press `F2` to toggle between the form and table views. Click the print icon as you view a form, and *AceFile* will ask whether you want to print the current record, a

HOT TIP

Figure 20: *AceFile keeps things clean and simple. To bring up the Print Form dialog box, just click on the printer icon when you are in the Edit/View Record mode.*

selection, or all of them. Do the same in table view, and you get a simple list printout of the whole database.

The main problem with *AceFile* is that it makes you use equationlike macro strings for queries, lookups, and data validation. A query-by-example system would have been far better than *AceFile*'s Build Filter Expression dialog box, which forces you to string together macros, field names, and operators—and to put field values in quotes. For data validation, you click the Edit/View Record icon, select Form//Layout, and choose Define Field from the resulting Layout menu. A dialog box appears, where you add validation by changing the default macros that *AceFile* automatically assigned to define each field's data type.

AceFile's reporting is simpler. Open the database you want to use, make sure you're not in edit mode, and select File//New//Report. From the resulting Report menu, choose Quick Report, and all the fields in the database will appear on the report layout where you can rearrange them, edit field names, create subtotals, change fonts, and so on. If you want to report on a subset of records, simply select Query//Define Filter at any time as you create the report.

HOT TIP

Alpha Four

Alpha Four is a DOS program with two claims to fame: relational power without programming, and direct access to *dBASE* files. If you're stuck with *dBASE* files, and you don't have the hardware for Windows (or the money or patience for *dBASE IV* or *FoxPro*), *Alpha Four* is your best choice. Otherwise, the interface in this program can get clumsy, and there are many better alternatives to choose from.

```
                    Set   Editor
HEADER -- Invoice header
     ┌─ CUST -- Customer list
     ├─ ITEMS ─── Invoice line items
     │        └──── INUTRY -- Inventory list




  HEADER ─→ CUST
Linked Database/Set      : C:\ALPHA4U3\INUOICE\CUST.DBF
Linking Index            : CUST_CST
Common Field/Expression: CUST_ID
Link to ?                : First
Child database editing options:
Can edit child database ?                : Yes
Can add new records to child database ? : Yes



  Set: C:\ALPHA4U3\INUOICE\INUCE

 Detach Link   Add Link   Integrity Rule   Switch windows   Save
```

In *Alpha Four*, you relate data files by defining a *set*. To do this, select Database/set design, Set commands, and then Create a set design. Then just walk through the menus and enter the names of the files you want to link, the linking index, and the field common to the files. (If you don't already have the right indexes, you can define them at this point.) Once you've defined a set, you can include any of its fields in forms and reports.

Figure 21: *Alpha Four has an awkward interface but strong relational capabilities. To relate files, you specify their linking fields and indexes with the Set Editor shown here.*

Here are some tips on where to find things in *Alpha Four:*

- **Adding data checks.** Select Database/Set design, choose Field rules, and simply pick the options you want.

- **Creating multitable forms and reports**. Choose Layouts from the main menu. You can use any field in the current set, so it's easy to create documents that show info from more than one file.

- **Setting the default form.** Use Layout//Forms//Select active form.

- **Working with selected records.** Choose Search/Sort lists from the main menu. From there, type in an expression for *Alpha Four* to use as it searches for records.

Going through menus as you use *Alpha Four* can get tedious, so it's a good idea to familiarize yourself with the program's keyboard shortcuts, especially when you design forms. You'll find many key combinations listed after commands on the menus. **HOT TIP**

Approach for Windows

Lotus's *Approach* claims to be a truly easy relational database program for nontechnical people. For the most part, it lives up to the hype. You can point and click your way through relating tables, setting up field validation, and creating buttons that run macros. *Approach* also lets you access *dBASE* and *Paradox* data directly, as well as communicate with SQL databases from Oracle and Microsoft, so you can play with data from a variety of sources without worrying about where it came from.

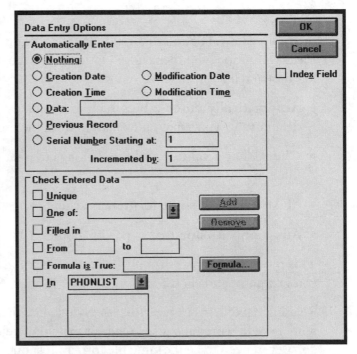

Figure 22: *With Approach, you can point and click your way to the relational power of a programmable database, instead of having to learn a language. This Data Entry Options dialog box is typical of the program's simplicity.*

Approach has four modes, each of which offers its own set of icons to provide easy access to commands:

- **Browse** is for looking at data.

- **Design** lets you relate files, as well as create forms, reports, mailing labels, and form letters.

- **Find** is for setting up searches.

- **Preview** shows a form or document layout on screen.

To change icons (called SmartIcons in Lotus lingo), click on the small blue grid at the bottom right of the screen to bring up a list of SmartIcon Sets, and pick the one you want. If you'd like to change the mix of icons on any bar, select Style//SmartIcons, and a dialog box will show you how.

Approach divides files into two types: *database files* and *view files*. Database files hold actual data and are displayed in table format, while each view file holds forms, reports, mailing labels, and form letters for a specific database file. To move between these different file types, choose View//Switch.

To apply data validation to a field, double-click on the field in Design mode, select Field Definition, and then chose Options. Use the resulting Data Entry Options dialog box to tell *Approach* to:

- **Automatically enter values** such as the date a record is created or modified, a default value you supply, information from the previous record, or a unique number

- **Check that a value is unique,** belongs to a set of values you define, or is simply filled in

- **Make sure that some formula is true**

- **Allow only a value that exists** in another database file

This process is simpler than in *AceFile*, because you don't need to write expressions— you just point and click.

Relating data files is easier with *Approach* than with any other relational program. You don't have to worry about key fields or matching field names or indexes. The data files don't even need to be the same file format. Just open the view file for the master database file, go into Design mode, choose Join from the File menu, click on Open, and select the file you want to join. Click on the linking fields in both field lists, and then click on Join. You can join several files by repeating these steps before you click OK to close the Join dialog box.

Approach makes creating a form that shows related files just as easy as joining tables. Follow these three steps:

1. Join the detail table to the master (if they're not already linked).

2. Open a new form and arrange the master file fields so there's room for the detail records.

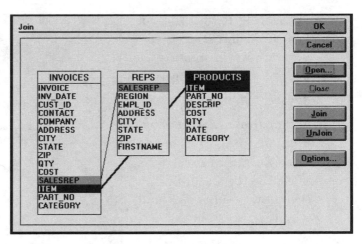

Figure 23: *Approach lets you link files using any two fields of the same data type, whether they're key fields or not.*

3. Select Design//Add Repeating Panel to open a dialog where you pick the detail database file, enter the number of detail lines, and pick fields for the panel.

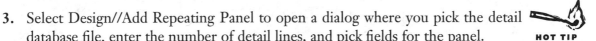

HOT TIP

Designing a report is almost exactly like designing a form. The difference is that you can't add a repeating panel (that is, a block of records from another file). Instead, Add Summary is activated on the Design menu. Use the Field icon to place your summary fields, and in the Field Definition dialog box, name the summary field and change the field type to Calculated. Click on Sum on the Function list to total a field, and then click on the name of the field you are totaling. Before you leave the dialog box, use the menu for Summarize on to specify whether *Approach* should total all the records or just groups of them.

FileMaker Pro for Windows

The original easygoing data manager, *FileMaker Pro* is my favorite program for handling simple lists. Unlike *AceFile*, it has query by example, and while it offers scripts, you don't need to string together commands for data validation or lookup tables. It has several unique features:

* **Free-form text fields.** Unlike with most programs, you don't have to set the length of text fields when you define a data file.

* **No distinction between forms and reports.** The same layouts are used to view, edit, and print data.

- **Repeating fields.** You can include a limited set of subsidiary records in a master record to handle projects like order entry.

- **Compatible Mac version.** *FileMaker* originated on the Mac, so the Mac version's files can be read by the Windows version's, and vice versa.

Although *FileMaker Pro* lacks *AceFile*'s ability to join tables, it provides lookup tables, plenty of Avery label layouts, and an excellent set of templates. You can even buy a set

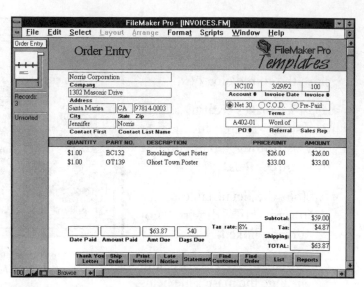

Figure 24: *Combine a friendly interface with a dollop of pseudo-relational capability and a strong macro language, and you have FileMaker Pro for Windows. In this template, repeating fields handle order entry and invoicing.*

of add-on templates, called *BizWorks*, that includes an order-entry system complete with accounts receivable, inventory reports, UPS zone charges, and so on. Not bad for a "personal" data manager.

In *FileMaker Pro*, data files, layouts (form/report designs), and scripts (to automate frequent tasks) are kept in a single file, so you can create descriptive names for any of these elements. One helpful feature is that you can add data validation and repeating fields as you set up data files, rather than having to go through a separate procedure.

FileMaker Pro has four modes. The current mode is always shown on the status bar at the bottom of the screen.

- **Browse** is for viewing multiple records *and* adding or editing records.

- **Find** lets you look for records.

- **Layout** is for creating form/report designs.

- **Preview** is for checking a layout on screen.

After you set up a *FileMaker Pro* data file, the program automatically kicks into Browse mode and presents you with a simple layout where you can start entering data. Remember to use (Tab) to move between fields—if you press (Enter) when you're in a text field, you'll just add a new blank line to the value. Note that the left side of the

HOT TIP

Browse window shows the Browse Status Area, which includes a Browse Book of records that you can page through by clicking on pages or dragging a bookmark.

Because layouts are both forms and reports, to print out records all you need to do is open the layout you want and select File//Print. To show summary information, switch to Layout mode, choose Select//Define Fields, and then choose Summary for the field type. When you click on Create, *FileMaker Pro* opens a dialog box where you can choose the kind of summary field you want. Once you do, you can drag it to any location in the layout. Drop the field into the Footer area to have summary results appear after all the layout's records have been printed.

HOT TIP

Q&A (for DOS and Windows)

Q&A is best known for its ability to "understand" English queries. Supposedly, you just ask the program's so-called Intelligent Assistant (otherwise known as Dave) for the records you want, and *Q&A* obliges. The problem is, you have to be careful how you word your question or it won't work, so the usual querying method ends up being easier. The Intelligent Assistant aside, the DOS and Windows versions of *Q&A* offer other interesting features, including:

- **Q&A Write,** a simple word processor

- **Automated forms** you can "program" with sophisticated macros

- **Network file sharing** and links to SQL data

- **Avery label formats** (more than 150 to choose from)

- **Truly easy file setup** with lots of data-checking options

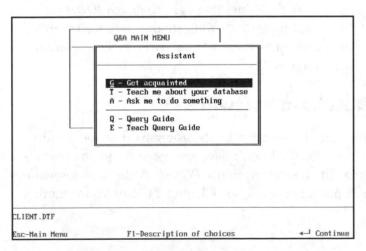

Q&A for Windows can create better-looking reports than the DOS version, and it offers some new features, like picture fields. But basically, both *Q&A*s are good for the same jobs—simple ones that use a single data file. You can add lookup tables to ensure that the values entered exist in

Figure 25: *Q&A's Intelligent Assistant begins by asking questions about your data, so later on you can run queries by typing questions in English. Too bad this works better in theory than in practice.*

another file, and with effort you can combine data from two files in reports, but that's as relational as *Q&A* gets.

The DOS version of *Q&A* has a very annoying convention: By default you always have to press Enter after you make each menu choice (which you do by typing a single letter). Select Utilities//Set global options and change Automatic Execution to Yes, and you can lay off the Enter key.

When you enter data in *Q&A*, keyboard shortcuts can really speed things up. To get a complete list, just press F1 while entering data. Here's a sampling:

- Alt F7 shows any restrictions on the current field.

- F10 saves the current record and calls up a blank form; Shift F10 saves and exits the program.

- F2 prints the current record.

- Alt F5 enters the current time; Ctrl F5 enters the date.

As with *AceFile*, adding data validation to a form involves working with macros. Choose File//Design file//Customize a file to bring up a menu with options for formatting and restricting values, for adding masks that fill in fixed characters, and for setting initial values. For example, if you choose Initial Values Spec, you can apply the @NUMBER functions to a field and *Q&A* will automatically enter a unique ID number in that field for each new record.

To retrieve records without using the program's Intelligent Assistant, select File//Search//Update, pick a data file, enter the values you want to match (*Q&A* calls them *retrieval specs*) into a blank form, and press F10. You can also look for records that don't match the spec, or that match only some of the criteria. Simply press Ctrl F7, change the default settings, and press F10.

Low-Cost Personal Database Software

These two personal data managers are inexpensive DOS programs that you'd only use on an old, low-powered 386 or 286 PC. I don't have the space to list the many shareware database programs that fit this description—*PC File* is the best known and can be acquired through most on-line services (see Chapter 21: *Utilities* for more on shareware).

Professional File

An old DOS standby for nonrelational file management, *Professional File* costs around $50 in stores and keeps things simple—you can apply data validation as you set up your database, for example. On the other hand, *Professional File* has accumulated some surprisingly powerful features over the years:

- **Extensive field formatting and validation,** including the ability to look up information in another file

- **An application generator** for creating applications without programming

- **dBASE III compatibility** for viewing and reporting on *dBASE* files

- **A macro recorder** for automating simple tasks

MyDatabase

At around $25, *MyDatabase* is quite a deal. Although this DOS program is limited—with only 45 fields per record and 5000 records per file—you can actually index files and search for records, plus take advantage of lots of label formats for mailings. You even get an on-screen calculator.

MyDatabase has a neat little feature that shows a single-field index on the left side of the screen that you can use to find records quickly. First press F2 and select the field whose values you want stored in the index. Then scroll through the index until the record you want is highlighted, and press Enter. When the record appears, use Tab to move between the index and the actual record.

HOT TIP

Contact Managers

Is the telephone your best friend *and* your worst enemy? Try a contact manager. These specialized database programs are designed for managing a steady stream of phone calls and appointments, offering phone books, schedulers, and auto-dialers (utilities that dial the phone for you with a modem). General database programs such as *AceFile* and *FileMaker Pro* come with contact manager templates, but none has as many specialized features as these programs.

The software described here is for professionals who engage in heavy phone work—and at $395 retail, it's priced that way. For a look at less powerful, less expensive programs, check out the section on personal information managers in Chapter 21.

Act! for Windows

Act! for Windows is for people who need to record every detail of phone calls, letters, and meetings. When you make a call using *Act!*'s auto-dialer, the program actually offers alternative calling times if you don't get through. The program's phone book can store a huge quantity of detail about each person, and a word processor and report writer are thrown in for the ride.

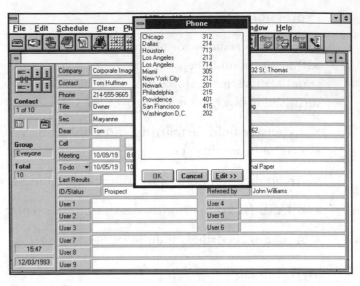

Figure 26: *Act! offers customizable, pop-up pick lists that speed data entry, such as this area code list.*

Act! stores contact information in files it calls *databases*. When you create a new database, *Act!* opens a dialog box so you can enter your own name, address, and phone number, which the program automatically drops into letters, memos, faxes, and other reports. You also have the option to password-protect your database.

Once you've entered names and addresses, you can use *Act!*'s lookup feature to search for specific records. Choose Lookup from the main menu and then select Last Name or whatever you want to search by. You don't have to enter the entire field value—the first few characters usually do the trick. To see all your records again, select Lookup/Everyone.

HOT TIP

As you move from field to field entering records, press [F2] to pop up pick lists for area codes, cities, zip codes, and so on. You can customize these lists to include whatever information you like, and you can attach pop-up lists to other fields. To accomplish the latter, choose Edit//Field Attributes as you view a contact form and click on Popup.

With *Act!* there are so many ways to check on what you have to do, it's tough to avoid responsibility:

- **For tasks related to a particular contact,** find that person's record and click on the Activities icon.

- **For all your tasks,** press [F7] or click on the Task List icon; then click on All in the Time Period panel.

• **For a prioritized list,** press F4 , or click on Data Range and complete the dialog box to show only the tasks you want on the list.

You can also get a list of the tasks for a certain date or a date range, or you can call up a list of completed tasks.

Act!'s built-in word processor can save time. Select Lookup to find the person you want to contact, and then click on the Letter icon. *Act!* will open a word processor window with the date, name, address, and salutation already filled in. If you use Lookup to summon several records (using *Act!*'s query-by-example method), you can send letters to all of those contacts by selecting Write/Form Letter, choosing a letter document, changing the setting for Use to Active Group in the Prepare Form Letter dialog box. When you print letters—or make any other type of contact—*Act!* automatically updates its history file.

Ecco Professional

Ecco Professional 2.0 is a Windows program that combines a calendar, a phone book, and to-do lists with a system of folders and outliners that enables you to shuffle names, dates, and notes in any combination—and share that information on a network. With *Ecco*, you organize things by project. Just create a folder to hold all the related details, from names and numbers to notes from phone calls. You can also include spreadsheets, graphics, document files, and so on, because *Ecco* can exchange data with other Windows programs.

In the PhoneBook Window you can stash away lots of specifics about any person—just click on the Column button and enter up to 50 columns' worth of data. To create a record for every call you make, for example, click on the Telephone button on the PhoneBook toolbar to bring up the Dialer/Call Logger dialog box. To view those notes later, enter the contact name in the text box

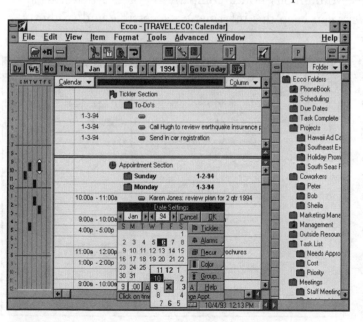

Figure 27: Ecco lets you add "columns" to your phone book, stretching the program's database capabilities.

on the PhoneBook toolbar, click the Search button, and then click on the Phone Log column (one of the columns *Ecco* automatically creates for you when you turn on the Columns feature).

The Calendar Window tracks both appointments and to-do lists. To enter an appointment, click on the time to open the Date Settings dialog box, where you can set reminder alarms as well as recurring dates for weekly or monthly appointments. If you're making an appointment with someone in your PhoneBook, click on the Calendar/PhoneBook icon, and you can simply drag that person's name and address into an appointment slot.

Ecco comes with several templates that already have folders for various projects built in, including one for managing people and another for research. To use a template, select File//Open and change the directory to \ECCO\ADVANCED. Each template includes a folder of instructions to get you started.

Textbases

There's another special kind of database, called a *textbase*, that's designed to handle free-form information. No fields and data types necessary here—basically, these programs are sophisticated search tools for text documents. If you need to maintain a database of reference materials, voluminous notes, company reports, articles, what have you, *askSam* and *Folio Views* can keep this information accessible and ready to combine into new documents.

askSam for Windows

askSam comes in both DOS and Windows versions. In keeping with its text orientation, each *askSam* database is a collection of documents instead of records. Although you don't need to define fields in these documents, you can if you like, and you can mix them in with blocks of text. *askSam*'s split personality gives you two modes for entering data, which you switch between by pressing Ctrl E. They are:

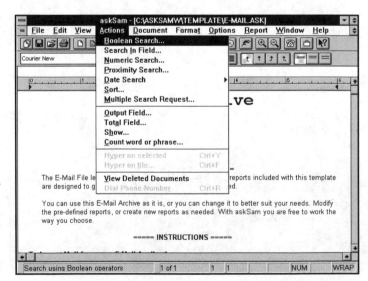

Figure 28: Essentially a sophisticated text search tool, askSam enables you to sift through documents for nuggets of information in almost any way imaginable.

- **Data Entry mode,** which lets you enter information only into fields you've defined, pressing [Tab] to move to the next field

- **Word Processing mode,** which lets you type anything anywhere in the form

This flexible program can serve a host of uses. It comes with templates for managing to-do lists, article extracts, E-mail archives, and phone contacts (it even has an auto-dialer). You can include graphics, sound, and video in a database, and a *hypertext* feature enables you to cross-reference information in different files and jump between those references easily.

If you're working with a free-form database, use [Ctrl][A] to bring up a blank page. Enter whatever information you like, or use File//Import to bring in text from existing files. If you import more than one file at one time, *askSam* will store each file as a separate document in the database.

To search an entire database for a word, or combination of words, open the database file and press [Esc]. *askSam* will move the cursor to the Command Line (just above the ruler), where you can type in words in any order. Press [Enter] to see if any documents include what you're looking for. When *askSam* finds a match, a Retrieval dialog box appears, enabling you to jump forward and back to each instance of the search value. [F6] toggles between the dialog box and the current document; [Esc] closes the dialog box.

HOT TIP

Of course, you can do the above with most word processors (though generally not with a group of documents at one time). For text search power approaching that of conventional database querying, use the Action menu. You can look for data in specific fields, perform AND/OR searches (such as searching for an article that includes both "carrot" and "vitamin A"), and find words a specified proximity from each other—by a specific number of words or within the same sentence or paragraph, for instance. By default, *askSam* searches are not case-sensitive. To change this and other settings, use Options//File Preferences.

Folio Views for Windows

This self-styled "infobase" combines free-form information management with tools for electronic publishing to yield a unique product. Besides the query and multiuser editing features that are standard in most databases of the '90s, *Folio Views* offers these extras:

- **Customizable "highlighters"** for pointing out hot spots in data

- **Shadow copies** that enable you to make notes without changing the original data

- **Cross-platform access** for DOS, Windows, and Mac users

- **Hypertext links** that let you "jump" all over documents, pop up windows for text or graphics, or start up other applications

- **Built in data compression** to save disk space

Besides the standard version, there's an inexpensive *Folio Views Lite* that lets users edit copies of infobases you give them, and a version for commercial use that has a bigger price to match its extra capabilities. If you want a shared database that lets users play with textbase data however they like, check out this product.

Product Directory

Access
FoxPro
FoxPro for Windows
Microsoft SQL Server
Microsoft Corp.
One Microsoft Way
Redmond, WA 98052
800/426-9400
206/936-8661

AceFile
Ace Software
1740 Technology Dr. #680
San Jose, CA 95110
800/345-3223
408/451-0100

Act! for Windows
Q&A
Q&A for Windows
Symantec
10201 Torre Ave.
Cupertino, CA 95014
800/441-7234
408/253-9600

Alpha Four
Alpha Software
168 Middlesex Tnpk.
Burlington, MA 01803
800/852-5750
617/229-2924

Approach for Windows
Lotus Development
55 Cambridge Pkwy.
Cambridge, MA 02142
800/346-4010
617/577-8500

askSam
askSam Systems
P.O. Box 1428
Perry, FL 32347
800/800-1997
904/584-6590

DataEase
DataEase for Windows
DataEase Express
  for Windows
DataEase Int'l
7 Cambridge Dr.
Trumbull, CT 06611
800/243-5123
203/374-8000

dBASE IV
Paradox
Paradox for Windows
Borland Int'l
1800 Green Hills Rd.
Scotts Valley, CA 95067
800/331-0877
408/431-1000

Ecco Professional
Arabesque Software
P.O. Box 3098
Bellevue, WA 98009-3098
800/457-4243
206/869-9600

FileMaker Pro for Windows
Claris
5201 Patrick Henry Dr.
Santa Clara, CA 95054
408/727-8227

Folio Views
2155 N. Freedom Blvd.
Provo, UT 84604
800/543-6546
801/344-3710

MyDatabase
MySoftware Co.
1259 El Camino Real #167
Menlo Park, CA 94025
415/325-9372

Professional File
Software Publishing
3165 Kiefer Rd.
Santa Clara, CA 95056
800/336-8360
408/986-8000

R:base
Microrim
15395 S.E. 30th Pl.
Bellevue, WA 98007
800/628-6990
206/649-9500

20

Communications

By Judy Heim

- Finding the right fax modem for your budget
- Connecting, swapping E-mail, downloading files
- Guide to on-line services and the best BBSs
- How to address E-mail to anyone in the world
- Tips and reviews for the top four communications programs
- Choosing a fax program and making it work
- When things go wrong: solving 13 common problems

In the past year I've used my PC to swap electronic mail with physics students in New Delhi, a graphic artist in mainland China, a computer nerd in Hong Kong, a journalist in Paris, a medical student in Cuba, a school-teacher in Russia, and a novelist in Saudi Arabia. I've never met any of these people face to face, yet I've learned more about their lives and their countries than I would have had I watched a PBS documentary. And the amazing thing is, I paid less to send that electronic mail than I would have on postage for paper mail.

Electronic mail (call it E-mail) is good business, too—I use it to keep in touch with all my clients—but it's only one of the many benefits of PC communications. Where do you start? For a couple hundred bucks or less, you buy a modem—a device that connects your PC to the telephone lines—and a communications program to make the modem work. Then, for a few dollars a month, you subscribe to one or more on-line services (information clearinghouses that link hoards of computers by phone line) that offer E-mail plus dozens of other things, including:

- Group "discussions" on almost any topic

- Stock market quotes and services

- Up-to-the-minute world news

- Financial data on thousands of businesses

- Complete sports scores and stats

- Travel information and reservations

- Access to public libraries

- Personal ads and introduction services

- Electronic catalog shopping

- Legal, medical, and other professional data

- Weather forecasts

- Games, utilities, and other software

HOT TIP

If you spend a little more and buy a *fax modem* and fax software, you get all of the above, plus the ability to turn your PC into a fax machine (though you can't transmit paper pages unless you own a scanner). Fax modems enable you to send crisp faxes right from your hard disk, so go ahead and pay the few extra dollars for a fax modem even if you already own a fax machine.

In this chapter, I'll explain the best way to select communications hardware and software, no matter what you want to do with them. I'll also demonstrate how to "get on line" (that is, how to use your modem and communications software to hook up with someone or something) and what to do once you're there. Along the way, you'll discover some great on-line deals, and what to do if you run into trouble.

How to Buy a Fax Modem

"Modem" is cyberspeak for *modulator/demodulator*. Whether transferring either faxes or data (that is, E-mail, files, software, and so on), a fax modem's basic job is simple: to turn digital signals from your PC into audio signals and send them over the phone lines, and to turn another modem's audio signals back into digital ones.

The nice thing about fax modems is that once you buy one and install it, you can usually forget about it. (Unless something goes wrong, which doesn't happen *too* often.) Fax modems dial out using the same tones telephones use, connect up to another computer's modem, exchange data, and hang up when they're done—all with very little intervention from you. There are three basic kinds of fax modems to choose from:

- **External fax modems** sit on your desk. They're usually small oblong boxes with headlights, slightly menacing looking—the sort of thing a customs agent might detain you for carrying.

- **Internal fax modems** slip into a slot inside your PC. They look like all expansion cards do—wee industrialized nations as seen from an airplane window.

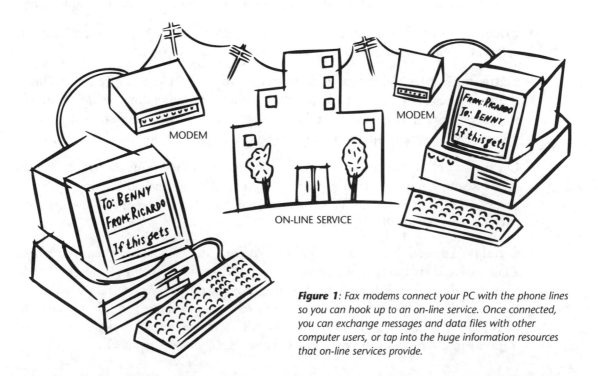

Figure 1: Fax modems connect your PC with the phone lines so you can hook up to an on-line service. Once connected, you can exchange messages and data files with other computer users, or tap into the huge information resources that on-line services provide.

- **Portable fax modems** are for laptops. Some fit in special laptop slots, while others screw onto an external connector. You'll find special buying advice on these later in this chapter.

Note that most fax modems come with communications software to get you started, but don't consider this a plus unless it's DCA's *Crosstalk Communicator.* You'll want to replace just about anything else with something better (toward the end of this chapter, the top communications programs are discussed).

Internal or External?

Assuming that you're buying a fax modem for a desktop PC, how do you decide whether to buy an internal or an external model? Well, if all your PC's expansion slots are occupied, you don't *have* a choice—you'll have to buy an external model unless you can live without one of the cards you already own. External fax modems only require a free *serial port*, which most PCs have.

A few other factors will affect your choice:

- **Installation.** An internal fax modem may cause hardware conflicts that—until you resolve them—can render your PC useless. If you don't like opening up your PC, reading instruction manuals, or flipping tiny switches, choose an external fax modem. To "install" an external model, you just connect it to a serial port with a cable.

- **Price.** An internal model typically costs between 15 and 20 percent less than an external model with the same capabilities from the same company.

- **Status indicators.** All fax modems worth buying have a speaker that reproduces the tones, clicks, bleats, and roars of modem communications, which indicate whether you're making a connection. External models also have status lights (or sometimes, message displays) to tell you what's happening on line.

HOT TIP

- **On/off switch.** Only externals have one. If your fax modem makes strange noises or refuses to hang up, turning your fax modem off and on and starting over is a crude but effective remedy. When an internal model is in a similar dilemma, you have to reboot your PC.

- **Serial port speed.** If you have an old PC, you may not be able to benefit fully from a fast external fax modem because the serial port may be too slow (you don't have to worry about internal modems, because they have their own serial ports). How can you tell? Call your PC manufacturer's technical support and ask. If your PC does have an old, slow serial port and you still want an external modem, you'll have to perform a serial port upgrade (see Chapter 8: *Upgrade It Yourself).*

The Reliability Question

The most critical factor in choosing a fax modem is one you can't evaluate in a store, namely, will it work reliably? This varies not only among brands, but also among models from the same manufacturer. Before you buy, do your homework and check out product reviews in the major computer magazines (*PC World, PC Magazine,* and *Byte*).

That said, the following companies sell particularly good products: Hayes, Microcom, Multi-Tech, and Telebit. On the downside, I've had bad experiences with modems from Zoom Telephonics, Boca Research, and Practical Peripherals. Whatever you do, avoid those send-only fax modems in the sale bins!

When fax modems fail, they usually do so in the first year, so don't buy anything with a warranty of less than a year, and don't pay more for an extended warranty. Free telephone technical support should be part of the deal.

One more proviso: Buying a fax modem with both Class 1 and Class 2 compatibility *should* mean it will work with any fax program, but there are no guarantees. Never trust a company's claims that its fax modem or fax software will work with something else. Ask them if they've actually tested it. And ask them for a money-back guarantee. Then take it home and see for yourself.

Which do I prefer? External fax modems are so much easier to install, it's no contest. **HOT TIP** And their status lights are often enough to diagnose what's going wrong with any connection. If you choose an external, look for one with a metal case, because metal dissipates heat better than plastic. Some flimsy plastic-cased fax modems start to mis-dial when they overheat. **DANGER**

How Fast for How Much?

Different fax modems have different speeds, and as with much else in life, you pay more for better performance. The faster the fax modem, the less time you spend waiting for a fax to appear, or for a book-length message to stroll across the phone lines. Higher speed also means lower long-distance charges. **REMEMBER**

It's easy to choose a fax modem fast enough at a price you can afford. Don't be intimidated by the ridiculous number of acronyms in fax modem ads and on fax modem boxes—I won't even attempt to define them all here, because (trust me) you don't need or want to know. But here are the basics you *should* look for on the box:

- **Bits per second (bps).** Sometimes called the *baud rate*, this is the basic speed measurement, the number of ones and zeros a fax modem can transfer each second. Fax modems often have different bps rates for faxes and data. Some salespeople talk about "9600 bps fax modems" that transmit faxes at 9600 but data at a slow 2400 bps, so watch out! It's hard to find fax modems that transfer data at 9600 bps anymore, because 14.4Kbps models cost just slightly more and deliver 50 percent more speed. My advice: **HOT TIP** Buy a 14.4Kbps fax modem.

The Best Deal in fax modems: 14.4Kbps				
Price[1]	$40 to $100	$100 to $200	$125 to $250	$300 to $500
Data rate	2400 bps	9600 bps[2]	14.4Kbps	28.8Kbps
Fax Rate	9600 bps	9600 bps	14.4Kbps	14.4Kbps
Modulation[3]	V.22bis	V.32	V.32bis	V.34
Error checking[4]	V.42	V.42	V.42	V.42
Compression[5]	MNP 5, V.42bis	MNP 5, V.42bis	MNP 5, V.42bis	MNP 5, V.42bis
Fax standards	Group III Class 1 and 2[6]	Group III Class 1 and2[6]	Group III Class 1 and2[6]	Group III Class 1 and2[6]

[1]Price ranges include both external and internal models; low end will not have all features.
[2]9600-bps models are rare because 14.4Kbps models are much faster and cost only a little more.
[3]Must have this spec or the modem may not work!
[4]Highly recommended for 9600 bps or faster.
[5]Increases speed, but not required.
[6]Class 1 works with more fax software; Class 2 delivers better performance.

Figure 2: *This table shows the specs to ask for when buying a modem in one of the major fax modem classes. While 2400-bps fax modems are dirt cheap, 14.4Kbps modems reduce phone charges (and frustration) in the long run.*

- **Modulation standards.** Modems need *standards*—technical specifications that manufacturers agree to comply with—or each modem would speak a different language and no one could communicate. Each speed class, represented by the *data rate* (see the preceding table), has its own modulation standard (V.32, V.32bis, and so on). Your modem *must* be certified as compliant with the modulation standard for its speed class or you could end up with a unit that talks only to itself.

DANGER

- **Error checking.** Sometimes errors occur in transmission that result in corrupted data—bad news if you've just received a huge program file. Error checking helps avert such problems, especially with noisy phone lines. The accepted error-checking standard is V.42, which should be built into your modem if it transfers data at 9600 bps or faster.

REMEMBER

- **Hardware data compression.** Yes, even more speed! If your modem and the one on the other end of the line use the same compression scheme, things proceed faster, because compressed files take less time to transmit. V.42bis compression delivers a 100 percent boost, while MNP 5 offers around 70 percent. Either scheme may add to the price. If you shop for a 14.4Kbps fax modem with V.42bis data compression, make sure the *DTE rate*—the speed at which the modem and the PC talk to each other—is listed as 57.6Kbps. That's the speed required by V.42bis.

REMEMBER

Hello? Is This Data, a Fax, or You?

If you have only one phone line, it's a pain to switch your fax modem into answer mode every time you want to receive a fax or data—and to remember to turn it off so your fax modem doesn't screech in callers' ears. *Intelligent-switching* fax modems purport to solve this problem. If a fax or data arrives, your software receives it automatically; if a voice call comes in, your phone rings (models with built-in voicE-mail are also available). Unfortunately, fax modem companies have yet to create intelligent-switching units that work reliably.

Until such units arrive, ask the local phone company to install two different phone numbers on your single line—one for voice, one for fax and data. The fax/data number will cause your phone to ring with a "distinctive" ring. For under $100, you can buy a gadget (available at most office supply stores) that plugs into the phone jack and routes the distinctive-ring calls to the fax-modem. To avoid having to listen to lots of rings, set your fax software to pick up the phone on an earlier ring than it normally would.

- **Fax standards.** If your fax modem complies with the Group III standard, it can swap faxes with most any fax modem or fax machine at either 9600 bps or 14.4Kbps (depending on your modem's fax rate). The *service class* indicates whether your fax software and fax modem will work together. Class 1 fax modems work with the most fax programs, while Class 2 fax modems offer better performance. Ideally, your fax modem should comply with both standards.

Beware of ads that describe a modem's speed with the phrase "effective throughput." That's a theoretical estimate of the amount of data the modem can pump down the phone line should its data compression be

DANGER

deployed and conditions be optimal. For a true gauge of the modem's speed, stay focused on the actual data and fax rates, the numbers that precede "bps" or "baud rate."

Portable Fax Modems

Like desktop models, portable fax modems come in internal and external varieties. When you take a laptop on the road, you know how important it is to save space and weight, so the rule for portable fax modems is simple: If your laptop can accommodate an internal model, and if you can afford it, buy an internal.

- **Internal portables.** Newer laptops have standard slots, called PCMCIA slots, that can hold a wide range of credit-card-size devices, including fax modems—at prices averaging a little less than twice those for internal desktop fax modems with comparable features (see Chapter 3: *Mobile Computing*). Older laptops and many current models have slots that hold only fax modems from the laptop's manufacturer, or from companies (MegaHertz is the largest) that specialize in creating accessories for popular laptop models. Pricing varies.

- **External portables.** Commonly known as *pocket fax modems*, external fax modems range in size from a cigarette case to an electric razor, and they either screw on or connect by cable to a laptop serial port. Like desktop externals, pocket fax modems have an external power supply—either batteries, an AC adapter, or both. This is an advantage, since internals steal juice from laptop batteries. Pocket fax modems are cheaper than internal portables, often costing only 15 or 20 percent more than similar desktop externals.

One advantage of buying an external is that you can use it on both your laptop and desktop, so you have to buy one modem instead of two. The best externals give you a choice between rechargeable or common AA-type batteries—and deliver at least two hours of connect time from either. A low battery light is a must, and an "on" light, a connect light, and a fax light are nice. Make sure the serial connector (usually a 9-pin female) is right for your laptop, or be prepared to pay a few bucks for an adapter. Two 14.4Kbps models worth a look are Microcom's MicroPorte and Practical Peripherals' PM14400FX PKT.

Opt for an internal model, and if you have a PCMCIA slot, you'll be amazed at the selection of PCMCIA fax modems. Newer models have a built-in phone jack that pops out, so you don't need to carry an adapter to hook your fax modem to the phone line. If your laptop has both a PCMCIA slot and a special slot just for fax modems made by the laptop manufacturer, fill the special slot and keep the PCMCIA slot free for other options. Accessories made for specific model laptops by third parties tend to be cheaper than comparable accessories from the laptop's manufacturer.

Getting Around On Line

Before you shop for a communications program, you need an idea of how you'll use the software to set up your modem, how to get on line, and what happens when you get there. This section offers basics and tips for connecting to a *bulletin board service* (BBS), an electronic forum where people swap messages, software, and so on. (There are thousands of BBSs for all kinds of interests; consult a local computer store to find some.) Once connected, you'll register, exchange E-mail, and *download* a file, that is, copy a file from the service to your computer over the phone lines.

Before you make your first call, you need to verify that your modem and PC are talking to each other. Head for the terminal screen in your communications program—

```
DIALING DIRECTORY: PCPLUS.DIR

    NAME                                NUMBER     BAUD PDS D P   SCRIPT
  1 MCI Mail (2400)                 1 800 456 6245  2400 N01 F D
  2 MCI Mail (1200)                 1-800-234-6245  1200 N81 F D
  3 CompuServe (300)                    256-5346     300 E71 F D
  4 CompuServe (2400)                   256-5346    2400 E71 F D
  5 GEnie                               274-2459    1200 N81 H D
  6 Exec-PC (USR)                   1-414-789-4337  9600 N81 F D
  7 Tim Pozar's BBS                 1-415-695-0759  2400 N81 F D
  8 Exec-PC (2400)                  1414-789-4210   2400 N81 F D
  9 Tymnet                              242-0227    2400 E71 F D
 10 Telenet                             257-8472    2400 N71 F D

 PgUp Scroll Up      Space Mark Entry      C Clear Marked     L Print Directory
 PgDn Scroll Dn      Enter Dial Selected   E Erase Entry(s)   P Dialing Codes
 Home First Page     D Dial Entry(s)       F Find Entry       X Exchange Dir
 End  Last Page      M Manual Dial         N Find Next        T Toggle Display
 ↑/↓  Select Entry   A Add Entry           G Goto Entry       S Sort Directory
 Esc  Exit           R Revise Entry        J Jot Notes

 Choice:

 Alt-Z FOR HELP| ANSI     | FDX | 9600 N81 | LOG CLOSED | PRINT OFF | OFF-LINE
```

Figure 3: *Procomm Plus for DOS offers a typical dialing directory for storing the phone numbers of the services you call. For each entry, you set such basic communications parameters as modem speed.*

that's the screen that's almost completely blank, usually the first screen that appears when you start the program. Type ATH0 and press (Enter). You should see the response OK or 0 appear beneath your entry—that's your modem talking back to you! If you don't get this response, see "Things That Go Wrong" at the end of this chapter.

Communications Settings

Every communications session begins with a phone number. If you've never dialed the BBS before, enter its name and number into your communication software's dialing directory, sometimes called a phone book, so you can dial the BBS again easily. If you're calling from the office and you have to dial 9 to get an outside line, remember to begin with that number followed by a comma (this adds a pause until an outside line kicks in).

The dialing directory has blanks not only for phone numbers, but also for various communications settings associated with each directory listing. Don't let a long list of settings intimidate you. Usually, all you need to do is select the speed—marked by "bps" or "baud rate"—and accept the default settings for everything else.

REMEMBER

- **Speed.** Let's say the BBS you want to connect with advertises 9600-bps access. (If you didn't know this, you could always connect up at 2400, and the BBS would advise you of higher-speed options.) If your modem lacks compression, or if you have an external modem and your PC has an old-style serial port, enter 9600. Otherwise, check out "Advanced Speed Settings" later in this chapter.

- **Parity, data bits, and stop bit.** Just accept the defaults. If you must know: *Parity* is a crude form of error checking; *data bits* describes the number of bits in the smallest unit of data exchanged; and *stop bit* refers to the bit that marks the end of that unit. These three values are commonly listed together; the near-universal setting is N-8-1 (for no parity, 8 data bits, and 1 stop bit). One big exception: CompuServe, the most popular on-line service, requires E-7-1 (for even parity, 7 data bits, and 1 stop bit).

HOT TIP

You may be offered other choices, which, depending on the software, are presented during installation or when you add an entry to the dialing directory. The choices I've noted will almost always be the defaults:

- **Full or half duplex?** Select full duplex. This keeps the remote computer from annoyingly "echoing back" what you type at the terminal.

- **Which port?** If you're asked to choose serial ports, select the one your modem is connected to (90 percent of the time, either COM1 or COM2).

- **What kind of terminal emulation?** This refers to the type of minicomputer or mainframe terminal your PC and its communications software should imitate if called upon to do so by whatever computer is on the other end of the line. The default here will probably be ANSI BBS, VT/ANSI, DEC VT-100 (ANSI), or some other variation on the ANSI theme. Accept it.

Making That First Call

When you select a number from the dialing directory, you'll hear a click, a dial tone, and your modem dialing the number. Then you'll hear another click as the modem on the other end of the line picks up the phone, followed by a "shwsssh!" that sounds like an off-the-air TV station. Expect a squawk, a tweet, and some signal from your software that you've connected. If you have an external modem, its CD light will flicker.

REMEMBER

The first thing you should do is press (Enter); a message will scroll by asking you to *log in* by entering your name. If you do, and the BBS can't find you in its database, it will ask you to register as a new user. Just go ahead and fill out the electronic questionnaire presented to you—don't worry about mucking up the BBS by typing something wrong. A subscription fee may be required, but all BBSs offer a free tour, which you should take before paying anything.

Advanced Speed Settings

If your modem uses V.42bis or MNP 5 compression and you have either an internal modem or a PC with a high-speed serial port, you should enter 57.6Kbps for every listing in your dialing directory. Your modem and whoever you call will still communicate at the maximum data rate for the slowest modem, but your PC and modem will talk to each other at super speed.

Here's what you need to do to perform this speed trick. For some settings, you'll need to check your communication program's manual or on-line help:

- **Turn off auto-baud detect.** This will keep the bps setting from automatically bumping back down to the actual modem speed. If your program doesn't have this option, don't worry about it.

- **Set your serial port to high speed.** To do this, you need to add a line to your AUTOEXEC.BAT file. Exit to the DOS prompt, change to your root directory, and type `EDIT AUTOEXEC.BAT`. Assuming your modem uses the first serial port (COM1) and your modem has V.32bis compression, add a line that reads `MODE COM1 576`. If your modem has *only* MNP 5 compression, add `MODE COM1` followed by a value twice that of the actual data rate (for example, if you had a 9600 bps connection, you'd add `MODE COM1 192` for 19.2Kbps). Save the file and reboot the PC.

- **Turn off XON/XOFF software flow control.** Designed to pace the flow of data and prevent data from being lost during a connection, software flow control is too slow for high-speed communications.

- **Activate RTS/CTS hardware flow control.** This does essentially the same thing as software flow control, but faster.

You may need to activate hardware flow control by adding a command to your *modem initialization string*—the string of commands your communications software sends to the modem when the software is loaded. Look for an option on your program's Setup menu (something like "Modem Commands"), and a screen will appear for editing the initialization string. Check your modem's manual to find the command you should add.

You'll also be asked to select a password. Choose it wisely. Don't use anything obvious like your name, your street, your city, or your PC brand. Ideally, you should use one word together with a numeral, like FLASH9. *Never* use the same password on two different services, or you're asking for trouble. You don't want someone reading your private E-mail, or posting messages under your name, do you?

DANGER

When the form-filling is out of the way, you'll get a menu of services. The average BBS offers:

- **Private E-mail** exchange among subscribers

- **Public message areas**, often called forums or special interest groups (SIGs), where people leave messages on specific topics (politics, science fiction, car repair, how to train your dog, you name it)

```
This is the WELL

Type newuser to sign up.

Type trouble if you are having trouble
logging in.

Type guest  to learn about the WELL.

If you already have a WELL account, type
your username.

login:
```

Figure 4: *This log-in screen for a popular Northern California BBS called The Well is typical of most. It's the first thing you see when you connect.*

- **Chat areas** where groups of people engage in typewritten conversation, so everyone sees each participant's input on screen as it's entered

- **Software**—some free, some shareware—that you can download

- **Sound and graphics files** including wild effects, photography, videos, and so on

- **Gateways** to other services, such as Internet, the world's biggest E-mail network

- **Miscellaneous services** such as on-line newsletters, personal ads, group games, X-rated material, whatever

HOT TIP

Sometimes, when you're on line and viewing a message or checking the contents of a file, things scroll by too fast for you to read them. When this happens, pause the display by pressing Ctrl S. Resume the scroll by hitting Ctrl Q To return to the previous prompt, press Ctrl C.

Exchanging Messages

Every BBS's message or mail system works a little differently, but the basic procedure is the same. To post a message in a public forum, you look over the messages already posted, find some that interest you, type in your own message, and check back maybe a day later and see if anyone has responded. Chat areas are often divided into "rooms," where you join in typewritten conversations that scroll off the screen continuously. In either case, people usually identify themselves by a *handle* (or pseudonym) to protect themselves from being harassed by weirdoes, of whom there are plenty on line.

What Your Modem's Lights Mean

One advantage of an external modem is that it has little lights to tell you what's going on. Here's what they mean:

- **EC (error control)** stays lit while the modem's built-in error checking and correction is in effect, ensuring a secure connection.

- **CS (clear to send)** lights up when the modem tells the PC that it can start transmitting data.

- **RS (request to send)** lights up when the PC asks the modem if it's ready for the PC to start transmitting data.

- **MR (modem ready)** is basically a "power on" light.

- **TR (terminal ready)** indicates that the PC has signaled to the modem that the PC is ready to send or receive data.

- **SD (send data)** lights up when the PC is sending data to the modem, to be forwarded to a distant computer.

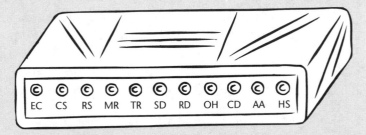

Figure 5: *The front of a top-of-the-line external modem looks like this, with status lights that signal various communications activities.*

- **RD (receive data)** lights up as the modem pumps data from a distant computer to the PC.

- **OH (off hook)** flashes as the modem picks up the phone.

- **CD (carrier direct)** flashes when the modem connects with a another modem. This is the light to watch!

- **AA (auto answer)** indicates that your modem has been set to pick up incoming calls.

- **HS (high speed)** stays lit when your modem is operating at the highest speed possible.

As you can tell, these lights tell you as much about the conversation between your modem and PC as the one between your modem and a distant system. If you're having trouble, lack of activity among the CS, RS, and TR lights indicates that the PC-to-modem connection may be at fault. You'll find the CD light useful, since this indicates whether you've established a connection at all.

Private E-mail is a little different. To send someone a message, you have to know the person's handle, which you'll probably get from a public forum. If you want to send a message, private or otherwise, remember that you don't have to be on line to compose it—nor do you *want* to be, if you're being charged for connect time. Here's how you prepare a message and *upload* it (that is, copy it from your PC to the service):

1. Start your word processor and open a new document. Make the margins fairly narrow—say, 50 characters wide—because long lines of text tend to break and look like a mess when you upload them. Don't bother with special fonts, since all you'll be sending is characters.

2. Save the file as straight text with line breaks (that is, with carriage returns at the end of the lines) so that none of your word processor's formatting will be included. You'll find the option in your word processor's Save As dialog box.

HOT TIP

3. Fire up your communications software. Fish around the help facility (or check the manual) to find a feature called *pacing*. You use pacing to inject pauses between uploaded words, lines, or even letters—if you *don't* use pacing, the BBS may be overwhelmed and not accept the message. Instruct your software to pause a half-second between each line.

4. Log on to the BBS and address the message.You can upload your text directly into the message.When you see the prompt asking you to type text into the message, invoke your software's ASCII upload feature. Invoke your software's text upload feature—or its ASCII file transfer feature, often found on the file transfer protocol list discussed later in this chapter—and send the message.

When you receive E-mail, you're usually asked if you'd like to retrieve it as soon as you log on to the BBS. Again, you can scroll through it on line, or you can download it to your hard disk and read it at your leisure.

Downloading Software, Etc.

Downloading shareware (or any file that isn't straight text) involves a few extra steps, because these types of files—called binary files—require special handling. Text files are generally small, and communications software can handle them without breaking a sweat. Binary files are not only larger, they're also more delicate—one tiny error in transmission, and a program may not run, an image may not display, a spreadsheet may not load, and so on.

So what extra steps do binary files require? Say you're nosing around the shareware area in your local BBS. You scroll through the list of programs, find some little utility that appeals to you, select it, and choose the download option. At this point, the BBS and/or your software will ask you what kind of file transfer protocol you want to use.

File Transfer Protocols

File transfer protocols are standard methods for safely transmitting binary data files. For a protocol to work, both your communications software and the on-line service or BBS must use the same one. Most protocols, but not all, have special error-checking and correction to guarantee the integrity of binary files.

E-mail Privacy

E-mail privacy is a relative concept. Many computer bulletin board operators post warnings on their log-on screens reminding callers that private messages are not necessarily private. Big on-line services like CompuServe insist that subscribers' mail is kept private, but the fact is that no E-mail is ever immune from prying eyes unless it has been encrypted by the sender prior to posting.

The lesson is: Never write an E-mail message that could be personally or professionally embarrassing. This is especially true when sending the E-mail through large public networks like Internet, where E-mail may be stored in multiple places before being forwarded. If you need to send a confidential message, encrypt it before uploading it (see Chapter 21: *Utilities* for information on file encryption programs).

When you're asked which protocol you want to use, which should you choose? That's easy—the fastest one the BBS and your communications software have in common. Here are the most common ones:

HOT TIP

- **Zmodem.** Frequently the only fast protocol offered by BBSs. The best choice for clean (that is, not noisy) phone lines.

- **Kermit.** Good for noisy lines, Kermit can be every bit as fast as Zmodem, but only if excellent versions (and there are many) are used on both ends. The Kermit found in most communications software is crummy.

- **Ymodem-G.** The only protocol here lacking error control, Ymodem-G should be used only when both your modem and the one on the other end of the line have hardware error control (such as V.42 or MNP). In that case, it's just as fast as Zmodem.

- **Xmodem.** Nearly universal—and slow. Don't use it unless the BBS and your communications software have no other protocols in common.

- **Ymodem.** Similar to Xmodem, but much faster, and you can transfer more than one file at a time. Ymodem is better than Zmodem on noisy phone lines.

Usually your software and/or the BBS will give you an estimate of the download time and the option to disconnect automatically when the transfer is complete so you don't have to wait around. When you upload a binary file to a BBS, you go through the same steps, but in reverse.

Software Data Compression

Not every modem has compression to speed things up. That's why you'll find that most BBSs and on-line services compress the files they offer for downloading with a software compression utility. When you download compressed files, you must have a copy of the compression utility (or a companion decompression utility) and decompress the files manually. The three most popular utilities used to compress files are themselves shareware:

- **PKZip** by PKWare is the most popular and the fastest at compressing. You can tell if a file has been "Zipped" by its ZIP extension.

- **LHA** by Haruyasu Yoshizaki compresses files the most. Look for the LZH extension.

- **ARC-E** by Vern Buerg and Wayne Chin has been around longest. Look for the ARC extension.

You can download the appropriate decompression utility from any on-line service that offers compressed files. You'll also run into self-extracting files, which usually have an EXE extension. You don't need a decompression program to unpack them—you simply type the file's name at the DOS prompt and the file decompresses itself.

Avoiding Hardware-Plus-Software Compression

If your modem already has compression built in, can it shrink software-compressed files further? In a word, no—it fact, the interaction between the two compression schemes actually slows transmission! Here's how to deal with this problem:

- If your modem has MNP 5 compression only, you need to turn off its compression manually when you download compressed files. You can find the command to do this in your modem's manual.

```
╔═╡ Download Protocols - 44072960 bytes free ╞═╗
║                                              ║
║   X) XMODEM                  A) ASCII        ║
║   Z) ZMODEM                  R) RAW ASCII    ║
║   Y) YMODEM (Batch)          T) TELINK       ║
║   G) YMODEM-G (Batch)        M) MODEM7       ║
║   O) 1K-XMODEM               W) WXMODEM      ║
║   E) 1K-XMODEM-G             I) IMODEM       ║
║   C) COMPUSERVE B+           1) [EXT 1]      ║
║   K) KERMIT                  2) [EXT 2]      ║
║   S) SEALINK                 3) [EXT 3]      ║
║                                              ║
║  Your Selection:    (press ENTER for XMODEM) ║
╚══════════════════════════════════════════════╝
```

Figure 6: Hit `Page Down` to start a download in Procomm Plus for DOS, and as with most programs, you get a wide choice of file transfer protocols.

PC-to-PC Communications

Most people use an on-line E-mail service to exchange files or E-mail. However, those who transfer gobs of data may want to avoid big online bills by connecting up over the phone lines directly with those with whom they want to exchange big files. There are two ways to do this. In both cases, the person who *receives* the call prepares for the connection:

- **Host mode.** If your communications software offers a host mode (most programs do), switch into it. This turns your PC into a mini BBS. When someone calls, he or she is greeted by menus for uploading or downloading files, swapping E-mail, or chatting with you by typing in stuff on the fly.

- **Auto-answer mode.** Every communications program has this mode. When outside callers connect, all they see is their blank terminal screen, along with anything typed at the keyboard once the connection is made. To transfer files, callers invoke their program's file download feature and choose the appropriate file transfer protocol. The sender then invokes the file upload feature on his or her PC and sends the file—which requires a bit of timing and coordination beforehand. Worse, auto-answer mode doesn't always work! If your modem won't pick up a ringing phone, turn auto-answer mode on by typing ATA [Enter] on your terminal screen. This forces the modem to pick up the phone.

Host mode is much better than auto-answer mode, which can be endlessly frustrating. You can even set up host mode so callers must enter a password to log on—a good idea, since most programs' host modes give callers unrestricted access to your hard disk. The better packages let you specify which directories callers can access.

- If your modem has V.42bis compression, you don't need to worry. V.42bis is smart enough to tell when a file is already compressed, and it turns off hardware compression automatically when transmitting compressed files.

- If your modem has both V.42bis and MNP 5 compression, add the command to turn off MNP 5 compression to your modem's initialization string. Most BBSs and on-line services that have compression offer either V.42bis or MNP 5, so you'll only need MNP 5 in rare circumstances.

HOT TIP

If your modem or your favorite BBS has MNP 5 only, *do not* modify your modem's initialization string to turn off MNP 5—you'll want the speed for reading E-mail, browsing forums, downloading uncompressed files, and so on. Instead, for quick access, use your communications software to assign the commands for turning MNP 5 off and on to a pair of function keys (or to a couple of special key combinations).

Guide to On-Line Services

HOT TIP

The three leading on-line services—CompuServe, Prodigy, and America Online—all provide the basics: E-mail, lots of public forums, shareware galore, international news, and access to specialized databases. If you're going to subscribe to only one service, make it CompuServe. You'll enjoy a huge array of services and be able to send E-mail to just about anyone who's on line.

Internet, the biggest on-line service of all, is in a class by itself. An international web of E-mail users, databases, forums, and just about anything else you can imagine, Internet defies definition and can take quite a bit of skill to navigate. If you want to chat with people around the world, this is the service for you. You can't tap into Internet directly, but many local BBSs and all the major on-line services (including CompuServe) offer at least partial access to it.

MCI Mail is the biggest service dedicated to E-mail, so if you want to exchange messages easily and cheaply with yet another universe of users, go ahead and subscribe. See the section "Guide to Global E-mail Addressing" to learn how to address E-mail messages to almost anyone on line, regardless of the service you or they use.

In this section, you'll get a quick tour of all the above services, plus GEnie (a budget alternative to CompuServe), Delphi (known for its cheap access to all of Internet), and Dow Jones/News Retrieval (the foremost source of stock market data). But first, here's some advice on where to go and what to see so you don't thrash around and waste too much money in connect charges.

On-Line Highlights and Lowlights

Despite what they may tell you, just because you subscribe to a few on-line services doesn't mean you can access any information in the world—at least, not cheaply. You'll find that much of what's out there is expensive, some of it is old, and in many instances you're better off going to the library.

HOT TIP

On-line services are information brokers. The best guide to on-line information is Don Rittner's *The Whole Earth Online Almanac*, published by Brady Books. It lists all databases available through the major on-line services and can give you an idea of whether you should link up to databases directly, instead of through a service.

Things Worth Doing On Line

Thanks to many sleepless nights wandering the phone lines, I can confidently recommend the following on-line activities:

- **Make travel plans.** On-line travel services are a terrific place to check out low airfares and plane schedules, make hotel and car rental reservations, and even find restaurants and places to look into once you arrive.

- **Get a job.** National on-line services aren't much good when you're job-hunting, but a local BBS can be better (and cheaper) than many employment agencies, especially for computer-related jobs.

- **Network.** In the noncomputer sense, that is. CompuServe can be a wonderful place to meet others in your field. If you're starting a business, GEnie is a great spot to share war stories with other entrepreneurs.

- **Organize politically.** On just about any on-line service, you can tap your way into a public forum devoted to issues you feel strongly about, be it the environment, animal rights, or the Young Republicans.

- **Read wire service news.** If you're a news junkie, you can't find stories that are more timely. CompuServe and Prodigy don't charge to read news from the wire services.   **HOT TIP**

- **Do research.** You can spend a bundle and get very little, or spend little and get a lot. The trick is knowing exactly what you want and the cheapest place to find it. Check out *The Whole Earth Online Almanac* for advice.

- **Manage investments.** Get free stock quotes, company reports, Standard & Poor's recommendations, and many other things financial from several major on-line services. You can also buy, sell, or trade stocks through such on-line discount brokers as E*Trade, Schwab, or Fidelity's FOX.

- **Download software.** You can find any software your heart desires, be it a medieval typeface for PostScript or financial portfolio software.

- **Get technical support.** The technical support you get in conferences like those for Microsoft or WordPerfect is often superior to what you get on the phone. The advice you get from other users is even better.

- **Join specialized forums.** Forums are one of the fastest growing areas of the major on-line services. They are where users share details about their hobbies, whether model rocketry, stamp collecting, or *Star Trek*. A few years ago Prodigy and GEnie were amazed to find that their sewing and quilting forums were the services' most frequented areas. The art and music forums of these services are also heavily trafficked.

Things to Avoid On Line

Aside from wandering aimlessly in $700-an-hour databases, here are some of the things you *don't* want to do on line:

- **Shop.** Do you really want to buy an overpriced suit based on a fuzzy computer picture on a $5-an-hour on-line service?

- **Bank.** Would you honestly pay your bank an extra $10 a month for the privilege of tapping out checks on line?

- **Read the encyclopedia.** I find on-line encyclopedias weak in content and generally exasperating. Tell your kids to go to the library instead.

Figuring On-Line Costs

I am always amused when consumers raise a ruckus about the tawdry billing practices of some cable TV companies. When it comes to hidden costs and tricky surcharges, on-line services leave cable companies in the dust. Here are some of the charges you'll find on line:

- **Subscription start-up fee.** Usually this is fairly low, like $10 to $25, but it can be much higher on some of the premium business database services.

- **Monthly or yearly membership fee.** This will run around $10 a month on services like CompuServe, more on premium business databases.

- **Hourly connect fee.** This can range from $3 an hour on GEnie to $100 or more on some of the premium law databases. All the major on-line services now have hourly fees, which typically double during business hours. Hourly connect fees also increase with the speed at which you connect—2400 bps may cost a fifth of what 9600 bps does.

- **Tymnet, Telenet, or other packet network charges.** Packet networks provide low-cost long-distance access to databases or on-line services. Access is billed by the hour, and prices vary a lot. Generally, the toll during evening hours is a fraction of what it is during the day.

- **Network charges.** Another hourly connect fee, usually to dial in to the service using its 800 number rather than Tymnet or Telenet.

- **Database surcharges.** Hourly fees to access a particular database or service that are charged in addition to the service's hourly connect fee and the Tymnet or network fee.

- **E-mail charges.** On-line services usually let you send a fixed number of electronic messages each month without incurring extra fees, then charge you for any messages that exceed that number. Some services will charge extra for copying messages, requesting receipts, or big file attachments.

The best way to keep on-line charges down is to be aware of all the costs before you call, and to tailor your on-line activities accordingly. When you subscribe to an on-line service, go through the above list with a customer rep—you won't learn about extra costs unless you ask a lot of questions. Also make sure you find out what you get for the basic connect rate (for instance, CompuServe has a Standard Plan for $8.95 per month that includes toll-free access to certain areas, but not to its popular forums). Before you sign up, take advantage of any free trial offers so you can learn your way around the service before the meter starts ticking.

REMEMBER

HOT TIP

Here's another tip: If in your first month as a subscriber you inadvertently rack up some hideously huge bill, some on-line services will forgive the bill if you whimper about it. Of course, not all services will do this, and the ones that do it won't do it more than once for you—but it never hurts to try.

HOT TIP

Finally, if *front-end software* is available for a service, buy it. Every major service offers communications software that is already set up to connect automatically. Without logging on, you can compose E-mail or peruse menus to find just the area you want to access. The program will then log you on to the service, download your mail, and even conduct searches you set up before going on line. Then the program logs off as quickly as it can, saving you money.

HOT TIP

The Great Virus Scare

Fears of contracting computer viruses on on-line services or BBSs are greatly exaggerated. You can't contract a virus by reading E-mail or dialing a system with general-purpose communications software. Unless you download software, you stand about zero chance of getting infected over the wire—and because most BBSs and all major on-line services screen the software they offer for downloading, the chances are still very, very low.

Follow these three rules, and no matter what you download, you should be OK:

1. Only download software from BBSs that you know screen software prior to posting it.

2. Never be the first to download a piece of software from a system. You'll usually find a number near the program's file name indicating how many people have downloaded it. Wait for the program to "age" a couple of weeks (in other words, let others take the chance and download it first).

3. Download software to a floppy disk and run a virus scanner on it before you do anything else (see Chapter 9: *Protect Your Data*).

CompuServe

The world's premier on-line service is full of charm, sass, lively intellects, and all manner of happenings. Hang out in one of its forums long enough and you'll run into just about everyone you've ever met. Because CompuServe has Internet access, you can send E-mail to users on literally any computer network in the world. You can also send E-mail to many private LANs.

CompuServe offers one of the world's biggest shareware collections. Associated Press news wire stories will fill you in on world events faster than TV. Public forums span from Rush Limbaugh's debate forum (he rarely reads the postings; if you care, his CompuServe ID is 70277,2502) to forums for UFOs, genealogy, Masonry, science fiction, and more. And many computer companies use CompuServe to provide superb technical advice.

Business users will find public conferences, along with databases containing demographic, credit, and marketing data. If your company files with the Securities and Exchange Commission, it can even file electronically through CompuServe. The legally minded will find a leading law database plus low-cost patent and trademark searching.

Subscription and Log-On Advice

HOT TIP

Sign up for the standard plan at $8.95 per month, and opt for the Executive Service option, which will give you discounts on stock quotes and some business databases. Try to access whatever you can through the Basic Services menu where lots of things are free of access charges.

CompuServe is reasonably priced—at night, you pay $4.80 per hour for 2400 bps access and $9.60 per hour for 9600 bps and 14.4kbps access. Still, you'll definitely want to use front-end software to speed up your time on line.

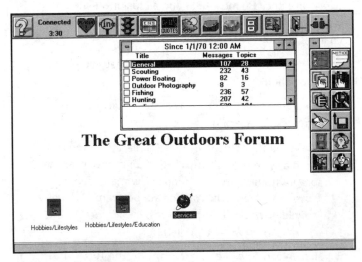

Figure 7: With CompuServe Information Manager for Windows, you can read and write E-mail off line, reducing your charges. The spiffy interface also enables you to dial up and access specific areas as soon as you connect.

Greatest Assets

Subscribers seem to go out of their way to help each other. It offers the greatest confluence of eggheads, artists, professionals, and generally charming people ever assembled. Users are much better behaved than on the academic discussion networks like Usenet. Subscribers in Paris throw great parties. Subscribers in Tokyo give impressive welcomes to visiting CompuServe users from abroad.

Greatest Flaws

Mysterious menus have been known to reduce powerful professional people to tears. Some of the business-oriented advice forums don't offer much advice at all. Searching for software can be hard and expensive.

Best Picks

Here are some particularly valuable or interesting areas I've encountered over the years. The Go commands I've listed take you directly to the areas described. If you use the DOS or Windows version of CompuServe Information Manager, CompuServe's front-end software, you'll find the Go option under the Services menu:

- **Medical advice.** If you have a family member who's ill and you need information fast, there's no better place to go. A variety of health databases and forums, some of which are toll-free, will provide the latest info on illness, treatment, and rehabilitation. Also on line is the National Library of Medicine's MedLine database (the world's biggest medical database), along with support groups, newsletters, and an orphan drug and disease database that lists current research projects with researcher contacts (type `go health`⌶Enter⌶.) **HOT TIP**

- **Investing.** If you're an armchair investor, you'll enjoy the free daily stock quotes—just remember to get them through the Basic Quotes menu or you'll pay a surcharge (type `go basicquotes`⌶Enter⌶). In the lively Investors' Forum, you can find advice on almost any investment and download loads of investment-related shareware (type `go invforum`⌶Enter⌶). For just $1 you can get a price-volume chart showing the price fluctuations of a specified issue (type `go trend`⌶Enter⌶). *Money Magazine*'s Fundwatch database will steer you to the best mutual funds, plus fill you in on particulars like annual fees and portfolio contents (type `go fundwatch`⌶Enter⌶). Want news and fundamental information on a specific company? You can get it free and fast if you know the company's ticker symbol (type `go glorep`⌶Enter⌶). **HOT TIP**

HOT TIP

- **Consumer Reports.** Check out *Consumer Reports'* toll-free database before you buy anything. This extensive database includes all the hard-hitting investigative reports from the magazine on everything from CD players to home owner's insurance (type `go csr-1`[Enter]).

- **Airline reservations.** The Eaasy Sabre on-line airfare reservation system can find you lower airfares than your travel agent can (type `go eaasy sabre`[Enter]).

- **Ziffnet.** The Ziffnet magazine forum provides lots of computer buying advice, plus product databases. It also offers an extensive cheap-to-search database that lists magazine articles on not just hardware and software, but on everything under the sun (type `go ziffnet`[Enter]).

Front-End Software

When you sign up, get a copy of *CompuServe Information Manager (CIM)* by CompuServe. (Or type `go order`[Enter] once you've logged on).

Although it costs $25, it comes with a certificate for free on-line time, so it's practically free. The Windows version is terrific.

You have a couple of free alternatives to *CIM*. Like *CIM*, *AutoSIG* will download your E-mail for you, along with public messages from forums you specify, so you can read messages and answer them off line. Ozarks West Software's *OzCIS* is a favorite of power users, with bells and whistles galore. You can download either program from the communications forum (type `go ibmcom`[Enter]).

Prodigy

Prodigy is so easy to use, I know three-year-olds who navigate it with ease. Its videogame-like screens look like they were drawn by kids using big crayons, and its on-line resources are dwarfed by the likes of CompuServe. Prodigy is also slow, full of annoying ads for shirts and pantyhose, and an object of criticism due to its censorship of public messages.

Prodigy is a family-oriented service. Public forums are screened for offensive material, and parents can set up their household account so that children can access only those areas that mom and dad see fit. Its information is *USA Today*-like, with colorful weather maps and headline news—don't expect hefty databases like you'd find on CompuServe. Instead, look for a guide to New England bed-and-breakfasts, on-line advice columnists like teen-parenting sage Dear Beth, best-

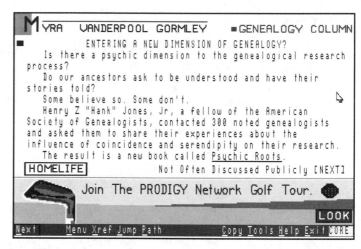

Figure 8: *Prodigy is a perfect resting place for those suffering brain death at the end of the day. Stories about psychics combine with festive ads for cars, pantyhose, and golf games to make your PC as escapist as tabloid TV.*

selling authors, and celebrities like James Earl Jones. Prodigy has even signed a deal with the NFL to get coaches and players on line.

America Online is cheaper, the software is free, and the family-oriented content is similar, so you may want to check out that service first.

Subscription and Log-On Advice

If you get your Prodigy software and start-up kit directly from Prodigy Services it won't cost you a dime.

HOT TIP

Sign up for the $14.95 per month value plan for your first month. You'll get unlimited toll-free access to news, weather, and reference services, plus two free hours of access to bulletin boards and stock quotes, and 30 free E-mail messages a month. After that you'll be billed $4.80 an hour for access to more popular services like the message conferences. Monitor your family's use of the service. When the novelty of Prodigy wears off, switch to the lower cost $7.95 per month plan. Since on-line rates are the same during the day and the evening, you can call anytime.

HOT TIP

Never run Prodigy software with memory-resident virus checkers or else you'll nuke Prodigy and jam its directory with what will look like Balto-Samoyedic cuss words the first time it tries to download from the service. For that matter, try not to run Prodigy with *any* memory-resident software. Except Windows. For some reason Prodigy works better in a DOS window under Windows than when run from the DOS prompt.

DANGER

HOT TIP

Greatest Assets

As easy to use as a pay TV in a bus station. So colorful and mindless it lets you zone out and experience life as a '60s psychedelic child.

Greatest Flaws

Snailish speed (so slow I embroider while menus are updating), combined with high hourly rates, make it a rip-off. Information content is superficial. People flit on and off, friendships made on the service tend to be fleeting, users don't answer E-mail as devotedly as they do on CompuServe and GEnie. The service suffers the cold impersonality of a shopping mall.

Best Picks

Prodigy may have its problems, but when it's good, sometimes it's *very* good:

- **Travel.** Prodigy has the most extraordinary collection of travel info and advice on line. You'll find restaurant and hotel guides, the Eaasy Sabre airline reservation system, and excellent advice from subscriber surveys on the best places to see and things to do when you reach your destination. Click on Jump at the bottom of the screen and type `travel` in the dialog box.

- **Investing.** For active investors, Wall St. Edge compiles tips and market insights from a variety of high-priced investment newsletters. Content changes daily. It costs $19.95 extra per month, or $1.95 to read a single day's issue. Click on Jump and type `Wall St Edge`.

- **The arts.** Prodigy's Arts Forum is a fun spot to share opinions on books, movies, politics, comics, and life in general. Click on Jump and type `artsbb`.

Front-End Software

Prodigy is its own front end, but it lacks the usual conveniences. If you're a heavy Prodigy user, you should get a copy of *Pro-Util* by Royston Utilities. This program, which runs on top of Prodigy software, may speed up your access to the service a bit, but, more important, it will give you capabilities that Prodigy's software won't, like the ability to save forum messages to a file and answer E-mail off line. That's a major advantage, since the service is so slow and the hourly connect rate so high.

General Electric's GEnie

GEnie is the poor man's CompuServe, with lots of fun people and the usual valuable on-line conversations about things like decoupage and gun collecting. It's the place to be if you're a Trekie. But its user interface is so blustery, you'll need to use GEnie's *Aladdin* navigation software to tame it.

Most GEnie features are followed by a "but...". It offers the Reuters news wire, but at a steep price. It delivers low-cost closing stock quotes daily, but no access to big data-bases. It has a large software collection, but it's a pain to search and download from. It offers an Internet mail link to the outside world, but it's known for its unreliability. WordPerfect, Borland, and Microsoft offer good tech support on line, but few other companies do.

Subscription and Log-On Advice

GEnie costs a flat $8.95 per month, which includes four hours of connect time. After that you're billed $3 per hour in the evening. Connection costs $9.50 an hour extra during the day, so always call at night. Never call at speeds higher than 2400 bps unless you want to pay a steep toll. Use *Aladdin* navigation software to bring costs down.

Greatest Assets

The public forums, or roundtables as they're called, offer more good chatter than on any other on-line service, thanks to low cost and lots of great people. Conversation is particularly vivacious in the entertainment and leisure areas (type `leisure` Enter at any prompt). A great place to get your feet wet on line.

Greatest Flaws

The ugly interface makes reading and downloading messages onerous. The E-mail feature, in particular, is a travesty. Some of GEnie's modems are hard to connect to at 2400 bps, so you may have to lower your speed to 1200 bps to get a good connection. Seems I can rarely get a file transfer going faster than 1200 bps running Xmodem.

DANGER

Best Picks

Once you get past the interface, you'll find some interesting attractions:

- **Trekie heaven.** Yes, this is the place to be if you're a Trekie. The *Star Trek* conferences are rich, and members of the production crew of *Next Generation* have been known to drop in from time to time. Lots of sci-fi writers are on line, too. Type `sfrt` Enter at any prompt.

- **Small business advice.** If you run a small business, you'll find lots of valuable information in the Home Office and Small Business Roundtable, which takes the prize as the best such conference available on line (type `hosb`⏎).

HOT TIP

- **Investing.** Investors will enjoy the investor's forum, which is every bit as good and sometimes better than the CompuServe offering. Daily closing market quotes can be had for the cost of downloading (type `invest`⏎).

- **Hobbies.** The hobby forum is always popular. It offers over a thousand different subject areas, ranging from model rocketry to Dickens Village bric-a-brac collecting (type `hobby`⏎).

- **BBS operator info.** Enthusiasts interested in setting up their own BBS will find extensive discussions on BBS software and modems (type `bbs`⏎).

HOT TIP

- **Internet info.** If you want to learn about this popular but often inscrutable network, the Internet Roundtable is the place to go. In addition, an Internet Archie function lets you search and retrieve files on Internet without ever leaving GEnie (type `internet-rt`⏎).

Front-End Software

HOT TIP

Be sure to get a copy of GEnie's *Aladdin* navigation software. It costs nothing, except for the cost of downloading from the service. Type `aladdin`⏎ and choose PC Aladdin Support Roundtable off the menu. *Aladdin* can be glitchy and so can GEnie, so keep an eye out for upgrades, which come out frequently.

America Online

America Online has a fun graphical interface and offers innovative attractions. You'll find the National Geographic Society on line, along with the Smithsonian museums, the Library of Congress, and National Public Radio. You'll also see publications like *Omni, The New Republic, Time, Consumer Reports,* and the *Chicago Tribune* available in their entirety in an easy-to-read format. Daily stories from UPI and *USA Today* are also available.

Though America Online has fewer subscribers than CompuServe or Prodigy, its forums are still good reading. Experts in various fields make on-line conversations informative: In the Pet Care forum, you can chat with veterinarians and animal behaviorists, while the Parent's and Teacher's Information Network features educators and child behavior experts. You won't find monster databases, but you can connect with on-line stock brokerages, exchange E-mail through an Internet link, and make airline reservations.

America Online is a lot like Prodigy, but the software is free and the hourly connect charges are lower. The service offers a ten-hour free trial, so you'd do well to check it out.

HOT TIP

Subscription and Log-On Advice

There's one basic plan, and it's not too shabby. Call America Online's 800 number and you'll get the service's software free, plus the first month of usage and ten hours on line free. After that a subscription costs $9.95 per month, which includes five hours of free connect time. After that connect time is billed at a flat $3.50 per hour.

Greatest Assets

A feel-good interface, good conferences, low price.

Greatest Flaws

American Online can be slow. You must read on line, that is, you usually can't save money by downloading and reading stories or messages off line.

Best Picks

Along with some pretty lively on-line forums, this light-duty service has several interesting diversions. Press Ctrl D after you log on to get a menu of the departments listed here:

HOT TIP

- **Browser's library.** The usual problem with on-line information is that you can't browse. America Online's Library of Congress Online solves that problem, offering fascinating articles on subjects ranging from early opera to the Dead Sea Scrolls, which you can flip through at your leisure. You can even download articles in order to save on-line charges. Go to the Learning & Reference department.

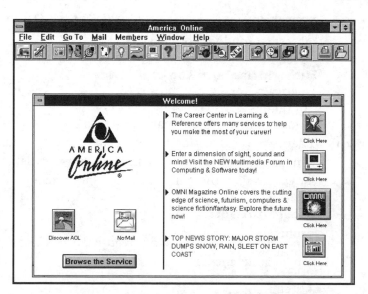

Figure 9: *Subscribe to America Online, and you get this engaging front end as part of the deal.*

- **SportsLink.** Sports aficionados, take note: You'll find scores, rosters, discussions, and even a software library that includes programs to manage the office football pool or track your golf handicap. Go to the Lifestyles & Interests department.

- **Pretend investing.** The Bulls & Bears stock market simulation game gives you a hypothetical $100K to invest. You compete with other users in playing the market. Go to the Games & Entertainment department.

Front-End Software

There's nothing you need besides the basic software to call this service.

MCI Mail

HOT TIP

Low rates and no hourly connect charges make this everyone's favorite E-mail service. Its low-cost links to other services mean you can send mail to literally anyone plugged into any computer network. Moreover, MCI Mail is available in just about every country in the world. MCI Mail also offers faxing. I hate to admit it, but I prefer to fax through MCI Mail rather then use my own fax-modem, because it's cheaper than making a long-distance call.

The service offers a wide range of messaging features. You can maintain mailing lists, request receipts, set the message priority, and send telexes or overnight hard copy letters. You can even maintain a computer bulletin board for your company.

MCI Mail has competitors, like SprintMail and AT&T Mail, but MCI has many more subscribers and it's cheaper.

Subscription and Log-On Advice

HOT TIP

MCI Mail's $10 per month preferred customer plan lets you send 40 messages or faxes a month with no additional charges—a great deal unless you have little use for E-mail. There's never a fee for receiving messages. Sporadic E-mail users should consider a standard membership at $35 per year, plus a variable per-message toll. These tolls will eat your wallet, though, if you send more than four or five messages a month.

Greatest Assets

Simplicity. Binary files like spreadsheets can be uploaded with Zmodem and sent as E-mail attachments.

Greatest Flaws

Its on-line editor is unpleasant, so it's best to read and write your E-mail off line.

Front-End Software

MCI Mail has no hourly connect fees, so a front end won't save you money, only time. A free program called *EMA*, which automates mail collecting, can be downloaded from CompuServe (type `go ziffnet`[Enter]). MCI sells *MCI Mail Xpress*, which automates mail retrieval, lets you attach files to messages easily, and includes a built-in spell checker.

Dow Jones/News Retrieval

Dow Jones/News Retrieval is a bargain for active individual investors who call after 8 p.m. You can access daily and historical market quotes going back two years, plus news wires, reports on insider trading, and fundamental data and analysis on companies—all for $29.95 per month with no connect charges. If you're in the market for this kind of data, skip the other on-line services (including *Money Magazine*'s Smart Investor) and log on here.

This service includes the largest collection of business news and data ever assembled on line. You'll find national and international business news wires, hundreds of regional business publications, and Securities and Exchange Commission filings. A tracking feature collects news on and prices of individual issues, and a clipping service retrieves stories on specific companies or industries from such publications as the *Wall Street Journal*, the *Boston Globe*, the *Washington Post*, and the *Los Angeles Times*. *Dunn's Financial Records* database, *Standard & Poor's* company profiles, and much more are available.

If you just want closing market quotes and a mutual fund database, you're better off going to CompuServe and signing up for its standard $8.95-per-month plan.

HOT TIP

Subscription and Log-On Advice

This is one of those services where you can easily run up a $50 bill trying to find the information you need. Before you sign up, determine *exactly* the sort of information you want. Do you want company 10K reports? Do you need news on the Japanese markets? Call Dow Jones and ask them if they have it, how timely it is, and if it's in a form you can use. Then set about determining the cheapest way to access it. Dow Jones costs approximately 75 cents per screenful of information that you read or download, with extra charges for certain special databases.

For a flat fee of $29.95 per month, the Market Monitor plan could be a better deal for you. You don't get access to the whole service, but you do get current day closing and two-year historical stocks, bonds, mutual fund, futures, and index quotes; Dow Jones averages; a so-so mutual fund database; five Dow Jones news wires and 500 business publications that you can search; daily accounts of insider transactions; company data that includes price changes, P/E ratio, earnings, dividends, debt, revenue, and other essentials; analysts' weekly buy-sell recommendations and company and industry earnings estimates; 6- to 12-line summaries of Investext reports on the outlook for major issues; and *Wall $treet Week* transcripts.

Greatest Assets

More financial information in one place than any other service offers.

Greatest Flaws

Professional investors like to grouse about the high number of errors they find in Dow Jones's market quotes (although it seems to me that the quotes have fewer errors than those on CompuServe and GEnie).

Front-End Software

Dow Jones sells several software packages for users who plan to download market quotes regularly. *Market Analyzer* and *Market Analyzer Plus* are portfolio management packages that will automatically dial up, download quotes, and chart them. One of the flaws of Dow Jones' Market Monitor plan is that in order to download historical quotes, you need to key in every date that you want a quote for—you can't just key in a date range. Give one of the *Analyzer* programs a range, though, and it will go on line and do the work. What does *Analyzer Plus* have that *Analyzer* lacks? You get 30 popular built-in price analysis formulas, a formula builder, the ability to import quotes from other applications, and a feature for retrieving news stories on issues.

Spreadsheet Link, also by Dow Jones, will similarly download quotes for you and feed them into a *Lotus*, *Excel*, or *Quattro Pro* spreadsheet. All these products are discounted 50 percent if you sign up for the Market Monitor plan.

Internet/Usenet

Outside of the fall of the Soviet empire, Internet is the most exciting thing to happen to democracy in this half of the twentieth century. Through Internet, computer users around the globe can exchange E-mail, usually for next to nothing. They can engage in uninhibited public discourse on politics, science, technology, anything they desire. Internet brought the world the first news of the student uprisings in China. It enables physicists in India to communicate with physicists in Cambridge. It allows doctors in Africa to log on to a computer in Boston and tap into the world's repositories of medical knowledge. It lets ordinary people like us screw around and make loads of friends.

Internet is bringing information and freedom of speech to countries in which phone service is a luxury. There is no nation that can stem the news and public discourse that Internet is wrapping around the globe. Originally a Department of Defense computer network linking the military, its contractors, and university researchers, Internet has blossomed into much more in the last decade. It's become both an electronic town hall and a public library. It is the world's digital highway.

Subscription and Log-On Advice

How do you tap into Internet? Individuals can't—unless they have a UNIX system and $10,000 or $20,000 to spend for special phone lines and membership fees.

Fortunately, if you're on a local area network (LAN), you may already have access to Internet via a university, business, or government agency with Internet links, so check it out. If so, you won't pay a dime for Internet access. If not, just sign up with an on-line service that offers Internet access, or subscribe to one of the many BBSs that are also connected. Several different kinds of Internet access are offered through BBSs and on-line services:

- **E-mail access.** You can exchange private E-mail with anyone who has an Internet address. Most commercial on-line and electronic mail services let you send Internet E-mail, including CompuServe, GEnie, and MCI Mail. Many BBSs also let you send Internet mail.

- **Usenet news.** Usenet news groups are the raucous, freewheeling forums that swirl through Internet. At last count there were nearly 5000 of them, although few services carry them all. Most participants seem to be college kids or professors with time on their hands, and discussions range from enlightening to childish. With no governing body, no sysops, and no censorship, Usenet is anarchy turned digital. Delphi, The Well, Portal, and many large BBSs carry the Usenet news groups.

- **Telnet and FTP access.** Telnet lets you log on to remote computers (like the one in your public library), scroll through the public file list, and even confer with others who've logged on. FTP access enables you to move files from one Internet computer to another. Delphi and Portal provide both Telnet and FTP access, as do several services, including HoloNet and a2i Communications. Performance Systems International of Reston, Virginia, links individuals as well as businesses to Internet.

- **Archie and gopher.** Archie will find a file for you on any Internet *public server* (a computer open for Internet users to access); gopher will retrieve it for you. GEnie offers archie and gopher services, along with a very good on-line forum with the latest information on using Internet.

If you plan on doing anything more than exchange Internet E-mail, get yourself one of the many primers on Internet commands available in your bookstore. The best one is Ed Krol's *The Whole Internet User's Guide and Catalog* from O'Reilly & Associates, Sebastopol, California. The book includes a guide to databases on Internet.

Greatest Assets

Access to everything at low cost. For a pittance, how else can you send E-mail to anyone in the world, engage in international discussions, and tap into the public electronic libraries of schools, universities, and government agencies?

Greatest Flaws

Tricky to figure out. Many messages posted on Usenet are rude. Internet has questionable value for non-high-tech businesses. Too much pornography.

Best Picks

Usenet offers so many forums, it's best to just get on line and have a look yourself. That said, a couple points of interest:

- **Talk.bizarre.** Pronounced "talk-dot-bizarre," this is undoubtedly the most offbeat public message forum in the world. Here, the greatest minds from academia, government, and private industry join forces to pontificate on rock 'n' roll, the pitfalls of cloning one's spouse, a sinister fictitious corporation known as "X-Industries," and other, well, bizarrities. Every tenth messages ends with the advice, "Getalife."

- **Oh no, not Star Trek again.** Believe it or not, Usenet's busiest electronic message forum is devoted to *Star Trek*. A particularly thought-provoking episode of a *Star Trek* spin-off can net a thousand new messages in a couple of days. Sobering, isn't it? The biggest traffic jam in the global data highway caused by a '60s TV show in which the aliens look liked dissipated Shakespearean actors. Getalife.

Front-End Software

So many different kinds of computers access Internet, no one has attempted to create a comprehensive front end to tame the Internet beast. There are, however, numerous *news readers*, which make reading Usenet forums easier. Contact the techie who runs the Usenet link for your BBS or on-line service and ask for a recommendation.

Delphi

A feisty little service that's been around since the dawn of on-line services, Delphi has been through many changes. Currently, it emphasizes low-cost Internet access, but who knows what the future holds for this mercurial perennial start-up. Delphi has some key advantages over the CompuServes of the world: It's dirt-cheap, and it offers full Internet access. It also lets users create their own public forums or mini on-line services for a small monthly fee.

Subscription and Log-On Advice

For $10 a month you get 4 free hours of evening and weekend access, and pay $4 an hour for every hour after that. Or, for $20 a month you get 20 hours of evening and weekend access, and pay $1.80 per hour after that. Add an extra $3 a month and you get full Internet access. Right now, those are the best prices going for a general-interest on-line service. And since Delphi is straightforward to use, you won't burn time getting tangled in menus.

Greatest Assets

Delphi certainly has its devotees. Every time I write a negative review of it, I get deluged with mail from offended subscribers. It's a nice, homey place, where it's easy to make friends and run into them frequently. And, of course, you can't beat the price.

Greatest Flaws

Delphi's content makes it look like a big BBS. It lacks the big message forums or shareware libraries of larger services, and it offers only a smattering of reference services, all of which you can find elsewhere for the same price or cheaper.

Best Picks

You'll find the usual reference stuff: Grolier's *Electronic Encyclopedia*, daily stock quotes at seven cents each, a register of public corporations, UPI and Reuters news, and on-line travel services like Eaasy Sabre and the Official Airline Guides. But these are the two features that may make subscribing worth it:

- **Full Internet access.** Delphi offers Telnet, FTP, archie, gopher, Usenet.

- **Your own BBS.** Delphi has a unique program whereby you can set up your own private message forum for a set-up fee of $39.95, plus $15 a month maintenance after the first three months. You can make your personal message forum private or public. There are already hundreds of them, most of them public. They range in topic from Equestrians Online to Dittoheads Unlimited, and they're generally more fun than the forums Delphi has established.

Computer Bulletin Boards

BBSs and their often anonymous operators, called *sysops*, are the unsung heroes of high tech. The media loves stories about hackers who use bulletin boards to distribute stolen credit card numbers, or about fiends who expose children to on-line pornography. Sure, unsavory stuff happens. But what about the time a poor family lost all its possessions in a fire—including a PC being used to earn a college degree—and BBS users all over the country banded together to build a new PC in 24 hours? Stories like that abound.

Full of camaraderie and possessed of a quirky subculture, your average local BBS is a slightly weirder on-line version of the bar in *Cheers*. Along with providing a venue for banter, many larger BBSs are like small on-line services, offering stock quotes, *USA Today* news stories, and access to Internet. Some specialize in particular professions or interests; others have representatives from companies like IBM providing tech support to callers.

But the BBS world resembles the Wild West. On BBSs you'll encounter jokers, braggarts, and con artists, and you'll probably get into a few brawls. Sometimes you'll yearn for the mannered drawing rooms of CompuServe; sometimes you'll think everyone is nuts. But if you spend enough time BBSing, you'll make friends you may keep for the rest of your life. You may even make a business contact or two, and you'll certainly learn a lot about using your PC. All from tapping in little messages on a screen.

Subscription and Log-On Advice

Local computer publications, computer stores, and user groups are all good places to find listings of local BBSs. There are tens of thousands of them in the United States— I've heard there are over 700 in Houston alone. You'll find thousands more in other countries (including Russia, the Philippines, even China), but the U.S. has the most, thanks to excellent, low-cost phone service. A few of the big BBSs charge annual fees, but most are free.

When you dial a BBS, think of it as walking into someone's family room. That is, after all, where most BBSs are kept. If you're logging on to a local BBS to get your feet wet on line, here are some things to keep in mind:

• Don't log on with a false name.

- When you log off, write the operator a message thanking him or her for letting you use the system. Most BBS owners run their systems as a hobby, at great time and expense.

REMEMBER

- If you download software from the board, always upload some in return. Never upload copyrighted software.

- Don't be rude to the sysop or other users. Never use four-letter words.

- Try to keep questions for the sysop to a minimum, since he or she is a busy person. If you're unsure about how to do something on the board, reread the help files and bulletins, or ask other users.

- If you call a board regularly and the owner asks for donations to keep it running, pitch in. In other words, act like a responsible adult.

A number of services let you dial BBSs around the country at low long-distance rates. Some are good, some are rip-offs. PC-Pursuit, which uses the SprintNet network (sometimes called Telenet), is an old favorite. It offers 30 hours of monthly long-distance modem calling at night for $30, plus a $30 setup fee, but you can only call 40 major metropolitan areas with it.

Global Access by G-A Technologies provides evening long-distance access to most cities in the United States for $4 per hour. MCI offers a program for participating BBSs and their callers dubbed PC Connect, which is kind of like a Friends and Family program for frequently called BBSs.

Greatest Assets

What's good, of course, depends on the BBS. Software collections on BBSs are usually better than the ones on big on-line services—and you can search and download from them faster and cheaper than from a commercial on-line service. Access to Usenet discussion groups, along with informal BBS networks, are big plusses for on-line raconteurs.

Echoes: Hot Links Between BBSs

Many BBSs have *echoes,* where messages are broadcast among a network of boards. In this way, callers to many different BBSs can participate in the same discussions and exchange E-mail around the country or around the world. Dial a BBS in New York, for instance, and you may be able to participate in discussions with BBSers in California or maybe even in London.

BBS echoes seem to be proliferating faster than BBSs. The biggest one is FidoNet, which reaches Europe, Asia, and Africa. It's also linked to Internet so that you can send a message from, say, MCI Mail, through Internet, to a FidoNet BBS in Australia. Other BBS echoes include ILINK, RIME, and SmartNet. Most BBSs say on their log-on screens whether they're part of an echo.

Greatest Flaws

Chronic busy signals on some small systems. On some boards, people can be pretty rude. The dark underbelly to the BBS world is that the distribution of pornography is the major stock-in-trade of many boards.

Best Picks

Based on my personal experience and the opinions of many users, here are the all-time great BBSs:

- **Exec-PC.** Bob and Tracey Mahoney's Exec-PC in Milwaukee takes the gold cup as the world's best and biggest BBS. Exec-PC has over 280 high-speed phone lines (so there's never a busy signal), a huge software library, FidoNet echo, and a classy menuing system a million times easier to navigate than that of any big on-line service. Exec-PC is a family business, so service is top-notch and the board's content is family oriented. For debate and general silliness, check out the Bull Roar and More conference. Cost is $60 a year, no connect fees. Dial 414/789-4210 to log on.

- **Sound of Music.** Not necessarily for music lovers, Paul Waldinger's Sound of Music is a favorite of New Yorkers. The content is decidedly family oriented, with lots of special-interest forums ranging from music to computers. Many software companies, including WordPerfect and Delrina, hang out and give free tech support. E-mail links stretch as far as Saudi Arabia. You get Usenet conferences, Internet mail, FidoNet, SmartNet, and ReshNet echoes. It's a pay-if-you-like board, and you will like. Dial 516/536-5630 to log on.

- **Channel One.** Boston's Channel One is the East Coast darling. A mom-and-pop operation, it offers a big software library, over 100 on-line games, 85 lines for conferencing, Internet E-mail, and 2500 Usenet discussion forums. You also get SmartNet, ILINK, and RIME echoes; plus daily

Kids and BBSs

Should you let your children call BBSs? If they're under 12, you should monitor them closely. I know a father who encourages some of his BBS friends to write his seven-year-old son, but he doesn't let the boy read the public conferences unless he's sitting beside him. Teenagers can handle themselves on line. Still, it would be a good idea to talk to your teens about what they're reading on bulletin boards, and advise them not to meet with any strangers they may encounter. Tell them that just because someone they meet on a BBS tells them they're 16 years old, doesn't mean they really are. Often people are not what they seem on BBSs. Adults should keep the same warning in mind.

stock quotes, market summaries, and horoscopes. Subscriptions run from $45 to $160 per year. Dial 617/354-7077 to log on.

- **The Well.** Many Californians won't dial any BBS but The Well. The electronic flagship of *The Whole Earth Catalog*, The Well is known for its memorable, only-in-Northern-California repartee. Eastern philosophies, cyberpunk, intellectual property law, the men's movement...it's all here, served up with the laid-back anarchy you expect from this part of the world. Usenet and Internet links are available, but dull in comparison to what goes on here. Subscription costs $15 per month plus $2 per hour access. Dial 415/332-6106 to log on.

Front-End Software

BBS *readers*, as they're called, automate message retrieval. They're tailored to work with the various breeds of BBS software, such as *PC Board* or *Fido*. Ask your BBS sysop to recommend the best reader for his or her board.

Guide to Global E-mail Addressing

When it comes to E-mail, you *can* get there from here. Want to send a message from CompuServe to someone on GEnie? No problem. From MCI Mail to AT&T's EasyLink? Whoosh—there it is! From a PC hooked to a LAN, you may even be able to send E-mail to Fido BBSs around the world.

Most of the time, the trick is to use Internet to route the message. As I've noted throughout this chapter, most BBSs, many local area networks (LANs), and all on-line services have access to Internet. This means that *almost everyone on line has an Internet address*, whether they know it or not. Most of the time, all you need to know are a few details about your addressee, how to plug him or her into the Internet address, and any special prefix you need to add if you're sending from an on-line service.

REMEMBER

- **If you're on a LAN, BBS, or on-line service with Internet access** (*except* CompuServe, MCI Mail, AT&T Mail, or GEnie), and you want to reach someone else on Internet, see "From Internet to Internet" later in this chapter.

- **If you're on a LAN, BBS, or on-line service with Internet access** (*except* CompuServe, MCI Mail, AT&T Mail, or GEnie), and you want to reach someone on a BBS *other than* your own, see "From Internet to FidoNet BBSs" later in this chapter.

- **If you're on any LAN, BBS, or on-line service with Internet access** (*except* CompuServe, MCI Mail, AT&T Mail, or GEnie), and you want to reach someone who has a mailbox on an on-line service *other than* Internet, see "From Internet to Other On-Line Services" later in this chapter.

- **If you're on CompuServe, MCI Mail, AT&T Mail, or GEnie,** and you want to reach someone on Internet or on an on-line service *other than* your own, see "From Your On-Line Service to Anywhere" later in this chapter.

From Internet to Internet

Seems like every university, government agency, and military organization has Internet access. So do an increasing number of private companies, because after they pay the start-up and membership fees, their employees can send jillions of E-mail messages around the world and incur no additional charges. All people need to do is specially address messages using their LAN's E-mail system (see Chapter 22: *About Networks*).

If you're on Internet and you want to send a message to someone on a LAN in an organization that has an Internet link, you always begin the Internet address with a *username* followed by an @ sign. How do you find out the username? You call the addressee and ask. The username is the same name the addressee has been assigned on the LAN E-mail system (if it's a first and last name, it will be connected by an underline, as in *user_name*). The structure of your basic Internet address is:

username@organization[.domain].suffix

The *organization* and the *domain* (the latter isn't always required) identify the LAN and department where the addressee is connected. The suffix identifies the type of organization: *.com* for a commercial concern; *.edu* for a school; *.mil* for a military organization, and *.gov* for a government agency.

Say you want to send a message to Jerry Jackson, who has a networked PC at a company called Ping-Pong Plastics. Before you address your message to Jerry, you have to give him a call and find out his username and his organization's abbreviation, including his domain, if any. When Jerry checks with his LAN administrator, he discovers that his Internet address is:

jerryj@pingpong.com

This is the address you use to reach Jerry, right through his company's Internet-capable LAN E-mail system. A few caveats:

- If you're addressing the message from *your own* organization's Internet-capable LAN E-mail system, you typically select INTERNET from the addressee list and type Jerry's address at the To: prompt.

> ### How to Send E-mail to Bill or Al
>
> That's right, you can reach the White House by E-mail. To send a message to Bill Clinton through Internet, use the address president@whitehouse.gov; to reach Al Gore, use vice.president@whitehouse.gov. To reach Bill on CompuServe, use the ID number 75300,3115; on America Online, address your message to CLINTONPZ.

- If you're on CompuServe, MCI Mail, AT&T Mail, or GEnie, this address contains all the information you need to reach Jerry on Internet, but the syntax will be different (consult Figure 11 for these variations).

- If you're on any other on-line service or BBS with Internet access—including America Online—you can use Jerry's Internet address as is.

From Internet to Other On-Line Services

Imagine that Jerry subscribes to so many on-line services that, for variety's sake, you like to send messages through a different service each time. (OK, no one would ever do this, but I have to set up this example somehow!) For each service, you need to know Jerry's unique ID—in some cases, this will be an ID number; in others, it will be a username that probably won't be the same as Jerry's LAN username. However, to make the addressing easier to understand, Figure 10 assumes Jerry will be able to keep his handle, jerryj, on every service.

On the following page, Figure 10 shows how to address E-mail to Jerry on 11 different on-line services. With this table, you can address messages from any LAN, BBS, or on-line service with Internet access—*except* CompuServe, MCI Mail, AT&T Mail, or GEnie. If you subscribe to any of these services, see Figure 11.

REMEMBER

Internet On-Line Service Addressing at a Glance		
Addressee subscribes to	**Address syntax**	**Example (using your pal Jerry, who is on every mail service)**
CompuServe	ID@compuserve.com	75300.713@compuserve.com[1]
GEnie	user ID@genie.geis.com	jerryj@genie.geis.com
MCI Mail	ID@mcimail.com.	3127737@mcimail.com[2]
America Online	username@aol.com	jerryj@aol.com
AppleLink	ID@applelink.apple.com	jerryj@applelink.apple.com
AT&T Mail	user ID@attmail.com	jerryj@attmail.com
AT&T EasyLink	address@eln.attmail.com	62123456@eln.attmail.com
BitNet	address@org.bitnet	jerryj@pingpong.bitnet
Connect	username@dcjcon.das.net	jerryj@dcjcon.das.net
Delphi	username@delphi.com	jerryj@delphi.com
Prodigy	username@prodigy.com	jerryj @prodigy.com
UUNet	username%org@uunet.uu.net	jerryj%pingpong@uunet.uu.net

[1]CompuServe ID numbers use a comma, but you must replace it with a period for Internet addressing!
[2]Remember not to include commas or dashes in the ID number.

Figure 10: *Use this table to address E-mail from any LAN, BBS, or on-line service with Internet access (except CompuServe, MCI Mail, AT&T Mail, or GEnie) to an addressee on any of these on-line services. Note that in real life, Jerry's username would probably vary from service to service.*

From Internet to FidoNet BBSs

As noted earlier in this chapter, FidoNet is the most popular BBS echo on earth. (An echo, you'll remember, is an informal BBS network.) Without even joining a FidoNet BBS, you can send mail to anyone who subscribes to one, as long as you know his or her username and which FidoNet BBS they're on. It's just like sending a message from Internet to someone on an on-line service, only a bit more complicated.

To figure out the FidoNet address, dial up the FidoNet BBS that the person subscribes to. You'll notice that on the log-on screen, the BBS identifies itself by a series of numbers that looks something like this: 4:88/2. This gobbledygook can be translated into an Internet address that you can use to send mail to callers on that BBS.

The first number in the string of numbers is the geographic zone, the second is the network number, the third is the node number. Translate them into an Internet address this way:

<username>@f<node number>.n<network number>.z<geographic zone number>.fidonet.org

So if your old pal Jerry was on the above BBS, the address would look like this:

jerryj@f2.n88.z4.fidonet.org

X.400: The Other Way to Send E-mail Wherever

While most people use Internet to get messages from here to there, in some cases you can't—for example, if you subscribe to CompuServe, MCI Mail, AT&T Mail, or SprintMail, you may not be able to go through Internet to send a message to any other service in this group. As you can see in Figure 11, the major services offer their own ways to exchange messages without using Internet as a throughway.

In several cases—say, sending a message from CompuServe to AT&T Mail—you use *X.400* addressing. An international electronic messaging standard without Internet's restrictions, X.400 routes messages faster than Internet, and it offers the added advantage of enabling you to attach binary files to messages. But X.400 addressing is also a lot more complicated, and the syntax varies with each on-line service. For foolproof X.400 addressing, carefully follow the instructions specified by the on-line service you subscribe to.

Addressing From Service to Service		
If you subscribe to	**And you want to reach Jerry on**	**Then use this address**
CompuServe	Internet	>INTERNET:jerryj@ping pong.com
	MCI Mail	MCIMAIL:3127737
	AT&T Mail	x400:(c=us;a=attmail;s=jackson;g=jerry;d=id:jerryj)
MCI Mail	Internet	To:Jerry Jackson (EMS) EMS:INTERNET MBX:jerryj@pingpong.com
	CompuServe	To:Jerry Jackson (EMS) EMS:Compuserve MBX:P= CSMAIL MBX:DDA=ID=75300,713 MBX:<Enter>
	AT&T Mail	To:Jerry Jackson (EMS) EMS:ATTMAIL MBX:DDA=ID=jerryj MBX:<Enter>
AT&T Mail	Internet	To:internet!pingpong.com!jerryj
	CompuServe	To:mhs!csmail/dd.id=75300.713
	MCI Mail	To:mhs!mci/pn=jerry_jackson/dda.id=3127737
GEnie	Internet[1]	To:jerryj@pingpong.com@inet

[1]You can use an Internet address to reach any recipient on any service, but you must add the @inet suffix. Consult Figure 10 for more Internet on-line service addresses.

Figure 11: *This table shows how to address a message to Jerry Jackson at Ping Pong Plastics—who happens to subscribe to five E-mail services—from any other E-mail service. If you subscribe to an Internet-capable service not listed here, just use Jerry's Internet address (see Figure 10).*

From Your On-Line Service to Anywhere

Since every on-line service offers access to Internet, you'd think you could reach any other on-line service using the Internet addresses in Figure 10. Not so fast!

Figure 11 explains the special addressing procedures required to send E-mail between the major on-line services (and to someone on Internet, since the major services usually require a special prefix). Note that if you subscribe to a service *not* listed in the table, you can use the basic Internet address in Figure 10 to get your message through to anywhere. For example, to send a message from CompuServe to Jerry on America Online, you'd simply enter the address in Figure 10 after CompuServe's Internet prefix:

HOT TIP   >INTERNET:jerryj@aol.com.

Communications Software

The communications software that comes packaged with your new modem will probably be crude stuff. It will let you dial out, download files, and store phone numbers in a dialing directory, but not much else. It may not even work with the modem it was packed with! Even if it does, you should go ahead and pay the extra $50 to $150 for new communications software. Why? For one thing, better software is less likely to lose a connection. Here are some other reasons:

- **Speed.** If you paid for a high-speed modem, you want to get the most out of it, don't you? Good software ensures that you can take full advantage of compression and includes the best selection of fast file transfer protocols.

- **Automation.** The best communications programs can "learn" as you log on to a service, download your mail, or whatever, and will perform those same actions again whenever you like. You can also create *scripts*—lists of commands you put together so your PC can log on to a service and do all sorts of things when you're not around. In addition, these programs enable you to attach modem commands (to turn MNP 5 compression on and off, for example) to function keys, saving time.

- **Easy operation.** Cheap communications software is often hard to use—some programs don't even have a decent dialing directory. Also, few modems come with Windows communications software, so you can't cut and paste between messages when answering E-mail.

In this section, you'll get my sterling recommendations on which program to buy, plus tips for getting set up and on line with the top four best-sellers. Remember, though, not to confuse communications software with fax software. Unfortunately, they are two separate items on your shopping list.

Which Program to Buy

I still prefer DOS communications software to Windows communications software, because connections are inherently faster and more stable. My recommendation? Buy Datastorm's *Procomm Plus* for DOS. It's easy, inexpensive, and includes all the features you need.

HOT TIP

For Windows communication, nothing beats DCA's *Crosstalk for Windows*. Its heavy-duty script language, function-key shortcuts, and wide range of configuration options endear it to power users.

HOT TIP

A few other communications programs bear consideration. Hilgraeve's *HyperAccess*, which comes in both DOS and Windows versions, is easy to use and offers everything *Procomm* does, plus better terminal emulations. Relay Technology's *Relay/PC* is a highly customizable Windows program with lots of point-and-click buttons. Mustang Software's *Qmodem* offers a *Procomm*-like DOS interface, plus a fax mode that lets you receive faxes, though not send them. The low-cost shareware program *Telemate* is a flashy DOS program that offers windowing plus cut and paste between messages.

Avoid these communications products: SoftKlone's *Mirror*, Hayes' *Smartcom* (which comes with Hayes modems), and *QuickLink*.

Procomm Plus for DOS

Procomm Plus for DOS fits most users like an old glove. Operations are easy to remember, from pressing ⎡Alt⎤⎡D⎤ for the dialing directory to ⎡Page Down⎤ for a download. Unlike the Windows programs, *Procomm Plus* for DOS won't let you cut and paste between E-mail messages or download files in the background while you do something else. But you can't argue with success: *Procomm Plus* is the world's most popular communications software.

Procomm Plus for DOS Tips

This program barely needs explaining. To get started, press ⎡Alt⎤⎡Z⎤ for a list of all of *Procomm*'s keyboard shortcuts. To access all the program's menus, press the apostrophe key.

HOT TIPS

- **Setup.** Press ⎡Alt⎤⎡S⎤ for the main setup screen. Don't forget to hit Save on the way out when you're done.

- **Dialing out.** Press ⎡Alt⎤⎡D⎤ for the dialing directory. To add an entry, press A; to revise one, press R. To dial an entry, cursor to it and press ⎡Enter⎤.

- **Capturing text.** Press ⎡Alt⎤⎡F1⎤ and enter a file name at the prompt.

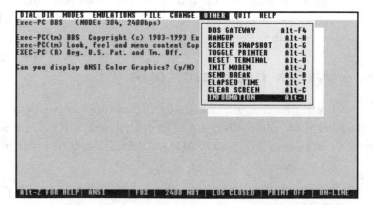

Figure 12: The easiest communications program going, Procomm Plus for DOS's pull-down menus give you all you need in one inexpensive package.

HOT TIPS

- **Uploading text.** Press [Page Up]. Choose the ASCII file transfer protocol from the list and press [Enter].

- **Downloading files.** Press [Page Down]. Choose the file transfer protocol you want from the list and press [Enter]. To view a downloaded text file, press [Alt][V].

- **Copying and pasting.** No, like I said, you can't cut and paste text between E-mail messages. But if you're scrolling through an on-line service's list of files and you see one you want to download, you can copy the file name temporarily so you don't have to remember it. Press [Alt][=], tab to the file name, and press C once it's highlighted. To paste it at the on-line system's download prompt, press [Alt][=] and then P.

- **Host mode.** Press [Alt][Q], and outside callers can dial into your system.

- **Hanging up.** Press [Alt][H]; [Alt][X][Y] gets you out of the program.

Procomm Plus for Windows

Procomm Plus for Windows is not as straightforward as its DOS brother, and as a *Windows* communicator, it's slower. Its virtues include mouseability, easy customization, a script language that enables you to grab data from other Windows programs, and a built-in viewer for graphics files.

Procomm Plus for Windows Tips

Talk about doing things the hard way. With *Procomm for Windows*, all the important stuff is hidden.

HOT TIPS

- **Setup.** To reach the main setup dialog box, press [Alt][S]. If you want to do something pretty simple, like change your modem's setup string, you select Connection, then Advanced, then Modem Setup, and type in your new settings. To store them, click OK, then Reconfigure, then Set as Default. What a nuisance, eh? But it's not over yet: Click on File, then Save, and then Settings, or you'll lose your changes!

- **Dialing out.** Press [Alt][D] to open the dialing directory. To add a new name and number, double-click on an empty entry. When you're done typing an entry, remember to press [Enter] or *Procomm* will lose it. Then select File//Save Directory to save it. To dial, click on the entry, and then click on the dial button.

- **Capturing text.** Click on the fishnet icon. Be warned, *Procomm* has the annoying habit of storing all captured text during an on-line session in a single file, even if you've specified more than one.

HOT TIPS

- **Uploading text.** Click on the file folder icon with the up arrow, choose the ASCII protocol, select the file, and then click OK. To slow down a text upload, click on Protocol, choose ASCII, and then click on Advanced. Under Upload Options, boost the value to 5 in Delay between lines.

- **Downloading files.** Click on the file folder icon with the down arrow, and downloading will chug into action automatically using

Figure 13: *To change any of Procomm for Windows' settings—even file transfer protocols—you need to bring up this setup screen. What a pain.*

the default file transfer protocol—so you'd better choose your protocol first. Press Alt S to bring up the setup box, click on Protocol, and pick your poison. Do the OK–Reconfigure–Set as Default routine, and then start downloading. To view a downloaded GIF file, press Alt V.

- **Copying and pasting.** Highlight the text; press Ctrl C to copy it, and Ctrl V to paste it.

- **Host mode.** Click on the Host button at the bottom of the screen, or press Alt 1.

- **Hanging up.** Click on the telephone icon.

Crosstalk Communicator

Crosstalk Communicator's easy setup makes it perfect for novices. Among its advantages: It's simple but fast and powerful, and it offers a full set of protocols and lots of scripts for logging on to on-line services. It also includes great terminal emulations, but no cutting and pasting between E-mail messages.

Crosstalk Communicator Tips

Communicator is almost as easy to use as *Procomm Plus* for DOS, but not quite. One quirk is that certain program functions are listed in the dialing directory. Technical problems? Then try DCA's excellent tech support.

Figure 14: With Crosstalk Communicator, this screen doubles as the dialing directory and the main menu. Works fine once you get used to it.

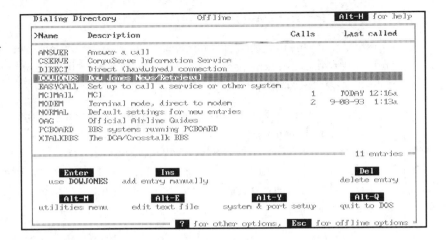

- **Setup.** Alt Y gets you to the setup menu, which is easier to use than that of any other communications program. To issue modem commands, cursor to the MODEM entry in the dialing directory and press Enter.

HOT TIPS

- **Dialing out.** As with *Procomm Plus* for DOS, you just cursor to a directory entry and press Enter. To create a new entry, cursor to EASYCALL, press Enter and follow the menus. Or press Insert to set up the entry yourself without the menus.

- **Capturing text.** Press Alt C.

- **Uploading text.** Press Alt U. To change or check upload settings, press Alt U a second time.

- **Downloading files.** Press Alt P, choose your protocol, and down comes the file. To view the contents of an archived file you've downloaded (one with a ZIP, ARC, or LZH extension), press Alt M, select PKGVIEW, and press Enter. To read a text file you've downloaded, press Alt M and select BROWSER.

- **Host mode.** Cursor to ANSWER and press Enter.

- **Hanging up.** Press Alt O.

Crosstalk for Windows

Crosstalk for Windows is the most powerful and versatile Windows communicator around, with a built-in editor, a robust programming language, a long list of quality terminal emulations, and panels of buttons that let you perform common tasks on several on-line services (such as checking news and research on Dow Jones/News Retrieval). But for a novice, mastering it can seem like learning Latin. You might find yourself craving something that doesn't leave you feeling lost and squinting at tiny icons.

Crosstalk for Windows Tips

Crosstalk for Windows doesn't include a dialing directory, and that can make both setup and day-to-day use confusing at times. Instead, you load *session files*, which generally hold more information than your average directory entry.

HOT TIPS

- **Setup.** In this program, you really configure things session file by session file. One thing you'll want to do right away, though, is change the program's unreadable default font to Courier (select Setting, then Terminal, then Font). To send commands to the modem, select File//Open and choose NORMAL.XWP from the list. When prompted for a phone number, press ⌊Enter⌋ and type your commands.

- **Dialing out.** To create a session file, click File//Open and scroll down to NEW-CALL.XWP. In the List Files of Type box, select Sessions (*.XWP) and click OK. When prompted, enter the name of the service or person you're calling, the phone number, the communications port, and the speed in bps. Press ⌊Alt⌋⌊F⌋ and the number of the session file on the list. Or load a session file using File//Open, then click on Action and then on Connect.

- **Capturing text.** Click on the video recorder icon.

- **Uploading text.** Click on the icon that has a page with an up arrow. Select the file you want to upload from the displayed directory.

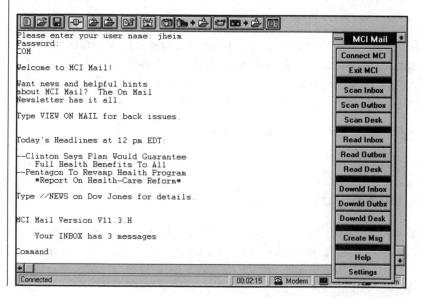

Figure 15: The nice buttons make Crosstalk for Windows look easy, and preset scripts that retrieve E-mail from MCI Mail and access other services make the impression partly true. But the program is a bear to set up.

HOT TIPS

Remote Software: Just Like Being There

A special breed of communications software called *remote software* lets you dial into a faraway PC and do anything you like, just as if you were sitting in front of it. It's especially helpful if you're on the road or at home and need files from your office PC, or if you're troubleshooting a distant client's system. The *host system* (that is, the one you're dialing into) stays on, you dial in and enter a password—and you're there, virtually.

The big problem with remote connections is that they're slow—especially if you use Windows. Make sure you have 14.4Kbps modems on either side of the connection, preferably with V.42bis compression—if you don't, you may want to stay in DOS while connected. And choose your modems carefully: The El Cheapo brands seem to collapse under the demands of remote software.

Another problem involves mismatched graphics hardware. If your graphics card is running at 800-by-600 resolution, and the host system has one running at standard VGA resolution, you may crash either system. If you can't match graphics standards, the next best thing is for the host PC's graphics card to be running at a higher resolution than the PC that's calling (see Chapter 5: *Monitors, Etc.* for more on graphics modes).

There are only two remote packages I recommend: *Close-Up* by Norton-Lambert and *Remote2* by Digital Communications Associates. *Close-Up*, while not a Windows program, does let you run Windows remotely—both better and faster than any other remote program. *Remote2* is fast, simple, and can translate between PCs with different graphics standards much cleaner than any other remote package. Both products offer password protection and call-logging, so you won't be afraid to leave your PC unattended.

- **Downloading files.** While on line, click on the file folder icon with the down arrow. If nothing happens, you haven't set your file transfer protocol properly. Click on Setting, then on File Transfer. Select the correct protocol from the list.

- **Cutting and pasting.** Highlight the desired text with the mouse, press Ctrl C to copy it, and press Ctrl V to paste it.

- **Host mode.** Select File//Open and click on ANSWER.XWP.

- **Hanging up.** Click on the icon of two cables separating.

~~~~~~

Fax Software

When fax software works, it's nothing short of miraculous. Sending a fax is as easy as printing a file, and receiving one doesn't interrupt your work—you just view the fax on screen or print it out at your leisure.

When fax software doesn't work, it's a curse. The problem is compatibility between fax software and fax modems. While both are supposedly designed according to certain standards (Class 1, Class 2, and so on), no one program or fax modem seems to comply with those standards in precisely the same way—which means some fax programs don't work, or work only grudgingly, with some fax modems they're *supposed* to work with.

REMEMBER

How can you be sure that the fax software you buy will work with your fax modem? You can't—you have to test it with your fax modem to be sure. (If you want to use a scanner to send paper faxes, you'll need to test that with your software, too.) That's why it's so important to buy fax software with a money-back guarantee.

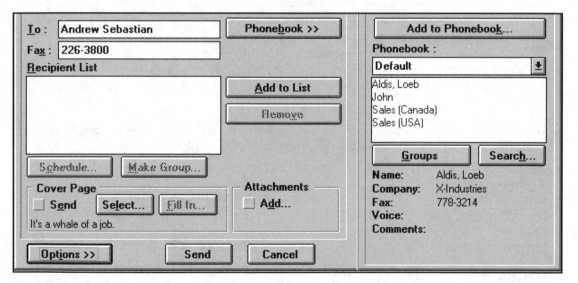

Figure 16: *With WinFax Pro, you choose all fax send options, from phone book entries to cover-sheet art, using this single pop-up screen.*

Which Program to Buy?

Here's my basic advice: Whatever you do, buy Windows fax software, not DOS fax software. Under Windows, your fax software conveniently becomes an alternate printer: To send a fax, you select Print Setup from your Windows application, choose the fax option, and print. The fax software's phone book pops up automatically, and you select the recipient for your fax. That's it, more or less, since receiving faxes under Windows happens automatically.

As usual, though, there are some ins and outs to consider:

- **Optical character recognition (OCR).** When you receive a fax, it arrives as a big graphics file—*not* as text you can edit. But if your fax software has OCR capability, it can convert received fax text into text you can crunch in any word processor, with the added bonus that faxes converted to text take up much less disk space. Unfortunately, OCR is never 100 percent accurate, and often much less so if the original fax was poor quality. OCR works best when the document comes from a high-resolution fax or fax modem.

- **Send and receive options.** Look for fax software that lets you schedule fax transmissions when you're not around. You should also be able to send the same fax to a whole list of recipients in one swoop and start a fax transmission after you initiate the call by voice—an important feature if you're faxing from a laptop and dialing through a hotel switchboard. On the receiving end, the program should alert you when a fax has arrived, automatically print faxes if you like, and let you forward a received fax to another fax machine or fax modem.

- **Document processing.** Look for a package that lets you preview faxes before sending them, and one that can rotate received faxes so you don't break your neck if they arrive upside down or sideways. A zoom feature for viewing fuzzy or small-font faxes is essential, and being able to view multiple pages can help you skim long faxes. Some products, like Delrina Technology's *WinFax Pro*, let you splice data from several applications into one fax. Also handy is the ability to mark up a fax and retransmit it.

My favorite fax software is *WinFax Pro*. I've gotten it to work with all the no-name fax modems piled up in my house. Its only flaw is that it can't transmit faxes when you initiate a call by voice. (This is more than made up for by a library of goofy cartoons that you can send as cover sheets.) I'm less impressed by Intel's popular *Faxability Plus*, or Alien Technology's *Faxit*.

HOT TIP

Things That Go Wrong

Want to know the best advice for avoiding problems? Buy a quality modem and some good software. The counterargument to this is that you can get schlocky modems and software much cheaper—and what's the big disaster if you drop a connection? Well, if you communicate a lot, broken connections are torture, and laggard performance wastes even more time. And there may be some connections you'll *never* make with a funky modem.

The following bits of advice are organized by the common symptoms of everyday communications problems. To avoid repeating myself, remember these two things in every case: If the cure for your symptoms doesn't seem to work, always go back and check the steps in "The Modem Doesn't Respond," below; Windows users should also check "Troubles With Windows" near the end of this section. If tech support is available, use it when in doubt.

The Modem Doesn't Respond

My new modem doesn't work. Help!

If it's an external modem, did you flip the On switch? (Sorry, I had to ask.) Is your external modem's little adapter securely plugged into an AC socket? If the power is on, the MR (modem ready) light should be lit. Next, make sure the cable between your modem and your PC's serial port is securely connected—if it is, the CR (clear to send) light should be on. Beyond this obvious stuff, try these other troubleshooting procedures:

HOT TIP

1. **Check serial port assignments.** If you have an external modem, make sure you've set your software to the same serial port that your modem is plugged into. Also, check that no other device is using the port you've chosen. If you have an internal model, remember that you have to go into your PC's setup utility and disable the port you've chosen for the modem.

2. **A simple hardware test.** Head for your communication software's terminal screen and type ATQ0V1 [Enter]. The modem should respond OK or 0 on the screen. If it doesn't respond at all, the PC and modem aren't talking and you should recheck the serial port assignments and cable connections. If the modem responds with "ERROR," you've got trouble—contact the modem's manufacturer because the modem may be defective. If you hear a buzz coming from inside your PC and you have an internal modem, either your PC or modem may have an electrical problem, and a technician should check them both right away.

3. **Another hardware test.** If you got an OK or 0 in the last test, type `ATDTxxx-xxxx`⌷Enter⌷, with your own phone number in place of those x's. If your modem has a speaker, you should hear it dialing. If it doesn't, and your phone is on the same line, pick up your phone and listen for the sound of dialing. If you hear it, everything is OK hardware-wise, and the problem is in your communications software.

HOT TIP

4. **A basic software test.** Head to your communication software's setup screen, and look for the area where you configure your modem. What you want to find is your software's modem *initialization string*, a piece of spaghetti beginning with "AT" (such as ATE1Q0V1X4&C1&D2 S7=60 S11=55 S0=0^M). Write down the string on a piece of paper, return to the terminal screen, type the whole string, and press ⌷Enter⌷. If the modem responds with OK or 0, call tech support. If it responds with something else, an errant command lurks in the string (see 5).

5. **The last-ditch software test.** To find the bad command, type each command in the modem initialization string individually on the terminal screen, preceding each one with `AT`. How can you tell where one command ends and another begins? If there's a letter followed by a numeral (and no ampersand precedes the letter), those two characters are a single command (so if you see "X4," type `ATX4`⌷Enter⌷). If an ampersand or a slash precedes an alphabetic character, that group of characters is one command (for &C1, type `AT&C1`⌷Enter⌷). If you see an S followed by a number, an equal sign, and another number, then all those characters are one command (for S7=60, type `ATS10=11`⌷Enter⌷).

If any commands *did not* elicit an OK or 0 from your modem, head back to the modem setup screen where you found the initialization string and delete those commands. If there's a `Z` in the string, erase that too. Insert at the beginning of the string, right after the AT, the command `&F` (this returns the modem to its factory settings and prepares it to be properly initialized). Now exit and restart the communications software. If the modem still won't work properly, well, I'm stumped.

Your Modem Isn't Listed in Your Software's Setup

I bought a new modem. The brand isn't listed in my communication software's modem list, and I can't get it to work with the software. The modem's manufacturer is no help.

Try installing the software for a Hayes 2400-bps modem. Set the phone book entries to the appropriate baud rate. Beyond that, you may need to do some fiddling with the modem's settings, but chances are the factory defaults will work.

d-Hand Modem

modem at a garage sale. It has no documentation. I can turn it on fine, but I can't
ork beyond that.

modem command &F to the beginning of the modem initialization string found in your communication software's modem setup screen (see 4 in "The Modem Doesn't Respond," earlier in this chapter). Also, if there's a Z in the string, erase it. Exit the communications software, start it up again, and things should work.

The Modem Won't Connect

There are certain modems I can't connect with. My modem dials their number, I hear hissing, but the connection is dropped or else gibberish spits across the screen.

A common problem. Try these steps, in order:

HOT TIP

1. **Turn on hardware flow control.** Flow control paces the exchange of data between your PC and modem, and it's necessary for high-speed (9600 bps or faster) communications. Check your software's modem setup screen, and turn on RTS/CTS handshaking if it isn't already enabled (this turns on hardware flow control). Then make sure XON/XOFF software flow control is turned *off*.

2. **Backpedal.** If you still can't connect, try dropping your modem's speed. If it's a 14.4Kbps modem, call at 9600 bps. Then at 2400 bps, then 1200. If the modems can communicate at a lower speed than their optimal one, one of them probably has a signaling problem. There's not much you can do about that.

3. **Turn off compression.** If the modems still won't connect, head to your communication software's terminal screen and type `ATDTxxx-xxxx`⌨Enter⌨ (with the other computer's phone number in place of the x's). If the modems connect and your modem has MNP 5 data compression, log off, disable MNP 5, and try dialing in the ordinary way, using your dialing directory. If that doesn't work, and your modem has V.42bis data compression, follow the same procedure for V.42bis.

If your modem has data compression, you'll find the commands to disable whichever compression schemes it has in your modem's manual. To disable data compression by default, add the disabling commands to the modem initialization string (see 4 in "The Modem Doesn't Respond," earlier in this chapter).

The Modem Won't Answer

The modem won't answer when I tell the software to pick up the phone, or else when it does, log-in prompts scroll all over the screen after it answers.

Most communications software offers two ways to get the modem to answer the phone when another computer calls in: host mode and auto-answer mode. If one doesn't work and the phone is ringing, you can always try the other, and usually it will work. Beyond this:

1. **Have you missed something?** Most problems with host mode are the result of missing some special setup procedure. For example, check to see if you have to enter passwords and set access levels for each caller.

2. **The brute force method.** If neither host nor auto-answer mode works, head to your software's terminal screen and type ATA Enter when another modem calls in. This *forces* the modem to answer.

3. **Stop those prompts!** If host mode answers the phone, but its log-in prompt scrolls over the screen, exit your software, restart it, and find the modem initialization string on your communication software's modem setup screen (see 4 in "The Modem Doesn't Respond," earlier in this chapter). Insert the command &D2 into the string. If you have an old modem with configuration switches (sometimes called DIP switches), check your manual and make sure the "DTR high" switch is off.

You See Funny Characters

I see funny characters on screen now and again when I'm connected to an on-line service or bulletin board. What's wrong?

The most likely explanation is telephone noise—you know, those crackles you hear over the line during long-distance calls. Some areas of the country suffer it worse than others, particularly rural areas with old telephone switching equipment (though city-dwellers aren't immune, either).

1. **Just try again.** If it's a long-distance call, the solution is to hang up and try calling again, or call at a different time, since phone calls get bounced around the country like budget air-flights. Your call will probably take a different, cleaner route to its destination the second time out.

2. **Add error control.** If line noise is a persistent problem, make sure you get a modem with V.42 error control (actually, you owe it to yourself to get one of these anyway). For file transfers, the Kermit or Xmodem-CRC protocols work well on windy lines.

3. **Turn off compression.** Another possibility is that the V.42bis data compression in your modem and the V.42bis data compression of the modem it's talking to are incompatible. See 3 under "The Modem Won't Connect," earlier in this chapter, for the procedure.

Text Uploads Go Berserk

Whenever I try to send an electronic message to an on-line service, the text spews across the screen, my PC starts beeping, and the on-line service broadcasts weird messages.

You need to slow down your text upload. See the "Getting Around On Line" section at the beginning of this chapter to find out how to do this.

If the message is a long one and will traverse multiple computers or mail systems before it reaches its destination (as it will on Internet or through BBS echoes), break it into chunks of less than 100 lines—and make those lines short. You never know what size limits your message may encounter in its travels. If it's too long, it could be truncated or come ping-ponging back to you.

File Transfers Are Lost

When I do a file transfer, it often cancels before it's done.

Experiment with different protocols. You never know, the version of the file transfer protocol you're using may not be compatible with the version of the same protocol on the other system. On the other hand, the trouble may be line noise, so try a noise-resistant file transfer protocol, such as Kermit or Xmodem-CRC (the system you're calling must have the same protocol, of course). If you're calling through a network like Tymnet or Telenet, you may have to use a "relaxed" protocol like "relaxed Xmodem" or "relaxed Kermit." Relaxed protocols do not rely on rigid timing in the sending and receiving of data.

Troubles With Windows

Under Windows, I keep losing characters; file transfers abort at speeds of 9600 bps or faster; things seem slower than under DOS; and so on, and so on....

When it comes to communications, Windows is a wimp. It can't keep up at high speeds. It will lose characters and slow down transfers. For that reason, many people prefer to run all their file transfers in DOS instead. But if you don't like to exit Windows, check out these special Windows tips:

1. **Check your serial port.** If you have an external modem, make sure your system has a high-speed serial port (more specifically, it must have a 16550A UART chip). If it doesn't, upgrade the serial port or get an internal modem that has its *own* 16550A UART. Actually, you should do this if you stick with DOS, too, but it's even more important under Windows (see Chapter 8: *Upgrade It Yourself*).

2. **Check your SYSTEM.INI file.** Assuming you run Windows in 386 Enhanced mode, edit Windows' SYSTEM.INI by adding the line COMxFIFO=1 to the [386Enh] section. In place of x, include the number of the communications port you're using (probably 1 for COM1). If the line already exists, change it if necessary.

HOT TIP

3. **For standard mode users only.** If you run Windows in Standard mode, remove the line DOS=HIGH from your CONFIG.SYS file. Load Windows' SYSTEM.INI in a text editor, find the [standard] section and add the line FasterModeSwitch=1, or edit the existing line to match.

4. **Check your software's serial port support.** Make sure that your communications software exploits high-speed serial ports. Most major communications programs can, including *Procomm Plus* for DOS, *Procomm Plus for Windows*, *Qmodem*, and all the DCA products. Funky programs—the kind you find packed in your modem's box—often cannot.

5. **Running DOS communications software in a window.** For better performance, run it full-screen instead. You should also replace Windows' *communications driver* (a little program called COMM.DRV that handles Windows' communications), because it won't let DOS communications programs exploit high-speed serial ports. Remove COMM.DRV (look in the /WINDOWS/SYSTEM directory) and install *TurboComm*, available for $47.50 from Pacific CommWare. Or download a copy of the shareware program *CHCOMB.EXE* from CompuServe or any of the major on-line services. You can also order it for $10 from Cherry Hill Software at 609/983-1414. To speed up things even more, add the line COMxBuf=0 to your SYSTEM.INI file, with the correct COM port number in place of x.

6. **Check those PIF files.** Make sure that all communications programs you run under Windows have a PIF file with proper settings (particularly any DOS ones). If you have problems with transfers aborting, try boosting the values of foreground and background priorities. Also, make sure the Lock application in memory box is checked.

7. **Clean house.** Cut out all but the most necessary RAM-resident programs and drivers.

8. **Backpedal.** If you have a high-speed internal modem, you may, alas, have to lower its speed to make sure Windows doesn't lose characters.

High-Speed File Transfers Seem Kinda Slow

I bought a 14.4Kbps modem, but when I transfer files, they run at only 550 characters per second (that is, s-l-o-w).

Here's a checklist of things you need to do to boost those transfer speeds:

1. **Check your serial port.** See 1 in the previous section "Toubles With Windows."

2. **Turn off MNP 5 compression.** If the you're transferring files that are already compressed, that is, if they end in .ZIP, .ARC, or .LHA—turn off the MNP 5 compression by adding the command that does this to the modem initialization string (see 4 under "The Modem Doesn't Respond" earlier in this chapter).

3. **Turn on hardware flow control.** And turn off software flow control (see 1 under "The Modem Won't Connect," earlier in this chapter).

4. **Jack up that bps.** Go to the dialing directory in your communications software, and for all high-speed entries, set the bps or baud rate to 4 times the speed at which you'll actually connect. If you're going to connect at 9600 bps, set the speed to 38.4Kbps.

5. **Clean house.** Remove unnecessary TSRs from memory, especially disk cachers and print spoolers. They can seriously degrade performance.

REMEMBER

6. **Use the fastest protocol for the job.** Try Zmodem first—it's fast. Several protocols, such as Ymodem-G, are just as fast. Remember that line noise will cause Zmodem to creep, so try Kermit, Ymodem, or 1K-Xmodem instead. For CompuServe connections, use CompuServe B+.

7   **Try DOS.** If you're using Windows, consider running high-speed file transfers in DOS, or at least using a DOS program under Windows with the communications software running full screen. If you opt for the latter, check out 5 under "Troubles With Windows," earlier in this chapter.

Call-Waiting Beeps Make the Modem Flip Out

I have call-waiting on my phone and it's disrupting communications.

Contact your local phone company and ask if there's a code you can enter—usually *70 or *71—to disable call-waiting temporarily. You need to add this code to every entry in your dialing directory, since call-waiting is reactivated after each call.

If there's no way to disable call-waiting, set the modem to ride out call-waiting beeps. To do this, add S10=55 to the modem initialization string (see 4 under "The Modem Doesn't Respond" earlier in this chapter).

Your Communications Program Kills Other Programs

After I use a certain communications program, my other communications programs refuse to work.

The first communications program is changing a modem setting and the other programs don't like it. Add the modem command &F to the beginning of the modem initialization string in each of your communications programs (see 4 under "The Modem Doesn't Respond" earlier in this chapter). If there's a Z anywhere in the string, erase it.

Certain communications programs, such as Prodigy's, seem to cause trouble no matter what. One remedy is to run this troublesome software in a DOS window under Windows, which seems to enable other communications programs to run error-free.

You Hear Rap Music Through the Modem's Speaker

Sometimes when my modem picks up the phone I hear music from a local radio station. This strange guy in my office keeps putting a metal vegetable strainer over the modem and telling me it's a Faraday cage.

Bizarre, but true. Michael Faraday was a 19th century British physicist who determined that a cage with holes of the proper diameter can block radio signals—and a nearby radio transmitter is your problem (you probably hear the same music on voice calls, too). But the vegetable strainer probably won't work because the mesh needs to be precisely the right width, and because your telephone cord, not your modem, is playing the role of antenna. You can try shortening the phone cord, or moving the modem out of hearing range. Or you can do all your modeming from under a thick concrete bridge.

You and Your Modem Need Counseling

Where's the best place to look for advice when I've tried all this stuff and my modem still doesn't work right?

All the on-line services offer communications forums where you can solicit help on modem woes from other users. These are dynamite sources of advice. The best spot is the IBM Communications Forum on CompuServe (type `go ibmcom`[Enter]).

CompuServe also offers technical support forums for many modem and communication software companies, and the advice you get is always better than what you get on the phone. To find support forums for a specific vendor, try typing `go`, the name of the vendor, and [Enter].

The second best source of advice is on General Electric's GEnie in the IBM PC Roundtable. Type `ibmpc`[Enter] at any prompt. At the forum's main menu type `set 23` [Enter]. There's also a communications forum on American Online. Type `telecom` and click on Message Boards. And don't forget BBSs, the watering holes of all the local computer geniuses.

Product and Service Directory

Major Modem Manufacturers

Hayes Microcomputers
  Products, Inc.
5835 Peachtree Corners East
Norcross, GA 30092-3405
404/441-1617

Microcom, Inc.
500 River Ridge Dr.
Norwood, MA
800/822-8224

Multi-Tech Systems Inc.
2205 Woodale Dr.
Mounds View, MN 55112
800/446-6336

Practical Peripherals, Inc.
375 Conejo Ridge
Thousand Oaks, CA 91361
800/442-4774

Telebit Corp.
1315 Chesapeake Terr.
Sunnyvale, CA 94089
800/835-3248

On-Line Services and BBSs

a2i Communications
1211 Park Ave. 202
San Jose, CA 95126
408/293-9010 (modem)

America Online
8619 Westwood Ctr. Dr.
Vienna, VA 22182
800/827-6364

Channel One BBS
P.O. Box 338
Cambridge, MA 02238
617/864-0100
617/354-3230 (V.32 modem)
617/354-7077 (2400 modem)

CompuServe Information
  Service
5000 Arlington Ctr. Blvd.
Columbus, OH 43220
614/457-8600

Delphi Internet Services Corp.
1030 Massachusetts Ave.
Cambridge, MA 02138
800/695-4005

Dow Jones/News Retrieval
Dow Jones & Company, Inc.
  Information Services Group
P.O. Box 300
Princeton, NJ 08543
800/815-5100

Exec-PC BBS
P.O. Box 57
Elm Grove, WI 53122
414/789-4200
414/789-4210 (modem)

Fidelity Online Xpress
Fidelity Electronic Product
  Information Center
161 Devonshire St.
Boston, MA 02110
800/544-0246

General Electric Information
  Service (GEnie)
401 N. Washington St.
Rockville, MD 20850
800/638-9636

Global Access
G-A Technologies, Inc.
P.O. Box 31474
Charlotte, NC 28231
800/377-3282
704/334-9030 (modem)

HoloNet
Information Access
  Technologies
46 Shattuck Sq. #11
Berkeley, CA 94704
510/704-0160
510/704-1058 (modem)
Internet address:
info@holonet.net

MCI Mail
MCI Mail Xpress
MCI PC Connect
1133 19th St., N.W. 700
Washington, DC 20036
800/444-6245

PC-Pursuit
SprintNet
12490 Sunrise Valley Dr.
Reston, VA 22096
800/736-1130

Portal
20863 Stevens Creek Blvd.
  #200
Cupertino, CA 95014
408/973-9111
800/827-7482

Prodigy Services Co.
P.O. Box 791
White Plains, NY 10601
800/776-3449

Sound of Music BBS
S.O.M. Ltd.
269 Waukena Ave.
Oceanside, NY 11572
516/536-5630 (modem)

The Well, or
The Whole Earth 'Lectronic Link
27 Gate Five Rd.
Sausalito, CA 94965
415/332-4335
415/332-6106 (modem)

Software

CHCOMB.EXE
Cherry Hill Software
300 E. Greentree Rd. #217
Marlton, NJ 08053
609/983-1414

CKCOMIRQ
Belkin Component
1303 Walnut Park Way
Compton, CA 90220
310/898-1100

Close-Up
Norton-Lambert Corp.
P.O. Box 4085
Santa Barbara, CA 93140
805/964-6767

Crosstalk Communicator
Crosstalk for Windows
Remote2
Digital Communications
  Associates
1000 Alderman Dr.
Alpharetta, GA 30202
404/442-4930

Faxability Plus
Intel Corp.
5200 N.E. Elam Young Pkwy.
Hillsboro, OR 97124
503/696-8080

HyperAccess
Hilgraeve Inc.
Genesis Centre
111 Conant Ave., Ste. A
Monroe, MI 48161
800/826-2760

Market Analyzer
Market Analyzer Plus
Spreadsheet Link
Dow Jones & Company, Inc.
800/815-5100

Norton Desktop for DOS
Symantec Corp.
10201 Torre Ave.
Cupertino, CA 95014
408 /253-9600

OzCIS
Ozarks West Software
14150 Gleneagle Dr.
Colorado Springs, CO 80921
719/260-7151 (fax)

PKZip
PKWare Inc.
9025 N. Deerwood Dr.
Brown Deer, WI 53223
414/354-8699

Procomm Plus
Procomm for Windows
Datastorm Technologies, Inc.
3212 Lemone Blvd.
Columbia, MO 65201
314/443-3282

Qmodem
Mustang Software
P.O. Box 2264
Bakersfield, CA 93303
800/999-9619

Relay/PC (formerly
MicroCourier)
Relay Technology, Inc.
1604 Spring Hill Rd.
Vienna, VA 22182
703/506-0500

TurboComm
Pacific CommWare
180 Beacon Hill Ln.
Ashland, OR 97520
503/482-2744

WinFax Pro
Delrina Technology, Inc.
6830 Via Del Oro 240
San Jose, CA 95119
800/268-6082

21 Utilities

By Michael Goodwin

- Programs for recovering lost data
- Software that doubles drive capacity
- How to snatch the last byte of RAM
- Programs to speed up your hard disk
- Software for customizing Windows
- Electronic address and appointment books
- Norton and PC Tools for DOS and Windows
- The top 20 shareware and freeware utilities

The question of what is, and what isn't, a utility, can lead to fist fights in bars. Let's just say a utility is an inexpensive software tool that helps you work faster, easier, and better. It might be a disk maintenance program, a virus scanner, a way to find lost files, a menu to change screen colors. Or it could be software that adds power, patches in missing features, or saves your data (not to mention your sanity) when disaster strikes. Or a million other handy things.

Most people are amazed when they discover how many utilities are available and how many cool things they do. Many of the best utilities are quite cheap, and some of the most useful ones are shareware, meaning you can download them from an on-line service with your modem, try them out for free, and pay a small fee only if you continue using them.

- **Recovery tools.** Whether you need to undelete a file or resurrect a dead hard disk, these utilities give you a fighting chance. The top two DOS utility libraries, The Norton Utilities and PC Tools Pro, specialize in data recovery.

- **Disk compression.** Even big hard disks can fill up fast. These popular products can nearly double the storage capacity of your drive.

- **Memory optimizers.** The latest applications eat RAM like a Caddy guzzles hi-test. When you start seeing grim "Out of Memory" error messages, one of these utilities can free up every possible byte.

- **Disk defraggers.** DOS has a bad habit of scattering data all over your hard disk. Disk defragmentation software reorganizes (or "defrags") that data for faster disk performance and less wear on moving parts.

- **Disk caches.** Reading and writing data to and from the hard disk is the worst PC performance bottleneck. Disk caching software breaks the jam by copying needed data into memory, where it can be accessed faster.

- **Windows shells.** Windows isn't *that* easy to use—which is why so many companies offer replacements for both the File Manager and the Program Manager. These utilities make Windows conform to *your* work style—not the other way around.

- **PIMs.** Personal Information Managers are grab bags of desktop tools that include various combinations of appointment calendars, Rolodexes, automatic phone dialers, to-do lists, note pads, and so on.

- **And more.** Want to synchronize your PC with the atomic clock at the Naval Observatory? Do you have a fondness for flying toasters? Or do you just need a good calculator? Read on...

DOS comes with its own versions of utilities in most of the above categories. Do you really need another undelete utility, say, or a different defragger? Sometimes yes, sometimes no—and you'll find out exactly why or why not in this chapter.

For the most part, I've chosen my favorite utilities, but you'll find critiques of popular utilities I don't like, too. I've covered almost every important type of utility, but some special-purpose ones made more sense to cover elsewhere in this book (particularly in Chapter 9: *Protect Your Data*).

As you go, you'll find that four products pop up again and again: Central Point's *PC Tools Pro* and *PC Tools for Windows*, and Symantec's *The Norton Utilities* and *Norton*

Desktop for Windows. That's no accident. These "libraries" have a bigger, better assortment of utilities than DOS, and they have proven themselves essential for almost every PC user. In fact, if you're in a hurry, you can skip reading the rest of this chapter and simply buy one of those packages.

But then, of course, you'll miss all the fun.

Recovery Tools

Like the song says, trouble comin' every day. Unless you're extraordinarily fortunate (and maniacally careful), at some point you *will* need to rescue a few damaged or accidentally deleted files. Maybe more than a few.

DOS can revive erased data, but can other utilities do better? If you simply want to resurrect a deleted file, or restore an accidentally formatted disk, the short answer is No. DOS can accomplish these tasks as well as its off-the-shelf competitors.

If you're faced with more serious problems, ones that involve actual damage to files, directories, or vital file allocation information, a utility in DOS 6.2 (and later DOS versions) called ScanDisk can help—but you'll stand a better chance with the recovery programs in *Norton* and *PC Tools*.

HOT TIP

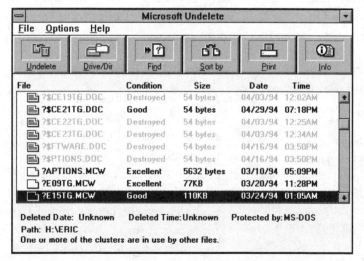

Figure 1: *Microsoft's Undelete comes with DOS and can even run under Windows. Like similar utilities from Symantec and Central Point, it estimates the probability of fully recovering a file.*

Bringing Files Back From the Dead

When DOS "deletes" a file, it doesn't really vaporize it. Instead, it deletes the marker for that file's name and location, leaving DOS free to write new data in that location when it needs to. In the meantime, the original data is still there, ready to be restored by an undelete utility. So if you accidentally delete a file, stop and undelete it immediately.

HOT TIP

DOS, *Norton*, and *PC Tools* all work basically the same way: You change directories to where you deleted the file, run the undelete utility, and pick from a list of recently deleted files the file you wish to resurrect.

It's fairly easy for undelete utilities to rescue short files. Longer files tend to scatter their data across the hard disk—and the more a file is fragmented, the harder it is for a utility to find and recover all the data. That's where undelete "helpers" can be invaluable.

Undelete Helpers

Two kinds of undelete helpers make it much more likely you'll recover accidentally deleted files, particularly long ones. DOS calls them Delete Sentry and Delete Tracker, but *Norton*, *PC Tools*, and other third-party undelete utilities have similar features, even if they use different names:

- **Delete Sentry** maintains complete copies of deleted files. It's foolproof and fail-safe. The downside is that it gobbles disk space, and deleting files takes a little longer.

- **Delete Tracker** won't help if the data has been overwritten, but it uses almost no disk space, and it vastly increases the chances of recovering long files.

To install either helper, you need to add a line to your AUTOEXEC.BAT file. For DOS's Delete Sentry, add undelete /s; for Delete Tracker, add undelete /tc (the second letter after the slash indicates the drive you want to protect). Alternatively, if you're using Windows, click on the Undelete icon in the Microsoft Tools group, and choose Configure Undelete Protection from the Options menu.

Hey! Is This a Hardware Problem or What?

Serious damage to your data—damage so bad you can't access your hard disk—is pretty rare. If you get a message like "Invalid drive specification" or "General failure reading drive C," it's likely that your PC's CMOS battery is weakening, your drive or controller is failing, or you've got a loose drive cable or corroded connector in there somewhere. Turn to Chapter 10: *When Things Go Wrong* to learn how to tell a hardware problem from a software problem, and how to troubleshoot from there.

Viewing Deleted Files

All undelete utilities show you a list of recently deleted files. But what if you don't remember the name of the file you want to revive? You can undelete them all, or you can take a look inside each deleted file before making up your mind. *Norton* and *PC Tools* let you do this, but DOS doesn't.

Critical Conditions, Risky Procedures

Sometimes a deleted file is the least of your worries. How bad can things get? Consider the following scenarios. Turn to Chapter 10: *When Things Go Wrong* to find the exact procedures for recovering from these disasters.

• **You accidentally delete a subdirectory.** DOS's Undelete for Windows (but not Undelete for DOS, strangely enough) may be able to recover an entire directory and its files, but the chances are much greater if you've been using one of the helpers. Both the DOS and Windows versions of *Norton* and *PC Tools* can handle this disaster, too.

• **You format drive C: by mistake.** Nice move! DOS's UNFORMAT command may save you, but unless you've prepared your hard disk with *Norton* or *PC Tools* first, your chances of successful recovery are slim.

HOT TIP

• **You find lost clusters.** Sometimes when you check the health of your hard disk, you get a message reporting *lost clusters*, which are scattered bits of data (usually caused by system crashes) no longer part of any file. DOS's ScanDisk, *Norton*'s Disk Doctor, and *PC Tools*' DiskFix all seem equally adept at testing for lost clusters and fixing them—that is, assembling them into files, which you can then comb for important data that would otherwise have been lost during a crash.

• **You discover cross-linked files.** Sometimes, DOS gets into a tangle and thinks two files are in the same location, a dangerous situation that can quickly destroy the contents of both files. DOS's ScanDisk, along with the DOS and Windows versions of *Norton* and *PC Tools*, can fix this problem much of the time, though you may lose segments of the files.

• **Your file allocation table (FAT) or root directory is corrupted.** Information corrupted in either of these key places means DOS's little

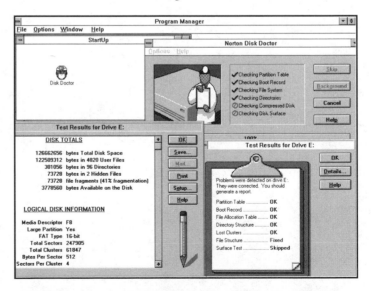

Figure 2: *S-o-o-o many things can happen to your data. Norton Disk Doctor, part of The Norton Utilities and Norton Desktop for Windows, runs a battery of seven tests and will do its best to fix the problems it detects.*

brain may lose track of data on your disk—maybe *all* your data—permanently. DOS's ScanDisk can help you reconstruct this information, but only up to a certain point (it won't help if your hard disk won't boot, for example). *Norton* and *PC Tools* do better, particularly if you've used one of those packages to create an "emergency disk," which you can use to boot your system and restore vital information to your hard disk.

Most experts find it hard to choose between *Norton* and *PC Tools* for major disk repairs, although the DOS versions seem to work better than the Windows versions. Sometimes *The Norton Utilities* works better, sometimes *PC Tools Pro* does. You may want to try both. Remember: The best data recovery insurance against disk disaster is an up-to-date backup (see Chapter 9: *Protect Your Data*).

Disk Compression

Like sex, money, and youth, you can never have too much space on your hard disk. That's where disk compression utilities come in. These programs use a special encoding scheme to compress data and free up disk space. Once you've installed a disk compression utility, you don't have to think about it. When you save a file, it's compressed automatically, and when you need it again, it's uncompressed.

Companies that sell disk compression utilities often claim their products double storage capacity. In reality, this depends almost entirely on file type. Program files shrink very little, while certain graphics files may crunch down to one-twentieth of their original size. Most people seem to end up with a little less than double capacity.

Still, it's megabytes for practically nothing, right? Not exactly. The big question is: Can you really get free disk space at no danger to your data?

File Compression Ratios			
File Type	**Extension**	**Percent Compression**	**100K File Compresses**
Application	EXE	31%	69K
Worksheet	XLS	70%	30K
Help	TXT	64%	36K
Graphics	TIF	95%	5K
Graphics	PCX	55%	45K
Graphics	BMP	70%	30K
Document	DOC	65%	35K
Compressed	ZIP	0%	100K

Figure 4: *Not all files compress equally. Text, worksheets, and most graphic files may shrink by 65 precent or more. Program files, which probably take up the lion's share of you hard disk, shrink far less.*

The Perils of Disk Compression

DANGER

The risk may be low, but it's far from nonexistent. In order to do their stuff, disk compression utilities create a huge file on your hard disk that contains all of your original files. If this doesn't make you nervous, it should. A disk error on an uncompressed disk will usually endanger only one file. A disk error in that huge compressed file puts all of your files at risk.

A few other factors put free disk space in the same category with free lunch:

DANGER

- **Utility incompatibilities.** Every compression utility uses a different encoding scheme, which means your defragger, disk cache, undelete utility, backup software, and other disk utilities may not work—or worse, they may screw up your data royally! You'll need to winnow your selection of disk utilities to those certified safe for your specific type of compression.

- **Slower disk performance.** Disk compression utilities take an instant to compress and decompress files, so you *will* experience a very slight slowdown.

DANGER

- **Mysterious drives.** Depending on which compressor you use, you may see an extra drive letter appear. Even though that uncompressed drive may appear to be empty, it holds files (usually *hidden* files, which means you won't see them if you do a DIR) that shouldn't be compressed, such as Windows' swap file. *Do not fool around with the hidden files on the new drive! If you do, all your compressed files may go up in smoke!*

- **Other software conflicts.** Weird interaction between compression utilities and who-knows-what software is a frequent cause of compressed disk disaster. It may never happen, particularly if you avoid all the known conflicts listed in documentation, but you never know.

HOT TIP

Here's my take on the matter: There are enough ways for data to become corrupted without adding extra ones. Any unnecessary risk to data is seldom worth it. So with the price of hard disks falling fast, why bother with compression? I wouldn't let any one of these products within ten feet of my hard disk.

Compression Insurance

If I haven't talked you out of the idea, and you *still* like the thought of all that extra disk space, the odds of things going smoothly are in your favor. Nonetheless, make sure you have a complete, up-to-date backup before you compress anything. Also look for these safety features:

REMEMBER

- **Surface scanning.** Before compression, the best utilities scan the entire hard disk for defects, mark any bad sectors, and move data to safe areas if necessary to ensure that no part of the huge, compressed file will be at risk.

- **Interruption protection.** When you install a compression utility, it may take hours to compress all the data on your drive. What happens if the AC power goes down during that time? You should be able to start up where you left off when the power comes back on. If the utility doesn't guarantee this, don't try running it, or you're gambling with your data.

- **Write verification.** If a software conflict causes the utility to encode compressed data incorrectly, the utility should be able to police itself and bring disk activity to a halt before serious damage is done.

- **Deinstallation.** Maybe you're having problems. Maybe you've just thought better of all this compression stuff. Either way, you should be able to deinstall the utility and decompress your drive (if you have the disk space to do so).

- **Recovery tools for compressed disks.** Utilities for undeleting files, rescuing lost clusters, repairing cross-linked files, and other data recovery procedures should be included with the compression utility.

DOS 6.22 includes a disk compression utility that has all of the preceding safety features. Since you get the utility for free with DOS, you'll probably be tempted to try it rather than turning to *Stacker*, the market leader before DOS moved in. Go right ahead!

HOT TIP

But watch out: If you have DOS 6.0 and you want to try its DoubleSpace disk compressor, *don't do it*—immediately upgrade to DOS 6.22 instead. The 6.0 version of DoubleSpace resulted in many reports of corrupted files, crashed systems, and lost data—especially with older disks.

DANGER

If DOS 6.0's bad rep makes you reluctant to try DOS 6.22's disk compression utility, give *Stacker* a whirl instead (800/522-7822). It has a full set of safety features, and it's been around longer than any other disk compression utility.

Memory Optimizers

Speaking of things you can't have too much of, let's talk about memory. This is one of the places in this book where there's no way to avoid a certain amount of nerdlike chat. If you find technical material offensive, feel free to ignore this section entirely.

Still with me? Then you may already know that DOS divides memory into five different types:

- **Base (or conventional) memory:** the first 640K, where applications are loaded

- **Upper memory:** memory between 640K and 1MB, reserved for drivers that control your video, hard disk, and so on

- **High memory:** the first 64K of RAM above 1MB, reserved for relocating parts of DOS where appropriate

- **Extended memory:** any memory above 1064K, used by Windows, print spoolers, disk caches, RAM disks, and a few clever DOS applications

- **Expanded memory:** extended memory that's been grabbed by an expanded memory manager (EMM) so it can be used by certain older DOS applications

While Windows and some DOS applications take advantage of extended memory, every application you run (including Windows applications) needs at least a little (and often a lot) of precious base memory. And if you run out of base RAM, you may not be able to load some of your everyday applications under DOS or Windows.

Do you use a mouse, a CD ROM drive, a RAM disk, or a print spooler? Are you on a network? All these items (and many more) require special programs, called *drivers*, that nibble away at base memory. Certain *memory-resident* or *TSR* (short for "terminate and stay resident") applications, such as DOS PIMs, gobble base memory, too.

Say you have a mere 500K of usable base RAM. Fire up a memory optimizer, and best case, you simply sit back for five minutes while your computer reboots a few times. Suddenly, you find yourself with *at least* 600K of base RAM—along with a RAM disk, disk cache, and mouse driver that still work perfectly.

How Memory Optimizers Liberate Base RAM

Figure 5: *In the Before diagram, drivers and TSRs gobble up nearly 100K of base RAM. The After diagram shows a memory optimizer that has stashed several drivers into upper memory, freeing up more base RAM for applications.*

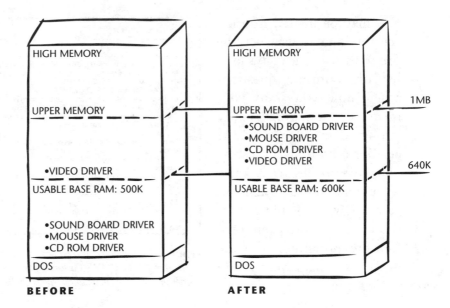

Instant Memory, If You're Lucky

The bad news is that memory optimizers, including DOS's own MemMaker, aren't always automatic. Run into problems, and you're expected to become a serious nerd overnight. It doesn't hurt to try troubleshooting, but if things start getting complicated, I recommend that you back out unless you really need the memory (that is, unless you can't load software for lack of base RAM).

To be safe in any situation, follow this procedure:

- **Before optimizing,** always print out your AUTOEXEC.BAT and CONFIG.SYS files and copy them to a floppy. Memory optimizers do their stuff by modifying those files, and if anything goes *really* wrong, you can copy the old versions to your root directory and go back where you started.

REMEMBER

- **After optimizing,** check the printout of your AUTOEXEC.BAT and CONFIG.SYS files and try out every one of the hardware devices and utilities listed in those two files. Make sure the mouse works, the RAM disk is still there, and your print spooler can print a page of text.

HOT TIP

The Easy Way vs. the Hard Way

Once you've installed the memory optimizer you'll be invited to run its optimizing routine. Just say yes. The most you'll need to do is watch the screen and turn the power switch off and on if one of the reboot sequences hangs up.

You may be invited to use a "custom" mode in which the program will ask you a long list of confusing questions about how you want your memory configured. My strong advice is to avoid the custom option at all costs—unless you really, really know what you're doing. You might gain a few bytes, but only if you know the correct answers. Let the program make the decisions. That's what you're paying it for.

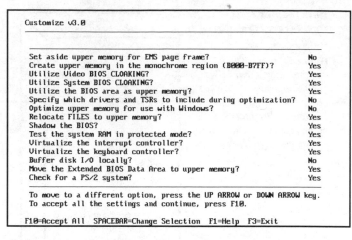

```
Customize v3.0
───────────────────────────────────────────────────────────────────

Set aside upper memory for EMS page frame?                      No
Create upper memory in the monochrome region (B000-B7FF)?       Yes
Utilize Video BIOS CLOAKING?                                    Yes
Utilize System BIOS CLOAKING?                                   Yes
Utilize the BIOS area as upper memory?                          Yes
Specify which drivers and TSRs to include during optimization?  No
Optimize upper memory for use with Windows?                     No
Relocate FILES to upper memory?                                 Yes
Shadow the BIOS?                                                Yes
Test the system RAM in protected mode?                          Yes
Virtualize the interrupt controller?                            Yes
Virtualize the keyboard controller?                             Yes
Buffer disk I/O locally?                                        No
Move the Extended BIOS Data Area to upper memory?               Yes
Check for a PS/2 system?                                        Yes
───────────────────────────────────────────────────────────────────
To move to a different option, press the UP ARROW or DOWN ARROW key.
To accept all the settings and continue, press F10.

F10=Accept All  SPACEBAR=Change Selection  F1=Help  F3=Exit
```

Figure 6: Don't panic? Hey, panic is permissible in the face of questions like these from NETROOM 3's Custom Optimizing screen. Avoid this screen altogether and let your memory optimizer make the decisions itself.

Troubleshooting

Occasionally, after the memory optimizer terminates successfully (and sends you a cheerful message about how much RAM it's reclaimed), one or more of your favorite applications won't run. Or you might discover that you can no longer use your floppy drives. Possibly you will have *less* RAM than you started with. Sometimes your system won't boot at all.

When you encounter problems like these, you have several ways to go:

- **Get lucky.** Run the memory optimizer again. Often (God knows why) it works perfectly the second time. Alternatively, you can restore your system to its original state and try another product.

- **The coward's way out.** Copy your original AUTOEXEC.BAT and CONFIG.SYS files (you backed them up to a floppy before, like I suggested, right?) to your root directory, reboot to restore your machine to its previous state, and forget about the damn thing.

- **The nerd's attack.** If a specific device won't work, open your CONFIG.SYS file with DOS's EDIT and look for the line that calls the driver for that device. If the line begins DEVICEHIGH, change it to DEVICE to put the driver back in base memory where it will work again.

- **The scattershot approach.** Having other system problems? Then "step through" your AUTOEXEC.BAT and CONFIG.SYS files by pressing F8 when you see the "Starting MS-DOS..." message. DOS will let you choose whether or not you want to execute each line, one by one, in each file. Start by saying no to one DEVICEHIGH line and say yes to the rest. If that doesn't work, try another DEVICE-HIGH line. If that doesn't work, do the same with AUTOEXEC.BAT lines that load drivers or TSRs. As soon as your system works right, you know the last line you said No to is the problem. Check the printout of your original CONFIG.SYS or AUTOEXEC. BAT and use DOS's EDIT to restore the line.

What's Going On in There, Anyway?

There's nothing mysterious about how memory optimizers work. If you're interested, here's what they do, step by step:

- They look in your CONFIG.SYS and AUTOEXEC.BAT files to see what kinds of drivers, utilities, and TSRs currently load into base memory.

- They scan upper memory to see if there's any RAM up there that's not being used. Usually, there is.

- They calculate the different ways they can load your drivers into the blocks of free upper memory.

- They reboot your PC a few times to try out various drivers in various upper-memory blocks and make sure they work.

- Sometimes, to free up the last few bytes of memory, they substitute their own versions of DOS drivers specially designed to work in upper memory. Not all DOS drivers like it up there.

- Finally, they rewrite your CONFIG.SYS and AUTOEXEC.BAT files to make the best arrangement permanent.

NETROOM 3 and QEMM: Better Than DOS

DOS's MemMaker has certain advantages: You've already got it, it's easy to use, and it works perfectly with Windows. (You may have to reconfigure Windows if you use a third-party memory optimizer like *NETROOM 3* or *QEMM*.) However, MemMaker is a bit more trouble-prone than some third-party alternatives, and it won't liberate as much memory. Most nerds agree: *QEMM* gets top score for freeing up the most memory, with *NETROOM 3* close behind.

HOT TIP

NETROOM 3

As long as you avoid the "custom" mode, in which you'll be forced to answer questions that might stymie a propeller-head, this package is fast and effective, and under

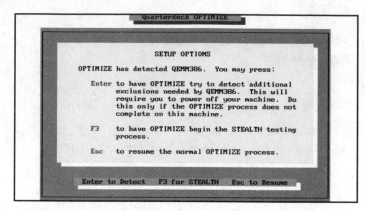

Figure 7: *Huh? Say what? Should you take the safe route and press* Esc *or take a chance on* F3 *or* Enter*? Only QEMM knows for sure. Oh well, if something goes wrong you can always start over with no harm done—as long as you have backup copies of AUTOEXEC.BAT and CONFIG.SYS.*

some circumstances produces more memory than *QEMM* does. It comes with its own video BIOS, screen saver, disk cache, RAM disk, and screen accelerator, all specially designed to work in upper memory.

QEMM 7.0

Long the industry standard for memory optimizers *QEMM* can still be a bit overwhelming. Some of its on-screen prompts are confusing, and sections of the manual are totally incomprehensible. Nonetheless, all you really need to do is install it, type `optimize`, and press Enter. Five minutes later (in most cases) your system will be automatically reconfigured. And experts agree: *QEMM* generally ferrets out more usable RAM than its rivals.

Disk Defragmenters

DOS is something of a mad housekeeper. It stores disk data in the first place it can find, which inevitably scatters bits of data from the same file all over the platter. This random storage scheme can slow performance, since the hard disk's read-write head has to bounce all over the disk to reunite the scattered sectors of a file every time you open it.

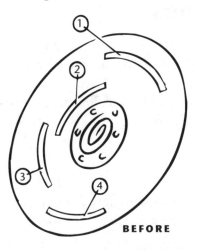

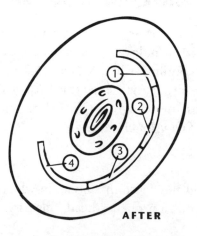

Figure 8: *In the first picture, file fragments have been randomly scattered around your hard disk. The second picture shows the file fragments after a defragging utility has placed them contiguously so the read-write head can read the entire file without skipping around the disk.*

BEFORE

AFTER

Disk defragmentation utilities, or "defraggers," find and reassemble the segments of a file into one contiguous area on the disk. Sort of like putting all the mad housekeeper's silverware back in the same drawer. Defragging can boost performance by as much as 30 percent on a badly fragmented disk, and it reduces wear and tear on the hard disk's moving parts.

DOS's Defragger vs. the Rest

A perfectly good defragger comes with DOS. There's little reason to look further—especially since all the defraggers I've ever tested deliver roughly the same speed-up benefits. True, some may do their actual defragging faster than DOS does, but since you'll probably defrag your disk on your lunch hour anyway, who cares if it takes 10 minutes or 12 minutes?

That said, DOS's defragger lacks a couple of key features:

- **Defrag protection.** If the power goes down during a defrag, you may lose data with DOS's defragger. *PC Tools'* Compress and *Norton's* SpeedDisk both include protection routines that safeguard your data, even if someone kicks out the plug.

- **Windows operation.** Windows addicts will appreciate *PC Tools for Windows* and *Norton Desktop for Windows*, both of which do their defragging in the background while Windows is running. It slows your system a bit, but you never have to stop work. Watch out, though: Constant defragging prevents you from undeleting files unless you use a Delete Sentry–style undelete helper.

HOT TIP

Defragging Strategies

At start up, defraggers do a quick scan of your disk and recommend one of three basic defragging strategies—the one the utility thinks will take the least time to achieve the best results. Feel free to ignore its suggestions. You're smarter than it is.

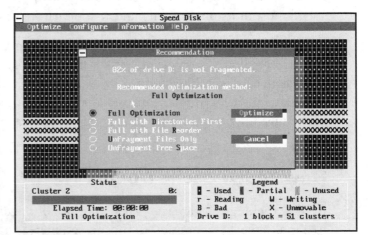

Figure 9: *Norton Utilities' SpeedDisk takes a look at your disk and recommends one of five defragging strategies. Forget the Directories First and File Reorder options—they offer no detectable advantage.*

- **Full defrag (files and free space).** The most time-consuming method, a full defrag is also the best, since it consolidates files *and* sucks out all the free space between them. This not only delivers full speed-up benefits, but it also keeps the disk defragged longer.

- **Quick defrag (files only).** This strategy gives you full speed-up benefits but ignores the space in between the files, in order to complete the job very quickly. The disk will refragment a little faster, but hey, all defragged disks eventually frag up again, so it's no big deal.

- **Space-only defrag.** Sometimes you don't care how fragmented your files are—you just want to collect all the free space at the back of the disk. This makes it easier for Windows to create temporary swap files, for instance, and produces significant speed-up for most Windows users. It's the least time-consuming strategy.

REMEMBER

Theoretically, the hard disk can read files a bit faster if they're located "at the front" of the disk, which is why some defraggers let you place selected files and directories there. Don't waste your time! I've never noticed any significant performance improvement after moving files or directories up front. Nor have any of my friends.

Disk Caching

The biggest performance bottleneck in your PC is in exactly the same place it's been for a decade: your hard disk. This is especially true for Windows, which seems to spend most of its time reading and writing hard disk data.

Disk caching software can deliver a huge speedup. As you probably know, it's a lot faster to read data from memory than from disk, so whenever your application calls for disk data, the caching utility kicks in. Caching utilities are designed to read more disk data than an application needs and store the extra data in cache memory. Hopefully, the next time the application needs data, it will find it in the cache instead of on the disk.

How Much Cache Do You Need?

All disk caching software lets you set the size of the disk cache from 256K all the way to a multimegabyte monster. In most cases, increasing the cache size much above the default delivers little (if any) speed improvement. If your program sizes its cache automatically, accept its judgment, at least for starters.

For example, I've never seen anyone really improve the performance of SmartDrive—which comes with both DOS and Windows—by tweaking it manually. But if you must fiddle, no matter what caching software you choose, set aside no more than one-quarter of your total memory for the disk cache. Otherwise, you'll waste precious RAM.

HOT TIP

Choosing the Best Cache

Tests show that there's very little performance difference between disk cache products. SmartDrive, another DOS freebie, is just as fast as any of the popular stand-alone disk caches. So you need look no further, right?

Well, almost right. While most people find SmartDrive to be all the disk cache they need, some applications on some systems don't run well with SmartDrive under certain conditions, and may damage data or cause a system crash. Check manuals and READ.ME files carefully to spot potential problems before you install any disk cache. If something weird starts happening anyway, disable the disk cache and see if that corrects the problem.

DANGER

Maybe you have a software conflict, or maybe you're just sick of Microsoft products. If so, try *Super PC-Kwik*, one of the most reliable disk caching programs you can buy. Like SmartDrive, *Super PC-Kwik* includes special features to optimize CD ROM performance, and it lets you disable or enable write caching with a keystroke. Its only drawback is that it eats 48K of base RAM, around 20K more than SmartDrive needs, and it's fairly pricey at $80 retail (the $129 *PC-Kwik Power Pak*, which includes a defragger, surface scanner, keyboard accelerator, print spooler, and more, is a better deal).

Delayed Writes: Danger!

Delayed writes (also known as *write-caching*) speed up hard disk performance a lot, sometimes a whole lot. Here, DOS not only *reads* data from memory instead of from the hard disk, it's fooled into thinking data is safely *written* to disk before it really is. In fact, the cache is storing the data, waiting until the CPU and the hard disk have a spare moment to complete the write.

If something goes wrong—say, a power failure—or you reboot the system before the cache dumps the data to disk, you may lose that data and discombobulate some key files. Many cautious people prefer to disable delayed writes, and if safety is your highest priority, you should probably follow suit.

Windows Fixers

Windows? Easy to use? If it were, then why would utilities designed to improve Windows' interface be such hot commodities? These programs, commonly called *Windows shells*, replace either the File Manager or the Program Manager or both, providing easier access to just about everything Windows has to offer.

Shells let you change Windows' interface just enough, and in just the right way, to suit your individual taste. Each offers its own visual metaphor, plus various techniques for making Windows shape up: button bars for file commands; file folders, groups, and menus; application launchers; and so on. *Norton Desktop for Windows* and *PC Tools for Windows* both provide shells, plus utility libraries that include backup programs, data recovery tools, defraggers, and much more.

Windows With Style

When you install and configure one of these Windows shells, you're doing something very similar to customizing the controls on your car. The main idea is to find something that feels exactly right to you, whether you're copying a file, launching an application, or backing up your hard disk. Fortunately, you'll find a profusion of shells offering every possible combination of benefits.

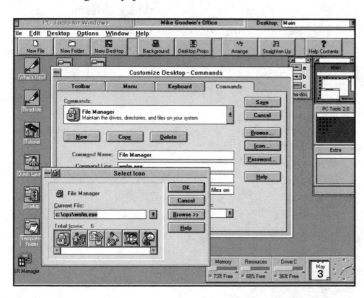

- **Program launching.** The Program Manager, with its clunky Program Groups, sometimes seems more trouble than it's worth. With Windows shells, you can quickly set up movable menus or rows of icons containing all the programs and files you use regularly. Or you can scroll through multiple desktops, each with its own array of applications and files.

Figure 10: Like most Windows shells, PC Tools for Windows is totally customizable. Of course, you still have to figure out what the icons mean.

- **Custom icons.** Need to create an icon for a brand-new database? Or has Windows assigned the *same* dumb icon to all your DOS apps? Then you need a shell with an icon editor. These tools work just like paint programs, only they create Windows icon files. You can edit an existing icon, pull one from an icon library, or create one from scratch.

- **File copying, moving, deleting, etc.** With its clumsy handling of multiple drives and directories, Windows' built-in File Manager

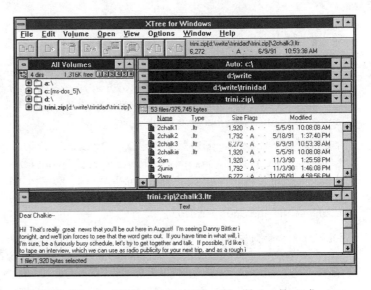

Figure 11: *XTree for Windows treats a ZIP archive file just like a directory. Click on the archive file in the file management window, and you can examine the contents of the compressed files.*

makes copying and moving files awkward. Many shells do it better. Some also let you delete files the Mac way—by dragging them with the mouse and dropping them into a trash can (or shredder, or dumpster, or black hole, or whatever). A few support long file names, so you can make those names descriptive.

- **File viewing.** Double-click on an XLS file in the File Manager's directory tree, and Windows obediently loads it into Excel. Yawn. For those of you with less time on your hands, many shells provide file viewing utilities for popular file formats, enabling you to see a file's contents without having to start the application. Most shells also let you view files stored in compressed ZIP files.

- **Added attractions.** *Norton*, *PC Tools*, and *NewWave* all let you record a series of mouse clicks or keystrokes, assign them to an icon, and play them back just by clicking the icon (for the ambitious, these three products also offer *scripts*, mini-programs that you create using a light-duty programming language). Others give you a constant readout of memory and disk space. And, of course, *Norton* and *PC Tools* come with a truckload of miscellaneous utilities.

The (Almost) Magic of Objects

Imagine you could pluck files off the File Manager's directory tree and arrange them any way you want. That's basically what some shells, such as *Norton Desktop for Windows,* let you do. Those free-floating files are more than files, they're *file objects,* so called because they're part file, part application, and load themselves when you double-click on them.

The trick is in the file extension—DOC, XLS, TXT, and so on. Several Windows shells (and even the File Manager) recognize common extensions and pop files into their applications automatically. If the shell encounters an extension it can't recognize, you need to open a dialog box and make the association between extension and application manually. After that, the shell remembers that those files always load into the app you specified.

Objects are fun, and in *Norton* and *PC Tools,* they go beyond files. For example, you can drop an entire drive or directory object on a virus scanner icon, a backup icon, or whatever, and the program will do its stuff to a whole group of files. A great way to combat boredom.

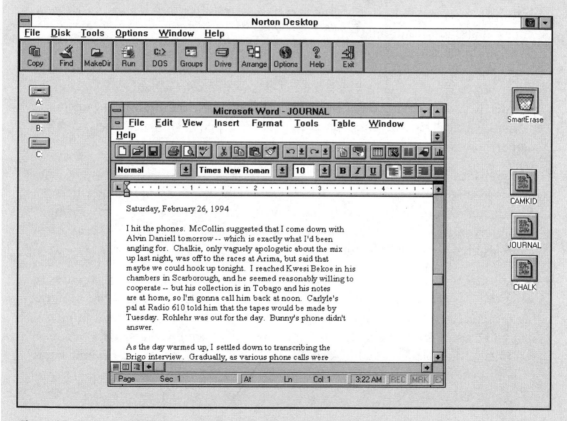

Figure 12: *These Norton Desktop for Windows file folders are "file objects." Double-click on one, and it loads itself into the application that created it—provided the file's extension is "associated" with an app.*

Norton Desktop vs. PC Tools for Windows

When it comes to Windows shells, *Norton Desktop for Windows* and *PC Tools for Windows* are the heavy hitters, with more customizable features and handy utilities than you'll ever use. Buy one, and you'll not only put a better face on Windows, you may also take care of all your utility needs at the same time.

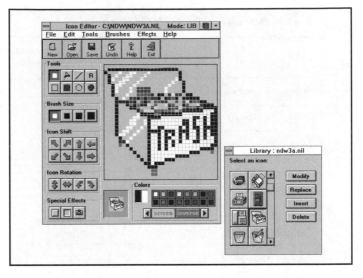

Figure 13: *Norton Desktop for Windows comes with an icon library and an icon editor so you can change Windows' standard icons. Custom icons are especially handy for distinguishing DOS applications under Windows.*

Both packages are so big, they share one serious problem: They take forever to load. Worse yet, once they're up and running, they can make Windows even more sluggish than usual, especially on older systems—so unless you have a 486 you may not want to use either one of them.

You'll find these packages very similar. Both offer objects, folders, and customizable program launchers, so you'll never have to mess with the Program Manager again. Both are true utility libraries as well, each offering its own backup program, virus scanner, defragger, and recovery tools—all of which are better than those included with DOS. Their File Manager replacements both make common file operations much easier. And both cost around $125 in stores.

So what's the diff? *PC Tools for Windows* takes a multiple-desktop approach, encouraging you to create several groups of applications, each one tailored to a different type of task. *Norton Desktop* sticks with a single desktop, but otherwise offers just as much customization. Then there's *PC Tools for Windows'* super diagnostic arsenal. CrashGuard gives a constant readout of disk and memory resources and sounds an alarm if Windows seems likely to go belly up. System Consultant checks your hardware and memory configuration, suggests improvements, and (when possible) makes the improvements itself. (Curiously, *The Norton Utilities* for DOS offers similar utilities, but not *Norton Desktop for Windows*.)

These are all great features to have—but I still maintain that the look and feel of a shell should inform your decision more than anything else. *Norton Desktop* feels better to me, especially its file management. But personal taste is what Windows shells are all about.

Norton Desktop vs. PC Tools for Windows

	Norton Desktop for Windows 2.0	PC Tools for Windows 3.0
Program Launching		
Replaces Program Manager	Y	Y
Nested groups/folders	Y	Y
Customizable button bar	Y	Y
Icon editor/library	Y	Y
Multiple desktops	N	Y
Application shortcut keys	Y	Y
File Features		
Replaces File Manager	Y	Y
Drag-and-drop file and drive objects	Y	Y
View ZIP files	Y	Y
Long file names	Y	Y
File finder with string search	Y	Y
Compress individual files	Y	Y
Data Recovery		
Undelete files and directories	Y	Y
Undelete files from compressed drives	Y	Y[1]
Unformat disk	Y	Y
Undelete sentry and tracker	Y	Y
View deleted files	Y	Y
Repair major disk problems	Y	Y
Repair problems on compressed drives	Y	Y[1]

(continued on next page)

Figure 14: *The Windows diagnostics in PC Tools for Windows offer a significant edge, but in the end you should base your choice on whether you like the way these programs change Windows' look and feel.*

(Figure 14, continued)	Norton Desktop for Windows 2.0	PC Tools for Windows 3.0
Safety Features		
Disk/tape backup	Y	Y
Antivirus	Y	Y
Windows resource/crash monitor	N	Y
Surface scanner	Y	N
Other Stuff		
Disk defragger	Y	Y
Defrag compressed drives	Y	Y[1]
INI file diagnostics	N	Y
Windows configuration analysis	N	Y
Macros	Y	Y
Calculator	Y	N
Personal information manager (PIM)	Y	N
Screen savers	Y	Y

[1] DoubleSpace drives only.

More Windows Shells

You don't have to buy a pet 500-pound gorilla like *Norton Desktop* or *PC Tools for Windows* to make Windows a better place to live. Except for *NewWave* (which may be a 1000-pound gorilla), the programs listed here are less ambitious and won't slow down your system. They also make Windows more fun.

Dashboard for Windows

Hewlett-Packard's *Dashboard for Windows* makes even the worst computerphobe feel right at home. Its charming dashboard facsimile has a clock, a gas gauge, and an odometer: The gas gauge measures system resources (which gives you an idea of how many more windows you can open), while the odometer shows system memory usage. (The clock just tells time.) Buttons along the top of the dash call up program groups, which appear as menus that list each application by name and icon. Other controls

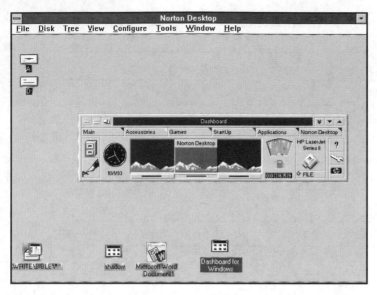

Figure 15: *Dashboard for Windows is a cleverly conceived program launcher. The panels can be customized, and clicking the push buttons along the top brings up application groups. Maybe the next version will include a CD player.*

pop you into Write, the File Manager, and so on. You can customize everything, of course, but no enhancements to the File Manager are offered.

hDC Power Launcher

This popular Windows shell combines all the advantages of menus, icons, and a command line. Whether you prefer its Power Bar, which floats at the top of your screen, or a customizable Task List, you can launch applications and have them start in custom-sized windows located just where you want them. You can launch multiple applications simultaneously, or have them start automatically at a predetermined time. A Virtual Desktop feature increases the size of your workspace up to 64 times by treating your screen as a window on a much larger desktop. Is there a catch? Well, *Power Launcher* isn't easy to learn, but that's because it gives you so many ways to customize.

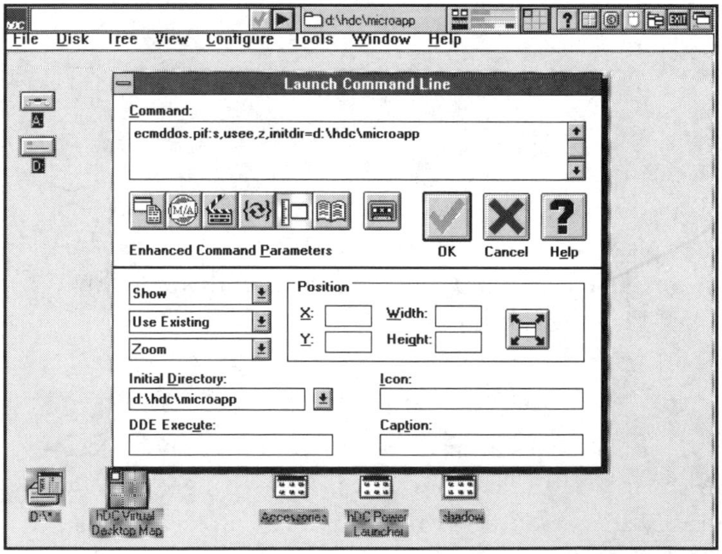

Figure 16: *hDC Power Launcher has so many customization options, it may take some getting used to. Here's how you prepare it to start up applications in presized and prepositioned windows.*

NewWave

Hewlett-Packard has been selling this package for several years as an "object-oriented environment." Now it's being pushed as a Windows shell. Despite the new packaging, it's still hard to customize, hard to learn, and hard to use. You'll need to learn new object-oriented terminology for many familiar concepts, but it provides all the basic features and reasonably fast performance, especially in a networked environment. Fact is, *NewWave* is really designed for developers who want to set up turnkey systems for large workgroups. Unless that's you, steer clear.

Outside In for Windows

Outside In started life as a file viewer, so you won't be surprised to hear that it comes with viewers for more than 120 different file types—including ZIP files, E-mail messages (and their file attachments!), Macintosh files, and most graphics formats. This inexpensive shell also lets you launch applications, as well as copy, move, and delete files, but its other file management capabilities are limited. After you look at a file, you can convert it to another file format, print it, search for text, and/or copy it (or a piece of it) to the Clipboard.

XTree for Windows

While this Windows version of the long-time DOS shell champ *will* replace the Program Manager, it's still primarily a file manager, and a very powerful one. You can run all your Windows applications, edit text files, create macros, and search for files. There's even a utility for copying files between your desktop and your laptop. And it lets you treat ZIP files like directories, so you can move individual files in and out of ZIP files as easily as if they weren't compressed.

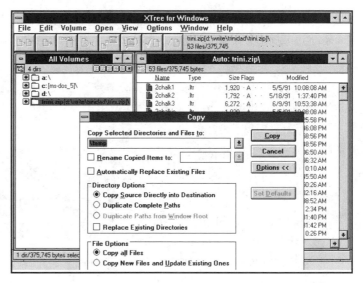

Figure 17: *XTree for Windows makes copying and moving files much easier. The ability to rename files as you move them is particularly handy.*

Personal Information Managers

Look, let me tell you something. I don't like learning new programs, even though it's my job, and I hate typing in addresses. But ever since I tried my first combination appointment calendar, notepad, and phone list (with built-in auto-dialer), I can't live without it. 'Nuff said?

Nowadays, these collections of "desktop" utilities are called *Personal Information Managers*, or *PIMs*. You'll find quite a few PIMs offering interesting combinations of functions, plus many single-purpose desktop utilities. Some run under DOS, others run under Windows. Some have as many functions as a Swiss Army knife, others specialize in calendar or dialing features.

Appointment Calendar

My electronic appointment calendar runs my life. If your paper appointment calendar runs *your* life, you'll probably discover that switching to a computerized version is a life-enhancing experience. Here's why:

- **Friendly reminders.** Set alarms to remind you about appointments a few minutes in advance. Most schedulers will even start up specified applications to help you prepare for a meeting.

- **Multiple views.** View your appointments by day, week, or month.

- **Quick searching.** Need to find the next free two hours? Looking for an appointment with someone whose name you only sort of remember? Most schedulers can find such information in a flash.

- **Recurring events.** Do you have a meeting every Wednesday from 1 to 4 p.m.? Most calendars let you set recurring appointments with a single entry.

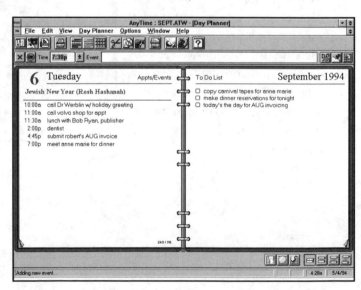

Figure 18: *AnyTime's to-do list pops up every day, so you won't forget to take the dog to the vet or pay your estimated income tax.*

- **Portable schedules.** Print out your appointments in a variety of formats and sizes.

Some PIMs also let you enter events that carry over from year to year, such as birthdays and anniversaries. The best let you specify how far in advance you want to be reminded of the event, so you have time to look for a decent gift, at least.

Between *Lotus Organizer* and *Ecco Simplicity*, I'd be hard pressed to choose my favorite appointment calendar. *Simplicity* has a few more features, such as the ability to warn you in advance about annual events, while *Organizer* is a little easier to use. Both come with address books, notepads, to-do lists with outlines, and other handy features. If a calendar is *all* you want, I recommend *AnyTime*. Delrina's *Far Side Daily Planner* is a worthy alternative, with plenty of features plus Gary Larsen's "Far Side" comics.

HOT TIP

Address Book

Call them what you like, they're basically electronic Rolodexes with names, addresses, and phone numbers. The simple ones work from a file you create with a text editor. The powerful ones have you fill in the blanks in a lengthy on-screen form, with places for fax numbers and work numbers and several addresses—*and* they let you search using a variety of criteria (all loudmouths in a certain area code, for example).

If you have a modem attached to your computer, most of these address books will function as an auto-dialer. Want to call your stockbroker? Search on either her first or last name, and when the information appears on screen, simply click on Dial. Some address books even log the time of the call automatically (which is handy if you bill your clients by the hour).

Once again, *Lotus Organizer* and *Ecco Simplicity* are tied for the top spot. *Organizer* is prettier, but *Simplicity* gives you a powerful system of outlines and folders that can help you get amazingly organized if you make a lot of calls.

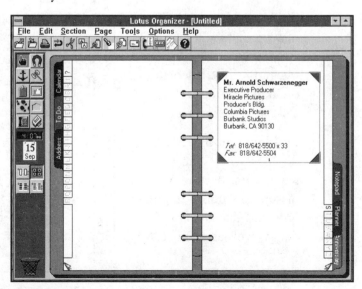

Figure 19: *Lotus Organizer provides one of the most intuitive, easy to use address books of any PIM. To pitch your latest movie idea to Arnie, just drag the phone number to the phone icon and Organizer will auto-dial the call.*

Notepads

If you get a brilliant idea, or a hot phone call, and need to take notes *right now*, you might not have time to load your word processor—so you pop up your notepad. Most PIMs come with these mini–word processors, which can even import and export text in a variety of formats.

Notepads are fine for DOS users, but if you use Windows, your word processor is only a click away, so what's the point? Personally, I wouldn't care if every notepad disappeared from the face of the earth tomorrow afternoon.

To-Do Lists

Those parts of my life that aren't run by my appointment calendar are run by a series of to-do lists. These crucial life-support tools give me the pleasant illusion that my personal and professional responsibilities are under control. A fully computerized list has many advantages:

- **Pop-up guilt.** A good to-do list will display your current responsibilities on screen, automatically, when you start your computer.

- **Anticipatory guilt.** You can arrange to be reminded of upcoming deadlines a set number of days in advance.

- **Shifting priorities.** If the manager lets you set priorities, the to-do list will rearrange itself depending on date, time, and which tasks you've finished.

- **Hidden agendas.** Most to-do lists work like outline generators, nesting a series of subtasks under the main one, and displaying only as many levels as you like.

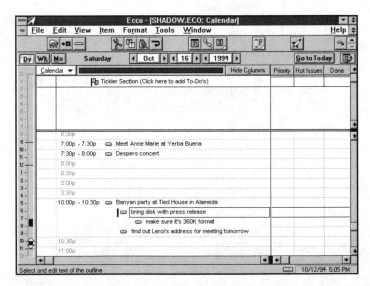

Figure 20: *Nesting items on a to-do list is one of the smartest ways to organize your tasks. Ecco's outlining abilities are among the best: Simply click on the bullet next to each item to conceal or reveal the subtasks hidden beneath.*

One of the very best to-do lists comes as part of a personal finance program called *Managing Your Money* (see Chapter 24). If you prefer an integrated PIM approach, either *Lotus Organizer* or *Ecco Simplicity* is a good place to start.

Printouts

PIMs are good at printing out hard copies of the nicely designed on-screen displays that show you your address book entries. Trouble is, they may insist on dumping only six simulated Rolodex cards per page. I don't know about you, but when I want a mobile dialing directory, I don't want it pretty, I want it short and small.

Fortunately, most address books will save their contents as an ASCII text file. Have your utility do so and load the file into a specialty printer utility, such as *ClickBOOK*. Using a small but readable font, *ClickBOOK* formats ASCII text files so that two pages print on each side of the paper, and orders pages so you can fold the printed sheets into a booklet (see the section "Printing Utilities" in Chapter 6).

Alternatively, you can load the file into your word processor and format the thing manually for duplex printing in the smallest readable typeface your printer will produce. A few minutes of massage will condense a phone book–size volume into six or eight pages.

HOT TIP

Recommended PIMs

As you'll notice, I've already mentioned these programs in my overall description of what to look for in a PIM. They're all reasonably priced and a pleasure to use.

AnyTime

AnyTime does only one thing—it schedules and tracks your appointments—but it does *that* as well as any full-fledged PIM, and for less money. This well-designed utility has all the bells and whistles you could want: You can schedule recurring events, add levels of detail to each appointment, set alarms on all your appointments, and switch from a daily view to a week, month, or year at the click of a mouse. It's available in both DOS and Windows versions.

Ecco Simplicity

Ecco Simplicity is an all-around good deal. This $149 Windows program is long on features: You get a powerful phone book, an outliner, and a great calendar with a to-do list and alarms. You can also cross-reference information between any of these functions. The user interface is intuitive, the price is affordable, and although the screen

Figure 21: With Delrina's Daily Planner, you get a different "Far Side" comic every day—plus a powerful appointment calendar with almost every feature you could want. There's even an electronic version of Trivial Pursuit.

is a little cluttered for my taste, my only real objection is that it's missing a long-range planner (see Chapter 19: *Databases* for information on *Ecco Professional*).

Far Side Daily Planner

The *Daily Planner* is a full-featured appointment calendar with the added attraction of pop-up comics from Gary Larsen's "Far Side"—some animated, some in color. It's a great way to take the chill off starting another work day. The DOS and Windows versions work similarly, though, of course, the graphics are better under Windows. If you prefer, you can get the same calendar at the same $60 retail price with a set of "Cathy" comics.

Lotus Organizer

Considering how many things you can do with *Lotus Organizer*, this Windows program is amazingly intuitive to use. A book appears on the screen; all you do is click on the colored tabs to jump from the phone book to the appointment calendar, to the long-range planner, or to the to-do list. Appointments can be displayed and printed by the day or week, and you can block out special events like vacations or off-site meetings and avoid scheduling conflicting appointments. Alarms? Of course! Considering its power, not to mention its notorious flaming wastebasket for deleting appointments, it's a steal at $149.

Miscellaneous Utilities

Sometimes it seems there are almost as many utility categories as there are utilities. In my experience, it's often the "little" utilities—inexpensive, unsung heroes of your hard disk—that make the biggest difference. Many utilities in this section may seem minor, but they make a major difference when you need them.

DOS Shells

These shells insulate you from the DOS prompt. You move, delete, copy, and rename files by picking them from a list instead of having to type in file names and remember complicated directory paths and commands. Of course, Windows does that too, more or less. And if you don't use Windows, you can fill in a little coupon in your DOS documentation for DOS's Supplemental disks, send in the coupon along with $5, and receive (among other things) one of the best DOS shells ever invented. So why bother paying real money for one?

HOT TIP

The answer is personal taste. Mine, in this case. My favorite DOS shell, which I find faster and more intuitive than either DOS's shell or most Windows-based file managers, is *XTree Gold*. You can perform virtually every DOS file function from an easy-to-use file window, and *XTree* supports both ZIP and ARC archive files. That means you can treat ZIP files like directories; *XTree Gold* displays the packed files and lets you manipulate them as easily as if they were uncompressed.

File Finders

Only those with photographic memories never forget which subdirectory they put their files in. The rest of us sometimes forget the *name* we gave a text or data file, and merely remember that it contains the phrase "Icon Stapler." For those awful moments, it's great to have a file-search utility.

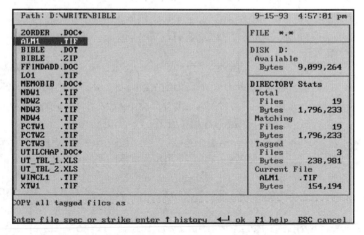

Figure 22: *A superb DOS shell, XTree Gold is so fast and easy to use that I run it under Windows in a DOS window! Here, you start a copying operation by tagging the files you want to copy.*

DOS's FIND searches for text strings if you already know the file name, and the File Manager's Search looks for filenames but not for text. Fortunately, there are good third-party products that not only look for files *and* text—some even search inside ZIP and ARC files, which neither DOS nor the File Manager can do. The DOS and Windows versions of *Norton* and *PC Tools* include excellent file finders. There's also a ton of fine shareware programs.

Print Spoolers

Unless you like staring at the screen during long print jobs, a print spooler is essential. Spoolers snatch print jobs from applications and load those jobs into a print cache—a temporary holding area on disk or in memory. While the spooler prints, the application is free, so you get back to work faster.

The best print spoolers let you choose between storing the text to be printed in base memory, high memory, or in a temporary disk file. Spooling to base memory is fast, but it eats up valuable RAM and may limit the size of other applications you can run. Spooling to disk uses virtually no memory, but it can be slow. Spooling to high (or extended) memory is usually best, but not all spoolers can do this trick.

HOT TIP

Windows comes with a built-in print spooler, Print Manager, that works pretty well. There are any number of commercial print-spooling products for DOS, including an excellent one in the *PC-Kwik Power Pak*, but my favorite is *PrintCache 3.1* from LaserTools. This powerful utility runs under DOS and Windows, offers more spooling options than any other, and is fast and reliable. There are also scores of shareware print spoolers, like *DMP*, waiting for you to download from an on-line service.

Macro Processors

If I had to choose my one favorite utility, *ProKey* would be it. I use this DOS macro processor to record command sequences both inside applications and at the DOS prompt. True, many applications these days come with their own macro processors. But few built-in macro functions enable you to create macros that suspend in mid-playback, wait for user input, and then resume playback. *ProKey* will do that, which makes it possible to create incredibly cool macros. There's also a Windows version of *ProKey*.

Whether you want to reprogram your function keys (so one press does your daily backup), or automate a series of find-and-replace-and-reformat operations in a DOS word processor, *ProKey* is up to the job. Its ability to accept input in mid-macro is unique, and you can save macros so they load every time an application starts. My only complaint is that *ProKey* eats up 47K of memory. Fortunately, my memory manager can load most of it into high memory.

Screen Savers

One of the most persistent PC legends is the Monitor Burn-In Chimera. Like Eskimos scaring each other with tales of the Wendigo ice-monster, many PC users believe that if you leave a monitor turned on with the same image displayed, that image will burn in and remain as a faint overlay forever. Personally, I've never seen a burnt-in color monitor, not even one—though monochrome monitors do occasionally suffer this fate.

Figure 23: *A legend in their own time, these flying toasters are one of many weird and entertaining screen savers included in the After Dark collection.*

The charm that supposedly wards off this imaginary burn-in monster is called a screen saver, a utility that notices when there's no keyboard activity and puts a series of changing images on the screen. There are scores of these inexpensive utilities, many of them very clever. Three of the most amusing screen savers come from Berkeley Systems: *After Dark, Star Trek: The Screen Saver,* and *The Disney Collection: The Screen Saver.*

Screen savers are really software toys, but there's nothing wrong with that. Remember, though, that if you elect a boring, black screen instead of those flapping toasters, you'll save around 30 percent on your monitor's electricity bill.

Figure 24: *Stop typing for a few minutes, and you'll boldly go with Star Trek: The Screen Saver.*

Timers

There are a few things computers are really good at, and timing is one of them. (They ought to be, since the damn things are full of clocks of one kind or another.) Whether you need to time a long-distance call for billing purposes, or keep track of the cassette you're recording in the front room, your PC ought to be able to help.

Figure 25: *Regress to your childhood effortlessly with The Disney Collection, yet another screen saver library from Berkeley Systems.*

But how? Since there's no stopwatch built into DOS, you may be tempted to simply push the button on your digital wrist chronometer—the one that costs $25 as opposed to $2500. If you'd rather push the stopwatch button on your PC, *Norton Utilities* comes with four different stopwatches that you can start and stop from the command line. *PC Tools Pro* has a few, too.

The best place to look for Windows timers is in the on-line shareware catalogs. Just search on keywords like TIMER, and take your pick.

Utility Libraries

Utility libraries hand you a huge bunch of inexpensive software tools in one neat package. Because the utilities in these collections come from a single company, they tend to look and work alike, which means you don't have to learn a new interface every time you fire up a new utility. And considering what you get, they're real bargains, usually costing less than $150 in stores.

My two favorite libraries have haunted this chapter from the beginning: Symantec's *The Norton Utilities* and Central Point's *PC Tools Pro*. I've discussed the major functions of these packages already: file recovery, defragging, disk caching, file finding, and both PIM and DOS shell features. However, the companies that create these packages are so bent on blowing your mind with bushels of features, you'll find even more. So let's discuss some of them here.

The Windows versions of these libraries, *Norton Desktop for Windows* and *PC Tools for Windows*, have many of the same utilities. But since the Windows versions are best known for improving Windows' interface, you'll find them compared in the "Windows Fixers" section earlier in this chapter.

Safety Features

Here's a quick sketch of software included in the leading libraries to keep your PC (or your meddlesome co-workers) from vaporizing your hard-earned data(see Chapter 9: *Protect Your Data*)

- **Backup software.** Eventually, *every* hard disk fails, and unless you have a recent backup, you *will* lose data. DOS includes both DOS and Windows backup utilities, though they're pretty bare bones. *The Norton Utilities* has no backup function, but *PC Tools Pro, Norton Desktop for Windows*, and *PC Tools for Windows* all offer better backup utilities than DOS provides.

- **Virus protection.** Viruses attack far less often than the media would have you believe—but it only takes getting hit once to make you wish you'd installed a virus protection utility for detecting and removing the little beasts. DOS comes with antivirus software that runs under both DOS and Windows, but all four libraries (except for *The Norton Utilities*) offer more virus-scanning options.

- **Crash recovery.** *PC Tools Pro* offers this unique feature, which it calls CPR. At intervals you specify, CPR saves the contents of RAM to disk, so if your system crashes you can recover all (or most of) your data up to the last save—even a Windows session with multiple open files and applications. The downside is that the save interrupts your work, and if your chief applications have an auto-save option already, you don't need CPR anyway.

- **Hard disk surface scanning.** Newer hard disks check the surfaces of hard disk platters on the fly and lock out damaged areas so you don't lose data—or even real-ize there's a problem. Many older drives lack this automatic feature, which is why you should run a surface scan utility from one of the libraries to be safe. DOS now comes with one, too: ScanDisk.

- **Low-level format.** On older hard disks, basic low-level information that marks the location of data can weaken, or hardware align-ment can "drift" 'til the head

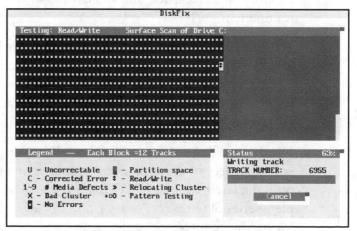

Figure 26 *Older hard disks are susceptible to surface flaws as bits of mag-netic oxide flake off. PC Tools' DiskFix checks every sector, and moves endan-gered data to safety if it can.*

can't find the low-level tracks. Eventually, the drive dies. Run a low-level format utility, and you'll ensure that this information is in good shape. The libraries have this; DOS doesn't.

- **File encryption.** Most people never think about PC security until someone sneaks in and copies a confidential file, or reads a passionate love letter. To use a file encryption utility, you password-protect the file you're worried about. Then the utility turns the file into gobbledygook—but very special gobbledygook, since anyone who knows the password can restore it to its original form. DOS doesn't offer this feature; the libraries do.

- **Total file eradication.** Deleting a file doesn't erase its data, at least not immediately. If the file was confidential, and you're worried about Boris and Natasha sneaking into your office and undeleting it, a file wiper will overwrite every single character of the original file. Wiped files cannot be recovered—by you or anyone else. They are ex-files. Deceased. Gone forever. Rest in peace.

Diagnostics

What happens when you use one of these libraries' diagnostic utilities to test every nook and cranny of your PC? Well, I've never seen them identify anything wrong, even when my PC was acting flaky. The more interesting diagnostic features have to do with software.

- **Windows resource/crash monitor.** Part of *The Norton Utilities*, this is basically the same feature offered by *PC Tools for Windows*. You get a constant readout of free memory and disk space, and an alarm sounds if resources sink too low and a crash is imminent.

- **INI file analysis and advice.** Offering another Windows utility reminiscent of *PC Tools for Windows*, *The Norton Utilities* helps you fine-tune your WIN.INI and SYSTEM.INI files, the two most difficult things about configuring Windows. It also keeps a log of changes you have made (or software you've installed), which can aid in tracking down problems.

- **Hardware diagnostics.** Library hardware diagnostic utilities generally provide only one piece of the puzzle when you're trying to track down a hardware problem. Still, the latest editions of *PC Tools Pro* and *The Norton Utilities* feature a very complete series of tests. *The Norton Utilities* is the only utility I've seen that actually tests for hardware interrupt conflicts, and while it's not foolproof, it could solve some knotty configuration problems.

Customizing Your DOS System

Windows' Control Panel gives you plenty of opportunity for personal color choices—just walk around an office full of Windows users and check out all the weird color schemes. However, unless you're comfortable messing with DOS's MODE command and ANSI.SYS, you'll be hard pressed to find anything close to that flexibility in DOS. Here again, the libraries can help.

- **Setting color and display options.** Prismatic color control under DOS is only a menu away. *The Norton Utilities*, for instance, lets you change DOS video modes, and set and save as many screen color combinations as you wish, so your custom colors will come up automatically when you turn on your PC.

- **Changing your cursor**. How you like your cursor to look is a highly individual matter. *The Norton Utilities* lets you adjust the cursor size and shape and save the results to a file, so the next time you turn on the system the cursor will automatically appear the way you like it.

- **Setting keyboard repeat rate.** Windows' Control Panel makes it simple to adjust how fast a key repeats if you hold it down, and how soon it starts repeating after you press it. DOS's MODE command does the same trick, but it won't work on every keyboard, and the syntax is complicated. *PC Tools Pro* and *The Norton Utilities* make it easy. So do several excellent shareware utilities, such as *KBFIX*.

Odds and Ends

A couple of handy library utilities don't fit into any pre-defined category.

- **Calculators.** While Windows has a fairly good calculator, DOS lacks one. *PC Tools Pro* provides several, including one designed specifically for programmers.

- **Viewing and changing file attributes.** Every file has four attributes that can be set and reset. Two of the four attributes, System and Hidden, needn't worry you. But knowing how to set the other two, Archive and Read-Only, can be very handy; changing the latter is the only way to delete files that give you the ominous message "Access Denied." DOS and all the libraries let you reset attributes, but *PC Tools Pro* gives you the easiest method.

Figure 27: Want to turn your $2000 PC into a $10 calculator? Easy! Here's one of several included with Norton Desktop for Windows.

The Bottom Line: Norton vs. PC Tools

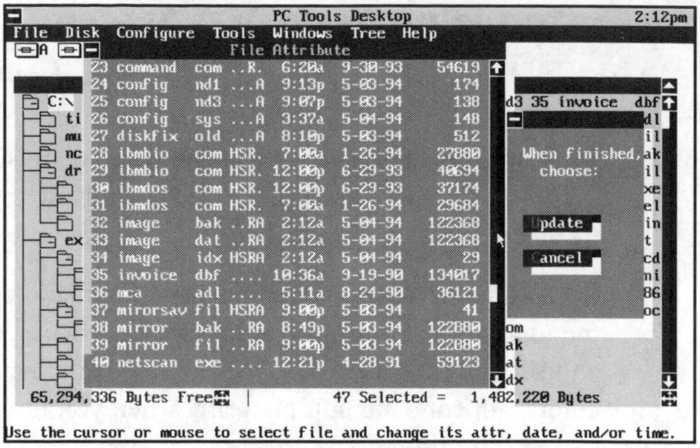

Big libraries. Truckloads of utilities. Which should you buy? Are the DOS or Windows versions of *Norton* and *PC Tools* better? Or, for that matter, should you stick with the latest version of DOS, which has many of the same utilities, some of which run under Windows?

The last question is easy to answer: Buy a library. DOS

Figure 28: *PC Tools Pro makes changing files attributes a snap. For example, to change a file's archive attribute (which tells backup programs whether to include a file in a backup), you simply highlight the file and click on "A." You can also change the file's date and time.*

has been beefed up with many capable utilities, but the libraries' recovery tools are better than DOS's when you've got serious problems, and they can be your last line of defense if you lack a viable backup. The real question is: Which library to buy?

- **If you're a Windows user,** buy *PC Tools for Windows*. It matches *Norton Desktop for Windows* pretty much feature for feature—and then trumps it by throwing in better virus protection and backup than DOS offers. The runner-up here is actually *The Norton Utilities*, because like *PC Tools for Windows*, it offers special Windows safety and tuning features that can improve performance and save you grief.

- **If you're a DOS user,** you should buy *PC Tools Pro* if you think you need crash recovery, or backup and antivirus that DOS can't touch (not to mention a calendar, a calculator, and a communications program). *The Norton Utilities* may not have all that extra stuff, but it has an easier interface, and its interrupt conflict detection will be useful for anyone who changes hardware configurations often.

	The Norton Utilities 8.0	PC Tools Pro 9.0	DOS 6.22
Data Recovery			
Undelete files/directories	Y	Y	Y[1]
Unformat disk	Y	Y	Y
Undelete sentry and tracker	Y	Y	Y
Repair lost clusters	Y	Y	Y
Repair cross-linked files	Y	Y	Y
Repair corrupted FAT	Y	Y	Y
View deleted files	Y	Y	N
Compressed data recovery	Y	Y	Y[2]
Data recovery under Windows	Y	N	Y[3]
Disk Defragger			
Full defrag/files-only defrag	Y	Y	Y
Space-only defrag	Y	Y	N
Includes Windows version	Y	N	N
Safety Features			
Disk backup	N	Y	Y
Tape backup	N	Y	N
Antivirus	N	Y	Y
Recover crashed data	N	Y	N
Surface scanning	Y	Y	Y
Low-level format	Y	Y	N
File encryption	Y	Y	N
File wiper	Y	Y	N

(continued next page)

Figure 29: *The Norton Utilities recovers data under DOS or Windows and comes with special Windows diagnostics, while PC Tools Pro has its own backup and antivirus programs, plus a special crash recovery feature.*

(Figure 29 continued)	The Norton Utilities 8.0	PC Tools Pro 9.0	DOS 6.22
Diagnostics			
Windows resource/crash monitor	Y	N	N
INI file analysis and advice	Y	N	N
Hardware diagnostics	Y	Y	Y
DOS Customization			
Color and display	Y	Y	Y[4]
Cursor size, shape, blink rate	Y	Y	Y[4]
Keyboard repeat rate	Y	Y	Y[4]
Other Stuff			
Memory manager	N	Y	Y
DOS shell	N	Y	Y
File finder with string search	Y	Y	Y
Compress individual files	N	Y	N
Disk cache	Y	Y	Y
Calculator	N	Y	N
Macros or scripts	Y	Y	Y[5]
View/change file attributes	Y	Y	Y
Address book/Auto-dialer	N	Y	N
Appointment calendar	Y	Y	N
Timer	Y	N	N

[1]With DOS's MS Windows Undelete only
[2]DoubleSpace disks only
[3]Undelete only
[4]Better learn DOS's MODE command syntax!
[5]Some limited macro capabilities available with DOSKEY

Shareware and Freeware Utilities

Shareware is software you can try before you buy. It's usually cheap, and some of it is of very high quality. You can use it, and even copy it for others to use, on a trial basis—usually for 30 days. If you like it and keep using it, you're expected to pay for it. Payment (on the honor system) is usually in the form of a registration fee, which may entitle you to other benefits, like a printed manual and free upgrades.

Freeware (or public domain software), as the name implies, is totally free.

Where to Find It

Most people get shareware and freeware from on-line services like CompuServe or America Online. Once you subscribe to these services, you can search through their huge shareware libraries, find a program you like, and retrieve a copy using your modem and communications software (a process called *downloading*).

The largest selection of shareware utilities is available on CompuServe, especially in its IBM forums, but many smaller services are catching up fast. The following services and BBSs are prime sources for shareware and freeware.

CompuServe: 800/848-8199

America Online: 800/827-6364

GEnie: 800/638-9636

Channel One BBS: 617/864-0100 (modem: 617/354-7077)

Exec-PC BBS: 414/789-4200 (modem: 414/789-4210)

Another great source for shareware is your local user group. Most groups have a broad selection of software available for members to try.

Searching On Line

Different on-line services have different software collections, and different search options. CompuServe, for instance, offers a sophisticated on-line file-searching utility, but in my experience it misses a lot of files. I prefer to do my searching myself.

- **By type.** If you know what *kind* of utility you're looking for, searching by keyword (SPOOLER, for instance, or MENU, or TIMER) is quite efficient.

- **By name.** You can search for a specific utility by name, if you know what it is. Remember that the name of the utility and the name of the downloadable file may not be the same.

- **By whim.** Simply browsing through the software libraries on line can be extremely enlightening, and fun.

Sometimes, your main problem will be an embarrassment of riches. If you're in the market for a screen saver and there are 75 of the damn things listed, where do you start? If the service you're using lists how many times a given program has been downloaded, use common sense and get the program with the largest number of downloads.

HOT TIP

Viruses

Most on-line services are pathologically careful about scanning shareware and freeware submissions for viruses before posting them. Nonetheless, do yourself a favor and download on-line software to a floppy—and check it with a virus scanner before you copy it to your hard disk, just to be safe.

HOT TIP

Money-Saving Tips for Downloading

While most on-line services and BBSs don't stick you with a surcharge for downloading shareware, you'll generally have to pay an hourly log-on fee. And if you're downloading a huge amount of data, those hourly charges can add up. If you don't have a local access number, you also have long-distance phone charges to worry about. Here's how to save a few bucks:

- **Use a fast modem.** Most services now offer 14.4Kbps access. You may have to pay more to log on at that speed, but in the long run it's worth it.

- **Use a fast error-checking protocol**, the fastest one your software supports. For instance, Zmodem is a good deal faster than Xmodem (see Chapter 21: *Communications* for more on error-checking protocols).

- **Log on at night.** Hourly on-line service and/or long-distance telephone charges are generally lower then.

- **Download a catalog.** If a catalog listing of all the files in the library is available as a downloadable text file, go ahead and snag it. Then you can do all your browsing and searching off line, using your word processor, without paying on-line charges at all.

Library and Archive Files

To save you precious minutes (and precious bucks), on-line services use several compression methods to make files shorter.

- **ARC.** You'll notice that some downloadable shareware files end in an *ARC* file extension (YESNO.ARC, for instance). That means they have been compressed by ARC, a shareware utility that's been in use for many years. It also means you'll need a copy of *ARC* or *ARC-E* to "unpack" those library files. Any on-line service that offers shareware also offers *ARC* and *ARC-E*.

- **PKZip/PKUnzip.** Most downloadable shareware files end in a ZIP file extension (BSTAT1.ZIP, for instance). That means they've been compressed with *PKZip*, the most popular archiving utility. It also means you'll need a copy of *PKUnzip*, its companion program, to decompress the files. Any service that offers shareware also offers *PKZip* and *PKUnzip* (see the top ten DOS list that follows).

- **Self-extracting EXE files.** You can use both *ARC* and *PKZip* to create self-extracting files with an EXE extension. If you download one of those files, you won't need *ARC* or *PKUnzip* to unpack them. Simply run the file. The archive will automatically unpack itself into its component files, after which you can delete the EXE file.

Licensing Fees: Do the Right Thing

There's nothing to stop you from using shareware forever without paying the licensing fee—except that it's wrong. In many cases, paying up gets you product support, not to mention the undying gratitude of the author. More important, if people pay shareware licensing fees, there's likely to be more shareware—and that works to everyone's advantage.

Top Ten DOS Shareware (and Freeware) Utilities

I use Windows, but that doesn't mean I'm a stranger to DOS—especially when there are so many cool shareware utilities to keep you entertained at the DOS prompt. Here are my favorites.

1. PKZip

Ask 100 people to name their favorite shareware utility, and I bet 83 of them will say "*PKZip*." This industrial-strength compression program lets you create shrunken archive files that hold other files inside them. Graphics files shrink the most, program files shrink the least, and text files usually end up less than half their original size.

HOT TIP

PKZip's companion utility, *PKUnzip*, lets you extract the stored files. A third utility, Zip2EXE, turns ZIP files into self-extracting EXE files that unpack themselves without *PKUnzip*. Download PK204G.EXE; it contains all three utilities, plus documentation, for a $25 registration fee. (Note: Some versions of the *Norton* antivirus program will report this file infected with the Amoeba virus. This is a false report.)

2. ARC

Like *PKZip* and *PKUnzip*, *ARC* lets you create archive files composed of many other files, and decompress those files when you want to use them. It's handy for sending and receiving files by modem, but it's also a great way to save disk space. However, it doesn't compress files as tightly as *PKZip*, so these days, you'll find many more ZIP files than ARC files. But you should still keep *ARC* around just in case. The latest version costs $35 and can be found in a self-extracting file called ARC602.EXE.

3. Split (free!)

Who you gonna call when you need to copy a file to a floppy, and it's bigger than 1.4MB? *SPLIT*, that's who. This life-saving utility splits any file into two or more output files of any specified size. To reassemble the original file, simply use DOS's COPY command to concatenate the fragments. Fast, easy, and brilliant. Look for the file SPLIT.ARC. (There are many similar shareware utilities on line. But I've tested this one, and it works.)

4. PC Clock

Do you want your PC to tell the *exact* time? This dandy little $20 program dials into the atomic clock at the U.S. Naval Observatory and resets your PC's clock/calendar,

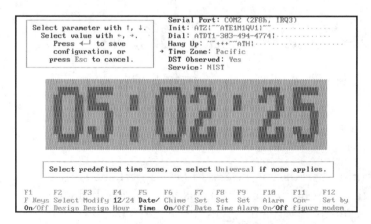

by modem, to the totally accurate time and date. After which it displays the new time in huge numbers so you can reset your watch—and your VCR. Look for the on-line file: PCK300.ZIP.

5. Signal (free!)

Sometimes it's handy to know when a time-consuming batch file has run through to the end. This tiny utility causes a loud,

Figure 30: *Want the really correct time? PC Clock calls up the atomic clock at the U.S. Naval Observatory and resets your PC's clock/calendar.*

wailing, three-note alarm to ring from your PC's speaker. Call it from the last line of your batch file and you'll always know when your coffee break is over. Download SIGNAL.COM.

6. ONCEADAY (free!)

Some tasks—a virus scan, say, or a quick disk defrag—are important enough to do every day. That's why many of us put a couple of start-up commands in AUTOEX-EC.BAT, so those housekeeping chores run automatically when we start up the PC in the morning. But if you boot your computer more than *once* a day (due to Windows crashes, say) you have to sit through tedious, time-consuming replays of these operations. *ONCEADAY* beats this problem. Add it to your AUTOEXEC.BAT file, and it will detect whether a program has already run today; if it has, *ONCEADAY* skips down to the next command. It can be found on line as DAILY.ZIP.

7. XT and XT302 (free!)

Want to delete every BAK file on your hard disk? There are quite a few shareware utilities that claim to run through every directory in your tree, executing the same DOS command (DEL *.BAK, for instance) in every one—but I can testify to the safe and reliable operation of Chris Dunford's shareware classic *XT*, which I've been using for years. Download XT.ARC. If you prefer a more recent implementation with a few more bells and whistles, look for Paul Whittemore's *XT302*, found on line as XT302.ZIP.

8. List Plus

You can page down through long text files using DOS's TYPE command (in conjunction with the MORE command), but if you want to page *up*, forget it. Vern Buerg's *LIST* will do this, and it lets you view popular word processing files without the formatting junk. You can also view some graphics files, and even look inside ARC and ZIP files. A telephone dialer is thrown in for yuks. Look for a file called LIST77.EXE. Suggested fee, $20.

9. DMP

One of my favorite print spoolers is *DMP*, a $29 item that's almost as versatile as *PrintCache*, and a lot cheaper. *DMP* spools to disk, RAM disk, and expanded, extended, or high memory. It will print to a file if you prefer, and it delivers fast output for all types of printers. The self-extracting library file to look for on line is called DMPLZH.EXE.

10. KBFIX (free!)

Adjusting the keyboard repeat rate can speed your work and make you a happier camper. If you'd rather not spend the dough for *PC Tools Pro* or *Norton Utilitie*s—or wrestle with DOS's MODE command, which may not work on your keyboard anyway—you'll find countless freeware and shareware keyboard utilities on line. My favorite is *KBFIX*. Download KBFIX2.ARC.

Top Ten Windows Shareware Utilities

These days, you can find more Windows shareware than DOS shareware. These are among the best and most useful I've seen.

1. Metz Task Manager

Designed to replace both Windows Task List and Program Manager, *Metz Task Manager* gives you push-button launching of as many as nine applications, with the ability to start up programs at preset times. You also get a touch of file management, including file searching. A terrific deal at $49.95. Look for MTM20.EXE

2. Almanac for Windows

Almanac is a powerful Windows calendar program, but it boasts so many desktop features—a daily schedule, notes, a to-do list, a variety of alarms, sunrise/sunset, moon phases, Gregorian and Jewish calendar modes—that it's more accurate to call this $49 utility a full-featured PIM. A wide array of recurring events are supported, including irregular holidays like Easter and Hanukkah. The file to look for on line is ALM30H.ZIP.

3. ClipMate for Windows

Every time you cut or copy a block of text, Windows' Clipboard vaporizes the last text you cut or copied. That's fine, until you need to reclaim a block you cut half a dozen edits back! *ClipMate* saves every item you copy to Windows' Clipboard, whether it's text, graphics, or a mix of both. You can view, edit, or combine all the Clipboard "saves," and then paste the result back into your application. Data is saved to disk between sessions. The registration fee is $25 and the file to download is CLIPMT.ZIP.

4. Detour (free!)

Double-click on a file in the File Manager, and Windows will automatically load that file into an application, based on the file's extension (TXT files load into Notepad, for example). But what happens if you'd rather load that TXT file into *Word for Windows*? You can start up *Word for Windows* first, of course. Or you can use Detour, which pops up a menu defined by you, giving you a choice of apps for each file type.

5. WinZip

Bored with shelling out to DOS every time you need to create or unpack a ZIP archive? For $29, *WinZip* will allow you to view, extract, run, and delete files within ZIP archives without ever leaving Windows. OK, *Norton Desktop for Windows* will do that too, but *WinZip* can handle *all* the archive formats: ARJ, LZH, ARC, and ZIP 2.0. Download WINZIP.ZIP.

6. Winclock

If you'd rather not spend $150 or more for a brand-name appointment scheduler, look what you can get for $16. This terrific, full-featured utility packs ten different alarms, two stopwatches, and two countdown timers to remind you of daily, weekly, or one-time-only appointments. Each alarm pops up with a note reminding you of whatever it was you promised to do, or you can set the alarms to run a program of your choosing. Scan for WINCLOCK.ZIP.

Figure 31: *Believe it! One of the best Windows shells is also shareware. Metz Task Manager makes organizing and launching Windows applications a snap.*

7. WinGrab

Quite a few computerized offices keep an IBM Selectric around to type envelopes. Why? Because irregular addresses or uncommon printers still confound most word processors, even the ones with pretty envelope icons at the top of the screen. At $49.95, *WinGrab* is relatively pricey for shareware, but it's everything an envelope-printing utility should be. It lets you capture an on-screen address and send it to your printer fully formatted for envelope printing, it works with almost all PostScript and LaserJet-compatible printers, and you can use it from within your Windows word processor. Look for GRAB61.ZIP.

8. Icon Manager

Remember "The Trouble With Tribbles," that classic *Star Trek* episode in which fuzzy aliens overran the *Enterprise*? Sometimes icons can be like that. If your PC has icons scattered across your hard disk, you can use *Icon Manager* ($19.95) to find and display all of them, dump the duplicates, and move the rest into their own directory. Look for IM11EX.ZIP, or (on some systems) ICONMGR.ZIP.

9. BizWiz

If you aren't crazy about Windows' built-in calculator, and you haven't invested in *Norton Desktop for Windows* (which comes with three nice ones), you might check out *BizWiz*, a $35 financial calculator designed to emulate the famous Hewlett-Packard HP-12C. A handy option keeps the calculator on top of other Windows applications. Look for BIZWIZ.ZIP.

10. Magic Screensaver

This Canadian screen blanker does only random geometric shapes (no toasters), but it's still fun, and you can use it to password-protect your PC if you want a little security while you're out to lunch. Not bad for only $25. The downloadable file is MAGIC.ZIP.

Product Directory

After Dark for DOS
After Dark for Windows
More After Dark
  for Windows
Star Trek: The Screen Saver
The Disney Collection:
  The Screen Saver
Berkeley Systems
2095 Rose St.
Berkeley, CA 94709
510/540-5535

AnyTime
Individual Software
5870 Stoneridge Dr. #1
Pleasanton, CA 94588
800/331-3313
510/734-6767

ClickBOOK
BookMaker Corp.
625 Emerson St. #200
Palo Alto, CA 94301
800/766-8531
415/617-1101

Dashboard for Windows
NewWave
Hewlett-Packard
974 E. Arques Ave.
Sunnyvale, CA 94086
800/554-1305

Ecco Simplicity
Arabesque Software
2340 130th Ave. N.E.
Bellevue, WA 98005
800/457-4243
206/869-9600

Far Side Daily Planner
Delrina Technology Inc.
6830 Via Del Oro #240
San Jose, CA 95119
800/268-6082
408/363-2345

hDC Power Launcher 2.0
Express Systems
2101 4th Ave. #303
Seattle, WA 98121
800/321-4606
206/728-8300

Lotus Organizer
Lotus Development Corp.
55 Cambridge Pkwy.
Cambridge, MA 02142
800/635-6887
617/577-8500

Managing Your Money
MECA Software, Inc.
55 Walls Dr.
Fairfield, CT 06430
203/255-1441

NETROOM 3
Helix Software Co.
47-09 30th St.
Long Island City, NY 11101
800/451-0551
718/392-3100

Norton Desktop
  for Windows
The Norton Utilities
Symantec Corp.
10201 Torre Ave.
Cupertino, CA 95014
800/441-7234
408/252-3570

Outside In for Windows
Systems Compatibility Corp.
401 N. Wabash #600
Chicago, IL 60611
800/333-1395
312/329-0700

PC-Kwik Power Pak
Super PC-Kwik
WinMaster
PC-Kwik Corp.
15100 S.W. Koll Pkwy.
Beaverton, OR 97006
800/759-5945
503/644-5644

PC Tools Pro
PC Tools for Windows
XTree Gold
XTree for Windows
Central Point Software
15520 N.W. Greenbrier Pkwy.
  #200
Beaverton, OR 97006
800/964-6896
503/690-8090

PrintCache
Laser Tools Corp.
1250 45th St. #100
Emeryville, CA 94608
800/767-8004
510/420-8777

ProKey for DOS
ProKey for Windows
CE Software
1801 Industrial Cir.
West Des Moines, IA 50265
800/523-7638
515/221-1801

QEMM
Quarterdeck Office Systems
150 Pico Blvd.
Santa Monica, CA 90405
800/354-3222
310/392-9851

Stacker
Stac Electronics
5993 Avenida Encinas
Carlsbad, CA 92008
800/522-7822
619/431-7474

22 About Networks

By Robert Lauriston

- What you can do with a network
- Picking a network operating system
- When to install a LAN yourself
- Fundamentals of network hardware
- Network support resources
- E-mail tips and PC-to-Mac file sharing

What a network means to you and how much you need to know (and worry) about it vary enormously depending on the kind of network you have and whether you or someone else is responsible for installing and maintaining the thing. Chances are you play one of these four basic roles:

1. User on a small network

2. Tiny cog in a big corporate network

3. Administrator of a big corporate network

4. Head user on a small network

If you fall into one of the first two categories, congratulations—you can skip the techie stuff and go straight to "Top Ten E-mail Tips" and "A Brief Guide to Guerrilla Networking" at the end of this chapter (though if you're curious you might find the rest of the chapter interesting anyway).

If you fall into group #3, you know most of this stuff already. To help you find answers to questions beyond your expertise, we've provided a handy guide to network support resources, also at the end of this chapter.

This chapter is aimed mostly at #4, the poor sucker stuck with installing, managing, and troubleshooting a small network. If you fit that description and you don't already have a network, this chapter will give you a good overview of the decisions you will need to make before taking the plunge.

Sharing Software

You hardly notice the freeway you're driving on unless there's a traffic jam or a bump in the asphalt. Likewise, except for the people who maintain LANs, nobody cares about network cabling, interface boards, or the network operating system until the network misbehaves. What people who *use* LANs really care about are the services provided by network *applications*. This software provides the main motive for installing and running a LAN.

Network Application 1: E-mail

Goodbye telephone tag. As users quickly discover, E-mail often works better than a phone call, since you can send and reply to messages even when the person at the other end is busy. You can "attach" word processing, spreadsheet, and other files to E-mail messages, eliminating the need to pass floppy disks around the office. And "broadcasting" electronic messages to the whole office replaces paper-wasting photo-copied memos.

There are dozens of network E-mail programs, but three turn up in the vast majority of installations: *cc:Mail* (from Lotus), *Microsoft Mail*, and *WordPerfect Office*. Several key features account for these programs' popularity:

- **Easy message and file exchange** for everyone on the network, whether the user has a DOS PC, a Windows PC, or a Mac

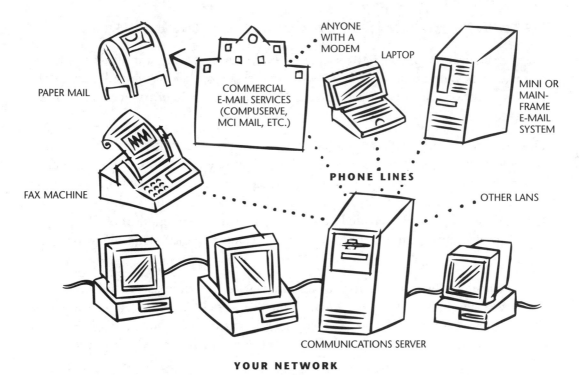

Figure 1: LAN E-mail to anywhere. *Using modems and phone lines, E-mail gateways extend the reach of LAN E-mail to faraway laptops, other LANs, and any user who subscribes to a commercial service like CompuServe or MCI Mail.*

- **Remote versions** that enable you to send and receive E-mail via modem from a laptop or home computer

- **E-mail gateways** that connect with such commercial services as Internet, MCI Mail, and CompuServe (and even minicomputer and mainframe mail systems like PROFS and All-in-One), enabling you to exchange E-mail with users in other locations just by adding a prefix or suffix to the address

- **Group scheduling,** a sort of multiuser calendar application, which makes it faster and easier for a busy group of people to set up meetings

- **E-mail links to other LANs,** which tie far-flung offices into one big E-mail system

Any capable PC user should be able to install and administer a basic E-mail system, though installing gateway software and managing a multi-LAN mail system may require special training.

Network Application 2: Multiuser Databases

Many organizations install networks because they need to run a multiuser database management system like *dBASE*, *Paradox*, *FoxPro*, or *Access*—or, more likely, a database application, such as an accounting program, an order entry system, or other custom program.

DANGER

Designing a custom database to hold important information like orders, inventory, accounts receivables, or payroll info is seldom a do-it-yourself job. Even configuring an off-the-shelf accounting program so multiple users can enter data simultaneously can be tricky, and if you set it up wrong you may lose data. That's why off-the-shelf applications are typically installed by a consultant, specialized applications by a value-added reseller, and custom applications by a developer (either a consultant or a staff programmer).

HOT TIP

An exception to the don't-do-it-yourself rule is when multiple users have no need to enter data simultaneously—things like phone directories and client contact lists typically fall into this category. You can easily set up a directory on any network so that all users have read-only access to its files, but only one person is allowed to edit them.

The Consultant From Hell

He talks a good game. He seems to know exactly what you want in a multiuser (check one) order entry system, accounting application, or customer database. But you're never really happy with the program he ends up writing. Then, after tens of thousands of records have been entered, the program starts crashing all over the place. *And the consultant from hell is the only one who can fix it. Again, and again, and again.*

The moral is: Always, always check reliable references before you hire a consultant to write a network application. Also, ask the vendor, consultant, or programmer if the software has any special requirements, so you don't end up having to replace software or hardware later on. Note that when you hire a database consultant to write a custom application, you may *not* need to buy a copy of the database program itself, since the consultant may have already paid for the right to distribute applications written in the program's language.

Other Network Applications

Networked *project management* programs help schedule and track the work of hundreds of people collaborating on complex engineering projects, like designing an airplane or building an automobile prototype. *Document management* systems help businesses with thousands of documents in progress (such as law firms or large contractors) track revisions, control access, and record word processing time for client billing or departmental charge-backs.

Working Together With Lotus Notes

Lotus Notes is in a category all its own. This unique program combines E-mail, a text-oriented database, and database-style programming tools. One popular use for *Notes* is to provide virtual "meeting rooms" for people who are too busy or geographically dispersed to meet in the flesh. Bulletin board software offers similar capabilities, but *Notes* is more flexible and significantly more secure (RSA public-key encryption, the best available outside the CIA, is built in and automatic).

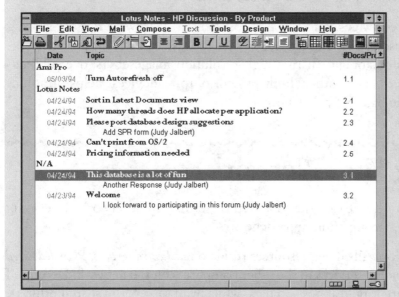

Other typical *Notes* applications help organize amorphous information, such as technical support updates or calls to customer support centers. *Notes* "work-flow" applications replace paper forms with digital equivalents that automatically route themselves from one desk to another as each bureaucrat "signs off" with an electronic signature.

Figure 2: *Many large companies swear by Lotus Notes, a network application that enables people to work collectively on documents and view only the information they need from a shared database.*

Sharing Hardware

If you're merely interested in sharing printers or other devices, the time and expense of setting up a network is just not worth the effort. But if you're setting up a LAN anyway, why miss the opportunity?

- **Shared printers** are more cost-effective than putting a printer on every desk, and they provide quick access to a variety of paper types. A typical setup is a pair of laser printers, one with letterhead, another with plain paper. Another common arrangement is a bank of dot matrix printers loaded with tractor-feed invoices, purchase orders, labels, and so on. People don't waste time swapping forms in and out of printers—they just select their printer of choice.

HOT TIP

- **Shared hard drives** are essential for running most network applications. They're also handy for storing shared files, like spreadsheet templates and boilerplate documents, or for holding huge files that won't fit on workstation hard disks. And, of course, when you're working at someone else's desk, you can access any file on the shared hard drive.

- **Shared tape drives** make it easy to back up your office's data. With the right software, you can back up a whole network—not just the shared hard drive, but each user's own hard drive as well—to a single set of tapes.

- **Sharing expensive devices** is a key LAN cost benefit. Hardware ripe for sharing includes optical disc drives and CD ROM "jukeboxes," which can provide hundreds of gigabytes of storage. Sharing high-resolution imagesetters, dye-sublimation color printers, and other high-priced output devices helps graphics workgroups get the hard copy they need.

Designing Your Network

Conventional wisdom has it that the first step in setting up a network is deciding between two distinct, incompatible approaches:

- **Total centralization.** All shared resources reside on *dedicated servers*, PCs *dedicated* exclusively to providing services to the other computers on the network. Dedicated *file servers* hold shared applications and data, while print servers run shared printers. Often a single PC plays both server roles. The file server, which no one touches except the network administrator, runs the *network operating system* (NOS), which enables servers and workstations to talk to each other. Such networks can be described as *server-based LANs*—or *NetWare LANs*, since *NetWare* is by far the most popular NOS for server-based LANs.

- **Total decentralization.** Shared applications, data, and printers can be located on any PC on the network; to put it another way, any PC can share its hard drive and printer with any other PC. Since each PC has an equal chance of being a server, such networks are described as *peer-to-peer LANs*. The "network operating system" isn't an operating system at all, but a memory-resident application that runs on each user's PC.

REMEMBER

In reality, server-based LANs and peer-to-peer LANs aren't mutually exclusive. These days even the most server-centric NOS (*NetWare* included) enables workstations to share their printers with the network. And peer-to-peer LANs often dedicate a server to storing applications.

The Bullet-Proof Server

It's worth spending money to make your file server reliable. Nothing puts a whole office in a worse mood than a crashed server. And if shared data has vaporized, everyone has to reconstruct that data as far back as the last server backup (which should be performed daily, of course). Here are some of the most common devices and techniques for protecting servers and their data:

- **Uninterruptible power supplies (UPSs)** use batteries to keep the server's juice flowing for a few minutes in the event of a power failure, while users are notified to save their work and log off (see Chapter 9: *Protect Your Data* for more on UPSs).

- **Disk mirroring** employs a second drive as a double of the first. The second drive reads and writes all the same data at the same time, so if the primary drive dies, nobody loses data.

- **Drive arrays** are multiple drives (four, typically) that act like a single drive. If one drive breaks down, the others collectively "remember" all the data on the broken drive, so users can still access the information. In some cases you don't even have to turn off the server to replace the failed drive. Because shared data spans multiple disks, drive arrays can handle more users with less loss of performance than can single or mirrored drives.

- **Server mirroring,** the ultimate in fault tolerance, uses twin servers connected by a high-speed fiber optic link. When the primary server fails, the backup kicks in, and users can keep working without interruption.

Since it's not an either/or choice between server-based and peer-to-peer LANs, you're really faced with two separate issues. How many servers do you need to dedicate, if any? And which peer-to-peer services do you need?

When You Need a Dedicated Server

Even on a peer-to-peer network, certain applications demand—and others benefit from—a dedicated server. Here are the main reasons for setting up a dedicated file server:

- **To run a multiuser database or accounting package.** Install a shared database on a peer-to-peer LAN workstation, and if that person's system crashes, the shared database goes down as well. Ditto if he or she forgets and flips the "off" switch. Installing the database on a dedicated server greatly reduces the likelihood of system crashes. In addition, server-based databases offer *transaction tracking*, which prevents half-completed operations from corrupting database files when crashes do occur.

- **To provide maximum network reliability.** Even if the NOS is rock-solid, power outages, disk failures, and other unexpected events can still crash the network. The

How to Configure a Server

	Workstation	Dedicated Server
CPU	486SX2-66 or better	Pentium-66 or better
RAM	8MB	16MB or more
Bus	Standard (with local bus)	EISA
Hard disk	340MB	1GB or larger
Hard disk interface	16-bit IDE	32-bit SCSI
Network adapter	16-bit	32-bit
Video	Super VGA	VGA color or mono
Case	Any	Full tower

Figure 3: Dedicated servers eat processing power and hard disk storage for breakfast. On the other hand, high-performance video would be wasted on a server.

best way to prevent such disasters is to dedicate a server to running the NOS and to make that server as reliable as possible.

- **To improve performance.** In a peer-to-peer LAN, dedicating a server to multi-user applications keeps operations from slowing to a crawl, since no workstation will have to divide its energies between, say, running a shared database for the network and loading its own huge spreadsheet file.

- **To simplify network administration.** It's often faster and easier to install a single shared copy of an application on a file server instead of installing a separate copy on each workstation. Ditto software upgrades. The bigger your network, the more time this approach will save.

Communications and Database Servers

File servers are the most common kind of dedicated server, but servers come in other flavors, too. For example, many offices set up *communications servers*, which are typically modem-equipped PCs dedicated to one or more specialized communications tasks. Your network may need a dedicated server to perform one of the following jobs:

- **To run E-mail gateway software.** An extension to the E-mail system you use locally, E-mail *gateway* software typically runs on a dedicated communications server and links to such commercial services as CompuServe, MCI Mail, and Internet—

or to remote LANs, mainframe terminals, and so on. For light traffic, E-mail gateways use regular modems and call each other at scheduled times or when triggered by a high-priority message. For heavy traffic, gateways are often permanently linked by special modems and high-speed leased lines.

- **To share modems and fax capabilities.** Modems may be cheap, but running a second phone line to every desk is an expensive proposition. A *modem server* enables everyone on the LAN to share modems and phone lines and link to on-line services, remote PCs, and so on. A simple fax server lets users send faxes directly from applications (see Chapter 21: *Communications* for more on fax modems). Sophisticated fax servers tie into the E-mail system, so sending a fax is just like sending a message, and incoming faxes arrive as file attachments to specially addressed messages.

- **To run software that connects with a wide area network.** Just as a LAN links workstations, a WAN hooks LANs together (usually over high-speed leased lines). Any workstation on either LAN enjoys complete access to the remote LAN's services, in effect creating a single network. Connecting to a WAN doesn't always

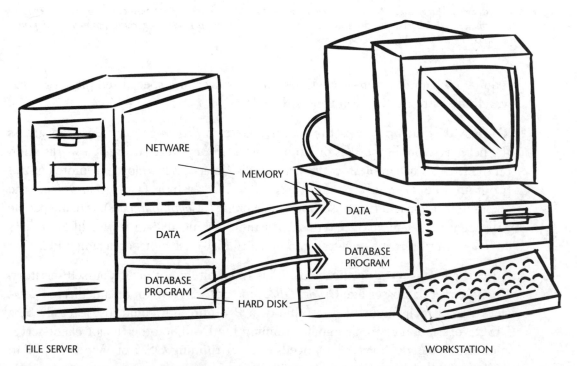

NETWARE

MEMORY

DATA

DATA

DATABASE
PROGRAM

DATABASE
PROGRAM

HARD DISK

FILE SERVER

WORKSTATION

Figure 4: Conventional network database. In conventional network databases, your PC does all the computing—the network server just stores the files and handles security. Run a database query, and the server sends the whole file across the network to your workstation, bogging down performance.

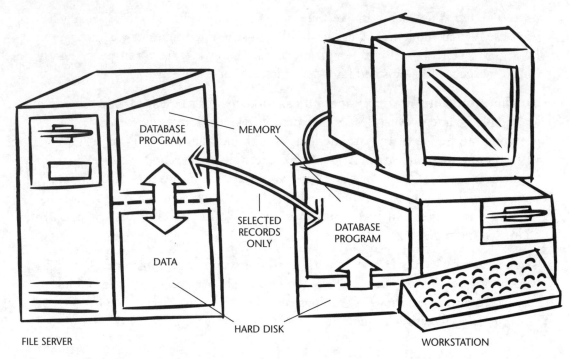

FILE SERVER

WORKSTATION

Figure 5: **Client-server database.** *In a client-server database, the database server does most of the computing. The application running on your PC sends the server a query, and the server sends back only the records that match the query criteria. This can cut network traffic dramatically.*

require a separate server—sometimes the file server or a specialized piece of hardware called a router box can handle the job.

HOT TIP

- **To provide dial-up access for remote users.** A *dial-in gateway* lets users access the network from home PCs or laptops just as if they were sitting at a workstation on the LAN. The simplest way to provide dial-in access is to load a remote control program like *Close-Up* or *Remote2* on a PC with a fast modem (see the "Communications Software" section of Chapter 21: *Communications*). If many people will need to dial in at once, consider a multitasking dial-in server like Novell's *NetWare Access Server*, which can run up to 16 dial-in sessions on a single PC.

- **To run client-server applications.** This is definitely not do-it-yourself territory. Client-server databases like *Oracle*, *DB/2*, and *SQL Server* run on a dedicated *database server*, which might be a fast 486 or a Pentium, but could just as easily be a RISC workstation or minicomputer running UNIX. The other major client-server application is *Lotus Notes*, which needs a server running OS/2 or Windows NT to deliver its full capabilities.

When You Need Peer-to-Peer Services

People choose peer-to-peer LANs for small installations because they're far easier and cheaper to set up and maintain than *NetWare* LANs. But all peer NOSs offer another inherent bonus: Unlike *NetWare*, they let you access other workstations' files and applications.

Printing Without a PC

All major network operating systems enable anyone on the network to use any printer hooked to any workstation (though many *NetWare* users prefer such third-party network printing utilities as Brightwork's *PS-Print*). However, you can also hook printers directly to the network using an inexpensive print server "box" like the Intel NetPort. A growing number of "network-ready" printers make even the box unnecessary, thanks to their built-in network adapters.

Peer-to-peer file and application sharing work best when security is a low priority. Users can easily offer the whole network access to a subdirectory containing, say, contact lists or a database application, but as soon as someone needs to restrict access, administrative nightmares loom. Every time an employee leaves or a new one arrives, it's up to whichever user has the shared app to edit authorized-user lists or distribute passwords. By contrast, *NetWare* LANs are designed to simplify such changes, because the network administrator simply edits a single, centralized user-access file.

DANGER

```
File Manager - [C:\WEP\*.* - [DOSV_5]]
 File   Disk   Tree   View   Options   Mail   Window   Help

 C: [DOSV_5]

 a    b    c    d

  mouse           abouttet.dll     10224    9/28/92    3:29:06pm   a
  placs            aboutwep.dll      9232    9/28/92    3:29:50pm   a
  qcwin            alert.wav        10400     9/7/92   12:00:00am   a
  rjl              bell.wav         10400     9/7/92   12:00:00am   a
  tk               blakjak.exe     136768     9/7/92   12:00:00am   a
  wconfig          blakjak.hlp      28272     9/7/92   12:00:00am   a
  wep              blip2.wav         1334     9/7/92   12:00:00am   a
  win31            boatrace.iw      22512    9/12/91    5:17:42pm   a
```

Figure 6: Windows for Workgroups offers an enhanced version of the File Manager, with added icons that enable you to make directories accessible to others, log on to your neighbors' directories, and so on.

Network Operating Systems

Once you have an idea of your network needs, you can get down to the nitty-gritty of picking a network operating system. Four NOSs account for the vast majority of PC network installations:

- **Artisoft's LANtastic** is by far the most common peer-to-peer NOS. It's a snap to set up and takes up relatively little workstation RAM.

- **Novell's NetWare Lite** is a peer-to-peer NOS used mostly in DOS environments. Don't confuse *NetWare Lite* with regular *NetWare*—except for its name and Novell logo, the two have nothing in common.

- **Microsoft's Windows for Workgroups** is a peer-to-peer NOS best suited for all-Windows environments. Each Windows for Workgroups workstation should be a 486 or a fast 386 with 8MB or more of RAM. Support for 286 and DOS systems is minimal—they can access shared resources but can't share their own.

- **Novell's NetWare** has the server-based category all wrapped up—by some estimates accounting for 90 percent of such installations.

For the future, keep an eye on Microsoft's Windows NT operating system, which offers peer-to-peer and server-based networking for both NT and Windows for Workgroups workstations. If you install Windows NT Advanced Server, which provides support for Macs, management tools for large networks, and a few other goodies, NT could be a practical alternative to *NetWare*. But it's still too early to tell. Microsoft's previous stab at competing with Novell was a major flop, so don't bet your business on NT quite yet.

DANGER

You should be aware of two other server NOSs just so some fast-talking consultant doesn't talk you into something you'll regret. A distant runner-up to *NetWare*, *OS/2 LAN Server* is a weak product used almost exclusively by large IBM customers. Banyan's *Vines* has a cult following in large corporations, but the company now seems to be concentrating on selling enhancements to other NOSs rather than promoting its own.

Picking the Right NOS

REMEMBER

LANtastic or a competing peer-to-peer NOS is the best choice for a small LAN when you only need to exchange E-mail and share documents and printers, not applications and databases. *NetWare* is the NOS of choice for large LANs or when you need top

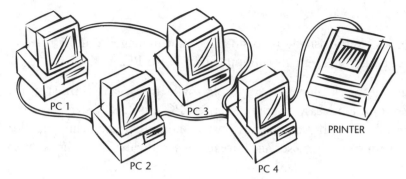

Figure 7: Peer-to-peer LAN
In a peer-to-peer network, people can share their applications, data, or hardware easily. For example, PC #1 could open a word processing document stored on PC #3's hard drive, and print it on PC #4's printer. PC #2 could use a copy of Excel stored on #1's hard drive...and so on.

performance from a multiuser database. If you need the performance of *NetWare* and the flexibility of peer-to-peer file sharing, you can get both by installing *NetWare* on the server and *LANtastic for NetWare* or Windows for Workgroups on workstations.

To help you make the right decision, here's a quick rundown of the key differences between the peer-to-peer NOSs and *NetWare:*

Installation

At each workstation on a peer-to-peer LAN, you run a setup utility and spend a few minutes swapping disks, just like installing any other application. That's no big deal if you've got a dozen workstations, but when you have 50 or more, software upgrades become a major time-waster.

NetWare is one of the most difficult pieces of PC software to install, since getting it up and running properly often involves making obscure changes to NOS defaults and installing bug fixes downloaded from Novell's bulletin board. Don't try this one at home.

DANGER

Figure 8: Server-based LAN
In server-based networks (which are usually NetWare LANs), a dedicated server holds the applications and data people need to share. For workstations to access each others' hard disks and printers, you need to run peer-to-peer network software (such as LANtastic) along with NetWare.

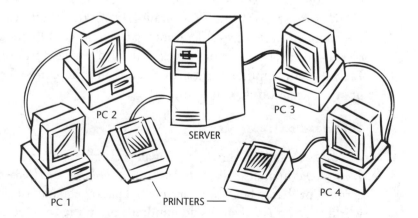

Administration

Peer-to-peer workstations must usually be configured and managed one by one, so adding new users or services often entails running from PC to PC.

NetWare's centralized network management tools make network administration efficient, but that doesn't mean it's easy. Even the sharpest PC user faces a steep learning curve. To handle the job, most big companies hire an administrator, while smaller companies often hire a consultant or a service bureau—a significant, ongoing expense either way.

Large Networks

NetWare's installation and management advantages make it a better choice for larger LANs. It's impossible to pinpoint the exact number of workstations, but if your LAN is so big somebody is spending half of his or her time managing it, you're probably better off with *NetWare* and a professional to maintain it.

LANtastic and other peer-to-peer LANs now offer *NetWare*-style management and installation tools, but if you're setting up a complicated LAN, you'll find it much easier to get training, consultants, and experienced network managers if you go with *NetWare*.

Performance

For top database and file server performance, you want *NetWare*. Lab tests consistently find *NetWare* faster than both its peer-to-peer and server-based competitors.

Connectivity

While the peer NOSs are strictly for DOS and Windows, *NetWare* also links Macs, UNIX workstations, and PCs running OS/2. (*LANtastic* can hook Macs and PCs, but the connection requires a dedicated gateway server.) Beyond that, there are thousands of add-ons available from Novell and third parties to hook *NetWare* LANs to other LANs, minicomputers, and mainframes, plus there are a battery of utilities for backup, troubleshooting, and so on.

Software Extras

LANtastic includes a very basic E-mail package and a remote control utility. *Windows for Workgroups* includes *Microsoft Mail* and *Schedule+*. *NetWare* comes with no such applications, probably because every E-mail package, database, and group scheduler in the world runs on *NetWare*, as do hundreds of utilities that add to the NOS's capabilities.

Network Installation

If you've decided that *NetWare* is the NOS for you, leave installation in the hands of an experienced consultant or dealer.

On the other hand, if you can install an internal modem, you can probably install a peer-to-peer NOS, although it may take a week or two of fiddling before everything runs smoothly. Expect to encounter problems that require vendor tech support, so don't assume you'll be able to accomplish anything when tech support is closed. Generally, that's weekdays after 5 p.m. and on weekends, exactly when you'd prefer to minimize disruptions—another reason to contract out the job.

HOT TIP

The trickiest part of most installations is the cabling. If you're networking several PCs in the same room and you don't mind a few wires running along the floor, go ahead and do it yourself. But if you're hooking up a whole building, need to run cables through walls, or want to hide the wires for aesthetic reasons, hire a professional. In that case, you might as well contract out the whole job.

REMEMBER

Network Hardware

If you plan to do your own installation, you need to know your way around network hardware. That means learning about network interface boards, cables, and possibly hubs (boxes that connect a bunch of cables together, kind of like a multioutlet power strip).

The Wireless Option

Wouldn't it be great to avoid running cable entirely? Well, you can, thanks to adapter boards that hook up to wireless transmitters and receivers instead of cable. The problem is, wireless LANs are comparatively slow and expensive, and you can actually crash some of them with a paper airplane.

Adapters that use *infrared light* are strictly line-of-sight—even a cloth cubicle divider will block transmission. *Low-power microwave* adapters have a range of about 120 feet and can sometimes penetrate drywall, but concrete stops 'em cold. *Spread-spectrum* adapters can penetrate almost any part of a building except steel-reinforced concrete (floors and some walls) and have a range of 100 to 800 feet, depending on how many walls are in the way.

So far, wireless adapters have proven cost-effective only in unusual situations, like older or landmark buildings where laying cable would be difficult and expensive, or in situations where the computers on the LAN are constantly being moved to new locations.

Ethernet or Bust

The first decision you need to make is barely a decision at all. You have an easy choice of network communications standards when you shop for hardware: Ethernet or everything else. Don't hesitate. Except in rare circumstances, you should go with Ethernet hardware. You'll enjoy the widest selection of boards and other devices, along with an abundance of support and service options.

HOT TIP

REMEMBER

Along with running cable, you'll need to install an Ethernet adapter card in every PC you want to network. Major manufacturers of Ethernet boards include 3Com, Intel, Novell/Eagle, and Standard Microsystems/Western Digital (SMC). If you have systems with Micro Channel or EISA slots, note that 16-bit Ethernet cards are all you need

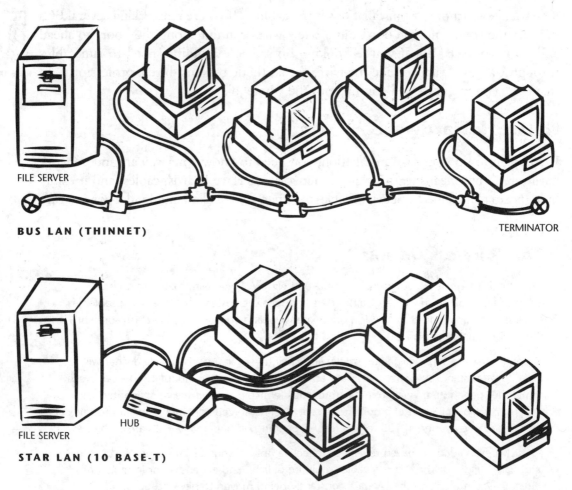

Figure 9: Bus vs. star topology. *When a cable breaks, all the PCs on a thinnet LAN cable (top) lose contact with the server. If a cable connecting a PC to the 10 Base-T hub (bottom) breaks, only that one PC will lose access to the server.*

PC to Mac and Back—Without a Net

If you don't have a network or if it's too much trouble to hook a couple of Macs to a PC LAN, PCs and Macs can still share files. For one thing, any Mac that can handle 1.44MB disks can read DOS disks.

Unfortunately, when you pop a DOS disk in a Mac, the Mac acts it as if it were a new, unformatted disk. To copy those DOS files to the Mac's hard disk, you need an unfriendly utility called Apple File Exchange (AFE). First, make sure AFE is on the hard disk. (If not, you'll find it on the System 7 Tidbits disk or the System 6 System Additions disk.) Then follow these three steps:

1. Launch AFE *before* inserting the DOS disk.

2. For plain ASCII files, choose Text Translation from the MS-DOS to Mac menu; for other files (including text in word processor format), choose Default Translation instead.

3. The Mac won't know what application created the file, so you won't be able to open it by double-clicking its icon. Instead, launch an application that can open or import the file (for example, *Excel for the Mac* for an *Excel for Windows* file) and use the File Open command.

This whole procedure can be avoided with a DOS disk-mounting utility like Insignia's *Access PC*, which makes DOS disks appear on the Mac's desktop, just like Mac disks.

So how do you get a 1.44MB PC floppy drive to read a Mac disk? Pick up a copy of Insignia's *MacDisk* (for DOS) or *MacDisk for Windows*, either of which enable you to read, write, and format Mac disks on your PC.

for workstations—there's no reason to spend the extra money for 32-bit cards except in EISA or Micro Channel servers.

Cable Wars: 10 Base-T vs. Thinnet

Ethernet cards come in two common varieties: those with jacks for *unshielded twisted-pair Ethernet* (also known as *10 Base-T*) cable and those with connectors for *thin coaxial Ethernet* (commonly called *thinnet*) cable. 10 Base-T cable resembles the cord that hooks your phone to the wall and uses similar jacks and plugs, while thinnet cable is virtually identical to the cable used to connect your TV to a cable service.

Your choice of cable is important because it determines your network layout. Networks with 10 Base-T cabling cost a little more than thinnet networks, but several advantages make them the best choice:

- **Reliability and troubleshooting.** 10 Base-T networks connect each PC to a central hub (a layout known as "star topology"), so hardware problems usually affect only a single workstation. Thinnet networks connect PCs along a single cable, so cable breaks can disrupt many PCs and make it hard to pinpoint the source of trouble.

- **No loose ends.** 10 Base-T networks don't require "terminators" at the beginning and end of cables, because all cables terminate at the hub. Missing or broken terminators on thinnet LANs can cause a mystifying array of network problems.

- **"Smart" hubs.** In larger 10 Base-T networks, special software lets you use these devices for remote configuration, management, and diagnostics.

Top Ten E-mail Tips

Even compared with word processing, E-mail is probably the easiest application to learn and use. However, using E-mail *well* isn't as simple as it seems. Here are ten tips to get you from novice to expert ASAP:

HOT TIPS

1. **Create folders.** Many people new to E-mail print out all the messages they mean to keep, a silly habit that wastes paper and printer time. Instead, create named "folders" to store and organize your messages, something all major E-mail packages enable you to do.

2. **Manage your messages.** Don't let more than one screenful of messages accumulate in your in-box. Once you've read a message, delete it or store it in the appropriate folder. If you're too busy to read junk mail, move it to a "To read" folder.

3. **Stay cool.** Don't write a message in the heat of anger. Stop and think: Would you say this to the person's face? Would you print out the message and leave it on the recipient's desk?

4. **Think before you address.** Be careful when you use mailing lists or reply to messages with many addressees. If the "Everyone" list includes people at other branch offices, do they really want to know that the blood bank truck is in the parking lot?

5. **Blind copy.** If you want to send a query to a number of people but want the responses to go only to you, use "bcc" (for "blind carbon copy") instead of "to" when addressing the message. The recipient can only reply to you, because that's the only name he or she will see. Great for party invitations.

6. **Make the subject clear.** Use descriptive headers for your messages. Instead of vague phrases like "A question" or "FYI," be specific: "Q1 figures ready yet?" or "FYI: laser printer out of service."

7. **What was the question?** Don't be too terse. If someone asks you a question by E-mail and you answer it a day later, a simple "yes" or "no" response may be incomprehensible. What was the question?

8. **Combine brief messages.** Everyone gets too many messages. So a whole message containing nothing but polite remarks ("Thanks," etc.) may not be appreciated. Try and fold them into a later message instead. ("Thanks for arranging today's meeting. Who's coming from your department?")

9. **Edit replies to group messages.** Group E-mail "discussions" can get confusing. Usually, a brief message copied to several people gets the ball rolling. Then each participant adds comments, until everyone has to scroll through one huge message to reach the latest comment at the end. Instead of adding to the mess, try copying only a few relevant portions from earlier messages and leave out the rest when you add your two cents.

10. **Compress file attachments.** When you send large files by modem (either because you're working on your home PC or laptop or sending to someone who is), compress the files with PKZip before attaching them to the E-mail message. This reduces connect time to a minimum. (For more on *PKZip*, see the "Shareware and Freeware Utilities" section of Chapter 21: *Utilities*.)

A Brief Guide to Guerrilla Networking

If you work in a company where a *NetWare* LAN is already in place, adding peer-to-peer capabilities for your own workgroup seems relatively simple. All you need to do is install *LANtastic for NetWare, Windows for Workgroups*, or some other peer-to-peer NOS on top, right?

Wrong. It's a bad idea to mess with LAN software without the cooperation of network administrators. Unfortunately, they probably won't want the extra work of managing your peer LAN. You may protest that you can manage it yourself, but the administrators will probably argue that you'll mess things up and they'll end up having to bail you out.

DANGER

They're probably right, too. Peer-to-peer installation utilities can change settings in some network boards, which may suddenly disconnect you from *NetWare*. Or after you install the peer software you may not have enough RAM left to run all your applications. Or the peer network may mess up some of your network drive mappings, and suddenly you'll be unable to access applications or databases on the *NetWare* server. Or...a host of other problems may await you. Are you capable of troubleshooting and resolving them on your own?

Network Support Resources

Finding good network support at a reasonable price can be difficult. If a consultant set up your network and then went out of business (an unfortunately common occurrence), you may not even know where to start looking. Here are a number of support options for the most popular NOSs. In general, you get the most for your money on line, where you benefit not only from the knowledge of the company's support staff but also from knowledgeable users as well.

LANtastic

Live phone support:
602/293-6363
900/555-8324
(immediate response)

Automated phone support:
602/884-1397

Phone support: 602/293-6363

BBS: 602/884-8648

CompuServe: go artisoft

NetWare

Phone support:
800/638-9273 (800/NETWARE),
801/429-5588

Referral to on-site support or
training in your area:
800/338-6272

CompuServe:
go ndsg (*NetWare Lite*),

go netw2x (*NetWare* 2.x)
go netw3x (*NetWare* 3.x)
go novlib (download files)

Usenet: comp.sys.novell

User groups and newsletters:
NetWare Users International
(run by Novell)
800/224-4684
801/429-7000
Affiliation of NetWare Users
(independent)
617/859-0859

Windows for Workgroups

Live phone support:
206/637-7098
(initial 90-day free support)
800/936-5700
(prepaid or credit card)
900/555-2000

Automated phone support:
800/936-4200

BBS: 206/936-6735
(download files)

CompuServe:
go mswrkg (support)
go mskb (support database)
go msl (download files)

America Online:
keyword "knowledge base"
(support database)

Usenet:
comp.os.ms-windows.misc

Internet: anonymous ftp to
ftp.microsoft.com
(IP address 131.107.1.11)
user login, "anonymous"
password, your Internet
E-mail address

Product Directory

Access PC
MacDisk
MacDisk for Windows
Insignia Solutions, Inc.
1300 Charleston Rd.
Mountain View, CA 94043
800/848-7677
415/694-7600

cc:Mail
Lotus Development Corp.
800 El Camino Real
Mountain View, CA 94041
800/448-2500
415/961-8800

Close-Up
Norton-Lambert Corp.
P.O. Box 4085
Santa Barbara, CA 93140
805/964-6767

LANtastic
LANtastic for NetWare
Artisoft, Inc.
2202 N. Forbes Blvd.
Tucson, AZ 85745
800/610-0001
602/670-7100

Lotus Notes
Lotus Development Corp.
55 Cambridge Pkwy.
Cambridge, MA 02142
800/346-1305
617/577-8500

NetPort II Print Server
Intel Corp.
5200 N.E. Elam Young Pkwy.
Hillsboro, OR 97124
800/538-3373
503/629-7354

NetWare
NetWare Lite
NetWare Access Server
Novell, Inc.
122 East 1700 South
Provo, UT 84606
800/453-1267
801/429-7000

PS-Print
Brightwork Development, Inc.
766 Shrewsbury Ave.
Tinton Falls, NJ 07724
800/552-9876
908/530-0440

Remote2
Digital Communications
Associates, Inc.
1000 Alderman Dr.
Alpharetta, GA 30202
800/348-3221
404/442-4000

Windows for Workgroups
Windows NT
Windows NT
Advanced Server
Microsoft Corp.
One Microsoft Way
Redmond, WA 98052
800/426-9400
206/882-8080

WordPerfect Office
WordPerfect Corp.
1555 N. Technology Way
Orem, UT 84057
800/526-5198
801/225-5000

23 | Multimedia

By Robert Lauriston

- What multimedia really is—and whether you need it
- How to buy a sound board for games or music
- Desktop video for professional productions
- Programs for developing multimedia applications

"Multimedia" isn't a straightforward term like "word processor" or "spreadsheet." It applies to a bunch of applications, lumped together because they use special hardware to extend the audio and/or video capabilities of a standard PC. Companies that make this hardware spend lots of money trying to convince us we all need microphones and TV cameras hooked to our PCs.

Don't believe the hype. Before you rush out and buy a bunch of multimedia hardware, you should have a good idea of what it can and can't do and whether you need or want its capabilities. It all depends on which applications catch your interest. Here's some of the possibilities:

- **Playing games** and running educational applications that provide music, sound effects, photographic images, and animation. Often this software comes on CD ROM instead of floppies, so there's room for rich backgrounds, colorful animated characters, and even digitized video clips (see Chapter 25: *Entertainment, Etc.*).

- **Spicing up Windows** by tying squawks, chimes, bits of movie soundtracks, and other sound effects to "events"—such as starting Windows or making a wrong move in an application. To enter commands, some people also use the toylike voice recognition software that comes with many sound boards.

- **Attaching voice messages** to documents or E-mail. Recipients click on the message icon to hear the recorded note. (This sounds like fun, until you realize that a one-paragraph message can occupy a couple of megabytes.)

- **Composing and playing music** with a synthesizer hooked to your PC's sound board using MIDI (Musical Instrument Digital Interface) hardware. With *sequencing* software you can compose music, choose synthetic instruments, change pitch, edit others' compositions, print out scores to be played by conventional instruments, and so on.

- **Producing videos** either for playback on PCs or for transfer to videotape. This ranges from jerky video clips in a little window to professional, computer-assisted videotape production.

- **Running interactive training and presentation software,** which can include animation, narration, and video sequences. Training materials usually come on CD ROM or laser disk, while simple presentations that include sound are often created and run on the same PC.

- **"Authoring,"** that is, *producing* your own interactive training materials, multimedia presentations, or educational software, or special-purpose applications like touchscreen "kioskware" for museums or trade shows (see the end of this chapter for more on authoring software).

In the real world, the vast majority of people encounter multimedia through games or educational software for kids. Authoring interactive applications, producing desktop video, and running laser training disks all require hardware so expensive, only developers, media professionals, and people with unusual instructional needs (such as ongoing training for large-scale manufacturing) are willing to make the investment.

Voice messaging, adding sound effects to Windows, and other fun activities require only a sound board and speakers (which together should cost you only a couple hundred bucks), but you'll also need a CD ROM drive if you want to play enhanced games. The following chart gives you an idea of the hardware you'd need for each of the basic multimedia applications.

Figure 1 (right): *The hardware you need all depends on your application. A basic multimedia PC with a CD ROM drive and sound costs a few hundred dollars more than an ordinary PC, while an authoring system could cost $20,000.*

Multimedia Hardware Guide

	Enhanced games	Voice notes and Windows sound effects	MIDI sequencing	Digital video playback	Digital video production	Running interactive multi-media	Authoring
System (1)							
Fast 486 or Pentium	p		p	p	x	p	x
Windows	o	x	p	p	x	o	x
8MB RAM	p	p	p	p	x	p	x
16MB RAM			p	p	p		p
Local bus	p			p	p	p	p
Storage (2)							
Huge hard disk		p		p	x		x
CD ROM drive	p				o	p	x
CD ROM recorder							o
DAT or optical drive					o		p
Sound							
Basic sound board	x	x				x	
High-quality sound board	p	p		x	x	p	x
Wavetable sound board or external MIDI devices	o		x			o	p
MIDI interface			x		o	o	o
Speakers	x	x	x	x	x	x	x
Microphone		x			x		x
Video (3)							
256-color VGA	x			x	x	p	x
True-color super-VGA				o	p		p
Video capture board					x		o
Hardware decompression				p	p	p	o
Video overlay board					o	o	o
Videotape recorder					o		o
Laser disk player						o	o

o = optional p = preferred x = usually required
1) See Chapter 2 for more on CPUs, memory, and buses.
2) See Chapter 4 for more on hard disks, CD ROM players, and other storage.
3) See Chapter 5 for more on graphics hardware.

Sound Hardware

Since your PC already has video, sound is really the "multi" in multimedia. Despite manufacturer rhetoric about "business audio" (who needs an E-mail message that croons, "Stop by my office, Bob"?), most people use sound boards for entertainment. Games are more engrossing when spiced up with good sound effects and music, and you can add some comic relief to your daily drudgery by replacing your PC's boring system beep with something more evocative. On my system, various Windows alerts trigger the theme from Psycho, Bevis and Butt-Head's creepy laughter, and Homer Simpson shouting, "d'oh!"

Choosing a Sound Board

Companies make choosing the right sound board difficult by burying the important facts in fine print on the back of the box. Prices range from under $50 to over $500 in stores, so it's worth knowing what you're buying.

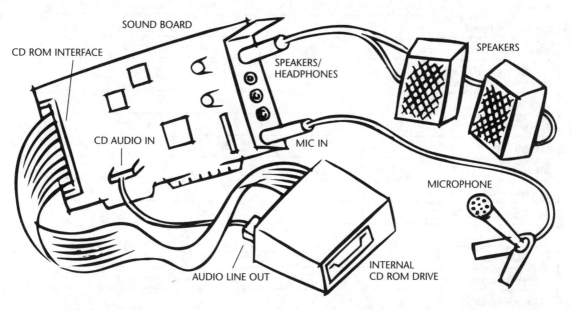

Figure 2: Sound connections. Here's how you hook up a typical sound board to a microphone, speakers, and CD ROM drive. If you don't want everyone to hear your game sound effects, substitute a pair of headphones for speakers.

Sound Quality

Sampling is the key to sound board audio quality. It's the method sound boards use to digitize audio signals from a microphone or other source. As it records, the board measures, or samples, microphone or line input thousands of times a second, producing digital values that describe the audio waveform. During playback, the board uses those values to approximate the original sound. The more data sampled per second, the better the digital sound quality.

What's All This About "CD Quality"?

The term "CD-quality sound" is often abused. Strictly speaking, it refers to 16-bit stereo with a sampling rate of 44.1 KHz, specs that only boards retailing for $200 and up generally offer. Note also that audio CD players have much better electronics than do PC sound boards or CD ROM drives. So when you play back CD-quality digital audio files or audio CD disks on your PC's CD ROM drive, the sound won't be as good as that produced by your stereo.

- **Sampling rate** is the number of times per second a board samples the incoming audio signal. Common sampling rates range from 2 KHz (lousy) to 48 KHz (excellent). Sound boards generally handle several different sampling rates and may be able to play back samples at higher rates than they can record them.

- **Sampling resolution** is the number of bits per sample. Sample resolution is either 8-bit, adequate for speech and crude sound effects, or 16-bit, which is not twice but 256 times the resolution of 8-bit. (Note: Don't confuse sampling resolution with the type of slot a board uses, which is also either 16 bit or 8 bit. The latter has no direct bearing on sound quality.)

REMEMBER

Most boards give you a choice between stereo and mono recording or playback. Read sampling specs carefully, because vendors often promote the mono sampling rate, which is twice that of stereo mode.

REMEMBER

Figure 3: Turning sound into numbers. The sampling resolution (vertical) and sampling rate (horizontal) determine sound quality. The more data sampled per second, the more the digital recording will sound like the original.

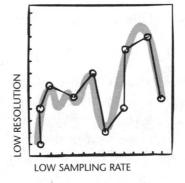

LOW RESOLUTION

LOW SAMPLING RATE

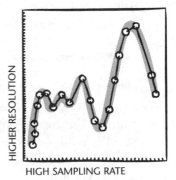

HIGHER RESOLUTION

HIGH SAMPLING RATE

How to Record a Windows Voice Note

Adding a voice note to a Windows document is easy, though the exact procedure varies depending on the application you're using to create or edit the document. Here are the basic steps using Sound Recorder, which comes with Windows:

1. Find your application's Sound option and click on it. (Some likely locations: on the Insert menu, on a scrolling list under Insert/Object, or under Insert/Object on the Edit menu.)

2. Click the microphone button (or press the spacebar) to start recording, and say your piece into the mike attached to your sound board.

3. Click the Stop button when you're through. Then close Sound Recorder and answer "Yes" to embed your sound in the document.

4. To play the sound, just double-click the microphone icon in the document.

While it's kind of fun to insert sounds in documents, it's not really a practical way to communicate. Sound files take two or three thousand times as much disk space as the same message in text, and you can't skim them or print them.

Figure 4: *With most sound boards, you use Windows' Sound Recorder utility (or a similar program) when you want to insert a voice note in a document. The buttons work just like those on an ordinary tape deck.*

Almost every board includes audio compression, which saves disk space but usually at some cost to sound quality. Due to the lack of a universal compression standard, commercial and shareware sound files are almost always distributed uncompressed.

CD ROM Hookup

Have you already installed a CD ROM drive? If not, and you have room enough for an internal one, choose a sound board with a built-in CD ROM interface and save yourself the cost of buying a separate interface with the drive. Look for a board that's SCSI II compatible, or you'll have little or no choice of drives. For example, most of the boards in Creative Labs' Sound Blaster series work only with the company's own CD ROM drives.

Whether or not your board has a CD ROM interface, you'll need to run a supplied cable between the drive's line out and the board's line in. This CD-audio connection is important but easy to overlook. It enables you to play standard audio CDs on your PC along with games and other software that use audio directly from the drive.

REMEMBER

Synthesizer

Sound boards commonly have a built-in MIDI synthesizer for playing music and synthesized sound effects. This synthesizer is usually pretty primitive—games use it to play MIDI files containing theme music, explosions, and so on. But MIDI is also a standard for connecting instruments to computers. If your board has a *MIDI port* (or you buy an external *MIDI breakout box*) you can plug in an external MIDI keyboard (such as those made by Yahama), play or compose a tune, and store it on your PC's hard disk in a file. There, you can edit the tune to make it sound like anything you want using one of many music sequencing programs on the market.

- **The number of voices** a synthesizer has indicates how many different notes it can play at once. Generally, most or all of these voices can be different sounds, so if set up properly, the synthesizer can act as a sort of band in a box. The typical sound board has 20 voices, more than enough for games.

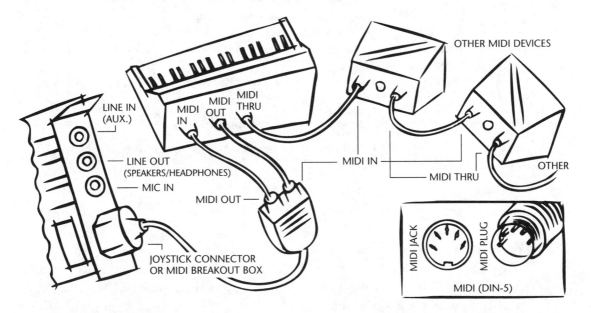

Figure 5: MIDI music hookups. *You hook your sound or MIDI interface board to your synthesizer with a pair of MIDI cables. Connect the board's MIDI Out to the instrument's MIDI In, and vice versa. If the instrument has a combination MIDI Out/Thru jack, set it to Out mode to avoid feedback.*

A Quick Guide to Music Software

Hooked together, a MIDI-compatible instrument and sound board open up a whole new world to musicians, professional and amateur alike. Here's a quick look at the main kinds of music software available.

- **Sequencers** turn your PC into the MIDI equivalent of a multitrack recording studio. Composers can create music for whole orchestras just by layering different voices for each instrument's part, one on top of the other. And because MIDI files contain descriptions of notes—volume, pitch, voice, duration—instead of actual recorded sound, they take up much less space than digital audio files do.

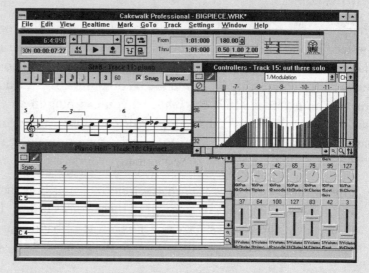

Figure 6: MIDI sequencers like Cakewalk Pro let you use your PC to record, edit, and play back music.

- **Sample editors** let you play with sampled sounds to make them sound better and more realistic, snipping out silences or noise, defining which section of a sound will be "looped" to create a sustained tone, and so on.

- **Patch editors** let you create or modify synthesizer sounds.

- **Librarians** organize hundreds or thousands of patches and/or samples stored on your hard drive.

- **Notation** programs turn MIDI data into sheet music.

- **Wavetable or ROM samples** are digital recordings of real instruments. They replace the cheesy synthesizer sounds that come with most sound boards. In some cases, these samples are identical to those used in the E-mu and Kurzweil keyboards used by professional musicians, and often they come as separate boards or add-on modules.

However, you don't need a fancy professional keyboard to mess around with music on your PC—Casio keyboards sold in department stores often have MIDI jacks. You don't even need to learn to play keyboards, since Casio also makes inexpensive, MIDI-equipped guitars and saxophones.

HOT TIP

Hardware and Software Extras

Sound boards frequently come with a microphone along with a pair of headphones and/or small speakers. Often they're just junk—you'd be better off buying your own at Radio Shack or a stereo store. Don't let a load of hardware extras determine which board you buy.

HOT TIP

The software extras can be more valuable, depending on what you plan to do:

- **Sound editors, mixers, and embedders.** Basically, these are improved versions of the sound utilities that already come with Windows. If you plan on recording voice notes or mixing music, sound effects, and recorded speech, this software can make such pursuits more fun.

- **Voice recognition.** Don't get excited—we're not talking dictation here. With a few popular applications you can voice-navigate menus, enter numeric data, and make simple edits. If you speak loudly, clearly, and slowly, it works fine—if you don't mind repeating yourself a few times.

- **Text to speech.** This ranges from a Stephen Hawking–like monotone to an actual recorded voice stringing words together like the 411 lady. Boards such as Microsoft's Windows Sound System feature the latter, so *Excel* can help verify a column of figures by reading it out loud. Impressive, huh?

- **Authoring.** Don't be fooled. The best authoring packages cost too much to be bundled with sound boards. The ones that are turn out to be toylike or too difficult to use.

- **Music sequencing.** Some higher-end boards, including some manufactured by Turtle Beach and Media Vision, come with good Windows-based sequencing software. You probably wouldn't want to use the rest.

The ultimate bundle is the *multimedia upgrade kit*, which is a sound board and CD ROM drive in one box. These kits can save you money, but check the specs carefully and price the components separately to make sure. Often such kits are bundled with a stack of CD ROM disks, which—based on wildly inflated list prices—the vendor may describe as worth $100 to $200 each. However, in most cases you can buy those disks for $25 to $40, and few are worth even that much.

Sound Board Compatibility

Which standards your board supports determines the software it can run. Here are the most important ones:

- **AdLib and Sound Blaster.** Many older DOS games support only these two sound boards, top sellers in the pre-Windows era. To enjoy those games' enhanced sound, you'll need a board that's compatible with one or the other. Almost all games and boards are Sound Blaster compatible.

HOT TIP

- **MPC.** The MPC (Multimedia PC) and MPC2 standards are two sets of minimum multimedia system requirements for Windows apps. The MPC or MPC2 logo on a piece of Windows software tells you the program will run with a sound board offering those specs or better, but it may also run on a sound board with worse specs. Read the fine print to find out exactly what hardware is required.

- **General MIDI.** If you plan to run games or play synthesized music, make sure you have general MIDI compatibility. Without it, you may end up with a crazy-sounding mess, the snare drum playing the clarinet part, a fuzz guitar playing the flute line, and so on.

- **Qsound.** This is a patented technique for creating 3-D surround effects in stereo recordings. Sound boards that offer it can make sounds seem to whiz around (or through!) your head. At the moment, most boards lack Qsound capabilities, so few games support it, but it's such cool technology it might catch on.

What MPC and MPC2 Really Mean

	MPC minimum requirements	MPC2 minimum requirements
CPU	386SX-20	486SX-25
Memory	2MB	4MB
Hard drive	30MB	160MB
Sample playback quality	22.05-KHz 8-bit mono	44.1-KHz 16-bit mono
Sample recording quality	11.025-KHz 8-bit mono	44.1-KHz 16-bit mono
Synthesizer	8-voice mono, General MIDI	8-voice mono, General MIDI
MIDI in/out	Yes	Yes
CD ROM sustained transfer	150Kbps	300Kbps
Read multisession PhotoCD	N/A	Yes
Video	640x480 resolution, 256 colors	640x480 resolution, 65,536 colors
Digital video playback	N/A	320x240 resolution, 15 frames per second

Figure 7: *The MPC or MPC2 logo on a software package is mostly hype. All it means is that the program will run on a Windows PC that has those specs, but a less powerful system may also do the trick. And the basic MPC spec is a joke: 8-bit sound is dreadful for music, and Windows itself is barely usable with a 386SX CPU, 4MB of RAM, and a 30MB hard drive.*

Desktop Video (DTV)

"Desktop video" is a catch-all term that applies to a panoply of software and hardware. At the low end, DTV can be as simple as playing back digitized video sequences from a CD ROM–based game. At the high end, DTV can be a professional videotape editing system based on an array of special video boards and peripherals worth $100,000 or more.

Playing Around With DTV

A sound board and a super-VGA adapter that supports 256 colors are all the hardware you need to play desktop video files on your Windows PC, although you'll probably want a CD ROM drive as well—video files are usually too large to fit on floppy disks. The only other requirement is a copy of Microsoft's *Video for Windows*, which comes free with Windows CD ROMs that include digitized video files. You can also fire up the modem and download *Video for Windows* with sample video files from Microsoft's Windows Multimedia forum on CompuServe (go winmm, library 4).

Video for Windows files have the extension AVI (for Audio-Video Interleaved, if you're interested). AVI is the definitive standard for PC motion video. A few vendors use their own motion video formats, and products that originated on the Mac sometimes use Apple's *QuickTime for Windows*, but you shouldn't need to worry about it. Such programs will either supply *Video for Windows* drivers or include their own software player.

Figure 8: *Video for Windows includes Windows' Media Player, which is all you really need to play digital video on your PC.*

Putting DTV to Work

If you want to do more than play back canned video sequences, you'll need a special video board. Here are the key capabilities of the products currently on the market. Frequently, a single board will include several of these functions.

TV to Hard Disk

Don't get rid of your VCR just yet. One second of grainy, jerky AVI video in a little window occupies 150K. Approach videotape quality, and you're talking 10 or 20 *megabytes* per second. And multimedia companies talk about zapping around personal "video notes" by E-mail? Well, maybe next century. In the meantime, turning camera or VCR output into digital video is only for a handful of specialized applications. And now, the devices that make it possible:

• **Video capture boards** let you create your own AVI files using a video camera, VCR, or other source. There's a serious trade-off between price and quality—inexpensive capture boards can record only 1/16- or 1/4-screen images at low frame rates, while a board that can capture full-screen, full-motion images may cost as much as your PC. (An alternative to buying an expensive capture board is to send videotapes to a service bureau for conversion to digital video files.) The low-end video might end up in a desktop presentation, while the high-end stuff could be used for an interactive training application or even a professional video production.

- **Frame grabbers** let you copy a single frame from a video signal and then paste it into a graphics or page layout program. This is a handy feature for desktop publishers, who can use it to grab illustrations from camcorder tapes, eliminating the cost and delays involved in processing and scanning film. Not magazine-quality, but fine for company newsletters and the like.

TV to Monitor

Two types of boards let you send TV signals directly to your monitor. The applications for this are limited, but at least you avoid the storage and performance problems of digital video.

> ## "Full-Motion" Video: A Slippery Term
>
> "Full-motion video" refers to digital video files recorded or played back at frame rates fast enough to keep the motion from looking jerky—about 12 to 15 frames per second or faster. Some hardware and software vendors use the term to refer to digital video with lower frame rates, for which "motion video" would be a more appropriate term. Video overlay boards are occasionally presented as full-motion, which is flat-out dishonest.
>
> You can play full-motion video on any standard super-VGA board, but the limited bandwidth of the ISA bus means the video window is the size of a couple of postage stamps. For larger video displays, you need an EISA or VL-bus video board, local-bus video built into the motherboard, or a special full-motion video board (see Chapter 2: *How to Buy a PC* for more on bus types).

- **Video overlay** boards let you patch in output from a TV, VCR, or laser disk player and send it directly to a window on your PC's screen. CNN on the PC is only one possibility. For example, you might use a video overlay board in a serious training application, where the software would call up instructional video clips from a laser disk player connected to the PC's serial port.

- **TV tuner** boards have only one purpose: to let you watch broadcast or cable TV on your monitor (say, the running ticker tape on the Financial News Network, or maybe Geraldo) without needing an external TV tuner. They plug into your super-VGA board's feature connector or hook to a video overlay board.

PC to TV

The size of video files makes distributing them a problem. You can spend big bucks and master your own CD ROM, or you can buy a board that turns your digital video production into *NTSC output*, which you can then record on a VCR and distribute on videocassette. Many DTV boards have NTSC outputs, but you can also get inexpensive VGA-to-NTSC converter boxes that let you record to videotape from any video board.

HOT TIP

Video Compression

Filling the PC's screen with full-motion digital video presents special storage problems. To achieve the kind of quality you're used to from videotape, you need VGA resolution (640 by 480) with millions of colors, running at 30 frames per second. This results in a data stream of over 25 megabytes per second, well beyond your hard disk's maximum transfer rate.

That's where compression comes in. In fact, due to digital video's hefty disk requirements, even small-size, low-frame-rate sequences are normally stored compressed. Microsoft's *Video for Windows* player includes three standard decompression *drivers*, which are small programs that expand files compressed by one of these compression methods:

- **Microsoft RLE** is useful mostly for computer-generated animation sequences. With images that have large blocks of solid colors, it can shrink the file size by 80 percent or more, with no degradation of image quality. Since no data is lost in the process, this is called *lossless* compression. Because real-world images don't contain large blocks of pure colors, RLE won't compress captured video very much. Also, Microsoft RLE is limited to 8-bit color (256 colors), not enough for good rendition of video images.

- **Microsoft Video 1** is Microsoft's general-purpose video compression method. On a 486 PC, Video 1 can deliver a small (160-by-120-pixel) image at 15 frames a second in 65,000 colors. Video 1 uses lossy compression—a technique that decreases file size by merging neighboring pixels of different colors into a single color. Like other lossy standards, Video 1 offers a range of compression ratios. Choosing a higher compression ratio merges more pixels and results in a smaller file, but it also results in a lower-quality image.

- **Intel Indeo** is a more powerful compression method that, on a 486 PC, can play back a 320-by-240-pixel image at 15 frames per second in 16.7 million colors. With a compatible hardware decompression board, the Indeo method can deliver a 640-by-480-pixel image at 30 frames per second—better quality than broadcast TV—even on an old, slow 386.

To play video files compressed using other methods, you'll need the appropriate *Video for Windows* driver. In most cases, this will be added automatically when you install a video capture or decompression board, or software that contains video sequences. (You can see which drivers are installed on your system by double-clicking on Drivers in Windows' Control Panel.) Other common compression methods include MPEG and Motion JPEG, SuperMac's Cinepak, Media Vision's Captain Crunch, and Apple's

Quicktime format. Some of these may require hardware decompression boards, particularly on slower PCs.

There are two ways to compress your own video. Most capture boards compress video signals on the fly, straight from camera or VCR to hard drive. This is fast and convenient, but you need a fairly expensive board to capture a full-screen image, and such real-time compression results in huge files. For more efficient compression, the computer needs more number-crunching time—20 seconds or more per frame. If you don't want to tie up your computer for days, video service bureaus can handle this chore in a matter of hours.

DTV Editing Systems

Just as desktop publishing took typesetting out of service bureaus and put it onto the PC, computer-based DTV editing systems are quickly making proprietary video editing decks, title generators, and special effects hardware obsolete. These new PC-based tools are much easier to learn and cost a fraction of what the old hardware did. The result? A continuing explosion in the number of amateur videographers and small businesses rolling their own videotape.

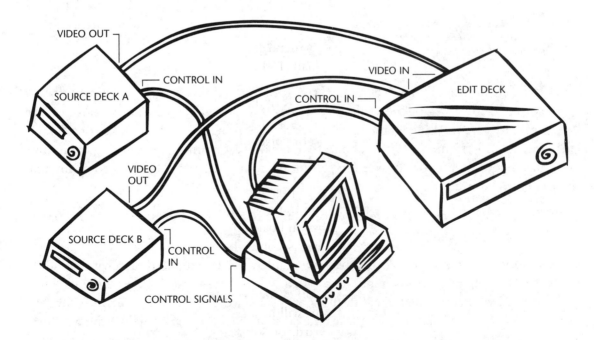

Figure 9: Linear (A-B roll) editing system. *Linear or A-B roll editing systems offer easy, precise control over special video-tape editing decks. These systems are relatively inexpensive, since you don't need special hardware to transfer video to the PC.*

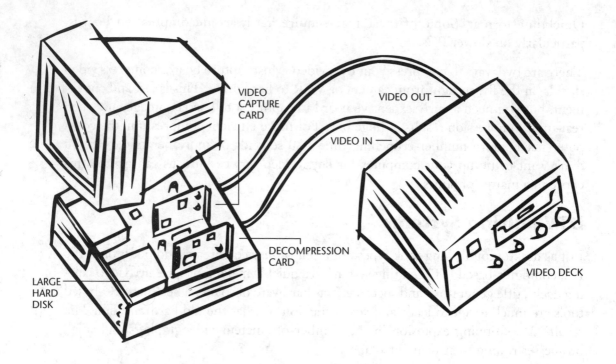

Figure 10: Offline editing system. Off-line nonlinear systems capture video sequences to disk, so you can edit them quickly without rewinding and fast forwarding. When you're finished, the software has the editing decks automatically duplicate your edits on tape.

REMEMBER

Before you rush out and buy a DTV rig, keep in mind that buying equipment doesn't automatically give you the ability to use it right. Just as good typesetting skills can take years to acquire, using a camera, writing scripts, editing, and the like take considerable talent and training. Think about that if you're dreaming of starting your own production house, or considering setting up an in-house facility for a company that used to farm out its video jobs.

DTV editing systems range in price from a few hundred bucks to over $100,000. These days, they group loosely into three categories:

• **Linear** systems are so called because you have to fast-forward or rewind to get to a particular edit in the tape. Also called A-B roll systems, they leave the video on tape, while the video signal displays on a standard TV monitor. The PC's involvement is minimal: Software makes the editing process easier by delivering easy, precise control over special playback and edit decks and (in some products) a special video processing board for adding titles and special effects. Not counting the video decks or PC, A-B roll systems start at under $500, and some don't require any special hardware beyond a serial port. This type of editor is likely to become extinct within the next few years as more sophisticated products drop in price. (A-X roll systems are similar, but they use only one playback deck instead of two.)

- **Off-line nonlinear** systems use a video capture board to store whole video sequences from source tapes on your hard disk. Once the video is on the hard drive, you don't need the video deck (hence *off-line*), and you can jump from one edit to another at will (hence *nonlinear*). You edit on your PC's screen, arranging and cropping the digital video sequences as desired. When you're finished, the software takes a list of the edits you've just done on the digital video sequence and automatically runs the editing decks to duplicate those same edits on the original videotapes—so it doesn't matter if the digitized video is low quality. These systems generally include very sophisticated titling and special effects capabilities.

- **On-line nonlinear** systems are the video equivalent of desktop publishing systems. Videotape is digitized at sufficient quality that editing can be done entirely in the PC and then transferred directly to the final tape. For industrial-quality output, the video capture board needs to do at least 640-by-480 resolution at 30 frames per second; broadcast quality demands even better digitization. Since high-quality digital video files are huge, an on-line system needs at least one and probably several gigabyte-size SCSI drives. Currently these systems cost upwards of $10,000—but then, so did laser printers, once. Within a few years, all video production will be done with on-line nonlinear editors, just as virtually all publishing is now done with page layout software.

Multimedia Authoring Software

Multimedia authoring packages let you combine a variety of digital media to create interactive presentations or training materials for playback from floppy, hard disk, or CD ROM. In one program, you can mix in text, graphics, animation, digitized sound and video clips, and MIDI music soundtracks. The most common uses for authoring packages are:

- **Computer-based training,** including interactive tutorials for businesses, and self-guided programs, study aids, and tests for schools

- **Multimedia presentations** for trade shows, sales presentations, product demos, and the like

- **"Kioskware"** for museums, public agencies, shopping centers, and other busy places, providing the public with self-guided access to maps, catalogs, and other information (often through use of a touch screen)

- **Commercial multimedia development** for software such as the multimedia CD ROM applications currently on the market

Most authoring software includes a *run-time engine*—a playback utility you can pass along to people who don't own the program so they can view your multimedia productions. In some cases you have to pay extra for the run-time engine, either via a one-time charge for an unlimited license to distribute copies or through a per-copy license fee for every disk you distribute.

There are a lot of authoring tools around, and a thorough survey of their capabilities is outside the scope of this book. Here's a brief look at a half-dozen of the authoring packages most popular among PC multimedia pros.

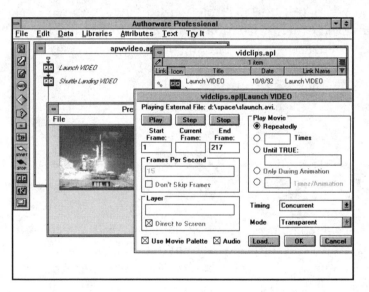

Figure 11: Authorware Professional for Windows. Macromedia's Authorware is an expensive program designed primarily for creating training materials. Its flowchart approach makes it fairly easy for you to create the kind of multiple-choice branching that's essential for self-guided tutorials.

Figure 12: IconAuthor for Windows.
AimTech's IconAuthor for Windows is similar in design, style, and price to Authorware, and it also targets users who plan to design computer-based training materials. The two programs are engaged in one of those "top this" upgrade battles, with the usual benefits of better features and lower prices.

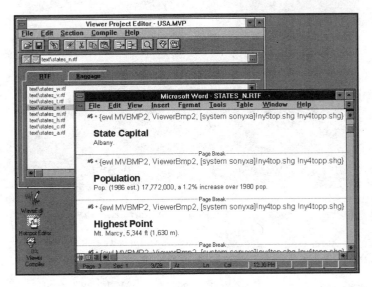

Figure 13: Microsoft Multimedia Viewer. Multimedia Viewer Publishing Toolkit is primarily for converting text documents—such as the Word for Windows document shown here—into on-line references like Microsoft's own Bookshelf, with graphics, sound, and video.

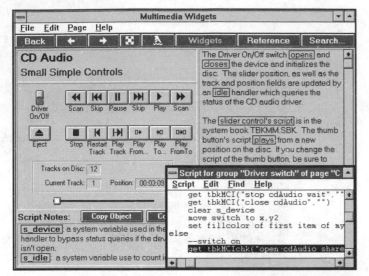

Figure 14: Multimedia ToolBook.
Asymetrix's ToolBook is patterned after the Mac's HyperCard. Like the original, ToolBook tries to make things easy for nonprogrammers. Most design tasks are performed visually, using mouse operations and dialog boxes. When you do need to write code, you do it in an English-like script language.

Figure 15: Multimedia Grasp.
This "kioskware" application was created with Paul Mace's Multimedia Grasp, one of the few PC multimedia tools that doesn't need Windows or a fast 486. That makes it a popular choice for developing multimedia apps for DOS or for older systems with slow CPUs. The downside is that Grasp requires a fair degree of programming skill.

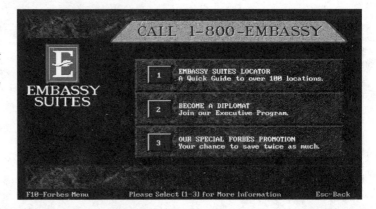

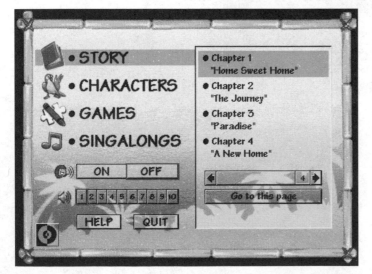

Figure 16: Macromedia Director.
Perhaps the single most popular authoring package is Macromedia Director, which was used to create the kids' application you see here. It combines excellent authoring tools with an equally good animation program. A Windows run-time engine allows you to play back Director productions on a PC.

Product Directory

Sound Cards

Microsoft Windows Sound System
Microsoft Corp.
One Microsoft Way
Redmond, WA 98052-6399
800/426-9400
206/882-8080

MultiSound Monterey
Turtle Beach Systems
P.O. Box 5074
York, PA 17405
800/645-5640
717/767-0200

Pro Audio Spectrum 16
Pro Audio Studio 16
Media Vision, Inc.
3185 Laurelview Ct.
Fremont, CA 94538
800/348-7116
510/770-8600

SoundBlaster 16 ASP
Sound Blaster Pro
Creative Labs, Inc.
1901 McCarthy Blvd.
Milpitas, CA 95035
800/998-5227
408/428-6600

Software

Authorware Professional for Windows
Macromedia Director Windows Player
Macromedia, Inc.
600 Townsend St. #310
San Francisco, CA 94103
800/288-4797
415/252-2000

IconAuthor for Windows
AimTech Corp.
20 Trafalgar Sq.
Nashua, NH 03063-1973
800/289-2884
603/883-0220

Microsoft Multimedia Viewer Publishing Toolkit
Microsoft Video for Windows
Microsoft Corp.
800/426-9400

Multimedia Grasp
Paul Mace Software, Inc.
400 Williamson Way
Ashland, OR 97520
800/944-0191
503/488-2322

Multimedia ToolBook
Asymetrix Corp.
110 110th Ave., NE #700
Bellevue, WA 98004
800/448-6543
206/462-0501

24 | Personal Finance and Tax Software

By Kathy Yakal

- When and how to choose a personal finance program
- The smart way to set up your personal accounts
- Quicken and Managing Your Money reviews and tips
- When to buy a tax program and how to use one

Who would use a powerhouse program like *Quicken,* the hottest-selling personal finance package, just to balance a checkbook?

In fact, few people do. Not many people use tax software to fill out a 1040EZ either—nor should they. Buying a program to help handle your own money makes sense only when investments, depreciation, or a home business become so complicated that you'll actually make life easier by biting the bullet and getting financially organized.

A tax program or a personal finance package won't create that organization for you. But if you take the time to pull your records together and set up some simple procedures, good software can cut the number of evenings and weekends devoted to paperwork, particularly around tax time.

If a CPA already does your books, your financial situation may be too complex for a tax or finance package alone to handle. But even in that case, you might consider using one. At worst, you'll have coherent records, so your CPA won't have to unravel your paperwork—and bill you for doing so. At best, you'll dig in and start creating budgets, turning up new tax deductions, figuring mortgage payments, and even paying bills electronically.

Personal Finance Software

Personal finance software is one of life's little bargains. The three top programs, Intuit's *Quicken*, MECA's *Managing Your Money*, and Computer Associates' *Simply Money*, all sell for well under $50 in stores. All except *Simply Money*, which runs only under Windows, come in both DOS and Windows versions. The packages differ in style and depth, but the core capabilities are so similar most people buy based on personal taste.

These leading programs come with clear instructions and friendly interfaces, so in every case you can learn how to handle bank accounts, credit card accounts, and even a little budgeting in a couple of hours. Teaching yourself how to track loans and

Was That Personal or Professional?

If you run a small business, a personal finance package may not cut it. Personal finance lies at the lowest end of accounting software, which extends to small business accounting and finally to expensive, multimodule packages that can handle businesses with tens of millions in revenue. Consider a higher-end package if you need any of the following:

- Invoicing with aging
- Audit trail
- Order-entry processing
- Multiple security levels
- Multiuser version

- General ledger
- Inventory tracking
- Multidepartment accounting
- Formal financial statements
- Flexible fiscal periods

Small business accounting programs take longer to learn than personal finance software, in part because they adhere more closely to traditional bookkeeping practices (good practices to follow when more than one person will be doing the books). Intuit offers a product in this category called *QuickBooks,* but you'll find a dozen or so worthy competitors from such companies as Peachtree, Computer Associates, and DacEasy. To decide for certain whether you need to step beyond personal finance software, talk to a CPA.

investments or print out custom reports will take a little longer. But that's the point of these easygoing programs—you learn new features as you need them.

If the Shoebox Fits...

Picture what your desk looks like when you pay bills or balance your checkbook. You're probably surrounded by stacks of old checks, receipts, bank statements, scribbled notes, and other miscellaneous slips of paper. You move from statement to checkbook, then to the calculator, then into a file folder or envelope to retrieve something, back to the checkbook, through a stack of old statements, and so on.

Personal finance software keeps all your records in one place. You'll still need to keep your paper documentation (old checks, car payment coupons, receipts, and so on), but once you've entered that information, you'll never have to scramble through junk drawers or shoeboxes again. Instead, you'll have quick access to data you can use for:

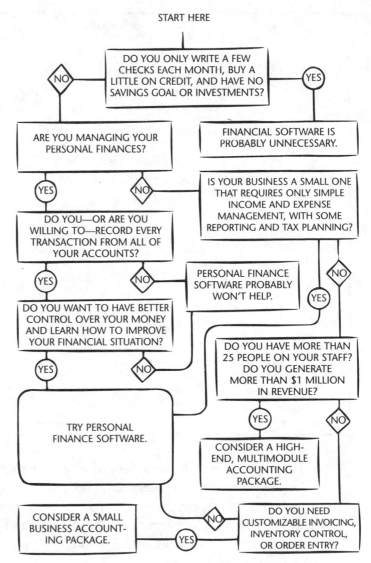

Figure 1 How To Choose Accounting Software: *Personal finance software isn't the only accounting solution. If you have a small business, you may need more; if your finances are simple, you may be better off with a calculator and a yellow pad.*

```
                    Cash Flow Report
                  7/14/94 Through 8/14/94
8/14/94                                                    Page 1
Checking

                                        7/14/94-
         Category Description           8/14/94
                                    ─────────────────
      INFLOWS
        Bonus                              500.00
        Invest Inc                       5,000.00
        Rent Income                        400.00
        Salary                           5,951.58

      TOTAL INFLOWS                      11,851.58

      OUTFLOWS
        Auto:
          Loan              250.00
          Service            55.37
                          ──────────
        Total Auto                         305.37
        Cash                               200.00
        Charity:
          Cash             250.00
                          ──────────
        Total Charity                      250.00
        Child Support                      650.00
        Childcare                          700.00
        Clothing                            89.95
        Groceries                          735.95
        Home Rpair                       2,895.05
        Housing                          1,020.00
        Insurance                          357.95
        Invest Exp                       7,000.00
        Meals & Entertn                    296.84
        Medical:
          Doctor           110.00
          Medicine          35.70
                          ──────────
        Total Medical                      145.70
        Telephone                           45.73
        Utilities:
          Gas & Electric    78.94
                          ──────────
        Total Utilities                     78.94
                                        ──────────
      TOTAL OUTFLOWS                     14,771.48

      OVERALL TOTAL                      -2,919.90
                                        ══════════
```

Figure 2:
Care to see where your money is going? Once you've entered your financial data, you can easily print a statement showing the bad news, as this Quicken report illustrates.

- **Instant reports.** Once you assign categories (such as food, clothing, medical, charitable donations) to transactions, you can quickly run reports that show where all the money is going, get precise income and expense breakdowns, and review any account balance whenever you like. If rows and columns of figures are Greek to you, pour them into charts and graphs.

- **Tax relief.** When tax time rolls around, you won't have to root around records that should have been in order to begin with. Personal finance software encourages you to flag tax-related categories, so you can run summary reports of tax-related transactions that match the order of IRS forms and schedules—or export the data directly to a tax program.

- **Faster bill paying.** Set up lists of regular transactions—the water bill, say, or that nagging credit card payment—and just change the amount when it's time to pay. Create a payment schedule, turn on the reminder feature, and you'll never forget to pay a bill again. If you have a modem, you can pay bills electronically through a service called CheckFree.

Figure 3: *A relatively simple chart can help you get a handle on investments, as this Simply Money graph illustrates.*

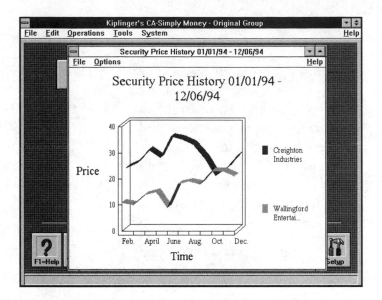

- **Practical budgeting.** Always running out of cash two days before payday? Create a budget based on data from your accounts and get constant updates on how you're adhering to it.

- **Quick account reconciliation.** This dreaded monthly activity is easier, too. You still have to mark the checks that have cleared, but the program makes all the calculations automatically.

- **Investment tracking.** Gauge the performance of stocks, bonds, mutual funds, and more. You may not get full-service advice, but you'll always know the value of your assets, which will enable you to buy and sell with more information under your belt. The best packages link to on-line stock quote services.

Setting Up Shop

Setup is the biggest stumbling block for people who keep haphazard manual records. Personal finance software cannot automatically "get you organized." If you constantly forget to enter your ATM withdrawals, stuff unopened bank statements in drawers, and misplace receipts for tax-deductible purchases, using a personal finance program will seem like twice the work.

You *must* change your ways and enter every check and every deposit, categorize every transaction, reconcile your accounts regularly, and earmark tax-related items. Otherwise, none of the reports or other helpful output will be accurate.

Step 1:
Preparing for Setup

REMEMBER

You'll breeze through your sessions a lot faster if you set up as much as you can up front. So grit your teeth and get through this unpleasant task in a few sessions, before you start entering transactions. To prepare for this first step, gather up:

- Your checkbook register and most recent statement

- Passbooks from any other accounts you might have

- All unpaid bills and stubs from the most recent paid ones

- Loan payment books

- Investment certificates

- A paycheck stub (or list of clients, if you're self-employed)

Step 2: Setting Up Accounts

HOT TIP

You'll have to enter opening balances as of a specific date for all of your bank and credit card accounts, along with information about other creditors and income sources. You don't have to start using your software on January 1st, your birthday, the vernal equinox, or any other significant date. But if it's August and you want a personal finance program to help you prepare your taxes next year, entering the previous eight months' transactions may be too tedious. In such a case, you might want to save the tax features for the next tax year.

Paying Bills Without Checks

Just as employers electronically deposit wages, you can pay your bills without ever writing a check. Simply fire up your modem and transfer funds to CheckFree, a nationwide system that pays your bills on the dates you specify, either with an electronic funds transfer or a laser-printed check.

Setup is a snap. Just get a copy of CheckFree's software (call 800/882-5280), enter information about the bills you want paid, and use the software to dial into a local or toll-free number. Tell CheckFree what recurring bills you want paid automatically and give four business days' notice for other bills. It doesn't matter what bank you use, since CheckFree works through the Federal Reserve System. The start-up kit costs $29.95 (free with *Quicken*) and you get one month free. After that, the monthly usage fee is $9.95.

Buy a lot on credit? Then consider *Quicken*'s IntelliCharge option. Apply for the *Quicken* VISA Gold Card, and instead of getting that dreaded window envelope every month, you can either have a disk mailed to you (for $4.50 a month) or download your monthly charges by modem (for $3 a month). Pop the data into *Quicken,* and it's automatically entered, categorized, and calculated. There's no annual fee and the variable interest rate is low. Call 800/242-9409 to apply.

Step 3: Customizing Your Categories

Every personal finance program includes a generous list of income and expense categories for classifying transactions. Each transaction must be categorized as you enter it, because categories enable you to group transactions for tax purposes and run reports that show you how much money you're spending on what—the two biggest benefits of personal finance software.

While the predefined category list may work fine for you, cruise through it before you start and see if any categories or subcategories are missing and add them. If you're planning to use the program to run a small business, you may want to enlist the services of a CPA to help with this part of the process.

Step 4: Backing Up Your Data

This isn't a "You might want to..." kind of thing. You *must* back up your financial records. Period. Businesses have folded when no one backed up a hard disk that decided to give up the ghost. All personal finance products instruct you how to back up your files, and some won't let you exit without reminding you to do so (See Chapter 9 for more information on backing up data).

DANGER

Also, keep a well-organized paper backup. Keep receipts, statements, check stubs, and so on in folders labeled by category or by month—you'll need the paper trail if you're ever audited. And if you run a detailed transaction report once a week, you'll have a last line of defense if your backup disks fry.

HOT TIP

Quicken

Spend more than a couple of minutes with *Quicken*, and you'll see why it's the top seller. To do basic financial chores, you barely have to learn anything— you can deposit money, write checks, and transfer funds using an electronic checkbook that probably looks like the one you use now. And instead of uptight accounting jargon, *Quicken* uses the same words you do: Payment. Deposit. Bill.

The Big Check Rip-Off

Although personal finance software itself costs little, preprinted forms purchased directly from the software vendor don't—particularly check blanks. Several third-party vendors sell forms compatible with popular packages like *Quicken* and *Managing Your Money*. You'll save money if you shop from these companies:

American Check Printers
2197 E. Bayshore Rd.
Palo Alto, CA 94303
800/262-4325

NEBS Computer Forms
500 Main St.
Groton, MA 01470
800/225-9550

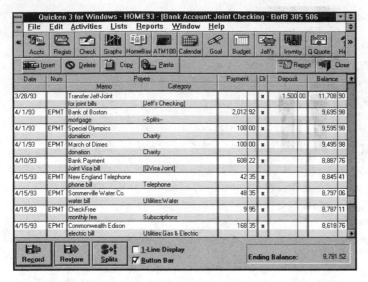

Figure 4: Quicken for Windows' intuitive checkbook metaphor, point-and-click toolbar, and lively screen graphics make bookkeeping fun (almost).

From the start both the DOS and Windows versions of *Quicken* hold your hand and won't let go. Set up an account, and a box pops up offering five account types: bank, credit, cash, asset, liability, or investment. If "liability account" has you scratching your head, a Post-it-like "Qcard" offers either on-line help or a page reference in the manual—a terrific idea every program should steal.

Automatic Bean Counting

Another nice thing about *Quicken* is that it remembers everything. Start making an entry, and the program suggests a matching payee or category based on what you've entered before during setup or on the fly. Press the Record button when you're done, and *Quicken* automatically posts the transaction to your checkbook register and adjusts the balance. Other bookkeeping and bill-paying features make the package a pleasure to use:

- **Electronic credit.** Sure, you can set up *Quicken* to work with CheckFree and pay bills electronically, just as you can with *Managing Your Money*. But Intuit also offers IntelliCharge, a special service for automating credit card payments. With a *Quicken* credit card, you get a monthly statement on disk that updates your account and pays your bill automatically.

- **Recurring transactions.** If you have several regular bills that are always due within a few days of each other, you can set up transaction groups and pay them all at once.

- **Account setup.** Each *Quicken* file holds up to 255 related accounts. If you use the program for both home and business data, set up a separate file for each, so you can create unique categories, run separate reports, and simplify tax preparation.

Beyond Bookkeeping

If you're wondering how you'll ever manage to send the kids to college and retire with some savings, *Quicken*'s financial planning calculators can at least give you some idea of how much money to sock away and where to put it. Advanced stuff like this makes personal finance software worth the effort.

Take investment management. You can use 17 different "yardsticks" to measure the performance of stocks, bonds, mutual funds, IRAs, and CDs and quickly calculate the value of your portfolio. Amortize a fixed- or variable-rate mortgage, and *Quicken* will do all the work, updating all balances every time you make a payment. And *Quicken*'s excellent Refinance Planner estimates how much you can save with today's low interest rates.

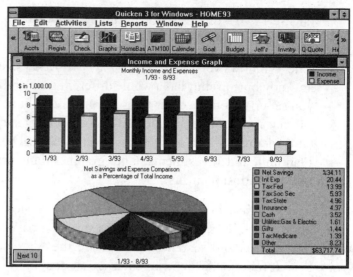

Figure 5: *Quicken for Windows can generate graphs like this one almost instantly. Click once on a pie slice, and you'll see the underlying dollar figure; click twice, and a graph pops up showing monthly subtotals.*

Reports and Graphs

Quicken comes with several canned reports that pop up on screen or print out at a mouse click, including net worth, cash flow, profit and loss, accounts payable, and accounts receivable. The first time you run a detailed transaction report, though, you may find categories and descriptions in strange places, forcing you to edit the category list. And creating custom reports isn't easy, because you have to hop around too many dialog boxes to find the options you need.

You may also get exasperated when you first try to print checks. If they're not aligned in the tray or feeder just right, you'll waste check blanks. So always use the Print Sample option before printing a whole run of checks. Graphs are more fun. Create an income and expense graph, for example, and you see in a flash how much you've spent this year on rent, groceries, car maintenance, and so on.

HOT TIP

Whatever capabilities you use, you'll get a lot for your money. Millions of people swear by *Quicken*. It's a powerhouse program that's so commonsensical, you'll barely need to crack the manual.

Managing Your Money

MECA's *Managing Your Money* is the brainchild of Andrew Tobias, financial guru and author of *The Only Investment Guide You'll Ever Need*. Tobias' snappy on-line advice is peppered throughout this program. In the middle of a boring 1090 form, he cracks you up with a joke about how many accountants it takes to screw in a lightbulb (answer: two—one to screw in the lightbulb and one to...). Sort of like your favorite unconventional-yet-effective teacher from high school.

The Windows version of *Managing Your Money* keeps the advice coming (it even has an Andy button) but has a whole different look and feel than the DOS version, where you set up accounts, enter transactions, create budgets, and so forth through a central Money menu. The Windows version spreads such functions among several icons (and menus), and also presents a cartoonlike Desk that groups them by Banking, Planning, and Investments. Cute graphics, but three paths to the same features can lead to confusion at first.

HOT TIP

Like *Quicken*, both *Managing Your Money* versions use the checkbook metaphor to good effect. To save time, and to ensure that payees are always entered the same way (for reports and searches), always use the Alert List, the Quick List, or the Payee Search functions when you enter a transaction.

More Advice, More Depth

Mouse around a little, and you'll realize that the day-to-day transaction stuff only hints at the power of this program. In several areas you'll find more depth here than in *Quicken*:

- **Tax estimation.** Predict tax liability for current and future years based on actual and budgeted income and expenses. You can export tax data directly to the popular *TurboTax* and MECA's own *TaxCut*.

- **Insurance estimation.** Decide how much life insurance you need by using a special calculator. Track and analyze policies and store information needed by your executor.

- **Financial planning.** Analyze retirement plans, refinancing, loans, annuities, tuition, and more with *Managing Your Money*'s impressive financial calculators. Compare the merits of, say, making your IRA contribution in January or April, or buying, leasing, or renting a home. Here, as with investments, you get lots of good advice from Tobias.

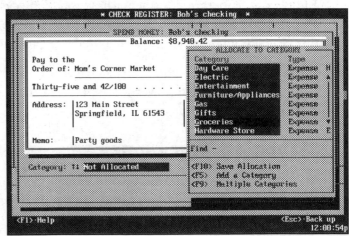

Figure 6: *The DOS version of Managing Your Money doesn't look as slick as the Windows version, but it's just as easy to use.*

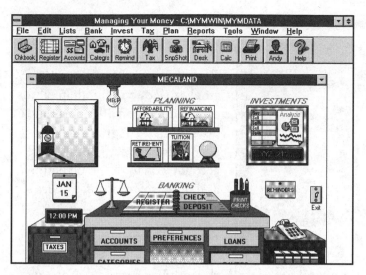

Figure 7: Some might argue that the new Windows version of Managing Your Money takes the desktop metaphor to extremes.

- **Investment management.** Update stock prices by modem, and have *Managing Your Money* alert you to significant price changes—the program will even dial up SkyTel and notify you via pager. To document an interaction with your broker, press F2 anywhere in the portfolio manager, and the memo area expands to hold unlimited notes.

HOT TIP

And Even More Stuff

Managing Your Money goes beyond dollars and cents to include a Rolodex, an auto-dialer, a simple word processor, and an appointment list. Without ever leaving the program, you can update your schedule, build a contact database, rearrange a to-do list, and set a reminder for an upcoming birthday.

Managing Your Money is a monster of an under-$50 program. Start with the basics, and with Tobias's on-line coaching you'll probably find yourself juggling scenarios and exploring investment possibilities just for the heck of it.

Other Personal Finance Software

The top two packages aren't the only ones worth considering. Newcomer *Simply Money* in particular is worth a look: It's clearly gone to school on the top two programs and then added an appealing new twist.

Simply Money

Simply Money from Computer Associates has a wildly innovative interface. Every account, payee, and income source gets its own icon, which you can drag and drop to do any number of things. To pay your phone bill, for example, you drag the checking account icon and drop it on the phone company icon, and up pops a check with the payee's name filled in. As you use the program, frequently used icons migrate to the top of the screen.

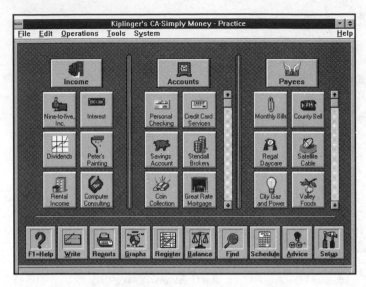

Figure 8: *Simply Money lets you drag and drop icons to initiate transactions and generate reports. It also borrows some of the best features from Quicken and Managing Your Money.*

Simply Money supplies copious on-line advice, courtesy of the folks who bring you *The Kiplinger Letter*. It also updates stock prices via modem and offers more than 50 reports and 30 graphs. To graph a year's account activity, drag the account icon to the graph button and release it. Poof! There's your graph.

Beyond the bells and whistles, *Simply Money* works much like the other programs. You get the usual account types and enter transactions via check-book register. You can create budgets, pay bills through CheckFree, and calculate amortization. But the Kiplinger advice adds value. Open a payroll account, and you'll get detailed setup instructions *plus* a clear idea of the program's limitations and how to obtain professional advice.

Don't let *Simply Money*'s inviting interface fool you. Underneath, you'll find personal finance power on par with *Quicken* and *Managing Your Money*. *Simply Money* imports data in *Quicken*'s native format, so if you're a *Quicken* user and decide you like *Simply Money* better, it's easy to make the switch.

HOT TIP

Microsoft Money

Windows-based *Microsoft Money* is a lightweight compared to the top three programs. It offers no portfolio-management functions per se, and its reporting is weak. Financial planning is limited to loan and mortgage calculators. And there's no on-line financial advice. It links to Prodigy's electronic bill-paying service, BillPay USA, but it doesn't support CheckFree (See Chapter 20 for more on Prodigy).

Money looks a lot like *Quicken* and uses a similar checkbook metaphor. All the basic banking stuff is there, along with a respectable set of graphs. On-line tutorials get you up and running, and you can quickly set up budgets based on past spending. But make no mistake: *Money* has some maturing to do before it's worth buying.

Money Counts for Windows

Parsons Technology's *Money Counts for Windows* is the only personal finance manager that lets you switch between single- or double-entry mode at the click of a menu item. In double-entry mode, you must post every transaction to a matching account, and you can run more complex, detailed reports. The security of balancing entries will appeal to CPA types, but the lack of invoicing, inventory, or payroll capabilities (even as add-ons) limits the program's usefulness as a small business accounting package.

Double-Entry Doublespeak

Unlike personal finance programs, business accounting packages use the *double-entry* system, which forces you to enter a matching *credit* for every *debit*. That is, if you pay a bill, you can't just write a check—you also have to record where that expense and cash originated.

Double-entry accounting has been the standard ever since a monk named Pacioli developed it hundreds of years ago, and it's still as confusing and complex as it must have been then. It also prevents fraud and error, which is why businesses with multiple bookkeepers and lots to lose prefer expensive double-entry packages. CPAs shrink in horror from programs like *Quicken* and *Managing Your Money*, which not only let you make single entries, but let you change previous entries without anyone being the wiser.

Five sample lists of accounts—for home, small business, farm, church, and nonprofit organizations—simplify setup. And getting around in *Money Counts* is just as easy as in other Windows personal finance managers. In trying to please both home users and small business operators, *Money Counts* falls short of being the best for either, but it's still a reasonable compromise.

Tax Software

Tax software cuts the time it takes you to fill out forms, prevents embarrassing errors, and may even help lower your liability. If you can fill out a 1040 on a lunch break, you don't need it. But if doing your taxes manually takes too much time, or you think you may be missing some deductions, tax software can help. The typical profile for a tax software user: a homeowner who has W-2 income, simple investments, and standard deductions (medical, day care, and so on).

Self-employed people, those with substantial investment income, and others with potentially complicated tax situations may want to think twice. Likewise, depreciation and rental property aren't always handled thoroughly or understandably by tax software. No software can handle complexity like a good tax accountant can.

If you're currently using the services of a tax accountant but want to take a crack at using tax software to reduce billable hours, ask your accountant how he or she would feel about checking over your return after you've completed it. If your accountant finds a missed deduction, you'll still be ahead, since reviewing your return should take fewer hours than doing it from scratch.

The Interview Circuit

Of all the PC-based tax programs available, ChipSoft's *TurboTax*, MECA's *TaxCut*, and Parsons Technology's *Personal Tax Edge* are the cream of the crop. All three offer the "interview" method of entering tax data. In other words, they ask you a series of questions that, based on your responses, progressively home in on your specific tax liabilities, just like a good CPA would do. When you're done you have a filled-in form—or forms, depending on your tax profile.

If this creeps you out, you can always fill in on-screen facsimiles of IRS forms, entering data as you would on paper. If you come to a line on the 1040 that requires a supporting document, the program will shunt to it and let you enter figures there. When you're finished, you can jump back to the 1040, and the total from the document you just completed will tag along with you.

Even if you opt for the straight data-entry option, it doesn't hurt to run quickly through the interview questions before you finalize your form, just in case you missed a deduction or some income you must claim. The interview identifies any additional worksheets, forms, and sched-

HOT TIP ules you may need.

As you go, instead of moaning about IRS instructions, you can pop up explanations of deductions, calculations, and exemptions that actually read like plain English. Again, neither the programs nor their technical support staff can give you tax advice. All they can do is ensure you understand what's being asked and suggest outside resources to consult for further clarification.

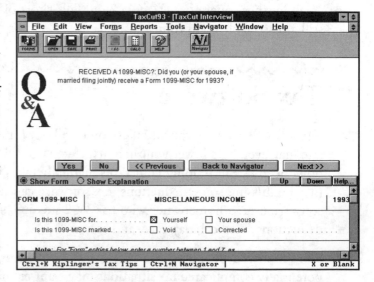

Figure 9: *Instead of merely presenting IRS forms on screen, tax software packages such as TaxCut simplify the whole nasty process by asking questions that ultimately direct you to the proper forms and schedules.*

But Is It Safe?

Using tax software is actually safer than filling out forms manually. Ever gotten a tax return back from the IRS with some corrections? Often, you simply miscopied a number from a schedule to your 1040. That kind of error can't happen if you're using tax preparation software. All data is automatically transferred to every field where it must appear.

In some situations you may need to override a particular number, and you can do so, but only after the program asks whether you're sure. Those warnings are there for a reason, so make sure you have valid grounds for overriding automatic entries. Log a note within the program to explain why, and double-check the entry when you review the final return.

You're probably tired of hearing this, but the ultimate reliability of tax software rests on you. You're the one who enters the data and signs the forms, so make sure you understand what you're doing, and call vendor tech support or enlist the services of a tax accountant if you don't. Software companies can't take any more responsibility than to guarantee they'll pay any penalties incurred from calculation errors made by the program, which are extremely unlikely.

While the best tax programs offer dozens of IRS forms, you may need one that's not supplied. Or you may be warned that a particular calculation—like depreciation—may be too complex to handle. Be forewarned that you may still need to pick up some extra forms, talk to a CPA, or consult other IRS documentation.

DANGER

Cutting Your Liability

If all tax preparation products did was automate filling out tax forms, they'd still be worth the money (usually less than $50). But they do more. Here's how they can actually help you cut your tax bill:

- **Hidden deductions.** If you select the interview option, the program may guide you toward deductions you're entitled to but haven't previously taken.

- **What-if scenarios.** It's too much paperwork for most of us to explore different ways of filing, such as comparing the merits of Married Filing Separately to Married Filing Jointly. Tax software makes it easy.

- **Tax forecasting.** Every program gives you some idea of your tax liability for the upcoming year based on your current income and expenses, along with projected tax rates, amounts, and regulations.

- **Built-in auditing.** This function checks for any discrepancies in forms and schedules, for fields that were left blank, and for figures that seem unusually high or low. The latter could save you the hassle of an IRS audit or the pain of a penalty if you entered a figure incorrectly.

Time to File

You have a couple of different filing options. Some people use their tax package like a souped-up calculator and fill in the actual IRS form by hand. Who knows why, since you can also print IRS-approved forms, all filled out and ready to sign. If you have a modem, you can file your return electronically. Processing centers charge a small fee for this service (less than $20), and programs that support it include clear instructions.

Most tax software vendors offer income tax forms for at least some states. Once you've filled out your federal form, you can export the pertinent data right into the state module. Which states a package supports will help you decide which one to buy.

TurboTax

HOT TIP

ChipSoft's *TurboTax*, the most popular tax program, gets a big thumbs-up for accuracy, maneuverability, and ease of use. While all tax preparation products produce a reliable set of forms and schedules, they don't all walk you through the process as capably—or offer as much help—as *TurboTax* in both its DOS and Windows versions.

Interview questions appear in a box that overlays the form you're working on. If you choose direct data entry, you'll find it easy to jump back and forth between your 1040 and supporting forms and schedules. You can also revisit any document at any time if you need to go back and check something.

Now Where Did That Receipt Come From?

So you think you've finished preparing your return. Well, what about those receipts and statements under the table? Don't despair. *TurboTax, TaxCut,* and *Personal Tax Edge* all offer a handy "shoe box" or "filing cabinet" feature. Indicate what kind of document you have, and the program will tell you exactly where it belongs, down to the line number.

DANGER

This is a terrific feature, but it comes with a warning: Tax software vendors treat this as a third method of data entry, but you shouldn't use it as such, or you may neglect to enter some income or expenses. Use it only as a supplement to the interview or straight fill-in-the-blanks method.

You get clear interpretations of tax law along with the verbatim IRS instructions themselves. Other highlights include pop-up lists of the figures behind totals, and a cross-reference feature that shows where a figure was originally generated, or where it jumped to after the original calculation.

One of the few problems with *TurboTax* is that switching between EasyStep and direct data entry can be confusing. Otherwise, this program's ease

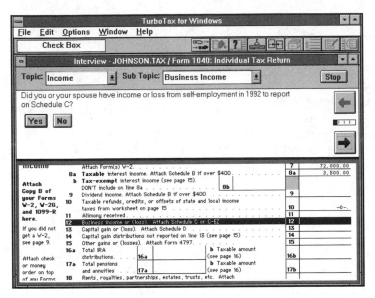

Figure 10: *TurboTax for Windows combines faithful facsimiles of IRS forms with the step-by-step interview approach.*

of use and adept handling of many scenarios make it the equal of *TaxCut*.

Andrew Tobias' TaxCut

As with *Managing Your Money*, one of the best reasons to consider buying *TaxCut* is Andrew Tobias. Tobias helped design *TaxCut*, and his sense of humor and financial savvy permeate the program.

TaxCut is available in both DOS and Windows versions. Its interview option is just as thorough as *TurboTax*'s, though *TaxCut* is a bit more honest about what its limitations are, warning you at some points that it's taken you as far as it can and that you might want to consult a professional or an IRS publication.

If you're a novice tax preparer, you'll appreciate the many levels of help, including occasional nudges during the interview process. If you're not sure how to answer a particular question, you'll get a "Most taxpayers will say..." response, plus further explanation.

TaxCut lets you skip around your entire tax return easily, thanks to convenient groupings of income and expense line items labeled Personal Information, For Employees, Retirement Plans, and so on. Navigation features like these, plus humor and plain-English advice, make this package hard to beat.

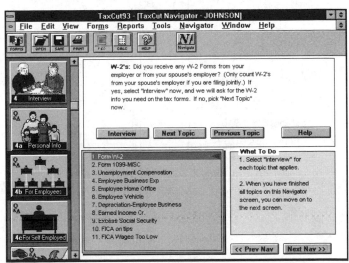

Figure 11: *With copious advice available at the click of a button, Andrew Tobias' TaxCut rarely leaves you scratching your head.*

Early Birds Catch the Deductions

Tax preparation software vendors release "early bird" editions of their programs every fall. Of course, until the final forms arrive in January, no one knows for sure how the tax laws will change, so you won't find finalized forms and schedules. However, some early bird editions also contain all the tax law changes known at the time. You can use these editions to estimate your tax liability for the current year, and, if you're lucky, you might be advised to spend more money to offset your income.

Personal Tax Edge

Compared to *TurboTax* and *TaxCut*, *Personal Tax Edge* includes fewer forms and schedules, imports from fewer personal finance packages, and has less capable printing, making it the least desirable of the top three products.

The program's interview option is too thorough in some ways; with joint returns, for example, it has an annoying habit of asking the same question twice—and it's not quite automatic enough in others. If you don't read some instructions carefully, you can easily end up filling out unnecessary fields.

HOT TIP

Like its competitors, *Personal Tax Edge* offers plenty of help along the way. And if you buy an early bird edition, you might benefit from looking at Tax Saver Tips, which contains more than 300 ideas for lowering your tax liability before the end of the year. Nonetheless, this package isn't in the same league as the other two.

Product Directory

Managing Your Money
Tax Cut
MECA Software, Inc.
55 Walls Dr.
Fairfield, CT 06430
203/255-1441

Microsoft Money
Microsoft Corp.
One Microsoft Way
Redmond, WA 98052
800/426-9400
206/435-9900

Money Counts
Personal Tax Edge
Parsons Technology
One Parsons Dr.
Hiawatha, IA 52233
800/223-6925
319/395-9626

Quicken
QuickBooks
Intuit, Inc.
P.O. Box 3014
Menlo Park, CA 94026
800/624-9060
415/322-0573

Simply Money
Computer Associates
   International, Inc.
One Computer Associates
   Plaza
Islandia, NY 11788
800/225-5224
516/342-5224

TurboTax
ChipSoft, Inc.
6256 Greenwich Dr. #400
San Diego, CA 92122
619/453-4446

25 | Entertainment, Etc.

by Gregg Keizer

- Games, games, games: from role-playing to twitch
- Kids' educational and reference software
- Graphic restaurant and entertainment finders
- Specialty joysticks and flight yokes

You just don't get it, do you? The PC's no juiced-up adding machine or typewriter. It's a game machine, stupid.

I should know. I spend more time playing games than the weirdest teenager. Games on video, games on boards, games on computers. All kinds of games. And for my money, the PC is the most powerful, most flexible game player ever. Not because of the hardware—that's far from state of the art, gamewise—but because its software backlist can turn the machine into *anything*.

Want to pretend Clinton gave you an F-16 jet fighter? Easy. Feel like taking on monsters that make subway muggers look like cute toddlers? You bet. Have an itch to see Michael Jordan's tongue flap like a wet blanket as you take him to the basket? Why not? The PC can do all that, and more. A whole lot more.

I'm here to lead you by the hand through a virtual games shop. I'm your guide to grown-up games, kids' software, home reference titles, and even some of the gamer's favorite gizmos. I'm the guy who's going to fill your head with buying pointers that will keep you electronic-entertainment literate long after Madonna is just a bad memory.

Let's get going. The sooner we get started, the sooner you'll get it.

The Games Gallery

PC games are cheap, and there are a million of 'em. Fortunately, they fall into a half-dozen broad categories. Get to know these classifications, and you'll never be awed by a 15-year-old's expertise again.

Role-Play: Which Way to the Castle?

With roots in literature like Tolkien's *Lord of the Rings* trilogy and paper-and-dice games like Dungeons & Dragons, PC role-playing games (called *RPGs* by dungeon junkies) rely on fantasy as a backdrop and player involvement as a hook. In the typical RPG, you run a group of characters on a heroic quest through a world where magic reigns and advanced armament means a sharp sword.

Role-playing games all share several traits, which include:

- **Human and nonhuman characters** who battle a blend of bizarre creatures like orcs, mages, and assorted mutants and monsters

- **Good vs. evil** plot line, where you fight to right a wrong

- **Puzzlelike problems** and a long play time, typically measured in dozens of hours

HOT TIP

That last means that you should steer clear of role-playing games unless you're a game vet, or at least incredibly patient.

Building a Better Dungeon

Like all games, most RPGs come, then go. I'm betting that some of the newest, though, will stick around. Think of them as the best dungeons on the block.

Origin's *Ultima Underworld*, now in its second episode, is one. This game popularized the first-person, 3-D perspective, where you see castle corridors and dank hallways as if through the main character's eyes. In *Ultima Underworld II: Labyrinth of Worlds*, you must defeat the Guardian, an evildoer, by finding a black gem as you make your way out of a complex prison. Fairly standard plot, but the too-excellent graphics make you forget all that.

Dynamix's *Betrayal at Krondor* is even better. The text descriptions and interludes are well written, which is unusual in RPGs, and the interface is a slick point-and-click affair. Even more impressive, *Krondor*'s scenery is superb. The bottom line is simple: *Krondor* is one of the best RPGs to hit the streets (or dungeons) in years.

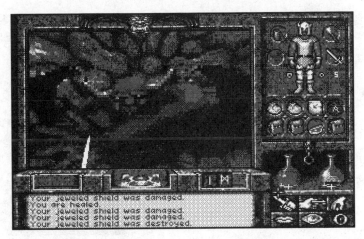

Figure 1: *Ultima Underworld II's 3-D look puts you right in the action.*

The Ultima Classics

The ultimate RPG line is *Ultima*, a longer-running (and different) series than *Underworld*. Now in its eighth game, *Ultima* runs you through a new plot each time, although the magic-encrusted land of Britannia keeps coming back. Interesting characters like Lord British (alter-ego of the games' designer, Richard Garriott), the sheer expanse of the games' worlds, and the constant updating of graphics and interface technologies mark *Ultima* as the RPG line to stay with.

Check out the Might & Magic, Magic Candle, and Wizardry series if you get addicted to RPGs. Might & Magic with *Eye of the Beholder III* and Wizardry with *DarkSide of Xeen* are especially strong.

Graphic Adventures: Comic Books for Grown-Ups

Graphic adventures may be the kissin' cousins of RPGs, but for the most part, they're more like grown-up comic books than morality plays. Rather than have you lead a crew through a good versus evil romp, adventures put you in the shoes of a single character heading through a set story line; they include these pieces:

- **Branching plots** that move you toward a fixed ending

- **As-real-as-software-gets stories,** like gritty cop dramas, science fiction scenarios, and tales of intrigue and mystery (they're often funny, intentionally or not)

- **Quick completion**, since they're much less time-consuming than a role-playing quest

Because of their wide-ranging stories, and because they're usually easier to play than RPGs, adventures are for first-time PC game players.

HOT TIP

Interactive Entertainment

It's no surprise that graphic adventures are the interactive age's answer to TV and movies.

Figure 2: *Indiana Jones and the Fate of Atlantis offers a state-of-the-art point-and-shoot interface so you can concentrate on the story.*

They all share common components, from a strongly defined character and a prepared plot line to dialog and a background score. No shock, then, that one of today's best graphic adventures steals a story from one of the all-time best action flicks.

Indiana Jones and the Fate of Atlantis comes from LucasArts, an arm of filmmaker George Lucas's empire, and features the man that Harrison Ford made famous. This interactive Indy takes you around the world in a race against Nazis for a strange and powerful metal once used by the inhabitants of the Lost Continent. As in most modern adventures, you can play without typing a stroke by clicking on icons to talk, grab objects, or move. And when you play the CD ROM version, Indy is an all-talkie.

Larry Rules

Like RPGs, some graphic adventures have long enough "legs" to keep coming back. One of the longest running, and strangest, is Sierra's *Leisure Suit Larry* series. Starring Larry Laffer, an inept make-out man, the five Larry adventures feature a bit of on-screen naughtiness (though nothing more risqué than what a kid would see at a PG-13 movie), lots of guy-stuff comedy, and enough ground to cover to keep you playing for a couple of solid days. If you can't stay away from graphic adventures, make sure you take in as many Larrys as you can stand.

Most of the other adventures of note come from Sierra, a publisher that specializes in the category. Its lines include *Space Quest*, *Police Quest*, *King's Quest*, and *Kitchen Quest* (OK, not that last one, but Sierra really covers the waterfront). Sierra's titles may not rank at the top in graphics or even plot sophistication, but they do provide a vast variety of stories and settings. You'll have no trouble finding *something* in the Sierra line that you'll like.

Simulations: Live Dangerously

Take out Saddam's Baghdad bunker. Run a metropolis and keep the little people happy. Or break every federal law and breed new life forms in a genetic laboratory right on your desktop. If the PC really is an adult's sandbox, that's mostly because of the machine's simulations. Most simulations feature:

- **Dangerous situations** that you'd never want to face in real life, like dodging missiles, driving at Monaco, or running Metropolis

- **Processor-hungry code** that demands the fastest PC possible or at least a math coprocessor to look good on the screen

- **Realistic views** of real-world situations through your PC's monitor

Because they need such high-powered hardware—not only a rabbit-fast processor, but also quick video—believable simulations are a relatively recent addition to PC gaming. In fact, if you're fascinated by simulations, buy the fastest PC you can afford. You won't regret it.

HOT TIP

Live and Die, Breed and Fly

Flight simulators took off like a rocket years ago, and they've never fallen off the pace. The PC's first sim, *Microsoft Flight Simulator*, boasts snappy—though not cutting-edge—graphics, both inside and outside the airplane. You can take the controls of several different aircraft, fly from airport to airport, and generally mimic a real pilot's chores.

Spectrum Holobyte's *Falcon* puts you in a plane, too, but rather than putter around, you fly combat against today's most advanced jets. Like the real thing, this virtual F-16 takes plenty of practice. (The most sophisticated flight sims are as much work as they are play; I'd head to a prop-driven sim like Dynamix's WWI-era *Red Baron* if you're a sim novice.)

HOT TIP

Figure 3: *Microsoft Flight Simulator puts you in a cockpit packed with the same dials and gauges you'd find in a real plane.*

Aerobatics isn't the only thing you can simulate on PCs. Maxis's *SimLife* lives even more on the edge, for it simulates the development and evolution of life, not the crash and burn of airborne annihilation. Here you create planets and their creatures, and then play God to keep them alive. You can change your handiwork (down to the genetic level), mess with the ecology, wipe it all out with natural disasters (the rain of comets is cool), and experiment all you want. Hey, it's your world, so do what feels good.

Raise Taxes, Build Roads, Run for Mayor

The classic simulation remains *SimCity*, an urban-development game where you build and then maintain a city and its infrastructure. That may sound dry, but *SimCity* is anything but, for it gives you complete control over something you have no control over in real life: government. You start a town, nurture its growth, raise taxes, build roads, and try to stay in the mayor's office and out of trouble.

Sports: Play Ball!

I was a jock once. But then I grew up and gave it up: too much pain. It's easy to skip the BenGay, though, when you sit your butt down in front of the PC and play sports the same way we watch them on TV—with our fingers on the controls.

You can define sports games almost as fast as Nolan Ryan throws home:

- **Arcade games,** where fast reaction times count most

- **Managerial contests** simulate the decisions a manager or coach makes from the dugout or sidelines

- **Hybrid titles** blend both for a more complete simulation

HOT TIP

This is one category where the PC beats the pants off the kiddy Nintendo or Sega video game machines. Unlike those systems, the PC can easily update its sports information. When you're scouting for a sports game, especially one as stats-intensive as baseball or course-different as golf, make sure that you're buying into a company that sells season updates or new courses.

Fore!

I hate golf. Who wants to dig a little ball out of the weeds all day long? But on the PC, golf is great. I can play 36 holes without losing a ball. *Links 386 Pro* and *Microsoft Golf*, both created by Access Software, may not be new but they are the best electronic links programs around. They've got crisp scenery, you can modify your swing and stance, and there's no chance of beaning somebody on the green.

Football fan? Check out *Front Page Sports: Football Pro*, a Dynamix simulation that built its teams from digitized versions of real players. The play-making editor is tops, and though the coaching can overwhelm beginners, its on-field action is slick.

For roadway mayhem, nothing beats MicroProse's *World Circuit: The Grand Prix Simulation*, a driving sim that not only turns the PC screen into a wind-

Figure 4: *Front Page Sports Football's players are built from video, so the action's much more realistic than in games with cartoon-style characters.*

shield, but also puts realistic scenery along the track. I really like the special options that let you "cheat" by having the program do the braking and shifting.

Bases Loaded, Two Out, Bottom of the Ninth

With new or updated sports titles less common than a good season for the Mets, classics such as *Tony LaRussa Baseball* are vital to your library. Tony's already gotten to second—*LaRussa II* has been on the shelves for over a year—and it's still the best digital baseball around. Fielding is especially simple: You just position the player under a shrinking spotlightlike circle to make the catch. Because it uses stats from real players to simulate the sport, Tony's publisher, SSI, releases season updates to keep the game current; it even sells a Fantasy League disk so you can build pretend teams and then send Pete Rose to the plate against Babe Ruth.

Strategy: War Is Hell

Back in the old days, people played war games on paper maps with little tokens. Low-tech stuff. Today, the PC puts combat on the computer by using:

- **Electronic maps** and pieces that don't get knocked around, and digital referees that make you play by the rules or hide the enemy's forces

- **Artificial generals** you wage war against, so you don't have to search for an opponent to beat up

- **Real-world campaigns and wars**—World War II is the most popular—that let you create Pentagon-style "what if" pseudohistories

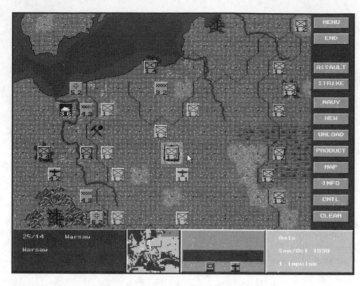

Figure 5: *Clash of Steel*, which replays WWII in Europe, isn't one of those monster games that take days to play. A nice one for beginners.

A few strategy games buck the trend and go for the abstract. They're still war games where you move tanks and ships and men around, but they take place on fake worlds. Each game is fresh, and with the terrain scrambled anew, you never know what's on the other side of that hill.

On to Berlin!

For sheer complexity, nothing beats Three-Sixty's *V for Victory* series. With four titles out and more on the way, *V for Victory* takes on World War II one battle at a time. You can fight on the Normandy beaches in two separate games, take on the Russians on the Eastern Front, or parachute into Holland behind German lines. You move small units around a gorgeous map while the PC takes the opposing side.

Battle neophytes should forget *V for Victory*, though: too much to manage, too much like work. Turn instead to one of SSI's many low-level war games, like *Clash of Steel*, a reproduction of WWII's European campaigns. Here you have fewer pieces to shove around, and you get to do Big Picture stuff like decide whether to build tanks, planes, or ships. It's good for greenhorns.

Bygone Battles

Few war or strategy games stick around long enough to become classics. One of the few that has is *Empire*, now in an enhanced version called *Empire Deluxe*. It's one of those make-a-fake-world games, where the map starts out black and the enemy is out there somewhere. Most of the fun is in exploring the world, building units furiously, and then beating up on your computer opponent. Great fun, especially for the occasional gamer.

HOT TIP

Another classic is *Civilization*, a MicroProse title that's not all war game (though there's plenty of combat), but at least partly an *Empire*-style simulation where you try to keep the barbarians away from the gates long enough to get literate.

Action: Twitch Games

Action games have taken a beating on the PC. Where once dozens of mindless arcade style shoot-'em-ups and martial arts games battled it out, only a handful bother to show up today. They've almost all moved to the video game machines, where millions of kids twitch thumbs.

A few buck the trend, usually because they're:

- **Short and sweet,** like Id Software's *Wolfenstein 3-D*, a classic shoot-'em-up with terrific three-dimensional graphics and fast play, even on the PC

- **Puzzle games** that appeal to older players, not kids

- **Hybrids** that combine lots of shooting with pieces from other PC categories, such as adventure games or simulations

Even then, the PC can't compete with current video game decks, much less the new CD-based machines like the one from 3DO that use special graphics chips to animate their games.

The Real Action's in Outer Space

If you shoot in space, are there sound effects? In PC games, you bet.

Maybe it's not realistic, but when it comes to games, nobody really cares. That's why *X-Wing*, an amalgam of space action and cinematic bits, can thumb its nose at the laws of physics. All that matters is that it's fun, graphically first-rate, and fast, fast, fast. You fly against the Empire vaporizing scads of moronic fighters in a battle of quantity, not artificial-intelligence quality.

Not all action happens in space. Dynamix's *The Even More Incredible Machine*, a puzzle game that has you building Rube Goldberg-like contraptions, is a scream. Using a toolbox of pieces—conveyor belts, ropes, ramps, and pulleys, among other things—you assemble a gadget that completes one of the dozens of chores in the game and takes you to the next level.

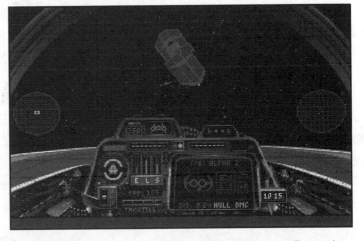

Figure 6: *X-Wing is one of the few worthwhile action games still around.*

Fun in the Future

It's tough enough to call the shots when you can see what you're aiming at, but with a moving target, prognosticating gets downright sticky. Who cares? Let's fire up the digital Ouija board and project what the future of PC fun holds.

- **Role-playing games** that integrate virtual-reality-like techniques. Interplay's *StoneKeep*, for example, shows battles up close and personal, and even uses some 3-D mouse movements as you wield your weapons.

- **Graphic adventures** that rely almost exclusively on CD ROM for their on-screen video, digitized speech, and film-quality scores.

- **Simulations** that use each technological leap in processing power to provide more complex, and thus more realistic, scenarios.

- **Sports** titles that steal flight sims' polygon-based graphics technology to smoothly animate players and put you right on the field.

- **War games** that use on-line services to bring together players in multiuser battles.

- **Action games** that go AWOL from the PC. If you're an action addict, my advice is to turn off the PC and slap a cartridge in a Sega Genesis or Super Nintendo.

Nor is *Wolfenstein 3-D* cast in a vacuum. This ultra-fast action game, where you hunt Nazis in a multifloor castle, features a first-person perspective, 3-D images that smoothly animate, and enough bullets, blood, and bodies to stock a Hollywood hit. More games using some of the same programming code are set to appear, including Id's own *Doom* and Origin's *SpellCaster*.

Tetris Forever

You've been out of touch if you haven't played *Tetris* in the past three years. This geo-metric puzzle game makes you rotate pieces that are dropping into a well to build level rows. The better you get, the faster the pieces drop, until even The Flash couldn't keep up. *Lemmings* isn't a pure puzzle, but its theme of little people with a suicidal bent can't be beat. The Lemmings are trying to do themselves in, and your job is to use their special skills to safely see them to the next level. *Lemmings II: The Tribes* is a reprise, with even more levels.

Kids' Stuff

Kids' games—those titles with at least *some* educational value—are different. Sure, it's easy enough to sort them out: math games, reading games, spelling games, geography games, history games. But more important—to parents *and* to their children—is the difference between programs that simply tutor and games that teach while they entertain.

- **Drill and practice** games are big on repetition, even bigger on basic skills. Like an electronic reading workbook or a digital math worksheet, they drum the facts into little heads.

- **Edutainment titles,** on the other hand, use breezy graphics and gameplay, sound effects and speech, and cute interfaces and kid-style storylines to keep children at the keyboard, and so keep them learning. The idea is to disguise the facts with fun.

Depending on what you're after—and depending on how still you can get your kid to sit at the PC—you'll want to consider both styles of kids' games.

HOT TIP

Preschool: Getting the Jump on the Joneses

With baby boomers seemingly flush with kids—and flush with money, too, think software publishers—tons of titles take aim at kids under the age of six. Most moms and dads want their tykes to excel and think that the PC's one way to give them a leg up on the world.

- **Basic skills** can be taught with drill-and-practice software, which covers everything from naming colors and counting to labeling shapes and rattling off the alphabet.

- **Prereading** tutoring is best left to edutainment software, which often puts a story on the screen and then sends digitized narration out through a sound card and some speakers.

Figure 7: *Putt-Putt Joins the Parade may not teach basic skills, but it's one of the best ways to keep a preschooler in front of the computer.*

To use what kids' software offers, especially in this age range, equip your PC with a sound board, speakers, and, if possible, a CD ROM drive. Almost all the worthwhile CD ROM games are squarely shot at children.

Living Books, Grinning Cars

If you have that CD ROM drive, your kids can pick up one of Broderbund's Living Books, a four-story series that's part passive read-along, part interactive exploration. *Grandma & Me* is a 12-screen talking story about Critter's trip to the beach with Grandma. As the narrator reads—in one of three languages, no less—each word is highlighted. Kids can turn the page to move on, head back for another look, or just sit back and listen to the music and dialogue. With just a dozen pages, though, it doesn't take long to exhaust *Grandma*'s entertainment value.

Putt-Putt Joins the Parade doesn't toss in much educational bang for the buck, but that doesn't mean it's not a terrific preschool program. Essentially a kiddy adventure, this title stars Putt-Putt, a happy-go-lucky car. He's heading to the parade and meets a slew of other animated characters in his travels through town. There are no wrong turns here, for like Broderbund's games, Humongous Entertainment rewards kids for exploring everything they see.

Elementary: Let Them Make It on Their Own

Older kids have more choices. In fact, kids in elementary school have a wider selection of educational and edutainment software to pick from than any other age group. That makes sense when you think about it: Children ages 6 to 11 are not only busy learning lots of basic facts—the core of drill-and-practice software—but typically they *really* like to learn.

- **Math software dominates** the drill-and-practice side for this age group. If your child needs the electronic equivalent of flash cards, there are dozens of programs to pick from, including Davidson's long-running *Math Blaster.*

- **Build-it software** rules in the edutainment category for elementary-age kids, who like nothing better than making something from scratch.

Pix and Prose

Count *KidPix* as one of the few must-haves in your home learning library. This paint program from Broderbund looks normal enough on the surface, but it's a fun digital canvas. Sound effects explode from the speakers when kids paint, erase, or draw, and scores of cute stickers can be stamped on the screen (they make noises, too). Get its companion program, *KidCuts*, too. This title lets kids make masks, stage puppet shows (scenery included), and print paper dolls.

Don't forget the program that started all this, either. *The New Print Shop Deluxe* runs in Windows and creates colorful banners, signs, and greeting cards. If you've ever walked through a school hallway and seen signs, they've probably come out of *Print Shop*. Your kids will love creating stuff and decorating their rooms and your whole house in like fashion.

Figure 8: *KidCuts lets junior artists print out paper dolls, scenery, and so on, for instant paper projects that require little more than a pair of scissors.*

For kids who would rather write than draw, let them experiment with Microsoft *Creative Writer*, a writing tool and tutorial that features helpful hints at every step and has options for building complex designs such as newspapers. It's a bit overloaded on the icons and slow on older PCs, but it'll get kids past any writer's block. When they're after more direct results, The Learning Company's *Children's Writing and Publishing Center* is a better bet. It's more of a stripped-down word processor than a *Creative Writer*, but it bundles tons of pictures that can be placed on the page and enough design options to create newsletters as well as straight-ahead reports.

Middle School: Interactive Education

As kids age, they're expected to learn without complaining, and without an elementary school program's bells and whistles. By the time they hit middle school or junior high (sixth or seventh grade, respectively), they've got study skills down pat, they know how to crack a textbook, and the games they like to play are probably on Nintendo, not the PC.

- Drill-and-practice is tough to find for this age range, but borderline programs like The Learning Company's *Spellbound* are expandable, since you can add words to this spelling game to keep it current with your kids.

- Interactive titles are the way to go with this group. Part simulation, part entertainment, these programs grab kids by the scruff of the neck and make them part of the action. Everyone likes to run things, and kids aren't any different.

HOT TIP

Carmen and California or Bust!

Where in the World Is Carmen Sandiego? started it all by posing kid players as detectives, and Carmen and her gang as thieves of famous objects.

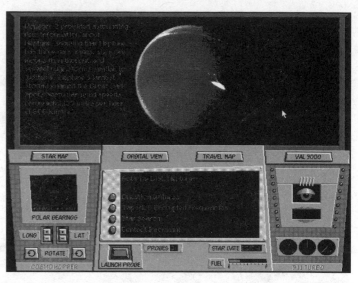

Figure 9: *Where in Space Is Carmen Sandiego? ups the age range of the series somewhat and helps fill the hole in science-related software for kids.*

Using an interface packed with investigative tools, the Carmen games take kids on jaunts around the world, across America, through Europe, and even back in time. In each game, the pint-size gumshoes must track a crook by asking questions and uncovering clues. Most are geography related, and all Carmen games come bundled with a paper-based reference book so that kids can look up the facts and find out where they need to travel next. In *Where in Europe Is Carmen Sandiego?*, for instance, a Fodor's guide comes in the box. If they can keep up with the criminal's frequent flying, kids eventually make an arrest.

Another interactive game for older children is MECC's *Oregon Trail*, a title that's been around about as long as personal computers. It's been updated several times, but even the most recent version looks retro—the graphics are not nearly as sharp or colorful as what you'll see in most games. Fortunately, its premise compensates. Kids take the part of a pioneer heading west across the plains and must make decisions at almost every step. Decision-making is the key here, and kids love it, especially when they play in groups.

High School: Test Time

By the time kids hit high school, they're using computers like the rest of us. Rather than using them to bone up on facts and figures, they're writing with word processors, crunching numbers with spreadsheets, and retrieving information from databases and on-line services.

The best thing you can do for a high schooler at home is to equip the PC with a capable word processor for writing the reports and papers teachers demand. Don't skimp by buying an entry-level package simply because it's for your child. At the least, the word processor should elegantly handle footnotes; even better are programs that help compile tables of contents, allow outlining, and ease the task of compiling bibliographies.

HOT TIP

Testing, One-Two-Three

One of the few nonproductivity software categories worth your high schooler's while is testing tutors, specifically those that prime students for the all-important Scholastic Aptitude Test (SAT), the exam that gets them into college.

- **Cliffs StudyWare for the SAT,** a tutoring package from the makers of the infamous Cliffs Notes, is typical. This self-paced program presents a pair of exams in either teaching or testing mode, then offers up an analysis of the test taker's strengths and weaknesses. An on-screen clock mimics the time limitations of the real SAT, but kids can turn it off.

- **Your Personal Trainer for the SAT** gives practice tests and quickly calculates scores, too. It also publishes a report that recommends a test-training schedule based on the student's demonstrated highs and lows.

Although both of these sample SAT tutors are inexpensive—certainly less money than one of those pay-to-study SAT cram sessions—neither is more than a workbook gone electronic. Kids can duplicate almost all of the elements in such software simply by picking up an SAT study guide or two, grabbing a kitchen timer, and sharpening a couple of number 2 pencils.

REMEMBER

Look It Up

Interactive. Multimedia. Tired buzzwords? Sure, but use them in the same breath as *encyclopedia*, and some parents go into a software feeding frenzy. Get rid of a bookcase full of paper encyclopedias, they shout, and look it all up on the PC. Good idea? Maybe, but not yet.

Three multimedia encyclopedias compete for parental dollars: Microsoft's *Encarta*, *Compton's Interactive Encyclopedia for Windows*, and *The New Grolier Multimedia Encyclopedia*. All sell for far less than what you'd pay for a full set of real encyclopedias. All are intriguing. None are worth the bucks. Here's why:

- **Photos and maps look blurry** when compared to what you see in a paper-based encyclopedia.

The Classroom at Home

All the software in the world won't do much good unless your kids use the PC. And they're not likely to sit at the keyboard if the computer is stuck away in that back bedroom you use for an office. That's mom and dad's workplace, not somewhere where kids can have fun. To build your home learning center, consider these suggestions:

- Put the PC in a place where everyone gathers, like the rec room or den.

- Plop it on a desk in a corner, then use a couple of low bookcases (for storing software, reference materials, and supplies) to separate the workspace from the rest of the clutter.

- Add some task lighting, like a lamp or track lights that focus on the desk.

- If you have several kids, consider putting the PC on a small, rolling cart, like the ones you can buy in an office supply store. Then you can move the machine between your kids' rooms when they use it to do homework.

- Get a mouse, sound card, and speakers. If the PC's in the same room as the TV or in a shared bedroom, pop for a pair of Walkman-style headphones so that your kids can listen to games without disturbing others.

- Buy a cheap color printer, like the HP DeskJet 500C. It'll do wonders when translating to paper what kids create on the screen.

- **Articles are generally academic lightweights** that rarely match *World Book*, much less the gorilla of encyclopedias, *Brittanica*.

- **Multimedia elements are limited,** with even the best—*Encarta*—showing only 45 short video clips. (It's got lots of sound, but that's what an audio CD is for.)

My recommendation? Spend the money on a paper-based encyclopedia instead. If you're set on getting something electronic, scout out the multimedia upgrade kits and CD ROM drive packages, for they usually toss in a bundle of discs. And most include an encyclopedia.

HOT TIP

Where Are We and When Do We Eat?

Reading a map or deciding what restaurant to go to can be as much of a game as any role-playing descent into dungeon hell. Maybe that's why the PC, by virtue of its display and data abilities, has been pressed into this kind of entertainment service.

Mapping software—which is what this stuff is, at heart—may be intriguing to some, but on today's PCs (even notebook and subnotebooks), it's not as portable as the alternatives: paper atlas, folding maps in the car's glove box, or the restaurant section of the Yellow Pages. The best way to use programs like these is to do your planning before leaving the house and then print out some maps or other info to stick in your briefcase.

Road Work

If you're dead set on using your PC as an electronic atlas, there *are* programs to satisfy a mild appetite:

- **PC Globe**, which includes lots of maps and facts and figures. The maps aren't nearly as detailed as those you find in a Rand McNally's, but you can view each country's terrain types, major features, and elevation changes. *PC Globe* isn't really suitable for anything but browsing, but it's not a bad pick when you have young geographers at home.

- **City Streets,** which is a bit more usable. You get extraordinarily detailed maps of midtown Manhattan, downtown D.C., downtown San Francisco, and a city of your choice (you pick from the more than 100 that are available). You can even search by address to find the cross street.

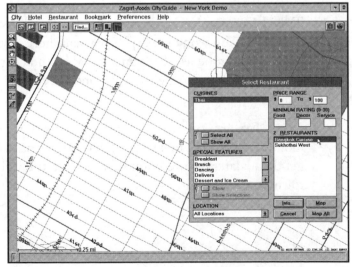

Figure 10: *Zagat-Axxis CityGuide lets you look up restaurants by food type. When you want to eat hot and spicy in Greenwich Village, it'll show you where to go.*

You may know where you are, but do you know where you're going to sleep? A slew of software offers the kind of restaurant, hotel, sightseeing, and entertainment information that you'd find in, say, a guidebook to a major city. Like electronic atlases, these city guides are best used beforehand as you plan your trip, though if you're convinced you need to have this info at your fingertips, you can squeeze some onto the hard disk of a notebook PC.

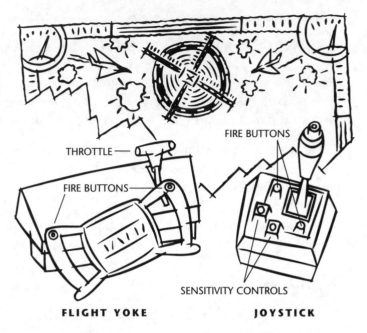

THROTTLE

FIRE BUTTONS

FIRE BUTTONS

SENSITIVITY CONTROLS

FLIGHT YOKE   **JOYSTICK**

Figure 11: Play twitch games with a mouse? Forget it. Joysticks work much better, and a yoke brings flight simulation to new heights. Either needs to plug into a joystick connector, which may require adding an expansion card.

- **Zagat-Axxis CityGuide,** a Windows program that offers maps and accompanying information for New York, Chicago, and San Francisco only. The guides are pricey, but they manage to provide a broad range of data. You can look up restaurants and hotels by searching for such criteria as food type, price, and how they rate on the Zagat scale. Warning: A single map can hog as much as a dozen megabytes on your hard disk.

DANGER

- **Travel Companion,** a DOS package from Software Toolworks, uses only 2MB of disk space. You won't see expansive maps here, but the basic outlines of its 25 cities are about as good as what you get at the rental car counter. The hotel database can be searched by price and ranking, and the restaurant listings can be perused by the type of food served.

- **Local Expert,** one of the few programs that stays current, offers inexpensive monthly updates. Unlike its competitors, it does a credible job (especially when you get the updates) of presenting the city's cultural side: It lists the happenings around town up to three months in advance.

Goofy Game Gear

The keyboard's for work and the mouse is for kids, role-playing, and some simulations. You need more than the bare bones if you're really going to kick back and play games on the PC. Fortunately, there's no lack of game gizmos and doodads that you can add to your computer.

Some of the best (or at least the strangest):

- **Joysticks,** like CH Products' FlightStick and Thrustmaster's Mark II Weapons Control System, industrial-strength peripherals solid enough to stay on the desk, but not too heavy for the lap. Perfect for combat flight simulators.

- **Flight yoke and rudder controls,** such as CH Products' Virtual Pilot. These resemble the control wheel of a small civilian airplane, perfect for the slower-going *Microsoft Flight Simulator.* Thrustmaster sells a heavy-duty rudder control add-on.

- **Voice recognition software,** like Covox's *Voice Blaster.* You get a microphone and software and just plug the former into any *SoundBlaster* or *SoundBlaster*-compatible board. Once you train the software to recognize your voice command, and link that command to a keyboard macro, you just yell "Fire!" instead of banging on the keyboard. Ultra cool.

An All-Game Network

If you own a modem, give The ImagiNation Network (formerly called The Sierra Network) a whirl. Once you connect with this on-line service, you can play against real people, not the dumb PC. Best of its bunch is a role-playing game, *The Shadow of Yserbius,* and a multipilot version of Dynamix's great *Red Baron,* a WWI flight sim. Watch the clock, though, for you can rack up some stupendous fees if you're not careful.

Figure 12: *You reach The ImagiNation Network's various areas through this Disneyland theme park–style interface. Call 800/743-7721 to subscribe.*

- **Big-screen picture,** something you'll get with GameBlaster, a hardware/software combo that lets you connect the PC to any television set sporting RCA or S-VHS video jacks. Resolution doesn't improve, of course, so you'll want to sit back a bit, but the increase in size makes it as close to the movies as we're likely to get until virtual reality comes home.

Product Directory

Games

Betrayal at Krondor
The Even More Incredible
  Machine
Front Page Sports:
  Football Pro
King's Quest
Leisure Suit Larry
Police Quest
Red Baron
The Shadow of Yserbius
Space Quest
Sierra/Dynamix
40033 Sierra Way
Coursegold, CA 93614
800/757-7707
209/683-4468

Clash of Steel
Eye of the Beholder III
Tony LaRussa Baseball 2
Strategic Simulations, Inc.
675 Almanor Ave. #201
Sunnyvale, CA 94086
800/245-4525
408/737-6800

Civilization
World Circuit: The Grand
  Prix Simulation
MicroProse
180 Lakefront Dr.
Hunt Valley, MD 21030
800/879-7529
410/771-0440

Darkside of Xeen
Empire
Empire Deluxe
New World Computing
20301 Ventura Blvd. #200
Woodland Hills, CA 91364
800/325-8898
818/999-0606

Doom
Wolfenstein 3-D
Id Software
18601 LBJ Freeway #615
Mesquite, TX 75150
800/434-2637

Falcon 3.0
Tetris
Spectrum Holobyte
2490 Mariner Square Loop
Alameda, CA 94501
800/695-4263
510/522-3584

Indiana Jones and the
  Fate of Atlantis
X-Wing
LucasArts Games
P.O. Box 10307
San Rafael, CA 94912
800/782-7927
415/721-3300

Lemmings II: The Tribes
Psygnosis
675 Massachussetts Ave.
Cambridge, MA 02139
617/497-5457

Links 386 Pro
Access Software
4910 W. Amelia Earhart Dr.
Salt Lake City, UT 84116
800/793-0073
801/359-2900

Microsoft Flight
  Simulator 5.0
Microsoft Golf
Microsoft Corp.
One Microsoft Way
Redmond, WA 98052
800/426-9400
206/882-8080

SimCity
SimLife
Maxis
2 Theatre Sq. #230
Orinda, CA 94563
800/336-2947
510/254-9700

SpellCaster
Ultima Underworld
Ultima Underworld II:
  Labyrinth of Worlds
Origin
12940 Research Blvd.
Austin, TX 78750
800/245-4525
512/335-5200

V for Victory
Three-Sixty Software
2105 Bascom Ave. #165
Campbell, CA 95008
408/879-9144

Education, Edutainment, and Reference

Children's Writing and
  Publishing Center
Spellbound
The Learning Company
6493 Kaiser Dr.
Fremont, CA 94555
800/852-2255
510/792-2101

Cliffs StudyWare
  for the SAT
Cliffs StudyWare
P.O. Box 80728
Lincoln, NE 68501
800/228-4078
402/423-5050

Compton's Interactive
  Encyclopedia
  for Windows
Compton's NewMedia, Inc.
2320 Camino Vida Roble
Carlsbad, CA 92009
800/862-2206
619/929-2500

Grandma & Me
KidCuts
KidPix
The New Print Shop Deluxe
Where in the World
  Is Carmen Sandiego?
Broderbund Software
500 Redwood Blvd.
Novato, CA 94948-6121
800/521-6263
415/382-4600

Math Blaster
Your Personal Trainer
  for the SAT
Davidson & Associates
19840 Pioneer Ave.
Torrance, CA 90503
800/545-7677
310/793-0600

Microsoft Creative Writer
Microsoft Encarta
Microsoft Corp.
800/426-9400

The New Grolier
  Multimedia Encyclopedia
Grolier Electronic
  Publishing, Inc.
Sherman Tnpk.
Danbury, CT 06816
800/285-4534
203/797-3530

Oregon Trail
MECC
6160 Summit Dr. North
Minneapolis, MN 55430
800/685-6322
612/569-1500

Putt-Putt Joins the Parade
Humongous Entertainment
13110 N.E. 177th Pl. #180
Woodinville, WA 98072
206/485-1212

Software Maps

City Streets
Road Scholar Software
2603 Augusta #1000
Houston, TX 77057
713/266-7623

Local Expert
Strategic Mapping, Inc.
3135 Kifer Rd.
Santa Clara, CA 95051
408/970-1991

PC Globe
Broderbund Software
800/521-6263

Travel Companion
The Software Toolworks
60 Leveroni Ct.
Novato, CA 94949
800/234-3088
415/883-3000

Zagat-Axxis CityGuide
Axxis Software, Inc.
644 Haverford Rd.
Haverford, PA 19041
215/896-0576

Hardware

FlightStick
Virtual Pilot
CH Products
970 Park Center Dr.
Vista, CA 92083
619/598-2518
800/624-5804

GameBlaster
Advanced Digital Systems
20204 State Rd.
Cerritos, CA 90701
310/865-1432

Mark II Weapons
  Control System
Thrustmaster, Inc.
10150 S.W. Nimbus Ave., #E-7
Tigard, OR 97223
503/639-3200

Voice Blaster
Covox
675 Conger St.
Eugene, OR 97402
800/432-8970
503/342-1271

Glossary

~~~~~~

Like this book, this glossary doesn't pretend to be fully comprehensive—but hey, a listing of more than 830 words is nothing to sneeze at, either. Beginners will find many basic words here, but if you're new to computers and find yourself back here looking up elementary stuff too often, you're better off reading Chapter 1: *For Beginners Only* first. It's got pictures, for one thing.

You'll notice many cross references to other definitions here, but very likely if you don't understand *any* word in a definition you'll find it defined elsewhere in the glossary. The exception to this are DOS commands. If you're looking for definitions of DOS commands or instructions on how to use them, turn to the Cookbook in Chapter 12: *Windows and DOS* or to Appendix C: *Important Stuff DOS's Help Doesn't Tell You.* If you're looking up a file extension—those three little letters after the period in file names—you'll find a few here, but for a comprehensive list turn to Appendix E: *Field Guide to File Formats.*

24-bit color Synonymous with *photorealistic* color, this term describes printers, graphics cards, and monitors that use 24 bits of color information per pixel or dot, producing up to 16.7 million colors per image.

286 An obsolete 16-bit CPU used in the original IBM AT and its clones. Incompatible with many contemporary applications and some Windows features.

386 DX Intel's first 32-bit CPU, now obsolete but still a key standard due to the millions of 386 systems in use and the ability of 486 and Pentium systems to run software written for the 386.

386SX A slightly slower version of the 386DX that accesses memory 16 bits rather than 32 bits at a time.

387 Intel's *math coprocessor* for 386 PCs.

3-D graphics Usually refers to graphics containing shapes that can be rotated and otherwise manipulated in three dimensions. For example, you could "walk through" a 3-D drawing of a building. Also used to refer to true stereo 3-D images (which usually require that you wear special glasses).

486DX Created by Intel, the 486DX is essentially a speeded-up 386 CPU with a built-in *math coprocessor* and an 8K memory cache.

486DX2 (see *DX2*).

486SL An obsolete version of the 486SX used in laptops.

486SX A 486DX without the built-in math coprocessor.

8086 An obsolete 16-bit variation on 8088 used in a few XT clones.

8088 An obsolete 8-bit CPU, used in original IBM PCs and PC-XTs and their clones. Incompatible with most contemporary software, including Windows.

8514A A proprietary IBM graphics standard for interlaced 1024 by 768 resolution (see *interlaced*).

A-B roll system A video editing system that uses three decks, two for playback (A and B) and one for recording.

A/B switch A box that enables you to attach two printers to one PC port (or two PCs' ports to one printer) and switch between them as desired.

accelerator card Any of several expansion cards designed to improve performance. For example, a *graphics accelerator card* hurries data to the screen, while a *CPU accelerator card* speeds up operations overall by replacing the current CPU with a faster one.

access control software A utility that blocks anyone without the proper password from accessing selected files on a PC's hard drive.

active-matrix LCD A brighter, sharper, and significantly more expensive alternative to *passive matrix* notebook displays (see *TFT*).

active window In Windows, the window you're currently working in.

add-on Any hardware or software designed to augment the capabilities of another product.

Adobe Type Manager (ATM) A Windows utility that enables you to display and print PostScript Type 1 fonts from within any Windows application, whether or not you have a PostScript printer.

algorithm A mathematical procedure for solving a problem, most often used to describe caching, compression, or encryption schemes.

allocation units To track data on disk, DOS divides disk space into groups of sectors called allocation units (also known as *clusters*). Depending on the size of the drive, allocation units usually range from 2K to 16K in size, but are always of equal size on any given drive. DOS's *file allocation table (FAT)* logs each allocation unit as available, damaged, or in use by a file. Only one file can use a particular allocation unit at one time (see *FAT, sectors, slack space*).

alphanumeric The set of characters that includes all letters, numbers, and punctuation marks.

AMD An Intel competitor that makes 486-compatible CPUs and other processors.

America Online (AOL) One of the most popular on-line services, offering E-mail, news wire reports, travel reservations, on-linc shopping, user forums, shareware, chat areas, a large reference library, and more (see *on-line service, shareware*).

ANSI Short for the *American National Standards Institute*, which develops standards in many fields. ASCII, terminal emulation, and SQL are only three of the many standards ANSI has set for the computer industry.

ANSI.SYS A *device driver* used to control screen display and keyboard remapping. For DOS use only; pretty much obsolete.

antivirus A type of program that scans your system and sounds the alarm if a computer virus is detected. Most antivirus programs also attempt to remove the infection (see *virus*).

app Short for *application*.

applet A small application, usually referring to the mini apps that come with Windows, such as the Notepad, Clock, PIF Editor, and so on.

application Any program with a user interface designed to be *applied* to a specific set of tasks. Most often refers to such "productivity" software as word processors, spreadsheets, draw programs, and so on (see *program, user interface*).

application generator Several data management programs come with an application generator, which enables you to create custom database applications without programming (see *database application*).

application launcher A Windows utility program that makes organizing and starting applications easier.

ARC A shareware utility that compresses files to save disk space and/or transmission time via modem. *ARC* does the compressing, while the companion program *ARC-E* does the decompressing. Both are available from most on-line services (see *compression, on-line service, shareware*).

archive Generally, any collection of data intended to be stored indefinitely and accessed infrequently (specifically, the type of file created by such compression utilities as *ARC* and *PKZip*—or the act of creating such files using these utilities. Archive files are also known as *library* files when composed of several files "packed" together by a compression utility; "unpacking" an archive file restores the original component files (see *ARC, compression*).

archive bit A file attribute used to indicate which files have been changed and which haven't since the last time you backed up your data (see *backup, file attribute*).

ASCII Short for the *American Standard Code for Information Interchange*, this is the international standard for turning characters (letters, numbers, and punctuation) into *binary* code. True ASCII uses only 7 bits of every byte for a total of 128 characters. However, a wide variety of 8-bit codes based on ASCII are used to support languages other than English and to create simple line graphics in character-based DOS programs.

ASIC Short for *application-specific integrated circuit*, an ASIC is a custom chip designed for a specific purpose. The size of motherboards has been radically reduced by the use of ASICs.

ASPI Short for *Advanced SCSI Programming Interface*, ASPI is a SCSI driver standard developed by Adaptec. In theory, any SCSI device that supports ASPI should work with any ASPI-compatible SCSI adapter card.

assembly language Also called *assembler*, the programming language closest to *machine language*, the only language understood by the CPU. Only crazy people write big programs in assembly language. These days, used mostly for fine-tuning the performance of programs written in easier, more sophisticated languages, such as C or C++.

asynchronous communications IBM-speak for using a modem.

AT See *IBM AT*.

AT commands A standard language developed by Hayes (the top modem manufacturer), used by communications software to tell modems what to do. The AT prefix starting all AT commands is short for "Attention!" or "Hey modem!" (see *communications software, modem*).

AT drive Originally, a hard drive compatible with the *controller* used in the IBM PC-AT; also the basis of the contemporary *IDE* standard.

audio compression A technique for reducing the size of sound files on disk. Depending on the compression scheme, it may reduce sound quality (see *lossy*).

audit trail Originally an accounting term, audit trail also applies to any log of a user's network or database activities.

auto-answer mode A setting that causes a modem to pick up incoming calls.

auto dialer A software utility that uses your modem to dial a phone number displayed on screen.

AUTOEXEC.BAT A batch file that executes automatically when you start your PC, telling your operating system where to look for application files, how to set up the C: prompt, which utilities to load, and so on. Along with CONFIG.SYS, it's one of the most important files on your PC's hard drive (see *batch file, CONFIG.SYS*).

automatic backup A backup utility that uses a software timer to trigger backups at set times, or a network utility that backs up local hard drives to a server without users having to do anything.

autosave An option found in many applications that saves your work automatically at specified intervals. A nice feature if you forget to save manually and experience a crash.

autotracing The imperfect process of converting *bit-mapped graphics* (such as a scanned drawing) into *vector graphics*, which can be easily manipulated by drawing software.

autodimensioning A feature used by CAD programs to draw lines, circles, and other drawing shapes of specific dimensions according to a scale factor defined by the user. For example, rather than calculate the X and Y end points of a 7-inch line at a 33-degree angle, you simply enter in a dialog box the angle, start point, and length of the line, and the software does the rest (see *CAD*).

average access time The average time it takes in milliseconds for a disk drive's read/write head (or a CD ROM drive's laser reader) to access any given point on a rotating disk.

average seek time The mean time it takes in milliseconds for a disk drive's read/write head (or a CD ROM drive's laser reader) to access any given point *along the radius* of a disk. Does not take into account the disk's rotation.

AVI Short for *Audio Video Interleaved*, Microsoft's standard file format for digital video.

B

background printing The process of printing behind the scenes while you work in another file or application. Windows comes with a *print spooler* called Print Manager, which enables you to use background printing with almost any Windows application (see *print spooler*).

backlighting Special lighting behind notebook *LCD* screens that increases contrast several times over; absolutely necessary for color LCDs (see *LCD, notebook computer*).

backup The process where you copy the contents of your hard disk to another medium, such as floppy disks or tape, in case the original data is lost or damaged (see *differential backup, full backup, incremental backup*).

backup set The disks or tapes on which you store your backup copies.

BAK file A backup copy of a data file. Many programs create files with a BAK extension automatically when you edit a file (for example, when you edit BUDGET.XLS, *Excel* creates a backup copy called BUDGET.BAK).

bandwidth The amount of information a piece of hardware (or a type of cable) can transfer during a given time interval.

bank switching Also known as *memory interleaving*, bank switching is a method used by system designers to sustain fast memory access while using relatively slow, cheap memory chips. A block of memory is divided in two, so that half the data is stored in one bank and half in the other. While one bank is being accessed, the other bank has time to recover, so the number of times any given memory chip is accessed per second is effectively cut in half, without degrading performance. You need twice as much bank-switched memory to achieve the same speed as that sustained by faster memory chips without bank switching (see *memory speed*).

bar chart A data chart designed to compare quantities at evenly spaced time intervals (by week, month, and so on). Bar charts emphasize each interval's *data point*, the individual numeric value represented by each bar's height (see *data chart*).

base memory See *conventional memory*.

BASIC *Short for Beginners All-purpose Symbolic Instruction Code*, a relatively simple programming language. Most versions of DOS include a BASIC interpreter (a program that lets you create and run BASIC programs).

batch file A file containing a series of DOS commands, each on its own line, that executes automatically when you type the name of the file at the DOS prompt and press Enter. Batch files enable you to speed up repetitive tasks (such as switching to a directory and launching a program). You can create a batch file with any text editor; all you do is give the file a BAT extension.

batch printing The ability to send several files to the printer in a single operation.

batch transfer To send a group of files by modem in a single batch (see *Ymodem, Zmodem*).

baud rate Indicates the speed of telecommunications transmissions. In PC jargon, generally synonymous with the preferable term *bps*.

BBS Short for *bulletin board service*, a home-brewed version of an on-line service such as CompuServe or America Online, where people dial up with their modems and leave messages or files for others to read or download. Anyone with a modem and the right (inexpensive) software can turn a PC into a BBS, and most small BBSs charge little (or nothing) for access (see *download, modem, on-line service, upload*).

bcc Short for "blind carbon copy," a typewriter-era term for a copy of a letter sent to someone whose name did not appear in the list of carbon copy (cc:) recipients below the signature. (For example, an attorney might send a paralegal a bcc for filing purposes.) Now used to refer to similar addressing options in E-mail programs.

benchmark A speed test performed under controlled conditions.

Bernoulli Box A type of *removable-media* drive that holds high-capacity disk cartridges (up to 150MB).

bidirectional Primarily used to describe a type of parallel port that can both send and receive data.

binary The numerical system (also known as base 2) used by computers. Binary logic employs only two numbers (0 and 1), which correspond to the two states (off and on) of each bit in memory or on disk. All data—text, numbers, pictures, sound, video—must be converted to binary code before your computer can process or store it (see *bit*).

binary file Any file containing nontext data, such as a program file, a spreadsheet, or a graphics file.

BIOS Short for *basic input/output system*, a small quantity of code used for controlling basic computer functions, stored permanently in a chip (or chips) on a PC's motherboard.

bit The smallest building block of computer data (see *binary, byte*).

BitBlt Short for *BitBlock Transfer*, a basic video operation often referred to in overly technical magazine articles. In theory, faster BitBlt performance means snappier performance when you move windows and icons around on screen.

bit-mapped graphics Images stored as a grid of dots. Paint programs, scanners, and fax modems save data as bit maps (see *vector graphics*).

bits per second (bps) The standard measure of modem speed. V.32bis modems run at a maximum speed of 14.4 kbps (kilobits per second), V.34 modems go up to 28.8 kbps.

bleed In design, layout, and desktop publishing circles, a bleed refers to any element (like a photo or a line of type) that runs off the edge of the page.

block copy Marking a block of text (in a spreadsheet or text document) and copying it to another location.

BMP Windows' own bit-mapped graphics file format.

board See *expansion card*.

body text The main body of type in a book or article. It specifically *excludes* headlines, captions, and special graphic elements (see *display type*).

boilerplate Text or graphics that are created once and inserted, unchanged, into a series of letters, articles, reports, and so on. A form letter, exclusive of the salutation and any other personalized touches, is boilerplate text.

bold Short for boldface, a dark, heavy version of a type font used for emphasis; the word **bold** at the beginning of this paragraph is set in boldface.

Boolean logic Refers to a set of logical commands (AND, OR, NOT, and so on) used in database queries and text searches.

bookmarks Placemarkers that let you move around rapidly in a long text document. Most word processors enable you to insert several bookmarks in a document, letting you jump from one to the next instead of scrolling.

boot The act of turning on your computer or of restarting it by pressing [Ctrl][Alt][Del]. Also refers to the moment when a PC finds the *operating system* on disk and loads it (see *cold boot*, *warm boot*, *operating system*).

boot sector A small section of your hard or floppy disk in which DOS looks for instructions about how to start your computer.

branch When discussing disks and files, a branch is a subsection of the directory tree (that is, a directory and all the subdirectories beneath it). In macros, batch files, or programming, it refers to a point where two or more different things can happen depending on the circumstances: For example, a macro might look to see whether a directory contains a particular file, then either open that file or create a new one (see *batch file*, *macro*).

bulletin board service See *BBS*.

buffer Memory used to improve performance by creating a small reservoir of readily accessible data. For example, hard disks have buffers to hold data likely to be needed by the PC, while printers have buffers to hold information received from the PC (see *disk cache*, *memory buffer*).

bug A mistake a programmer made when writing software that shows up on your end as some unexpected event, usually an unpleasant one.

burst mode A special mode used by a disk drive or other device to quickly transfer a large block of data (see *bus*).

burst transfer rate The speed (usually in MB per second) of a burst-mode transfer. With disk drives, the burst transfer rate usually reflects the best possible performance under optimum circumstances; for a more realistic measure, look to the *sustained transfer rate*.

bus Any electrical circuit that transfers data. The term *bus* most often refers to the kind of slots (ISA, VL, PCI, EISA, MCA) found on a PC's expansion bus, but it may also refer to other connections within a PC: the memory bus, SCSI bus, and so on.

bus arbitration The scheme by which a system prioritizes requests from multiple devices on the same expansion bus.

bus mastering When an intelligent expansion card enhances performance by taking control of the expansion bus, usually to transfer a large quantity of data in a short period of time without involving the CPU.

bus topology A network cable design where all workstations share a common cable (similar to the way all houses in a block are connected to the same water main).

button A graphic representation of a push button with an icon on it, used by most Windows programs to provide easy access to commands; an array of buttons is usually called a *toolbar* or *button bar*. Also one of the two or three switches on your mouse.

byte The standard unit for measuring disk storage and memory. Each byte contains 8 bits. The characters you see on your computer screen are usually composed of 2 bytes, but if you're not a programmer you never have to worry about such matters.

C

cache See *disk cache*, *memory cache*.

CAD Short for *computer-aided design*. Essentially computerized drafting, CAD may also refer to programs that do complex materials analysis. CAD software ranges from $50 programs used mostly for space planning to engineering programs that cost hundreds of thousands of dollars. *AutoCAD* is far and away the most popular CAD program for PCs.

calculated field In database lingo, a field whose value is determined by using a formula that usually refers to data in another field. For example, in a payroll database, the net pay field might be calculated by subtracting tax and insurance from the gross salary.

card See *expansion card*.

carpal tunnel syndrome One of the most common repetitive strain injuries (RSIs), carpal tunnel syndrome is an often painful compression of the median nerve in the wrist, caused by repeated bending of the wrist and/or by swelling of nearby tendons and their sheaths. Computer users are frequent victims of carpal tunnel syndrome (see *RSI*).

carriage return A term left over from typewriter technology, where the typewriter carriage had to be "returned" to start a new line. On a computer, a carriage return simply moves the cursor to the beginning of the next line (see *hard carriage return, line feed, text wrap*).

carrier detect (CD) When a modem connects with another modem, the CD light on an external modem lights up.

CASE Short for *computer-aided software engineering*. Using software to write software; that is, automated programming. Talked about far more often than it's done successfully.

CCITT Short for Comite Consultatif International Telephonique et Telegraphique *(International Telephone and Telegraph Consultative Committee)* (see *ITU*).

CD-I Short for *compact disk interactive*, a CD ROM standard used by the Philips CD-I player (a gadget you hook to your TV). Not relevant to PC CD ROMs.

CD ROM A disk that stores hundreds of megabytes of data in laser-readable form. Although Short for *compact disk read-only memory*, CD ROM is a type of storage, *not* of memory. You need a CD ROM drive to read CD ROM disks (see *read-only*).

cellular modem A modem that connects to a cellular phone (see *modem*).

CGA Short for IBM's first color graphics card, the *Color Graphics Adapter*. The CGA standard is long obsolete, offering a mere 320-by-200 resolution in four colors.

CGM Short for *Computer Graphics Metafile*, a somewhat quirky file format for storing various kinds of graphics.

character A single letter, number, punctuation mark, or symbol.

chat area BBS systems and on-line services often have areas where everyone who's currently logged on can exchange written messages in real time. This is called a chat area, or sometimes a CB simulator (see *BBS, on-line service*).

checkboxes A group of boxes (usually found in Windows dialog boxes) that enable you to "check off" the options you want, letting you select all, none, or a few items from a list at one time.

chip Also called an *integrated circuit*, a chip refers to any complex combination of transistors and other circuitry etched onto a silicon die. Chips make computers possible, handling everything from data storage to number crunching. Chip is also slang for *CPU*.

CIS See *CompuServe*.

CISC Short for *complex instruction set computing*, a term used to distinguish CPUs that process longer instructions (particularly Intel's 486, Motorola's 68040, and their predecessors) from RISC (reduced instruction set computing) CPUs that process shorter instructions faster, such as the Intel i960 and the AMD 29000.

click To press and release a mouse button—usually the left one. When you *click on* something (a menu item, a graphic, whatever), you move the pointer to it and click the left mouse button.

click and drag To hold down the left mouse button and move the mouse at the same time. Generally, you click and drag to move an object (such as a program icon) or to highlight a block of text (see *drag and drop*).

client-server Any network application (usually a database or accounting program) where most of the processing is done on the server, while workstations (clients) do relatively little work. In conventional network applications, the file server holds the data files, but all the processing is done by the workstations (see *network server*).

clip art Any collection of drawings or other ready-made images you can insert into your documents to liven them up.

Clipboard The place in Windows where text and graphics go when you cut or copy them. There they wait, ready to be pasted, until you cut or copy something else, in which case the previous contents are overwritten.

clock speed Also known as *clock rate*, the speed of a CPU, motherboard, or expansion bus expressed in megahertz (or millions of cycles per second). Often, the CPU and motherboard have different clock speeds—for example, a 486DX2-66 CPU runs at 66 MHz internally, but its motherboard runs at only 33 MHz.

clone An old-fashioned term that refers to an IBM-compatible PC.

clusters See *allocation units*.

CMOS Short for *complementary metal oxide semiconductor*, a special kind of memory chip that requires very little power. Most PCs use battery-powered CMOS chips to store basic system configuration info, such as the type of hard disk and the amount of memory installed. You change those settings with a setup utility—hence the term *CMOS setup*.

CMYK Short for cyan, magenta, yellow, and key (usually black), the colors of the inks used in the four-color printing process. CMYK is one of several systems for combining primary colors to produce a full-color image.

codec Short for *compression/decompression*, codec refers to an audio or video compression method. Indeo and Cinepak are common video codecs.

cold boot When you turn your PC off and on, or press the reset button, you've just performed a cold boot, which is usually the last resort when a warm boot fails (see *boot, warm boot*).

color matching A software and/or hardware system for making a PC's display approximate the colors of the final printed page. Some monitors have color matching features built in.

color separation A process used in desktop publishing for separating a color image into four single-color images, one for each ink (cyan, magenta, yellow, black) used in four-color printing.

color temperature A technical measure of the color displayed by a video tube. Variations in color temperature can give a monitor a slight yellow, blue, or red tint.

COM A file extension for a type of program file. Also used to designate a serial port, as in COM 1 and COM 2 (see *executable file, serial port*).

command An instruction you issue that tells your computer what to do. In Windows or most apps, you pick commands from menus, push a button on a tool bar, or hit a keyboard shortcut (like Ctrl C for Copy). At the DOS *command line*, commands are short words (COPY, MOVE, FORMAT) that you type at the C: prompt.

command line See *DOS prompt*.

COMMAND.COM The most vital DOS file, COMMAND.COM contains most of the code needed to start your PC, as well as many basic DOS commands like DIR and COPY.

communications server A PC or special box hooked to a network to provide communications services, such as *Internet* access or E-mail connections to people on other LANs.

communications software A program that lets you use your modem to send or receive files or log onto on-line services like CompuServe (see *modem, on-line service*).

compact desktop PC A PC with a case smaller than that used in the original IBM PC-AT.

compiler Software that takes all the high-level instructions in a program and converts them wholesale into *machine language*, the language understood by the CPU. The compiled version of the program must then be *decompiled* for any modifications to be made (see *interpreter*).

compression The process of shrinking files to conserve disk space or reduce modem transmission time. Archiving utilities such as *ARC* and *ZIP* and disk compression utilities such as *Stacker* compress files to approximately half their size on average, but the degree of compression varies widely depending on the file type. Programs that perform video and audio compression usually give you a choice of several compression ratios, depending on how much of the original quality you're willing to lose (see *archive, disk compression, lossy*).

CompuServe Officially called the CompuServe Information Service (CIS), the biggest commercial on-line service. Offers hundreds of on-line forums on any topic imaginable, along with E-mail, games, thousands of shareware programs, free medical advice, on-line air reservations, up-to-the-minute news, on-line shopping, and access to hundreds of business, financial, and technical databases (see *on-line service, shareware*).

CONFIG.SYS One of the two files your PC looks for at start-up, CONFIG.SYS is principally responsible for two key configuration tasks: loading device drivers necessary to run various peripherals and allocating your PC's memory. Other key DOS options are set here as well. You can customize CONFIG.SYS using DOS's Edit (or any program that saves files as unformatted text), but you should know what you're doing (see *AUTOEXEC.BAT, device driver*).

configuration A general term for the process of setting up hardware or software the way you want it (for example, to configure Windows to work at a resolution sharper than 640 by 480). Also refers to the specific combination of hardware installed in a system or to the layout of a LAN. Most PCs come with a configuration utility that prepares the system for a new floppy drive, an additional hard disk, a math coprocessor, and so on. Windows applications store their configuration settings in INI files; DOS stores its configuration information in CONFIG.SYS (see *SYSTEM.INI, WIN.INI*).

connectivity A geeky term often used to make anything having to do with networks or modems sound more impressive. In this book, we've reserved the term to describe hooking Macs, minicomputers, and other alien systems to a network of PCs.

contact manager A sophisticated program that keeps track of names, addresses, phone numbers, appointments, correspondence, and virtually everything else for people who make their living on the phone. It usually includes an electronic Rolodex, a powerhouse appointment calendar, and the ability to link information in various ways (see *PIM*).

continuous-form paper Also known as fan-fold paper, this is the folded stuff that feeds through most dot matrix printers, with perforations between the pages and little holes on the outside (see *dot matrix printer, tractor-feed*).

Control Panel A Windows utility for setting a wide variety of options: selecting printers, changing the desktop's appearance, adjusting mouse response, and so on.

control point The small dots or boxes that appear when you select a line, curve, polygon, or other object in a drawing program. Dragging a control point with the mouse changes the object's shape and/or size.

controller The electronics that control the workings of a hard drive or a monitor. A controller may be mounted either on an expansion card or on the motherboard.

conventional memory All memory under 640K (also known as *base memory*).

coprocessor See *math coprocessor.*

counter fields A database term used to describe a field that stamps a unique identification number on each record (see *field, record*).

CPU Short for *central processing unit*, the chip that does most (if not all) the computing in your PC. Most PC models derive their names from the name of the CPU inside the system (486SX, DX2, Pentium, and so on). The CPU is usually located on the motherboard, the main circuit board that lines the bottom of your PC.

crash A general term for a serious malfunction. In the most common type of crash, your computer *locks up* (synonymous with *hangs* or *freezes*) and refuses to accept keyboard or mouse input, so that you have to reboot in order to resume working. In some cases, only one of several applications will stop functioning, or Windows disappears and leaves you staring at the DOS prompt (system crashes obliterate any data not saved to disk).

CRC Short for *cyclical redundancy checking*, this is a common technique for detecting errors when transmitting data by modem.

CRT Short for *cathode ray tube*, the picture tube in your monitor or TV set. Also jargony synonym for monitor.

cross-linked files When a disk error or system crash damages the *FAT*, one common result is that two files sort of merge into one big mess (kind of like a bad car wreck). *Norton, PC Tools*, or DOS's ScanDisk can often repair this problem.

cursor The small flashing rectangle, vertical line, or underline that shows you where the characters you type will appear. Not to be confused with the little arrow (called the *pointer*) or I-beam (called the *insertion point*) in Windows, both of which are controlled by the mouse.

cut and paste The term for a procedure used to move text or graphics from one place to another. In Windows, you can cut and paste data within the same file, between different files, or between applications (see *Clipboard*).

cut-sheet A single sheet of paper, like that used in most photocopiers and laser printers.

Cyrix An Intel competitor that makes 486-compatible CPUs and other processors.

D

DAC Short for *digital-to-analog converter*, a chip used in sound cards, graphics cards, and other devices to transform digital signals into sound, video, and other things readily appreciable by humans.

daisy-chaining Hooking several devices (usually *SCSI* drives) together with a series of cables. The second device plugs into the first, the third plugs into the second, like strings of Christmas tree lights.

DAT Short for *digital audio tape*, a tape cassette format developed by the consumer electronics industry for use in tape decks for stereo systems, later adapted for use in tape backup drives for computers.

data A vague term that usually refers to the stuff you create or work with—text in a word processor, numbers in a spreadsheet, database records, and so on. Data may also refer to anything stored on disk or residing in memory.

data bits A basic modem setting that specifies the number of bits in the smallest unit of data exchanged (usually seven or eight bits).

data chart A presentation graphics term used to describe bar charts, line charts, pie charts, and other graphs based on numeric data (see *word chart*).

data file The place where you keep your data—as opposed to a *program file*, which holds the programming code from which software is constructed.

data manager See *database program*.

data recovery What you do when you discover you've deleted the wrong file or that your hard disk is corrupted. Plenty of software utilities (such as the undelete and disk repair tools included in DOS and most utility libraries) are available to make this job easier (see *undelete*, *utility library*).

data transfer rate The amount of data that can be hustled from disk to memory in one second, usually applied to hard disks and CD ROM drives. Not necessarily a good measure of hard disk performance, but a telling spec for a CD ROM drive.

data type In a database, refers to the kind of data stored in a field: text, date, number, logical, and so on. In programming languages, basic data types are integers (whole numbers), floating-point values (other numbers), and strings (usually text).

database Basically, any collection of information, but most often used to describe a file or a group of related files created by a data manager. Sometimes used as shorthand for *database program*.

database application A complete custom program created using a database program. Usually written by a professional programmer to handle a specific task (such as order entry, billing, or sales tracking), the typical database application is designed to run on a network, so that an entire department or small business can enter and retrieve information.

database program Any application that stores data in fields and records and enables users to retrieve that data using queries or reports. Also known as a *database* or *data manager* (see *field*, *record*, *query*).

database programming language The core of any programmable data manager, a database programming language is a set of commands that, used in specific combinations, can complete any database task, from sorting a group of records to creating a complex report. Most people use a database program's menus to accomplish simple tasks, while professionals employ a programming language to create database applications. The most widely used database programming languages are *dBASE* and its *Xbase* dialects.

database server A network server that does the processing in a client-server database (see *client-server*).

DBMS Short for for *data base management system* (see *database program*).

DDE A term describing a type of data link between Windows applications (see *OLE*).

DEC VT-100 A terminal once produced by Digital Equipment Corporation, the VT-100 has become a popular standard for terminal emulation software. VT-102 is a slight variation (see *terminal emulation*).

dedicated server A PC used exclusively for supplying services (like communications or printing) to a network. Nondedicated servers provide services to the network but are also used as workstations.

default The computer equivalent of "factory settings," or how things will happen normally unless you decide otherwise. For instance, with most word processors, you insert text by default, and you must press the [Ins] key to overtype text. Usually, a menu enables you to change this default setting.

defragger See *disk defragmenter.*

Delete To remove or erase, usually by highlighting the thing to be deleted and pressing the [Del] key.

Delete Sentry An undelete "helper" utility that come with DOS, Delete Sentry makes it easier to recover accidentally deleted files by maintaining complete copies of them. It's foolproof but gobbles disk space, and deleting files takes a little longer (see *data recovery, undelete*).

Delete Tracker The other DOS "helper" utility intended to increase the likelihood that you can recover deleted files. Unlike Delete Sentry, Tracker uses almost no disk space but still improves the chances of recovering long files (see *data recovery, undelete*).

delimiter Usually a comma, used to separate words in a text file into fields for use by a database program.

desktop A loose metaphor for the background of Windows and other graphical user interfaces, designed to make new computer users more comfortable. More obviously, the type of PC that goes *on* your desk as opposed to under it.

desktop publishing (DTP) The process of using word processing and page layout (desktop publishing) software—plus a laser printer or phototypesetter—to produce professional-looking reports, newsletters, brochures, and other publications. Most Windows word processors include many DTP features, which means that using DTP software is often a professional endeavor.

desktop video (DTV) Recording and editing video on your PC.

device driver A small program than enables a specific peripheral device (such as a CD ROM drive or a printer) to communicate with DOS, Windows, or a DOS application (see *CONFIG.SYS, peripheral*).

diagnostic utility A software tool that checks the health of your PC, usually by testing memory, disk drives, the motherboard, the CPU, the communications ports, and so on. Better diagnostic utilities alert you to problems with IRQs and other hardware conflicts (see *IRQ*).

dial-in gateway A PC or special box attached to a LAN that enables users to dial in by modem from their home PC or laptop and access the network as if they were sitting at a regular workstation (also known as a *dial-up* or *remote access* gateway).

dialog box A window that pops up on screen in response to a command, system error, or alert, asking for input from the user. Dialog boxes can be as simple as two buttons (OK and Cancel), or they may contain dozens of buttons, checkboxes, list boxes, and sliders.

differential backup One of several kinds of daily backups. A differential backup makes copies of every file that has changed since the last full backup (see *backup*).

digitize The process of converting analog input, such as photographs or sound waves, to digital output such as scanned images or audio CDs (see *scanner, sound card*).

dingbats Decorative typeface characters (also known as ornaments), such as arrows, stars, and yin-yang symbols, used to spiff up boring text. TrueType and PostScript Dingbats can be printed at any size. For a starter set, install Windows' Wingdings font.

DIP switch A tiny toggle switch mounted on expansion cards, motherboards, modems, and other devices. Used to configure the hardware and avoid conflicts between devices.

direct memory access See *DMA*.

directory The basic tool for organizing information on your hard disk, a directory is intended to hold related files, such as all the data files created with an application. If your hard disk is a filing cabinet, then a directory is a file folder—which is why Windows' File Manager represents directories this way. A *subdirectory* is a directory beneath another directory on the *directory tree* (see *File Manager, directory tree*).

directory listing A list of all files and subdirectories within (or "beneath") a directory. In Windows, clicking on a directory folder in File Manager displays a directory listing; in DOS, typing DIR and pressing [Enter] does the same thing, but the listing is harder to read (see *File Manager*).

directory tree A full listing of your hard disk's directory structure, showing subdirectories as branches off the root (or main) directory. To view a directory tree from the DOS prompt, type TREE and press [Enter]; if you're in Windows, simply run File Manager.

disk Any small discus-shaped medium for storing data. Usually refers to a *hard disk* (the disks are inside the hard disk casing) or *floppy disk*.

disk cache A software utility that speeds up performance by keeping recently accessed data in RAM instead of on disk.

disk compression A scheme in which all (or most of) the data on an entire disk is scrunched to gain more space, usually by a software utility such as DOS's DriveSpace. Disk compression utilities compress and decompress files on the fly, without intervention from you (see *compression*).

disk defragmenter A utility (also known as a *defragger*) that gathers up all the fragments of files that DOS has scattered across the surface of your hard disk and reassembles them, so that each file's data is contiguous. The defragging usually improves disk performance (see *full defrag*).

disk mirroring A system where identical data is written to two separate drives in order to keep data safe and accessible if one drive dies. Usually used on network servers (see *RAID*).

diskette See *floppy disk*.

display Usually refers to the monitor (or LCD panel on a notebook) that shows you the big picture; sometimes also refers to the CRT plus the graphics card. As a verb, it describes the PC's ability to show something on the screen (see *LCD, monitor*).

display type A design, layout, and desktop publishing term for headlines, subheads, pull-quotes, captions, and other prominent text (see *body text*).

dithering Simulating colors (or shades of gray) not available on a monitor or printer by mixing pixels or dots of other colors (or shades). For example, a monitor could simulate yellow-green by mixing yellow and green dots.

DMA Short for *direct memory access*, whereby an expansion card or other device accesses system memory directly, without involving the CPU.

DOC A file extension used by many word processors.

docking station An optional desktop platform for plugging in a notebook computer, so that connecting with a network, printer, full-size keyboard, desktop monitor, or any other peripheral can be accomplished all at once. Not all notebooks have optional docking stations (see *notebook computer*).

document file Usually refers to a text file created by a word processor or desktop publishing program, but may also apply to a worksheet or a saved database report.

document management system A network application that helps large organizations track documents through many revision cycles. Most common in legal and corporate word processing centers.

documentation The manual and any other sheets of instructions that come with hardware or software, plus any software (tutorials, and so on) that helps you use the product in question.

DOS Short for *disk operating system*, DOS is the essential set of software programs that enables your computer to run, used by all IBM-compatible PCs. DOS also comes with many useful utilities (see *operating system, utility*).

DOS prompt Also known as the command line, the place on screen where you type in DOS commands (like COPY or DEL) and launch applications. It usually looks something like C:\>.

dot matrix printer A printer that uses tiny metal pins (usually 24 of them) and an inked ribbon to tap letters, numbers, and graphics onto the printed page. Dot matrix printers are the cheapest you can buy, and are still essential for multipart forms.

dot pitch A basic measure of monitor sharpness, the dot pitch is the distance, measured as a fraction of a millimeter, between phosphor dots of the same color on the inner surface of a CRT's screen. (On Trinitron monitors, which do not use phosphor dots, the equivalent measure is aperture pitch.)

double-click To tap the left mouse button twice in quick succession, usually to launch programs or execute commands (see *mouse*).

download Usually, to receive a file via modem from a BBS or on-line service. Also to send downloadable fonts, such as TrueType or PostScript fonts, from the PC to a printer (see *BBS, modem*).

downloadable font A font that can be sent directly to a printer, without the PC having to create a bit-mapped image of the text (see *bitmapped graphics, PostScript, TrueType*).

dpi (dots per inch) A measure of resolution used for printers, scanners, and other devices. Generally, the higher the dpi, the better a printed page or scanned image will look (see *resolution*).

DPMS Short for *DOS Protected Mode Services*, a Novell DOS feature that can load some device drivers and TSRs into extended memory, freeing conventional and upper memory for use by other software.

draft mode A low-quality but generally fast mode for printing or displaying documents.

drag and drop A mouse move that usually refers to selecting text or graphics within a document, dragging it by holding down the left mouse button, and dropping it in a new location by releasing the button. Also refers to dragging a file icon and dropping it on an application (or command) icon to perform some action (see *click and drag*).

DRAM Short for *dynamic random access memory*, this term applies to the most common type of memory chip, almost always used for a PC's main memory (see *RAM, SIMM*).

draw program An application that enables you to create and edit images—from simple lines and shapes to full-color illustrations—using lines, shapes, and patterns (see *vector graphics*).

drawing layer Some spreadsheets and word processors and many drawing programs enable you to draw on transparent overlays that "float" above the document (or over other drawing layers). Although common applications usually have a single drawing layer, CAD programs often have hundreds.

drawing node See *control point*.

drive Generic term for peripheral device that handles data stored on disk or tape (see *disk*, *tape backup drive*).

drive arrays Systems using two or more hard drives (see *RAID*).

drive bay Space inside your computer reserved for holding a floppy drive, hard disk, CD ROM drive, or tape drive. Different computers accommodate different numbers and sizes of drives.

drop cap A typesetting term for the first letter in a paragraph when set in extra-large or decorative display type, where the base of the letter drops below the rest of the line. Drop caps are typically used to indicate the first page of a new chapter or the beginning of a new section.

DSP Short for *digital signal processor* a special kind of processor designed for ultra-fast manipulation of audio, video, and other analog data.

DTP See *desktop publishing*.

duplex printing The process of printing on both sides of a sheet of paper.

duty cycle The amount of time a piece of hardware is expected to be active. For example, if a printer has a 25 percent duty cycle, then the manufacturer expects it to be printing for 6 hours out of 24. Printer duty cycles are often expressed in pages per day or month.

DVI Short for *Digital Video Interactive*, an Intel video codec that requires special hardware. DVI-RTV (real-time video) can be captured by a PC as it is recorded or broadcast, while DVI-PLV (production-level video) must be compressed from videotape.

Dvorak An alternative keyboard layout that puts the most frequently used letters on the home row.

DX2 Intel's successor to the 486DX, a "clock doubling" version of the 486DX whose internal processing speed is twice that of a 486DX installed in the same motherboard (see 486DX). Formerly known as the 486DX2.

DX4 A "clock tripling" (*not* quadrupling) version of the 486DX whose internal processing speed is three times that of a 486DX in the same motherboard.

DXF The *AutoCAD* vector file format (see *vectors graphics*).

dye sublimation The best and most expensive color printing method used by desktop color printers.

E

ECC memory Short for *error correction code* memory, an expensive type of memory used in some fancy network servers to help prevent crashes.

echo Copying BBS messages from one system to another automatically. For example, FidoNet messages are echoed around the world.

EEPROM Short for *electronic erasable programmable read-only memory*, a special type of memory chip that holds information even when the PC is turned off. Can be erased by applying electric voltage; typically used for system BIOSs.

EGA Short for *Enhanced Graphics Adapter*, an obsolete IBM graphics card. The EGA standard is 640 by 350 resolution with 16 colors.

EISA Short for *Extended Industry Standard Architecture*, an aging 32-bit standard for expansion buses and cards still popular in network servers.

electron beam A stream of finely focused electrons that impact on the inside face of the CRT, causing the color phosphors to glow.

electronic mail See *E-mail*.

electronic presentation A slide show displayed on a monitor or LCD panel, often combining word and data charts with sound, music, and animation.

ELF Short for *extremely low frequency*, which describes a type of electromagnetic radiation emitted by most electric and electronic devices, including computer monitors. May pose a health risk (see *VLF*).

E-mail Short for electronic mail, this term refers to private messages that can be sent and received via a local area network (LAN), BBS, or on-line service such as CompuServe or the Internet (see *on-line service*).

embedded When applied to hardware, this term refers to built-in devices such as video controllers, SCSI adapters, serial ports, and so on. When applied to software, it refers to fonts, graphics, sound clips, and so on that have been saved within a document (see *font embedding*).

emergency disk A floppy disk that contains essential DOS files (like COMMAND.COM) and data recovery utilities, which you can use to boot up your computer if your hard disk becomes badly corrupted or infected with a virus. Most utility libraries create an emergency disk for you (see *boot*, *data recovery*, *utility library*).

EMI See *RFI*.

EMM386 DOS's *expanded memory manager*, used to help old DOS apps (and some device drivers) access memory over 640K.

EMR Short for *electromagnetic radiation*, a broad term that refers to any radiation emitted at a frequency below that of light, including radio waves and monitor emissions.

EMS Short for *expanded memory specification*, a largely outdated specification developed to enable applications to use memory beyond 640K. DOS 5 and later versions can emulate EMS for applications that require it.

emulated keys Notebook computer keyboards have fewer keys than a standard keyboard, so some of the keys must do double duty. For instance, if there's no (Page Up) key, the notebook may emulate that key by having you press (F)(N) and (Home) simultaneously.

encryption Protecting confidential files by turning them into gobbledygook. Encryption utilities let you assign passwords to encrypted files, so anyone who knows the password can restore the file to its original form.

Energy Star A set of specifications developed by the Environmental Protection Agency for energy-saving "green" PCs.

Enhanced IDE A recent augmentation of the IDE (Integrated Drive Electronics) standard, the most popular hard disk interface specification. Supports drives larger than 500MB, promises increased performance, and lets one adapter handle up to four devices (see *IDE*).

enhanced parallel port A type of parallel port capable of sending data to and receiving data from hard disks and other devices at high speed. Enhanced Capabilities Ports (ECP) is the matching Windows software standard.

EPROM Short for *erasable programmable read-only memory*. Like an *EEPROM*, except to erase the chip you must remove its cover and expose it to ultraviolet light. Generally used to produce small quantities of custom ROM chips (see *ROM*).

EPS Short for *Encapsulated PostScript*, a high-quality, PostScript-based file format used by some drawing programs (see *PostScript*).

ergonomic A buzzword that means easy and comfortable to use.

error-checking protocol In modem communications, nearly all file transfer protocols check for errors to ensure the integrity of the data being transmitted or received. However, some file transfer protocols, such as Ymodem-G and 1K-Xmodem-G, leave out the error checking to speed transmission and let an error-checking modem do the work (see *file transfer protocol, V.42*).

error message Software's snippy way of telling you that you (or hardware or software) screwed up without giving you enough information to figure out what to do about it.

ESDI Short for *enhanced small device interface*, a defunct hard disk interface standard.

Ethernet The most popular kind of network card; also refers to the matching cables. The most common versions are thinnet (also known as Cheapernet or 10Base2), which uses thin coax cable and round metal snap-on connectors; and 10BaseT, which uses the same kind of cable used by telephones, and similar plastic snap-in plugs.

EXE A file extension used solely for executable files.

executable file Basically, a program that you can start yourself. When you type an application's name at the DOS prompt or double-click on its icon in Windows, you're running an executable file. Most executable files end in an EXE extension, but some end in COM or BAT (see *program file*).

expanded memory Memory that has been grabbed by a memory manager such as DOS's EMM386 so it can be used by certain older DOS applications and device drivers (see *extended memory, memory manager*).

expansion card Also known as an *expansion board*, an add-in circuit board that plugs into one of your PC's expansion slots and provides additional capability (as with a sound card), or supports a peripheral device such as a monitor or CD ROM drive (see *expansion slots, ISA*).

expansion slots The slots in your computer that hold expansion cards, known collectively as the *expansion bus*.

extended memory All memory above 1064K, exploited by Windows and some DOS applications (see *conventional memory*).

external memory cache See *secondary memory cache*.

F

fan-fold paper See *continuous-form paper*.

Fast ATA A term used by Seagate to identify a recent enhancement of the IDE hard disk interface standard (see *Enhanced IDE*).

FAT Short for *file allocation table*, the tracking system DOS uses to monitor the status (available, in use, or damaged) of every *sector* on a hard or floppy disk (see *sectors*).

fax-back An automated product-support system where you punch buttons on your touch-tone phone to order documents, which are sent to your fax machine.

fax modem A modem capable of sending and receiving faxes as well as the usual computer files (see *modem*).

fax server A PC hooked to a network to provide fax modem services to workstations on the LAN. Sometimes tied in to an E-mail system.

FDDI Short for *Fiber Distributed Data Interface*, an *ANSI* standard for 10MB-per-second network adapters using fiber-optic cable.

fiber-optic link Fiber-optic cables used as a faster alternative to Ethernet, most commonly to link network servers (also known as a *network backbone*).

field In databases, the basic building block of a data file. Each field holds a specific kind of information, such as a street address or a dollar amount. The contents of each field is called a *field value* (see *database, record*).

file The basic unit you use to store anything—text, data, computer instructions, all are saved in files (see *directory*).

file association A link established between a file extension and a particular application (for example, XLS with *Excel*, DOC with *Word*, and so on). Enables Windows to open files in the proper application when you double-click on them in the File Manager.

file attribute One of the four settings DOS uses to indicate whether a file is read-only (and cannot be deleted), an operating system file (like MSDOS.SYS), a hidden file (that won't appear when you run a DIR command), or a file that has been backed up (see *archive bit*).

file extension The part of a file name that comes after the period, such as DOC or EXE (see *file, file name*).

file folder In Windows, a graphical representation of a *directory*.

file format A type of program or data file, often indicated by the file extension.

File Manager In Windows, the File Manager lets you use your mouse to move, copy, rename, and delete files and directories.

file name DOS file names have two parts separated by a period. The part that comes before the period can contain up to eight characters. The part that comes after the period, called the *extension*, is optional and can contain up to three characters. In WS.EXE, *EXE* is the extension.

file server A PC that stores data and program files for a network.

file transfer protocol A software routine included with communications software, designed to ensure error-free transmission of files by modem. The most popular file transfer protocols are Xmodem, Zmodem, Ymodem, Kermit, and Ymodem-G. For files to be transferred, both the sender and receiver must use the same protocol (see *error-checking protocol, Ymodem-G*).

file transfer utility A program, such as *Laplink* or DOS's INTERLNK, that lets you quickly copy files between two computers hooked together with a parallel or serial cable (see *parallel port, null modem cable*).

file viewer A utility found in many Windows shells that lets you view files created by popular word processors, spreadsheets, and other applications.

film recorder Primarily used by people who create professional presentations, film recorders transfer computer graphics output to 35mm slide film.

flash memory A type of memory chip, commonly used to create a kind of permanent RAM disk for notebooks, that can retain data after the system is turned off (see *RAM disk*).

flat file database A *data manager* that stores all its data in a single table. Sometimes applied to any easy-to-use database that does not require programming (see *relational database*).

flat-panel display Basically any display that doesn't use a picture tube. The most popular technology for this is the liquid crystal display (LCD), used in virtually all notebook computers.

flicker free A hyperbolic marketing term used by manufacturers to describe displays that run at *refresh rates* higher than 70 Hz to reduce perceived flicker.

floating point unit See *FPU*.

floppy disk A removable disk used to store computer data. The vast majority of floppies come in $3^1/2$-inch (720K or 1.44MB), and $5^1/4$-inch (360K or 1.2MB) formats.

floppy drive The drive that reads and writes data to and from a floppy disk. Floppy drives come in $3^1/2$-inch and $5^1/4$-inch varieties.

floptical drive A 3^1/$_2$-inch floppy drive that uses a laser to pack 21MB on a single disk. Floptical drives also accept standard 3^1/$_2$-inch floppies with 720K and 1.44MB capacities.

flowchart A diagram that uses lines, boxes, circles, arrows, and other shapes to demonstrate a process or other activity. Most popular presentation graphics programs let you create simple flowcharts.

font Originally referred to a specific point size and weight of a particular typeface. In computer terminology, a font is an electronic file that contains a *typeface*.

font cartridge Before Windows had scalable TrueType fonts, the best way to get fonts was to buy a cartridge containing them and plug the thing into the printer (see *scalable font, TrueType*).

font converter A utility for converting a font from one format into another—for example, PostScript Type 1 to TrueType.

font embedding Storing a font within a document. Some embedded fonts can only be printed, while others can be edited or used in other documents.

font manager A utility that helps organize a large number of fonts.

font rasterizer A program used to scale fonts for printing and to display fonts on screen almost exactly as they'll appear in print. The TrueType rasterizer comes with Windows and makes scalable TrueType fonts available in all Windows applications. The *Adobe Type Manager* rasterizer does the same thing, but provides access to the larger universe of PostScript Type 1 fonts.

footer Most word processors allow you to print a line or two of type at the bottom of every page called a footer. Footers may include text and/or a page number.

footprint The space a computer or a peripheral device takes up on your desk. If a computer is designed to stand on end, for instance, it is said to have a small footprint.

form factor Most often used to refer to the size of an internal disk drive. The most common form factors are 5^1/4-inches and 3^1/$_2$-inches, which describe the widths of the internal platters, not the widths of the drives themselves.

format To prepare a disk to receive data—or to apply fonts, indents, margins, colors, and so on to a document (see *file format*).

formatting The end result of creating a page layout and applying text attributes (see *desktop publishing, word processor*).

forms In a database, a screen display that shows a subset of the database's fields, often with explanatory labels and instructions. Database applications typically include a variety of forms for various functions, such as entering data and browsing records.

forum Special interest area on a BBS or on-line service, sometimes called a special interest group or SIG (see *BBS, on-line service*).

FPU Short for *floating point unit* (see *math coprocessor*).

fractal A mathematical formula that produces graphics that look like (often beautiful) natural textures and shapes.

frame In desktop publishing or word processing, a box that can be filled with graphics or text and positioned anywhere on the page. In video, one of many discrete images in a video sequence (standard video is 30 frames per second).

frame grabber A video board and matching software that enable you to isolate individual frames in a video sequence and copy them into a graphics or page layout program.

freeware Free software, usually available through a BBS or on-line service.

front end Usually just another way of saying user interface. Sometimes refers to the "client" end of a client-server network application (see *client-server, user interface*).

full backup Making a safety copy of every file on your hard disk (see *backup*).

full defrag A mode used by a disk defragger, in which all your files are reassembled and all the empty spaces between them removed (see *disk defragmenter*).

full duplex A type of modem communications where data travels in both directions simultaneously. Communications standards for modems that run at 9600 bps or faster stipulate full duplex operation (see *half duplex*).

full-motion video Strictly speaking, TV-quality or better moving video images displayed in a window or full screen on your PC. Term often misused to refer to jerky, postage-stamp-size images.

function key The 12 (or fewer) "F" keys, usually lining the top of the keyboard. Different applications use them for different things, but F1 usually triggers the Help menu.

G

gateway A PC or special box hooked to a network to connect it to another system, such as the *Internet*, a remote LAN, or a commercial E-mail system.

GIF Short for *Graphic Interchange Format*, a graphics format popular with CompuServe users.

gigabyte (GB) 1024 megabytes

glare screen An antiglare covering that goes over the front of your monitor to reduce eye-straining reflections.

glitch A small problem with hardware or software, usually less serious than a bug but annoying nonetheless.

glossary In word processing, a list of words that you can quickly insert into a document.

graphics card Also known as the video card (or video board), an expansion card that contains the graphics controller. A connector on the card's rear bracket connects to the monitor.

graphics controller The circuitry that produces the image you see on your screen, the graphics controller may reside either on a card or on the PC's motherboard. Also used to refer to the single chip that does most of the work in producing an image.

graphics file Any file that holds an image rather than text, such as a drawing, a scanned photo, a bit map, or clip art.

graphics mode One of several combinations of color density and resolution produced by your graphics card (such as 640 by 480 resolution in 256 colors, 1024 by 768 resolution in 16 colors, and so on). Also used to describe a display mode distinct from *text mode* (also known as *character mode*).

graphics tablet A flat panel (also known as a graphics pad) that enables you to draw using a stylus instead of a mouse. A pressure-sensitive tablet lets you vary the width or color of the line on screen by pressing harder, providing a close simulation of working with a pencil or brush.

grayscale A term used to describe an image containing a number of gray shades as well as black and white. Also describes hardware (usually scanners) that produce grayscale images.

green computing Using a PC with the environment in mind, typically involving computers and peripherals designed to use less power, plus a commitment to recycling paper, batteries, and toner cartridges.

Group III fax Supporting speeds up to 9600 bps, this is the standard to which almost every fax machine and fax modem conforms. Group I and II are long obsolete, while Group IV (which requires a *leased line*) is extremely rare.

GUI (graphical user interface) Pronounced *gooey*, this unfortunate acronym describes a way to use your computer by mousing and clicking on icons and pull-down menus, instead of typing text-based commands at the DOS prompt. On PCs, Windows is the GUI almost everyone uses.

H

half duplex A modem communications method where data travels in only one direction at a time (see *full duplex*).

halftone A type of image produced using screens (patterns of dots) to simulate grays on black-and-white printers, or to simulate a full range of colors from the 3 or 4 inks used by color printers.

handle The nickname people use when they log onto a BBS, used to preserve privacy and sometimes to adopt a strange persona (see *BBS*).

hard carriage return Pressing the Enter key puts two invisible characters into a text file: a line feed and a carriage return. Together they are called a *hard carriage return*. They make the cursor move down one line and back to the left end of the new line.

hard copy A paper print out.

hard disk Also known as a *hard drive*, the basic data storage device in most computers. A hard disk may store up to 2GB of data on one or more (usually four) metal platters coated with a magnetic medium (see *magnetic media*).

hard disk interface A term that variously refers to the circuitry employed by a hard disk to communicate with a PC; an expansion card containing that circuitry; or a hard disk connector either on the motherboard, an expansion card, or on the hard disk itself. IDE, Enhanced IDE, and SCSI are the three most popular hard disk interface standards.

hardware disk cache Works just like a software disk cache, except that it's an expansion card with its own on-board memory chips, so it doesn't use any of your PC's RAM (see *disk cache, expansion card*).

Hayes command set See *AT commands*

header A line or two of type at the top of every page, usually including a small amount of text and/or a page number (see *footer*).

Hertz (Hz) A standard measure of frequency, synonymous with cycles per second (cps). One megahertz (MHz) equals 1,000,000 Hz.

hidden file A file that won't display when you run a directory listing. You can set the file attribute to hide a file using DOS's ATTRIB command or Windows' File Manager (see *file attribute, directory listing*).

high-level programming language A *programming language* that's somewhat Englishlike, although only a programmer would think that. The ultimate *low-level* programming language is assembly language, which is kind of like programming with the 1s and 0s of binary math.

high memory The first 64K of RAM above 1MB, reserved for relocating parts of DOS where appropriate (see *memory manager*).

High Performance ATA A term used by Maxtor to identify a recent enhancement of the IDE hard disk interface standard (see *Enhanced IDE*).

horizontal scan rate Measures how fast a video board or monitor can draw a line from one side of the screen to the other. The higher the horizontal scan rate, the higher the maximum resolution at a given *refresh rate*.

host mode If you leave your communications software in host mode, outside users can call in via modem and download files, upload files, leave messages, and (if you give them the secret password) even rummage around your hard disk. Sort of like setting up your own cheesy little BBS (see *BBS, download, upload*).

I

IBM AT An ancient IBM personal computer, introduced in 1985 and built around Intel's 286 CPU (see *CPU*).

IBM PC The first IBM personal computer, released in 1981. Built around Intel's 4.77-MHz 8088 CPU, it originally shipped with 64K of RAM.

IBM XT The first IBM system with a hard disk, otherwise nearly identical to the IBM PC.

icon A little picture that represents an application, file, or command in Windows or another graphical user interface (see *GUI*).

IDE Short for *Integrated Drive Electronics*, currently the most popular type of hard drive used in PCs. A standard IDE adapter can handle a maximum of two hard drives (see *Enhanced IDE, SCSI*).

IEEE Short for the *Institute of Electrical and Electronics Engineers*, a professional organization that (among other things) develops and publishes communications standards, notably those for Ethernet networks.

image editor In desktop publishing parlance, an image editor is a tool used to touch up or enhance a *bit-mapped* image, such as a scanned photograph.

imagesetter An expensive, high-resolution PostScript printer often used in desktop publishing (see *PostScript printer*).

incremental backup A backup that duplicates every file that has changed since the *last* incremental backup; usually performed every day (see *backup*).

Indeo Intel's video compression scheme (see *codec*).

infrared Light below the visible spectrum, used in some wireless mice, printer sharing devices, and network adapters.

INI An extension used by Windows and Windows applications for the files used to store program initialization settings.

ink jet printer An inexpensive alternative to laser printers, an ink jet printer sprays liquid ink onto the paper. Color printers using liquid ink jets are the least expensive and lowest quality. Solid ink jet color printers are comparable to more expensive *thermal wax* printers.

insertion point The I-beam shaped mouse pointer that appears in Windows text documents.

instruction In programming, instructions are the equivalent of commands. Fundamentally, a program is simply a long list of instructions.

Intel The largest microprocessor manufacturer in the world, responsible for setting all the important standards in PC CPUs, including the 286, 386, 486, and Pentium lines.

interactive A buzzword in the computer gaming and multimedia business, it implies that your input will affect what's happening on the screen. But since that's true of almost all computer applications, including word processors, the term is a bit too general to be very useful.

interface A connector, such as a serial port or a hard disk interface; also any specification that enables hardware devices to communicate. When applied to software, a shortened form of *user interface* (see *hard disk interface, user interface*).

interlaced A video mode that draws the even lines on the screen in one pass, the odd lines on the next. Allows a higher resolution display than a monitor would otherwise be able to support, but usually results in an irritating flicker.

interleave Once upon a time, you had to set a hard drive's disk interleave (the number of rotations required to read a track from disk) to match the speed of the computer in which it was installed. With today's hard disk drives, this is a nonissue (see *bank switching*).

Internet The world's biggest on-line service. A worldwide network of computers and BBSs with more E-mail users, forums, databases, brilliant academics, and borderline personalities than there are modems. You can't subscribe to Internet directly—access requires a UNIX system and high installation and subscriber fees—so most people log on through their company, a university, an on-line service, or their local BBS.

interpolated resolution A technique used primarily by scanners to increase the sharpness of scanned images (see *scanner*).

interpreter Software that converts *high-level* programming instructions in a program into the *machine language* understood by your computer—on the fly, as the program is running. A program that uses an interpreter is said to be *uncompiled*, and runs slower than one that's been compiled (see *compiler*).

interrupt A PC's hardware interrupts work a little like valves in a car's engine, routing the CPU's attention to various pieces of hardware as necessary. Most expansion cards need exclusive access to one or more of your PC's 15 interrupt request (IRQ) lines. There are also software interrupts, but only programmers need to mess with them.

interrupt conflict When two or more devices attempt to use the same IRQ.

I/O Computerese for *input/output*. The term *I/O port* describes any port on your PC, but is often used to refer specifically to a serial port (see *port, serial port*).

IRQ Short for *interrupt request line*, an exclusive communications channel between an expansion card and the CPU.

ISA Short for *Industry Standard Architecture*, the most popular specification for expansion slots. Any PC you buy should have at least a couple of these slots, so that you can select from the vast number and variety of ISA expansion cards. However, ISA slots run at a slow 8 MHz and transmit data 16 bits or 8 bits at a time, so make sure the PC has a couple of local bus slots, too (see *expansion slots, local bus*).

ISDN Short for *Integrated Services Digital Network*, a digital phone standard that enables high-speed data transmission. ISDN is available in some areas of the U.S., but not all, which limits its practical use.

ITU Short for the *International Telecommunications Union*, the successor to the CCITT. This United Nations agency sets major modem and fax standards such as V.32bis and Group II (see *Group III fax*).

J

jargon What people who know something about computers use to intimidate others who know less.

joules See *watt*.

joystick A throttle-like input device that moves the cursor in computer games, usually outfitted with a couple of "fire" buttons and sensitivity controls.

JPEG Short for *Joint Photographic Experts Group* and the name of a compression standard for still images. *Motion JPEG* is a digital video standard that compresses each frame with JPEG (see *lossy*).

jumper A bit of plastic the size of a match head containing a metal connector, designed to fit over a pair of pins on a circuit board. Many expansion cards, disk drives, and motherboards enable you to configure them by moving a jumper from one pair of pins to another pair (see *configuration*).

justified text Text that aligns perfectly on the right *and* left margins. Most word processors and desktop publishing programs can justify text with the click of a mouse.

K

K See *kilobyte*.

Kermit A widely used *file transfer protocol* with several variants, most of them slow.

kerning Adjusting the space between two adjacent letters so they look more pleasing to the eye.

keyboard accelerator Software that lets you adjust the keyboard repeat rate (how fast a key repeats if you hold it down) and repeat delay (how long it takes for a key to start repeating after you press it). The Keyboard program in Windows' Control Panel is a keyboard accelerator.

keystroke A single key-press.

kilobyte (K or Kb) 1024 bytes. See *byte*.

kilohertz (kHz) One thousand cycles per second.

kioskware Slang term for multimedia applications run on terminals with touchscreens or membrane keyboards. Commonly found in museums, public transit hubs, and shopping malls.

L

LAN Short for *local area network*, a group of computers connected so they can swap files, exchange E-mail messages, share peripherals (printers, hard disks, modems), and sometimes run workgroup software such as *Lotus Notes* or a multiuser database application (see *network operating system, peer-to-peer LAN, server-based LAN*).

landscape orientation Printed sideways on a page, so the page is wider than it is tall (see *portrait orientation*).

laptop The predecessor to the notebook, the laptop is a mobile PC usually weighing somewhere between 8 and 15 pounds (see *portable computer*).

laser printer The most popular printer for getting sharp printouts, a laser printer produces one page at a time by scanning an image onto an electrostatically charged drum with a laser. Toner clings to the image and is fused to the page, similar to the way a photocopier produces copies.

LaserJet Hewlett-Packard's trade name for its popular line of laser printers.

LCD Short for *liquid crystal display*, a flat panel of tiny cells, used on most mobile computers in place of a monitor. Each cell contains a substrate that blocks or admits light depending on the electric charge; together these cells produce the image on screen (see *active-matrix LCD*).

LCD panel An LCD that sits atop an overhead projector, so images can be projected against a wall or screen. Plugs into any monitor connector (usually a notebook's, for convenience).

leading The amount of space, measured in points, between two lines of type. In the old days of manual typesetting, lines were divided by thin strips of lead—hence the name.

leased line Telephone line permanently connecting two locations, with a much higher *bandwidth* than a conventional phone line.

LED Short for *light-emitting diode*, an LED is a sort of tiny electronic light bulb. Used in a PC's front panel, external modems, smoke alarms, and so on.

ligature A character composed of two letters, as in the combination a/e in *encyclopædia*.

line chart A graph that shows continuous change over time, intended to emphasize trends rather than the individual values that make up the line.

line conditioner A device designed to protect your PC from such electrical problems as brownouts, surges, and spikes. More sophisticated and expensive than a *surge protector*.

line feed On a computer, a nonprinting character that moves the cursor down one line (see *hard carriage return*).

list boxes A Windows term for pull-down menus in dialog boxes.

lithium ion storage (LIS) Describes a fairly new kind of battery used in many notebooks. Offers longer life than other batteries (see *nickel-cadmium* and *nickel metal-hydride*).

load A general term that refers to copying software or data from disk to memory. Synonymous with *start*, *run*, or *launch* when applied to programs; the same as *open* when applied to a data file. The only term used to describe copying a device driver from disk to memory, a task usually performed by the CONFIG.SYS file (see *CONFIG.SYS*, *device driver*).

local area network See *LAN*.

local bus Strictly speaking, the bus where the CPU resides, which may include slots that enable expansion boards to run at the same clock speed as the CPU. The VL bus is a true local expansion bus, but the PCI bus is slightly different, because a special controller chip isolates PCI slots from the CPU. The performance difference between VL and PCI buses is insignificant (see *PCI bus*, *VL bus*).

log in Synonymous with *log on*, to enter your name and password when you connect with a LAN or dial into an on-line service or BBS via modem (see *BBS*, *LAN*, *on-line service*).

logical drive A drive that DOS recognizes, instead of the actual, physical drive. For example, when some people buy a new hard disk, they split it into multiple logical drives (C:, D:, E:, and so on) of varying sizes using DOS's FDISK utility. Creating these drives is called *partitioning*.

logical format Preparing a disk to store data using DOS's FORMAT command. Most people just say "format," for short.

logical operators See *Boolean logic*.

lookup tables A lookup table is a multi-column table used (primarily in databases) to define correlations between different types of data. For example, you could use a lookup table to generate grades from test scores: The first column would contain break points for the scores (90 percent, 80 percent, and so on), while the second column would have the grades (A, B, and so on).

lossy A compression scheme typically used with graphics, sound, and digital video that saves disk space by reducing the amount of information in the original file. High compression ratios result in smaller files but lower quality images or sound due to data loss.

low-level format The basic grid of *sectors* and *tracks* that DOS uses to store data on a hard disk. New hard disks come with the low-level format already in place, but some old hard disks may need their low-level format "refreshed" in order to work properly. A hard disk needs its low-level format in order to be *partitioned* and *logically formatted* with DOS.

M

macro A series of keystrokes, commands, and/or mouse actions that can be "played back" using a special key combination.

macro language A simple programming language that goes beyond recording keystrokes and/or mouse actions, enabling you to add special features, such as branching (see *branch*).

macro processor A utility that lets you create macros that work in different applications.

macro recorder A feature found in many applications that records your keystrokes and/or mouse actions and saves them as a macro. This is the way most people create macros.

magnetic media Anything that stores information in magnetic form: diskettes, cassette tapes, reel-to-reel tapes in a recording studio, the strip on the back of your credit card.

magneto-optical (MO) drive A type of removable-media drive that enhances the capacity of conventional magnetic drives using a laser. The most common type of MO cartridge holds 128MB, but capacities go up to 1.3GB.

mail merge A word processing feature that inserts information from a data file (usually a list of names and addresses) into pre-selected positions in a text file (such as a form letter) in order to print a series of customized documents. As its name implies, mail merge is most often used to create mass mailings.

main memory Also called *system memory*, the large block of memory chips in your PC where computing happens. When you start an application or open a file, that information is copied from its storage area on disk into main memory, the place where you create or change data (an E-mail message, a long report, whatever). Adding to main memory can make your PC run faster, although most people who use Windows need no more than 8MB. When people say "memory" or "RAM," they usually mean main memory (see *DRAM*, *memory*).

mainframe An old-fashioned computer that lives in its own air-conditioned tomb, attended by geek priests in lab coats. Now useful mostly for giant processing tasks like airline reservation systems and insurance claims processing.

mask In a database, a mask is used to ensure that data entered in a field is formatted in exactly the desired way. For example, a mask for a phone number might be (###) ###-####. The # characters will take only numbers, and the database will automatically add the parentheses, space, and hyphen.

master page An electronic page that holds the text and graphics you want to appear on every page of a desktop publishing document or on every slide of a presentation.

math coprocessor Also known as a floating point unit (FPU), a math coprocessor is specifically designed to accelerate certain mathematical operations. Most useful for high-end CAD, graphics, and statistical software, as well as for some complex spreadsheet applications, math coprocessors come as stand-alone chips, but are most often combined with CPUs. Intel's 486DX, DX2, and Pentium CPUs all have built-in math coprocessors.

MCA Short for *Micro Channel Architecture*, an obsolete expansion bus standard employed in some IBM PS/2s.

MCI Mail The largest commercial E-mail service.

mean time between failure (MTBF) A largely meaningless statistic suggesting how long a device, such as a hard disk or printer, will run before breaking down.

megabyte (MB) 1024 kilobytes or 1,048,576 bytes.

megahertz (MHz) One million cycles per second.

MemMaker The *memory optimizer* that comes with DOS.

memory Usually refers to *main memory*, the biggest bank of memory chips in your PC—the place where data gets processed. Click a command in your word processor, and your computer shuffles 1s and 0s in memory at a frightening pace; turn off your PC, and everything in memory vaporizes, which is why you need to save any changes to disk before you turn off your PC. In the stricter, techier sense, memory refers to any chips that hold data or software in the form of minuscule electrical charges (see *main memory*, *RAM*, *ROM*, *storage*).

memory buffer This catchall term describes a small area of a memory on a wide range of devices, but it's most often used in conjunction with CD ROM drives and hard disks. Data immediately ahead of the drive's laser or read/write head is copied into the memory buffer for fast access. Generally, the bigger the memory buffer, the faster the data throughput (see *disk cache*).

memory cache A small chunk of fast RAM that holds a copy of whatever data the CPU most recently used. A PC's *main memory* is too slow for the CPU to access directly without incurring debilitating *wait states*; a memory cache keeps wait states to a minimum. Most

CPUs have a small memory cache right on the chip (see *main memory, secondary memory cache, wait state*).

memory manager A utility that configures memory above 640K as extended or expanded. DOS comes with HIMEM.SYS to configure extended memory (usually so Windows can use it) and EMM386 to configure expanded memory (for old DOS applications and some device drivers).

memory optimizer A utility that can load device drivers and even parts of DOS into upper, high, and extended memory, maximizing your usable base memory (see *conventional memory, device driver*).

memory-resident Synonymous with *terminate and stay resident (TSR)*, describes a type of DOS application (such as a calendar or a print spooler) or device driver that hangs around in RAM and "pops up" over other DOS programs at the press of a key or two.

memory speed The speed at which a memory chip can be accessed by a processor without causing errors, measured in nanoseconds (ns). The most common memory speeds are 80ns, 70ns, and 60ns; the fewer the nanoseconds, the faster the memory.

menu A list of commands you choose from, as you'd choose an entrée.

menu bar The place at the top of a Windows application where the pull-down menus (File, Edit, and so on) are found.

MGA Short for the long-dead *Monochrome Graphics Adapter*, IBM's first video card for the PC, which could only produce characters.

MHz See *megahertz*.

Micro Channel See *MCA*.

microprocessor Generally, a computer (or most of one) on a single chip. Many PCs contain several microprocessors: the CPU, the graphics controller, the math coprocessor, and so on.

Microsoft Video 1 A Microsoft video compression scheme.

MIDI Short for *Musical Instrument Digital Interface*, this standard was created by musical instrument manufacturers. If you install MIDI-in and MIDI-out ports in your PC, you can hook up with any MIDI-compatible device (such as a synthesizer) and, with the aid of MIDI sequencer software turn your PC into an electronic recording studio.

MIDI breakout box A box that hooks to a sound board's joystick port to add MIDI-in and MIDI-out ports.

millisecond (ms) One thousandth of a second, a measurement often used to describe a disk drive's *average seek time*.

minicomputer A relatively expensive and powerful computer, such as an IBM AS/400 or a DEC VAX, often used as a *database server* for PC networks. As PCs have gotten more powerful, the once-clear distinction between microcomputers (PCs and Macs), workstations (from Sun, IBM, and other manufacturers), and minicomputers has gotten fuzzy.

MIPS Short for *million instructions per second*, an abstract (and therefore pretty useless) measure of CPU performance.

MIPS R4000 and R4400 A family of RISC CPUs developed by MIPS, now owned by Silicon Graphics. MIPS systems can run Windows NT.

MNP 5 A standard developed by Microcom for compressing data transferred by modem. More or less superseded by V.42bis compression.

MNP 10 Microcom standard for modem error control specifically intended for use with cellular phones.

mobile computer Any PC designed for portability. Common mobile computer categories include *palmtops*, *PDAs*, *notebooks*, *subnotebooks*, and *laptops*.

modem Short for *modulator/demodulator*, the device that enables your PC to send and receive data over the phone lines.

modem initialization string A series of commands sent to your modem to set it up for use with a particular communications or E-mail program.

modem server A PC or a special gadget hooked to a network to give users access to one or more shared modems.

monitor The TV-like box that shows you what's going on. Without one, you'd feel pretty dumb staring at the top of your computer. Sometimes referred to as the *display*.

monochrome Single-color video card or monitor that usually displays white, green, or amber characters against a dark background. Usually refers to the original IBM Monochrome Display Adapter (MDA) or Hercules Graphics Card (HGC).

monospaced A typeface, such as Courier, in which all the letters are spaced equally, no matter how fat or thin each letter is (the *i* gets as much space as the *w*). See *proportionally spaced*.

motherboard The main circuit board in your PC. Usually includes the memory, CPU, and expansion slots (see *CPU*, *expansion slots*).

motion video A term used to distinguish TV-style moving pictures from computer "video" (graphics cards and monitors).

mouse A handheld device with two or three buttons sprouting a taillike cord, which you slide around your desktop to move a pointer on screen.

mouse port A connector on the back of the PC where the mouse plugs in.

MPC Short for *Multimedia PC*. The MPC specification suggests now-obsolete minimum hardware requirements for multimedia, while the succeeding MPC 2 spec is somewhat more realistic.

MPEG Short for *Motion Picture Experts Group*. A number of video compression schemes (MPEG 1, MPEG 2, and so on) are named after the industry group that defined them. MPEG can be either *lossy* or lossless; in all its variations, it saves disk space by saving only data that changes from one frame to another. A bad format for desktop video editing.

MPR II Concerned about health risks, the Swedish government established the MPR II standard, a maximum exposure level for electromagnetic monitor emissions. Most (but not all) new monitors come with specially engineered components that bring them in line with MPR II (see *VLF* and *ELF*).

multimedia Probably the vaguest term in the PC industry, freely applied to anything that involves CD ROM, sound, or motion video.

multiscan Synonymous with *multifrequency*, this term describes a monitor that can handle more than one video mode. Except for a few cheap VGA-only monitors, pretty much everything on the market today is a multiscan.

multitasking Running more than one application at the same time. Windows can do this handy trick, as can OS/2.

multiuser Network applications that enable more than one person to work on them at the same time.

N

nanosecond (ns) A billionth of a second, most often used to describe the speed ratings of memory chips.

NetWare The most popular *network operating system*.

network A group of PCs (and sometimes other devices) hooked together by a network operating system and cable in order to share information and devices such as printers and modems.

network administrator The person who makes sure the network is working properly and who assigns access rights to users. Also the person you blame when something goes wrong (see *LAN, network operating system*).

network application Any application that requires a network to run—E-mail, multiuser databases, *Lotus Notes*, and so on.

network card The expansion card used to connect your PC with a LAN.

network node Synonymous with *network workstation*, a single PC on a LAN.

network operating system (NOS) Loose term for any software that ties PCs together into a network, such as *NetWare, LANtastic*, or Windows for Workgroups.

network server Generally, any PC that shares its hard drive with the network. See *dedicated server, database server*.

nickel-cadmium (NiCd) The least expensive type of rechargeable battery, commonly used in notebooks.

nickel metal-hydride (NiMH) The most popular type of notebook battery, NiMH batteries run longer on a single charge than NiCd batteries, but not as long as LIS batteries.

noninterlaced See *interlaced*.

notebook computer The most popular type of mobile computer. Usually the size of a ream of paper, notebooks weigh between four and eight pounds and offer performance approaching that of the most powerful desktop systems.

Notepad The simple text editor that comes with Windows (see *text editor*).

Novell DOS An MS-DOS compatible operating system from Novell that includes networking and multitasking.

NTSC Short for *National Television Standard Committee*. Describes the U.S. standard for broadcast TV, which provides for 525 scan lines and 30 frames per second.

null modem cable A cable specially wired to connect two computers together via their serial ports. Not compatible with a regular modem cable.

numeric keypad The 17 numeric keys on the right of most computer keyboards, arranged in a layout similar to that of an old 10-key adding machine. If you turn off [Num Lock], these keys also do double duty as cursor movement keys ([Page Up], [Home], [Ins], and so on).

O

object In Windows or other graphical operating systems, an icon or other item on the screen that does something when you click on it with a mouse. In programming, a self-contained chunk of code that can be used in a variety of contexts without modification.

object-oriented In Windows and other graphical operating systems, a term for executing commands or creating links between files by moving *objects* with the mouse. In programming, a modular approach to program design. These two meanings are often confused, but they have nothing to do with each other (see *OLE*).

OCR Short for *optical character recognition*, a technology that takes a scanned image of a printed page and converts it into editable text, usually with a small percentage of errors.

OEM Short for *original equipment manufacturer*, the company that actually made the hardware as opposed to the company whose name is on it. Also used to refer to the *OEM market*— companies that buy and resell original equipment under their own name.

Off-line nonlinear A type of desktop video editing using digital video files to define and preview edits, although the final tape is composed using conventional *A-B roll* hardware.

OLE Short for *Object Linking and Embedding*, a Windows standard for combining data from different applications. Creating an OLE link is like cutting and pasting between documents, except the pasted data is updated automatically to reflect any changes made to the original.

on-line service Similar to a BBS except larger and more expensive to access, on-line services such as CompuServe and America Online are information clearinghouses where members dial in via modem and exchange E-mail, ask questions, get help, download useful utility programs, and generally hang out. Most services charge a monthly membership fee and an hourly fee for connect time (see *America Online, CompuServe, Internet*).

on-site service If something goes wrong with your PC, the repair person will come to your door to fix it (or, worst case, pick it up for servicing).

operating system A program (usually DOS) that enables your PC to read and write data to and from disk, send pictures to your monitor, and accept keyboard commands. Without an operating system, your PC is just an expensive paperweight.

org chart A treelike diagram showing managerial responsibilities in a company, usually rendered with lines and boxes.

ornaments Also known as dingbats, ornaments are pictorial characters, as opposed to alphabetic or numeric characters.

orphan record A record in a database table that refers to information that has been deleted from another table (see *referential integrity*).

OS/2 An IBM operating system, functionally similar to a seamless combination of Windows and DOS, that can run most of the same software Windows 3.1 can. In some ways superior to Windows and DOS, OS/2 has suffered incompatibilities that have kept it from gaining wide acceptance.

OverDrive A whole product line of Intel upgrade processors, which can boost the speed of 486, DX2, and Pentium systems. Also refers to the socket required for OverDrive processors.

overhead transparencies Paper-size sheets of clear plastic, which you write on or run through your printer and then plop on an overhead projector, which projects the text or graphics on a wall or screen.

P

page layout The design decisions that affect the way a printed page will appear, including margins, columns, picture placement, typefaces, and so on.

paint program A graphics application that lets you create colorful images using your mouse or a drawing tablet. Unlike draw programs, paint images are saved as bitmaps, which makes them hard to edit (see *bit-mapped graphics*).

palette Available screen colors; also, a grid showing these colors, which you can use to pick the colors you want. May also refer to groups of command buttons, such as the floating "icon palettes" in some Windows applications.

palmtop Toylike mobile computers that weigh a pound or less and come with tiny keyboards and screens. Not for serious computing.

parallel port Sometimes called the *printer port*, the 25-pin socket on the back of your PC into which you plug a parallel cable (there's usually a printer on the other end). A PC can have a maximum of two parallel ports, referred to as LPT 1 and LPT 2 by DOS. Parallel ports move data 8 bits at a time (see *enhanced parallel port*, *serial port*).

parity bit An extra bit added to each byte that helps control errors by letting the operating system or modem software know whether the information in the byte is valid or corrupted.

passive-matrix display The most common and least expensive LCD, which uses an invisible grid of wires embedded in glass to send electrical pulses to individual liquid crystal cells, turning them on or off. (see *active-matrix LCD, LCD*).

path More properly called the *search path*, this is a list of the directories you want DOS to look in when you enter a command at the DOS prompt—for example, if your C:\WINDOWS directory is in your search path, entering win at the DOS prompt starts Windows, no matter what directory you're in. The list of directories follows the PATH command in your AUTOEXEC.BAT (see *AUTOEXEC.BAT, directory*).

path name Same as the *directory name*.

PC-DOS IBM's version of MS-DOS.

PC-to-PC communications This term normally refers to direct modem communications between two PCs over the phone lines, but it can also apply to two side-by-side PCs linked by a *null modem cable*.

PCI bus A fast industry-standard expansion bus that runs at 33 MHz, common in Pentium systems but also used in many 486 and DX2 computers (see *local bus, VL bus*).

PCL The page description language used by HP printers, including LaserJets. An application must have a PCL driver in order to tell PCL printer how a document should be printed. Widely cloned (with varying degrees of success) by other printer manufacturers.

PCMCIA Short for *Personal Computer Memory Card International Association*, this acronym refers to three notebook expansion specifications (Type I, Type II, and Type III), which describe slots and expansion cards no larger in width and height than a credit card (but varying in thickness depending on the Type). Memory cards, modems, hard disks, and more have all been squeezed onto PCMCIA cards.

PCX The *PC Paintbrush* graphics format, widely supported by other applications.

peer-to-peer LAN A network without a *dedicated server*, where every PC can share its drives and printers with others on the network.

pen computing Using an electronic stylus to check menu choices or enter handwritten information, usually on a notebook or *PDA*'s screen.

Pentium Intel's high-speed successor to the 486, able to run virtually all software written for previous Intel CPUs.

peripheral Any hardware that installs in or connects to your PC, such as disk drives, monitors, modems, scanners, printers, CD ROM drives, and so on.

personal data manager A database program lacking a programming language and designed to handle a single user's data, such as a mailing list or a phone log (see *programmable data manager*).

personal digital assistant (PDA) A term coined by former Apple chief John Sculley to refer to Apple's Newton and similar mobile computers designed to accept handwritten instead of keyboard input.

personal laser printer A small, inexpensive, and relatively slow laser printer intended to be used by one or two individuals rather than a large group.

phosphors A layer of phosphorescent material on the inside of your monitor's picture tube that glows when struck by an *electron beam*.

photosensitive drum The key component of a laser printer. The laser draws the image of the page on the drum, creating a static charge that picks up toner only in the areas that are supposed to be black.

pick list A database feature (or programming technique) that enables you to enter data in a field by picking entries from a list.

pie chart A circular data chart designed to show proportions (usually percentages) of a whole quantity.

PIF Short for *program information file*. PIFs are used to help control the behavior of DOS applications under Windows. To create or modify a PIF, you use the PIF Editor, which comes with Windows.

PIM Short for *personal information manager*, an all-in-one program that keeps track of names and addresses, appointments, phone calls, to-do lists, and so on. Less powerful and expensive than a contact manager.

pixel Short for *picture element*, one of the tiny points of glowing phosphor that combine to create the image on your computer (or TV) screen.

plotter An output device that uses colored pens to literally draw on the page with a robotic arm. Used almost exclusively to produce engineering and architectural drawings; expensive models can draw full-size blueprints.

plug and play A standard developed by Microsoft, Intel, and other vendors that will allow future PCs running Windows 4 and its successors to configure themselves automatically, theoretically making it easier to install expansion boards, CD ROM drives, and the like.

PMS Short for Pantone Matching System, this is a method of precisely selecting *spot colors* by referring to numbered samples, just like picking paint hues at a hardware store.

pocket modem A modem small enough to be carried comfortably in your pocket that attaches to your serial port (see *modem, fax modem*).

point The standard measure for type size. One point is approximately $1/72$ of an inch.

pointer The little arrow you move around the screen with your mouse.

pointing device A mouse, trackball, or drawing tablet used to move an arrow-shaped pointer on screen.

polymorphic virus A computer virus that continually mutates, enabling it to avoid detection by antivirus software (see *virus*).

port A connector, usually on the back of your PC, through which data leaves and/or enters the computer, such as a serial port, parallel port, keyboard connector, or mouse port (see *parallel port, serial port*).

portable computer Synonymous with the umbrella term *mobile computer*, which applies to any PC designed to stray from the desktop. May also refer to the large, heavy mobile computers of yore that ran off AC power.

portrait orientation A page on which text and graphics are positioned normally—that is, the page is taller than it is wide (see *landscape orientation*).

PostScript Most often used to describe a type of font (see *PostScript Type 1*). More accurately, a complex page description language that enables software to control exactly how and where printed elements—lines, type, graphics, colors—will appear on the page. Used on Macs much more than on PCs.

PostScript printer A printer capable of printing PostScript documents, such as those produced by *QuarkXPress* or *Adobe Illustrator*.

PostScript Type 1 The most widely used type of scalable font in professional typesetting. If *Adobe Type Manager* is installed in your system, you can use any of the thousands of excellent Type 1 fonts available, without having to use a PostScript printer to print them (see *scalable font*).

power glitch A surge, spike, or other variation in line current that causes a problem for your PC (see *surge supressor*).

power management Software built into most notebook computers that conserves battery power by shutting down the hard disk, dimming the display, or idling the CPU when you're not using them.

power spikes A momentary jump in the amount of power a wall socket puts out. In some cases, power spikes can cause crashes or damage your hardware.

power supply The device in your PC that converts AC house current into the DC current your PC's innards need in order to function.

presentation software Applications aimed at producing overhead transparencies or 35mm slides with graphics, display type, and lots of color.

print buffer A small area of memory in a printer intended to speed up printing. Also a separate hardware device that can hold several print jobs in its memory, where they hang around in a queue until the printer is ready.

print spooler A utility that takes over print jobs from applications, so you can continue working while a file prints. Print Manager is the print spooler built into Windows (see *background printing*).

printer port An informal name for the parallel port, the 25-pin female connector on the back of your PC into which you usually plug your printer.

private key See *public key encryption*.

process colors Colors produced by separating a color image into three or four colors, and then recombining those colors to reproduce the original hues (see *CMYK, color separation*).

processor Frequently used to refer to the main processor in a PC, the *central processing unit (CPU)*. Actually, your PC has many little processors inside it (your microwave oven and TV also have a few), all of them carrying out their tasks based on instructions received from the CPU. Generally synonymous with the term *microproccessor*.

Prodigy The information superhighway's answer to *USA Today*, a commercial on-line service offered by IBM in partnership with Sears.

program A group of instructions that tell the computer what to do. Programs range from weeny *batch files* to huge Windows applications (which, strictly speaking, are collections of many small programs). More or less interchangeable with the term *software*.

program file A file that holds software instructions instead of your data.

program groups Program Manager windows in which you keep related program icons.

Program Manager Windows' control center, a place where you organize and start up all your applications.

programmable data manager A database program that includes (and usually requires extensive knowledge of) a programming language.

programming code Programmers use different languages (BASIC, C, C++) to write the applications you use every day. Because these languages employ esoteric commands a cryptographer might balk at, the result is called code, or programming code.

project management software Timeline-based applications that help managers track complicated construction or engineering projects.

proprietary Denotes software or hardware features created by a company that are not compatible with industry standards.

proportionally spaced A typeface (such as the one you're reading) in which letters are spaced according to the width of each individual character.

protocol In communications, any set of standard procedures that enables computers to talk to each other (see *error-checking protocol*).

public key encryption An encryption scheme that uses two keys: a public key, which you distribute to anyone you wish, and a private key, which you keep to yourself. If someone wants to send you a secure message, that person encrypts it using your public key, resulting in a file that can be decrypted only by your private key.

pull-down menus In most applications, you can "pull down" a menu of choices by clicking your mouse on a menu bar at the top of the screen.

QIC-40/QIC-80 The most popular backup tape format for DC2000 cartridges. QIC-40 tapes hold up to 120MB of compressed data, QIC-80 tapes as much as 250MB.

QIC-3010 New format for DC2000 tape cartridges that enables you to cram as much as 680MB of compressed data on a single tape.

Qsound A patented technique for simulating 3-D sound on stereo speakers.

query In databases, to ask a question about your data, usually by entering field values (a last name, an area code) in a blank record.

query by example (QBE) The most common method for finding data in a database. You define your query by entering the values (or ranges of values) in the appropriate fields. For example, to find all the checks you've written to the IRS since 1982, you'd enter >1981 in the date field, and IRS in the payee field.

QWERTY Refers to the standard keyboard layout.

R

radio button A standard dialog box element that enables you to pick only one choice from several entries (like a bank of car radio buttons that only allows you to choose one station).

RAID Short for *Redundant Array of Inexpensive Drives*, RAID refers to any of several methods where two or more disk drives are used to improve speed and/or reliability of network hard disk storage. Raid 1 is also known as *disk mirroring*.

RAM Short for *random access memory* (an archaic phrase not worth explaining), RAM usually refers to *main memory*, the large group of RAM chips where the computer does its computing. In the narrower, nerdy sense, RAM refers to the most common class of memory chip, which comes in several varieties (see *DRAM, main memory, SRAM, VRAM*).

RAM disk A section of system memory set up to emulate a super-fast disk drive. Data stored on a RAM disk disappears when you turn off the power.

range In spreadsheets, this term refers to any group of (usually contiguous) cells.

RCA jacks The type of jacks used by most stereo equipment. They look like small raised cylinders shaped like a pencil eraser with a hole in the middle, often color-coded red for right channel, white for left.

READ.ME file A file that installs alongside most applications and contains the latest information on troubleshooting and installation. You can use your word processor to read it.

read-only Describes any data that cannot be edited or deleted (see *file attribute*).

read/write head The part of every disk or tape drive that records data on the magnetic media and reads it back later.

reboot Restarting your computer, usually after a crash, or to put into effect some change you've made to your AUTOEXEC.BAT or CONFIG.SYS file. You can reboot by pressing Ctrl Alt Del simultaneously, by pressing the reset button, or by turning the power off and back on.

record A group of fields in a database that relate to a single entity: a person, an event, a place, a financial transaction, whatever. A record is like a single row in a table: a single product's name, description, and price on an inventory sheet, for example (see *field*).

referential integrity This ensures that users modifying a relational database cannot perform actions that would "orphan" data. For example, an inventory program might block you from deleting the account of a customer with pending orders.

refresh rate The number of times per second a monitor displays a complete screen of information. The faster the rate, the steadier the image, and the less likely you are to suffer eyestrain.

relational database A controversial term often used to refer to any database program that enables information in multiple tables to be linked. Sophisticated database programmers use a narrower definition.

remote When two PCs are in communication, the distant one is the remote PC.

remote control software Applications that let you operate a remote PC via modem, providing access to all files and applications. Nice idea, but slow.

removable media Any disk or drive designed to be removed without opening up a PC, including floppy disks, backup tapes, SyQuest cartridges, magneto-optical discs, and so on.

repeater A device that amplifies (repeats) signals on a cable, allowing the data to travel longer distances.

report generator A database feature or separate utility that performs a query, then organizes and formats the results for printing.

repro paper A high-gloss paper used in phototypesetting machines. Often employed by professional printing services to print high-resolution master documents from which volume copies are reproduced.

resolution On a monitor, the dimensions of an image in *pixels*, the tiny dots that create what you see (VGA resolution is 640 by 480 pixels, for example). On the printed page, the sharpness of the printout measured in dots per inch (standard laser printer output is 300 dots per inch, for example).

resolution enhancement A technique used by some laser printers to make their printed characters smoother and better-looking.

resource sharing Making a hard drive, printer, or other goodies available to users on a network.

restocking fee Even when a product is offered with a money-back guarantee, you may be stuck paying a small charge called a restocking fee, which supposedly covers the vendor's expense in replacing the unit you bought and then returned. Is this bogus or what?

restore Copying a file from a floppy or tape backup onto your hard disk (see *backup*).

RFI Short for *radio frequency interference*, RFI is electrical noise—generated by computers, monitors, printers, and other electronic devices—that can interfere with radio, television, and cordless phone reception. An FCC Class B rating on a piece of equipment means its EMI emissions are low enough for use in residential areas. An FCC Class A rating means it's legal to use the equipment only in business and industrial areas.

RGB Short for red-green-blue, the primary colors used by monitors to create the images you see on screen. Sometimes refers to the obsolete CGA video standard.

RISC Short for *reduced instruction set computing*, which describes a class of processor that executes smaller, simpler instructions at a faster rate than CISC processors. Windows NT, Microsoft's successor to Windows, can run on many RISC processors (see *CISC*).

RLE *Run-length encoding*, a lossless compression algorithm for bit-mapped graphics. Also used by both IDE and SCSI hard disks.

RMA number Short for *return merchandise authorization*, this is the number you write on the box (and sometimes give to your credit card company) when you ship a piece of unsatisfactory or broken equipment back to the factory.

role-playing games A vague category of computer games defined primarily by what it *excludes*: shoot-em-up, kick-em-down arcade action. Role playing games include strategic war games, dungeon and dragon adventures, fantasy games, and a broad variety of interactive "movies" where the user pretends to be one or more characters in the game.

ROM Short for *read-only memory*, a type of memory that retains its information whether the computer is on or off. ROM chips are built into a variety of hardware devices and usually contain little pieces of software that give the hardware enough smarts to do its job. Your computer uses ROM to store basic start-up information, like where to look for an operating system and how to load it into RAM (see *BIOS*).

root directory The "top" directory where the directory tree begins, containing the DOS files necessary for your PC to boot, vital information DOS needs to locate all files on a drive, and your all-important CONFIG.SYS and AUTOEXECBAT files. Every logical drive (there can be more than one per hard disk—C:, D:, E:, and so forth) has its own root directory.

RS-232C The official spec (developed by the Electronics Industry Association) on which standard PC serial ports are based.

RS-422, RS-423 Two RS-232–compatible standards that specify shielding or twisted pairs of wire to extend the length of a serial cable.

RSI Short for *repetitive strain injury*, one of several cumulative traumas resulting from repeated motion of the hands and forearms (you know, what you do with your keyboard and mouse every day). Includes tendinitis, tennis elbow, de Quervain's disease, tenosynovitis, and carpal tunnel syndrome. Computer users are frequent victims of RSI, which can be quite debilitating (see *carpal tunnel syndrome*).

rules Thin, straight lines used to set off blocks of text on a printed page.

run-time engine A stripped-down version of a program that can be distributed free without copyright violation, such as software than enables a multimedia application to run.

S

sampling The process of turning sound into a digital audio file. The sampling rate is the number of times per second your sound board measures the amplitude of incoming sound. Typical sampling rates are 8 kHz (worst) to 48 kHz (best); 44 kHz is standard. The sampling resolution determines how much data is collected at each sampling interval. The two common *sampling resolutions* are 8 bit (lousy) and 16 bit (best).

sans serif Refers to a group of typefaces that lack the squiggles (used to make type more readable) you see in the body type here. The bold words at the beginning of the entries in this glossary are sans serif. Arial is a typical sans serif typeface.

scalable font An electronic typeface that you can adjust in size, often from barely readable to poster size (see *font*, *PostScript*, *TrueType*).

scan lines The horizontal lines on a computer monitor.

scanner A device that takes a digital snapshot of a page (or part of one) and saves it as a graphics file. *Flatbed* scanners have photocopierlike windows and scan an entire page at one time; hand scanners are like little Dustbusters that you drag across the page (see *digitize*, *graphics file*).

screen saver Some people believe that if the image on a monitor screen doesn't change often, the image will "burn in." To avoid this (probably mythical) fate, screen saver utilities notice when there's no keyboard activity and send a series of changing images to the screen: flying toasters, Captain Picard, kittens chasing butterflies.

script A list of commands that execute one after another, similar to a batch file or a macro. Communications programs usually have a *script language*, so you can write scripts that automate such activities as logging onto a BBS and collecting E-mail.

scroll arrows The arrows at either extreme of a scroll bar. Clicking on one and holding down the left mouse button is the way people usually scroll the contents of a window.

scroll bars The basic navigation system in Windows: Two bars, one at the bottom of a window and the other on the right, that enable you to move the contents of a window up and down or side to side with the mouse to reveal parts of a document not currently displayed.

scroll box The little square in the middle of a scroll bar—drag it with the mouse, and you can jump around a big document fast.

SCSI Pronounced *scuzzy*, but short for *Small Computer Systems Interface*, SCSI is the second-most popular interface standard for hard disks. Most scanners and CD ROM drives, along with some tape drives, are SCSI devices. You can hook up as many as seven SCSI devices to a single SCSI interface card if nothing goes wrong (it usually does).

secondary memory cache Most CPUs (including all Intel 486s and Pentiums) have a fast, built-in memory cache. If the CPU can't find what it needs in its own cache, it tries the secondary memory cache—also known as the *external* memory cache—an array of *SRAM* chips on the motherboard between the CPU and main memory. The idea is to keep the CPU from accessing main memory directly, which would slow things down (see *memory cache*, *CPU*).

sectors The basic units of disk storage—so basic you only rarely need to know about them. At the factory, hard disks are divided into a grid of 512-byte sectors (see *allocation units*).

self-extracting file A compressed file that decompresses automatically when you type its name at a DOS prompt. Both *ARC* and *PKZIP* are capable of creating self-extracting files (see *ARC*, *archive*, *compression*).

serial port Also known as a COM port, a 9-pin or 25-pin connector on the back of your PC usually used to connect an external modem or a mouse. A PC can have a maximum of four serial ports, but it's usually a pain in the butt to try using more than COM 1 and COM 2 (see *I/O*).

serif Refers to a group of typefaces, like the lighter-weight typeface in the text you're reading, whose characters end in little squiggles instead of clean lines. Also refers to the little squiggles themselves.

server See *network server*.

server-based LAN A network where all shared files reside on a *file server*.

server mirroring Synchronizing two servers so that if the first one fails, the backup takes over automatically. In NetWare, this is also called SFT Level III.

service bureau A shop that provides a variety of services for desktop publishing: scanners and fancy printers you can rent by the hour, Linotronic output, slide scanning, and so on.

service class A standard for fax communications with four successive variations—Group I, Group II, Group III, and Group IV—each one intended to supersede the previous one. Only Groups III and IV are currently in use (see *Group III fax*).

shadow mask A thin, finely perforated sheet of metal that covers the inside of a monitor's screen. The shadow mask allows the CRT's electron beam to pass through and strike a selected color dot while blocking electrons that might strike neighboring dots and cause the screen to appear fuzzy.

shareware Software you can try out for free. If you like it, you're requested to send a small payment to the author. The most common way to get shareware is to download it via modem from an on-line service such as CompuServe (see *download, on-line service*).

SIMM Short for *single in-line memory module*, the standard PC memory component. Although they have many different capacities, SIMMs come in two basic varieties: 30 pin (also known as 9 bit) and 72 pin (also known as 36 bit).

slack space Even if a file occupies only a fraction of an allocation unit, the FAT registers the unit as "in use," which means that (on average) half an allocation unit is wasted per file. This wasted capacity is called *slack space*. The larger the drive, the larger the allocation unit—and the more slack space created.

SLED Short for *single large expensive disk*, this half-joking, half-serious term was coined to refer to the alternative to *RAID*.

sleep mode Also known as *suspend mode*, a state of battery-saving hibernation that notebook computers go into when you press a button—everything shuts down except for the trickle of power required to preserve data in memory, which may stay there intact for weeks. Press the suspend button again, and you pick up where you left off (see *notebook computer, power management*).

slide sorter view Offered by most presentation graphics applications, this bird's eye view displays all the slides (or pages) in a presentation. Good for rearranging the sequence of slides.

slot See *expansion slots*.

software piracy To make an unauthorized copy of commercial software without permission.

sound card An expansion card that vastly improves a PC's sound capabilities. Sound boards connect to headphones or speakers and typically offer the ability to record and play back digital audio (WAV) files. Most also include a synthesizer that can play MIDI music, an input for a CD ROM drive's audio output, and a mixer to put all that together.

Sound Recorder A standard Windows utility for recording digital audio (WAV) files.

source directory The directory from which you are copying a file or group of files (see *directory*).

spot color A term used by desktop publishers to describe solid colors that can be produced without the multiple overlays required by *process colors*. Spot color can be reproduced on low-end color printers with good results.

special interest group (SIG) See *forum*.

spread A page layout term for two facing pages.

spreadsheet An application that performs a wide variety of mathematical, logical, financial, and statistical calculations, using an on-screen grid that looks a little like an accountant's paper spreadsheet. Spreadsheets are great for making complicated financial projections, but most people employ a fraction of their power and use them to maintain simple lists.

spread-spectrum LANs Wireless network adapters that use a special kind of low-power radio instead of a cable.

SRAM Short for *static random access memory*, static RAM is faster but more expensive than DRAM. Often used for memory caching, where speed is of the essence (see *secondary memory cache*).

standby mode The notebook computer equivalent of taking a nap. If you don't touch the keyboard for awhile, the little machine's screen goes dark, the hard disk stops spinning, and (in some cases) the CPU throttles down, giving you a few extra hours of battery life.

star topology A network layout where each workstation is connected to a central hub. 10-BaseT LANs use star topology (see *Ethernet*).

stealth virus A type of computer virus designed to defeat antivirus software by covering its tracks (see *virus, antivirus, polymorphic virus*).

stop bit Technically, a bit that divides data bits when communicating by modem. As a practical matter, it's a setting you seldom need to think about, since it's almost always set to 1 (as in N-8-1 or E-7-1).

storage Usually refers to your hard disk, but may also apply to floppy disks, tape cartridges, optical disks, or any other place where your data stays intact when you turn off your PC.

Structured Query Language (SQL) A standard language for database queries, supported by all client-server and most conventional database programs. Standard SQL is often ignored in favor of powerful proprietary variations or alternatives.

style In word processing and desktop publishing, a collection of formats (for example: bold, italic, 18-point Times Roman, 1/4-inch indent) that you can save together under a single name. Later, you can pick that name from a list and apply the style to any paragraph with a couple of mouse clicks.

stylus The penlike tool used with a *drawing tablet*.

subdirectory Almost synonymous with *directory*, except that it's sometimes used to refer to a directory "beneath" another one on the directory tree (see *directory*).

subnotebook A class of mobile computer immediately beneath that of notebooks in size, weight, and computing power.

super VGA Video modes better than 640 by 480 at 16 colors, and the graphics cards and monitors that support those modes. Popular resolutions include 800 by 600, 1024 by 768, 1280 by 1024, and 1600 by 1200; the number of colors ranges from 256 to 16.7 million.

surface scan Some diagnostic utilities check the surface of your hard disk, looking for—and marking off—physically damaged sectors.

surge suppressor A protective electrical device you put between your PC and the wall plug that keeps your PC from getting fried from sudden voltage spikes or power surges.

suspend mode See *sleep mode*.

sustained data transfer rate The amount of data a device can transfer per second for sustained periods of time. See also *burst transfer rate*.

swap file A file on your hard disk that Windows uses as a temporary holding area. You can choose between a temporary swap file (created every time you start Windows) or a permanent swap file that remains there even when you're not running Windows. A permanent swap file produces better performance.

swash characters Letters or numbers having one or more strokes ending in an extended flourish.

switches Things you add to a DOS command to change its behavior. For example, adding the /P switch to the DIR command results in a pause after each screenful of files.

SX2 Same as the DX2, except without a math coprocessor (see *DX2*).

sysop Short for *system operator;* the person in charge of a BBS or of a forum on a large on-line service like CompuServe or America Online (see *BBS, on-line service*).

system disk See *boot sector*.

SYSTEM.INI Windows configuration file, which stores mostly hardware-related settings.

system unit The PC itself—the main boxlike chassis to which the keyboard and monitor connect.

T

tape backup drive A device reminiscent of a stripped-down car cassette player, designed to copy data from your hard disk to little cassette tapes for safekeeping (see *backup, restore*).

target directory The directory to which you are copying a file or group of files (see *directory*).

tech support Usually a telephone number, but sometimes a BBS, where you can get help, advice, and troubleshooting tips for an application or piece of hardware that isn't working right. Tech support is usually staffed by live techies, but occasionally you may run into an automated voice mail or fax-back system (see *BBS*, *fax-back*, *on-line service*).

telecommunications In PCs, another word for modem communications over the phone lines.

template In word processing, desktop publishing, and presentation graphics, a document where most of the layout and formatting decisions have been made for you, so all you need to do is enter text or graphics.

terminal A keyboard and monitor attached to a multiuser system, usually a minicomputer or mainframe.

terminal emulation The process of fooling a minicomputer or mainframe into believing your PC is one of the big guy's terminals, so you and the larger system can communicate over the phone lines using a modem. All communications software can emulate some kind of terminal, typically DEC's VT-100, which is usually all you need (see *mainframe*).

text editor A simple word processor designed for editing batch files, INI files, and other ASCII text files used by your computer. DOS's Edit and Windows Notepad are both text editors (see *ASCII*, *batch file*).

text file Usually refers to a file containing plain text without formatting, also known as an ASCII file (which may have an ASC or TXT extension), but the term is also used to differentiate a word processing file from a spreadsheet, database, or graphics file (see *ASCII*, *file*, *text editor*).

text mode A method of displaying images on your monitor, commonly employed by DOS applications, which uses ASCII characters exclusively (see *ASCII*).

textbase A database program designed to handle large text documents and retrieve information with sophisticated search tools.

TFT Short for *thin film transistor*, the tiny device used to control a single cell in an *active-matrix LCD*, the best screen type available for notebook computers (see *LCD*).

thermal wax A popular method used by color printers to print color on plain paper, whereby colored wax is actually melted onto the page. Less expensive and lower quality than *dye sublimation*.

third-party Describes a piece of hardware or software designed to be used with another product, but sold by a different company.

thinnet See *Ethernet*.

TIFF Short for *Tagged Image File Format*, TIFF is the bitmapped graphics format of choice among graphics professionals. There are many variations on TIFF, and it's likely that no program can read them all.

TIGA Short for *Texas Instruments Graphics Architecture*, a graphics programming language supported by graphics cards that have a Texas Instruments 34010 or 34020 graphics coprocessor. Primarily used in CAD systems.

tilt-and-swivel The ball-joint base of a monitor that allows you to adjust it for the most convenient viewing angle (see *monitor*).

TMP files Temporary files created by applications to hold scratch data.

toggle Derived from *toggle switch* (like a light switch), a toggle is a command or a key on the keyboard that turns something on or off. For example, the [Ins] key toggles between inserting and overtyping text.

Token-Ring Most common alternative to *Ethernet*, used mostly by large IBM customers (or former customers).

tombstoning In design, layout, and desktop publishing circles, this refers to a bad layout in which boxed elements are lined up across the page.

toner cartridge Laser printers use replaceable cartridges containing a black powdered "ink" called toner; the cartridge saves you the messy task of refilling the toner by hand (see *laser printer*).

toolbars Many Windows applications place icons representing frequently used commands in a row of buttons along the top or side of the screen. This is a toolbar, and in most cases you can customize it easily.

tower system Most computers are designed so the PC lies flat. Tower systems are usually designed to stand on end and fit under the desk, using less space.

trackball A popular pointing device, commonly described as a mouse "on its back." Instead of moving the pointer by rolling a mouse on your desk, you rotate a stationary ball with your fingers or the palm of your hand.

tracks The concentric rings in which data is stored on floppy and hard disks.

tractor-feed The sprocketed mechanism that feeds continuous-form paper through a dot matrix printer (see *dot matrix printer*).

transaction tracking A process that helps protect multiuser databases from becoming corrupted. If a database crashes in the middle of a transaction, its tables may no longer be synchronized (for example, an employee's withholding taxes might have been subtracted from the payroll table, but not yet added to the tax-paid table). Transaction tracking allows the database to be "rolled back" to the point before any incomplete transactions started or "rolled forward" to complete the transactions.

transparent Anything that happens in software that's so seamless you don't even know it's happening. For example, if you wanted to browse the hard disk of someone in Tallahassee, and all you had to do was click on an icon that looked like ordinary drive E:, the process of connecting to that hard disk would be termed *transparent*.

Trojan horse A program that pretends to be something nice (say, a game, or an update to a popular shareware utility) but is actually designed to do mischief. Often confused with a *virus*.

TrueType The scalable font format used by Windows, TrueType is much more popular on the PC than PostScript Type 1. Also the name for the *font rasterizer* in Windows that scales TrueType fonts and sends them to the printer.

TSR Short for *terminate and stay resident* (see *memory-resident*).

typeface A complete set of letters, numbers, punctuation marks, and special characters in a particular style, such as Times Roman or Helvetica (see *font*).

U

undelete To recover an accidentally deleted file. An *undelete utility*, such as DOS's Microsoft Undelete, will restore the file in most cases (see *data recovery*).

undo A function available in many applications than enables you to reverse your last action or series of actions.

unformat To recover the data on a disk that you've accidentally formatted. The unformatting tools in the top two utility libraries, *The Norton Utilities* and *PC Tools*, do a much better job of recovering from this serious and very destructive mistake than DOS's UNFORMAT command.

uninterruptible power supply See *UPS*.

UNIX Probably the most popular operating system after DOS, Windows, and the Mac's System 7. The name isn't really an acronym; it's just an example of nerd humor, which is probably why it comes in so many incompatible varieties.

upgrade To buy a newer version of an application you already own, to add hardware that increases the performance or capacity of your PC, or to buy a new computer more powerful than your old one.

upload To send a file to a BBS or on-line service using your modem and communications software (see *BBS*, *on-line service*).

upper memory Memory between 640K and 1MB, reserved for drivers that control your video, hard disk, and so on.

UPS Short for *uninterruptible power supply*, a data protection device that you plug into the wall socket. Then you plug your PC into it. If the power fails, a built-in rechargeable battery will keep your computer running long enough for you to save your work and shut down safely. It also protects your PC from potentially destructive power surges.

user group A kind of a computer club for people interested in computers in general, a particular type of computer, or a specific application. Memberships are often a wild mix of techies and beginners, all of them interested in learning more about PCs for work or play. Most user groups are nonprofits independent of any computer company; they exert substantial influence in the computer industry.

user interface The overall layout of software as it appears to the person who uses it—the arrangement of its menus, the positioning of its toolbars, the design of its dialog boxes. The user interface determines how easy a given application is to learn and use.

utility An inexpensive software tool that helps you accomplish some small but often important task, such as backing up your data, searching for files, tuning up your system in some way, and so on.

utility library A collection of useful utilities, usually including an undelete utility, other data recovery tools, a disk defragmenter, and a host of other handy software (see *disk defragmenter, data recovery, utility*).

V

V.22bis The modulation specification for 2400 bps modems. Must be supported in hardware, or the modem may not be able to link up with other modems.

V.32 The modulation standard for 9600 bps modems. Must be supported in hardware, or the modem will fail to communicate at 9600 bps with modems from other manufacturers.

V.32bis The modulation standard for 14.4 kbps modems. Must be supported hardware, or the modem won't communicate at 14.4 kbps with modems from other manufacturers.

V.32terbo An outdated AT&T modulation standard for this company's 28.8 kbps modems. Supplanted by V.34.

V.34 The prevalent modulation standard for 28.8 kbps modems. If you want to communicate at 28.8 kbps with a wide range of other 28.8 kbps modems, your modem must support this standard.

V.42 Widely accepted standard for modem error control. Includes the earlier error-control standards MNP 2, MNP 3, and MNP 4.

V.42bis The highest-speed standard for modem data compression. Requires V.42 error control (and a modem on the other end of the line that supports V.42bis and V.42).

vector graphics Easily edited graphics based on lines, curves, and shapes described by mathematical formulas. The type of graphics produced by draw programs.

vertical scan rate The speed at which the monitor's electron beam moves from the top of the screen to the bottom, measured in cycles per second (Hz). The higher the vertical scan rate, the faster the phosphors in the screen are "refreshed."

VESA Short for the *Video Electronics Standards Association*, a trade organization of graphics hardware manufacturers that devised and published the popular *VL Bus* specification and developed guidelines for resolutions beyond standard VGA.

VGA Short for *Video Graphics Array*, the most widely accepted IBM graphics hardware standard and the lowest common denominator for all graphics cards and monitors manufactured in the last few years. Virtually all current graphics cards and monitors can handle resolutions higher than standard VGA's 640 by 480 at 16 colors (see *super VGA*).

video board See *graphics card*.

video capture card An expansion card that enables you to convert analog video from a VCR or camera into digital video and store it on disk.

video card Sometimes used to refer to a card with multimedia video capabilities, but more commonly a synonym for *graphics card*.

video compression A technique for reducing the amount of data a video capture card sends to the PC and/or for reducing the size of digital video files on disk (see *codec*).

video overlay Video from a VCR, laserdisc player, video tuner, or camera displayed in a window on your PC.

video projector A device that accepts video input from a computer or VCR and projects it onto a large screen suitable for meetings.

virtual memory Not memory at all, but disk space treated as memory to enable you to run more applications at one time. Windows uses this technique when it runs out of application memory, a state of affairs that slows things down considerably.

virus A nasty bit of software expressly designed to damage the data on your hard disk. A virus can infect your computer when you load new software, innocently accept a neighbor's floppy disk, or download a file via modem, and may lie quiet for months before becoming active (see *antivirus*).

VL bus The *VESA local bus*, a very popular expansion bus specification designed primarily to provide fast graphics performance for 486 PCs at low cost (see *expansion bus, local bu*s). Runs at speeds up to 66 MHz.

VLF Short for *very low frequency* radiation, a range of frequencies emitted by monitors and other devices. A possible health hazard (see *ELF*).

voice recognition A computer's ability to recognize and respond to spoken commands or to take dictation. Works OK...if...you...talk...like...this (and repeat yourself a few times).

voices The different instruments a sound board's synthesizer can imitate simultaneously.

volume Anything to which DOS assigns a drive letter (also known as a logical drive). Note that a single hard disk can be partitioned into multiple logical drives, or volumes.

VRAM Short for *video random access memory*, a type of memory chip that costs more and runs faster than DRAM. VRAM is used in about half of all graphics cards.

VT-100 See *terminal emulation*.

W

wait state A brief pause in the CPU's operation as it waits for a slower component (such as memory or the expansion bus) to finish doing something.

wallpaper Windows lets you set a decorative pattern, or even a photographic image, as the background of the Windows desktop. This is called *wallpaper*. You can install wallpaper by double-clicking on the Desktop icon, found in Windows' Control Panel.

WAN Short for *wide area network*, this usually refers to geographically dispersed LANs linked by *leased lines* or the *Internet*, but it is also used to describe LANs linked by occasional E-mail exchanges between E-mail servers.

warm boot Restarting your computer by pressing Ctrl Alt Del . This has an effect similar to turning your PC off and on again, except it's a bit faster and easier on the power supply. You'll lose all unsaved data (see *boot, cold boot*).

watermark In desktop publishing, any image electronically "faded" and used as a background.

watt The standard measure of electric consumption, equal to one *joule* per second. A joule, the standard measure of work in the metric system, is roughly equal to the amount of energy expended moving one kilogram one meter.

wavetable A method used in some sound boards to store the sampled sounds of real instruments in ROM, resulting in much better sounds than those produced by the usual cheesy synthesizer.

weight A typesetting term that indicates the thickness of the lines that make up the characters in a font. A blocky, boldface font would be said to have more weight than a delicate italic character.

white space White space refers to margins and other parts of a printed page unoccupied by text or graphics.

wide carriage printers Dot matrix printers designed to handle extra-wide paper, usually 16 or 17 inches across.

wildcards In certain DOS commands, characters like * and ? function as wildcards. They mean "all" and can be used to process many files at the same time. For instance. DEL *.BAK will delete every file with a BAK file extension.

Winchester drive An old-fashioned term for *hard disk*.

window In Windows, applications run inside boxes called windows, which you can open, close, size, overlap, and otherwise have a ball with.

Windows Not an application itself, but an icon-crazy, mouse-happy environment where you'll find the best applications that run on PCs—the best word processors, the best spreadsheets, you name it. Thanks to certain conventions, Windows applications tend to look and work alike, making it easier to learn another if you already know one. For all that, Windows isn't nearly as easy to use as it pretends to be (see *icon, mouse*).

Windows NT Microsoft's high-end alternative to Windows, currently most prevalent on network servers.

Windows shell A program that replaces Windows' File Manager or Program Manager or both, providing easier access to just about everything Windows has to offer. Each shell offers its own visual metaphor, plus various techniques for making Windows shape up (see *application launcher, File Manager, Program Manager*).

WIN.INI A Windows configuration file, in which settings not directly related to hardware are stored.

wireless LANs Network adapters that use infrared, microwave, or radio transceivers instead of cables.

WMF Short for *Windows metafile*, Windows' own vector graphics file format (see *vector graphics*).

word chart A presentation graphics term used to describe a chart that uses words instead of numeric data to convey information (see *data chart*).

word processor An application designed to let you create, edit, and print documents. These days, most word processors offer so many advanced formatting features they're hard to distinguish from desktop publishing programs (see *formatting*, *desktop publishing*).

word wrap In a word processor, when you type to the end of a line, the next line automatically begins flush with the left margin. That's word wrap.

workgroup Marketing slang for a group of coworkers who share data on a LAN.

workgroup software Any application that couldn't run without a network, such as a group scheduler, or Lotus's popular *Notes* product.

Workplace-OS IBM's successor to OS/2.

worksheet A document created by a spreadsheet.

workstation Usually means a PC that's hooked to a network. Also used to describe high-end computers running UNIX. Sometimes just a synonym for PC.

WORM Short for *write once/read many*, a term describing an optical disk that can be written to only once. Useful for creating archive disks of data that you don't want changed.

write-back cache A memory cache that enables the CPU to write to fast cache memory instead of to main memory, avoiding wait states and keeping performance high (see *wait state*).

write caching Also called *delayed write*, this somewhat risky function is offered by some disk caching software: The PC is fooled into thinking it's storing (or *writing*) data to disk, when in fact it's writing to the disk cache—which holds the data in memory temporarily, until the computer has nothing better to do than write to disk. This speeds things up, but if there's a crash or power failure before the disk cache writes to disk, the data in memory is lost and the file or files being written to may be trashed (see *disk cache*).

write protected Describes a floppy disk that's been set up so you can only read its contents, not save anything. On 3^1/$_2$-inch floppies, pushing up a little switch on one corner prevents the disk from being written to; on 5^1/$_4$-inch floppies, you need to cover a notch near one corner of the disk with tape.

write-through cache A memory cache that speeds up memory reads but not writes, since the CPU must write directly to main memory, incurring wait states. Slower than a write-back cache.

write verification A scheme to check data after it's been written to disk to verify that no errors occurred.

WYSIWYG A silly acronym for "what you see is what you get"—that is, a representation on screen that closely approximates what you'll see in print. Once, only desktop publishing programs were WYSIWYG; now virtually all Windows programs are WYSIWYG.

X

XGA Short for *Extended Graphics Array*, a proprietary IBM graphics standard for 1024 by 768 resolution.

XLS files The file name extension for Excel worksheet files (see *file extension*).

Xmodem The lowest common denominator of file transfer protocols, offered by nearly all communications and BBS software. Slower than Ymodem or Zmodem.

XMS Short for *extended memory specification*, the set of official rules that applications (and Windows) employ when they use extended memory. XMS is also a cool way of saying "extended memory"; it's one of those terms that makes it sound as if you know something (see *extended memory*).

XON/XOFF An older modem communications protocol that uses ASCII characters to control the flow of data so that the sender and receiver stay in sync. While it's supported by most communications software, it's been all but supplanted by newer, faster protocols (see *protocol, ASCII*).

Y

Y-connector A Y-shaped cable that splits a source input into two output signals.

Ymodem Based on Xmodem, but faster, Ymodem includes the ability to transfer more than one file at a time. Better than Zmodem on noisy phone lines but not as fast.

Ymodem-G A faster version of Ymodem that leaves out error checking for speed's sake, relying on modems to fulfill that essential function. Requires modem with MNP or V.42.

Z

zero-wait state An exaggerated term implying that a system's CPU is accessing main memory without any wait states whatsoever, which is impossible. In fact, if a CPU is running at zero wait states, it's probably accessing its own built-in cache (see *wait state*).

ZIF socket Short for *zero insertion force* socket, a socket for CPUs that makes replacing a chip easy: Lift a little lever, and the chip comes out; push it back, and the chip is locked in tight. ZIF sockets are great for CPU upgrades.

ZIP file A file compressed with the *PKZIP* utility; usually has the ZIP file extension.

Zmodem A fast and widely supported file transfer protocol, Zmodem offers both high-speed transmission and *batch transfers*. If a transfer is interrupted, it can be resumed later without having to start from scratch.

A

Tuning AUTOEXEC.BAT and CONFIG.SYS

By Robert Lauriston

Installing, configuring, and troubleshooting software frequently requires modifying DOS's CONFIG.SYS and AUTOEXEC.BAT files. These are simply text files containing a series of commands or settings used to configure your system. Both are stored in the root directory of the drive your PC boots from. Here are the three most important things to remember when editing them:

1. Make a backup copy of the file before editing it, so you can return to the original settings if your changes cause problems.

2. Every command or setting must go on a line by itself (a single CONFIG.SYS line is known as a statement).

3. To temporarily disable an entry for troubleshooting, insert `rem` at the beginning of the line.

To edit CONFIG.SYS and AUTOEXEC.BAT in DOS, use the MS-DOS Editor— enter `edit c:\config.sys` or `edit c:\autoexec.bat`. Alternatively, you can use your favorite word processor; just be sure to save the file as text (also known as DOS text or ASCII) *without* line breaks. Never save a configuration file in a word processor format or as text with line breaks.

DANGER

In Windows, use Notepad or the SysEdit utility. The latter is more convenient, as it automatically opens both CONFIG.SYS and AUTOEXEC.BAT along with Windows' two main configuration files, WIN.INI and SYSTEM.INI, all at once. To use SysEdit, choose Run from Program Manager's File menu and enter `sysedit`.

In the following section, you'll find a fairly typical CONFIG.SYS and AUTOEXEC.BAT. The lines appear in the order you normally see them listed, with explanations that can help you create and edit your own configurations.

CONFIG.SYS

The CONFIG.SYS file is primarily a list of hardware *device drivers*—small programs that add capabilities to DOS or allow it to work with particular hardware. A few other basic DOS options are also set here, some by special commands that can be used only in CONFIG.SYS.

```
device=c:\dos\himem.sys
device=c:\dos\emm386.exe ram x=a000-c7ff
dos=umb
```

These three entries set up DOS's memory management. DOS's MemMaker usually creates these lines automatically, but sometimes you have to tweak them manually to troubleshoot software or hardware problems (see the section "Memory Optimizers" in Chapter 21: *Utilities* for an explanation of the various types of memory). The statement DEVICE= is the CONFIG.SYS command for loading a device driver.

HIMEM.SYS lets applications share *extended memory* (XMS). In practical terms, that means you need HIMEM.SYS to run Windows or any DOS program that requires a 386. If you use a third-party memory manager like QEMM, you'll use its memory manager instead.

REMEMBER

EMM386 does two things: It can emulate expanded memory (EMS) for older DOS applications that require it, and it can set up the upper memory area so you can use

DEVICEHIGH and LH commands to make more conventional memory available (allowing you to run larger DOS apps and make Windows run better). EMM386.EXE by itself does only the first; EMM386.EXE NOEMS does only the second; and EMM386.EXE RAM does both. (In DOS 5.0 and 6.0, you had to put a number after RAM indicating the amount of memory in KB you wanted to dedicate to EMS. Starting with DOS 6.2, EMM386 shifts memory between EMS and XMS on the fly.) Which setting is best depends on what programs you run; see the "Making More Memory Available" chapter of your DOS manual for tips on optimizing these settings.

DOS=UMB tells DOS to manage the upper memory area set up by EMM386. If you use EMM386 with the NOEMS or RAM options, you need "dos=umb" as well.

REMEMBER

REMEMBER

Windows can emulate EMS for DOS applications, so if you don't need EMS outside of Windows, and you don't use DEVICEHIGH or LOADHIGH, you can leave EMM386 and DOS=UMB out of your CONFIG.SYS.

```
dos=high
```

This line moves some DOS code out of conventional memory and into the high memory area, making room in conventional memory for larger DOS applications and giving Windows a little more elbow room to run more applications faster. DOS=HIGH requires HIMEM. You can combine DOS=HIGH and DOS=UMB into the single command DOS=HIGH,UMB.

```
devicehigh=c:\dos\setver.exe
```

The SETVER command fools older DOS apps into thinking that they're running under the version of DOS they expect to find. You may never run a program that needs SETVER, but you should include the statement just to be safe. DEVICE-HIGH= works just like DEVICE=, except it loads device drivers into the upper memory area. Some drivers don't like it up there, so if MemMaker or a similar utility makes any of your hardware devices unusable, the first thing you should do is to find the CONFIG.SYS line that loads the driver for that hardware and try changing the command from DEVICEHIGH to DEVICE (see DOS Help for more on DEVICEHIGH).

HOT TIP

```
buffers=4
```

This statement creates a sort of crude disk cache by telling DOS to copy a small quantity of data on disk into memory. If you already use SmartDrive or a third-party disk cache, you can save a little memory by setting it to a low value, like 4. (If you set it to 1, check to make sure it doesn't slow down floppy disk operations.) With no disk cache, 20 is usually adequate.

```
files=50
```

HOT TIP

This controls how many files DOS can have open at once; 50 is a conservative setting if you're using Windows. If you're just using DOS, you can probably get away with 20. If you get an error message about "file handles" from DOS, Windows, or one of your applications, try raising this value.

```
lastdrive=F
```

DOS allocates a little memory for each potential drive letter. You can recover some of that by setting LASTDRIVE to the last drive letter in your system.

```
shell=c:\dos\command.com c:\dos\ /e:1024 /p
```

SHELL tells DOS where to look for COMMAND.COM, its *command interpreter* (the program that enables DOS to run commands and batch files). SHELL is also used to load alternate command interpreters, such as *The Norton Utilities*'s NDOS, which adds extra capabilities to the command line. If you encounter the error message, "out of environment space," you can resolve it using the /e: switch to increase the amount of memory DOS sets aside to store the path and other variables displayed by the SET command (see Chapter 10: *When Things Go Wrong* for instructions on determining the right environment size).

```
device=c:\dos\smartdrv.exe /double_buffer
```

Under some circumstances this is required to use SmartDrive with some hard drives. For more information, see the Notes section of DOS Help for SMARTDRV.EXE.

```
fcbs=16
stacks=20,256
```

These arcane entries are required by some programs. If a program says it needs two numbers after FCBS, like FCBS=16,0, you can leave off the second number (unless you're using DOS 4 or an earlier version). If two programs need different STACKS settings, use the highest value for both numbers. For example, if one program wants STACKS=9,512 and another wants STACKS=32,256, set it to 32,512.

Depending on what kind of hardware you have installed in your system, you may have a number of device drivers installed in your CONFIG.SYS. Here are two from my system:

```
device=c:\apps\fax\satisfax.sys ioaddr=0350
devicehigh=c:\utils\tscsi\tslcdr.sys /d:tslcd /r
```

The first is used by my fax modem, the second by my SCSI adapter. There are thousands of drivers out there, so it's impossible to provide a guide to all of them. In most cases, installation software will add these statements automatically. Often the path will make clear what device is using the driver.

AUTOEXEC.BAT

The AUTOEXEC.BAT file loads memory-resident utilities, executes any commands that need to be run at startup, and sets various DOS options. When it finishes with those tasks, it usually starts Windows.

```
@echo off
```

This suppresses messages that would otherwise display on the screen as DOS executes the AUTOEXEC.BAT sequence.

```
prompt $p$g
```

Without this command, the DOS prompt won't show the path to the current directory.

REMEMBER

```
path c:\windows;c:\dos
```

The PATH command lets you start programs just as if they were in the current directory. Simply add the program's directory name to the PATH, and DOS will search that directory and see if the command you entered at the DOS prompt starts anything. The shorter your path, the faster DOS finds the program whose startup command you've entered.

REMEMBER

Here are two tips for keeping your path short: In Windows, instead of adding a program to your path, define its Working Directory in the Program Manager (select the icon and press [Alt][Enter]) or its Start-Up Directory in the program's PIF file. In DOS, start apps using batch files (see Appendix D: *Batch Files* for more information).

HOT TIP

```
set temp=c:\temp
echo y | del c:\temp\.
```

The SET command followed by a \TEMP OR \TMP directory tells programs that need to create temporary files where to put those files. Adding this line to your AUTOEXEC.BAT isn't absolutely necessary, but it's a good idea, or else programs may scatter useless temporary files all over your hard disk. The DEL command automatically deletes everything in C:\TEMP when you boot your PC; ECHO Y | bypasses DOS's usual delete confirmation. This prevents temp files in the directory from accumulating and wasting hard drive space.

```
set pctools=c:\apps\pctools\data
set wpc=/d-d:\temp
set dircmd=/ogne /l /p
```

Some applications and DOS commands use the SET command to store special settings. The PCTOOLS entry tells *PC Tools* where to find certain settings used by that program, while the WPC entry tells WordPerfect Corporation programs to store temp files in C:\TEMP. The DIRCMD entry changes the default options for the DIR command, so that DIR gives lists files in a format that would otherwise require DIR /OGNE/L/P.

```
lh /L:0;1,45456 /s c:\dos\smartdrv /x
```

LH is shorthand for LOADHIGH (see DOS Help for more on this command). According to DOS Help, SmartDrive loads itself into upper memory without LOADHIGH's help, but MemMaker adds LH (and its /L: and /S switches) anyway. When you install DOS 6.2, it adds /X to turn off write-buffering, a measure that may keep you from losing data (see the section "Windows Tips" in Chapter 12: *DOS and Windows* for more SmartDrive advice).

```
c:\dos\mscdex /d:tslcd /m:20 /L:f /e
```

DOS needs this to read CD ROM discs. MSCDEX should come after SMARTDRV in your AUTOEXEC.BAT—otherwise, SmartDrive won't speed up CD ROM performance.

```
lh c:\windows\mouse.com
```

You need MOUSE.COM if you use a mouse with DOS applications outside of Windows. Some mouse drivers use upper memory automatically, even without LH, while others won't load high even *with* LH (in which case you should just leave LH out). Depending on what mouse you use, the driver may have a slightly different name (like LMOUSE for Logitech mice), or reside in a different directory. In some cases it may use a MOUSE.SYS driver in your config, instead.

As in CONFIG.SYS, depending on what hardware and software you've installed, there are a seemingly infinite variety of entries that might show up in your autoexec. Here are a couple from mine:

```
c:\utils\hercules\setcrt  c:\utils\hercules\myscreen.crt
c:\apps\fax\casmgr.exe c:\apps\fax\casmgr.cfg
```

The first sets my super-VGA board's output to match my monitor's capabilities, and the second loads some memory-resident software used by my fax modem.

```
call pctools
```

CALL lets you run a batch file (in this case, PCTOOLS.BAT) then continue with the rest of the commands in your AUTOEXEC.BAT. If you don't use CALL, DOS will execute the commands in the batch file and stop without finishing the rest of the autoexec commands.

```
win :
```

Generally, the last entry in your autoexec should load Windows. If you don't run Windows, enter the startup command for your primary DOS app or your favorite DOS shell (see the "Miscellaneous" section of Chapter 21: *Utilities* for more on DOS Shells).

DOS's Default CONFIG.SYS and AUTOEXEC.BAT

After installing DOS and Windows and running MemMaker (as described in the "Setting Up a New Hard Disk" section of Chapter 12: *DOS and Windows*), CONFIG.SYS and AUTOEXEC.BAT will look pretty much like this. If you ever need to create a set of configuration files from scratch, this is a good place to start.

CONFIG.SYS

```
device=c:\dos\himem.sys
device=c:\dos\emm386.exe ram
buffers=15,0
files=30
dos=umb
lastdrive=H
fcbs=4,0
devicehigh=C:\dos\setver.exe
dos=high
stacks=9,256
```

AUTOEXEC.BAT

```
lh c:\dos\smartdrv.exe /x
@echo off
prompt $p$g
path C:\windows;c:\dos
set temp=c:\dos
```

The one objectionable setting here is the last line, SET TEMP=C:\DOS. Under some circumstances this can lead to your DOS directory getting cluttered with abandoned temp files. A much better approach is to create a directory dedicated to temporary files, so you should replace this line with SET TEMP=C:\TEMP.

B Editing Windows' INI Files

By Robert Lauriston

Windows uses text files referred to as *INI* (short for "initialization") files to maintain special software and hardware settings. For example, any changes you make to the File Manager's configuration using menus or dialog boxes are stored in WINFILE.INI. Here are some INI files you're likely to have in your \WINDOWS directory:

CONTROL.INI	Control Panel
DOSAPP.INI	DOS applications
MOUSE.INI	Windows' mouse program
PROGMAN.INI	Program Manager
SYSTEM.INI	General hardware
WIN.INI	General software
WINFILE.INI	File Manager
WINHELP.INI	Windows Help

Windows apps usually create INI files in \WINDOWS as well—for example, 123R4.INI (*1-2-3*), EXCEL5.INI (*Excel*), and QPW.INI (*Quattro Pro*). However, you seldom have to worry about applications' INI files, since you can almost always adjust a program's settings using its menus and dialog boxes.

Windows normally manages INI files without any intervention from you. However, troubleshooting software problems or changing an obscure setting may require you to edit INI files manually. Most of the time, when you need to edit an INI file, it will be either WIN.INI or SYSTEM.INI—the former holds software settings, the latter hardware configuration.

To edit either WIN.INI or SYSTEM.INI, use the SysEdit utility: Just pick Run from the Program Manager's File Menu and enter `sysedit`; the utility will serve up WIN.INI and SYSTEM.INI (along with AUTOEXEC.BAT and CONFIG.SYS) in separate windows, ready to edit. To edit other INI files easily, use Notepad, and associate INI files with it: Select an INI file, choose Associate from File Manager's File Menu, select Text File [notepad.exe], and click OK. From then on, when you double-click an INI file in File Manager, the file will automatically load itself into Notepad.

HOT TIP

WIN.INI and SYSTEM.INI are long, often complicated files, and discussing all the ins and out of them would require a book in itself. To help get you acquainted with INI files, I've chosen a simpler example. Here's a quick look at a sample WIN-FILE.INI that exemplifies how INI files work:

```
[Settings]
undelete.dll=c:\dos\mstools.dll
LowerCase=1
Save Settings=0
ConfirmDelete=0
ConfirmSubDel=0
ConfirmReplace=1
ConfirmMouse=0
ConfirmFormat=0
StatusBar=1
Window=0,0,508,276, , ,1
dir1=0,0,522,249,-1,-1,1,0,201,1905,174,c:\windows\*.*

[AddOns]
MS-DOS Tools Extentions=c:\dos\mstools.dll
Mail File Manager Extension=c:\windows\system\sendfile.dll
```

Entries in Windows INI files are grouped into sections with bracketed headings. In WINFILE.INI, the [Settings] section stores changes you make to File Manager's options using its menu commands and dialog boxes, as well as settings for its directory windows. The [AddOns] section defines any enhancements you or your applications have added to File Manager—here, the Tools menu added by DOS and the File//Send command added by *Microsoft Mail*. (For no good reason, DOS adds the File//Undelete command in the [Settings] section instead.)

Add a line to an INI file yourself, and you *must* put that line in the right section, or your change won't do anything. When you need to add a line, it's often because the people who designed a piece of hardware or software missed something in an automatic installation routine. The specs for adding a line manually are often found in a README file containing installation afterthoughts (see "To install an application..." in Chapter 12's Cookbook).

REMEMBER

Entries in INI files have two parts, divided by an equal sign (=) in the middle. To the left of the = is a label (the *keyname*) that describes—often cryptically—what option the entry sets. To the right of the = is the setting (the *value)* that the INI assigns to the keyname. Values can be anything, but typically are numbers, file names, paths, font names, or on/off switches. As you can see in the Window= and dir1= entries, values can contain a number of settings, separated by commas or spaces.

On/off values are usually stored as 1/0, so LowerCase=1 means the Lowercase box is checked in the Options/Font dialog box, and SaveSettings=0 means Save Settings on Exit is *not* checked on the Options menu. Other ways of indicating on/off values you may encounter: yes/no, true/false, and on/off. You're supposed to be able to use all of these interchangeably, but in practice that doesn't always work—so always use whichever one the instructions you're following tell you to use.

REMEMBER

Now that you have an idea of how INI files work, remember these five rules as you edit them:

1. Make a backup copy of the INI file before editing it, so you can return to the original settings if your changes cause problems. (An easy way to back up INI files is to create a \BAK subdirectory beneath \WINDOWS, and enter `copy \windows\*.ini` to make the copies.)

2. Windows INI files are divided into sections indicated by bracketed headings, such as [386Enh] or [Desktop]. When you add a setting to an INI file, be sure you put it under the right section heading.

3. Every entry must go on a line by itself.

4. INI files can be very long, so before adding a new entry to a long section of an INI file, use the Find command to make sure you didn't overlook an existing entry. Search only for the keyname (the part before the =).

5. To temporarily disable an entry, insert a semicolon at the beginning of the line.

If you need more information about Windows' INI files, get a copy of Microsoft's *Windows Resource Kit* ($15), a reference manual that documents most of the entries in WIN.INI and SYSTEM.INI. There should be an order form included in the envelope with your Windows registration card. If you can't find it, call 800/642-7676 to find out where you can get one.

C Important Stuff DOS Help Doesn't Tell You

By Robert Lauriston

The HELP command in recent versions of DOS will tell you most of what you need to know about DOS commands—at the DOS prompt, just enter help followed by the command you want to learn about (or enter help by itself if you just want to browse and see what's there). HELP is terrific—use it whenever you're stuck—but it won't tell you everything.

Neither will we, but at least we can fill in a few important gaps. Here's a selection of essential warnings, tricks, tips, examples, and explanations that Microsoft left out. It's also a pretty complete list of commands, if you forget what any of them do. Note that all references to DOS 6 also apply to DOS 6.2, DOS 6.22, and later versions.

ANSI.SYS. Some older DOS applications might require that you add this to your CONFIG.SYS. You can also use ANSI.SYS to customize DOS in fancy ways (such as a color background in DOS), but it's seldom worth the effort.

APPEND. This works just like the PATH command, only for data files instead of for programs. For example, if you enter the command APPEND C:\DATA, and that directory contains the file REPORT.TXT, entering the command EDIT REPORT.TXT would open the file, even if the current directory is not C:\DATA (unless there's a REPORT.TXT in the current directory, in which case that file would be opened instead).

HOT TIP

ASSIGN. This command was removed from DOS 6. It's used to trick software that will only run from a particular drive into thinking that's where it is. For example, if you're installing an application from disks that fit your B: drive, but the setup utility is designed to work only from drive A:, the command ASSIGN B: A: will usually make it work properly. If your version of DOS has SUBST, enter `subst b: a:\` instead.

DANGER

ATTRIB. HELP explains this command pretty well (you use it to hide files, make hidden files visible again, make files read-only, or make read-only files writable again), but neglects to mention that if you don't know what you're doing, using this command on hidden or system files can seriously screw up your system.

BACKUP. This command was removed from DOS 6, because Microsoft Backup made it obsolete. However, DOS 6 and later versions *do* include RESTORE, which you can use to restore files backed up with previous DOS versions.

BUFFERS. If for some strange reason you can't use a disk cache, you can add a second parameter to create a primitive substitute for one. Try adding the line BUFFERS=50,8 to your CONFIG.SYS and see if it improves performance.

CALL. Use this command in a batch file if you want to start a program, exit it, and resume the batch file (see Appendix D).

CD. This stands for "change directory" (see "To move from one directory to another..." in Chapter 12's Cookbook).

CHDIR. This is identical to CD, which you should enter instead because it's shorter.

CHKDSK. This checks disks for certain data errors and fixes some of them. DOS 6's ScanDisk is vastly superior, so use it instead.

COMP. This command was removed from DOS 6. It compares two files to see if they are identical, which you may want to do if, say, you've just copied a very important file to a floppy. FC is similar, but COMP is better if you just want to know if files are identical.

For example, COMP C:\DOS\COMMAND.COM A: will check to see if the copy of COMMAND.COM in your DOS directory matches the one on a boot floppy (see "What's on the Supplemental Disk").

COPY. Use this command to copy files (see "To copy or move files or directories..." in Chapter 12's Cookbook).

DEFRAG. Defragments your hard drive (see the section "Safety Check" in Chapter 12: *Windows and DOS*).

DEL. This commands deletes files (see "To delete files or directories..." in Chapter 12's Cookbook).

What's on the Supplemental Disk

Microsoft left a dozen commands found in earlier releases out of DOS 6.0: ASSIGN, BACKUP, COMP, CV, EDLIN, EXE2BIN, GRAFTABL, JOIN, MIRROR, MSHERC, and RECOVER. They also pulled DOSSHELL from DOS 6.2 (though the manual still discusses it in detail). If you upgraded from an earlier version of DOS, these commands will still be in your DOS directory, but they're not covered in HELP. Otherwise, these files are available on a supplemental disk—there's an order form in the back of your DOS manual—or you can download them from one of Microsoft's on-line libraries. While most of these commands are obscure or obsolete, COMP, DOSSHELL, and MIRROR are worth having around. If the others have been left in your DOS directory after upgrading, you can delete them to recover wasted disk space.

DELOLDOS. After you upgrade DOS, you can use this command to delete the backup copy of the old version from your hard drive. Then you can delete DELOLDOS.EXE itself from your DOS directory to save space.

DELTREE. This deletes a directory, all directories underneath it, and all the files they contain (see "To delete files or directories..." in Chapter 12's Cookbook).

DIR. This displays a list of file names (see "To see what files are in a directory..." in Chapter 12's Cookbook).

DISKCOPY. This makes a copy of a floppy disk (see "To copy a floppy disk..." in Chapter 12's Cookbook).

DOSKEY. If you use DOSKEY, which lets you recall and edit the last few DOS commands you entered, you'll probably want to add it to your AUTOEXEC.BAT (see the section "DOS Shortcuts" in Chapter 12: *Windows and DOS*).

DOSSHELL. This excellent file manager was unfortunately removed from DOS 6.2, though it's still discussed in detail in the manual (see "What's on the Supplemental Disk").

EDLIN. This horrible antique editor was removed from DOS 6, and good riddance. Use EDIT instead.

ERASE. Use DEL, it's shorter.

EXE2BIN. This obsolete programmers' tool was removed from DOS 6.

EXPAND. EXPAND copies files from DOS's setup disks onto your hard drive. (HELP's example, EXPAND A:\SORT.EX_ C:\DOS\SORT.EXE, is unnecessarily complicated; you could drop the second file name and just use EXPAND A:\SORT.EXE C:\DOS.) EXPAND will look for A:\SORT.EXE; when it doesn't find it, it will look for SORT.EX_ instead, expand it as it copies it, and change the _ to an E in the expanded file. HELP mistakenly refers to "files," but in fact EXPAND can only work on one file at a time. If you have access to *PC Magazine*'s PCMAGNET CompuServe forum, download Michael Bee's MEXPAND.BAT, which resolves this problem.

HOT TIP

FDISK. This utility is used by DOS SETUP to create logical volumes on a new hard drive (see "How to Set Up a New Hard Disk" in Chapter 12: *Windows and DOS*). Don't use FDISK if you don't know what you're doing, as it can erase everything on your hard drive. If you accidentally do wipe your drive screwing around with FDISK *do nothing* to the drive until you get your hands on a copy of *The Norton Utilities* or *PC Tools*, which may be able to recover your data intact.

HOT TIP

FORMAT. Use this command to prepare a new disk or erase an already formatted one (see "To format a floppy..." in Chapter 12's Cookbook).

GORILLA. This sample QBasic file was removed from DOS 6.

GRAFTABL. Obsolete video utility removed from DOS 6.

GRAPHICS. This is supposed to let you print the current screen by pressing Shift Print Screen when the display is in graphics mode (say, when you're running Windows), but it often doesn't work.

INTERLNK AND INTERSVR. You can use this pair of utilities to copy files between two computers over a file transfer cable connecting their serial or parallel ports (the latter is considerably faster). It's most often used for copying files between a desktop and a laptop. The DOS manual and on-line help explain both these commands well enough, but they don't do a great job of giving the big picture. First, decide which computer you want to work at; DOS calls this the "client," and the other computer the "server." Contrary to the DOS manual's advice, it's usually best to make the desktop the client and the laptop the server. Add the line `device=c:\dos\interlnk.exe` to the client's CONFIG.SYS, and reboot. On the server, enter the command `intersvr`. The server's drives then show up on the client as

HOT TIP

additional drive letters, and you can copy files using DOS commands, File Manager, or whatever file management tools you like.

JOIN. This not-so-useful command was removed from DOS 6. It "joins" the contents of a drive and a directory. For example, JOIN A: C:\UTILS would make the contents of A: appear in C:\UTILS. Enter the command `join /d` and A: and C:\UTILS resume their normal, separate roles.

MD. Short for "make directory," this command creates a directory immediately beneath the directory in which the command is entered (see "To create a directory..." in Chapter 12's Cookbook).

MEM. This command, for techies mostly, displays various information about your PC's memory. You can abbreviate MEM's switches—for example `mem /c/p` to page a moderately detailed display, or `mem /d/p` to page maximum details.

Mirror. This command was removed from DOS 6. It stores information that allows Microsoft Unformat to recover more data. To store unformat information for drive C:, enter `mirror c:`. For more help on using MIRROR, enter `help mirror`. This command would be obsolete, since the FORMAT command now stores this information automatically, but since Windows' File Manager's Disk//Format Disk command does not, MIRROR is worth having (see "What's on the Supplemental Disk").

MKDIR. Use MD, it's shorter.

MONEY. This sample QBasic file was removed from DOS 6.

MORE. DOS HELP's example, TYPE CLIENTS.NEW | MORE, makes no sense, since it's more efficient to type MORE < CLIENTS.NEW. Use *command* | MORE to page command output, as in TREE | MORE, and MORE < *filename* to page files, as in MORE < AUTOEXEC.BAT.

MOVE. This command moves or renames files or directories (see "To copy or move files or directories..." in Chapter 12's Cookbook).

MSAV. This utility scans for and removes viruses (see "Safety Check" in Chapter 12: *Windows and DOS*).

MSBACKUP. This command backs up your hard disk to floppy disk (see "Safety Check" in Chapter 12: *Windows and DOS*).

MSD. Displays a wide variety of information about your system (see Chapter 8: *Upgrade It Yourself*). Running MSD under Windows sometimes interferes with applications currently using COM ports, such as a communications program performing a file transfer.

MSHERC. This command was removed from DOS 6. It supported graphics compatible with the original monochrome Hercules graphics board.

NIBBLES. This sample QBasic file was removed from DOS 6.

PRINTER.SYS. This obsolete printer driver was removed from DOS 6.

PROMPT. One example missing from HELP is how to set the prompt to display the time. For the format (12:30) C:\DOS>, use the command prompt (thhhhh) pg.

RD. Deletes a directory, but only if it's empty (see "To delete files or directories..." in Chapter 12's Cookbook).

RECOVER. This command was removed from DOS 6, and about time. Over the years, this badly designed data recovery tool has done far more harm than good.

REMLINE. This sample QBasic file was removed from DOS 6.

REN. Use this command to rename files (see "To rename files or directories..." in Chapter 12's Cookbook).

RENAME. Use REN, it's shorter.

RMDIR. Use RD, it's shorter.

SCANDISK. This tells DOS to search for and repair disk errors (see "Safety Check" in Chapter 12: *Windows and DOS*).

SETVER. This lets older apps work with DOS 6 by making them think they're running under an older DOS version. This should usually be added to your AUTOEXEC.BAT.

SHARE. This allows applications to share files, which is a good feature. But if you've installed a recent Windows program that includes VShare, you have this capability already—and you should be able to remove SHARE, which wastes memory. To find out if VShare is installed, see if the file VSHARE.386 is in your \WINDOWS\SYSTEM directory. If it is, make sure the entry DEVICE=VSHARE.386 appears in the [386Enh] section of your SYSTEM.INI.

SMARTDRV. DOS's disk cache speeds up disk operations (for some tips on using it, see the section "Windows Tips" in Chapter 12: *Windows and DOS*).

SWITCHES. Adding the command SWITCHES=/F to the beginning of your CONFIG.SYS will supposedly eliminate the pointless two-second delay after the "Starting MS-DOS ..." message—but my stopwatch doesn't detect any difference.

UNDELETE. This recovers files after you accidentally delete them (see "To retrieve accidentally deleted files or directories..." in Chapter 12's Cookbook).

UNFORMAT. This recovers data from a disk you formatted by mistake (see "To recover data from an accidentally formatted disk..." in Chapter 12's Cookbook).

VERIFY. This tells DOS whether to check if data is correctly written to disk. It slows operations a bit, so the default is OFF.

VSAFE. This protects against virus infections (see "Safety Check" in Chapter 12: *Windows and DOS*).

XCOPY. This copies entire directories—and the directories beneath them, if you like (see "To copy or move files or directories..." in Chapter 12's Cookbook).

D ⦚ Batch Files

By Robert Lauriston

Batch files contain lists of DOS commands. You create batch files with a text editor such as DOS's EDIT or Windows' Notepad and save them using a BAT extension. That extension essentially turns your text list of commands into a mini-program: Enter the name of the batch file at the prompt, and DOS executes the commands you saved in the order you listed them.

With batch files, you can automatically start programs, change directories, archive files, rename commands...anything repetitive you'd prefer a batch file did instead of you. In this Appendix, you'll find several batch files I use regularly. Some may be useful for your own applications if you modify them a bit, but in any case you'll learn a few batch file tricks if you follow closely.

To learn about AUTOEXEC.BAT, the batch file that runs automatically when you start your computer, turn to Appendix A.

~~~~~~

Start Programs Fast

I have lots of simple batch files in my C:\UTILS directory that start DOS programs and utilities. I could just add the names of the directories containing these programs to my PATH, but this slows down DOS by forcing it to search a long list of directories every time you enter a command (see Appendix A for more on the PATH command).

Batch Files for PKZip and UnZip

PKZIP.EXE and PKUNZIP.EXE are the file compression and decompression components of *PKZip*, the most popular file archiving utility, which squeezes down individual files to a fraction of their normal size (for more on *PKZip* see "Shareware and Freeware Utilities" in Chapter 21). *PKZip* has over a dozen files, so for organization's sake I've installed the utility in its own directory, C:\UTILS\PKZIP. Instead of adding this directory to my path, I created these two batch files, which I store in C:\UTILS (which is in my path):

ZIP.BAT

```
c:\utils\pkzip\pkzip %1 %2 %3 %4 %5 %6 %7 %8 %9
```

UNZIP.BAT

```
c:\utils\pkzip\pkunzip %1 %2 %3 %4 %5 %6 %7 %8 %9
```

%1, %2, and so on are replaceable parameters that pick up whatever you type after the batch file name at the DOS prompt and plug it into the batch file. Every time you type a space, DOS assigns what follows to the next parameter. For example, if I entered this at a DOS prompt:

```
pkzip reports -rP *.doc
```

I would have replaced three of the nine replaceable parameters in ZIP.BAT. REPORTS replaces %1 and tells *PKZip* to create an archive file by that name. -rP replaces %2 and tells *PKZip* to include all subdirectories beneath the current directory. *.DOC replaces %3 and tells *PKZip* to include all DOC files in the archive file. The final result is the equivalent of entering this command:

```
c:\utils\pkzip\pkzip reports -rP *.doc
```

Change Directories, Then Start a Program

Some apps won't work right unless you are in their directory when you start them. Here's a batch file for such a program:

FAX.BAT

```
c:
cd \apps\fax
fax
cd\
```

I always have batch files like this switch back to the root at the end, so I never have to waste time thinking about what subdirectory I might be in.

Turn Off Caching, Then Start a Program

Sometimes you need to do something tricky before you start an app, like load or disable a memory-resident utility. This batch file shuts off a disk cache that conflicts with a Mac-to-DOS file conversion utility, then turns caching back on after the utility is finished:

MACINDOS.BAT

```
c:
cd \utils\macindos
superpck /d
clink
superpck /e
```

SUPERPCK /D unloads the disk cache, while CLINK starts the file conversion utility.

Command Entries

It's often tedious—and occasionally impossible—to enter certain combinations of commands at the DOS prompt. Here are a couple of batch files that help me out in these situations.

Simplify or Rename a Command

If you enter a complicated command over and over, or tend to make typos while entering a command, you can use a batch file to simplify or rename it. Since I spend a lot of time testing software, I'm constantly checking memory with the command MEM /C /P, which I can never seem to type without making a mistake. So I just put those slashes and letters in a batch file:

MEMC.BAT

```
mem /c /p
```

Enter a Command DOS Won't Let You Type

Batch files can be useful for entering commands you can't type at the DOS prompt. For example, the command to reset a LaserJet printer is the escape command (a special directive for printers) followed by an E. Since you can't enter an escape command at the DOS prompt, I use this batch file to reset my LaserJet:

RESET-HP.BAT

```
echo ←E > lpt1
```

Getting an escape command (represented by the ← character) into a batch file can be kind of tricky. To do this in DOS's text editor, enter this special character by pressing Ctrl -P, then Esc.

Easy Automation

Why not take the hard work out of long command sequences you enter over and over? Someday when you have time, make a list of these sequences, and see how many of them could be rolled up into batch files. Here are some of my favorites.

Archive, Rename, Delete

When I'm archiving old files, I often store them in *PKZip* files with the same name as the directory they were stored in. This batch file zips all the files in a directory, then deletes the directory. It must be run from the directory immediately above the one you're archiving. I could simplify this macro using DELTREE, but using RD (the "remove directory" command) prevents me from accidentally deleting subdirectories

I might have forgotten about (for more on deletion see "To delete a file or directory..." in Chapter 12's Cookbook).

ZIPNDEL.BAT

```
c:\utils\pkzip\pkzip %1.zip %1\*.*
echo y | del %1\*.*
rd %1
```

Enter the command `zipndel february`, and the batch file will replace every occurrence of %1 with that month's name. Without the batch file, you'd have to enter the following:

```
c:\utils\pkzip\pkzip february.zip february\*.*
echo y | del february\*.*
rd february
```

Double Decompression

Here's a fairly complicated batch file I use regularly to decompress the on-line versions of *PC Week* and *Macweek* that I download from CompuServe every week. CompuServe compresses the first publication with *PKZip*, the second with its Mac counterpart, *StuffIt*. (The line numbers are for reference only; they're not part of the batch file.)

ZIFFNEWS.BAT

```
(1)     d:
(2)     cd\info\pcweek
(3)     cd c:\download
(4)     call pkunzip c:pcweek
(5)     c:
(6)     del pcweek.zip
(7)     call noheader macweek.sit macweek2.sit
(8)     del macweek.sit
(9)     d:
(10)    cd ..\macweek
(11)    call unstuff c:macweek2.sit
(12)    del c:macweek2.sit
(13)    ed macweekn.ews /m-repl-cr
```

Lines 1 through 6 decompress the *PC Week* file into C:\DOWNLOAD, store it in the file D:\INFO\PCWEEK, and delete the ZIP file. Lines 7 and 8 create a copy of the *StuffIt* file without the Mac file system header and delete the original. Lines 9 through 12 decompress the *Macweek* file into D:\INFO\MACWEEK. The last line loads the *Macweek* file into a text editor and runs a REPL-CR macro I wrote that converts the text file's carriage returns from Mac to DOS format.

Writing a batch file this complicated is kind of a pain, but in the long run it's easier than performing the same series of commands every week. To make it even easier, I've set things up so I can run this batch file under Windows. To do this with any batch file, choose File//New from the Program Manager's menu and enter the usual information, with the batch file's name in the Command Line box. File Manager will create an icon for the batch file, which you can double-click on to start just like you would any other program.

HOT TIP

E Field Guide to File Formats

A file's extension is the clue to what program the file is part of or which application created it. To help you identify the myriad mystery files out there, we present this guide to no less than 169 file extensions.

$$$	Temporary
ADP	Sound
ARC	*ARC-E* archive
ASC	Text
ASM	Assembler source code
AVI	Windows video
BAK	Backup copy
BAS	BASIC program
BAT	Batch file
BFX	Fax
BK	Backup copy
BK!	Backup copy
BMP	Windows bitmap
C	C source code
CAL	*SuperCalc* or Windows Calendar
CDR	*CorelDraw*
CFG	Settings
CGM	Drawing (metafile)
CHK	Data recovered by CHKDSK
CHP	*Ventura Publisher* chapter
CLP	Windows or *Quattro Pro* clipboard
CMD	*dBASE II* program
COM	Program

CPL	Windows Control Panel application
CPP	C++ source code
CRD	Windows cardfile
CSV	Comma-delimited text
CTX	*FoxPro* index
CUT	*Dr. Halo* bitmap
DAT	data or settings
DB	*Paradox*
DBF	*dBASE* (and compatible) data
DBK	Backup copy of DBF file
DBT	*dBASE* memo
DCX	Fax
DDF	*BTrieve* data definition
DIB	Bitmap
DIF	Spreadsheet interchange (*VisiCalc*)
DLL	Program overlay
DOC	*Word for Windows, Word for DOS, DisplayWrite, MultiMate*
DOT	*Word for Windows* template
DOX	*MultiMate 4.0*
DRV	Windows device driver
DRW	*Micrografx Draw* graphic
DTF	*Q&A* data
DVP	*DesqView* settings
DWG	*AutoCAD*
DXF	*AutoCAD*
EPS	Encapsulated PostScript graphic
EXE	Program
F	*Paradox* form
FAX	Fax image
FLI	*AutoDesk Animator* animation
FM	*FileMaker Pro* database
FM3	*1-2-3 3.x* formatting data
FMT	*1-2-3 2.x* formatting data
FON	Font
FOR	FORTRAN source code
FOT	TrueType font (path to TTF file)
FXG	Fax
GIF	Bitmap
H	C header
HDR	Assembler header

HGL	HPGL graphic
HLP	Windows Help
IDX	*Q&A* index
IMG	*GEM Paint* bitmap
INI	Windows program settings
JIF	JPEG bitmap
JPG	JPEG bitmap
LBM	*Deluxe Paint* bitmap
LDB	*Microsoft Access* locking file
MAC	*MacPaint* bitmap
MDA	*Microsoft Access* add-in
MDB	*Microsoft Access* database
MDX	dBASE IV index
MID	MIDI data
MMM	*Macromedia Director* animation
MP	*Multiplan*
MSP	*Microsoft Paint* bitmap
MVB	*Microsoft Viewer* document
NDX	*dBASE III* index
NTX	*Clipper* index
OBJ	Object file (for *LINK*)
OVL	Program overlay
PAL	Color palette
PCD	PhotoCD bitmap
PCM	Sound
PCT	Macintosh PICT
PCX	*PC Paintbrush* bitmap
PDF	*Acrobat* document
PFA	PostScript font ASCII
PFB	PostScript font binary
PFM	PostScript font metric
PIC	*1-2-3* chart, *PC Paint* bitmap, or Macintosh PICT
PIF	Windows settings for DOS program
PLT	HPGL or *AutoCAD* graphic
PM3	*PageMaker 3.x*
PM4	*PageMaker 4.x*
PRD	Printer driver
PRG	*dBASE III* or *dBASE IV* program
PRN	*1-2-3* formatted text
PSD	*Photoshop*

PUB	Desktop publishing document
PX	*Paradox* primary index
QRY	Database query
QXD	*QuarkXPress* document
R	*Paradox* report
RAW	Sound
REC	Windows Recorder macro file, sound
REG	*RegEdit* data
RFT	DCA-RFT (word processing interchange format)
RIF	Multimedia document
RLE	Bitmap
RPL	*Replica* document
RTF	Rich text (word processing interchange format)
SAM	*Ami Pro* sound
SC	*Paradox* script
SDS	MIDI sample dump
SET	Settings
SLD	*AutoCAD* slide
SLK	Spreadsheet interchange (*Multiplan*)
SND	SoundBlaster sound
SNG	MIDI data
SOU	Sound
STY	Style sheet
SYS	Device driver
TGA	Targa bitmap
TIF	Bitmap
TMP	Temporary file
TRM	Windows' Terminal settings
TT	TrueType font (distribution format)
TTF	TrueType font (installed)
TXT	Text
VAL	*Paradox* validity checks
VOC	SoundBlaster sound
W51	*WordPerfect 5.1*
WAV	Windows sound
WB1	*Quattro Pro* notebook
WK!	*1-2-3* (SQZ compressed)
WK1	*1-2-3 2.x*
WK3	*1-2-3 3.x, 1-2-3 for Windows*
WK4	*1-2-3 for Windows 4.0*

WKQ	*Quattro Pro 3.x*
WKS	*1-2-3 1.x, Microsoft Works*
WKZ	*Quattro Pro* (SQZ compressed)
WLL	DLL for *Microsoft Word*
WMF	Windows graphics (metafile)
WPD	*WordPerfect* document
WPG	*WordPerfect* or *DrawPerfect* graphic
WPS	*Microsoft Works*
WPT	*WordPerfect* template
WQ1	*Quattro Pro 1.x, 2.x*
WR1	*Symphony 2.x*
WRI	*Windows Write*
WRK	*Symphony 1.x*
WSP	*Quattro Pro* workspace
X##	*Paradox* secondary index
XLA	*Excel* add-in
XLB	*Excel* toolbar
XLC	*Excel* chart
XLL	*Excel* add-in
XLM	*Excel* macro sheet
XLS	*Excel* spreadsheet or workbook
XLT	*Excel* template
XLW	*Excel 4.0* worksheet or *3.0* workspace
XXT	*QuarkXPress* add-on
Y##	*Paradox* secondary index
ZIP	*PKZip* archive

Index

N

T